# Distributed Shared Memory
## Concepts and Systems

# Distributed Shared Memory
## *Concepts and Systems*

Jelica Protić

Milo Tomašević

Veljko Milutinović

IEEE

# COMPUTER SOCIETY

Los Alamitos, California

Washington   •   Brussels   •   Tokyo

**Library of Congress Cataloging-in-Publication Data**

Distributed shared memory: concepts and systems / [edited by] Jelica Protić, Milo Tomašević,
  Veljko Milutinović.
        p.   cm.
    Includes bibliographical references (p.  ).
    ISBN 0-8186-7737-6
      1.  Memory management (computer science).      2.  Distributed shared memory.
  I. Protić, Jelica.      II. Tomašević, Milo.      III. Milutinović, Veljko.
  QA76.9.M45D58        1998
  005.4 ' 25—dc21                                                          97-11392
                                                                              CIP

IEEE Computer Society Press Order Number BP07737
Library of Congress Number 97-11392
ISBN 0-8186-7737-6


Additional copies can be ordered from

IEEE Computer Society Press
Customer Service Center
10662 Los Vaqueros Circle
P.O. Box 3014
Los Alamitos, CA 90720-1314
Tel: (714) 821-8380
Fax: (714) 821-4641
Email: cs.books@computer.org

IEEE Service Center
445 Hoes Lane
P.O. Box 1331
Piscataway, NJ 08855-1331
Tel: (908) 981-1393
Fax: (908) 981-9667
mis.custserv@computer.org

IEEE Computer Society
13, avenue de l'Aquilon
B-1200 Brussels
BELGIUM
Tel: +32-2-770-2198
Fax: +32-2-770-8505
euro.ofc@computer.org

IEEE Computer Society
Ooshima Building
2-19-1 Minami-Aoyama
Minato-ku, Tokyo 107
JAPAN
Tel: +81-3-3408-3118
Fax: +81-3-3408-3553
tokyo.ofc@computer.org


Publisher: Matt Loeb
Technical Editor: Jon Butler
Acquisitions Editor: Bill Sanders
Developmental Editor: Cheryl Smith
Advertising/Promotions: Tom Fink
Production Editor: Lisa O'Conner
Cover Design: Alex Torres

IEEE
COMPUTER
SOCIETY     IEEE

# CONTENTS

# Preface

Distributed shared memory (DSM) systems represent a successful hybrid of two parallel computer classes: shared memory multiprocessors and distributed computer systems. They provide the shared memory abstraction in systems with physically distributed memories, and consequently combine the advantages of both approaches. Because of that, the concept of distributed shared memory is recognized as one of the most attractive approaches for building large-scale, high-performance multiprocessor systems. The increasing importance of this subject imposes the need for its thorough understanding. To this end, our tutorial book covers and discusses many relevant issues, and presents a survey of both research DSM efforts and commercial DSM systems.

Problems in this area logically resemble the cache coherence-related problems in shared memory multiprocessors. The closest relation can be established between algorithmic issues of DSM coherence maintenance strategies and cache coherence maintenance strategies in shared memory multiprocessors. Therefore, the reader may consider this tutorial a follow-up to two previous IEEE tutorials:

1. M. Tomašević and V. Milutinović, eds., *Cache Coherence Problem in Shared Memory Multiprocessors: Hardware Solutions,* IEEE Computer Society Press, Los Alamitos, Calif., 1993.

2. I. Tartalja and V. Milutinović, eds., *Cache Coherence Problem in Shared Memory Multiprocessors: Software Solutions,* IEEE Computer Society Press, Los Alamitos, Calif., 1996.

This book compiles the broad knowledge of the DSM field, and provides state-of-the-art information for the interested reader. Consequently, it is useful to novices in this area, and also to the architects, designers, and programmers of DSM systems, as a research and development reference. Also, it can serve as a textbook for university courses in parallel processing and distributed systems.

This tutorial consists of six chapters. Chapter 1 gives a general introduction to the DSM field, and provides a broad survey of various approaches and systems. It consists of the papers that present basic DSM concepts, mechanisms, design issues, and systems. Chapter 2 concentrates on basic DSM algorithms, their enhancements, and their performance evaluation. Chapter 3 provides an overview of memory consistency models. Chapter 4 includes a number of papers that employ DSM solutions at the software level. Hardware implementations of DSM are covered in Chapter 5, together with an evaluation study. A description of DSM systems based on the hybrid hardware/software approach can be found in Chapter 6.

The decision to prepare this tutorial came after the authors had completed the design of a board that enables a personal computer to become a node in a distributed shared memory system based on the concept of reflective memory (for details, see suggestions for further reading in the section on hardware implementations); many of the included papers helped the authors achieve their design goal successfully.

We must mention that some valuable papers have been omitted, primarily because of their excessive length and owing to the space limitations of the tutorial. Therefore, suggestions for further reading are included in each chapter introduction. We strongly believe that this selection of papers covers essential issues in the field, and contributes to the widening of the general knowledge of distributed shared memory concepts and systems.

Jelica Protić
Milo Tomašević
Veljko Milutinović
June 1997

# Editors' Introduction

As the need for more computing power (demanded by new applications) constantly increases, systems with multiple processors are becoming a necessity. However, it seems that the programming of such systems still requires significant effort and skill. The commercial success of multiprocessors and distributed systems will be highly dependent on the programming paradigms they offer. Thus numerous ongoing research efforts are focused on an increasingly attractive class of parallel computer systems—distributed shared memory systems, which are the main topic of this tutorial.

The gap between processor and memory speed is apparently widening, and that is why memory system organization has become one of the most critical design decisions to be made by computer architects. Depending on the memory system organization, systems with multiple processors can be classified into two large groups: shared memory systems and distributed memory systems.

In a shared memory system (often called a *tightly coupled multiprocessor*), a single global physical memory is equally accessible to all processors. The ease of programming owing to a simple and general programming model is the main advantage of this kind of system. However, it typically suffers from increased contention in accessing the shared memory (especially if the single bus topology is used), which limits the scalability. In addition, the design of the memory system tends to be more complex.

A distributed memory system (often called a *multicomputer*) consists of a collection of autonomous processing nodes, having an independent flow of control and local memory modules. Communication between processes residing on different nodes is achieved through a message-passing model, via a general interconnection network. Such a programming model imposes a significant burden on the programmer, and induces considerable software overhead. On the other hand, these systems are claimed to have better scalability and cost-effectiveness.

A relatively new concept—distributed shared memory (DSM)—tries to combine the best of these two approaches. A DSM system logically implements a shared memory model in a physically distributed memory system. This approach hides the mechanism of communication between remote sites from the application writer, so the ease of programming and the portability typical of shared memory systems, as well as the scalability and cost-effectiveness of distributed memory systems, can be achieved

1

with less engineering effort. Considerable research endeavors have been devoted to the building of DSM systems, although the vast majority of DSM systems are implemented only as experimental prototypes in the laboratories of prominent universities. The overview of those systems, together with a presentation of the fundamental concepts and algorithms, represents the main subject of this tutorial.

## Problem Statement

The main problems that every DSM approach must address are (1) mapping of a logically shared address space onto the physically distributed memory modules, (2) locating and accessing a needed data item, and (3) preserving the coherent view of the overall shared address space.

The crucial objective in solving those problems is the minimization of the average access time to the shared data. With this goal in mind, two strategies for distribution of shared data are most frequently applied: *replication* and *migration*. Replication allows multiple copies of the same data item to reside in different local memories, in order to increase the parallelism in accessing logically shared data. Migration implies a single copy of a data item that must be moved to the accessing site, counting on the locality of reference in parallel applications. Besides that, just as in shared memory systems with private caches, systems with distributed shared memory must deal with the consistency problem, when replicated copies of the same data exist. To preserve the coherent view of shared address space, according to strict consistency semantics, a read operation must return the most recently written value. Therefore, when one of multiple copies of data is written, the others become stale, and must be invalidated or updated, depending on the applied coherence policy. Although strict coherence semantics provides the most natural view of shared address space, various weaker forms of memory consistency can be applied in order to reduce latency.

As a consequence of applied strategies and distribution of shared address space across different memories, on a memory reference, the data item and its copies must be located and managed according to a mechanism that is appropriate for such an architecture. The solutions to the above problems are incorporated into the DSM algorithm, which can be implemented at the hardware and/or software level. The implementation level of a DSM mechanism is regarded as the basic design decision, since it profoundly affects system performance. Other important issues include structure and granularity of shared data; the memory consistency model, which determines allowable memory access orderings; the coherence policy (invalidate or update); the responsibility for DSM management; the organization of system-wide tables; and so on. A broad description of the DSM field is given in Chapter 1.

## Importance of the Problem

The cost of parallel software development is an enormous obstacle to the widespread use of parallel computing. The distributed shared memory paradigm is able to reduce this cost effectively, since it can ease the programming of new applications and enable the reuse of those intended for shared memory environment, with appropriate modifications. At the same time, this approach inherits good scalability of the underlying distributed system, making it possible to build parallel machines with very high computing power. In addition to numerous research projects, commercial systems have also appeared on the market, proving the viability of the concept.

## Solutions to the Problem

Possible classifications of DSM systems can be based on (1) the level of DSM implementation (where and how), (2) the type of DSM algorithm (which reflects the adopted strategy), and (3) the organization of DSM management (centralized or distributed). The last two criteria are usually closely related, while the first criterion seems to be the most important design decision in building a DSM system.

The presentation of DSM solutions in this tutorial attempts to introduce general DSM concepts and illustrate their implementation in existing systems. It begins with an elaboration of algorithmic issues and memory consistency models, followed by an exhaustive overview of DSM systems, classified as hardware-level, software-level, and hybrid DSM implementations.

### Distributed Shared Memory Algorithms

The overall performance of a DSM system is highly dependent on the correspondence between the applied DSM algorithm and the access patterns generated by the application. One of the possible classifications of DSM algorithms distinguishes between SRSW (single reader/single writer), MRSW (multiple reader/single writer), and MRMW (multiple reader/multiple writer). The SRSW algorithms prohibit replication, and migration can be allowed if the distribution of shared address space over distributed memories is not static. The MRSW algorithms are most often encountered in DSM systems. On the basis of the realistic assumption that in some applications the read operation is generally more frequent than the write operation, and that the read operation cannot cause inconsistency, they allow multiple read-only copies of data items, in order to decrease read latency. Finally, the MRMW algorithms allow the existence of multiple copies of data items, even while being written to, but in some cases, depending on the consistency semantics, write operations must be globally sequenced.

The responsibility for DSM management can be centralized or distributed. Centralized management is easier to implement, but the central manager can become a bottleneck of the system. The responsibility for distributed management can be defined statically or dynamically, in order to eliminate bottlenecks and provide scalability. Basic DSM algorithms, as well as their improvements, and performance evaluation are covered in Chapter 2.

## Memory Consistency Models

The simultaneous existence of multiple copies of the same data, allowed by some DSM algorithms, imposes an additional problem in keeping those copies consistent.

- *Strict consistency* is the most intuitive model of memory consistency. It requires that each read operation returns the most recently written value. Since this is possible only in systems with a global notion of time, DSM systems based on underlying distributed systems use weaker forms of consistency.

- *Sequential consistency* provides that all processors in the system observe the same ordering of reads and writes issued in sequence by individual processors.

- *Processor* consistency assumes that the order in which memory operations can be seen by two processors need not be identical, but the order of writes issued by any particular processor must be preserved.

- *Weak consistency* distinguishes between ordinary accesses and synchronization accesses, and requires that memory become consistent only on synchronization accesses.

- *Release consistency* further divides synchronization accesses into acquire and release operations, so that protected accesses can be performed between acquire–release pairs. Ordinary accesses must wait for completion of prior acquire operations; as well, release operations must wait until all previous ordinary accesses become visible to other processors. Synchronization accesses are processor consistent.

- *Lazy release consistency* represents a refinement of release consistency. It further postpones propagation of modifications to the shared address space, so that only those writes associated with the chain of preceding critical sections need to be propagated at the time of the acquire operation.

- *Entry consistency* is, finally, a variant of release consistency that requires explicit protection of shared data with synchronization variables, using language-level annotations. Modifications to the shared variables are propagated selectively, only on the acquire operation of the corresponding synchronization variable.

Weakening of consistency semantics represents one of the key sources for performance improvements of DSM systems, since it allows overlapping and reordering of memory accesses. However, it puts an additional burden on the programmer to take care of synchronization. In any case, different applications have different requirements for data consistency, and it is not easy to resolve all of them at the system level. Therefore, involvement of the programmer is sometimes inevitable in resolving those problems at the application level. Detailed formal definitions of memory consistency models, as well as some evaluation results, are given in Chapter 3.

## Software Solutions

The early research projects that explored the innovative concept of DSM started with the idea of hiding the message-passing mechanism in the loosely coupled systems, typically on a network of workstations. The goal was to provide the abstraction of shared memory to the programmer. Some software-based solutions try to integrate the DSM mechanism by using an existing virtual memory management system. Because of that, and also because of the typically high cost of communications in those systems, they use large physical blocks as units of sharing (equal to the virtual memory page, or its multiple). The overhead introduced by building an additional software layer on top of message passing can be amortized to some extent with an increased locality inherent to applications with coarse-grain sharing. On the other hand, larger granularity of sharing increases the probability that multiple processors will require access to the same block simultaneously, even if they actually access unrelated parts of that block. This phenomenon is referred to as *false sharing*. This can cause *thrashing*—a behavior characterized by an extensive exchange of data between sites competing for the same data block—so frequent that it becomes the predominant activity, which considerably slows down useful processing in the system. To prevent false sharing and thrashing, some software solutions introduce logical units of sharing, such as objects, language types, and so on.

Software support for DSM is generally more flexible and convenient for experiments than hardware implementations, but in many cases cannot compete with hardware solutions in performance. Nevertheless, the majority of DSM systems described in the open literature are based on software mechanisms, since networks of workstations are becoming more popular and more powerful. Therefore, the use of the DSM concept seems to be an appropriate, and relatively low-cost, solution for their use as parallel computers. Ideas and concepts that originally appeared in software-oriented systems often migrate to hardware implementations. Some DSM systems rely on special runtime libraries that are to be linked with the application that uses a DSM paradigm. Software-based DSM mechanisms can also be implemented at the level of programming language, since the compiler can detect shared accesses and insert calls to synchronization and coherence routines into the executable code. Another class of approaches finds it appropriate to incorporate a DSM mechanism into the distributed operating system, inside or outside the kernel. Selected representatives of all these implementations are presented in Chapter 4.

## Hardware Solutions

Hardware-level implementation of DSM mechanisms can be seen as a natural extension of cache coherence mechanisms used in shared memory multiprocessors with private caches. The hardware approach has two very important advantages: complete transparency to the programmer, and generally better performance than other approaches. Since hardware implementations typically use a smaller unit of sharing (for example, cache block), they are less susceptible to false sharing and thrashing effects. Hardware implementations are particularly superior for applications that exhibit a high level of fine-grain sharing. These solutions are predominantly based on directory schemes, in order to achieve scalability. The use of the snooping method is limited to systems with the appropriate type of network (for example, bus or ring) and smaller bus-based system components (for example, clusters).

Hardware-level DSM implementations are presented in Chapter 5 of this tutorial. They are classified into three groups: CC-NUMA (cache coherent nonuniform memory access) architecture, COMA (cache-only memory architecture), and RMS (reflective memory system) architectures.

In CC-NUMA systems, parts of shared address space are statically distributed among the local memories in the clusters of processors, where improved locality of accesses is expected. In COMA architectures, the distribution of data is dynamically adaptable to the application behavior, so parts of the overall workspace can freely migrate according to their usage. However, as there is no *home* in the main memory for each data item, and cache *(attraction)* memories can run out of space, an appropriate replacement policy must be applied.

In both COMA and CC-NUMA architectures, invalidation-based protocols are predominantly used for coherence maintenance. In reflective memory architectures, all write operations to the globally shared regions are immediately followed with updates of all other copies of the same data item. Read operation in this class of systems does not introduce any additional overhead. The reflective memory concept is sometimes referred to as "mirror memory."

The hardware-oriented DSM mechanism appears to be a very promising DSM approach, owing to its superior performance and the transparency it offers to the programmer. It is expected to be more frequently used in future, since recently adopted standards, such as SCI (Scalable Coherent Interface), assume a hardware implementation.

## Hybrid Solutions

To achieve both the speed and transparency of hardware schemes, as well as the flexibility and sophistication of software solutions, designers sometimes choose to implement a suitable combination of hardware and software methods. Some level of software support can be found even in the entirely hardware solutions, with the goal of better suiting the application behavior. For example, software-controlled prefetching, which brings data to the local memory before actually being used, is one possible software refinement of the hardware-oriented systems. Also, some hardware support, such as dedicated accelerators for specific operations, can be added, in order to achieve a better performance of complex software solutions. However, only those systems that use a combination of hardware and software features as the basic design principle are regarded as hybrid solutions in this tutorial. A set of systems built with these ideas in mind is described in Chapter 6.

Not only a hybrid of hardware and software means, but also a combination of invalidate and update mechanisms, as well as an integration of message-passing and DSM paradigms, have been implemented in systems developed recently. As none of the design choices in the world of DSM has proven to be absolutely superior, it seems that the integration of various approaches will be intensively pursued in future by system architects, in their efforts to gain better performance.

## Distributed Shared Memory in Heterogeneous Systems

As computer systems of various classes already coexist in many environments, the efforts to make them cooperate in solving complex problems become more and more important. Furthermore, computer architects have realized that real-world problems can be successfully decomposed into components suitable for different architectures, so heterogeneous computing has become a hot topic in the computer community.

Research efforts focused on heterogeneous computing have also influenced the field of DSM, resulting in a few research projects striving to implement the DSM paradigm in the environment of various computer systems, widely different in data representation, virtual memory management, and operating system. For all these reasons, the implementation of the DSM model in heterogeneous systems seems to be quite a challenge. Data conversions that may affect numerical precision represent an inevitable part of DSM algorithms for heterogeneous systems. Some existing solutions to the problem of implementing the DSM paradigm in heterogeneous systems are also presented in this tutorial.

## Conclusion

This tutorial covers many relevant topics in an increasingly important area—distributed shared memory computing. In addition to providing the elaboration of basic concepts and algorithms, as well as a broad overview of proposed and existing approaches, this book gives a comprehensive survey of this attractive and promising field of parallel systems. The papers included in this tutorial are organized to follow the implementation level of the DSM mechanism as the basic classification criterion, although different approaches to classification could have served the same purpose. If there had been no limitations on the size of this book, the following six chapters could have included other relevant papers, as well.

In spite of many interesting experimental and research implementations in the field of DSM, commercial systems employing this paradigm are still rare. The strong impact of the appropriate DSM design choices on overall system performance and the potential for scalability require continuing efforts to develop systems with significant prospective benefits. Therefore, we strongly believe that DSM systems will remain the focus of considerable research attention, and promise to become a crucial source of advances in multiprocessor and parallel computing performance in the future.

# Chapter 1

# An Introduction to Distributed Shared Memory Concepts

## Editors' Introduction

A general survey of distributed shared memory (DSM) principles, algorithms, design issues, and existing systems is given in the following two papers, included in Chapter 1:

1. J. Protić, M. Tomašević, and V. Milutinović, "An Overview of Distributed Shared Memory" (*originally developed for this tutorial, 1996*).

2. B. Nitzberg and V. Lo, "Distributed Shared Memory: A Survey of Issues and Algorithms," *Computer,* Vol. 24, No. 8, Aug. 1991, pp. 52–60.

The first research efforts in the area of distributed shared memory systems started in the mid-1980s. This interest has continued to the present, with the increasing attention of the research community. Having in mind the primary goal of providing a shared memory abstraction in a distributed memory system, in order to ease the programming, designers of the early DSM systems were inspired by the principles of virtual memory, as well as the cache coherence maintenance in shared memory multiprocessors.

On the one hand, networks of workstations are becoming more and more popular and powerful nowadays, so they represent the most suitable platform for many programmers entering the world of parallel computing. Communication speed is still the main obstacle preventing these systems from reaching the level of performance of supercomputers, but weakening of the memory consistency semantics can significantly reduce the communication needs. On the other hand, designers of shared memory multiprocessors are striving for scalability, by physical distribution of shared memory and its sophisticated organization such as clustering and hierarchical layout of the overall system. For these reasons, as the gap between multiprocessors and multicomputers (that early DSM intended to bridge) narrows, and both classes of systems seemingly approach each other in basic ideas and performance, more and more systems can be found that fit into a large family of modern DSM. In spite of many misunderstandings and terminology confusion in this area, we adopted the most general definition, which assumes that all systems providing shared memory abstraction in a distributed memory system belong to the DSM category.

The main purpose of this chapter is to elaborate the distributed shared memory concept and closely related issues. The papers in this chapter define the fundamental principles and effects of DSM memory organization on overall system performance. Insight is also provided into the broad variety of hardware, software, and hybrid DSM approaches, with a discussion of their main advantages and drawbacks. Chapter 1 serves as a base for an extensive elaboration of DSM concepts and systems in Chapters 2–6.

The paper "An Overview of Distributed Shared Memory," by Protić, Tomašević, and Milutinović, covers all of the topics incorporated in this tutorial. In the first part of the paper, an overview of basic approaches to DSM concepts, algorithms, and memory consistency models is presented, together with an elaboration on possible classifications in this area. The second part of the paper briefly describes a relatively large number of existing systems, presenting their essence and selected details, including advantages, disadvantages, complexity, and performance considerations. The DSM systems are classified according to their implementation level into three groups: hardware, software, and hybrid DSM implementations. Relevant information about prototypes, commercial systems, and standards is also provided. The overall structure of the paper is quite similar to the layout of this tutorial. The paper also presents an extensive list of references covering the area of distributed shared memory.

In the paper "Distributed Shared Memory: A Survey of Issues and Algorithms," Nitzberg and Lo introduce DSM concepts, algorithms, and some existing systems. They consider the relevant choices that a DSM system designer must make, such as structure and granularity of shared data, as well as the coherence semantics. The issues of scalability and heterogeneity in DSM systems are also discussed. The authors explain the essential features of the DSM approach—data location and access, and coherence protocol—and illustrate general principles by a more detailed description of coherence maintenance algorithms used in the Dash and PLUS systems. Other issues such as replacement strategy, synchronization, and the problem of thrashing are also mentioned. The paper provides an extensive list of DSM systems, available at the time of writing, with a brief description of their essence, and a survey of the design issues for some of them.

## Suggestions for Further Reading

1. V. Lo, "Operating System Enhancements for Distributed Shared Memory," *Advances in Computers*, Vol. 39, 1994, pp. 191–237.

2. D.R. Cheriton, "Problem-Oriented Shared Memory: A Decentralized Approach to Distributed System Design," *Proc. 6th Int'l Conf. Distributed Computing Systems*, IEEE CS Press, Los Alamitos, Calif., 1986, pp. 190–197.

3. M. Dubois, C. Scheurich, and F.A. Briggs, "Synchronization, Coherence, and Event Ordering in Multiprocessors," *Computer*, Vol. 21, No. 2, Feb. 1988, pp. 9–21.

4. J. Hennessy and D. Patterson, *Computer Architecture: A Quantitative Approach*, Morgan Kaufmann Publishers, San Mateo, Calif., 1990.

5. K. Hwang, *Advanced Computer Organization: Parallelism, Scalability, Programmability*, McGraw-Hill, New York, N.Y., 1993.

6. M.J. Flynn, *Computer Architectures: Pipelined and Parallel Processor Design*, Jones and Bartlett, Boston, Mass., 1995.

# An Overview of Distributed Shared Memory

Jelica Protić
Milo Tomašević
Veljko Milutinović

*Department of Computer Engineering*
*School of Electrical Engineering*
*University of Belgrade*
*Belgrade, Yugoslavia*
*{jeca,etomasev,emilutiv}@ubbg.etf.bg.ac.yu*

## I. Concepts

### A. Introduction

Significant progress has been made in the research on and development of systems with multiple processors that are capable of delivering high computing power satisfying the constantly increasing demands of typical applications. Systems with multiple processors are usually classified into two large groups, according to their memory system organization: shared memory and distributed memory systems.

In a shared memory system (often called a *tightly coupled multiprocessor*), a global physical memory is equally accessible to all processors. An important advantage of these systems is the general and convenient programming model that enables simple data sharing through a uniform mechanism of reading and writing shared structures in the common memory. Other programming models can be readily emulated on those systems. The cost of parallel software development is reduced owing to the ease of programming and portability. However, shared memory multiprocessors typically suffer from increased contention and longer latencies in the accessing of shared memory, resulting in a somewhat lower peak performance and limited scalability compared to distributed systems. In addition, the design of memory systems tends to be complex. A detailed discussion of shared memory multiprocessors is provided in [FLYNN95].

On the other hand, a distributed memory system (often called a *multicomputer*) consists of multiple independent processing nodes with local memory modules, connected by means of some general interconnection network. Distributed memory systems are claimed to be scalable, and systems with very high computing power are possible. However, communication between processes residing on different nodes is achieved through a message-passing model, which requires explicit use of send/receive primitives; most programmers find this more difficult to achieve, since they must take care of data distribution across the system, and manage the communication. Also, process migration imposes problems because of different address spaces. Therefore, compared to shared memory systems, the hardware problems are easier and software problems more complex in distributed memory systems.

A relatively new concept—distributed shared memory (DSM), discussed in [LO94] and [PROTI96]—tries to combine the advantages of the two approaches. A DSM system logically implements the shared memory model in a physically distributed memory system. The specific mechanism for achieving the shared memory abstraction can be implemented in hardware and/or software in a variety of ways. The DSM system hides the remote communication mechanism from the application writer, so the ease of programming and the portability typical of shared memory systems are preserved. Existing applications for shared memory systems can be relatively easily modified and efficiently executed on DSM systems, preserving software investments while maximizing the resulting performance. In addition, the scalability and cost-effectiveness of underlying distributed memory systems are also inherited. Consequently, the importance of the distributed shared memory concept comes from the fact that it seems to be a viable choice for building efficient large-scale multiprocessors.

The ability to provide a transparent interface and a convenient programming environment for distributed and parallel applications has made the DSM model the focus of numerous research efforts. The main objective of current research in DSM systems is the development of general approaches that minimize the average access time to shared data, while maintaining data consistency. Some solutions implement a specific software layer on top of existing message-passing systems, while others extend strategies applied in shared memory multiprocessors with private caches, described in [TOMAS94a], [TOMAS94b], and [TARTA95], to multilevel memory systems.

Part I of this paper provides comprehensive insight into the increasingly important area of DSM. As such, Sections I.B–D cover general DSM concepts and approaches. Possible classifications of DSM systems are discussed, as well as various important design choices in building DSM systems. Section I.E presents a set of DSM algorithms from the open literature, and differences between them are analyzed under various conditions. Part II of this paper represents a survey of existing DSM systems, developed either as research prototypes or as commercial products and standards. It consists of three sections dedicated to DSM implementations on the hardware level, software level, and using a hybrid hardware/software approach. Although not exhaustive, this survey presents extensive and up-to-date information on several key implementation schemes for maintaining data in DSM systems. In the description of each DSM system, the essentials of the approach, implementation issues, and basic DSM mechanism are highlighted.

## B. General Structure of a Distributed Shared Memory System

A DSM system can be generally viewed as a set of nodes or clusters, connected by an interconnection network (Figure 1). A cluster can be a uniprocessor or a

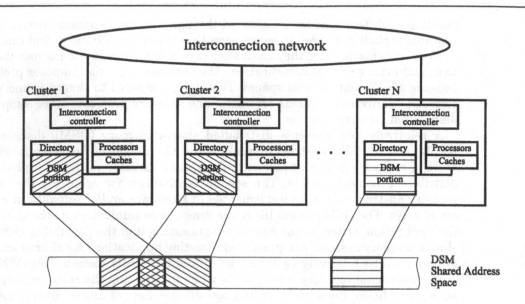

Figure 1. Structure and organization of a DSM system.

multiprocessor system, usually organized around a shared bus. Private caches attached to the processors are inevitable for reducing memory latency. Each cluster in the system contains a physically local memory module, which is partially or entirely mapped to the DSM global address space. Regardless of the network topology (for example, a bus, ring, mesh, or local area network), a specific interconnection controller within each cluster is needed to connect it into the system.

Information about states and current locations of particular data blocks is usually kept in the form of a system table or directory. Storage and organization of directory are among the most important design decisions, with a large impact on system scalability. Directory organization varies from a full-map storage to different dynamic organizations, such as single- or double-linked lists and trees. No matter which organization is employed, the cluster must provide the storage for the entire directory, or just a part of it. In this way, the system directory can be distributed across the system as a flat or hierarchical structure. In hierarchical topologies, if clusters on intermediate levels exist, they usually contain only directories and the corresponding interface controllers. Directory organization and the semantics of information kept in directories depend on the applied method for maintaining data consistency.

## C. Classifications of Distributed Shared Memory Systems

Since the first research efforts in the area of DSM in the mid-1980s, the interest in this concept has increased continuously, resulting in tens of systems developed predominantly as research prototypes. Designers of the early DSM systems were inspired by the principle of virtual memory, as well as by the principle of cache coherence maintenance in shared memory multiprocessors.

On the one hand, networks of workstations are becoming more and more popular and powerful nowadays, so they represent the most suitable platform for many programmers entering the world of parallel computing. However, communication speed is still the main obstacle preventing these systems from reaching the level of performance of high-end machines. On the other hand, designers of shared memory multiprocessors are striving for scalability, by physical distribution of shared memory and its sophisticated organization such as clustering and hierarchical layout of the overall system. For these reasons, as the gap between multiprocessors and multicomputers (that early DSM intended to bridge) narrows, and both classes of systems seemingly approach each other in basic ideas and performance, more and more systems can be found that fit into a large family of modern DSM. In spite of many misunderstandings and terminology confusion in this area, we adopt the most general definition, which assumes that all systems providing shared memory abstraction on a distributed memory system belong to the DSM category. This abstraction is achieved by specific actions necessary for accessing data from global virtual DSM address space, which can be shared among the nodes. Three important issues are involved in the performance of these actions, which bring the data to the site where accessed, while keeping them consistent (with respect to other processors); each of these actions leads to a specific classification of DSM systems:

- *How* the access actually executes   &rarr;   **DSM algorithm**
- *Where* the access is implemented   &rarr;   **Implementation level of DSM mechanism**
- *What* the precise semantics of the word *consistent* is   &rarr;   **Memory consistency model**

Having in mind these most important DSM characteristics, we next discuss three possible classifications of DSM approaches.

## 1. The First Classification: According to the DSM Algorithm

DSM algorithms can be classified according to the allowable existence of multiple copies of the same data, also considering access rights of those copies. Two strategies for distribution of shared data are most frequently applied: *replication* and *migration*. Replication allows that multiple copies of the same data item reside simultaneously in different local memories (or caches), in order to increase the parallelism in accessing logically shared data. On the other hand, migration implies a single copy of a data item that must be moved to the accessing site for exclusive use, counting on the locality of references in parallel applications. DSM algorithms can be classified as:

1. SRSW (single reader/single writer)
   a. Without migration
   b. With migration
2. MRSW (multiple reader/single writer)
3. MRMW (multiple reader/multiple writer)

Replication is prohibited in SRSW, while it is allowed in MRSW and MRMW algorithms. The complexity of coherence maintenance is strongly dependent on the introduced classes. To adapt to the application characteristics on the basis of typical read/write patterns, while keeping the acceptable complexity of the algorithm, many solutions have been proposed. Among them, MRSW algorithms are predominant. More details on DSM algorithms are given in Section I.E.

## 2. The Second Classification: According to the Implementation Level of the DSM Mechanism

The level at which the DSM mechanism is implemented is one of the most important decisions in building a DSM system, since it affects both the programming and the overall system performance and cost. Possible implementation levels are:

1. Software
   a. Runtime library routines
   b. Operating system
      i.  Inside the kernel
      ii. Outside the kernel
   c. Compiler-inserted primitives
2. Hardware
3. Hardware/software combination (hybrid)

Software-oriented DSM started with the idea of hiding the message-passing mechanism and providing a shared memory paradigm in loosely coupled systems. Some of these solutions rely on specific runtime libraries that are to be linked with the application that uses shared data. The others implement DSM on the level of programming language, since the compiler can detect shared accesses and insert calls to synchronization and coherence routines into the executable code. Another class of approaches finds it appropriate to incorporate a DSM mechanism into the distributed operating system, inside or outside the kernel. Operating system- and runtime library-oriented approaches often integrate the DSM mechanism with an existing virtual memory management system. However, existing DSM systems usually combine elements of different software approaches. For example, IVY is predominantly a runtime library solution that also includes modifications to the operating system, while Midway implementation is based on a runtime system and the compiler for code generation that marks shared data as dirty when written into.

Some DSM systems use dedicated hardware responsible for locating, copying shared data items, and keeping their coherence. Those solutions extend traditional caching techniques typical of shared memory multiprocessors to DSM systems with scalable interconnection networks. They can for the most part be classified into three groups according to their memory system architecture: CC-NUMA (cache coherent nonuniform memory access) architecture, COMA (cache-only memory architecture), and RMS (reflective memory system) architecture. In a CC-NUMA system, DSM address space is statically distributed across local memory modules of clusters, which can be accessed both by the local processors and by processors from other clusters in the system, although with quite different access latencies. COMA provides the dynamic partitioning of data in the form of distributed memories, organized as large second-level caches (attraction memories). RMS architectures use a hardware-implemented update mechanism in order to propagate immediately every change to all sharing sites using broadcast or multicast messages. This kind of memory system is also called "mirror memory."

Because of possible performance/complexity trade-offs, the integration of software and hardware methods seems to be one of the most promising approaches in the future of DSM. Some software approaches include hardware accelerators for frequent operations in order to improve the performance, while some hardware solutions handle infrequent events in software to minimize complexity. An example of a hybrid solution is to use hardware to manage fixed size fine-grain data units, in combination with the coarse-grain data management in software. To gain better performance in DSM systems, recent implementations have used multiple protocols within the same system, and even integrate message passing with the DSM mechanism. To handle the complexity of recent, basically software solutions, special programmable protocol processors can also be added to the system.

While hardware solutions bring total transparency of the DSM mechanism to the programmer and software layers, and typically achieve lower access latencies, software solutions can take better advantage of application characteristics through the use of various hints provided by the programmer. Software systems are also very suitable for experimenting with new concepts and algorithms. As a consequence, the number of software DSM systems presented in the open literature is considerably higher; however, the ideas generated in software-based solutions often migrate to hardware-oriented systems. Our presentation of DSM systems in Part II follows the classification of hardware, software, and hybrid DSM implementations and elaborates extensively on these issues.

### 3. The Third Classification: According to the Memory Consistency Model

A memory consistency model defines the legal ordering of memory references issued by some processor, as observed by other processors. Different types of parallel applications inherently require various consistency models. Performance of the system in executing these applications is largely influenced by the restrictiveness of the model. Stronger forms of the consistency model typically increase the memory access latency and the bandwidth requirements, while simplifying programming. Looser constraints in more relaxed models that allow reordering, pipelining, and overlapping of memory consequently result in better performance, at the expense of higher involvement of the programmer in synchronizing the accesses to shared data. To achieve optimal behavior, systems with multiple consistency models adaptively applied to appropriate data types have been proposed.

Stronger memory consistency models that treat synchronization accesses as ordinary read and write operations are *sequential* and *processor consistency* models. More relaxed models that distinguish between ordinary and synchronization accesses are *weak, release, lazy release,* and *entry consistency* models. A brief overview of memory consistency models can be found in [LO94]. Sufficient conditions for ensuring sequential, processor, weak, and release memory consistency models are given in [GHARA90].

*Sequential consistency* provides that all processors in the system observe the same interleaving of reads and writes issued in sequences by individual processors. A simple implementation of this model is a single-port shared memory system that enforces serialized access servicing from a single first in–first out (FIFO) queue. In DSM systems, similar implementation is achieved by serializing all requests on a central server node. In both cases, no bypassing of read and write requests is allowed. Conditions for sequential consistency hold in the majority of bus-based shared memory multiprocessors, as well as in early DSM systems, such as IVY and Mirage.

*Processor consistency* assumes that the order in which memory operations can be seen by different processors need not be identical, but the sequence of writes issued by each processor must be observed by all other processors in the same order of issuance. Unlike sequential consistency, processor consistency implementations allow reads to bypass writes in queues from which memory requests are serviced. Examples of systems that guarantee processor consistency are VAX 8800, PLUS, Merlin, RMS, and so on.

*Weak consistency* distinguishes between ordinary and synchronization memory accesses. It requires that memory becomes consistent only on synchronization accesses. In this model, requirements for sequential consistency apply only on synchronization accesses themselves. In addition, a synchronization access must wait for *all* previous accesses to be performed, while ordinary reads and writes must wait *only* for completion of previous synchronization accesses. A variant of weak consistency model is used in SPARC architecture by Sun Microsystems.

*Release consistency* further divides synchronization accesses into acquire and release, so that protected ordinary shared accesses can be performed between acquire–release pairs. In this model, ordinary read or write access can be performed only after all previous *acquires* on the same processor are performed. In addition, *release* can be performed only after all previous ordinary reads and writes on the same processor are performed. Finally, acquire and release synchronization accesses must fulfill the requirements that processor consistency imposes on ordinary read and write accesses, respectively. Different implementations of release consistency can be found in Dash and Munin DSM systems.

An enhancement of release consistency, *lazy release consistency*, is presented in [KELEH92]. Instead of propagating modifications to the shared address space on each release (as in release consistency—sometimes called *eager release*), modifications are further postponed until the next relevant acquire. In addition, not all modifications need to be propagated on the acquire—only those associated to the chain of preceding critical sections. In this way, the amount of data exchanged is minimized, while the number of messages is also reduced by combining modification with lock acquires in one message. Lazy release consistency was implemented in the DSM system TreadMarks.

Finally, *entry consistency* is a new improvement of release consistency. This model requires that each ordinary shared variable or object be protected and associated to the synchronization variable using language-level annotation. Consequently, modification to the ordinary shared variable is postponed to the next acquire of the associated synchronization variable that guards it. Since only the changes for associated variables need be propagated at the moment of acquire, the traffic is significantly decreased. Latency is also reduced since a shared access does not have to wait for the completion of other nonrelated acquires. Performance improvement is achieved at the expense of higher programmer involvement in specifying synchronization information for each variable. Entry consistency was implemented for the first time in the DSM system Midway.

## D. Important Design Choices in Building Distributed Shared Memory Systems

In addition to the DSM algorithm, implementation level of DSM mechanism, and memory consistency model, a set of characteristics that can strongly affect the overall performance of a DSM system includes:

**Cluster configuration**—Single/multiple processor(s), with/without (shared/private) (single/multiple level) caches, local memory organization, network interface, etc.

**Interconnection network**—Bus hierarchy, ring, mesh, hypercube, specific LAN, and so on

**Structure of shared data**—Nonstructured or structured into objects, language types, and so on

**Granularity of coherence unit**—Word, cache block, page, complex data structure, and so on

**Responsibility for DSM management**—Centralized, distributed fixed, distributed dynamic

**Coherence policy**—Write-invalidate, write-update, type-specific, and so on

*Cluster configuration* varies greatly across different DSM systems. It includes one or several (usually off-the-shelf) processor(s). Since each processor has its local cache (or even cache hierarchy) the cache coherence on a cluster level must be integrated with the DSM mechanisms on the global level. Parts of a local memory module can be configured as private or shared (mapped to the virtual shared address space). In addition to coupling the cluster to the system, the network interface controller sometimes integrates some important responsibilities of DSM management.

Almost all types of *interconnection networks* found in multiprocessors and distributed systems can also be used in DSM systems. The majority of software-oriented DSM systems are network independent, although many of them happened to be built on top of an Ethernet network, readily available in most environments. On the other hand, topologies such as a multilevel bus, ring hierarchy, or mesh have been used as platforms for some hardware-oriented DSM systems. The topology of the interconnection network can offer or restrict good potential for parallel exchange of data related to DSM management. For the same reasons, topology also affects scalability. In addition, it determines the possibility and cost of broadcast and multicast transactions, very important for implementing DSM algorithms.

*Structure of shared data* represents the global layout of shared address space, as well as the organization of data items in it. Hardware solutions always deal with nonstructured data objects, while some software implementations tend to use data items that represent logical entities, in order to take advantage of the locality naturally expressed by the application.

*Granularity of coherence unit* determines the size of data blocks managed by coherence protocols. The impact of this parameter on overall system performance is closely related to the locality of data access typical for the application. In general, hardware-oriented systems use smaller units (typically cache blocks), while some software solutions, based on virtual memory mechanisms, organize data in larger physical blocks (pages), counting on coarse-grain sharing. The use of larger blocks results in saving space for directory storage, but it also increases the probability that multiple processors will require access to the same block simultaneously, even if they actually access unrelated parts of that block. This phenomenon is referred to as *false sharing*. This can cause *thrashing*—a behavior characterized by extensive exchange of data between sites competing for the same data block.

*Responsibility for DSM management* determines which site must handle actions related to the consistency maintenance in the system; the management can be centralized or distributed. Centralized management is easier to implement, but the central manager represents a bottleneck. The responsibility for distributed management can be defined statically or dynamically, eliminating bottlenecks and providing scalability. Distribution of responsibility for DSM management is closely related to the distribution of directory information.

*Coherence policy* determines whether the existing copies of a data item being written to at one site will be updated or invalidated at other sites. The choice of coherence policy is related to the granularity of shared data. For very fine-grain data items, the cost of an update message is approximately the same as the cost of an invalidation message. Therefore, the update policy is often used in systems with word-based coherence maintenance. On the other hand, invalidation is largely used in coarse-grain systems. The efficiency of an invalidation approach increases when the read and write access sequences to the same data item by various processors are not highly interleaved. The best performance can be expected if coherence policy dynamically adapts to the observed reference pattern.

## E. Distributed Shared Memory Algorithms

The algorithms for implementing distributed shared memory deal with two basic problems: (1) static and dynamic distribution of shared data across the system, in order to minimize their access latency, and (2) preserving a coherent view of shared data, while trying to keep the overhead of coherence management as low as possible. Replication and migration are the two most frequently used policies that try to minimize data access time, by bringing data to the site where they are currently used. Replication is mainly used to enable simultaneous accesses by different sites to the same data, predominantly when read sharing prevails. Migration is preferred when sequential patterns of write sharing are prevalent in order to decrease the overhead of coherence management. The choice of a suitable DSM algorithm is a vital issue in achieving high system performance. Therefore, is must be well adapted to the system configuration and characteristics of memory references in typical applications.

Classifications of DSM algorithms and the evaluation of their performance have been extensively discussed in [LIHUD89], [STUM90], [BLACK89], and [KESSL89]. This presentation follows a classification of algorithms similar to the one found in [STUM90].

### 1. Single Reader/Single Writer Algorithms

Single reader/single writer (SRSW) algorithms prohibit the possibility of replication, while the migration can be, but is not necessarily, applied. The simplest algorithm for DSM management is the *central server* algorithm [STUM90]. The approach is based on a unique central server that is responsible for servicing all access requests from other nodes to shared data, physically located on this node. This algorithm suffers from performance problems since the central server can become a bottleneck in the system. Such an organization implies no physical distribution of shared memory. A possible modification is the static distribution of physical memory and the static distribution of responsibilities for parts of shared address space onto several different servers. Some simple mapping functions (for example, hashing) can be used to locate the appropriate server for the corresponding piece of data.

More sophisticated SRSW algorithms additionally allow for the possibility of migration. However, only one copy of the data item can exist at any one time and this copy can be migrated on demand. In [KESSL89] this kind of algorithm is referred to as *Hot Potato*. If an application exhibits high locality of reference, the cost of data migration is amortized over multiple accesses, since data are moved not as individual items, but in fixed size units—blocks. It can perform well in cases where a longer sequence of accesses from one processor uninterrupted with accesses from other processors is likely to happen, and write after read to the same data occurs frequently. In any case, the performance level of this rarely used algorithm is restrictively low, since it does not take advantage of the parallel potential of multiple read-only copies, in cases when read sharing prevails.

### 2. Multiple Reader/Single Writer Algorithms

The main intention of multiple reader/single writer (MRSW) (or *read-replication*) algorithms is to reduce the average cost of read operations, by counting on the fact that read sharing is the prevalent pattern in parallel applications. To this end, they allow read operations to be simultaneously executed locally at multiple hosts. Permission to update a replicated copy can be given to only one host at a time. On the occurrence of write to a writable copy, the cost of this operation is increased, because the use of other replicated stale copies must be prevented. Therefore, the MRSW algorithms are usually invalidation based. Protocols following this principle are numerous.

A variety of algorithms belong to this class. They differ in the way the responsibility for DSM management is allocated. Several MRSW algorithms are proposed in [LIHUD89]. Before discussing those algorithms, the following terms must be defined:

**Manager**—The site responsible for organizing the write access to a data block

**Owner**—The site that owns the only writable copy of the data block

**Copy set**—A set of all sites that have copies of the data block

A list of algorithms proposed by Li and Hudak includes the following.

a. **Centralized Manager Algorithm.** All read and write requests are sent to the manager, which is the only site that keeps the identity of the owner of a particular data block. The manager forwards the request for data to the owner, and waits for confirmation from the requesting site, indicating that it received the copy of the block from the owner. In the case of a write operation, the manager also sends invalidations to all sites from the copy set (a vector that identifies the current holders of the data block, kept by the manager).

   b. **Improved Centralized Manager Algorithm.** Unlike the original centralized manager algorithm, the owner, instead of the manager, keeps the
   copy set in this version of the centralized algorithm. Copy set is sent together with the data to the new owner, which is also responsible for invalidations. In this case, the overall performance can be improved because of the
   decentralized synchronization.

   c. **Fixed Distributed Manager Algorithm.** In the fixed distributed manager algorithm, instead of centralizing the management, each site is predetermined to manage a subset of data blocks. The distribution is done according to some default mapping function. Clients are still allowed to over-
   ride it by supplying their own mapping, tailored to the expected behavior of
   the application. When a parallel program exhibits a high rate of requests for
   data blocks, this algorithm performs better than the centralized solutions.

   d. **Broadcast Distributed Manager Algorithm.** There is actually no
   manager in the broadcast distributed manager algorithm. Instead, the requesting processor sends a broadcast message to find the true owner of the
   data block. The owner performs all actions just like the manager in previous algorithms, and keeps the copy set. The disadvantage of this approach
   is that all processors must process each broadcast, slowing down their own
   computations.

   e. **Dynamic Distributed Manager Algorithm.** In the dynamic distributed
   manager algorithm, the identity of the probable owner, not the real owner,
   is kept for each particular data block. All requests are sent to the probable
   owner, which is also the real owner in most cases. However, if the probable
   owner does not happen to be the real one, it forwards the request to the node
   that represents probable owner according to the information kept in its own
   table. For every read and write request, forward, and invalidation messages,
   the probable owner field is changed accordingly, in order to decrease the
   number of messages to locate the real owner. This algorithm is often called
   the Li algorithm. For its basic version, where the ownership is changed on
   both read and write fault, it is shown in [LIHUD89] that the performance of
   the algorithm does not worsen as more processors are added to the system,
   but rather degrades logarithmically when more processors contend for the
   same data block.

   A modification of the dynamic distributed manager algorithm, also proposed in
[LIHUD89], suggests a distribution of the copy set, which should be organized as
a tree rooted at the owner site. This is a way to distribute the responsibility for
invalidations, as well.

### 3. Multiple Reader/Multiple Writer Algorithms

The multiple reader/multiple writer (MRMW) algorithm (also called the *full-
replication* algorithm) allows the replication of data blocks with both read and
write permission. To preserve coherence, updates of each copy must be distributed to all other copies at remote sites, by multicast or broadcast messages. This
algorithm tries to minimize the cost of write access. Therefore, it is appropriate
for write sharing and it is often used with write-update protocols. This algorithm

can produce high coherence traffic, especially when the update frequency and the number of replicated copies are high.

Protocols complying to the MRMW algorithm can be complex and demanding. One possible way to maintain data consistency is to sequence the write operations globally, in order to implement reliable multicast. When a processor attempts to write to the shared memory, the intended modification is sent to the sequencer. The sequencer assigns the next sequence number to the modification and multicasts the modification with this sequence number to all sites having the copy. When the modification arrives at a site the sequence number is verified, and if it is not correct a retransmission is requested.

A modification of this algorithm proposed in [BISIA88] distributes the task of sequencing. In this solution, writes to any particular data structure are sequenced by the server that manages the master copy of that data structure. Although the system is not sequentially consistent in this case, each particular data structure is maintained in a consistent manner.

## 4. Avenues for Performance Improvement

Considerable effort has been dedicated to various modifications of the basic algorithms, in order to improve their behavior and gain better performance by reducing the amount of data transferred in the system. Most of these ideas have been evaluated by simulation studies, and some of them have been implemented in existing prototype systems.

An enhancement of Li's algorithm (named the Shrewd algorithm) is proposed in [KESSL89]. It eliminates all unnecessary page transfers with the assistance of the sequence number per copy of a page. On each write fault at a node with a previously existing read-only copy, the sequence number is sent with the request. If this number is the same as the number kept by the owner, the requester will be allowed to access the page without its transfer. This solution shows remarkable benefits when the read-to-write ratio increases.

All solutions presented in [LIHUD89] assume that a page transfer is performed subsequent to each attempt to access a page that does not reside on the accessing site. A modification proposed in [BLACK89] employs a competitive algorithm and allows page replication only when the number of accesses to the remote page exceeds the replication cost. A similar rule is applied to migration, although the fact that, in this case, only one site can have the page makes the condition to migrate the page more restrictive and dependent on the other site's access pattern to the same page. The performance of these policies is guaranteed to stay within a constant factor from the optimal.

Another restriction to data transfer requests is applied in the system Mirage, in order to reduce thrashing—an adverse effect that occurs when an alternating sequence of accesses to the same page issued by different sites makes its migration the predominant activity. The solution to this problem is found in defining a time window Δ in which the site is guaranteed to uninterruptedly possess the page after it has acquired it. The value of Δ can be tuned statically or dynamically, depending on the degree of processor locality exhibited by the particular application.

There are a variety of specific algorithms implemented in existing DSM systems, or simulated extensively using appropriate workload traces. Early DSM implementations found the main source of possible performance and scalability improvements in various solutions for the organization and storage of system tables, such as copy set, as well as the distribution of management responsibilities. In striving to gain better performance, recent DSM implementations have relaxed memory consistency semantics, so the algorithms and the organization of directory information must be considerably modified. Implementations of critical operations using hardware accelerators and a combination of invalidate and update methods also contribute to the better performance of modern DSM systems.

## II. Systems

### A. Introduction

A distributed shared memory system logically implements a shared memory model on physically distributed memories, in order to achieve ease of programming, cost-effectiveness, and scalability [PROTI96]. Basic DSM concepts are discussed extensively in Part I of this paper. Part II represents a wide overview of existing systems, predominantly developed as research prototypes. Since the shared address space of DSM is distributed across local memories, on each access to these data a lookup must be performed, in order to determine if the requested data is in the local memory, and if not, an action must be taken to bring it to the local memory. An action is also needed on write accesses in order to preserve the coherence of shared data. Both lookup and action can be performed in software, hardware, or the combination of both. According to this property, systems are classified into three groups: *software*, *hardware*, and *hybrid* implementations. The choice of implementation level usually depends on price/performance trade-offs. Although typically superior in performance, hardware implementations require additional complexity, allowable only in high-performance large-scale machines. Low-end systems, such as networks of personal computers, based on commodity microprocessors, still do not tolerate cost of additional hardware for DSM, and are limited to software implementation. For the class of mid-range systems, such as clusters of workstations, low-cost additional hardware, typically used in hybrid solutions, seems to be appropriate.

### B. Software Distributed Shared Memory Implementations

Until the last decade distributed systems widely employed the message-passing communication paradigm. However, it appeared to be much less convenient than the shared memory programming model since the programmer must be aware of data distribution and explicitly manage data exchange via messages. In addition, they introduce severe problems in passing complex data structures, and process migration in multiple address spaces is aggravated. Therefore, the idea of building a software mechanism that provides the shared memory paradigm to the programmer on top of message passing emerged in the mid-1980s. Generally, this can be achieved in user-level runtime library routines, the operating system, or the programming language. Some DSM systems combine the elements of these three approaches. Larger grain sizes (on the order of a kilobyte) are typical for software solutions, since DSM management is usually supported through a virtual memory mechanism. It means that if the requested data are not present in local memory, a page fault handler will retrieve the page either from the local memory of another cluster or from disk. Coarse-grain pages are advantageous for applications with high locality of references and also reduce the necessary directory storage. On the other hand, parallel programs characterized by fine-grain sharing are adversely affected, owing to false sharing and thrashing.

Software support for DSM is generally more flexible than the hardware support and enables better tailoring of the consistency mechanisms to the application behavior. However, in most cases it cannot compete with hardware implementations in performance. Apart from trying to introduce hardware accelerators to solve the problem, designers also concentrate on relaxing the consistency model, although this can put an additional burden on the programmer. The fact that research and experiments can rely on widely available programming languages and operating systems on the networks of workstations resulted in numerous implementations of software DSM.

### 1. User-Level and Combined Software Distributed Memory System Implementations

IVY [LI88] is one of the first proposed software DSM solutions, implemented as a set of user-level modules built on top of the modified Aegis operating system on the Apollo Domain workstations. IVY is composed of five modules. Three of them, from the client interface (*process management, memory allocation,* and *initialization*), consist of a set of primitives that can be used by application programs. *Remote operation* and *memory mapping* routines use the operating system low-level support. IVY provides a mechanism for consistency maintenance using an invalidation approach on 1-Kbyte pages. For experimental purposes, three algorithms for ensuring sequential consistency were implemented: the improved centralized manager, the fixed distributed manager, and the dynamic distributed manager. Performance measurements on a system with up to eight clusters have shown linear speedup in comparison with the best sequential solutions for some typical parallel programs. Although IVY performance could have been improved by implementing it at the system level rather than at the user level, its most important contribution was in proving the viability of the DSM concept in real systems with parallel applications.

A similar DSM algorithm is also used in Mermaid [ZHOU90]—the first system to provide a DSM paradigm in a heterogeneous environment (HDSM). The prototype configuration includes the SUN/Unix workstations and the DEC Firefly multiprocessors. The DSM mechanism was implemented at the user level, as a library package which is to be linked to the application programs. Minor changes to the SunOS operating system kernel included setting the access permission of memory pages from the user level, as well as passing the address of a DSM page to its user-level fault handler. Because of the heterogeneity of clusters, in addition to data exchange, the need for data conversion also arises. Besides the conversion of standard data types, for user-defined data types conversion routines and a table for mapping data types to particular routines must be provided by the user. A restriction is that just one data type is allowed per page. Mermaid ensures the variable page size that can be suited to data access patterns. Since the Firefly is a shared-memory multiprocessor, it was possible to compare physical versus distributed shared memory. The results showed that the speedup is increased far less than 20 percent when moving from DSM to physically shared memory for up to four nodes. Since the conversion costs are found to be substantially lower than page transfer costs, it was concluded that the introduced overhead caused by heterogeneity was acceptably low—page fault delay for the heterogeneous system was comparable to that of the homogeneous system with only Firefly multiprocessors.

The Munin [CARTE91] DSM system includes two important features: type-specific coherence mechanisms and the release consistency model. The 16-processor prototype is implemented on an Ethernet network of SUN-3 workstations. Munin is based on the Stanford V kernel and the Presto parallel programming environment. It can be classified as a runtime system implementation, although a preprocessor that converts the program annotations, a modified linker, some library routines, and operating system support are also required. It employs different coherence protocols well suited to the expected access pattern for a shared data object type (Figure 2). The programmer is responsible for providing one of several annotations for each shared object, which selects appropriate low-level parameters of coherence protocol for this object. The data object directory is distributed among nodes and organized as a hash table. The release consistency model is implemented in software with delayed update queues for efficient merging and propagating of write sequences. Evaluation using two representative Munin programs (with only minor annotations) shows that their performance is less than 10 percent worse compared to their carefully hand-coded message passing counterparts.

Another DSM implementation that counts on significant reduction of data traffic by relaxing consistency semantics according to the lazy release consistency model is TreadMarks [KELEH94]. This is a user-level implementation that relies on Unix standard libraries in order to accomplish remote process creation, interprocess communication, and memory management. Therefore, no

| Data object type | Coherence mechanism |
| --- | --- |
| Private | None |
| Write-once | Replication |
| Write-many | Delayed update |
| Results | Delayed update |
| Synchronization | Distributed locks |
| Migratory | Migration |
| Producer-consumer | Eager object movement |
| Read mostly | Broadcast |
| General read-write | Ownership |

Figure 2. Munin's type-specific memory coherence.

modifications to the operating system kernel or particular compiler are required. TreadMarks runs on commonly available Unix systems. It employs an invalidation-based protocol, which allows multiple concurrent writers to modify the page. On the first write to a shared page, DSM software makes a copy *(twin)* that can later be compared to the current copy of the page in order to make a *diff*—a record that contains all modifications to the page. Lazy release consistency does not require *diff* creation on each release (as in the Munin implementation), but allows it to be postponed until next acquire in order to obtain better performance. Experiments were performed using DECstation-5000/240s connected by a 100-Mbps ATM network and a 10-Mbps Ethernet, and good speedups for five SPLASH programs were reported. Results of experiments have shown that latency and bandwidth limitations can be overcome using more efficient communication interfaces.

Unlike Munin, which uses various coherence protocols on a type-specific basis, Midway [BERSH93] supports multiple consistency models (processor, release, entry) that can be dynamically changed within the same program, in order to implement a single consistency model—release consistency. Midway is operational on a cluster of MIPS R3000-based DEC stations, under the Mach OS. At the programming language level, all shared data must be declared and explicitly associated with at least one synchronization object, also declared as an instance of one of Midway's data types, which include locks and barriers. If the necessary labeling information is included, and all accesses to shared data done with appropriate explicit synchronization accesses, sequential consistency can also be achieved. Midway consists of three components: a set of keywords and function calls used to annotate a parallel program, a compiler that generates code that marks shared data as dirty when written to, and a runtime system that implements several consistency models. Runtime system procedure calls associate synchronization objects to runtime data. The control of versions of synchronization objects is done using the associated timestamps, which are reset when data are modified. For all consistency models, Midway uses an update mechanism. Although less efficient with the Ethernet connection, Midway shows close to linear speedups of chosen applications when using the ATM network.

Blizzard is another user-level DSM implementation that also requires some modifications to the operating system kernel [SCHOI94]. It uses Tempest—a user-level communication and memory interface that provides mechanisms necessary for both fine-grained shared memory and message passing. There are three variants of this approach: Blizzard-S, Blizzard-E, and Blizzard-ES. The essence of Blizzard-S, an entirely software variant, is the modification of executable code by inserting a fast routine before each shared memory reference. It is intended for state lookup and access control for the block. If the state check requires some action, an appropriate user handler is invoked. Blizzard-E, on the other hand, uses the machine's memory ECC (error correction code) bits to indicate an *invalid* state of the block by forcing uncorrectable errors. However, a *read-only* state is maintained by enforcing read-only protection at page level by the memory management unit (MMU). Otherwise, *read-write* permission is assumed. The third variant, Blizzard-ES, combines the ECC approach of Blizzard-E for read instructions, and software tests of Blizzard-S for write instructions. Performance evaluation of the three variants for several shared memory benchmarks reveals that Blizzard-S is the most efficient (typically within a factor of two). When compared to a hardware DSM implementation with fine-grain access control (the KSR1 multiprocessor), the typical slowdown of Blizzard is severalfold depending on the application.

## 2. Operating System Software Distributed Shared Memory Implementations

In Mirage [FLEIS89], coherence maintenance is implemented inside the operating system kernel. The prototype consists of VAX 11/750s connected by Ethernet network, using the System V interface. The main contribution introduced by Mirage is that page ownership can be guaranteed for a fixed period of time, called *time window* $\Delta$. In this way thrashing is avoided, and inherent processor locality can be better exploited. The value of the $\Delta$ parameter can be tuned statically or dynamically. Mirage uses the model based on page segmentation. A process that creates a shared segment defines its size, name, and access protection, while the other processes locate and access the segment by name. All requests are sent to the site of segment creation, called the *library site* (Figure 3) where they are queued and sequentially processed. The *clock site*, which provides the most recent copy of the page, is either a writer or one of the readers of the requested page, since the writer and the readers cannot possess copies of the same page simultaneously. Performance evaluation of the worst case example, in which two processes interchangeably perform writes to the same page, has shown that the throughput increase is highly sensitive to the proper choice of the parameter $\Delta$ value.

Clouds [RAMAC91] is an operating system that incorporates software-based DSM management and implements a set of primitives either on top of Unix, or in the context of the object-based operating system kernel Ra. Clouds is implemented on SUN-3 workstations connected via Ethernet. The distributed shared memory consists of objects, composed of segments, that have access attributes: *read-only*, *read-write*, *weak-read*, or *none*. Since the *weak-read* mode allows the node to obtain a copy of the page with no guarantee that the page will not be modified during read, the memory system behavior of Clouds without any specific restrictions leads to inconsistent DSM. Fetching of segments is based on *get*

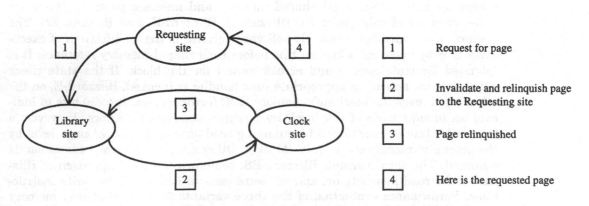

| | |
|---|---|
| 1 | Request for page |
| 2 | Invalidate and relinquish page to the Requesting site |
| 3 | Page relinquished |
| 4 | Here is the requested page |

Figure 3. Write request for a page in Mirage.

and *discard* operations provided by a distributed shared memory controller (DSMC). This software module also offers P and V semaphore primitives as separate operations. The DSMC is, therefore, a part of the Clouds operating system, but implemented outside its kernel Ra. It is invoked by a DSM partition that handles segment requests from both Ra and user objects, and determines whether the request for segment should be satisfied locally by disk partition, or remotely by the distributed shared memory controller. Both DSM and DSMC partitions are also implemented on top of Unix, with minor changes due to the operating system dependencies.

## 3. Programming Language Concepts for Software Distributed Shared Memory

An architecture-independent language, Linda, is introduced in [AHUJA86]. Distributed shared memory in Linda is organized as a "tuple space"—a common pool of user-defined tuples (basic storage and access units consisting of data elements) that are addressed by logical names. Linda provides several special language operators for dealing with such distributed data structures, such as inserting, removing, and reading tuples, and so on. The consistency problem is avoided since a tuple must be removed from the tuple space before an update, and a modified version is reinserted again. By its nature, the Linda environment offers possibilities for process decoupling, transparent communication, and dynamic scheduling. Linda offers the use of replication as a method for problem partitioning. Linda is implemented on shared memory machines (Encore Multimax, Sequent Balance) as well as on loosely coupled systems (S/Net, an Ethernet network of MicroVAXes).

Software DSM implementations are extensively elaborated on in [BAL88]. A new model of shared data objects is proposed (passive objects accessible through predefined operations), and used in the Orca language for distributed programming. The distributed implementation is based on selective replication, migration, and an update mechanism. Different variants of update mechanism can be chosen, depending on the type of communication provided by the underlying distributed system (point-to-point messages, reliable multicast and unreliable multicast messages). Orca is predominantly intended for application programming.

| Name and reference | Type of implementation | Type of algorithm | Consistency model | Granularity unit | Coherence policy |
|---|---|---|---|---|---|
| IVY [LI88] | User-level library + OS modification | MRSW | Sequential | 1 Kbyte | Invalidate |
| Mermaid [ZHOU90] | User-level library + OS modifications | MRSW | Sequential | 1 Kbyte, 8 Kbytes | Invalidate |
| Munin [CARTE91] | Runtime system + linker + library + preprocessor + OS modifications | Type-specific (SRSW, MRSW, MRMW) | Release | Variable-size objects | Type-specific (delayed update, invalidate) |
| Midway [BERSH93] | Runtime system + compiler | MRMW | Entry, release, processor | 4 Kbytes | Update |
| TreadMarks [KELEH94] | User level | MRMW | Lazy release | 4 Kbytes | Update, invalidate |
| Blizzard [SCHOI94] | User-level + OS kernel modification | MRSW | Sequential | 32–128 bytes | Invalidate |

| Mirage [FLEIS89] | OS kernel | MRSW | Sequential | 512 bytes | Invalidate |
|---|---|---|---|---|---|
| Clouds [RAMAC91] | OS, out of kernel | MRSW | Inconsistent, sequential | 8 Kbytes | Discard segment when unlocked |
| Linda [AHUJA86] | Language | MRSW | Sequential | Variable (tuple size) | Implementation dependent |
| Orca [BAL88] | Language | MRSW | Synchronization dependent | Shared data object size | Update |

[AHUJA86]    S. Ahuja, N. Carriero, and D. Gelernter, "Linda and Friends," *Computer,* Vol. 19, No. 8, May 1986, pp. 26–34.

[BAL88]    H.E. Bal and A.S. Tanenbaum, "Distributed Programming with Shared Data," *Proc. Int'l Conf. Computer Languages '88,* IEEE CS Press, Los Alamitos, Calif., 1988, pp. 82–91.

[BERSH93]    B.N. Bershad, M.J. Zekauskas, and W.A. Sawdon, "The Midway Distributed Shared Memory System," *Proc. COMPCON '93,* IEEE CS Press, Los Alamitos, Calif., 1993, pp. 528–537.

[CARTE91]    J.B. Carter, J.K. Bennet, and W. Zwaenepoel, "Implementation and Performance of Munin," *Proc. 13th ACM Symp. Operating Systems Principles,* ACM Press, New York, N.Y., 1991, pp. 152–164.

[FLEIS89]    B. Fleisch and G. Popek, "Mirage: A Coherent Distributed Shared Memory Design," *Proc. 14th ACM Symp. Operating System Principles,* ACM Press, New York, N.Y., 1989, pp. 211–223.

[KELEH94]    P. Keleher et al., "TreadMarks: Distributed Shared Memory on Standard Workstations and Operating Systems," *Proc. USENIX Winter 1994 Conf.,* 1994, pp. 115–132.

[LI88]    K. Li, "IVY: A Shared Virtual Memory System for Parallel Computing," *Proc. 1988 Int'l Conf. Parallel Processing,* Penn State Press, University Park, Pa., 1988, pp. 94–101.

[RAMAC91]    U. Ramachandran and M.Y.A. Khalidi, "An Implementation of Distributed Shared Memory," *Software Practice and Experience,* Vol. 21, No. 5, May 1991, pp. 443–464.

[SCHOI94]    I. Schoinas et al., "Fine-Grain Access Control for Distributed Shared Memory," *Proc. 6th Int'l Conf. Architectural Support for Programming Languages and Operating Systems,* ACM Press, New York, N.Y., 1994, pp. 297–306.

[ZHOU90]    S. Zhou, M. Stumm, and T. McInerney, "Extending Distributed Shared Memory to Heterogeneous Environments," *Proc. 10th Int'l Conf. Distributed Computing Systems,* IEEE CS Press, Los Alamitos, Calif., 1990, pp. 30–37.

## C. Hardware-Level Distributed Shared Memory Implementations

A hardware-implemented DSM mechanism ensures automatic replication of shared data in local memories and processor caches, transparently for software layers. This approach efficiently supports fine-grain sharing. The nonstructured, physical unit of replication and coherence is small, typically cache line. Consequently, a hardware DSM mechanism usually represents an extension of the principles found in cache coherence schemes of scalable shared-memory architectures. Communication requirements are considerably reduced, since detrimental effects of false sharing and thrashing are minimized with finer sharing granularities. Searching and directory functions implemented in hardware are much faster compared to the software-level implementations, and memory access latencies are decreased. However, advanced techniques used for coherence maintenance and latency reduction usually make the design complex and difficult to verify. Therefore, hardware DSM is often used in high-end machines where performance is more important than cost.

According to the memory system architecture, three groups of hardware DSM systems are regarded as especially interesting:

**CC-NUMA**—Cache coherent nonuniform memory access architecture

**COMA**—Cache-only memory architecture

**RMS**—Reflective memory system architecture

### 1. CC-NUMA Distributed Shared Memory Systems

In a CC-NUMA system (Figure 4), the shared virtual address space is statically distributed across local memories of clusters, which can be accessed both by the local processors and by processors from other clusters in the system, although with quite different access latencies. The DSM mechanism relies on directories with organization varying from a full map to different dynamic structures, such as singly or doubly linked lists and trees. The main effort is to achieve high performance (as in full-map schemes) and good scalability provided by reducing the directory storage overhead. To minimize latency, static partitioning of data should be done carefully, so as to maximize the frequency of local accesses. Performance indicators are also highly dependent on the interconnection topology. The invalidation mechanism is typically applied in order to provide consistency, while some relaxed memory consistency model can be used as a source of performance improvement. Typical representatives of this type of DSM approach are Memnet, Dash, and SCI.

Memnet (MEMory as NETwork abstraction)—a ring-based multiprocessor—is one of the earliest hardware DSM systems [DELP91]. The main goal was to avoid costly interprocessor communication via messages and to provide an abstraction of shared memory to applications directly from the network, without kernel OS intervention. The Memnet address space is mapped onto the local memories of each cluster *(reserved area)* in an NUMA fashion. Another part of each local memory is the *cache area,* which is used for replication of 32-byte blocks whose reserved area is in some remote host. The coherence protocol is

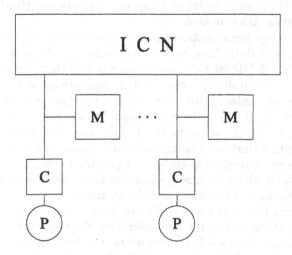

Figure 4. CC-NUMA memory architecture. P, Processor; C, cache; M, memory; ICN, interconnection network.

implemented in hardware state machines of the Memnet device in each cluster—a dual port memory controller on its local bus, and an interface to the ring. On a miss in local memory, the Memnet device sends an appropriate message that circulates on the ring. The message is inspected by each Memnet device on the ring in a snooping manner. The request is satisfied by the nearest cluster with a valid copy, which inserts requested data in the message before forwarding. The write request to a nonexclusive copy results in a message that invalidates other shared copies as it passes through each Memnet device that has a valid copy of that block. Finally, the message is received and removed from the ring by the interface of the cluster that generated it.

Dash (Directory Architecture for SHared memory), a scalable cluster multiprocessor architecture using a directory-based hardware DSM mechanism [LENOS92], also follows the CC-NUMA approach. Each four-processor cluster contains an equal part of the overall system's shared memory (*home* property) and corresponding directory entries. Each processor also has a two-level private cache hierarchy where the locations from other clusters' memories *(remote)* can be replicated or migrated in 16-byte blocks (unlike Memnet, where a part of local memory is used for this purpose). The memory hierarchy of Dash is split into four levels: (1) processor cache, (2) caches of other processors in the local cluster, (3) home cluster (cluster that contains directory and physical memory for a given memory block), and (4) remote cluster (cluster marked by the directory as holding the copy of the block). Coherence maintenance is based on a full-map directory protocol. A memory block can be in one of three states: *uncached* (not cached outside the home cluster), *cached* (one or more unmodified copies in remote clusters), and *dirty* (modified in some remote cluster). In most cases, owing to the property of locality, references can be satisfied inside the local cluster. Othewise, a request is sent to the home cluster for the involved block, which takes some action according to the state found in its directory. Improved performance is achieved by using a relaxed memory consistency model—release consistency, as well as some memory access optimizations. Techniques for reducing memory latency, such as software-controlled prefetching, update, and deliver operations, are also used in order to improve performance. Hardware support for synchronization is also provided.

Memory organization in an SCI-based CC-NUMA DSM system is similar to Dash and data from remote memories can be cached in local caches. Although the IEEE P1596 Scalable Coherent Interface (SCI) [JAMES94] represents an interface standard, rather than a complete system design, among other issues, it defines a scalable directory cache coherence protocol. Instead of centralizing the directory, SCI distributes it among those caches that are currently sharing the data, in the form of doubly linked lists. The directory entry is a shared data structure that may be concurrently accessed by multiple processors. The home memory controller keeps only a pointer to the head of the list and a few status bits for each cache block, while the local cache controllers must store the forward and backward pointers, and the status bits.

A read miss request is always sent to the home memory. The memory controller uses the requester identifier from the request packet to point to the new head of the list. The old head pointer is sent back to the requester along with the data block (if available). It is used by the requester to chain itself as the head of the list, and to request the data from the old head (if not supplied by the home cluster). In the case of write to a nonexclusive block, the request for the ownership is also sent to the home memory. All copies in the system are invalidated by forwarding an invalidation message from the head down the list, and the requester becomes the new head of the list. However, the distribution of individual directory entries increases the latency and complexity of the memory references. To reduce latency and to support additional functions, the SCI working committee has proposed some enhancements, such as converting sharing lists to sharing trees, request combining, support for queue-based locks, and so on.

## 2. COMA Distributed Shared Memory Systems

Cache-only memory architecture (Figure 5) uses local memories of the clusters as huge caches for data blocks from virtual shared address space (attraction memories). There is no physical memory home location predetermined for a particular data item, and it can be replicated and migrated in attraction memories on demand. Therefore, the distribution of data across local memories (caches) is dynamically adaptable to the application behavior. The existing COMAs are characterized by hierarchical network topologies that simplify two main problems in these types of systems: location of a data block and replacement. They are less sensitive to static distribution of data than are NUMA systems. Owing to its cache organization, attraction memories are efficient in reducing capacity and conflict miss rates. On the other hand, the hierarchical structure imposes slightly higher communication and remote miss latencies. A somewhat increased storage overhead for keeping the information typical of cache memory is also inherent to COMA systems. The two most relevant representatives of COMA systems are KSR1 and DDM.

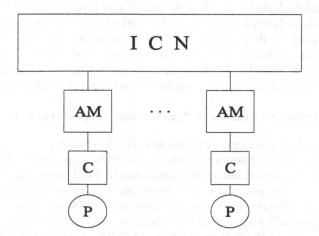

Figure 5. Cache-only memory architecture (COMA). P, Processor; C, cache; AM, attraction memory; ICN, interconnection network.

The KSR1 multiprocessor represents one of the early attempts to make DSM systems available on the market [FRANK93]. It consists of a ring-based hierarchical organization of clusters, each with a local 32-Mbyte cache. The unit of allocation in local caches is a page (16 Kbytes), while the unit of transfer and sharing in local caches is a subpage (128 bytes). The dedicated hardware responsible for locating, copying, and maintaining coherence of subpages in local caches is called the ALLCACHE engine, and it is organized as a hierarchy with directories on intermediate levels. The ALLCACHE engine transparently routes the requests through the hierarchy. Missed accesses are most likely to be satisfied by clusters on the same or next higher level in the hierarchy. In that way, the ALLCACHE organization minimizes the path to locate a particular address. The coherence protocol is invalidation based. Possible states of a subpage within a particular local cache include the following: *exclusive* (only valid copy), *nonexclusive* (owner; multiple copies exist), *copy* (nonowner; valid copy), and *invalid* (not valid, but allocated subpage). Besides these usual states, an *atomic* state is provided for synchronization purposes. Locking and unlocking the subpage are achieved by special instructions. As in all architectures with no main memory, where all data are stored in caches, the problem of the replacement of cache lines arises. There is no default destination for the line in the main memory, so the choice of a new destination and the directory update can be complicated and time consuming. Besides that, propagation of requests through hierarchical directories is responsible for longer latencies.

The DDM (Data Diffusion Machine) is another COMA multiprocessor [HAGER92]. The DDM prototype is made of four-processor clusters with an attraction memory and an asynchronous split-transaction bus. Attaching a directory on top of the local DDM bus, to enable its communication with a higher level bus of the same type, is the way DDM builds a large system with directory/bus-based hierarchy (as opposed to the KSR1 ring-based hierarchy). The directory is a set-associative memory that stores the state information for all items in attraction memories below it, but without data. The employed coherence protocol is of the snoopy write-invalidate type, which handles the attraction of data on read, erases the replicated data on write, and manages the replacement when a set in an attraction memory is full. An item can be in seven states; three of them correspond to Invalid, Exclusive, and Valid (typical for the snoopy protocols), while the state Dirty is replaced with a set of four transient states needed to remember the outstanding requests on the split-transaction bus. Transactions that cannot be completed on a lower level are directed through the directory to the level above. Similarly, the directory recognizes the transactions that need to be serviced by a subsystem and routes them onto the level below it.

## 3.  Reflective Memory Distributed Shared Memory Systems

Reflective memory systems are DSM systems with a hardware-implemented update mechanism designed for fine data granularity. The global shared address space is formed out of the segments in local memories, which are designated as shared, and mapped to this space through programmable mapping tables in each cluster (Figure 6). Hence, the parts of this shared space are selectively replicated ("reflected") across different clusters. Coherence maintenance of shared regions is based on the full-replication, MRMW algorithm. Each write to an address in this shared address space in a cluster is propagated using a broadcast or mul-

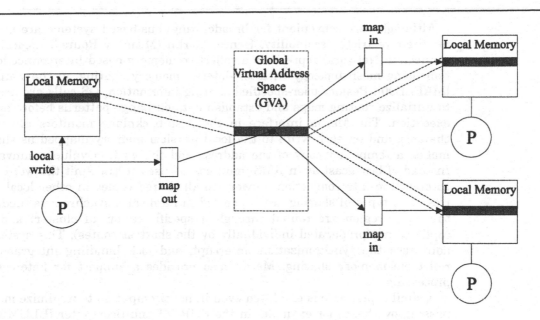

Figure 6. Reflective memory system (RMS) architecture.

ticast mechanism to all other clusters to which the same address is mapped, to keep it updated in a nondemand, anticipatory manner. The processor does not stall on writes, and computation is overlapped with communication. This is the source of performance improvement typical of relaxed memory consistency models. Also, there is no contention and long latencies as in typical shared memory systems, since unrestricted access to shared data and simultaneous accesses to local copies are ensured. On the other hand, all reads from the shared memory are local, with a deterministic access time. The principle of this DSM mechanism is similar to the write-update cache coherence protocols. Typical reflective memory systems are RMS and Merlin.

The reflective memory concept is applied in some existing systems with different clusters and network topologies. Since broadcast is the most appropriate mechanism for updating of replicated segments, the shared bus topology is especially convenient for the reflective memory architecture. A number of bus-based reflective memory systems (RMS), for example, the Encore Infinity [LUCCI95], have been developed by the Encore Computer Corporation for a wide range of applications. These systems typically consist of a lower number of minicomputer clusters connected by an RM bus—a "write-only" bus since traffic on it consists only of word-based distributed write transfers (address + value of the data word). Some later enhancements also allow for block-based updates (memory channel). The unit of replication is an 8-Kbyte segment. Segments are treated as "windows" that can be open (mapped into reflective shared space) or closed (disabled for reflection and exclusively accessed by each particular cluster). A replicated segment can be mapped to different addresses in each cluster. Therefore, the translation map tables are provided separately for the transmit (for each block of local memory), and receive (for each block of reflected address space) sides.

Although very convenient for broadcasting, bus-based systems are notorious for their restricted scalability. Hence, Merlin (MEmory Routed, Logical Interconnection Network) represents a reflective memory-based interconnection system using mesh topology with low-latency memory sharing on the word basis [MAPLE90]. Besides user-specified sharing information, OS calls are necessary to initialize routing maps and establish data exchange patterns before program execution. The Merlin interface in the host backplane monitors all memory changes, and on each write to the local physical memory mapped as shared it makes a temporary copy of the address and the written value noninvasively. Instead of broadcast as in RMS, multicast is used to transmit the word packet through the interconnection network to all shared copies in other local memories. Two types of sharing are supported in hardware: synchronous (updates to the same region are routed through a specific canonical cluster) and rapid (updates are propagated individually by the shortest routes). This system also addresses the synchronization, interrupt, and lock handling integrated with reflective memory sharing. Merlin also provides a support for heterogeneous processing.

A similar principle is employed even in multicomputers to minimize message-passing overhead, for example, in the SHRIMP multicomputer [BLUMR94]. A virtual memory-mapped network interface implements an "automatic update" feature in hardware. On analyzing communication patterns, it was noticed that most messages from a send buffer are targeted to the same destination. Therefore, after some page (send buffer) is mapped out to some other's cluster memory (receive buffer), each local write (message) to this page is also immediately propagated to this destination. There are two implementations of automatic updates: single-write and block-write. In this way, passing the message avoids any software involvement.

| Name and reference | Cluster configuration | Network | Type of algorithm | Consistency model | Granularity unit (bytes) | Coherence policy |
|---|---|---|---|---|---|---|
| Memnet [DELP91] | Single processor, Memnet device | Token ring | MRSW | Sequential | 32 | Invalidate |
| Dash [LENOS92] | SGI 4D/340 (4 PEs, 2-L caches), local memory | Mesh | MRSW | Release | 16 | Invalidate |
| SCI [JAMES94] | Arbitrary | Arbitrary | MRSW | Sequential | 16 | Invalidate |
| KSR1 [FRANK93] | 64-bit custom PE, I+D caches, 32-Mbyte local memory | Ring-based hierarchy | MRSW | Sequential | 128 | Invalidate |
| DDM [HAGER92] | 4 MC88110s, 2-L caches, 8- to 32-Mbyte local memory | Bus-based hierarchy | MRSW | Sequential | 16 | Invalidate |
| Merlin [MAPLE90] | 40-MIPS computer | Mesh | MRMW | Processor | 8 | Update |
| RMS [LUCCI95] | 1–4 processors, caches, 256-Mbyte local memory | RM bus | MRMW | Processor | 4 | Update |

[DELP91]     G. Delp, D. Farber, and R. Minnich, "Memory as a Network Abstraction," *IEEE Network*, July 1991, pp. 34–41.

[FRANK93]    S. Frank, H. Burkhardt III, and J. Rothnie, "The KSR1: Bridging the Gap between Shared Memory and MPPs," *Proc. COMPCON '93*, IEEE CS Press, Los Alamitos, Calif., 1993, pp. 285–294.

[HAGER92]    E. Hagersten, A. Landin, and S. Haridi, "DDM—A Cache-Only Memory Architecture," *Computer*, Vol. 25, No. 9, Sept. 1992, pp. 44–54.

[JAMES94]    D.V. James, "The Scalable Coherent Interface: Scaling to High-Performance Systems," *Proc. COMPCON '94: Digest of Papers*, IEEE CS Press, Los Alamitos, Calif., 1994, pp. 64–71.

[LENOS92]    D. Lenoski et al., "The Stanford Dash Multiprocessor," *Computer*, Vol. 25, No. 3, Mar. 1992, pp. 63–79.

[LUCCI95]    S. Lucci et al., "Reflective-Memory Multiprocessor," *Proc. 28th IEEE/ACM Hawaii Int'l Conf. System Sciences*, IEEE CS Press, Los Alamitos, Calif., 1995, pp. 85–94.

[MAPLE90]    C. Maples and L. Wittie, "Merlin: A Superglue for Multicomputer Systems," *Proc. COMPCON '90*, IEEE CS Press, Los Alamitos, Calif., 1990, pp. 73–81.

## D.  Hybrid Level Distributed Shared Memory Implementations

During the evolution of this field, numerous entirely hardware or software implementations of DSM mechanism were proposed. However, even in entirely hardware DSM approaches, there are software-controlled features explicitly visible to the programmer for memory reference optimization (for example, prefetch, update, and deliver in Dash; prefetch and poststore in KSR1). On the other side, many purely software solutions require some hardware support (for example, virtual memory management hardware in IVY; error correction code in Blizzard-E). As can be expected, neither approach has all the advantages. Therefore, it seemed quite natural to employ hybrid methods, with predominantly or partially combined hardware and software elements, in order to balance the cost/complexity trade-offs. A solution implemented in some industrial computers provided a DSM-like paradigm in software executed by a microcontroller located on a separate communication board [PROTI93].

One of the typical hybrid approaches is to achieve replication and migration of data from a shared virtual address space across the clusters in software, while their coherence management is implemented in hardware. PLUS is an example of such a system [BISIA90]. In PLUS, software is responsible for data placement and replacement in local memories in units of 4-Kbyte pages. However, memory coherence for replicated data is maintained on the 32-bit word basis by a nondemand, write-update protocol implemented in hardware. Replicated instances of a page are chained into an ordered, singly linked list, headed with the *master* copy, in order to ensure the propagation of updates to all copies. Since a relaxed consistency model is assumed, writes are nonblocking, and the *fence* operation is available to the user for explicit strong ordering of writes. In order to optimize the synchronization, PLUS provides a set of specialized interlocked read-modify-write operations called *delayed* operations. Their latency is hidden by splitting them into *issue* and *verify* phases, and allowing them to proceed concurrently with regular processing.

Some solutions to DSM issues in another hybrid DSM system—Galactica Net [WILSO94]—are similar to those applied in PLUS. Pages from virtual address space are replicated on demand under control of virtual memory software, implemented in the Mach operating system. In addition, there is hardware support for the virtual memory mechanism, realized through a block transfer engine, which can rapidly transfer pages in reaction to page faults. A page can be in one of three states: *read-only, private,* and *update,* denoted by tables maintained by the OS. The coherence for writable shared pages (*update* mode) is kept by a write-update protocol implemented entirely in hardware. All copies of a shared page in *update* mode are organized in a *virtual sharing ring*—a linked list used for forwarding of updates. Virtual shared rings are realized using update routing tables kept in the network interface of each cluster, and also maintained by software. Therefore, write references to pages in update mode are detected by hardware and propagated according to the table. Because of the update mechanism, for some applications, broadcast of excessive updates can produce a large amount of traffic. Besides that, the unit of sharing is quite large, and false sharing effects can adversely affect performance. On recognizing an actual reference pattern, Galactica Net can dynamically switch from a hardware update scheme to software invalidate coherence (another hybrid and adaptive feature), using a competitive protocol based on per-page update counters. When remote updates to a page far exceed local references, an interrupt is raised, and the OS invalidates this page and removes it from its sharing ring in order to prevent the unnecessary traffic to unused copies.

MIT's Alewife is a specific hybrid system that implements the LimitLESS directory protocol. This protocol represents a hardware-based coherence scheme supported by a software mechanism [CHAIK94]. Directory entries contain only a limited number of hardware pointers, in order to reduce the storage requirements—the design assumes that it is sufficient in the vast majority of cases. Exceptional circumstances, when more pointers are needed, are handled in software. In those infrequent cases, an interrupt is generated, and a full-map directory for the block is emulated in software. A fast trap mechanism provides support for this feature, and a multiple context concept is used for hiding the memory latency. The main advantage of this approach is that the applied directory coherence protocol is storage efficient, while performing about as well as the full-map directory protocol.

Unlike Alewife, the basic idea behind the FLASH multiprocessor is to implement the memory coherence protocol in software, but to move the burden of its execution from the main processor to an auxiliary protocol processor—MAGIC (Memory And General Interconnection Controller) [KUSKI94]. This specialized programmable controller allows for efficient execution of protocol actions in a pipelined manner, avoiding context switches on the main processor. This approach, which also ensures great flexibility in experimenting and testing, is followed in some other systems, for example the network interface processor (NP) in Typhoon [REINH94]. The NP uses a hardware-assisted dispatch mechanism to invoke a user-level procedure to handle some events.

To improve performance, a hybrid approach called *cooperative shared memory* is based on programmer-supplied annotations [HILL93]. The programmer identifies the segments that use shared data with corresponding *Check-In* (exclusive or shared access) and *Check-Out* (relinquish) annotations, executed as memory system directives. These performance primitives do not change program semantics (even misapplied), but reduce unintended communication caused by thrashing and false sharing. Cooperative *prefetch* can also be used to hide the memory latency. The CICO programming model is completely and efficiently supported in hardware by a minimal directory protocol $Dir_1SW$. Traps to the system software occur only on memory accesses that violate the CICO.

A hybrid DSM protocol presented in [CHAND93] tries to combine the advantages of a software protocol for coarse-grain data regions and a hardware coherence scheme for fine-grain sharing in a tightly coupled system. The software part of the protocol is similar to Midway. The programmer is expected to identify explicitly the *regions*—coarse-grain data structures. Usage annotations (for example, *BeginRead/EndRead, BeginWrite/EndWrite*) are then provided to identify program segments where the data from a certain region are safely referenced (without modification from other processors). Coherence of annotated data is kept by library routines invoked by these annotations. Coherence of nonannotated data is managed by means of a directory-based hardware protocol. Both software and hardware components of the protocol use the invalidation policy. The variable-size coherence unit of the software part of the protocol eliminates the problem of false sharing, while reducing remote misses by efficient bulk transfers of coarse-grain data and their replication in local memories. The protocol is also insensitive to initial data placement. Just like in Midway, Munin, and CICO, the main disadvantage is the burden put on the programmer to insert the annotations, although this appears to be not so complicated since this information about the data usage is naturally known.

The implementation of automatic update release consistency (AURC) turns Shrimp [BLUMR96] into an efficient hybrid DSM system. In this approach, only one copy of a page is kept consistent, using fine-grain automatic updates performed by hardware, after necessary software mappings. All other copies are kept consistent using an invalidation-based software protocol. An AURC refinement called *scope consistency* [IFTOD96] represents a successful compromise between entry and lazy release consistency.

Finally, since message passing and shared memory machines have been converging recently, some efforts have been made to integrate these two communication paradigms within a single system (Alewife, Cray T3D, FLASH, Typhoon). In addition to the above-mentioned coherence protocol, Alewife also allows explicit sending of messages in a shared memory program. Messages are delivered via an interrupt and dispatched in software. Cray T3D is also a physically distributed memory machine with hardware-implemented logically shared memory. It also integrates message passing extensively supported by DMA. Besides the Dash-like software-implemented directory cache coherence protocol, FLASH also provides message passing with low overhead, owing to some hardware support. Accesses to block transfer are allowed to the user without sacrificing protection, while the interaction of message data with cache coherence is ensured. Typhoon is a proposed hardware implementation especially suited for the Tempest interface—a set of user-level mechanisms that can be used to modify the semantics and performance of shared memory operations. Tempest consists of four types of user-level mechanisms: low-overhead messages, bulk data transfers, virtual memory management, and fine-grain access control. For example, user-level transparent shared memory can be implemented using *Stache*—a user library with Tempest fine-grain access mechanisms. *Stache* replicates the remote data in part of a cluster's local memory according to a COMA-like policy. It maps virtual addresses of shared data to local physical memory at page granularity, but maintains coherence at the block level. A coherence protocol similar to LimitLESS is implemented entirely in software.

| Name and reference | Cluster configuration and network | Type of algorithm | Consistency model | Granularity unit | Coherence policy |
|---|---|---|---|---|---|
| PLUS [BISIA90] | M88000, 32-Kbyte cache, 8- to 32-Mbyte local memory, mesh | MRMW | Processor | 4 Kbytes | Update |
| Galactica Net [WILSO94] | 4 M88110s, 2-L caches, 256-Mbyte local memory, mesh | MRMW | Multiple | 8 Kbytes | Update/Invalidate |
| Alewife [CHAIK94] | Sparcle PE, 64-Kbytes cache, 4-Mbyte local memory, CMMU, mesh | MRSW | Sequential | 16 bytes | Invalidate |
| FLASH [KUSKI94] | MIPS T5, I+D caches, MAGIC controller, mesh | MRSW | Release | 128 bytes | Invalidate |
| Typhoon [REINH94] | SuperSPARC, 2-L caches, NP controller | MRSW | Custom | 32 bytes | Invalidate custom |
| Hybrid DSM [CHAND93] | FLASH-like | MRSW | Release | Variable | Invalidate |
| Shrimp [IFTOD96] | 16 Pentium PC nodes, Intel Paragon routing network | MRSW | AURC, Scope | 4 Kbytes | Update/Invalidate |

[BISIA90]   R. Bisani and M. Ravishankar, "PLUS: A Distributed Shared-Memory System," *Proc. 17th Ann. Int'l Symp. Computer Architecture*, IEEE CS Press, Los Alamitos, Calif., 1990, pp. 115–124.

[CHAIK94]   D. Chaiken, J. Kubiatowicz, and A. Agarwal, "Software-Extended Coherent Shared Memory: Performance and Cost," *Proc. 21st Ann. Int'l Symp. Computer Architecture*, IEEE CS Press, Los Alamitos, Calif., 1994, pp. 314–324.

[CHAND93]   R. Chandra et al., "Performance Evaluation of Hybrid Hardware and Software Distributed Shared Memory Protocols," CSL-TR-93-597, Stanford University, Stanford, Calif., Dec. 1993.

[IFTOD96]   L. Iftode, J. Pal Singh, and K. Li, "Scope Consistency: A Bridge between Release Consistency and Entry Consistency," *Proc. 8th Ann. Symp. Parallel Algorithms and Architectures*, 1996, pp. 277–287.

[KUSKI94]   J. Kuskin et al., "The Stanford FLASH Multiprocessor," *Proc. 21st Ann. Int'l Symp. Computer Architecture*, IEEE CS Press, Los Alamitos, Calif., 1994, pp. 302–313.

[REINH94]   S. Reinhardt, J. Larus, and D. Wood, "Tempest and Typhoon: User-Level Shared Memory," *Proc. 21st Ann. Int'l Symp. Computer Architecture*, IEEE CS Press, Los Alamitos, Calif., 1994, pp. 325–336.

[WILSO94]   A. Wilson, R. LaRowe, and M. Teller, "Hardware Assist for Distributed Shared Memory," *Proc. 13th Int'l Conf. Distributed Computing Systems*, IEEE CS Press, Los Alamitos, Calif., 1993, pp. 246–255.

## E.  Conclusion

This survey provides extensive coverage of relevant topics in an increasingly important area—distributed shared memory computing. A special attempt has been made to give a broad overview of various approaches, presented according to the implementation level of the DSM mechanism. Because of the combined advantages of the shared memory and distributed systems, DSM approaches appear to be a viable step toward large-scale high-performance systems with reduced cost in parallel software development. In spite of this, the building of successful commercial systems that follow the DSM paradigm is still in its infancy; and research prototypes still prevail. Therefore, the DSM field remains a very active research area. Some of the promising research directions include (1) improving the DSM algorithms and mechanisms, and adapting them to the characteristics of typical applications and system configurations, (2) synergistic combining of hardware and software DSM implementations, (3) integration of the shared memory and message-passing programming paradigms, (4) creating new and innovative system architectures (especially in the memory system), (5) combining multiple consistency models, and so on. From this point of view, further investments in exploring, developing, and implementing DSM systems seem to be quite justified and promising.

# References

[BLACK89]   D.L. Black, A. Gupta, and W. Weber, "Competitive Management of Distributed Shared Memory," *Proc. COMPCON '89*, IEEE CS Press, Los Alamitos, Calif., 1989, pp. 184–190.

[BLUMR94]   M. Blumrich et al., "Virtual Memory Mapped Network Interface for the SHRIMP Multicomputer," *Proc. 21st Int'l Symp. Computer Architecture*, IEEE CS Press, Los Alamitos, Calif., 1994, pp. 142–153.

[FLYNN95]   M.J. Flynn, *Computer Architecture: Pipelined and Parallel Processor Design*, Jones and Bartlett Publishers, Boston, Mass., 1995.

[GHARA90]   K. Gharachorloo et al., "Memory Consistency and Event Ordering in Scalable Shared-Memory Multiprocessors," *Proc. 17th Ann. Int'l Symp. Computer Architecture*, IEEE CS Press, Los Alamitos, Calif., 1990, pp. 15–26.

[HILL93]   M. Hill, J. Larus, and S. Reinhardt, "Cooperative Shared Memory: Software and Hardware for Scalable Multiprocessors," *ACM Trans. Computer Systems*, Nov. 1993, pp. 300–318.

[KELEH92]   P. Keleher, A.L. Cox, and W. Zwaenepoel, "Lazy Release Consistency for Software Distributed Shared Memory," *Proc. 19th Ann. Int'l Symp Computer Architecture*, IEEE CS Press, Los Alamitos, Calif., 1992, pp. 13–21.

[KESSL89]   R.E. Kessler and M. Livny, "An Analysis of Distributed Shared Memory Algorithms," *Proc. 9th Int'l Conf. Distributed Computing Systems*, IEEE CS Press, Los Alamitos, Calif., 1989, pp. 498–505.

[LIHUD89]   K. Li and P. Hudak, "Memory Coherence in Shared Virtual Memory Systems," *ACM Trans. Computer Systems*, Vol. 7, No. 4, Nov. 1989, pp. 321–359.

[LO94]   V. Lo, "Operating System Enhancements for Distributed Shared Memory," *Advances in Computers*, Vol. 39, 1994, pp. 191–237.

[PROTI93]   J. Protić and M. Aleksić, "An Example of Efficient Message Protocol for Industrial LAN," *Microprocessing and Microprogramming*, Vol. 37, Jun. 1993, pp. 45–48.

[PROTI95]   J. Protić, M. Tomašević, and V. Milutinović, "A Survey of Distributed Shared Memory: Concepts and Systems," Technical Report No. ETF-TR-95-157, Department of Computer Engineering, Univ. Belgrade, Belgrade, Yugoslavia, July 1995.

[PROTI96]   J. Protić, M. Tomašević, and V. Milutinović, "Distributed Shared Memory: Concepts and Systems," *Parallel & Distributed Technology*, Vol. 4, No. 2, 1996, pp. 63–79.

[STUM90]   M. Stumm and S. Zhou, "Algorithms Implementing Distributed Shared Memory," *Computer*, Vol. 23, No. 5, May 1990, pp. 54–64.

[TARTA95]   I. Tartalja and V. Milutinović, "A Survey of Software Solutions for Maintenance of Cache Consistency in Shared Memory Multiprocessors," *Proc. 28th Ann. Hawaii Int'l Conf. System Sciences*, IEEE CS Press, Los Alamitos, Calif., 1995, pp. 272–282.

[TOMAS94a]   M. Tomašević and V. Milutinović, "Hardware Approaches to Cache Coherence in Shared-Memory Multiprocessors, Part 1 (Basic Issues)," *IEEE MICRO*, Vol. 14, No. 5, Oct. 1994, pp. 52–59.

[TOMAS94b]   M. Tomašević and V. Milutinović, "Hardware Approaches to Cache Coherence in Shared-Memory Multiprocessors, Part 2 (Advanced Issues)," *IEEE MICRO*, Vol. 14, No. 6, Dec. 1994, pp. 61–66.

# Distributed Shared Memory: A Survey of Issues and Algorithms

Bill Nitzberg and Virginia Lo, University of Oregon

**Distributed shared-memory systems implement the shared-memory abstraction on multicomputer architectures, combining the scalability of network-based architectures with the convenience of shared-memory programming.**

As we slowly approach the physical limits of processor and memory speed, it is becoming more attractive to use multiprocessors to increase computing power. Two kinds of parallel processors have become popular: tightly coupled shared-memory multiprocessors and distributed-memory multiprocessors. A tightly coupled multiprocessor system — consisting of multiple CPUs and a single global physical memory — is more straightforward to program because it is a natural extension of a single-CPU system. However, this type of multiprocessor has a serious bottleneck: Main memory is accessed via a common bus — a serialization point — that limits system size to tens of processors.

Distributed-memory multiprocessors, however, do not suffer from this drawback. These systems consist of a collection of independent computers connected by a high-speed interconnection network. If designers choose the network topology carefully, the system can contain many orders of magnitude more processors than a tightly coupled system. Because all communication between concurrently executing processes must be performed over the network in such a system, until recently the programming model was limited to a message-passing paradigm. However, recent systems have implemented a shared-memory abstraction on top of message-passing distributed-memory systems. The shared-memory abstraction gives these systems the illusion of physically shared memory and allows programmers to use the shared-memory paradigm.

As Figure 1 shows, distributed shared memory provides a virtual address space shared among processes on loosely coupled processors. The advantages offered by DSM include ease of programming and portability achieved through the shared-memory programming paradigm, the low cost of distributed-memory machines, and scalability resulting from the absence of hardware bottlenecks.

DSM has been an active area of research since the early 1980s, although its foundations in cache coherence and memory management have been extensively studied for many years. DSM research goals and issues are similar to those of research in multiprocessor caches or networked file systems, memories for nonuniform memory access multiprocessors, and management systems for distributed or replicated databases.[1] Because of this similarity, many algorithms and lessons learned in these domains can be transferred to DSM systems and vice versa.

Reprinted from *Computer*, Vol. 24, No. 8, Aug. 1991, pp. 52–60.

However, each of the above systems has unique features (such as communication latency), so each must be considered separately.

The advantages of DSM can be realized with reasonably low runtime overhead. DSM systems have been implemented using three approaches (some systems use more than one approach):

(1) hardware implementations that extend traditional caching techniques to scalable architectures,

(2) operating system and library implementations that achieve sharing and coherence through virtual memory-management mechanisms, and

(3) compiler implementations where shared accesses are automatically converted into synchronization and coherence primitives.

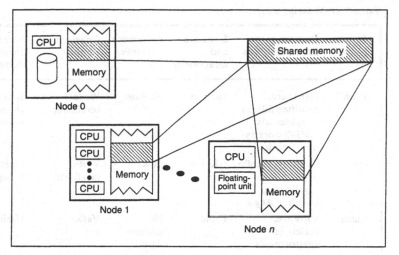

**Figure 1. Distributed shared memory.**

These systems have been designed on common networks of workstations or minicomputers, special-purpose message-passing machines (such as the Intel iPSC/2), custom hardware, and even heterogeneous systems.

This article gives an integrated overview of important DSM issues: memory coherence, design choices, and implementation methods. In our presentation, we use examples from the DSM systems listed and briefly described in the sidebar on page 55. Table 1 compares how design issues are handled in a selected subset of the systems.

## Design choices

A DSM system designer must make choices regarding structure, granularity, access, coherence semantics, scalability, and heterogeneity. Examination of how designers handled these issues in several real implementations of DSM shows the intricacies of such a system.

**Structure and granularity.** The structure and granularity of a DSM system are closely related. Structure refers to the layout of the shared data in memory. Most DSM systems do not structure memory (it is a linear array of words), but some structure the data as objects, language types, or even an associative memory. Granularity refers to the size of the unit of sharing: byte, word, page, or complex data structure.

Ivy,[2] one of the first transparent DSM

systems, implemented shared memory as virtual memory. This memory was unstructured and was shared in 1-Kbyte pages. In systems implemented using the virtual memory hardware of the underlying architecture, it is convenient to choose a multiple of the hardware page size as the unit of sharing. Mirage[3] extended Ivy's single shared-memory space to support a paged segmentation scheme. Users share arbitrary-size regions of memory (segments) while the system maintains the shared space in pages.

Hardware implementations of DSM typically support smaller grain sizes. For example, Dash[4] and Memnet[5] also support unstructured sharing, but the unit of sharing is 16 and 32 bytes respectively — typical cache line sizes. Plus[6] is somewhat of a hybrid: The unit of replication is a page, while the unit of coherence is a 32-bit word.

Because shared-memory programs provide locality of reference, a process is likely to access a large region of its shared address space in a small amount of time. Therefore, larger "page" sizes reduce paging overhead. However, sharing may also cause contention, and the larger the page size, the greater the likelihood that more than one process will require access to a page. A smaller page reduces the possibility of *false sharing*, which occurs when two unrelated variables (each used by different processes) are placed in the same page. The page appears shared, even though the

original variables were not. Another factor affecting the choice of page size is the need to keep directory information about the pages in the system: the smaller the page size, the larger the directory.

A method of structuring the shared memory is by data type. With this method, shared memory is structured as objects in distributed object-oriented systems, as in the Emerald, Choices, and Clouds[7] systems; or it is structured as variables in the source language, as in the Shared Data-Object Model and Munin systems. Because with these systems the sizes of objects and data types vary greatly, the grain size varies to match the application. However, these systems can still suffer from false sharing when different parts of an object (for example, the top and bottom halves of an array) are accessed by distinct processes.

Another method is to structure the shared memory like a database. Linda,[8] a system that has such a model, orders its shared memory as an associative memory called a *tuple space*. This structure allows the location of data to be separated from its value, but it also requires programmers to use special access functions to interact with the shared-memory space. In most other systems, access to shared data is transparent.

**Coherence semantics.** For programmers to write correct programs on a shared-memory machine, they must understand how parallel memory updates are propagated throughout the

Table 1. DSM design issues.

| System Name | Current Implementation | Structure and Granularity | Coherence Semantics | Coherence Protocol | Sources of Improved Performance | Support for Synchronization | Hetero-geneous Support |
|---|---|---|---|---|---|---|---|
| Dash | Hardware, modified Silicon Graphics Iris 4D/340 worksta-tions, mesh | 16 bytes | Release | Write-invalidate | Relaxed coherence, prefetching | Queued locks, atomic incre-mentation and decrementation | No |
| Ivy | Software, Apollo workstations, Apollo ring, modified Aegis | 1-Kbyte pages | Strict | Write-invalidate | Pointer chain collapse, selec-tive broadcast | Synchronized pages, sema-phores, event counts | No |
| Linda | Software, variety of environments | Tuples | No mutable data | Varied | Hashing | | ? |
| Memnet | Hardware, token ring | 32 bytes | Strict | Write-invalidate | Vectored in-terrupt support of control flow | | No |
| Mermaid | Software, Sun workstations DEC Firefly multiprocessors, Mermaid/native operating system | 8 Kbytes (Sun), 1 Kbyte (Firefly) | Strict | Write-invalidate | | Messages for semaphores and signal/wait | Yes |
| Mirage | Software, VAX 11/750, Ether-net, Locus dis-tributed operat-ing system, Unix System V interface | 512-byte pages | Strict | Write-invalidate | Kernel-level implementa-tion, time window coherence protocol | Unix System V semaphores | No |
| Munin | Software, Sun workstations, Ethernet, Unix System V kernel and Presto paral-lel programming environment | Objects | Weak | Type-specific (delayed write update for read-mostly protocol) | Delayed update queue | Synchronized objects | No |
| Plus | Hardware and software, Motorola 88000, Caltech mesh, Plus kernel | Page for sharing, word for coherence | Processor | Nondemand write-update | Delayed operations | Complex synchronization instructions | No |
| Shiva | Software, Intel iPSC/2, hypercube, Shiva/native operating system | 4-Kbyte pages | Strict | Write-invalidate | Data structure compaction, memory as backing store | Messages for semaphores and signal/wait | No |

system. The most intuitive semantics for memory coherence is *strict consistency*. (Although "coherence" and "consistency" are used somewhat interchangeably in the literature, we use coherence as the general term for the semantics of memory operations, and consistency to refer to a specific kind of memory coherence.) In a system with strict consistency, a read operation returns the most recently written value. However, "most recently" is an ambig-uous concept in a distributed system. For this reason, and to improve perfor-mance, some DSM systems provide only a reduced form of memory coherence. For example, Plus provides processor consistency, and Dash provides only release consistency. In accordance with the RISC philosophy, both of these systems have mechanisms for forcing coherence, but their use must be explicitly specified by higher level software (a compiler) or perhaps even the programmer.

Relaxed coherence semantics allows more efficient shared access because it requires less synchronization and less data movement. However, programs that depend on a stronger form of coherence may not perform correctly if executed in a system that supports only a weaker form. Figure 2 gives brief definitions of strict, sequential, processor, weak, and release consistency, and illustrates the hierarchical relationship among these types of coherence. Table 1 indicates the coherence semantics supported by some current DSM systems.

**Figure 2. Intuitive definitions of memory coherence. The arrows point from stricter to weaker consistencies.**

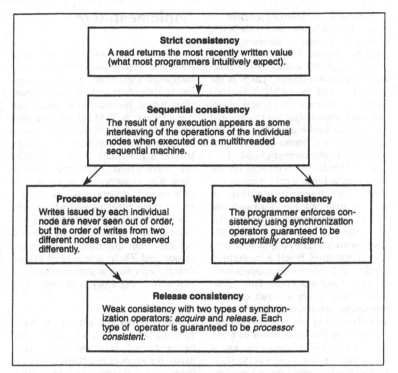

**Strict consistency**
A read returns the most recently written value (what most programmers intuitively expect).

**Sequential consistency**
The result of any execution appears as some interleaving of the operations of the individual nodes when executed on a multithreaded sequential machine.

**Processor consistency**
Writes issued by each individual node are never seen out of order, but the order of writes from two different nodes can be observed differently.

**Weak consistency**
The programmer enforces consistency using synchronization operators guaranteed to be *sequentially consistent*.

**Release consistency**
Weak consistency with two types of synchronization operators: *acquire* and *release*. Each type of operator is guaranteed to be *processor consistent*.

## DSM systems

This partial listing gives the name of the DSM system, the principal developers of the system, the site and duration of their research, and a brief description of the system. Table 1 gives more information about the systems followed with an asterisk.

**Agora** (Bisiani and Forin, Carnegie Mellon University, 1987- ): A heterogeneous DSM system that allows data structures to be shared across machines. Agora was the first system to support weak consistency.

**Amber** (Chase, Feeley, and Levy, University of Washington, 1988- ): An object-based DSM system in which sharing is performed by migrating processes to data as well as data to processes.

**Capnet** (Tam and Farber, University of Delaware, 1990- ): An extension of DSM to a wide area network.

**Choices** (Johnston and Campbell, University of Illinois, 1988- ): DSM incorporated into a hierarchical object-oriented distributed operating system.

**Clouds** (Ramachandran and Khalidi, Georgia Institute of Technology, 1987- ): An object-oriented distributed operating system where objects can migrate.

**Dash\*** (Lenoski, Laudon, Gharachorloo, Gupta, and Hennessy, Stanford University, 1988- ): A hardware implementation of DSM with a directory-based coherence protocol. Dash provides release consistency.

**Emerald** (Jul, Levy, Hutchinson, and Black, University of Washington, 1986-1988): An object-oriented language and system that indirectly supports DSM through object mobility.

**Ivy\*** (Li, Yale University, 1984-1986): An early page-oriented DSM on a network of Apollo workstations.

**Linda\*** (Carriero and Gelernter, Yale University, 1982- ): A shared associative object memory with access functions. Linda can be implemented for many languages and machines.

**Memnet\*** (Delp and Farber, University of Delaware, 1986-1988): A hardware implementation of DSM implemented on a 200-Mbps token ring used to broadcast invalidates and read requests.

**Mermaid\*** (Stumm, Zhou, Li, and Wortman, University of Toronto and Princeton University, 1988-1991): A heterogeneous DSM system where the compiler forces shared pages to contain a single data type. Type conversion is performed on reference.

**Mether** (Minnich and Farber, Supercomputing Research Center, Bowie, Md., 1990- ): A transparent DSM built on SunOS 4.0. Mether allows applications to access an inconsistent state for efficiency.

**Mirage\*** (Fleisch and Popek, University of California at Los Angeles, 1987-1989): A kernel-level implementation of DSM. Mirage reduces thrashing by prohibiting a page from being stolen before a minimum amount of time (Δ) has elapsed.

**Munin\*** (Bennett, Carter, and Zwaenepoel, Rice University, 1989- ): An object-based DSM system that investigates type-specific coherence protocols.

**Plus\*** (Bisiani and Ravishankar, Carnegie Mellon University, 1988- ): A hardware implementation of DSM. Plus uses a write-update coherence protocol and performs replication only by program request.

**Shared Data-Object Model** (Bal, Kaashoek, and Tannenbaum, Vrije University, Amsterdam, The Netherlands, 1988- ): A DSM implementation on top of the Amoeba distributed operating system.

**Shiva\*** (Li and Schaefer, Princeton University, 1988- ): An Ivy-like DSM system for the Intel iPSC/2 hypercube.

**Scalability.** A theoretical benefit of DSM systems is that they scale better than tightly coupled shared-memory multiprocessors. The limits of scalability are greatly reduced by two factors: central bottlenecks (such as the bus of a tightly coupled shared-memory multiprocessor), and global common knowledge operations and storage (such as broadcast messages or full directories, whose sizes are proportional to the number of nodes).

Li and Hudak[2] went through several iterations to refine a coherence protocol for Ivy before arriving at their dynamic distributed-manager algorithm, which avoids centralized bottlenecks. However, Ivy and most other DSM systems are currently implemented on top of Ethernet (itself a centralized bottleneck), which can support only about 100 nodes at a time. This limitation is most likely a result of these systems being research tools rather than an indication of any real design flaw. Shiva[9] is an implementation of DSM on an Intel iPSC/2 hypercube, and it should scale nicely. Nodes in the Dash system are connected on two meshes. This implies that the machine should be expandable, but the Dash prototype is currently limited by its use of a full bit vector (one bit per node) to keep track of page replication.

**Heterogeneity.** At first glance, sharing memory between two machines with different architectures seems almost impossible. The machines may not even use the same representation for basic data types (integers, floating-point numbers, and so on). It is a bit easier if the DSM system is structured as variables or objects in the source language. Then a DSM compiler can add conversion routines to all accesses to shared memory. In Agora, memory is structured as objects shared among heterogeneous machines.

Mermaid[10] explores another novel approach: Memory is shared in pages, and a page can contain only one type of data. Whenever a page is moved between two architecturally different systems, a conversion routine converts the data in the page to the appropriate format.

Although heterogeneous DSM might allow more machines to participate in a computation, the overhead of conversion seems to outweigh the benefits.

## Implementation

A DSM system must automatically transform shared-memory access into interprocess communication. This requires algorithms to locate and access shared data, maintain coherence, and replace data. A DSM system may also have additional schemes to improve performance. Such algorithms directly support DSM. In addition, DSM implementers must tailor operating system algorithms to support process synchronization and memory management. We focus on the algorithms used in Ivy, Dash, Munin, Plus, Mirage, and Memnet because these systems illustrate most of the important implementation issues. Stumm and Zhou[1] give a good evolutionary overview of algorithms that support static, migratory, and replicated data.

**Data location and access.** To share data in a DSM system, a program must be able to find and retrieve the data it needs. If data does not move around in the system — it resides only in a single static location — then locating it is easy. All processes simply "know" where to obtain any piece of data. Some Linda implementations use hashing on the tuples to distribute data statically. This has the advantages of being simple and fast, but may cause a bottleneck if data is not distributed properly (for example, all shared data ends up on a single node).

An alternative is to allow data to migrate freely throughout the system. This allows data to be redistributed dynamically to where it is being used. However, locating data then becomes more difficult. In this case, the simplest way to locate data is to have a centralized server that keeps track of all shared data. The centralized method suffers from two drawbacks: The server serializes location queries, reducing parallelism, and the server may become heavily loaded and slow the entire system.

Instead of using a centralized server, a system can broadcast requests for data. Unfortunately, broadcasting does not scale well. All nodes — not just the nodes containing the data — must process a broadcast request. The network latency of a broadcast may also require accesses to take a long time to complete.

To avoid broadcasts and distribute the load more evenly, several systems use an owner-based distributed scheme.

This scheme is independent of data replication, but is seen mostly in systems that support both data migration and replication. Each piece of data has an associated owner — a node with the primary copy of the data. The owners change as the data migrates through the system. When another node needs a copy of the data, it sends a request to the owner. If the owner still has the data, it returns the data. If the owner has given the data to some other node, it forwards the request to the new owner.

The drawback with this scheme is that a request may be forwarded many times before reaching the current owner. In some cases, this is more wasteful than broadcasting. In Ivy, all nodes involved in forwarding a request (including the requester) are given the identity of the current owner. This collapsing of pointer chains helps reduce the forwarding overhead and delay.

When it replicates data, a DSM system must keep track of the replicated copies. Dash uses a distributed directory-based scheme, implemented in hardware. The Dash directory for a given cluster (node) keeps track of the physical blocks in that cluster. Each block is represented by a directory entry that specifies whether the block is *unshared remote* (local copy only), *shared remote*, or *shared dirty*. If the block is shared remote, the directory entry also indicates the location of replicated copies of the block. If the block is shared dirty, the directory entry indicates the location of the single dirty copy. Only the special node known as the *home cluster* possesses the directory block entry. A node accesses nonlocal data for reading by sending a message to the home cluster.

Ivy's dynamic distributed scheme also supports replicated data. A *ptable* on each node contains for each page an entry that indicates the probable location for the referenced page. As described above, a node locates data by following the chain of probable owners. The copy-list scheme implemented by Plus uses a distributed linked list to keep track of replicated data. Memory references are mapped to the physically closest copy by the page map table.

**Coherence protocol.** All DSM systems provide some form of memory coherence. If the shared data is not replicated, then enforcing memory coherence is trivial. The underlying network automatically serializes requests in the order they

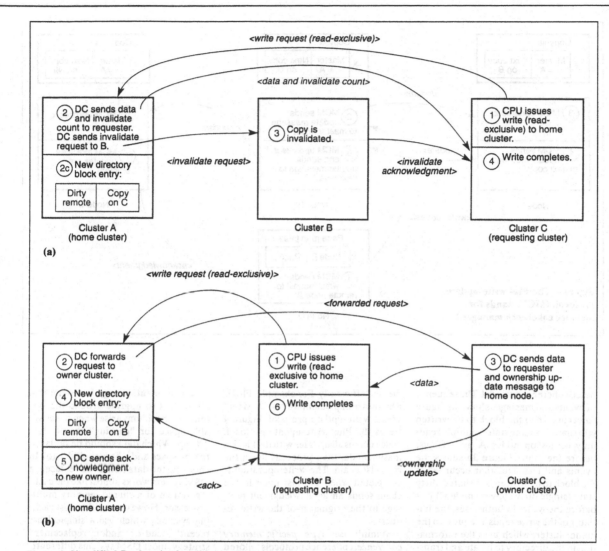

**Figure 3. Simplified Dash write-invalidate protocol: (a) Data is shared remote; (b) data is dirty remote (after events depicted in Figure 3a). (DC stands for directory controller.)**

occur. A node handling shared data can merely perform each request as it is received. This method will ensure strict memory consistency — the strongest form of coherence. Unfortunately, serializing data access creates a bottleneck and makes impossible a major advantage of DSM: parallelism.

To increase parallelism, virtually all DSM systems replicate data. Thus, for example, multiple reads can be performed in parallel. However, replication complicates the coherence protocol. Two types of protocols — write-invalidate and write-update protocols — handle replication. In a write-invalidate protocol, there can be many copies of a read-only piece of data, but only one copy of a writable piece of data. The protocol is called write-invalidate because it invalidates all copies of a piece of data except one before a write can proceed. In a write-update scheme, however, a write updates all copies of a piece of data.

Most DSM systems have write-invalidate coherence protocols. All the protocols for these systems are similar. Each piece of data has a status tag that indicates whether the data is valid, whether it is shared, and whether it is read-only or writable. For a read, if the data is valid, it is returned immediately. If the data is not valid, a read request is sent to the location of a valid copy, and a copy of the data is returned. If the data was writable on another node, this read request will cause it to become read-only. The copy remains valid until an invalidate request is received.

For a write, if the data is valid and writable, the request is satisfied immediately. If the data is not writable, the directory controller sends out an invalidate request, along with a request for a copy of the data if the local copy is not valid. When the invalidate completes, the data is valid locally and writable, and the original write request may complete.

Figure 3 illustrates the Dash directory-

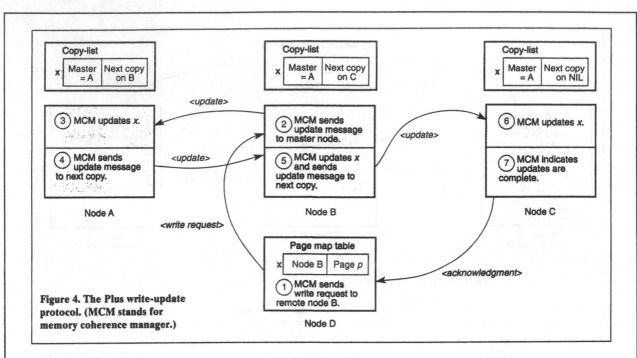

**Figure 4. The Plus write-update protocol. (MCM stands for memory coherence manager.)**

based coherence protocol. The sequence of events and messages shown in Figure 3a occurs when the block to be written is in shared-remote state (multiple read-only copies on nodes A and B) just before the write. Figure 3b shows the events and messages that occur when the block to be written is in shared-dirty state (single dirty copy on node C) just before the write. In both cases, the initiator of the write sends a request to the home cluster, which uses the information in the directory to locate and transfer the data and to invalidate copies. Lenoski et al.[4] give further details about the Dash coherence protocol and the methods they used to fine-tune the protocol for high performance.

Li and Hudak[2] show that the write-invalidate protocol performs well for a variety of applications. In fact, they show superlinear speedups for a linear equation solver and a three-dimensional partial differential equation solver, resulting from the increased overall physical memory and cache sizes. Li and Hudak rejected use of a write-update protocol at the onset with the reasoning that network latency would make it inefficient.

Subsequent research indicates that in the appropriate hardware environment write-update protocols can be imple-

mented efficiently. For example, Plus is a hardware implementation of DSM that uses a write-update protocol. Figure 4 traces the Plus write-update protocol, which begins all updates with the block's master node, then proceeds down the copy-list chain. The write operation is completed when the last node in the chain sends an acknowledgment message to the originator of the write request.

Munin[11] uses *type-specific memory coherence*, coherence protocols tailored for different types of data. For example, Munin uses a write-update protocol to keep coherent data that is read much more frequently than it is written (read-mostly data). Because an invalidation message is about the same size as an update message, an update costs no more than an invalidate. However, the overhead of making multiple read-only copies of the data item after each invalidate is avoided. An eager paging strategy supports the Munin producer-consumer memory type. Data, once written by the producer process, is transferred to the consumer proce where it remains available until the consumer process is ready to use it. This reduces overhead, since the consumer does not request data already available in the buffer.

**Replacement strategy.** In systems that allow data to migrate around the system, two problems arise when the available space for "caching" shared data fills up: Which data should be replaced to free space and where should it go? In choosing the data item to be replaced, a DSM system works almost like the caching system of a shared-memory multiprocessor. However, unlike most caching systems, which use a simple least recently used or random replacement strategy, most DSM systems differentiate the status of data items and prioritize them. For example, priority is given to shared items over exclusively owned items because the latter have to be transferred over the network. Simply deleting a read-only shared copy of a data item is possible because no data is lost. Shiva prioritizes pages on the basis of a linear combination of type (read-only, owned read-only, and writable) and least recently used statistics.

Once a piece of data is to be replaced, the system must make sure it is not lost. In the caching system of a multiprocessor, the item would simply be placed in main memory. Some DSM systems, such as Memnet, use an equivalent scheme. The system transfers the data item to a "home node" that has a statically allocated space (perhaps on disk) to store a copy of an item when it is not needed elsewhere in the system. This method is simple to implement, but it wastes a lot of memory. An improvement is to have the node that wants to delete the item simply page it out onto disk. Although this does not waste any memory space, it is time consuming. Because it may be faster to transfer something over the network than to transfer it to disk, a better solution (used in Shiva) is to keep track of free memory in the system and to simply page the item out to a node with space available to it.

**Thrashing.** DSM systems are particularly prone to thrashing. For example, if two nodes compete for write access to a single data item, it may be transferred back and forth at such a high rate that no real work can get done (a Ping-Pong effect). Two systems, Munin and Mirage, attack this problem directly.

Munin allows programmers to associate types with shared data: write-once, write-many, producer-consumer, private, migratory, result, read-mostly, synchronization, and general read/write. Shared data of different types get different coherence protocols. To avoid thrashing with two competing writers, a programmer could specify the type as write-many and the system would use a delayed write policy. (Munin does not guarantee strict consistency of memory in this case.)

Tailoring the coherence algorithm to the shared-data usage patterns can greatly reduce thrashing. However, Munin requires programmers to specify the type of shared data. Programmers are notoriously bad at predicting the behavior of their programs, so this method may not be any better than choosing a particular protocol. In addition, because the type remains static once specified, Munin cannot dynamically adjust to an application's changing behavior.

Mirage[3] uses another method to reduce thrashing. It specifically examines the case when many nodes compete for access to the same page. To stop the Ping-Pong effect, Mirage adds a dynamically tunable parameter to the coherence protocol. This parameter determines the minimum amount of time ($\Delta$) a page will be available at a node. For example, if a node performed a write to a shared page, the page would be writable on that node for $\Delta$ time. This solves

the problem of having a page stolen away after only a single request on a node can be satisfied. Because $\Delta$ is tuned dynamically on the basis of access patterns, a process can complete a write run (or read run) before losing access to the page. Thus, $\Delta$ is akin to a time slice in a multitasking operating system, except in Mirage it is dynamically adjusted to meet an application's specific needs.

**Related algorithms.** To support a DSM system, synchronization operations and memory management must be specially tuned. Semaphores, for example, are typically implemented on shared-memory systems by using spin locks. In a DSM system, a spin lock can easily cause thrashing, because multiple nodes may heavily access shared data. For better performance, some systems provide specialized synchronization primitives along with DSM. Clouds provides semaphore operations by grouping semaphores into centrally managed segments. Munin supports the synchronization memory type with distributed locks. Plus supplies a variety of synchronization instructions, and supports delayed execution, in which the synchronization can be initiated, then later tested for successful completion. Dubois, Scheurich, and Briggs[12] discuss the relationship between coherence and synchronization.

Memory management can be restructured for DSM. A typical memory-allocation scheme (as in the C library malloc()) allocates memory out of a common pool, which is searched each time a request is made. A linear search of all shared memory can be expensive. A better approach is to partition available memory into private buffers on each node and allocate memory from the global buffer space only when the private buffer is empty.

R esearch has shown distributed shared memory systems to be viable. The systems described in this article demonstrate that DSM can be implemented in a variety of hardware and software environments: commercial workstations with native operating systems software, innovative customized hardware, and even heterogeneous systems. Many of the design choices and algorithms needed to implement DSM are well understood and

integrated with related areas of computer science.

The performance of DSM is greatly affected by memory-access patterns and replication of shared data. Hardware implementations have yielded enormous reductions in communication latency and the advantages of a smaller unit of sharing. However, the performance results to date are preliminary. Most systems are experimental or prototypes consisting of only a few nodes. In addition, because of the dearth of test programs, most studies are based on a small group of applications or a synthetic workload. Nevertheless, research has proved that DSM effectively supports parallel processing, and it promises to be a fruitful and exciting area of research for the coming decade. ■

## Acknowledgments

This work was supported in part by NSF grant CCR-8808532, a Tektronix research fellowship, and the NSF Research Experiences for Undergraduates program. We appreciate the comments from the anonymous referees and thank the authors who verified information about their systems. Thanks also to Kurt Windisch for helping prepare this manuscript.

## References

1. M. Stumm and S. Zhou, "Algorithms Implementing Distributed Shared Memory," *Computer*, Vol. 23, No. 5, May 1990, pp. 54-64.

2. K. Li and P. Hudak, "Memory Coherence in Shared Virtual Memory Systems," *ACM Trans. Computer Systems*, Vol. 7, No. 4, Nov. 1989, pp. 321-359.

3. B. Fleisch and G. Popek, "Mirage: A Coherent Distributed Shared Memory Design," *Proc. 14th ACM Symp. Operating System Principles*, ACM, New York, 1989, pp. 211-223.

4. D. Lenoski et al., "The Directory-Based Cache Coherence Protocol for the Dash Multiprocessor," *Proc. 17th Int'l Symp. Computer Architecture*, IEEE CS Press, Los Alamitos, Calif., Order No. 2047, 1990, pp. 148-159.

5. G. Delp, *The Architecture and Implementation of Memnet: A High-Speed Shared Memory Computer Communication Network*, doctoral dissertation, Univ. of Delaware, Newark, Del., 1988.

6. R. Bisiani and M. Ravishankar, "Plus: A Distributed Shared-Memory System," *Proc. 17th Int'l Symp. Computer Archi-*

*tecture*, IEEE CS Press, Los Alamitos, Calif., Order No. 2047, 1990, pp. 115-124.

7. U. Ramachandran and M.Y.A. Khalidi, "An Implementation of Distributed Shared Memory," *First Workshop Experiences with Building Distributed and Multiprocessor Systems*, Usenix Assoc., Berkeley, Calif., 1989, pp. 21-38.

8. N. Carriero and D. Gelernter, *How to Write Parallel Programs: A First Course*, MIT Press, Cambridge, Mass., 1990.

9. K. Li and R. Schaefer, "A Hypercube Shared Virtual Memory System," *Proc. Int'l Conf. Parallel Processing*, Pennsylvania State Univ. Press, University Park, Pa., and London, 1989, pp. 125-132.

10. S. Zhou et al., "A Heterogeneous Distributed Shared Memory," to be published in *IEEE Trans. Parallel and Distributed Systems*.

11. J. Bennett, J. Carter, and W. Zwaenepoel. "Munin: Distributed Shared Memory Based on Type-Specific Memory Coherence," *Proc. 1990 Conf. Principles and Practice of Parallel Programming*, ACM Press, New York, N.Y., 1990, pp. 168-176.

12. M. Dubois, C. Scheurich, and F.A. Briggs. "Synchronization, Coherence, and Event Ordering in Multiprocessors," *Computer*, Vol. 21, No. 2, Feb. 1988, pp. 9-21.

# Chapter 2

# Distributed Shared Memory Algorithms

## Editors' Introduction

This chapter presents papers describing different algorithms intended to provide a distributed shared memory (DSM) abstraction. The following papers are included:

1. M. Stumm and S. Zhou, "Algorithms Implementing Distributed Shared Memory," *Computer,* Vol. 23, No. 5, May 1990, pp. 54–64.

2. R.E. Kessler and M. Livny, "An Analysis of Distributed Shared Memory Algorithms," *Proc. 9th Int'l Conf. Distributed Computing Systems,* IEEE CS Press, Los Alamitos, Calif., 1989, pp. 498–505.

3. D.L. Black, A. Gupta, and W.-D. Weber, "Competitive Management of Distributed Shared Memory," *Proc. COMPCON '89,* IEEE CS Press, Los Alamitos, Calif., 1989, pp. 184-190.

One of the essential issues in building DSM systems is the choice of an appropriate algorithm for providing the shared memory abstraction, since the matching of a DSM algorithm to the memory access behavior of applications largely determines system performance.

The task of an efficient DSM algorithm is to provide a static and/or dynamic distribution of shared data, in order to minimize the memory access latency. This is usually achieved using replication and migration strategies. Replication is mainly used to enable simultaneous accesses to the same data by different sites, predominantly when read sharing prevails. Migration is preferred when a sequential pattern of write sharing is characteristic, in order to decrease the overhead of coherence management. Both policies try to reduce the data access time, by bringing the data to the site where they are currently used. The effectiveness of an

51

algorithm is also reflected in its ability to decrease the number of data transfers and the amount of coherence overhead. Responsibility for DSM management and the choice of memory consistency model affect the implementation of the DSM algorithm, as well.

Chapter 2 includes papers that describe fundamental algorithms based on replication and/or migration strategy, presenting their essence, advantages, and drawbacks. Many viable modifications and enhancements of the basic algorithms are proposed. The papers also deal with performance evaluation of DSM algorithms, using either analytical or simulation methodologies. Their results indicate the conditions necessary for the best performance of the algorithms considered, in terms of memory reference characteristics of parallel applications.

The paper entitled "Algorithms Implementing Distributed Shared Memory," by Stumm and Zhou, considers four basic distributed shared memory algorithms, categorized according to the possibilities of data replication and migration: central-server, migration, read-replication, and full-replication algorithms. After detailed descriptions, a performance comparison is performed, in order to unveil and explore the relationship between the access patterns of applications and the DSM algorithms used to maintain the consistency. The evaluation is based on a simple analytical model that expresses the average cost per data access, as a function of only a few parameters. Multiple pairs of DSM algorithms are compared by generating the equal-performing curves, and it is concluded that the read-replication algorithm is often a good compromise for many applications. The paper further discusses the relation between shared data access patterns of some concrete typical applications and their expected performance, using suitable algorithms. Finally, some variations and enhancements of basic algorithms (full replication with delayed broadcasts, an optimistic full replication, application-level control with locking) with potentials to improve performance are also considered.

The results of a simulation study of some DSM algorithm issues are given in the paper "An Analysis of Distributed Shared Memory Algorithms," by Kessler and Livny. Four different algorithms are considered: a basic "multiple reader/single writer" protocol (Base), a naive scheme that allows for only one copy of a page at a time (Hot Potato), IVY's "dynamic distributed manager" with the transfer of ownership on both read and write faults (Li), and an algorithm that uses a sequence number per copy of a page in order to eliminate unnecessary page transfers (Shrewd). A simulation methodology employing synthetic address traces is used to compare the performance of the algorithms under various conditions (read/write ratio, number of nodes). The analysis focuses mainly on the double faulting problem (a read followed by a write fault to the same page). The authors conclude that the algorithms that allow multiple read-only copies solve the double faulting problem (third and fourth contender) and have superior performance. Therefore, they propose combining the features of these algorithms to achieve better performance for different application characteristics.

Black, Gupta, and Weber present and evaluate two DSM algorithms in their work, "Competitive Management of Distributed Shared Memory."

They propose that the decisions for the replication of read-only pages and the migration of write-only pages should be based on past observed usage. The algorithms are strongly competitive, which means that their costs are guaranteed to be within a small constant factor of optimal, on any sequence of accesses (two for replication and three for migration). Incorporation of these algorithms into the memory management part of the Mach VM operating system is shown to be feasible without major problems. Hardware support consists of two reference counters per processor for each page. Trace-driven simulations demonstrate that a significant improvement in performance relative to the random assignment of pages can be achieved using the proposed approach. Some possible improvements of the algorithms and extensions to other hardware architectures are also briefly discussed.

## Suggestions for Further Reading

1.  K. Li and P. Hudak, "Memory Coherence in Shared Virtual Memory Systems," *ACM Trans. Computer Systems*, Vol. 7, No. 4, Nov. 1989, pp. 321–359.

2.  O. Krieger and M. Stumm, "An Optimistic Algorithm for Consistent Replicated Shared Data," *Proc. 1990 Hawaii Int'l Conf. System Sciences*, IEEE CS Press, Los Alamitos, Calif., 1990, pp. 367–375.

# Algorithms Implementing Distributed Shared Memory

**Michael Stumm and Songnian Zhou**

**University of Toronto**

Traditionally, communication among processes in a distributed system is based on the *data-passing model*. Message-passing systems or systems that support remote procedure calls (RPCs) adhere to this model. The data-passing model logically and conveniently extends the underlying communication mechanism of the system; port or mailbox abstractions along with primitives such as Send and Receive are used for interprocess communication. This functionality can also be hidden in language-level constructs, as with RPC mechanisms. In either case, distributed processes pass shared information by value.

In contrast to the data-passing model, the *shared memory model* provides processes in a system with a shared address space. Application programs can use this space in the same way they use normal local memory. That is, data in the shared space is accessed through Read and Write operations. As a result, applications can pass shared information by reference. The shared memory model is natural for distributed computations running on shared memory multiprocessors. For loosely coupled distributed systems, no physically shared memory is available to support such a model. However, a layer of software can provide a shared memory abstraction to the

**This article compares several algorithms for implementing distributed shared memory. It shows that the performance of these algorithms is sensitive to the memory access behavior of applications.**

applications. This software layer, which can be implemented either in an operating system kernel or, with proper system kernel support, in runtime library routines, uses the services of an underlying (mes-

sage passing) communication system. The shared memory model applied to loosely coupled systems is referred to as *distributed shared memory*.

In this article, we describe and compare basic algorithms for implementing distributed shared memory by analyzing their performance. Conceptually, these algorithms extend local virtual address spaces to span multiple hosts connected by a local area network, and some of them can easily be integrated with the hosts' virtual memory systems. In the remainder of this section, we describe the merits of distributed shared memory and the assumptions we make with respect to the environment in which the shared memory algorithms are executed. We then describe four basic algorithms, provide a comparative analysis of their performance in relation to application-level access behavior, and show that the correct choice of algorithm is determined largely by the memory access behavior of the applications. We describe two particularly interesting extensions of the basic algorithms and conclude by observing some limitations of distributed shared memory.

**Advantages of distributed shared memory.** The primary advantage of distributed shared memory over data passing

Reprinted from *Computer*, Vol. 23, No. 5, May 1990, pp. 54–64.

is the simpler abstraction provided to the application programmer, an abstraction the programmer already understands well. The access protocol used is consistent with the way sequential applications access data, allowing for a more natural transition from sequential to distributed applications. In principle, parallel and distributed computations written for a shared memory multiprocessor can be executed on a distributed shared memory system without change. The shared memory system hides the remote communication mechanism from the processes and allows complex structures to be passed by reference, substantially simplifying the programming of distributed applications. Moreover, data in distributed shared memory can persist beyond the lifetime of a process accessing the shared memory.

In contrast, the message-passing models force programmers to be conscious of data movement between processes at all times, since processes must explicitly use communication primitives and channels or ports. Also, since data in the data-passing model is passed between multiple address spaces, it is difficult to pass complex data structures. Data structures passed between processes must be marshaled and unmarshaled by the application. (Marshaling refers to the linearizing and packing of a data structure into a message.)

For these reasons, the code of distributed applications written for distributed shared memory is usually significantly shorter and easier to understand than equivalent programs that use data passing.

The advantages of distributed shared memory have made it the focus of recent study and have prompted the development of various algorithms for implementing the shared data model.[1-8] Several implementations have demonstrated that, in terms of performance, distributed shared memory can compete with direct use of data passing in loosely coupled distributed systems.[2-4,9]

In a few cases, applications using distributed shared memory can even outperform their message-passing counterparts (even though the shared memory system is implemented on top of a message-passing system). This is possible for three reasons:

(1) For shared memory algorithms that move data between hosts in large blocks, communication overhead is amortized over multiple memory accesses, reducing overall communication requirements if the application exhibits a sufficient degree of locality in its data accesses.

(2) Many (distributed) parallel applications execute in phases, where each computation phase is preceded by a data-exchange phase. The time needed for the data-exchange phase is often dictated by the throughput limitations of the communication system. Distributed shared memory algorithms typically move data on demand as they are being accessed, eliminating the data-exchange phase, spreading the communication load over a longer period of time, and allowing for a greater degree of concurrency.

(3) The total amount of memory may be increased proportionally, reducing paging and swapping activity.[4]

**Similar systems.** Distributed shared memory systems have goals similar to those of CPU cache memories in shared-memory multiprocessors, local memories in shared memory multiprocessors with nonuniform memory access (NUMA) times, distributed caching in network file systems, and distributed databases. In particular, they all attempt to minimize the access time to potentially shared data that is to be kept consistent. Consequently, many of the algorithmic issues that must be addressed in these systems are similar.

Although these systems therefore often use algorithms that appear similar from a distance, their details and implementations can vary significantly because of differences in the cost parameters and in the ways they are used. For example, in NUMA multiprocessors, the memories are physically shared and the time differential between accesses of local and remote memory is lower than in distributed systems, as is the cost of transferring a block of data between the local memories of two processors. Hence, some of the algorithms we discuss in this article will be relevant to designers of NUMA memory management systems, but the algorithms they chose as most appropriate may differ.

Similarly, in bus-based shared memory multiprocessors, replication in the CPU caches (to avoid the much higher delays of accessing main memory and to reduce bus congestion) can be implemented cost effectively because of the reliability and broadcast properties of the bus. On the other hand, in distributed systems where communication is unreliable, we show that algorithms without replication can benefit certain types of applications. As a third example, distributed file systems and databases must provide for persistent data and, in the case of distributed databases, reliability and atomicity. These requirements can significantly affect the choice of algorithm.

**Model and environmental assumptions.** In our discussions and analyses, we make certain assumptions with respect to the environment in which the algorithms are implemented. These are described here. The extrapolation of our results to other environments is left for future work.

In general, the performance of distributed and parallel applications is dictated primarily by communication costs, which in turn are dictated by the underlying hardware. Here, we assume a distributed system environment consisting of a cluster of hosts connected by a local area network, such as an Ethernet. In this environment, communication between processors is unreliable and slow relative to local memory access. We assume that broadcast and multicast communication, where a single message can be sent (unreliably) to multiple receivers in a single network transaction, is available. Most bus and ring networks fit this description.

For performance analysis, communication costs are abstracted in terms of the number of messages sent and the number of packet events. A packet event is the cost associated with either receiving or sending a small packet (about 1 millisecond on a Sun-3/50). A point-to-point message transfer therefore requires one message, a packet event at the sending site, and a packet event at the receiving site. A multicast or broadcast message transmission requires one message, a packet event at the sending site, and a packet event at each receiving site.

The shared memory model provides two basic operations for accessing shared data:

    data := read( address )
    write( data, address )

Read returns the data item referenced by Address, and Write sets the contents referenced by Address to the value of Data. For simplicity, the algorithms for implementing shared data are described in terms of these two operations. We assume that the distributed applications call these functions explicitly, although this may not always be necessary with suitable compiler and/or operating-system support, and that the data item accessed is always a single word.

Of course, variations in the syntax and semantics of these operations are possible. For instance, the operations may be called by a number of different names, such as

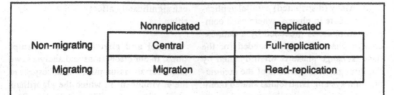

| | Nonreplicated | Replicated |
|---|---|---|
| Non-migrating | Central | Full-replication |
| Migrating | Migration | Read-replication |

**Figure 1. Four distributed memory algorithms.**

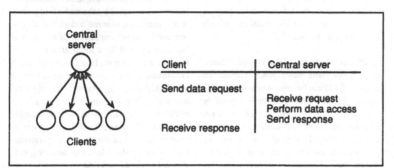

| Client | Central server |
|---|---|
| Send data request | Receive request |
| | Perform data access |
| | Send response |
| Receive response | |

**Figure 2. The central-server algorithm.**

fetch/store and in/out. The type of the data being accessed can also vary and include integers, byte arrays, or more complex user-defined types. Finally, the semantics of the memory access functions can go beyond those offered by traditional memory systems and can include atomic enqueuing or dequeuing operations, or even entire database operations. For example, Linda[10] is a programming language that directly supports a shared data space by providing a shared tuple space and three basic operations: Read reads an existing data item called "tuple" from the tuple space, Out adds a new tuple, and In reads and then removes an existing tuple. Linda's tuples are addressed by content rather than by location.

## Basic algorithms

This section describes four basic distributed shared memory algorithms. For each of these algorithms, we consider the cost of read and write operations and issues in their implementation. The algorithms described can be categorized by whether they migrate and/or replicate data, as depicted in Figure 1. Two of the algorithms migrate data to the site where it is accessed in an attempt to exploit locality in data accesses and decrease the number of remote accesses, thus avoiding communication overhead. The two other algorithms replicate data so that multiple read accesses can take place at the same time using local accesses.

Implementations of distributed shared memory based on replication should make this replication transparent to the applications. In other words, processes should not be able to observe (by reading and writing shared data) that all data accesses are not directed to the same copy of data.

More formally,[11] the result of applications using shared data should be the same as if the memory operations of all hosts were executing in some sequential order, and the operations of each individual host appear in sequence in the order specified by its program, in which case the shared memory is said to be *consistent*.

Shared memory in a shared memory multiprocessor is expected to behave this way. This definition of consistency should not be confused with a stricter definition requiring read accesses to return the value of the most recent write to the same location, which is naturally applicable to concurrent processes running on a uniprocessor but not necessarily to those on shared

memory multiprocessors with CPU caches and write-back buffers.[12] If the stricter definition holds, then so does the weaker definition (but the converse is not true).

**Central-server algorithm.** The simplest strategy for implementing distributed shared memory uses a central server that is responsible for servicing all accesses to shared data and maintains the only copy of the shared data. Both read and write operations involve the sending of a request message to the data server by the process executing the operation, as depicted in Figure 2. The data server executes the request and responds either with the data item in the case of a read operation or with an acknowledgment in the case of a write operation.

A simple request-response protocol can be used for communication in implementations of this algorithm. For reliability, a request is retransmitted after each time-out period with no response. This is sufficient, since the read request is idempotent; for write requests, the server must keep a sequence number for each client so that it can detect duplicate transmissions and acknowledge them appropriately. A failure condition is raised after several time-out periods with no response.

Hence, this algorithm requires two messages for each data access: one from the process requesting the access to the data server and the other containing the data server's response. Moreover, each data access requires four packet events: two at the requesting process (one to send the request and one to receive the response), and two at the server.

One potential problem with the central server is that it may become a bottleneck, since it has to service the requests from all clients. To distribute the server load, the shared data can be distributed onto several servers. In that case, clients must be able to locate the correct server for data access. A client can multicast its access requests to all servers, but this would not significantly decrease the load on all servers, since every server would incur the overhead of a packet event for each such request. A better solution is to partition the data by address and use some simple mapping function to decide which server to contact.

**Migration algorithm.** In the migration algorithm, depicted in Figure 3, the data is always migrated to the site where it is accessed. This is a "single reader/single writer" (SRSW) protocol, since only the threads executing on one host can read or write a given data item at any one time.

Instead of migrating individual data items, data is typically migrated between servers in a fixed size unit called a *block* to facilitate the management of the data. The advantage of this algorithm is that no communication costs are incurred when a process accesses data currently held locally.

If an application exhibits high locality of reference, the cost of data migration is amortized over multiple accesses. However, with this algorithm, it is also possible for pages to *thrash* between hosts, resulting in few memory accesses between migrations and thereby poor performance. Often, the application writer will be able to control thrashing by judiciously assigning data to blocks.

A second advantage of the migration algorithm is that it can be integrated with the virtual memory system of the host operating system if the size of the block is chosen equal to the size of a virtual memory page (or a multiple thereof). If a shared memory page is held locally, it can be mapped into the application's virtual address space and accessed using the normal machine instructions for accessing memory. An access to a data item located in data blocks not held locally triggers a page fault so that the fault handler can communicate with the remote hosts to obtain the data block before mapping it into the application's address space. When a data block is migrated away, it is removed from any local address space it has been mapped into.

The location of a remote data block can be found by multicasting a migration request message to all remote hosts, but more efficient methods are known.[3] For example, one can statically assign each data block to a managing server that always knows the location of the data block. To distribute the load, the management of all data blocks is partitioned across all hosts. A client queries the managing server of a data block, both to determine the current location of the data block and to inform the manager that it will migrate the data block.

**Read-replication algorithm.** One disadvantage of the algorithms described so far is that only the threads on one host can access data contained in the same block at any given time. Replication can reduce the average cost of read operations, since it allows read operations to be simultaneously executed locally (with no communication overhead) at multiple hosts. However, some of the write operations may

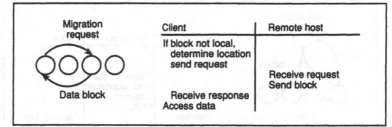

Figure 3. The migration algorithm.

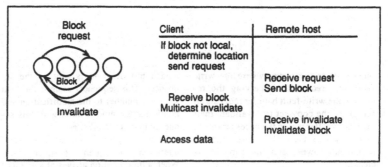

Figure 4. The write operation in the read-replication algorithm.

become more expensive, since the replicas may have to be invalidated or updated to maintain consistency. Nevertheless, if the ratio of reads over writes is large, the extra expense for the write operations may be more than offset by the lower average cost of the read operations.

Replication can be naturally added to the migration algorithm by allowing either one site a read/write copy of a particular block or multiple sites read-only copies of that block. This type of replication is referred to as "multiple readers/single writer" (MRSW) replication.

For a read operation on a data item in a block that is currently not local, it is necessary to communicate with remote sites to first acquire a read-only copy of that block and to change to read-only the access rights to any writable copy if necessary before the read operation can complete. For a write operation to data in a block that is either not local or for which the local host has no write permission, all copies of the same block held at other sites must be invalidated before the write can proceed. (See Figure 4.)

This strategy resembles the write-invalidate algorithm for cache consistency implemented by hardware in some multiprocessors.[13] The read-replication algorithm is consistent because a read access always returns the value of the most recent write to the same location.

This type of replication has been investigated extensively.[3,4] In Li's implementation, each block has a server designated as its *owner* that is responsible for maintaining a list of the servers having a read-only copy of that block. This list is called the block's *copy set*.

A read (or write) access to a block for which a server does not have the appropriate access rights causes a read (or write) fault. The fault handler transmits a request to the server that has ownership of the appropriate block. For a read fault, the owning server replies with a copy of the block, adds the requesting server to the copy set of the requested block and, if necessary, changes the access rights of its local copy to read-only.

When a write fault occurs, ownership for the block is transferred from the previ-

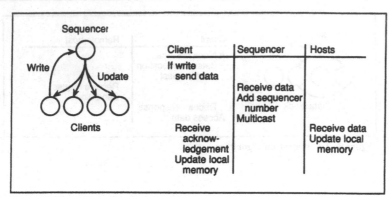

**Figure 5. The full-replication algorithm.**

| Client | Sequencer | Hosts |
|---|---|---|
| If write send data | | |
| | Receive data Add sequencer number Multicast | |
| Receive acknow- ledgement Update local memory | | Receive data Update local memory |

## Performance comparisons

All four algorithms described in the previous section ensure consistency in distributed shared memory. However, their performance is sensitive to the data-access behavior of the application. In this section, we identify the factors in data-access costs and investigate the application behaviors that have significant bearings on the performance of the algorithms. Based on some simple analyses, we compare the relative merits of the algorithms in an attempt to unveil the underlying relationship between access patterns of applications and the shared memory algorithms that are likely to produce better performance for them.

ous owner to the server where the write fault occurred. After receiving the response, the write-fault handler requests all servers in the copy set to invalidate their local copy, after which the access rights to that block are set to write access at the site of the new owner and the copy set is cleared.

**Full-replication algorithm.** Full replication allows data blocks to be replicated even while being written to. The full-replication algorithm therefore adheres to a "multiple readers/multiple writers" (MRMW) protocol. Keeping the data copies consistent is straightforward for non-replicated algorithms, since accesses to data are sequenced according to the order in which they occur at the site where the data is held. In the case of fully replicated data, accesses to the data must either be properly sequenced or controlled to ensure consistency.

One possible way to keep the replicated data consistent is to globally sequence the write operations, while only sequencing the read operations relative to the writes that occur local to the site where the reads are executed. For example, the *write update* algorithm for cache consistency implemented by hardware in some multiprocessors[13] maintains consistency in this fashion; that is, its reads occur locally from the cache while writes are broadcast over the bus that sequences them automatically.

A simple strategy based on sequencing uses a single global gap-free sequencer, depicted in Figure 5, which is a process executing on a host participating in distributed shared memory. When a process attempts a write to shared memory, the intended modification is sent to the sequencer. This sequencer assigns the next sequence number to the modification and multicasts the modification with this sequence number to all sites.

Each site processes broadcast write operations in sequence number order. When a modification arrives at a site, the sequence number is verified as the next expected one. If a gap in the sequence numbers is detected, either a modification was missed or a modification was received out of order, in which case a retransmission of the modification message is requested. (This implies that somewhere a log of recent write requests be maintained.) In effect, this strategy implements a negative acknowledgment protocol.

In the common case within our assumed environment, packets arrive at all sites in their proper order. Therefore, a write requires two packet events at the writing process, two packet events at the sequencer, and a packet event at each of the other replica sites, for a system total of $S+2$ packet events with $S$ participating sites.

Many variants to the above algorithms exist. For example, Bisiani and Forin[1] described an algorithm for full replication that uses the same principle as the sequencing algorithm to ensure individual data structures remain consistent. However, rather than using a single server to sequence all writes, writes to any particular data structure are sequenced by the server that manages the master copy of that data structure. Although each data structure is maintained in a consistent manner, there is no assurance with this algorithm that updates to multiple data structures are made consistently.

**Model and assumptions.** The parameters in Figure 6 characterize the basic costs of accessing shared data and the application behaviors. Among them, the two types of access fault rates, $f$ and $f'$, have the greatest impact on performance of the corresponding algorithms but, unfortunately, are also the most difficult to assess since they vary widely from application to application. We should also point out that these parameters are not entirely independent of one another. For instance, the size of a data block and therefore the block transfer cost, $P$, influences $f$ and $f'$, in conflicting directions. As the block size increases, more accesses to the block are possible before another block is accessed; however, access interferences between sites become more likely. $S$ also has direct impact on the fault rates. Nevertheless, the analyses below suffice to characterize the shared memory algorithms.

To focus on the essential performance characteristics of the algorithms and to simplify our analyses, we make a number of assumptions:

(1) The amount of message traffic will not cause network congestion. Hence, we will only consider the message-processing costs, $p$ and $P$, but not the network bandwidth occupied by messages.

(2) Server congestion is not serious enough to significantly delay remote access. This is reasonable for the algorithms we study, since there are effective ways to reduce the load on the servers (see the "Central-server algorithm" section).

(3) The cost of accessing a locally available data item is negligible compared to remote access cost and therefore does not

show up in our access cost calculations below.

(4) Message passing is assumed to be reliable, so the cost of retransmission is not incurred. Note, however, that the cost for acknowledgment messages, required to determine whether a retransmission is necessary or not, is included in our models.

To compare the performance of the distributed shared memory algorithms, we need to define a performance measure. Distributed shared memory is often used to support parallel applications in which multiple threads of execution may be in progress on a number of sites. We therefore choose the average cost per data access to the entire system as the performance measure. Hence, if a data access involves one or more remote sites, the message-processing costs on both the local and remote site(s) are included.

Using the basic parameters and the simplifying assumptions described above, the average access costs of the four algorithms can be expressed as follows:

Central server: $C_c = (1 - \frac{1}{S}) * 4p$

Migration: $C_m = f * (2P + 4p)$

Read replication: $C_{rr} = f' * [2P + 4p + \frac{Sp}{r+1}]$

Full replication: $C_{fr} = \frac{1}{r+1} * (S + 2)p$

Each of these expressions has two components. The first component, to the left of the *, is the probability of an access to a data item being remote. The second component, to the right of the *, is equal to the average cost of accessing a remote data item. Since the cost of local accesses is assumed to be negligible, the average cost of accessing a data item therefore equals the product of these two components.

In the case of the central-server algorithm, the probability of accessing a remote data item is $1-1/S$, in which case four packet events are necessary for the access (assuming that data is uniformly distributed over all sites). The overall cost, $C_c$, is therefore mainly determined by the cost of a packet event, as long as the number of sites is more than four or five.

For the migration algorithm, $f$ represents the probability of accessing a nonlocal data item. The cost of accessing a data item in that case equals the cost of bringing the data block containing the data item to the local site, which includes a total of one block transfer ($2P$) and four packet events distributed across the local, manager, and server sites. We assume here that the local, manager, and server sites are all distinct,

---

$p$: The cost of a packet event, that is, the processing cost of sending or receiving a short packet, which includes possible context switching, data copying, and interrupt handling overhead. Typical values for real systems range from one to several milliseconds.

$P$: The cost of sending or receiving a data block. This is similar to $p$, except that $P$ is typically significantly higher. For an 8-kilobyte block, where often multiple packets are needed, typical values range from 20 to 40 milliseconds.

For our analyses, only the ratio between $P$ and $p$ is important, rather than their absolute values.

$S$: The number of sites participating in distributed shared memory.

$r$: Read/write ratio, that is, there is one write operation for every $r$ reads on average. This parameter is also used to refer to the access pattern of entire blocks. Although the two ratios may differ, we assume they are equal in order to simplify our analyses.

$f$: Probability of an access fault on a nonreplicated data block (used in the migration algorithm). This is equal to the inverse of the average number of consecutive accesses to a block by a single site, before another site makes an access to the same block, causing a fault. $f$ characterizes the locality of data accesses for the migration algorithm.

$f'$: Probability of an access fault on replicated data blocks used in the read-replication algorithm. It is the inverse of the average number of consecutive accesses to data items in blocks kept locally, before a data item in a block not kept locally is accessed. $f'$ characterizes the locality of data accesses for the read-replication algorithm.

**Figure 6. Parameters that characterize the basic costs of accessing shared data.**

---

and that the request is forwarded by the manager to the server. The sequence of packet events is send (on local site), receive (on manager site), forward (on manager site), and receive (on server site).

For read replication, the remote access cost approximates that of the migration algorithm except that, in the case of a write fault (which occurs with a probability of $1/(r + 1)$), a multicast invalidation packet must be handled by all $S$ sites. The block transfer cost is always included in our expression, although it may not be necessary if a write fault occurs and a local (read) copy of the block is available.

Finally, for the full-replication algorithm, the probability of a remote access equals the probability of a write access. The associated cost for this write is always a message from the local site to the sequencer (two packet events), followed by a multicast update message to all other sites ($S$ packet events).

**Comparative analyses.** The discussion above prepares us to make some pair-wise comparisons of the algorithms' performance to illustrate the conditions under which one algorithm might outperform another. Each comparison is made by equating the average costs of the two algorithms concerned, to derive a curve along which they yield similar performance.

This curve, which we call the *equal-performing curve*, divides the parameter space into two halves such that in each half one of the algorithms will perform better than the other. For example, in the following comparison between migration and read replication, the equation on the right of Figure 7 is that of the equal-performing curve, derived from $C_m = C_{rr}$ (with some rearrangement). Since all of the cost formulas include packet cost $p$, only the ratio between $P$ and $p$ matters in the following comparative analyses. We assume the value of $P/p$ to be 20. Based on these

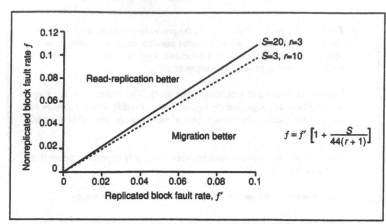

**Figure 7. Performance comparison: migration versus read replication.**

$$f = f' \left[1 + \frac{S}{44(r+1)}\right]$$

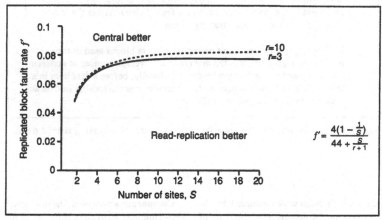

**Figure 8. Performance comparison: central server versus read replication.**

$$f' = \frac{4(1 - \frac{1}{S})}{44 + \frac{S}{r+1}}$$

comparisons, we will be able to make some general comments on performance.

*Migration versus read replication.* The only difference between these two algorithms is that replication is used in the read-replication algorithm to allow interleaved reads on several sites without block movements, but at the expense of multicasting invalidation requests upon updates. Interestingly, as shown in Figure 7, the invalidation traffic does not have a strong influence on the algorithms' relative performances. As long as the cost of a block transfer is substantially higher than

that of a small message, the curves for different values of $S$ and $r$ cluster closely together and are very close to the $f=f'$ line.

Typically, read replication effectively reduces the block fault rate because, in contrast to the migration algorithm, interleaved read accesses to the same block will no longer cause faults, so the value of $f'$ is smaller than $f$. Therefore, one can expect read replication to outperform migration for a vast majority of applications.

*Central server versus read replication.* Figure 8 compares the central-server and read-replication algorithms. The equal-

performing curve is almost flat, that is, insensitive to the number of sites. Moreover, the influence of the read/write ratio is also minimal. Hence, the key consideration in choosing between the two algorithms is the locality of access. Typically, a block fault rate of 0.07 (14 accesses between faults) is considered very high (faults very frequent). Therefore, read replication appears to be more favorable for many applications.

*Read replication versus full replication.* Both algorithms use read replication. The full-replication algorithm is more aggressive in that multiple copies are maintained even for updates. Figure 9 shows that the relative performance of the two algorithms depends on a number of factors, including the degree of replication, the read/write ratio, and the degree of locality achievable in read replication. The full-replication algorithm is not susceptible to poor locality, since all data is replicated at all sites. On the other hand, the cost of multicast increases with $S$. Therefore, full replication performs poorly for large systems and when update frequency is high (that is, when $r$ is low).

*Central server versus full replication.* These two algorithms represent the two extremes in supporting shared data: one is completely centralized, the other is completely distributed and replicated. Except for small values of $S$, the curve shown in Figure 10 is almost linear. For $S$ values of up to about 20, the aggressive replication of full replication seems to be advantageous, as long as the read/write ratio is five or higher. For very large replication, however, the update costs of full replication catch up, and the preference turns to the simple central-server algorithm.

*Remaining comparisons.* The two remaining pairs not yet considered are summarized as follows. The comparison between central server and migration resembles that between central server and read replication, with a rather flat curve beneath $f = 0.09$. Thus, unless the block fault rate is very high, migration performs better. The comparison between migration and full replication reveals no clear winner, as in the case of read replication versus full replication, with the key deciding factors being $S$ and $r$.

*Comments.* Based on the comparisons above, we can make a few observations. The central-server algorithm is simple to implement and may be sufficient for infrequent accesses to shared data, especially if the read/write ratio is low (that is, a high percentage of accesses are writes). This is often the case with locks, as will be discussed further below. However, locality of reference and a high-block-hit ratio are present in a wide range of applications, making block migration and replication advantageous.

The fault rate of the simple migration algorithm may increase due to interleaved accesses if different data items that happen to be in the same block are accessed by different sites. It thus does not explore locality to its full extent. The full-replication algorithm is suitable for small-scale replication and infrequent updates.

In contrast, the read-replication algorithm is often a good compromise for many applications. The central-server and full-replication algorithms share the property of insensitivity to access locality, so they may outperform the read-replication algorithm if the application exhibits poor access locality.

A potentially serious performance problem with algorithms that move large data blocks is *block thrashing*. For migration, it takes the form of moving data back and forth in quick succession when interleaved data accesses are made by two or more sites. For read replication, it takes the form of blocks with read-only permissions being repeatedly invalidated soon after they are replicated.

Such situations indicate poor (site) locality in references. For many applications, shared data can be allocated and the computation can be partitioned to minimize thrashing. Application-controlled locks can also be used to suppress thrashing (see the section entitled "Application-level control with locking"). In either case, the complete transparency of the distributed shared memory is compromised somewhat.

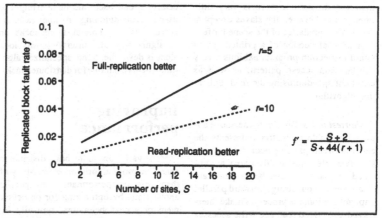

$$f' = \frac{S+2}{S+44(r+1)}$$

**Figure 9. Performance comparison: read replication versus full replication.**

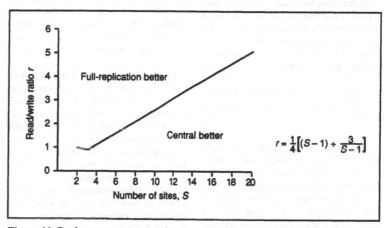

$$r = \frac{1}{4}\left[(S-1) + \frac{3}{S-1}\right]$$

**Figure 10. Performance comparison: central server versus full replication.**

**Applications.** From the above comparisons, it is clear that strong interactions exist between the shared data access patterns of applications and their expected performance using the various algorithms. To make our discussion more concrete, we study such interactions further in this section, based on our experience implementing the algorithms and measuring their performance. We do this by examining a few types of applications and the consistency algorithms that might suit them.

*Numerical subroutines and other applications.* The Blas-III package contains a

frequently used set of matrix manipulation subroutines implemented in Fortran. Typically, one or more (large) matrices are used as input to generate a result matrix of the same dimension. The amount of computation, usually substantial, can be sped up by assigning processors to compute subregions of the result matrix. This results in the input data being widely read-shared and the individual regions of the result matrix being updated by a single site.

Thus, read replication is highly desirable, whereas update multicast for write replication is unnecessary and too costly.

We observed excellent speedup using the read replication algorithm. Li studied similar applications in his thesis, and also reported very good speedup.[3]

Interestingly, this data-access pattern is widespread. For example, we converted a graphics application to use distributed shared memory. This application uses a three-dimensional description of a set of objects to compute the visible scene. Again, the scene description is input to the master process and read-shared among all the slave processes, which compute parts of the scene. Once the parts are completed, the master displays the entire scene. Like matrix computation, there is very little interference between the slaves except at the block boundaries of the scene buffer.

A parallel version of a printed circuit board inspection program exhibits a very similar data-access pattern, as well as excellent speedup using the read-replication algorithm.

*Shortest paths.* Similar to the above applications, a large matrix represents the paths between pairs of nodes in a graph. However, elements of this matrix are updated in place as new, better paths are discovered. In our straightforward parallel implementation, the processes make interleaved and mixed read and write accesses to the matrix, with the update rate being high at the beginning and declining as better paths become harder and harder to find. The central-server algorithm is inappropriate because, like the applications above, accesses are frequent.

On the other hand, since access locality is poor, large numbers of block transfers due to thrashing are unavoidable if either the migration or the read-replication algorithm is used. Full replication appears to perform better, especially for the later stages of the computation. Instead of transferring or invalidating a whole block when one entry is updated, only that entry is distributed.

*Hypermedia and distributed game playing.* Although these two types of applications serve very different purposes, they often share the characteristics of making interactive, concurrent accesses to shared data, with updates to moving, focused regions of the data space as the participants cooperate on or fight over the same areas. The read-replication algorithm may exhibit block thrashing as a result, and full replication again shows its merits.

*Distributed locks.* Locks are often used in parallel applications for synchronization. Typically, locks require little storage and exhibit poor locality, so that algorithms using block transfers — migration and read replication — are inappropriate. If the demand on a lock is light, a thread will usually find the lock free and may simply lock it, perform the relevant operation, and then unlock it.

Since such operations are relatively infrequent, a simple algorithm such as central server is sufficient. However, if a lock is highly contended for, a process might repeatedly attempt to lock it without suc-

cess, or a "call-back" mechanism might be used to avoid spinning. In either case, the cost of accessing remotely stored locks can be significant, and migrating this lock alone is desirable. Some specialized algorithm seems desirable for distributed locks.

# Improving performance

Many variations to the basic distributed shared memory algorithms exist. Many of them improve performance for specific applications by optimizing for particular memory access behaviors, typically by attempting to reduce the amount of communication since costs are dominated by communication costs. Here, we describe two particularly interesting variations and also describe how applications can help improve performance by controlling the actions of the distributed shared memory algorithm. The largest improvements to performance can probably be achieved by relaxing consistency constraints,[2] something we do not consider here.

**Full replication with delayed broadcasts.** The full-replication algorithm incurs $S + 2$ packet events on each write operation, where $S$ is the number of participating sites. A slight modification to this algorithm can reduce the number of packet events per write to four, while read operations continue to be executed locally (with no communication overhead).

Instead of broadcasting the data modifications to each site, the sequencer only logs them. A write sent to the sequencer by process $P$ is acknowledged directly and a copy of all modifications that arrived at the sequencer since the previous time $P$ sent a write request is included with the acknowledgment. Thus, the shared memory at a site is updated only when a write occurs at that site. As in the full-replication algorithm, read operations are performed locally without delays.

This variation on the full-replication algorithm still maintains consistency, but has at least two disadvantages. First, it refrains from updating shared memory for as long as possible and therefore does not conform to any real-time behavior. Programs cannot simply busywait, waiting for a variable to be set. Second, it places an additional load on the (central) sequencer, which must maintain a log of data modifications and eventually copy each such modification into a message $S$-1 times.

**An optimistic full-replication algorithm.** All of the basic algorithms described in the "Basic algorithms" section are *pessimistic* in that they ensure a priori that a process can access data only when the shared data space is and will remain consistent. Here, we describe an algorithm[7] that is *optimistic* in that it determines a posteriori whether a process has accessed inconsistent data, in which case that process is *rolled back* to a previous consistent state. This algorithm evolved from attempts to increase performance of the full-replication algorithm by coalescing multiple write operations into a single communication packet.

Instead of obtaining a sequence number for each individual write operation, a sequence number is obtained for a series of consecutive writes by a single process. Obviously, this may lead to inconsistent copies of data, since writes are made to the local copy and only later transmitted (in batch) to other sites. If the modified data is not accessed before it reaches a remote site, temporary inconsistencies will not matter. Otherwise, a conflict has occurred, in which case one of the processes will have to roll back.

To roll back a process, all accesses to shared data are logged. To maintain the manageability of the size of these logs (and the operations on them efficient), it is convenient to organize the data accesses into transactions, where each transaction consists of any number of read and write operations bracketed by a begin_transaction and a end_transaction.

When end_transaction is executed, a unique gap-free sequence number for the transaction is requested from a central sequencer. This sequence number determines the order in which transactions are to be committed. A transaction $T$ with sequence number $n$ is aborted if any concurrently executed transaction with a sequence number smaller than $n$ has modified any of the data that transaction $T$ accessed. Otherwise, the transaction is committed and its modifications to shared data are transmitted to all other sites. These transactions will never have to roll back. The logs of a transaction can then be discarded.

Clearly, the performance of this optimistic algorithm will depend on the access behavior of the application program and the application program's use of transactions. If rollbacks are infrequent, it will easily outperform the basic full-replication algorithm. It will also outperform the read-replication algorithm for those applications that suffer from thrashing, since the optimistic algorithm compares shared memory accesses at the per-data-item level (as opposed to a per-data-block level). The primary drawback of this algorithm, however, is the fact that the shared memory is no longer transparent to the application because the memory accesses must be organized into transaction and because roll backs must be properly handled by the application.

**Application-level control with locking.** Locks can be used by the application not only for its synchronization needs, but also to improve the performance of the shared memory algorithms. For example, in the case of the migration and read-replication algorithms, locking data to prevent other sites from accessing that data for a short period of time can reduce thrashing.

In the case of the full-replication algorithm, the communication overhead can be reduced if replica sites only communicate after multiple writes instead of after each write. If a write lock is associated with the data, then once a process has acquired the lock, it is guaranteed that no other process will access that data, allowing it to make multiple modifications to the data and transmitting all modifications made during the time the lock was held in a single message without causing a consistency problem. That is, communication costs are only incurred when data is being unlocked rather than every time a process writes to shared data.

Having the application use locks to improve the performance of the shared memory has a number of disadvantages, however. First, the use of locks needs to be directed towards a particular shared memory algorithm; the shared memory abstraction can no longer be transparent. Second, the application must be aware of the shared data it is accessing and its shared data-access patterns. Finally, in the case of those algorithms that migrate data blocks, the application must be aware of the block sizes and the layout of its data in the memory.

Despite the simplifying assumptions made in the performance analyses, the essential characteristics of the four basic algorithms are captured in the models used. The concept of distributed shared memory is appealing because, for many distributed applications, the shared memory paradigm leads to simpler (application) programs than

when data is passed directly using communication primitives. Moreover, with respect to performance, numerous implementations have shown that distributed shared memory can compete with and, in some cases, even outperform data-passing programs.

On the negative side, the performance of the algorithms that implement distributed shared memory are sensitive to the shared memory access behavior of the applications. Hence, as we have shown, no single algorithm for distributed shared memory will be suitable for most applications. The performance-conscious application writer will need to choose an appropriate algorithm for an application after careful analysis or experimentation.

In some cases, he or she will want to use different algorithms (for different data) within a single application. Moreover, because these algorithms are sensitive to the access behavior of the applications, it is possible to improve their performance significantly either by fine-tuning the application's use of the memory or by fine-tuning the shared memory algorithm for the access behavior of the particular application, thus eliminating the advantages of transparent shared memory access. We should also emphasize that distributed shared memory may be entirely unsuitable for some applications.

Further work is still needed to make distributed shared memory as versatile as its data-passing counterparts. For example, the distributed shared memory algorithms we have described are not tolerant of faults. Whenever a host containing the only copy of some data items crashes, critical state is lost. Although the central-server and the full-replication algorithms can be made tolerant of single-host crashes (for example, by using a backup server in the case of the central-server algorithm), it is not clear how to make the migration and read-replication algorithms equally fault tolerant.

Compared to data passing, distributed shared memory does not appear to be as suitable for heterogeneous environments at this time, although several research efforts on this problem are currently under way.[7,9] Consider, for example, the migration algorithm in an environment consisting of hosts that use different byte orderings and floating-point representations.

When a page is migrated between two hosts of different types, the contents of the page must be converted before it can be accessed by the application. It is not possible for the distributed memory system to

convert the page without knowing the type of the application-level data contained in the page and the actual page layout. This complicates the interface between the memory system and the application.

If noncompatible compilers are used for an application to generate code for the different hosts such that size of the application-level data structures differs from host to host, then conversions on a per-page basis become impossible. For example, an additional problem for numerical applications is that, since the application has no control over how often a block is migrated or converted and since accuracy may be lost on floating-point conversions, the result may become numerically questionable.

For these reasons, we consider distributed shared memory to be a useful paradigm for implementing a large class of distributed applications, but do not expect it to become widely available in the form of a single standardized package, as has been the case for remote procedure calls, for example. Rather, we expect that distributed shared memory will be made available in a number of forms from which the application writer can choose. ∎

## Acknowledgments

Many thanks go to Tim McInerney, who did most of the work implementing the migration and read-replication algorithms for the Sun and DEC Firefly workstations, and to Orran Krieger, who designed and implemented the optimistic full-replication algorithm. The anonymous reviewers and the editors provided numerous valuable suggestions for improvements.

## References

1. R. Bisiani and A. Forin, "Multilanguage Parallel Programming of Heterogeneous Machines, *IEEE Trans. Computers*, Vol. 37, No. 8, Aug. 1988, pp. 930-945.

2. D.R. Cheriton, "Problem-Oriented Shared Memory: A Decentralized Approach to Distributed System Design, *Proc. Sixth Int'l Conf. Distributed Computing Systems*, May 1986, pp. 190-197.

3. K. Li, *"Shared Virtual Memory on Loosely Coupled Multiprocessors,"* PhD thesis, Dept. of Computer Science, Yale Univ., 1986.

4. K. Li and P. Hudak, "Memory Coherence in Shared Virtual Memory Systems," *ACM Trans. Computing Systems*, Vol. 7, No. 4, Nov. 1989, pp. 321-359.

5. A. Forin et al., "The Shared Memory Server," *Proc. 1989 Winter Usenix Conf.*, Jan. 1989, pp. 229-243.

6. R.E. Kessler and M. Livny, "An Analysis of Distributed Shared Memory Algorithms," *Proc. 9th Int'l. Conf. Distributed Computing Systems*, CS Press, Los Alamitos, Calif., Order No. 1953, June 1989, pp. 498-505.

7. O. Krieger and M. Stumm, "An Optimistic Algorithm for Consistent Replicated Shared Data," *Proc. 1990 Hawaii Int'l Conf. on System Sciences*, CS Press, Los Alamitos, Calif., Order No. 2009, Vol. 2, 1990, pp. 367-375.

8. B.D. Fleisch and G.J. Popek, "Mirage: A Coherent Distributed Shared Memory Design," *Proc. 12th ACM Symp. Operating System Principles*, Dec. 1989, pp. 211-222.

9. S. Zhou, M. Stumm, and T. McInerney, "Extending Distributed Shared Memory to Heterogeneous Environments," *Proc. 10th Int'l. Conf. Distributed Computing Systems*, CS Press, Los Alamitos, Calif., Order No. 2048, May-June 1990.

10. S. Ahuja, N. Carriero, and D. Gelernter, "Linda and Friends," *Computer*, Vol. 19, No. 8, Aug. 1986, pp. 26-34.

11. L. Lamport, "How to Make a Multiprocessor Computer that Correctly Executes Multiprocess Programs," *IEEE Trans. Computers*, Vol. 28, No. 9, Sept. 1979, pp. 690-691.

12. M. Dubois, C. Scheurich, and F.A. Briggs, "Synchronization, Coherence, and Event Ordering in Multiprocessors," *Computer*, Vol. 21, No. 2, Feb. 1988, pp. 9-21.

13. J. Archibald and J.L. Baer, "Cache Coherence Protocols: Evaluation Using a Multiprocessor Simulation Model, *ACM Trans. Computing Systems*, Vol. 4, No. 4, Nov. 1986, pp. 273-298.

# An Analysis of Distributed Shared Memory Algorithms

*R. E. Kessler[†], Miron Livny*

The University of Wisconsin-Madison
Computer Sciences Department
Madison, WI 53706

### ABSTRACT

This paper describes results obtained in a study of algorithms to implement a Distributed Shared Memory in a distributed (loosely coupled) environment. Distributed Shared Memory is the implementation of shared memory across multiple nodes in a distributed system. This is accomplished using only the private memories of the nodes by controlling access to the pages of the shared memory and transferring data to and from the private memories when necessary. We analyze alternative algorithms to implement Distributed Shared Memory, all of them based on the ideas presented in [Li86b].

The Distributed Shared Memory algorithms are analyzed and compared over a wide range of conditions. Application characteristics are identified which can be exploited by the Distributed Shared Memory algorithms. We will show the conditions under which the algorithms analyzed in this paper perform better or worse than the other alternatives. Results are obtained via simulation using a synthetic reference generator.

## 1. Introduction

Two major models of interprocess communication are: message passing and shared memory. In the first model, processes communicate and synchronize by sending and receiving messages whereas in the latter model processes interact by storing and retrieving data from a common address space. Shared memory can be considered a more flexible means of interprocess communication, if for no other reason than the ease at which message passing can be implemented given a shared memory. Moving in the opposite direction, namely from a system that only supports message passing to a shared memory system, is not a simple task. It requires the development of algorithms that will provide a consistent view of the shared space with an affordable overhead. We call algorithms which maintain this view Distributed Shared Memory (DSM) algorithms. The logical advantages of a single address space along with the physical advantages of a loosely coupled message based system have triggered efforts to develop and evaluate such algorithms.

In a distributed system each processor has its own virtual address space that is mapped to its local (private) memory. A processor can access only its local memory, unlike multiprocessor systems such as Cm* [Oust80] and RP3 [Pfis85] which allow different processors to access the same physical memory. As a performance optimization in these local/remote architectures one may migrate data from remote to local memories [Holl88]. Migration is a necessity, not an optimization, when supporting shared memory in a distributed system. One processor can read the content of a location in the shared space that was written by another process only if its content has been transferred by a message from the local memory of the writer to the local memory of the reader. With the help of the

access control provided by virtual memory hardware, the need for such a transfer can be detected. It is the responsibility of the DSM algorithm to provide the right information to the virtual memory control hardware and to control the node to node message exchange when implementing a DSM.

Kai Li [Li86a, Li86b, Li88] developed an implementation of a DSM for Apollo workstations and observed good performance for parallel algorithms using the DSM for interprocess communication. Subsequently, DSM implementations have been considered for the Mach [Youn87], and LOCUS [Flei87] operating systems. The increasing interest in DSM algorithms has motivated us to study the performance tradeoffs of this type of distributed algorithms. The DENET [Livn86] discrete event simulation environment allowed the implementation of a detailed simulation model of a distributed system, as well as a flexible synthetic access pattern generator. We feel the generator captures some characteristics of parallel programs which may use shared memory in a distributed environment. Using this simulator, we analyzed the performance of an algorithm introduced by Li as well as several variants of the algorithm. In Section 3, following a section that is devoted to the basic concepts which allow the implementation of a DSM, we describe the four algorithms we analyzed and discuss the differences between them. The flexibility of the simulation model and synthetic access pattern generator enabled us to observe the performance of the algorithms for a wide range of system and access pattern parameters. Section 4 describes the synthetic access pattern generator and the simulation model. Section 5 describes the simulation results from which we derive the conclusions we draw in Section 6.

## 2. How Does Distributed Shared Memory Work?

DSM algorithms are implemented in software, but, are very similar to hardware *directory* [Agar88, Cens78], and *snooping cache* [Arch86, Good83] schemes used to maintain cache coherency in multiprocessor systems. A strong definition of a coherent memory system is: a system in which a read from a location of the shared memory will return the value of the latest store to that location. A weaker definition would be that a read will eventually return the value of the latest store. Hardware cache coherency schemes maintain coherency on the cache block, which is the basic unit of memory controlled by the cache hardware. The major difference between DSM and hardware cache coherency schemes is that the cost of maintaining a coherent DSM can be much higher since coherency is maintained on pages, not cache blocks, and network transfers are required to transfer pages. Not only are virtual memory pages typically considerably larger than a cache block, but, network communications will lead to much higher latencies than that of bus-based hardware coherency schemes. An interesting variation of cache coherency schemes is the software and hardware control of coherency in the VMP [Cher86, Cher88] multiprocessor, in which software manages coherency control and caching with hardware support.

DSM algorithms utilize four major ideas to maintain an image of a coherent shared memory:

[†] This work has been supported by graduate fellowships from the National Science Foundation and the University of Wisconsin-Madison

(1)   The DSM is partitioned into pages, the granularity afforded by virtual memory.

(2)   The page is the unit on which coherency is maintained. Writes to a given page are strictly ordered and eventually propagated to all nodes.

(3)   Copies of each page of the DSM will exist on one or more nodes as per the coherency constraints. At any time at least one copy of each page exists.

(4)   Virtual Memory hardware is used to restrict access to shared data. At any time a processor may have: no access, read access, or read&write access to a given page of the DSM. Page faults will occur when a process violates access rights.

The rules enforced by DSM algorithms to efficiently maintain coherency are:

(1)   A node should have read&write access to a page of the shared memory if and only if the given node has *the one and only* current copy of the given page.

(2)   A node should have only read access to a page if and only if multiple copies of the page exist on different nodes.

In order to maintain these invariants, DSM algorithms keep track of the location of all copies of a given page. The easiest way to do this is to have an *owner* for each page who will know which nodes retain a copy of the page. All requests for changes in access rights to the page will then go through the owner of that page. Ownership can be assigned dynamically and transferred from one node to another.

Two types of faults can occur when access rights are violated: read faults, and write faults. Read faults will occur when a process attempts to read a page to which it has no access (i.e. the node does not have a copy of the page). Write faults will occur when a process attempts to write to a page to which it does not have read&write access (it has either no access or read access).

The *Base* protocol followed upon a **read fault** for a page of the DSM is as follows:

(1)   The faulting node requests a copy of the page from the owner of the page.

(2)   The owner of the page sends a copy to the faulting node, notes the location of the new copy and changes its local access rights to read-only.

(3)   The faulting node receives the page and sets the local access rights of it to read-only.

The Base protocol followed for a **write fault** is as follows:

(1)   The faulting node requests read&write access from the owner of the page.

(2)   The owner of the page sends the page (if necessary) and the list of nodes with copies of the page to the faulting node (that is, ownership of the page is transferred to the faulting node).

(3)   The faulting node sends invalidation messages to all other nodes with a copy of the given page. On receipt of an invalidation message, the copy of the given page is destroyed.

(4)   The faulting node sets the local access rights to read&write access and notes that it is the new owner of the page.

Note that with this algorithm it may be possible for read-only noncurrent copies of a given page to exist for a *short length of time* after another node has obtained write access to the page, depending on whether writes can proceed before invalidations are completed (i.e. acknowledged). If writes are not allowed until the invalidations are completed, the strong definition of a coherent memory given above will be implemented. If execution can continue before the invalidations are completed, higher efficiency may be obtained, but, only the weak definition of coherency can be enforced, and the property of sequential consistency [Lamp79] may be violated.

So far we have not addressed the question of how to locate the current owner of a page during a fault. Li has used both a distributed and a centralized mechanism for finding the current owner of a given page. In the distributed case (the "Dynamic Distributed Manager" [Li86a]) the owner of a page is determined when a page fault occurs by retaining, at each node, a *hint* (or guess) of who the owner of the page is. Requests for changes in access rights are sent to the node that the given hint indicates. When the hint is wrong, the node receiving the request simply forwards the request to the node it thinks is the owner. The hint at a node is changed to point to the node which is obtaining ownership when it is recognized that ownership of a page will be transferred. Li has shown that no loops or deadlocks occur in the distributed tree which develops as a result of these hints.

The centralized mechanism (the "Improved Centralized Manager" and "Fixed Distributed Manager" [Li86a]) uses a known manager for each page to locate the current owner of the page. All request for changes in access rights and ownership are forwarded to the current owner only after passing through the node which is the manager of the page. The manager for a page is then always aware of the current owner of the page. Our analysis of the distributed and centralized mechanisms to determine the owner of the pages has shown the performance difference to be small as compared to the differences in the DSM algorithms specified in the next section. We have therefore decided to consider the method used to determine the owner of a page to be separate and distinct from the solution to the *double faulting* problem, which is defined in the next section. All the algorithms analyzed in this paper could use either a centralized manager or hints to determine the owner of a page. For consistency, however, all of them use hints.

### 3.  Double Faulting and Distributed Shared Memory Algorithms

Our *Base* algorithm follows the protocol outlined in the previous section for read and write faults and uses hints to determine ownership. With this algorithm, a location in an invalid DSM page that is read and then written by two successive references will incur a pair of faults, a read fault followed by a write fault. We refer to this (read, write) pair of faults to the same page as a *double faulting pair*. If the DSM algorithm could predict that the read fault were to be quickly followed by the write fault, the write fault could be eliminated by taking the equivalent of a write fault when the read fault occurs. Information could be provided by the application to indicate that a page to be read would soon be written (by a hint to the operating system). Prediction without help from the application would require interpretation of the instruction stream causing the fault, particularly difficult since the two faults can be generated from different instructions.

In such a double faulting situation, a node to node page transfer will occur as a result of both the read and the write fault when using the Base algorithm or the "Improved Centralized Manager" algorithm of Li [Li86a]; the difference in these algorithms is that they use different methods to determine the owner of a given page: centralized and hints, respectively. When the access rights to a page are updated from read-only to read&write (during a write fault), an unnecessary page transfer can occur if the transferred page is the same as the previous read-only copy held at the faulting node.

To give an example of why the Base algorithm performs a page transfer during all write faults, whether a previous read-only copy exists at the node or not, consider the following scenario: Two nodes have read-only copies of a page which is owned by a third node. Both nodes write fault on that page at the same time and send request messages to the owner of the page. There may be a very long path from these nodes to the current owner of the page, and, assuming an arbitrary network between the nodes (we only assume that all messages from one node to another are received in the order sent), the delay for each of the messages to reach the owner is undetermined. One of the nodes will receive read&write access (and ownership) to the page first, invalidate other copies of the page, and modify its own copy. The other requesting node may still be waiting to obtain write access to the page, but, unbeknownst to the request message still outstanding, the requesting node no longer has a current copy of the page. A page transfer is completed on every write fault without considering whether the requesting node had an up to date read-only copy of the page at the time the message requesting write access (and ownership) was sent since it is possible for the read-only copy to be invalidated during the time the request for write access is outstanding.

There are alternatives to this double page transfer scenario. One alternative is to adapt a single bus hardware cache coherency scheme to a DSM implementation; the possibility is mentioned in [Good83]. A single bus serves as an excellent broadcast media and serializes all coherency requests. The "owner" of a cache block (page) can be determined by only a single broadcast message, with all of the nodes receiving the message and deciding if they are the owner. A block (page) transfer can be eliminated when writing to a block (page) of which a current read-only copy is held when the request to write (an invalidation of all other copies and transfer of ownership) appears on the broadcast media and the block (page) is not invalidated before the request appears. Such a broadcast scheme is much less appropriate for a DSM implementation than for single bus hardware coherency schemes for the following reasons: (1) Large amounts of processor time would be required to respond to all the broadcast requests; and (2) Ethernet message transfer is not as reliable as single bus messages. As a final comment, when the communication media is not inherently broadcast, even hardware schemes require double block transfers on successive reads and writes to a block[1] since there is no broadcast serialization of the requests.

Another potential cure to the double faulting problem is the naive one given by the *Hot Potato* algorithm. This algorithm solves the problem by treating all faults (read or write) as if they were a write fault. The implication of this algorithm, however, is that *one and only one* copy of each page may exist at a given time. This copy is stored and owned by the node who has read&write access rights to the page. In case of a double faulting pair, the first (read) fault gains read&write access to the page. The second (write) fault does not occur since the page has been granted read&write access after the first fault.

The Hot Potato algorithm shows us how to solve the double faulting problem if we are willing to live with a single copy DSM. The question which then arises is whether it is necessary to give away the advantages of a multi-copy (read-only) DSM in order to solve the double faulting problem? The next algorithms indicate that the double page transfer can be eliminated in a multi-copy DSM.

The "Dynamic Distributed Manager" algorithm of Li [Li86a], which we will call the *Li* algorithm, allows for multiple read-only copies to exist. The Li algorithm differs from the Base algorithm only in when ownership of a page is transferred. The Li algorithm transfers ownership during both a read and a write fault, whereas, the Base algorithm transfers ownership only during a write fault. When a node first reads and then writes to the same page, the first (read) fault will obtain both a copy of and ownership to the page. On a write fault occurring soon after the read fault, an invalidation of other pages is all that is necessary to allow read&write access since the local node is the owner of the page.

The Li algorithm is an improvement over the Base algorithm when considering double faulting pairs in that it eliminates the page transfer necessary for the write fault when it occurs soon after the read fault. Unfortunately, it does not minimize the number of page transfers when the write does not occur soon after the read. When a write fault is taken at a node which has a read-only copy of the page, but, is not the owner, unnecessary page transfers can still result. Furthermore, transferring ownership on a read fault is not always the best decision. When single-writer/multiple-readers (producer-consumers) sharing is taking place, the ownership transfer is a poor choice. In this case, ownership is transferred to the readers when they obtain copies of the page, whereas, it would be preferable for the single writer to remain owner at all times.

The *Shrewd* algorithm eliminates *all* unnecessary page transfers with the help of a sequence number per copy of a page. Each time read&write access is newly obtained, the sequence number of the new copy is the sequence number of the previous copy incremented by one. Each time read-only access to a page is obtained, the sequence number of the new copy is the same as the sequence number of the old copy. On each write fault at a node with a previously existing read-only copy, the sequence number of the copy is sent with the request for read&write access. When arriving at the node which is the owner of the page, the owner compares the sequence number of its copy of the page to the sequence number in the incoming request. If they are equivalent, the requesting node can be allowed read&write access to the page without a page transfer. Page transfer minimization is *guaranteed* since the sequence number is a direct indication of the validity of the previously existing copy of the page at the requesting node. In the case of a double faulting pair, the first (read) fault gains a copy of the page, while the second (write) fault is likely to find that a page transfer is unnecessary since the sequence numbers are equivalent.

Alternative algorithms which provide the guaranteed page transfer minimization of the Shrewd algorithm while transferring ownership on write faults were also considered. A particular possibility is an *optimistic* algorithm in which it is assumed that a page transfer will be unnecessary when a node is requesting write access to a page which it already has a read-only copy of. Ownership transfer would occur during the write fault. If the copy were still available (not invalidated) after the write request returned from the previous owner of the page to the requesting node, it would be the current copy of the page. It is possible that the copy at the requesting node could be invalidated before ownership is transferred to the requesting node. In that case, the requesting node would retrieve the up to date copy of the page from the previous owner. This optimistic algorithm would thus require separate transfers for the ownership to and copy of the page in that situation, whereas, the Shrewd algorithm transfers both at the same time. We do not consider this optimistic algorithm further since it can only require more messages than the Shrewd algorithm.

The difference between the Shrewd and Base algorithms is that the Shrewd algorithm eliminates page transfers when a node faults on a page which it has an up to date copy of. The difference between the Shrewd and Li algorithms is the means by which the double faulting problem is solved; the Shrewd algorithm solves it by sequence numbers and the Li algorithm solves it by ownership transfer. Neither the Shrewd or the Li algorithm can be said to be superior to the other in all cases. Our simulations, in section 5, help to highlight the differences between the two algorithms and the conditions which make one or the other perform better.

---

[1] The hardware coherency protocol of the Wisconsin Multicube [Good88] is one which requires a double block transfer on successive reads and writes to the same block.

## 4. The Simulation Model

When faced with the choice between alternative algorithms, the most important question a system designer must ask is: what algorithm is best for my system? The answer to that question depends on many factors within the system, as well as the characteristics of the applications using the system. The goal of this study is to understand the implications of the differences in the Base, Hot Potato, Li, and Shrewd algorithms presented in section 3 and to determine under what conditions these algorithms perform better or worse.

A simulation model has been developed which consists of a synthetic reference generator, a processor model, and a network model. This model, described below, was used to analyze the performance of the different DSM algorithms. The major advantage of this simulation model is its flexibility. It can be used to simulate many potential distributed system configurations and it allowed us to uncover the behavior of the DSM algorithms under widely varying application access patterns as well.

### 4.1. The Synthetic Reference Generator

The generator views the parallel program as executing localities [Denn72], or *phases*. The execution of each process in the program is considered to be a sequence of phases through which it flows. Each phase references a subset of the address space of the program in a characteristic pattern. The memory references of a process are considered to access one of two types of memory: *private*, and *shared*. The private memory can only be accessed by the process to which it belongs and is assumed to be mapped to the local memory of a node without causing any page faults. The shared memory of the program is mapped to the DSM. References to this type of memory can and will cause page faults.

The reference string of a process is assumed to consist of two types of phases: shared and private. The duration of a phase is called a *burst*. Each burst has the following characteristics: *percentage, placement, read to write ratio, locality,* and *length*. During a private burst the process accesses only its private memory whereas both shared and private references are made during a shared burst. The burst percentage determines how many accesses during a shared burst are to shared memory. Each shared burst has a placement around which the references to the shared memory will be centered. The distribution of the placement for different shared bursts is uniform across the shared memory space. The address of each shared memory reference during a shared memory burst is determined by a normal distribution with the mean being the placement of the burst and the locality of the burst being the standard deviation. Note that the placement is constant during a given burst. By increasing (decreasing) the locality of a burst, a larger (smaller) locality of reference within a burst is simulated. Each shared memory reference is chosen to be either a read or a write according to the read to write ratio.

Shared and private bursts are of the same length on the average. On completing a burst, a choice is made as to the type, length, and placement of the next burst depending upon the *private/shared ratio, mean burst length,* and placement distribution (uniform across the shared memory), respectively. The burst length of a shared burst is the number of accesses to the shared memory. Since shared accesses occur interleaved with private accesses, the actual number of processor references during a burst is larger than the burst length.

Although the shared memory is only accessed during shared bursts; since bursts appear back to back over the long term it will appear as though private and shared memory references occur interspersed over all time. Locality of reference is simulated within, but not across, shared bursts.

This synthetic access pattern is not intended to be, nor should it be taken as, a realistic access pattern. It is a tunable tool used to determine how the various DSM algorithms perform under varying circumstances to gain insight as to the conditions under which one

Table 1. Parameters for the Workload and the CPU Time Taken.

| Parameters | | | |
|---|---|---|---|
| Workload | | CPU Time Taken | |
| Name | Default | Operation | Time |
| Number of Nodes | 5 | Forward Message | .8 msec |
| Reference Rate | 1 MHz | Send Page | 5 msec |
| Page Size | 4 Kbytes | Invalidate Page | .5 msec |
| Shared Memory Size | 50 pages | Page Fault | .5 msec |
| Burst Percentage | 25 % | Receive Page | 5 msec |
| Private/Shared Ratio | 40 to 1 | | |
| Mean Burst Length | 100 Accesses | | |
| Locality | 20 Bytes | | |
| Placement Distribution | Uniform | | |

algorithm performs better than another. It is unlikely that the synthetic access pattern can realistically be said to characterize any given real access patterns. However, it contains interesting characteristics which will be exploited in the simulations, emphasizing the differences in the DSM algorithms. The absence of an attempt to model interprocess synchronization and primitives may be the most limiting characteristic of this synthetic application model.

### 4.2. The Processor and Network

The network models a multicast message passing network (token ring, bus, or ethernet) which can send messages at the rate of 10 Mbit/sec with a channel dead time of 3 microseconds between each message. Messages can be of arbitrary length, though in this simulation they are assumed to be either a short packet or a page packet. A short packet is 32 bytes, includes all header information necessary to transfer a message on the network, and is assumed of sufficient size to carry all messages other than page transfers. The size of a page packet is the size of a short packet plus the size of a page (in all the simulations here, 4 Kbytes). The channel is assumed to be error free and nodes are assumed to buffer each and every message without error[2]. Acknowledges are assumed unnecessary. The network model could be extended to account for acknowledgements and random channel errors; however, it is unlikely that this would change the fundamental results of this study.

References by the processor to its local memory are assumed to take a fixed amount of time per reference (except on a page fault). The processor model attempts to take into account the processor time necessary to receive and return page requests, forward page requests, invalidate pages, and page fault. Page transfers (both to and from a node) are assumed to take a considerable amount of processor time due to needed copying of data.

## 5. Results

The simulations isolate the effects of the values of the workload parameters of table 1 by changing the value of a parameter while holding others constant. In so doing, specific characteristics of the DSM algorithms can be analyzed in detail. It was difficult to choose the "correct" values of the parameters in the model since there is no published information to guide us. We simply chose values we thought were appropriate.

The performance metric used in this paper, *processing power*, is intended to indicate the effective number of processors of the parallel synthetic access pattern running on the system using the given DSM algorithm. Processing power is defined here as the sum of the processor references of the synthetic access pattern at all nodes divided by the maximum number of references achievable by a single processor in the same amount of time running at the memory access rate (assuming no page faults, of course).

---

[2] That is, it is assumed that the network interface at a node can buffer multiple incoming messages without error.

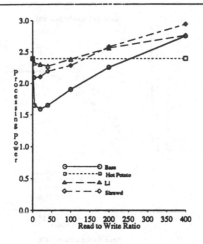 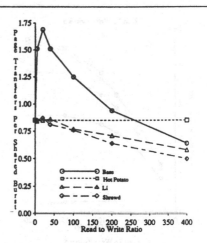

Figure 1. Performance vs. Read to Write Ratio.

This figure shows the performance of the algorithms for varying read to write ratios with a five node synthetic access pattern. The left graph shows the processing power for the varying read to write ratios, the right shows the number of page transfers per shared burst for the read to write ratios.

## 5.1. Read to Write Ratio

Simulation results for varying read to write ratios are shown in Figure 1. Varying the read to write ratio is important in examining the effectiveness of the algorithms in solving the double faulting problem. It also is important to determine what can be gained by allowing multiple read-only copies of a given page of the DSM to exist at multiple nodes. The curve for the Hot Potato algorithm is a straight line since its performance is independent of the read to write ratio. The characteristic trough[3] in the Base, Shrewd, and Li curves of Figure 1 is due to the presence of double faulting pairs. In the lower portions of the trough double faulting pairs are more frequent. Pages faulted on a burst are first being faulted as a read fault; soon after a write fault is taken in the same burst. This is opposed to either the situation where the write fault is the only fault taken during a burst (since a write occurs before a read), or a read fault is taken during a burst and no subsequent write fault occurs within the same burst. The better performance to the left of the trough is because the first fault is more often a write fault during a burst, due to the low read to write ratio. The better performance to the right of the trough is because more often a read fault occurs and no write fault occurs, allowing for the increased concurrency which multiple read-only copies allows.

The Base algorithm requires more network page transfers than the other algorithms, particularly at small read to write ratios, resulting in its poor performance in this area. Figure 1 shows that the Base algorithm near the peak is forcing approximately twice the number of page transfers per shared memory burst as the other algorithms. The Hot Potato algorithm performs poorly at large read to write ratios since it does not allow for read-only copies of the pages of the DSM to exist at multiple nodes in the system. Both the Li and Shrewd algorithms reduce the number of page transfers per shared burst, yet retain the potential for parallel access which is allowed by multiple read-only copies.

The Li algorithm performs better than the Shrewd at smaller read to write ratios since write faults (just after a read fault) can often be handled without request from a remote node, simply by

invalidating other copies of the page. This can be done particularly quickly in this simulation since invalidations are not acknowledged. Note, however, how the Shrewd algorithm performs better than the Li algorithm at larger read to write ratios. This occurs since nodes are write faulting on pages which they have read-only copies of, but don't have ownership of. The Li algorithm is unable to detect that page transfer is unnecessary in this situation, often the case when a write fault does not occur during the same burst as the read fault which obtained the read-only copy of the page.

## 5.2. Number of Nodes

Performance of the algorithms versus the number of nodes is indicated by Figure 2. It shows the Hot Potato and Li algorithms are close in performance at a read to write ratio of 5, with a slight advantage to the Hot Potato. They are followed by the Shrewd algorithm, then the Base algorithm. The Base algorithm performs only about half as well as the leaders for large numbers of nodes. For a read to write ratio of five the double faulting problem is prevalent so the algorithms which solve this the best, the Hot Potato and the Li, perform the best. At a read to write ratio of 400 the Shrewd and Li algorithms perform best since they allow multiple read-only copies, followed by the Base and Hot Potato algorithms. Figure 2 shows that the network is being saturated around 15 nodes, which is roughly where the processing power curves saturate as well, indicating how network utilization is very important to the performance of a DSM algorithm. The Shrewd and Li algorithms have lower network utilizations than the Base algorithm. It is for this reason that they perform better than the Base algorithm over the range of conditions studied.

The fact that the Li algorithm is superior in performance to the Shrewd algorithm for a read to write ratio of 5 in Figure 2 (reference the upper left graph) indicates that transferring ownership on a read fault is a good idea under those conditions. The performance difference is due to the fact that the Shrewd algorithm must transfer ownership during the write fault of a double faulting pair, whereas, the Li algorithm simply needs to invalidate other copies of the page.

---

[3] Note that the curve of all algorithms pass through the same point at a read to write ratio of 0.

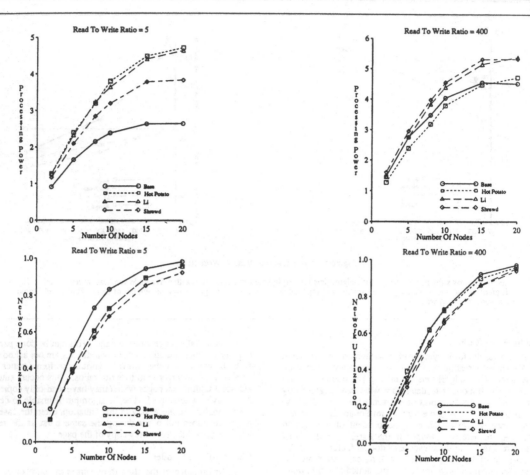

Figure 2. Performance vs. Number of Nodes.

This figure shows the performance of the algorithms versus the number of nodes for read to write ratios of 5 (left) and 400. The top figures show the processing power and the bottom figures show the network utilization.

### 5.3. Other Relationships

The relationship of burst length to processing power is indicated in Figure 3. An access pattern with a longer burst length will make longer, less frequent accesses to the DSM. A longer burst length results in a large improvement in performance for the given synthetic access pattern. This occurs since the longer burst length means that there are less bursts per unit time. Since a burst typically implies a page transfer, less bursts result in a big win. Applications using DSM will likely perform better if they limit their accesses to the shared memory to less frequent, longer accesses. The algorithms intended to solve the double faulting problem performed well over the spectrum of burst lengths for a read to write ratio of five. At a read to write ratio of 400, the algorithms which allow multiple read-only copies perform well for small burst lengths since most of the bursts are read-only. As the burst length increases above the read to write ratio, the double faulting problem becomes prevalent, so the algorithms which solve it perform better.

Figure 4 indicates that performance decreases as the size of the locality of reference increases. One reason for this is that it is likely that multiple pages may have to be transferred during a given burst. Another is that it is likely to increase contention among nodes for a page. That is, multiple nodes may be accessing the same page

of the DSM at the same time. The general downward slope of the curves is due to the multiple page transfers needed per burst. The performance of the Shrewd, Li and Base algorithms increases relative to the performance of the Hot Potato algorithm as the size of localities increase. This is an indication that these algorithms perform better in the presence of this contention since they allow multiple read-only copies of a page to exist.

The fact that the Shrewd algorithm outperforms the Li algorithm at a read to write ratio of 400 in Figure 4 is an indication that the Li algorithm performs some unnecessary page transfers. Note how the Li algorithm performs closer to the Base algorithm in this case. The guaranteed page transfer minimization of the Shrewd algorithm is very useful when pages are being read and will not soon be written.

### 6. Conclusions

This study brings out major characteristics of DSM and issues a DSM implementation should address. Several algorithms were presented here to implement DSM: Base, Hot Potato, Shrewd, and Li, each has its tradeoffs. The algorithms analyzed other than the Base algorithm attempt to minimize the implications of the double faulting problem outlined in section 3. Solving the double faulting

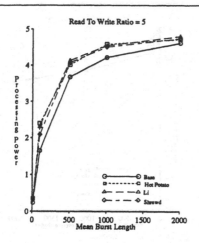
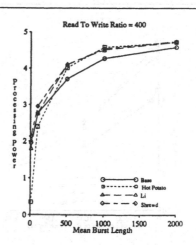

Figure 3. Performance vs. Mean Burst Length.

This figure shows the Performance of the algorithms versus the mean burst length for read to write ratios of 5 (left) and 400 on five node synthetic access patterns.

problem reduces the number of page transfers and decreases network utilization. Reducing usage of the network is important since network operations are expensive and often the major determinant of the performance of distributed systems.

The naive Hot Potato algorithm provides a very good solution to the double faulting problem, but, performs poorly as compared to the other algorithms when read sharing can occur since it does not allow multiple read-only copies of a page to exist. This is due to the implication of the Hot Potato algorithm that at any time one and only one copy of any given page of the DSM exists. A pathological scenario for the relative performance of the Hot Potato algorithm is the case when areas of the shared memory are accessed read-only, likely a common occurrence.

The Shrewd algorithm retains the parallel potential of multiple read-only copies, yet significantly reduces the number of node to node page transfers as compared to the Base algorithm since pages rarely need be transferred on write faults. The Shrewd algorithm will consistently outperform the Base algorithm. In our simulations it performs best when the read to write ratio is high.

The Li algorithm performs very well in our simulations, particularly for small read to write ratios. It is a good solution to the double faulting problem, but, the ownership transfer on read faults it requires can be counter-productive. When a node is obtaining a read-only copy of a page and will not subsequently write that page, it is preferable that the node does not become the owner of the page. The Li algorithm, however, will always make the node the owner of the page. Nevertheless, our simulations show that algorithms which allow multiple read-only copies of a page while solving the double faulting problem will perform well.

A simple variant of the Shrewd and Li algorithms would be one which combines the properties of both to achieve the advantages of both. Since they use separate mechanisms to solve the double faulting problem and reduce network utilization, the ideas of both can be combined into an algorithm which has the good performance of the Li algorithm at lower read to write ratios while retaining the page transfer minimization provided by the Shrewd algorithm at higher read to write ratios. We are confident that this variant will prove useful and expect to examine it in the future.

Our simulations have shown the Shrewd and Li algorithms to have superior performance to the Base algorithm over a wide range of application characteristics. In some cases we observed they obtained twice the performance of the Base algorithm. The algorithms consistently perform over 10-20 percent better than the Base algorithm under most conditions studied. While our synthetic access pattern generator is not a real application, we feel it captures significant characteristics of applications which will use a DSM, notably, locality of reference and sharing. Its tunability was most useful in bringing out the differences in the DSM algorithms. We expect performance gains will be seen in practice by using the algorithms which solve the double faulting problem rather than the Base algorithm.

Finally, we present some general application characteristics which can be exploited by all DSM algorithms:

(1) Designating certain areas of the shared memory as read-only. This allows the pages of the DSM to exist on multiple nodes.

(2) Less frequent, longer term shared memory access. This can reduce the level of contention among nodes for the shared memory and the number of page transfers needed.

(3) Differing locality of reference across nodes. This allows the pages of the DSM to be partitioned among the nodes. It is helpful for applications to place independent objects on separate pages in order to reduce contention for pages.

### 7. Acknowledgements

The authors would like to thank Mark Hill for his reviewing and suggested improvements. The authors would also like to thank the reviewers for pointing out some serious flaws in a previous version of this paper.

### 8. References

[Agar88]  A. Agarwal, R. Simoni, J. Hennessy and M. Horowitz, An Evaluation of Directory Schemes for Cache Coherence, *The 15th Annual Symposium on Computer Architecture*, Honolulu, Hawaii (1988), 280-289.

[Arch86]  J. Archibald and J. Baer, Cache Coherence Protocals: Evaluation Using a Multiprocessor Simulation Model, *ACM Transactions on Computer Systems*, 4, 4 (November, 1986), 273-298.

[Cens78]  L. M. Censier and P. Feutrier, A New Solution to Coherence Problems in Multicache Systems, *IEEE*

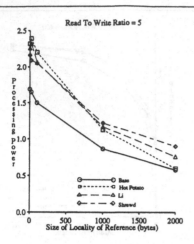
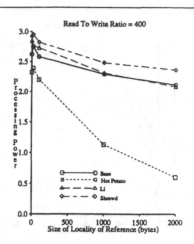

Figure 4. Performance vs. Locality of Reference.

This figure shows the Performance of the algorithms versus the locality of reference for read to write ratios of 5 (left) and 400 on five node synthetic access patterns.

*Transactions on Computers,* c-27, 12 (December, 1978), 1112-1118.

[Cher86]  D. R. Cheriton, G. A. Slavenburg and P. D. Boyle, Software-Controlled Caches in the VMP Multiprocessor, *Proceedings of the 13th International Symposium on Computer Architecture*(1986), 366-374.

[Cher88]  D. R. Cheriton, A. Gupta, P. D. Boyle and H. A. Goosen, The VMP Multiprocessor: Initial Experience, Refinements, and Performance Evaluation, *The 15th Annual Symposium on Computer Architecture,* Honolulu, Hawaii (1988), 410-421.

[Denn72]  P. J. Denning, On Modelling Program Behavior, *Proceedings of the AFIPS Spring Joint Computer Conference*(1972), 937-944.

[Flei87]  B. D. Fleisch, Distributed Shared Memory in a Loosely Coupled Distributed System, *Proceedings of the ACM SIGCOMM '87 Workshop,* Stowe, Vermont (August 1987), 317-327.

[Good83]  J. R. Goodman, Using Cache Memory to Reduce Processor-Memory Traffic, *Proceedings of the 10th International Symposium on Computer Architecture*(1983), 124-131.

[Good88]  J. R. Goodman and P. J. Woest, The Wisconsin Multicube: A New Large Scale Cache-Coherent Multiprocessor, *The 15th Annual International Symposium on Computer Architecture*(1988), 422-431.

[Holl88]  M. A. Holliday, Page Table Management in Local/Remote Architectures, *International Conference on Supercomputing*(1988), 1-8.

[Lamp79]  L. Lamport, How To Make a Multiprocessor Computer That Correctly Executes Multiprocess Programs, *IEEE Transactions on Computers*(September 1979), 690-691.

[Li86a]  K. Li and P. Hudak, Memory Coherence in Shared Virtual Memory Systems, To appear in ACM Transactions on Computer Systems. *Proceedings of the 5th Annual ACM Symposium on Principles of Distributed Computing*(August 1986), 229-239.

[Li86b]  K. Li, *Shared Virtual Memory on Loosely Coupled Multiprocessors,* Ph.D. dissertation, Yale University, Department of Computer Science, YALEU/Dept. of Computer Science/RR-492, (September 1986).

[Li88]  K. Li, IVY: Shared Virtual Memory System for Parallel Computing, *International Conference on Parallel Processing*(1988).

[Livn86]  M. Livny, *DENET Users Guide, Version 1.0,* Computer Sciences Department, University of Wisconsin-Madison, (1986).

[Oust80]  J. K. Ousterhout, D. A. Scelza and P. S. Sindhu, Medusa: An Experiment in Distributed Operating System Structure, *Communications of the ACM,* 23, 2 (February, 1980), 92-105.

[Pfis85]  G. F. Pfister, W. C. Brantley, D. A. George, S. L. Harvey, W. J. Kleinfelder, K. P. McAuliffe, E. A. Melton, V. A. Norton and J. Weiss, The IBM Research Parallel Processor Prototype (RP3): Introduction and Architecture, *Proceedings of the 1985 International Conference on Parallel Processing*(1985), 764-771.

[Youn87]  M. Young, A. Tevanian, R. Rashid, D. Golub, J. Eppinger, J. Chew, W. Bolosky, D. Black and R. Baron, The Duality of Memory and Communication in the Implementation of a Multiprocessor Operating System, *11th Symposium on Operating Systems Principles*(November 1987).

# Competitive Management of Distributed Shared Memory

**David L. Black**
Carnegie-Mellon University
Pittsburgh, PA 15213

**Anoop Gupta** and **Wolf-Dietrich Weber**
Stanford University
Stanford, CA 94305

## Abstract

This paper presents and analyzes algorithms for managing the distributed shared memory present in non-uniform memory access multiprocessors and related systems. The competitive properties of these algorithms guarantee that their performance is within a small constant factor of optimal even though they make no use of any information about memory reference patterns. Both hardware and software implementation concerns are covered. A case study of the Mach operating system indicates that integration of these algorithms into operating systems does not pose major problems. On the other hand, hardware support is required to obtain the full functionality of the algorithms. We also sketch possible extensions to the algorithms to support additional hardware architectures and software programming models.

Trace driven simulations are used to evaluate our approach and compare it to other alternatives. Speedups of 5 to 10 over random assignment of pages on production applications are achieved without modifying the applications for *non-uniform memory access* (NUMA) architectures. We compare our proposed hardware support with the more aggressive approach of fully-consistent caches. An additional factor of 2 to 3 in performance can be obtained from the cache approach, but at the cost of much more hardware. These results indicate that the algorithms and their hardware support may represent a viable cost/performance tradeoff.

## 1  Introduction

The widespread use of *uniform memory access* (UMA) multiprocessors has sparked interest in using uniform shared memory programming models on *non-uniform memory access* (NUMA) multiprocessors. Use of a common programming model enhances the portability of applications among such machines, and can reduce the effort required to fit or tune applications to NUMA multiprocessors. New techniques are required to manage the distributed physical memory found in a NUMA multiprocessor because the location of memory used by an application (with respect to the processor(s) executing the application) directly affects performance. Optimizing the use of physical memory to minimize access costs is a major issue that must be faced by any implementation of a shared memory programming model on such machines. This paper presents techniques and algorithms for this problem, along with preliminary performance results from trace-driven simulations.

Our algorithms are strongly competitive in a theoretic sense. An informal statement of this property is that the algorithms are essentially the best that can be achieved in the absence of information about future memory reference behavior. The techniques of competitive algorithm analysis are particularly useful for this work because they explicitly address the constant factors ignored by standard complexity analysis, and because they are well-suited to the analysis of resource management problems. Previous work has developed competitive algorithms for the related problems of

optimizing the use of snoopy caches [8].

The performance results for these algorithms are based on trace-driven simulations of several production applications from UMA multiprocessors. These results show that the proposed algorithms attain total speedups of 5 to 10 over random assignment of pages. This indicates that significant locality (both code and data) may exist in a large class of multiprocessor applications, and that this locality can be detected and exploited automatically. As a result such applications may not require extensive design changes or modifications for use on NUMA multiprocessors; no such changes or modifications were made to our applications.

This paper concentrates on the application aspects of our work. Proofs of the competitive properties of the algorithms can be found in [2]. The next section presents a basic model that covers the systems to which our algorithms are applicable. This is followed by an introduction to competitive algorithms. Section 4 breaks down the basic problem and presents our competitive algorithms for solving it. Sections 5 and 6 continue with a discussion of implementation concerns including the difficulties imposed by most current hardware. Section 7 presents our performance results from trace driven simulations. Sections 8, 9, and 10 briefly discuss extensions of this work. Sections 11 and 12 conclude the paper with a review of related work and a short summary of results.

## 2  Processor-Memory Model

This section presents the basic memory model for which our algorithms were developed. We assume an idealized machine composed of processor-memory clusters, with physical memory divided entirely among the clusters. A processor-memory cluster consists of one or more processors with local memory that is equally accessible (in terms of latency) to all processors. Our idealized machine has two distinct memory access latencies; the latency to access memory in the same cluster, and a significantly larger latency to access memory in another cluster. As a result all memory within a single cluster is equivalent, and all processors within a cluster have identical memory access characteristics (latency in terms of the cluster in which the accessed memory is located). Finally all memory locations outside the cluster have the same access latency from any processor in the cluster.

This basic model subdivides memory into pages and pages into locations. Pages are the fundamental unit of memory management; locations are the fundamental unit of memory access. We assume the existence of virtual memory mapping mechanisms, and therefore distinguish between virtual pages (in the address space of some program or the operating system) and physical pages (actual memory in the clusters). Mapping virtual pages to physical pages is one of the responsibilities of a memory management facility. Sharing may result in more than one virtual page in one or more address spaces being mapped to the same physical page. The page size used by our algorithms can be no smaller than the hardware page size if mapping is used, but it may be a multiple thereof.

Reprinted from *Proc. COMPCON*, 1989, pp. 184-190.

We normalize our model by assuming the difference in cost between an in-cluster memory access and a remote-cluster memory access is 1; this cost includes the effects of both increased latency and use of interconnection bandwidth. This cost only applies to accesses that actually use the interconnection network. In addition, we assume that read and write costs are identical; all of our work generalizes to cases in which these costs are not identical.

This model permits us to analyze techniques for managing the performance impact of distribution in a shared memory system. We concentrate on two major tools for this management; *replication* and *migration* of virtual memory. Replication consists of making a copy of a virtual page in another cluster and updating mappings that benefit from this copy (in reduced access time). Migration consists of moving a virtual page from one cluster to another and updating all mappings to that page. We formalize the costs of replication and migration as $r$ and $m$ respectively in terms of access costs. These costs include latency and overhead components, but do not include the additional costs of allocating a physical page in a cluster with a page shortage (i.e. causing pageout) or the additional benefits of freeing a physical page in such a cluster (i.e. avoiding pageout). We separate the issues involved in page reclaim from migration and replication; these are addressed in section 5.1.

Our basic model applies to any machine that can implement NUMA memory. This includes NUMA machines that implement the model directly (e.g. Butterfly [5]), *no remote memory access* (NORMA) machines with uniform access costs, and network shared memory implementations on networks with uniform communication costs. For the last two classes of machines, it is essential that the system (hardware and/or software) support access forwarding so that accesses to pages that are not in local memory can be satisfied at remote memory *without* moving the entire page to local memory (an expensive operation). Most current NORMA machines (e.g. hypercubes) and network shared memory implementations [4,9,20] do not support this functionality.

## 3   Basic Problem

The problem we address here is the management of distributed shared memory in architectures conforming to our model. For architectures utilizing a single copy of the operating system (NUMA multiprocessors), this includes not only memory shared explicitly, but also memory shared implicitly via copy-on-write techniques. Since we rely on replication and migration to perform this management, the problem can be restated as "When and under what circumstances should (virtual) pages be replicated into or migrated to memory in other clusters?"

There is a significant difference between this problem and the related problem of snoopy caching; our model and its realizations do not have broadcast, invalidate, or snooping mechanisms that can maintain consistency among multiple copies of a virtual page when writes occur. This prohibits replication of writable pages. Because we have separated the issue of page reclamation, migration of read-only pages make little sense; replication is less costly, and provides the benefits of local access to two clusters instead of one. As a result the overall problem splits into two sub-problems:

- Replication of read-only pages.
- Migration of writable pages.

If a virtual page is both read-only and writable at different times during the execution of an application, we consider each segment (read-only or read/write) of the page's existence to be a separate instance of the corresponding problem.

## 4   Basic Algorithms

Effective use of replication and migration presents an enigma. Replicating or migrating a page that will never be referenced again is very costly, but so is failing to replicate or migrate a page that will be used heavily in a remote cluster. Avoiding these situations seems to require knowledge of the future that is not available when decisions must be made; this results in a situation where any decision about replication or migration could be both wrong and costly. Problems that require these decisions to be made (affected by future system behavior, but must be made without any knowledge about this behavior) and algorithms that make these decisions are called *on-line*.

Results obtained from the analysis of competitive algorithms provide a solution to this enigma. An on-line algorithm is called *competitive* if its cumulative cost on any sequence is within a constant factor of the cost of an optimal algorithm that may examine the entire sequence in advance. If this constant is the smallest possible, then the algorithm is called *strongly competitive*. Competitive algorithms have been found for a number of problems, including list management [15], snoopy caching [8], and some server problems [10]. This paper extends past work by presenting strongly competitive algorithms for managing distributed shared memory.

### 4.1   Replication

The on-line replication problem consists of determining when in a sequence of accesses a page should be replicated into other clusters, without look-ahead. Under our model all clusters are uniformly equidistant; if a page is not resident locally, the cost to access it does not depend on the cluster in which it is accessed. As a result the decision to replicate a page into a given cluster is independent of the decisions to replicate into any other clusters. Hence the general replication problem reduces to the replication problem for two clusters with the page initially resident in only one cluster. Algorithm R is our algorithm for this problem.

**Algorithm R:**

> Count remote accesses from the cluster that does not have the page. When this count exceeds the replication cost, $r$, replicate the page into the cluster.

**Results:**

1. Any on-line algorithm for this problem must have a cost that is at least twice the cost incurred by an optimal off-line algorithm on some sequence of accesses.

2. Algorithm R is strongly competitive, i.e. its cost is always within a factor of two of optimal on any sequence of accesses.

Algorithm R (and algorithm M to be presented later) are algorithms that perform well across the entire spectrum of possible sequences. If the specific sequence that will occur is known in advance, an on-line algorithm can be constructed that performs well on that particular sequence, but will perform worse than our algorithm on many other sequences. This embodies the optimality property of our competitive algorithms; they are essentially the best possible in the absence of knowledge about what will happen in the future.

Copy on reference is a major alternative to our replication approach. It should be used where enough locality is known (e.g. from previous experimentation) or expected (e.g. code) to exist to cause replication by algorithm R; if replication is going to occur, it is always more efficient to do it in response to the first reference.

The proposed algorithm R, however, has an advantage in cases where read-only data may not be accessed enough to cause replication; systems that manage large amounts of data for which locality cannot be assumed are an example. The choice of approach is situation-dependent; copy on reference is probably more applicable to the most common situations.

## 4.2 Migration

The on-line migration problem consists of determining when in a sequence of accesses a page should be migrated to another cluster without look-ahead. Unlike the replication problem, migration depends on the number of clusters; of all the clusters that would benefit from having the page, only one can actually have the page. Decisions to migrate different pages are still independent, so the migration problem reduces to migration of a single page in response to accesses to that page. Algorithm M is our algorithm for this multiple cluster page migration problem.

**Algorithm M:**

> Associate a counter with each cluster; initialize the counts to zero. Access from a cluster that does not have the page increments that cluster's counter, and decrements some other cluster's counter, but not to less than zero. When a cluster's counter reaches twice the migration cost (i.e. $2m$) migrate the page to that cluster and zero its counter. Access from a cluster that has the page decrements some other cluster's counter, but not to less than zero.

All of the counters for a page will be zero after a migration due to the way they are maintained by algorithm M.

**Results:**

1. Any on-line algorithm for this problem must have a cost that is at least three times the cost incurred by an optimal off-line algorithm on some sequence of accesses.

2. Algorithm M is strongly competitive, i.e. its cost is always within a factor of three of optimal on any sequence of accesses.

# 5  Operating Systems Issues

There are two sets of operating systems issues that must be addressed in implementing our algorithms: (i) how do we take into account the limited size of physical memory; and (ii) what are the interactions between the proposed algorithms and the memory management portion of an operating system. The second issue arises primarily if the algorithms are implemented in the operating system kernel; this is an attractive choice both because it permits direct access to mapping information and also because it makes the resulting benefits available to all applications on the system, instead of just those that are modified to use our algorithms.

## 5.1  Limited Physical Memory Size

Since there are many other demands on physical memory besides those generated by replication and migration (e.g. memory allocation, file mapping, internal use by the operating system, etc.), extending the replication and migration algorithms to control memory usage is not appropriate. We believe that the operating system should separate reuse of physical memory (pageout or page reclaim) from replication and migration issues. Even the fallback

position of dedicating a fixed amount of physical memory to replication/migration and managing that is not a good idea; this prevents reallocation of memory to the uses for which it is in greatest demand.

We propose the use of independent pageout daemons for the management of various cluster memory pools. These daemons can respond appropriately to the potentially different memory demands from cluster to cluster. Any of several standard paging algorithms can be used to implement the daemons [17]. The migration and replication costs can be dynamically modified to feed information about page availability back into the replication and migration algorithms. These modifications should be restricted to increasing costs above their basic levels to reflect page shortages and hence discourage future use of memory in clusters with page shortages. Decreasing migration costs to encourage freeing memory in clusters with shortages, and cost-based reclamation of replicates are fraught with potential danger; this is because not all system components that use memory are or can be sensitive to costs – hence these cost-driven alternatives may result in heavily used pages being evicted in order to retain lightly used ones for cost-insensitive components.

## 5.2  Memory Management Interactions

Algorithms M and R can be incorporated into the operating system's memory management code on a NUMA multiprocessor. Implementing these algorithms inside the operating system allows their benefits to accrue to all uses of the machine, but also results in interactions with other memory management functions that must be dealt with as part of the implementation.

We use the virtual memory management portion of the Mach operating system [12] as a base for a case study of these interactions. Mach is a multiprocessor operating system developed at Carnegie-Mellon University; its VM system provides advanced memory management functionality including flexible sharing (both read/write and virtual copy), mapped files, and external memory management. This functionality stresses the interactions of our algorithms with the remainder of the operating system, and serves to expose potential problems.

The Mach VM implementation is cleanly split into machine-dependent and machine-independent portions. The machine-dependent portion consists of a single module, the *pmap* module, that is responsible for all physical map operations. The machine-independent portion of the system associates a pmap with each address space and invokes the pmap module as needed to perform mapping operations. Mach supports parallel execution of multiple threads within a single task's address space; this parallel execution can result in a single pmap being used simultaneously by more than one processor.

Mach envisions support for non-uniform physical memory by adding a NUMA layer between the machine-dependent and machine-independent portions of the VM system [17]. This layer hides the non-uniformity of the memory structure by translating *logical pages* (manipulated by the machine-independent portion of the VM system) to physical pages (in the hardware) in order to implement architecture-specific memory management policies (e.g. replication, migration). A similar translation process is needed for pmaps to allow replication within a single address space if its threads are spread across multiple clusters; in this case each cluster would have its own physical map, but the collection of these pmaps would appear as a single logical pmap to the machine-independent portion of the VM system. This adds additional complexity to the NUMA layer to better support multi-threaded applications, and may complicate interfaces that allow users to modify replication and migration behavior because an address space no longer uniquely specifies a cluster.

There are two other minor interactions of the NUMA layer with the remainder of the Mach VM system, and one major interaction. The two minor interactions are:

- Pageout functionality must be moved into the NUMA layer and redesigned to use multiple pageout daemons as discussed in Section 5.1. The resulting daemons must cope with system-wide (logical) page shortages as well as page shortages in the individual clusters.

- There must be a physical page available for every free logical page. Therefore use of a physical page for replication may require stealing a logical page from the resident page subsystem to maintain this invariant. Freeing of such a replicate should cause the stolen logical page to be returned to the resident page subsystem's free list.

Neither interaction poses great difficulties for an implementation.

The major interaction involves replication and copy-on-write. If the system has replicated a shared page that must be copied if written, then the replicates can be used to satisfy write faults on the page; this avoids the costs of creating an extra copy, but imposes extra costs if the replicate was used by more than one address space and has to be recreated as a result. The easy case is if there is a replicate that is only being used by the address space that caused the write fault; this replicate can always be used to satisfy the fault. For multiple address spaces, we would propose always using the replicate unless one of the other spaces has indicated that the replicate is needed (cf. the **always replicate** operation in section 10). An additional primitive must be added to Mach's machine-dependent interface to implement this functionality; the fault handler must be able to find out if the NUMA layer has a replicate that can be used to satisfy a write fault.

## 6   Hardware Support

Existing multiprocessor hardware will not allow a sufficiently accurate implementation of the NUMA memory management schemes discussed in this paper. Software systems that impose a level of indirection on all accesses to memory or shared memory can not hope to recover from this performance penalty. Thus we propose an architecture with hardware support for our algorithms. For each page, a set of two reference counters is required per processor in the system. Together with increment/decrement logic these maintain the counts required by algorithms R and M. An exception is caused when a pre-loaded threshold for migration or replication is reached. The operating system then deals with the copying and remapping operations required.

The counters are kept with their associated memory page. For a 64-processor system and 16-bit counters, we thus require 256 bytes of memory per page. This translates to 50% overhead for 512-byte pages, 25% overhead for 1K pages, 6.25% for 4K pages and 3.125% for 8K pages. The overhead seems quite acceptable for pages in the 4K - 8K range.

For replication, we only need to increment a single counter. Migration, on the other hand, requires updating two counters, one of which must be chosen from the non-zero counters for that page (local references only update the latter counter). Since the updating of the counters must take place transparently and at the same rate as memory references, a sequential search for non-zero counters is not acceptable. An alternative is to pick a counter and decrement it if it is non-zero. This is much simpler to implement and our simulations indicate that its performance is similar to the original migration algorithm.

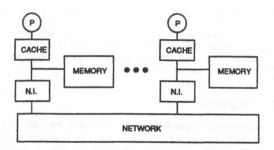

Figure 1: Architectural model

A major alternative to the replication of code is the use of instruction caches. Since code can be assumed to be read-only, the global cache consistency problem does not arise. However, unlike the schemes proposed in this paper, instruction caches do not help with replicatable data.

## 7   Performance Analysis

### 7.1   Architectural Model and Assumptions

The architectural model shown in Fig 1 was used for the analysis of the algorithms presented in this paper. It consists of several nodes linked by an interconnection network. Each node has a network interface (N.I.), its share of the global memory, a processor and a cache. In the case of the NUMA architecture, the cache is write-through and is only used to cache memory locations in the local portion of the global memory. Global cache consistency is thus assured.[1] The following costs were used for the various operations in our simulations:

| Operation | Time |
| --- | --- |
| local reference | 0.1 $\mu$s |
| remote reference | 4.0 $\mu$s |
| replication of a page | 1200 $\mu$s |
| migration of a page | 2100 $\mu$s |

The access costs are loosely based on those found in the Butterfly; replication and migration costs were estimated by examining page fault overheads in Mach (e.g. replication is very similar to a copy on write fault). These times include the overhead of updating page tables; this results in larger migration costs because more page tables must be changed by a migration than by a replication.

We also evaluate a system that allows the caches to cache *all* memory locations and uses a directory-based scheme to keep the caches coherent [1]. The hardware requirements of this scheme are greater, both in terms of memory requirements and in terms of complexity of the directory controller. We assume the cache scheme has the following costs for comparison with the NUMA scheme:

| Operation | Time |
| --- | --- |
| cache hit | 0.1 $\mu$s |
| cache miss | 4.0 $\mu$s |
| invalidation | 4.0 $\mu$s |

The invalidation cost is a *per remote invalidation* cost. Thus if a write reference results in invalidations in three remote caches, the

---

[1]Note that to make algorithms R and M work with caches, counters also need to be associated with translation buffer entries.

total cost would be 12 $\mu$s.

The algorithms were evaluated using multiprocessor traces of three parallel applications: LocusRoute [13], MP3D [11] and P-THOR [16]. LocusRoute is a standard cell global router, which exploits parallelism at a fairly coarse grain. MP3D is a 3-dimensional particle simulator. It uses distributed loops and is a typical example of parallel scientific code. P-THOR is a parallel logic simulator.

The traces were gathered on a VAX 8350, using a combined hardware/software scheme [7]. All traces were 8-processor runs and contained about half a million references per processor (4 million references total).

A simulator was used to keep track of the location of every memory page and the values of the various counters. The initial placement of each page was random. Code pages were allowed to replicate while data pages could only migrate.

## 7.2    Results

Figure 2 shows the performance increases gained by applying replication and migration. We are plotting the overall runtime for four schemes. "Neither" designates a random placement of memory pages in the nodes with neither replication nor migration allowed. The other points show the effect of allowing only migration, only replication and then both. Each curve shows the results for one of the three applications. When both replication and migration are allowed, the overall runtime decreases by a factor of 5 to 10.

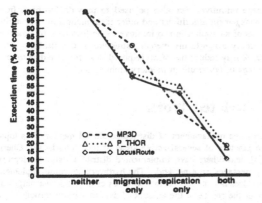

Figure 2: Performance Improvements

We also explored variations of three parameters: page size, replication threshold and migration threshold. The results from varying the page size are shown in Figure 3. We plot the effect of varying page size against the simulated run time of the trace. This time is shown as a percentage of the time required to execute the trace with replication and migration turned off (i.e. "neither" in Fig. 2).

Two effects are important when deciding the most efficient page size. Smaller pages are basically smaller units of replication/migration and would be expected to efficiently track the sharing needs of a program. At the same time, however, the fixed portion of remapping overhead makes larger pages more efficient. These two effects result in a U-shaped curve as seen in Figure 3. Although the position of the curves for the different applications varies vertically, their shape is basically identical. In every case the best page size was 512 bytes, but the effect of using larger pages was not significant.

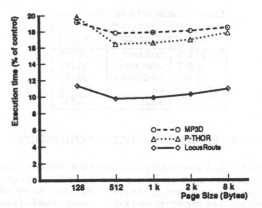

Figure 3: Effect of page size

Tuning the thresholds in these algorithms to match expected access patterns may improve average case performance without sacrificing constant factor bounds on the worst case performance. Tuning increases the constant factors in the bounds (i.e. the resulting algorithms are competitive instead of strongly competitive), but the increases may be offset by the improved average case behavior. For example changing the replication threshold in algorithm R from $r$ to $0.5r$ or $2r$ increases the constant factor in the performance bound from 2 to 3. In each case lowering the threshold increases performance by a very small amount. Most of the pages are replicated or migrated just once, so the sooner the movement takes place, the lower the overall cost.

In the results presented above, each page was allowed to migrate any number of times. We also explored a variation where only a single migration per page was allowed – this basically allowed the program to achieve a good initial page assignment. The performance of this variation was just as good as when multiple migrations were allowed, indicating that a good initial assignment is the most critical factor. This may be due in part to the length of the traces. Longer traces may show a larger benefit for dynamic migration, as the program moves from one "working set" to another.

Tables 1 and 2 compare the performance of the NUMA memory management scheme to that of a directory-based cache scheme. Due to space limitations, only results for LocusRoute are shown, but the relative performance was similar for the other two applications. The data shows that the cache scheme does about twice as well as the NUMA scheme. While cost for local references are comparable, the extra cost of remote references in the NUMA scheme is not offset by the extra cost of misses and invalidations in the cache scheme.

Table 1: NUMA scheme performance

| NUMA | | |
|---|---|---|
| Count | Operation | Cost ($\mu$s) |
| 36 | replication | 43,200 |
| 86 | migration | 180,600 |
| 227,304 | remote ref | 909,216 |
| 4,114,180 | local ref | 411,418 |
| | Total | 1,544,434 |

Table 2: Cache scheme performance

| CACHE | | |
|---|---|---|
| Count | Operation | Cost ($\mu$s) |
| 31,435 | read miss | 125,740 |
| 8,547 | write miss | 34,188 |
| 5,192 | invalidation | 20,768 |
| 4,301,493 | hit | 430,149 |
| | Total | 610,845 |

## 8   Extensions to Other Architectures

Competitive replication and migration algorithms have been found for certain extensions to our basic architectural model. A companion paper [2] presents strongly competitive algorithms for replication and migration in arbitrary trees and architectures based on trees including hypercubes and meshes. The related topologies of rings and torii handle replication easily, but pose problems for migration.

Migration on rings and torii (products of rings) is problematic. Bidirectional rings exhibit the phenomenon of *pinning* [14] in which accesses in both directions from the far side of the ring can pin a page in place and prevent it from migrating closer to the accesses. Unidirectional rings or unidirectional routing structures imposed on bidirectional rings avoid this problem, but instead exhibit the phenomenon of *cycling* in which a static access pattern distributed over the ring can cause a page to cycle around the ring interminably (using up ring bandwidth) when it should stay put. More sophisticated algorithms that keep additional information about the pattern and history of accesses may avoid these problems, but the cost of maintaining the additional state may affect the utility of such algorithms.

## 9   Replication of Writable Pages

So far we have not allowed the replication of writable pages. For portions of shared memory that are rarely written (called *mostly-read objects* in [19]), the amortized costs of the atomic updates required by the writes may not be prohibitive. Such a scheme can be implemented by using hardware mechanisms to cause a trap if a write occurs to any of the replicates. The handler for this trap can then perform the update by obtaining an exclusive lock on the logical page structure and propagating correct data to all copies. The resulting serialization of writes preserves sequential consistency. Relaxed consistency constraints are preferable if the data has to be updated frequently. On the other hand, if the memory is never written after some point, then replication is a very good idea. Researchers working on the ACE project at IBM Hawthorne have found this to be the case for a parallel shortest path program; the data structures describing the graph to be searched are never written after the initialization phase, but are read heavily during the search. Replicating these structures into local memories on their machine produced major improvements in the run time of the application [3].

Algorithm R may not be appropriate for managing replicated writable shared memory because it ignores the costs of updating other replicates in response to a write. The *General-Snoopy-Caching* algorithm in [8] is a better choice if these costs are important because it takes them into account; this algorithm is strongly competitive with a factor of 3. If update costs depend on the number of replicates (e.g. if individual messages are required to update each replicate), then the algorithm must be modified accordingly in order to remain strongly competitive.

## 10   Input and Feedback

If additional information is available about the access patterns for a page, the algorithms M and R can be further improved upon. We propose four primitives to help specify this additional memory usage information:

**Never replicate:** On average, this page is used so infrequently in this cluster that it should never be replicated, even if it accumulates $r$ accesses.

**Always replicate:** On average, this page will be used enough in this cluster to justify replication as early as possible. Alternatively, this page is read-only due to the use of copy-on-write techniques and is going to be written (which will require a copy to be made).

**Never migrate:** On average, this page is used so infrequently that it should not be migrated to this cluster even if it accumulates enough accesses to justify migration.

**Anchor:** This page will be so heavily used in this cluster that it should be anchored here and not allowed to migrate until further notice. An option to reverse this effect is also needed.

Lazy evaluation can be used to delay the effects of always replicate until the memory in question is actually accessed. This is done by unmapping the page in hardware and performing the operation in response to the page fault generated by the first access. This permits greater flexibility in the use of this primitive, as no additional cost is imposed for pages that are not used; similar functionality is provided by copy on reference.

These primitives can also be used to provide feedback from the management algorithms and other instrumentation over multiple runs of an application to improve its performance by adapting its memory usage to the memory structure of the machine. This feedback may reduce the effort required to restructure data to take advantage of non-uniform memory architectures.

## 11   Related Work

Competitive management of distributed shared memory is a topic at the juncture of several active areas of research. Li [9], Cheriton [4], and others have implemented distributed shared memory using messages on a network. The hardware for these implementations does not support remote accesses or access forwarding; this removes the choice of the amount of data to send in response to a request that is critical to our work. Most research projects in the area of NUMA architectures have implemented a shared memory programming model; the best known is BBN's Uniform System [18], and it typifies them in that it directly exports the non-uniform memory structure to users. Our work supports automatic management mechanisms that free users from some of the details involved in managing non-uniform memory, and should make these machines easier to program. Scheurich and Dubois [14] have independently discovered an extension of our migration algorithm to mesh-connected machines and hypercubes, but not its competitive properties. They also note the pinning problem for bidirectional rings, but not the cycling problem for unidirectional rings. Our work also makes contributions to the area of competitive algorithms; the migration algorithms are competitive solutions to several cases of the 'one server with excursions' problem [10]. While we would like to solve this problem in full generality (i.e. for any topology), we are of the opinion that any such solution must maintain too much state to be applicable to real systems. Finally the techniques of competitive algorithm analysis may be applicable to other resource management problems that occur in distributed systems and multiprocessors, such as load balancing [6].

## 12   Conclusion

This paper has presented and analyzed algorithms for managing memory in NUMA multiprocessors and related systems. Competitive algorithm analysis was used to obtain small constant factor bounds on performance with respect to optimal algorithms that require information on future memory reference behavior. A case study of the Mach VM system indicates that incorporation of these algorithms into an operating system kernel should not pose any great difficulties. In contrast, hardware support is required to obtain the full functionality of our approach on most multiprocessors. We have also sketched extensions of our approach to additional hardware architectures (e.g. hypercubes) and software programming models (e.g. weak consistency).

We used trace driven simulations to evaluate our approach and compare it to other alternatives. Speedups of 5 to 10 over random assignment of pages are achieved on production applications without modifying the applications for NUMA architectures. These results indicate that significant instruction and data locality may be present in many shared memory multiprocessor applications, and that this locality can be exploited automatically. We also compare our proposed hardware support with the more aggressive approach of fully-consistent caches. An additional factor of 2 in performance can be obtained from the cache approach, but at the cost of greater hardware complexity.

## Acknowledgements

Most of the theoretical results in this paper represent joint work with Daniel Sleator; complete proofs and details can be found in [2]. David Black is supported by DARPA contract N00039-87-C-0251. Anoop Gupta and Wolf-Dietrich Weber are supported by DARPA contract N00014-87-K-0828. Anoop Gupta is also supported by a faculty award from Digital Equipment Corporation.

## References

[1] A. Agarwal, R. Simoni, J. Hennessy, and M. Horowitz. An Evaluation of Directory Schemes for Cache Coherence. In *15th International Symposium on Computer Architecture*, 1988.

[2] D. Black and D. Sleator. *Competitive Algorithms for Management of Distributed Shared Memory.* Technical Report, Computer Science Dept., Carnegie Mellon University, Pittsburgh, PA, 1988. to appear.

[3] W. Bolosky. Personal Communication, September 1988.

[4] D. Cheriton. *Unified Management of Memory and File Caching Using the V Virtual Memory System.* Technical Report STAN-CS-88-1192, Computer Science Dept., Stanford University, Stanford, CA, 1988.

[5] W. Crowther, J. Goodhue, E. Starr, R. Thomas, W. Milliken, and T. Blackadar. Performance Mmeasurements on a 128-node Butterfly Parallel Processor. In *Intl. Conf. on Parallel Processing*, pages 531–540, 1985.

[6] A. Ezzat. Load Balancing in NEST: a Network of Workstations. In *Fall Joint Computer Conference (FJCC)*, November 1986.

[7] S. Goldschmidt. Simulating Multiprocessor Memory Traces. Dec. 1987. EE390 Report, Stanford University.

[8] A. Karlin, M. Manasse, L. Rudolph, and D. Sleator. *Competitive Snoopy Caching.* Technical Report CMU-CS-86-164, Computer Science Dept., Carnegie Mellon University, Pittsburgh, PA, 1986. Preliminary version appeared in 27th FOCS, 1986.

[9] K. Li and P. Hudak. Memory Coherence in Shared Virtual Memory Systems. In *5th Symp. on Principles of Distributed Computing*, pages 229–239, 1986.

[10] M. Manasse, L. McGeoch, and D. Sleator. Competitive Algorithms for Server Problems. In *20th Symp. on Theory of Computing*, pages 322–333, 1988.

[11] J. McDonald. A Direct Particle Simulation Method for Hypersonic Rarified Flow on a Shared Memory Multiprocessor. March 1988. CS411 - Final Project Report, Stanford University.

[12] R. Rashid, A. Tevanian Jr., M. Young, D. Golub, R. Baron, D. Black, J. Chew, and W. Bolosky. Machine-Independent Virtual Memory Management for Paged Uniprocessor and Multiprocessor Archtectures. *IEEE Trans. Comput.*, 37(8):896–908, August 1988.

[13] J. Rose. LocusRoute: A Parallel Global Router for Standard Cells. In *Design Automation Conference*, pages 189–195, June 1988.

[14] C. Scheurich and M. Dubois. Dynamic Page Migration in Multiprocessors with Distributed Global Memory. In *Int. Conf. on Distributed Computer Systems*, pages 162–169, 1988.

[15] D. Sleator and R. Tarjan. Amortized Efficiency of List Update and Paging Rules. *Commun. ACM*, 28(2):202–208, February 1985.

[16] L. Soule and T. Blank. Parallel Logic Simulation on General Purpose Machines. In *Design Automation Conference*, pages 166–171, June 1988.

[17] A. Tevanian Jr. *Architecture-Independent Virtual Memory Management for Parallel and Distributed Environments: The Mach Approach.* PhD thesis, Carnegie Mellon University, Pittsburgh, PA, December 1987.

[18] R. Thomas and W. Crowther. The Uniform System: An approach to runtime support for large scale shared memory multiprocessors. In *Proc. of 1988 Int. Conf. on Parallel Processing, Vol II*, pages 245–254, 1988.

[19] W. Weber and A. Gupta. Analysis of Cache Invalidation Patterns in Multiprocessors. In *Third International Conference on Architectural Support for Programming Languages and Operating Systems (ASPLOS III)*, Apr. 1989.

[20] M. Young, A. Tevanian, R. Rashid, D. Golub, J. Eppinger, J. Chew, W. Bolosky, D. Black, and R. Baron. The Duality of Memory and Communication in the Implementation of a Multiprocessor Operating System. In *11th Symp. on Operating Systems Principles*, pages 63–76, 1987.

# Chapter 3

# Memory Consistency Models

## Editors' Introduction

Three papers explaining memory consistency models, as well as some innovative solutions in this field, are included in Chapter 3:

1. K. Gharachorloo, D. Lenoski, J. Laudon, P. Gibbson, A. Gupta, and J. Hennessy, "Memory Consistency and Event Ordering in Scalable Shared-Memory Multiprocessors," *Proc. 17th Ann. Int'l Symp. Computer Architecture*, IEEE CS Press, Los Alamitos, Calif., 1990, pp. 15–26.

2. P. Keleher, A.L. Cox, W. Zwaenepoel, "Lazy Release Consistency for Software Distributed Shared Memory," *Proc. 19th Ann. Int'l Symp. Computer Architecture*, IEEE CS Press, Los Alamitos, Calif., 1992, pp. 13–21.

3. B.N. Bershad, M.J. Zekauskas, and W.A. Sawdon, "The Midway Distributed Shared Memory System," *Proc. COMPCON '93*, IEEE CS Press, Los Alamitos, Calif., 1993, pp. 528–537.

In all systems that allow replication of data, the memory consistency problem must be solved. The first research efforts in this area were done by designers of shared memory multiprocessors with private caches, and the most recent contributions have been made by the designers of distributed shared memory (DSM) systems based on underlying networks of workstations. No matter which platform is being used, memory consistency semantics has a significant influence on system performance and on the complexity of its design, as well. Generally, relaxed forms of consistency require more programming effort, in order to preserve the correct execution of applications. The three papers in Chapter 3 explain the semantics of known memory consistency models, and compare them for a set of representative applications.

An overview of three previously proposed memory consistency models (sequential, processor, and weak) and the proposal of a new, more relaxed model (release consistency) are presented by Gharachorloo et al. in their paper "Memory Consistency and Event Ordering in Scalable Shared-Memory Multiprocessors." Event-ordering requirements for all models analyzed in this paper are precisely defined in a formal manner. Different types of shared memory accesses (important for release consistency) are distinguished. The notion of *properly labeled programs* is also introduced, and the equivalence between release consistency and sequential consistency for those programs is shown. The similarities and differences among the models for certain classes of programs are particularly discussed. Practical implementation techniques, using a set of *fence* operations, and performance implications are also presented. The release consistency model described in this paper is applied in the Stanford Dash multiprocessor.

To reduce the latency in DSM systems by decreasing the number of messages and the amount of data that should be transmitted, a new relaxed consistency model is proposed in the paper "Lazy Release Consistency for Software Distributed Shared Memory," by Keleher, Cox, and Zwaenepoel. Unlike Munin's eager release consistency (ERC), which makes all modifications to the shared address space globally visible at the release operation, the lazy release consistency (LRC) model guarantees only that the processor acquiring the lock will see all modifications that logically precede the lock acquire. Logical precedence is determined by a chain of release and acquire operations on the same lock, ending with the current acquire. After formal definitions of ERC, LRC, and the alternatives of the data movement protocol, the results of simulation analysis are presented. Lazy update, lazy invalidate, eager update, and eager invalidate protocols have been simulated for five SPLASH programs. The results show that the advantages of LRC are particularly visible in those applications that suffer from false sharing and heavily use locks.

A new consistency model, called entry consistency, that further relaxes event-ordering requirements of release consistency, is introduced by Bershad, Zekauskas, and Sawdon in their paper "The Midway Distributed Shared Memory System." The entry consistency model is implemented in a system called Midway, together with other consistency models such as the processor and release consistency models. Shared data are guarded by synchronization objects that must be sequentially consistent themselves. Explicit association of shared data with synchronization objects must be done at the programming language level. The Midway system consists of three components: a set of keywords and function calls used to annotate a parallel program, a compiler for code generation that marks shared data as dirty when written into, and a runtime system that implements several consistency models. The unique characteristic of Midway is its ability to dynamically change the consistency model for a particular data unit. In spite of the good performance figures reported in this paper, entry consistency is more demanding, since consistency requirements should be well understood and made explicit by the programmer.

## Suggestions for Further Reading

1. L. Lamport, "How to Make a Multiprocessor Computer That Correctly Executes Multiprocess Programs," *IEEE Trans. Computers*, Vol. 16, No. 6, Sept. 1979, pp. 690–691.

2. S. Adve and M Hill, "Weak Ordering: A New Definition," *Proc. 17th Ann. Int'l Symp. Computer Architecture*, IEEE CS Press, Los Alamitos, Calif., 1990, pp. 2–14.

3. M. Dubois, C. Scheurich, and F.A. Briggs, "Synchronization, Coherence, and Event Ordering in Multiprocessors," *Computer*, Vol. 21, No. 2, Feb. 1988, pp. 9–21.

4. S. Dwarkadas et al., "Evaluation of Release Consistent Software Distributed Shared Memory on Emerging Network Technology," *Proc. 20th Ann. Int'l Symp. Computer Architecture*, IEEE CS Press, Los Alamitos, Calif., 1993, pp. 144–155.

5. K. Gharachorloo, A. Gupta, and J. Hennessy, "Performance Evaluation of Memory Consistency Models for Shared-Memory Multiprocessors," *Proc. 4th Symp. Architectural Support for Programming Languages and Operating Systems*, ACM Press, New York, N.Y., 1991, pp. 245–257.

6. L. Iftode, J. Pal Singh, and K. Li, "Scope Consistency: A Bridge between Release Consistency and Entry Consistency," *Proc. 8th Ann. Symp. Parallel Algorithms and Architectures*, 1996, pp. 277–287.

7. J. Protić, I. Tartalja, and M. Tomašević, "Memory Consistency Models for Shared Memory Multiprocessors and DSM Systems," *Proc. 8th Mediterranean Electrotechnical Conf.: Melecon '96*, 1996, pp. 1112–1115.

# Memory Consistency and Event Ordering in Scalable Shared-Memory Multiprocessors

Kourosh Gharachorloo, Daniel Lenoski, James Laudon, Phillip Gibbons,
Anoop Gupta, and John Hennessy

Computer Systems Laboratory
Stanford University, CA 94305

## Abstract

Scalable shared-memory multiprocessors distribute memory among the processors and use scalable interconnection networks to provide high bandwidth and low latency communication. In addition, memory accesses are cached, buffered, and pipelined to bridge the gap between the slow shared memory and the fast processors. Unless carefully controlled, such architectural optimizations can cause memory accesses to be executed in an order different from what the programmer expects. The set of allowable memory access orderings forms the memory consistency model or event ordering model for an architecture.

This paper introduces a new model of memory consistency, called *release consistency*, that allows for more buffering and pipelining than previously proposed models. A framework for classifying shared accesses and reasoning about event ordering is developed. The release consistency model is shown to be equivalent to the sequential consistency model for parallel programs with sufficient synchronization. Possible performance gains from the less strict constraints of the release consistency model are explored. Finally, practical implementation issues are discussed, concentrating on issues relevant to scalable architectures.

## 1   Introduction

Serial computers present a simple and intuitive model of the memory system to the programmer. A load operation returns the last value written to a given memory location. Likewise, a store operation binds the value that will be returned by subsequent loads until the next store to the same location. This simple model lends itself to efficient implementations—current uniprocessors use caches, write buffers, interleaved main memory, and exploit pipelining techniques. The accesses may even be issued and completed out of order as long as the hardware and compiler ensure that data and control dependences are respected.

For multiprocessors, however, neither the memory system model nor the implementation is as straightforward. The memory system model is more complex because the definitions of "last value written", "subsequent loads", and "next store" become unclear when there are multiple processors reading and writing a location. Furthermore, the order in which shared memory operations are done by one process may be used by other processes to achieve implicit synchronization. For example, a process may set a flag variable to indicate that a data structure

it was manipulating earlier is now in a consistent state. Consistency models place specific requirements on the order that shared memory accesses (*events*) from one process may be observed by other processes in the machine. More generally, the consistency model specifies what event orderings are legal when several processes are accessing a common set of locations.

Several memory consistency models have been proposed in the literature: examples include sequential consistency [7], processor consistency [5], and weak consistency [4]. The *sequential consistency* model [7] requires the execution of a parallel program to appear as some interleaving of the execution of the parallel processes on a sequential machine. While conceptually simple, the sequential consistency model imposes severe restrictions on the outstanding accesses that a process may have and effectively prohibits many hardware optimizations that could increase performance. Other models attempt to relax the constraints on the allowable event orderings, while still providing a reasonable programming model for the programmer.

Architectural optimizations that reduce memory latency are especially important for scalable multiprocessor architectures. As a result of the distributed memory and general interconnection networks used by such multiprocessors [8, 9, 12], requests issued by a processor to distinct memory modules may execute out of order. Caching of data further complicates the ordering of accesses by introducing multiple copies of the same location. While memory accesses are atomic in systems with a single copy of data (a new data value becomes visible to all processors at the same time), such atomicity may not be present in cache-based systems. The lack of atomicity introduces extra complexity in implementing consistency models. A system architect must balance the design by providing a memory consistency model that allows for high performance implementations and is acceptable to the programmer.

In this paper, we present a new consistency model called *release consistency*, which extends the weak consistency model [4] by utilizing additional information about shared accesses. Section 2 presents a brief overview of previously proposed consistency models. The motivation and framework for release consistency is presented in Section 3. Section 4 considers equivalences among the several models given proper information about shared accesses. Section 5 discusses potential performance gains for the models with relaxed constraints. Finally, Section 6 discusses implementation issues, focusing on issues relevant to scalable architectures.

# 2 Previously Proposed Memory Consistency Models

In this section, we present event ordering requirements for supporting the sequential, processor, and weak consistency models. Although the models discussed in this section have already been presented in the literature, we discuss them here for purposes of completeness, uniformity in terminology, and later comparison. Readers familiar with the first three models and the event ordering terminology may wish to skip to Section 3.

To facilitate the description of different event orderings, we present formal definitions for the stages that a memory request goes through. The following two definitions are from Dubois *et al.* [4, 10]. In the following, $P_i$ refers to processor $i$.

> **Definition 2.1: Performing a Memory Request**
> A LOAD by $P_i$ is considered *performed with respect to* $P_k$ at a point in time when the issuing of a STORE to the same address by $P_k$ cannot affect the value returned by the LOAD. A STORE by $P_i$ is considered *performed with respect to* $P_k$ at a point in time when an issued LOAD to the same address by $P_k$ returns the value defined by this STORE (or a subsequent STORE to the same location). An access is *performed* when it is performed with respect to all processors.

Definition 2.2 describes the notion of *globally performed* for LOADs.

> **Definition 2.2: Performing a LOAD Globally**
> A LOAD is *globally performed* if it is performed *and* if the STORE that is the source of the returned value has been performed.

The distinction between performed and globally performed LOAD accesses is only present in architectures with non-atomic STOREs. A STORE is atomic if the value stored becomes readable to all processors at the same time. In architectures with caches and general interconnection networks, a STORE operation is inherently non-atomic unless special hardware mechanisms are employed to assure atomicity.

From this point on, we implicitly assume that uniprocessor control and data dependences are respected. In addition, we assume that memory is kept coherent, that is, all writes to the same location are serialized in some order and are performed in that order with respect to any processor. We have formulated the conditions for satisfying each model such that a process needs to keep track of only requests initiated by itself. Thus, the compiler and hardware can enforce ordering on a per process(or) basis. We define *program order* as the order in which accesses occur in an execution of the single process given that no reordering takes place. When we use the phrase *"all previous accesses"*, we mean all accesses in the program order that are before the current access. In presenting the event ordering conditions to satisfy each model, we assume that the implementation avoids deadlock by ensuring that accesses that occur previously in program order eventually get performed (globally performed).

## 2.1 Sequential Consistency

Lamport [7] defines *sequential consistency* as follows.

> **Definition 2.3: Sequential Consistency**
> A system is sequentially consistent if the result of any execution is the same as if the operations of all the processors were executed in some sequential order, and the operations of each individual processor appear in this sequence in the order specified by its program.

Scheurich and Dubois [10, 11] have described event order restrictions that guarantee sequential consistency. Condition 2.1 presents sufficient conditions for providing sequential consistency (these differ slightly from conditions given in [10]).

> **Condition 2.1: Sufficient Conditions for Sequential Consistency**
> (A) before a LOAD is allowed to perform with respect to any other processor, all previous LOAD accesses must be *globally* performed and all previous STORE accesses must be performed, and
> (B) before a STORE is allowed to perform with respect to any other processor, all previous LOAD accesses must be *globally* performed and all previous STORE accesses must be performed.

## 2.2 Processor Consistency

To relax some of the orderings imposed by sequential consistency, Goodman introduces the concept of *processor consistency* [5]. Processor consistency requires that writes issued from a processor may not be observed in any order other than that in which they were issued. However, the order in which writes from two processors occur, as observed by themselves or a third processor, need not be identical. Processor consistency is weaker than sequential consistency; therefore, it may not yield 'correct' execution if the programmer assumes sequential consistency. However, Goodman claims that most applications give the same results under the processor and sequential consistency models. Specifically, he relies on programmers to use explicit synchronization rather than depending on the memory system to guarantee strict event ordering. Goodman also points out that many existing multiprocessors (e.g., VAX 8800) satisfy processor consistency, but do not satisfy sequential consistency.

The description given in [5] does not specify the ordering of read accesses completely. We have defined the following conditions for processor consistency.

> **Condition 2.2: Conditions for Processor Consistency**
> (A) before a LOAD is allowed to perform with respect to any other processor, all previous LOAD accesses must be performed, and
> (B) before a STORE is allowed to perform with respect to any other processor, all previous accesses (LOADs and STOREs ) must be performed.

The above conditions allow reads following a write to bypass the write. To avoid deadlock, the implementation should guarantee that a write that appears previously in program order will eventually perform.

## 2.3 Weak Consistency

A weaker consistency model can be derived by relating memory request ordering to synchronization points in the program. As an example, consider a processor updating a data structure within a critical section. If the computation requires several STORE accesses and the system is sequentially consistent, then each STORE will have to be delayed until the previous STORE is complete. But such delays are unnecessary because the programmer has already made sure that no other process can rely on that data structure being consistent until the critical section is exited. Given that all synchronization points are identified, we need only ensure that the memory is consistent at those points. This scheme has the advantage of providing the user with a reasonable programming model, while permitting multiple memory accesses to be pipelined. The disadvantage is that all synchronization accesses must be identified by the programmer or compiler.

The *weak consistency* model proposed by Dubois *et al.* [4] is based on the above idea. They distinguish between ordinary shared accesses and synchronization accesses, where the latter are used to control concurrency between several processes and to maintain the integrity of ordinary shared data. The conditions to ensure weak consistency are given below (slightly different from the conditions given in [4]).

> **Condition 2.3: Conditions for Weak Consistency**
> (A) before an ordinary LOAD or STORE access is allowed to perform with respect to any other processor, all previous *synchronization* accesses must be performed, and
> (B) before a *synchronization* access is allowed to perform with respect to any other processor, all previous ordinary LOAD and STORE accesses must be performed, and
> (C) *synchronization* accesses are sequentially consistent with respect to one another.

## 3 The Release Consistency Model

This section presents the framework for release consistency. There are two main issues explored in this section—performance and correctness. For performance, the goal is to exploit additional information about shared accesses to develop a memory consistency model that allows for more efficient implementations. Section 3.1 discusses a categorization of shared accesses that provides such information. For correctness, the goal is to develop weaker models that are equivalent to the stricter models as far as the results of programs are concerned. Section 3.2 introduces the notion of properly-labeled programs that is later used to prove equivalences among models. Finally, Section 3.3 presents the release consistency model and discusses how it exploits the extra information about accesses.

### 3.1 Categorization of Shared Memory Accesses

We first describe the notions of *conflicting accesses* (as presented in [13]) and *competing accesses*. Two accesses are conflicting if they are to the same memory location and at least one of the accesses is a STORE.[1] Consider a pair of conflicting accesses $a_1$ and $a_2$ on different processors. If the two accesses are not ordered, they may execute simultaneously thus causing a race condition. Such accesses $a_1$ and $a_2$ form a *competing pair*. If an access is involved in a competing pair under any execution, then the access is considered a *competing access*.

A parallel program consisting of individual processes specifies the actions for each process and the interactions among processes. These interactions are coordinated through accesses to shared memory. For example, a producer process may set

---
[1] A read-modify-write operation can be treated as an atomic access consisting of both a load and a store.

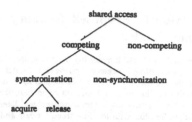

Figure 1: Categorization of shared writable accesses.

a flag variable to indicate to the consumer process that a data record is ready. Similarly, processes may enclose all updates to a shared data structure within lock and unlock operations to prevent simultaneous access. All such accesses used to enforce an ordering among processes are called *synchronization accesses*. Synchronization accesses have two distinctive characteristics: (i) they are competing accesses, with one process writing a variable and the other reading it; and (ii) they are frequently used to order conflicting accesses (i.e., make them non-competing). For example, the lock and unlock synchronization operations are used to order the non-competing accesses made inside a critical section.

Synchronization accesses can further be partitioned into *acquire* and *release* accesses. An acquire synchronization access (e.g., a lock operation or a process spinning for a flag to be set) is performed to gain access to a set of shared locations. A release synchronization access (e.g., an unlock operation or a process setting a flag) grants this permission. An acquire is accomplished by reading a shared location until an appropriate value is read. Thus, an acquire is always associated with a read synchronization access (atomic read-modify-write accesses are discussed in Section 3.2). Similarly, a release is always associated with a write synchronization access.

Not all competing accesses are used as synchronization accesses, however. As an example, programs that use chaotic relaxation algorithms make many competing accesses to read their neighbors' data. However, these accesses are not used to impose an ordering among the parallel processes and are thus considered *non-synchronization* competing accesses in our terminology. Figure 1 shows this categorization for memory accesses.

The categorization of shared accesses into the suggested groups allows one to provide more efficient implementations by using this information to relax the event ordering restrictions. For example, the purpose of a release access is to inform other processes that accesses that appear before it in program order have completed. On the other hand, the purpose of an acquire access is to delay future access to data until informed by another process. The categorization described here can be extended to include other useful information about accesses. The tradeoff is how easily that extra information can be obtained from the compiler or the programmer and what incremental performance benefits it can provide.

Finally, the method for identifying an access as a competing access depends on the consistency model. For example, it is possible for an access to be competing under processor consistency and non-competing under sequential consistency. While identifying competing pairs is difficult in general, the following conceptual method may be used under sequential consistency. Two conflicting accesses $b_1$ and $b_2$ on different processes form

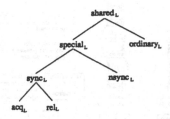

Figure 2: Labels for memory accesses.

a competing pair if there exists at least one legal interleaving where $b_1$ and $b_2$ are *adjacent*.

## 3.2 Properly-Labeled Programs

The previous subsection described a categorization based on the intrinsic properties of an access. We now describe the labelings for an access. The label represents what is asserted about the categorization of the access. It is the responsibility of the compiler or the programmer to provide labels for the accesses. Figure 2 shows possible labelings for memory accesses in a program. The labels shown correspond to the categorization of accesses depicted in Figure 1. The subscript $L$ denotes that these are labels. The labels at the same level are disjoint, and a label at a leaf implies all its parent labels.

The release consistency model exploits the information conveyed by the labels to provide less strict event ordering constraints. Thus, the labels need to have a proper relationship to the actual category of an accesses to ensure correctness under release consistency. For example, the $ordinary_L$ label asserts that an access is non-competing. Since the hardware may exploit the $ordinary_L$ label to use less strict event orderings, it is important that the $ordinary_L$ label be used only for non-competing accesses. However, a non-competing access can be conservatively labeled as $special_L$. In addition, it is important that *enough* competing accesses be labeled as $acq_L$ and $rel_L$ to ensure that the accesses labeled $ordinary_L$ are indeed non-competing. The following definition provides a conceptual model for determining whether enough $special_L$ accesses have been categorized as $sync_L$ (again assuming the sequential consistency model).

> **Definition 3.1: Enough $Sync_L$ Labels**
> Pick any two accesses $u$ on processor $P_u$ and $v$ on processor $P_v$ ($P_u$ not the same as $P_v$) such that the two accesses conflict, and at least one is labeled as $ordinary_L$. Under any legal interleaving, if $v$ appears after (before) $u$, then there needs to be at least one $sync_L$ write (read) access on $P_u$ and one $sync_L$ read (write) on $P_v$ separating $u$ and $v$, such that the write appears before the read. There are *enough* accesses labeled as $sync_L$ if the above condition holds for all possible pairs $u$ and $v$. A $sync_L$ read has to be labeled as $acq_L$ and a $sync_L$ write has to be labeled as $rel_L$.

To determine whether all labels are appropriate, we present the notion of properly-labeled programs.

> **Definition 3.2: Properly-Labeled (PL) Programs**
> A program is *properly-labeled (PL)* if the following hold: (shared access) $\subseteq$ $shared_L$, competing $\subseteq$ $special_L$, and *enough* (as defined above) $special_L$ accesses are labeled as $acq_L$ and $rel_L$.

An $acq_L$ or $rel_L$ label implies the $sync_L$ label. Any $special_L$ access that is not labeled as $sync_L$ is labeled as $nsync_L$. In addition, any $shared_L$ access that is not labeled as $special_L$ is labeled as $ordinary_L$. Note that this categorization is based on access and not on location. For example, it is possible that of two accesses to the same location, one is labeled $special_L$ while the other is labeled $ordinary_L$.

Most architectures provide atomic read-modify-write operations for efficiently dealing with competing accesses. The load and store access in the operation can be labeled separately based on their categorization, similarly to individual load and store accesses. The most common label for a read-modify-write is an $acq_L$ for the load and an $nsync_L$ for the store. A prevalent example of this is an atomic test-and-set operation used to gain exclusive access to a set of data. Although the store access is necessary to ensure mutual exclusion, it does not function as either an acquire or a release. If the programmer or compiler cannot categorize the read-modify-write appropriately, the conservative label for guaranteeing correctness is $acq_L$ and $rel_L$ for the load and store respectively (the operation is treated as both an acquire and a release).

There is no unique labeling to make a program a PL program. As long as the above subset properties are respected, the program will be considered properly-labeled. Proper labeling is not an inherent property of the program, but simply a property of the labels. Therefore, any program can be properly-labeled. However, the less conservative the labeling, the higher is the potential for performance benefits.

Given perfect information about the category of an access, the access can be easily labeled to provide a PL program. However, perfect information may not be available at all times. Proper labeling can still be provided by being conservative. This is illustrated in the three possible labeling strategies enumerated below (from conservative to aggressive). Only leaf labels shown in Figure 2 are discussed (remember that a leaf label implies all parent labels).

1. If competing and non-competing accesses can not be distinguished, then all reads can be labeled as $acq_L$ and all writes can be labeled as $rel_L$.

2. If competing accesses can be distinguished from non-competing accesses, but synchronization and non-synchronization accesses can not be distinguished, then all accesses distinguished as non-competing can be labeled as $ordinary_L$ and all competing accesses are labeled as $acq_L$ and $rel_L$ (as before).

3. If competing and non-competing accesses are distinguished and synchronization and non-synchronization accesses are distinguished, then all non-competing accesses can be labeled as $ordinary_L$, all non-synchronization accesses can be labeled as $nsync_L$, and all synchronization accesses are labeled as $acq_L$ and $rel_L$ (as before).

We discuss two practical ways for labeling accesses to provide PL programs. The first involves parallelizing compilers that generate parallel code from sequential programs. Since the compiler does the parallelization, the information about which accesses are competing and which accesses are used for synchronization is known to the compiler and can be used to label the accesses properly.

The second way of producing PL programs is to use a programming methodology that lends itself to proper labeling. For example, a large class of programs are written such that accesses to shared data are protected within critical sections. Such programs are called *synchronized programs*, whereby writes to shared locations are done in a mutually exclusive manner (no other reads or writes can occur simultaneously). In a synchronized program, all accesses (except accesses that are part of the synchronization constructs) can be labeled as *ordinary$_L$*. In addition, since synchronization constructs are predefined, the accesses within them can be labeled properly when the constructs are first implemented. For this labeling to be proper, the programmer must ensure that the program is synchronized.

Given a program is properly-labeled, the remaining issue is whether the consistency model exploits the extra information conveyed by the labels. The sequential and processor consistency models ignore all labels aside from *shared$_L$*. The weak consistency model ignores any labelings past *ordinary$_L$* and *special$_L$*. In weak consistency, an access labeled *special$_L$* is treated as a synchronization access and as both an acquire and a release. In contrast, the release consistency model presented in the next subsection exploits the information conveyed by the labels at the leaves of the labeling tree.

From this point on, we do not distinguish between the categorization and the labeling of an access, unless this distinction is necessary.

### 3.3 Release Consistency

Release consistency is an extension of weak consistency that exploits the information about acquire, release, and non-synchronization accesses. The following gives the conditions for ensuring *release consistency*.

> **Condition 3.1: Conditions for Release Consistency**
> (A) before an ordinary LOAD or STORE access is allowed to perform with respect to any other processor, all previous *acquire* accesses must be performed, and
> (B) before a *release* access is allowed to perform with respect to any other processor, all previous ordinary LOAD and STORE accesses must be performed, and
> (C) *special accesses* are processor consistent with respect to one another.

Four of the ordering restrictions in weak consistency are not present in release consistency. The first is that ordinary LOAD and STORE accesses following a release access do not have to be delayed for the release to complete; the purpose of the release synchronization access is to signal that previous accesses in a critical section are complete, and it does not have anything to say about ordering of accesses following it. Of course, the local dependences within the same processor must still be respected. Second, an acquire synchronization access need not be delayed for previous ordinary LOAD and STORE accesses to be performed. Since an acquire access is not giving permission to any other process to read/write the previous pending locations, there is no reason for the acquire to wait for them to complete. Third, a non-synchronization special access does not wait for previous ordinary accesses and does not delay future ordinary accesses; a non-synchronization access does not interact with ordinary accesses. The fourth difference arises from the ordering of special accesses. In release consistency, they are only required to be processor consistent and not sequentially consistent. For all applications that we have encountered, sequential consistency and processor consistency (for special accesses) give the same results. Section 4 outlines restrictions that allow

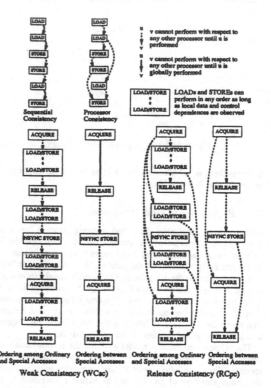

Figure 3: Ordering requirements for different consistency models.

us to show this equivalence. We chose processor consistency since it is easier to implement and offers higher performance.

## 4   Model Equivalences

The purpose of this section is to provide more insight into the similarities and differences among the consistency models presented in Sections 2 and 3 by showing relations and equivalences among the models.

We have presented four consistency models: sequential consistency (SC), processor consistency (PC), weak consistency with special accesses sequentially consistent (WCsc), and release consistency with special accesses processor consistent (RCpc). Two other models that fit within this framework are weak consistency with special accesses processor consistent (WCpc) and release consistency with special accesses sequentially consistent (RCsc). Figure 3 depicts the event orderings imposed by Conditions 2.1 through 2.3 for SC, PC, WCsc, and Condition 3.1 for RCpc. The WC and RC models have fewer restrictions on ordering than SC and PC, and RC has fewer restrictions than WC. Of course, a hardware implementation has the choice of enforcing the stated conditions directly or imposing some alternative set of conditions that guarantee the executions of programs appear as if the stated conditions were followed.

We define the relations $\geq$ (stricter) and $=$ (equal) for relating the models. If $A$ and $B$ are different consistency models, then relation $A \geq B$ says that results of executions of a program under model A will be in accordance to legal results for the program under model B, but not necessarily vice versa. The stricter relation is transitive. The relation $A = B$ says that for a certain program, models A and B cannot be distinguished based on the results of the program. Given $A \geq B$ and $B \geq A$, we know $A = B$. Some obvious relations that hold for any parallel program are: $SC \geq PC$, $SC \geq WCsc \geq RCsc$, $SC \geq WCpc \geq RCpc$, $PC \geq RCpc$, $WCsc \geq WCpc$, and $RCsc \geq RCpc$. However, the stricter relation does not hold among the following pairs: (PC,WCsc), (PC,RCsc), (PC,WCpc), and (RCsc,WCpc).

Due to the more complex semantics of the weaker models, it is desirable to show that the weaker models are equivalent to the stricter models for certain classes of programs. Such equivalences would be useful. For example, a programmer can write programs under the well defined semantics of the sequential consistency model, and as long as the program satisfies the restrictions, it can safely be executed under the more efficient release consistency model.

Let us first restrict the programs to PL programs under sequential consistency. Given such programs, we have proved the following equivalences: $SC = WCsc = RCsc$. This is done by proving $RCsc \geq SC$ for PL programs and using the relation $SC \geq WCsc \geq RCsc$. Our proof technique is based on an extension of the formalism presented by Shasha and Snir [13]. We have included the proof for $RCsc \geq SC$ in the appendix. A similar proof can be used to show $PC = WCpc = RCpc$ for PL programs under the processor consistency model.

More equivalences can be shown if we restrict programs to those that cannot distinguish between sequential consistency and processor consistency ($SC = PC$). Given a set of restrictions on competing LOAD accesses, it can be shown that $SC = PC$.[2] The restrictions are general enough to allow for all implementations of locks, semaphores, barriers, distributed loops, and task queues that we are interested in. Given competing LOAD accesses have been restricted (therefore, $SC = PC$) and shared accesses are properly labeled to qualify the program as a PL program under SC, it is easily shown that $SC = PC = WCsc = RCsc = WCpc = RCpc$. Therefore, such a program could be written based on the sequential consistency model and will run correctly under release consistency (RCpc).

The above equivalences hold for PL programs only. In some programs most accesses are competing (e.g., chaotic relaxation) and must be labeled as special for proper labeling. While this will make the equivalences hold, the program's performance may not be substantially better on RCsc than on SC. However, such applications are usually robust enough to tolerate a more relaxed ordering on competing accesses. For achieving higher performance in these cases, the programmer needs to directly deal with the more complex semantics of release consistency to reason about the program.

---

[2]Given such restrictions, one can allow an atomic test-and-set used as an acquire to perform before a previous special write access (e.g., unset) has been performed. We are currently preparing a technical report that describes the details.

## 5   Performance Potentials for Different Models

The main purpose of examining weaker models is performance. In this section, we explore the potential gains in performance for each of the models. Realizing the full potential of a model will generally depend on the access behavior of the program and may require novel architectural and compiler techniques. Our goal is to provide intuition about how one model is more efficient than another.

The performance differences among the consistency models arise from the opportunity to overlap large latency memory accesses with independent computation and possibly other memory accesses. When the latency of an access is hidden by overlapping it with other computation, it is known as access *buffering*. When the latency of an access is hidden by overlapping with other accesses, it is known as access *pipelining*. To do buffering and pipelining for read accesses requires prefetch capability (non-blocking loads).

We provide simple bounds for the maximum performance gain of each model compared to a base execution model. The base model assumes that the processor is stalled on every access that results in a cache miss. It is easily shown that sequential consistency and processor consistency can at best gain a factor of 2 and 3, respectively, over the base model. This gain arises from the opportunity to buffer accesses. In practice though these two models are not expected to perform much better than the base model, since access buffering is not effective when the frequency of shared accesses is high.

The weak and release consistency models can potentially provide large gains over the base model, since accesses and computation in the region between two adjacent synchronization points can be overlapped freely as long as uniprocessor dependences are respected. In this case, the maximum gain over the base model is approximately equal to $t_{lat}/t_{ser}$, where $t_{lat}$ is the latency of a miss and $t_{ser}$ is the shortest delay between the issue of two consecutive accesses that miss in a cache. Intuitively, this is because ordinary accesses within a region can be pipelined. Unlike the maximum gains for SC and PC, the potential gains for WC and RC are more realizable. For example, several numerical applications fetch and update large arrays as part of their computations. The pipelining of reads and writes in such applications can lead to large performance gains.

The difference in performance between WC and RC arises when the occurrence of special accesses is more frequent. While weak consistency requires ordinary accesses to perform in the region between two synchronization points, release consistency relaxes this by allowing an ordinary access to occur anywhere between the previous acquire and the next release. In addition, an acquire can perform without waiting for previous ordinary accesses and ordinary accesses can perform without waiting for a release. Figure 4 shows an example that highlights the difference between the two models (assume that there are no local dependences).

To illustrate the performance gains made possible by the release consistency model, we consider the example of doing updates to a distributed hash table. Each bucket in the table is protected by a lock. A processor acquires the lock for a bucket first. Next, several words are read from records in that bucket, some computation is performed, and several words are written based on the result of the computation. Finally, the lock is released. The processor then moves on to do the same se-

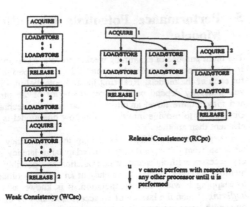

Figure 4: Possible overlap difference between WCsc and RCpc.

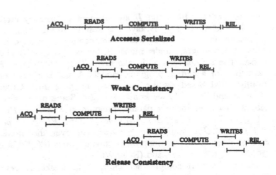

Figure 5: Overlap in processing hash table buckets.

quence of operations on another bucket. Such operations are common in several applications (for example, token hash tables in OPS5 [6]). The locality of data in such an application is low since the hash table can be large and several other processors may have modified an entry from the last time it was accessed. Therefore, the read and write accesses will miss often.

Under sequential consistency, all accesses and computation become serialized. With weak consistency, the reads can be pipelined. Of course, this assumes the architecture allows multiple outstanding reads. All reads need to complete before the computation. Once the computation completes, the writes occur in a pipelined fashion. However, before releasing the lock, all writes need to complete. The lock for the next record can not be acquired until the previous lock is released.

Release consistency provides the most opportunity for overlap. Within a critical section, the overlap is the same as in weak consistency. However, while the release is being delayed for the writes to complete, the processor is free to move on to the next record to acquire the lock and start the reads. Thus, there is overlap between the writes of one critical section and the reads of the next section.

To make the example more concrete, assume the latency of a miss is 40 cycles. Consider read miss, write miss, acquiring a lock, and releasing a lock as misses. Assume $t_{ser}$ is 10 cycles and the computation time is 100 cycles. Assume three read misses and three write misses in each record lookup and update. If all accesses are serialized, each critical section takes 420 cycles. With weak consistency, the read misses before the computation and the write misses after the computation can be pipelined. The three read misses will complete in 60 cycles. The same is true for the write misses. Therefore, the critical section completes in 300 cycles on an implementation with weak consistency. Under release consistency, the same overlap is possible within a critical section. In addition, there is overlap between critical sections. Therefore, the processor can move on to the next critical section every 230 cycles. Figure 5 shows the overlap differences among sequential, weak, and release consistency. The segments shown span the time from the issue to the completion of an access. An access may be initiated by the processor several cycles before it is issued to the memory system.

# 6 Implementation Issues

The two most important issues from an implementation point of view are correctness and performance. The consistency model determines what a correct implementation of the memory system must provide. The challenge for a correct implementation is to achieve the full performance potential of the chosen consistency model. This section presents practical implementation techniques, focusing on issues relevant to scalable architectures that use caches, distributed memory, and scalable interconnection networks.

In the following subsections, we outline the techniques for ordering accesses under the various consistency models. The problem is split between ordering accesses to the same memory block and those to different memory blocks. General solutions to achieve the proper ordering are given along with the particular solutions employed in the DASH prototype system [8]. Our discussion focuses on invalidation-based coherence protocols, although the concepts can also be applied to update-based protocols.

## 6.1 Inter-Block Access Ordering and the FENCE Mechanism

As a result of the distribution of the memory and the use of scalable interconnection networks, requests issued by a processor to distinct memory modules may execute out of order. To maintain order among two accesses, we need a mechanism to delay the issue of one access until the previous one has been performed.[3] This requires each processor to keep track of its outstanding accesses. Due to multiple paths and variable delays within the memory system, acknowledge messages from target memories and caches are required to signal the completion of an access.

We refer to the mechanism for delaying the issue of accesses as a *fence* [3, 5, 13]. We define a general set of fence operations and demonstrate how these fence operations can be used to implement the consistency models presented earlier. While

---

[3]There is a subtle difference between delaying issue and delaying an access from being performed with respect to any other processor. Instead of delaying the issue of a write, the processor can delay making the new value visible to other processors. The write is considered performed when the new value is made visible to other processors. This allows write accesses to be pipelined. We are studying hardware techniques that exploit this distinction for write accesses in invalidate-based machines. However, we do not consider such techniques in this paper.

| Model | Operation Preceded by Fence | Fence Type | Previous Accesses that must be performed | |
|-------|-----------------------------|------------|------|-------|
| | | | LOAD | STORE |
| SC | LOAD | full | G | P |
| | STORE | full | G | P |
| PC | LOAD | full | P | |
| | STORE | write | P | P |

Figure 6: Fence operations to achieve sequential and processor consistency. P denotes performed while G denotes globally performed.

fence operations are described here as explicit operations, it is possible, and often desirable, to implicitly associate fences with load, store, and special (e.g., acquire, release) accesses.

For generality, we assume that load operations are non-blocking. The processor can proceed after the load is issued, and is only delayed if the destination register of the load is accessed before the value has returned. In contrast, a blocking load stalls the processor until it is performed.

Fence operations can be classified by the operations they delay and the operations they wait upon. Useful operations to delay are: (i) all future read and write accesses (*full fence*); (ii) all future write accesses (*write fence*), and (iii) only the access immediately following the fence (*immediate fence*). Likewise, useful events to wait for are a combination of previous load accesses, store accesses, and (for the weaker models) special accesses.

Figure 6 shows the placement and type of fence operations required to achieve sequential and processor consistency. For example, the first line for SC in the figure indicates that the fence prior to a load is a full fence waiting for all previous loads to globally perform and all previous stores to perform. Figure 7 shows the fence operations necessary to achieve weak consistency (WCsc) and release consistency (RCpc). The implementations outlined are the most aggressive implementation for each model in that only the delays that are necessary are enforced. Conservative implementations are possible whereby hardware complexity is reduced by allowing some extra delays.

To implement fences, a processor must keep track of outstanding accesses by keeping appropriate counters. A count is incremented upon the issue of the access, and is decremented when the acknowledges come back for that access (an acknowledge for a read access is simply the return value). For full and write fences, the number of counters necessary is a function of the number of different kinds of accesses that need to be distinguished. For example, RCpc needs to distinguish four groups of accesses: ordinary, nsync load, acquire, and special store accesses. Therefore, an aggressive implementation requires four counters. However, only two counters are required if special loads are blocking. For immediate fences, the same number of counters (as for full or write fence) is required for each outstanding immediate fence. Therefore, we have to multiply this number by the number of immediate fences that are allowed to be outstanding. Slightly conservative implementations of release consistency may simply distinguish special load accesses from other accesses by using two counters (only one if special loads are blocking) and limit the number of outstanding immediate fences to a small number.

Full fences can be implemented by stalling the processor until the appropriate counts are zero. A write fence can be implemented by stalling the write buffer. The immediate fence, which is only required in release consistency (for an aggressive implementation), requires the most hardware. Each delayed operation requires an entry with its own set of counters. In addition, accesses and acknowledges need to be tagged to distinguish which entry's counters should be decremented upon completion. In the DASH prototype (discussed in Section 6.3), a write fence is substituted for the immediate fence (load accesses are blocking), thus providing a conservative implementation of release consistency.

## 6.2 Intra-Block Ordering of Accesses

The previous section discussed ordering constraints on accesses to different memory blocks. When caching is added to a multiprocessor, ordering among accesses to the same block becomes an issue also. For example, it is possible to receive a read request to a memory block that has invalidations pending due to a previous write. There are subtle issues involved with servicing the read request while invalidations are pending. Cache blocks of larger than one word further complicate ordering, since accesses to different words in the block can cause a similar interaction.

In an invalidation-based coherence protocol, a store operation to a non-dirty location requires obtaining exclusive ownership and invalidating other cached copies of the block. Such invalidations may reach different processors at different times and acknowledge messages are needed to indicate that the store is performed. In addition, ownership accesses to the same block must be serialized to ensure only one value persists. Unfortunately, the above two measures are not enough to guarantee correctness. It is important to distinguish between dirty cache lines with pending invalidates versus those with no pending invalidates. Otherwise, a processor cache may give up its ownership to a dirty line with invalidates pending to a read or write request by another processor, and the requesting processor would not be able to detect that the line returned was not performed. The requesting processor could then improperly pass through a fence operation that requires all previous loads to be globally performed (if access was a read) or all previous stores to be performed (if access was a write). Consequently, read and ownership requests to a block with pending invalidates must either be delayed (by forcing retry or delaying in a buffer) until the invalidations are complete, or if the request is serviced, the requesting processor must be notified of the outstanding status and acknowledges should be forwarded to it to indicate the completion of the store. The first alternative provides atomic store operations. The second alternative doesn't guarantee atomicity of the store, but informs the requesting processor when the store has performed with respect to all processors. In the next subsection, we will discuss the specific implementation technique used in DASH.

The issues in update-based cache coherence schemes are slightly different. In an update-based scheme, a store operation to a location requires updating other cache copies. To maintain coherence, updates to the same block need to be serialized at a central point and updates must reach each cache in that order. In addition, SC-based models are difficult to implement because copies of a location get updated at different times (it is virtually impossible to provide atomic stores). Consequently, a load may return a value from a processor's cache, with no indication of whether the responsible store has performed with respect to all

| Model | Operation Preceded by Fence | Fence Type | Previous Accesses that must be Performed | | | |
|---|---|---|---|---|---|---|
| | | | LOAD | STORE | SPECIAL LD | SPECIAL ST |
| WCsc | first LOAD/STORE after SPECIAL | full | | | P | P |
| | SPECIAL LD | full | P | P | G | P |
| | SPECIAL ST | full | P | P | G | P |

| Model | Operation Preceded by Fence | Fence Type | Previous Accesses that must be Performed | | | | | |
|---|---|---|---|---|---|---|---|---|
| | | | LOAD | STORE | NSYNC LD | ACQUIRE | NSYNC ST | RELEASE |
| RCpc | first LOAD/STORE after ACQUIRE | full | | | | P | | |
| | NSYNC LD | immediate | | | P | P | | |
| | ACQUIRE | full | | | P | P | | |
| | NSYNC ST | immediate | | | P | P | P | P |
| | RELEASE | immediate | P | P | P | P | P | P |

Figure 7: Fence operations to achieve weak consistency and release consistency. P denotes performed while G denotes globally performed.

processors. For this reason, PC-based models are an attractive alternative for update-based coherence schemes.

## 6.3 The DASH Prototype

The DASH multiprocessor [8], currently being built at Stanford, implements many of the features discussed in the previous sections. The architecture consists of several processing nodes connected through a low-latency scalable interconnection network. Physical memory is distributed among the nodes. Each processing node, or *cluster*, is a Silicon Graphics POWER Station 4D/240 [2] consisting of four high-performance processors with their individual caches and a portion of the shared memory. A bus-based snoopy scheme keeps caches coherent within a cluster while inter-cluster coherence is maintained using a distributed directory-based protocol. For each memory block, the directory keeps track of remote clusters caching it, and point-to-point messages are sent to invalidate remote copies of the block.

Each cluster contains a directory controller board. This directory controller is responsible for maintaining cache coherence across the clusters and serving as the interface to the interconnection network. Of particular interest to this paper are the protocol and hardware features that are aimed at implementing the release consistency model. Further details on the protocol are given in [8].

The processor boards of the 4D/240 are designed to work only with the simple snoopy protocol of the bus. The base, single-bus system implements a processor consistency model. The single bus guarantees that operations cannot be observed out of order, and no acknowledgements are necessary. Read operations are blocking on the base machine.

In the distributed DASH environment, the release consistency model allows the processor to retire a write after it has received ownership, but before the access is performed with respect to all other processors. Therefore, a mechanism is needed to keep track of outstanding accesses. In DASH, this function is performed by the remote access cache (RAC). Corresponding to each outstanding access, the RAC maintains a count of invalidation acknowledges pending for that cache block and keeps track of the processor(s) associated with that access. In addi-

tion, the RAC maintains a counter per processor indicating the number of RAC entries (i.e., outstanding requests) in use by each processor.

To ensure proper intra-block ordering, the RAC detects accesses to blocks with pending invalidates by snooping on the cluster bus. In case of a local processor access, the RAC allows the operation to complete, but adds the new processor to the processor tag field of the RAC. Thus, the processor that has a copy of the line now shares responsibility for the block becoming performed. For remote requests (i.e., requests from processors on a different cluster) the RAC rejects the request. The RAC does not attempt to share a non-performed block with a remote processor because of the overhead of maintaining the pointer to this remote processor and the need to send an acknowledgement to this processor when the block has been performed. Rejecting the request is not as desirable as queuing the requests locally, but this would require extra buffering.

To ensure proper inter-block ordering, DASH again relies on the acknowledges in the protocol and the RAC. The per processor counter indicates the number of outstanding requests for each processor. When this count is zero, then the processor has no outstanding operations and a fence operation can complete. There are two types of fence operations in DASH: a full fence and a write fence. The full fence is implemented by stalling the processor until all previous memory operations are performed (i.e., the RAC count is zero for that processor). The less restrictive write fence is implemented by stalling the output of the processor's write-buffer until all previous memory operations are performed. This effectively blocks the processor's access to the second level cache and cluster bus.

DASH distinguishes lock and unlock synchronization operations by physical address. All synchronization variables must be partitioned to a separate area of the address space. Each unlock (release) operation includes an implicit write fence. This blocks the issuing of any further writes (including the unlock operation) from that processor until all previous writes have been performed. This implicit write fence provides a sufficient implementation for release consistency. The explicit forms of full and write fence operations are also available. These allow the programmer or compiler to synthesize other consistency models.

## 7    Concluding Remarks

The issue of what memory consistency model to implement in hardware is of fundamental importance to the design of scalable multiprocessors. In this paper, we have proposed a new model of consistency, called release consistency. Release consistency exploits information about the property of shared-memory accesses to impose fewer restrictions on event ordering than previously proposed models, and thus offers the potential for higher performance. To avoid having the programmer deal directly with the more complex semantics associated with the release consistency model, we presented a framework for distinguishing accesses in programs so that the same results are obtained under RC and SC models. In particular, we introduced the notion of properly-labeled (PL) programs and proved the equivalence between the SC and the RCsc model for PL programs. This is an important result since programmers can use the well defined semantics of sequential consistency to write their programs, and as long as the programs are PL, they can be safely executed on hardware implementing the release consistency model.

To implement the various consistency models, we propose the use of fence operations. Three different kinds of fence operations – full fence, write fence, and immediate fence – were identified. Careful placement of these multiple types of fences enabled us to minimize the duration for which the processor is blocked. We also discussed subtle ordering problems that arise in multiprocessors with caches and provided solutions to them. Finally, practical implementation techniques were presented in the context of the Stanford DASH multiprocessor.

We are currently building the prototype for the DASH architecture, which supports the release consistency model. We are using a simulator for the system to quantify the performance differences among the models on real applications and to explore alternative implementations for each model. We are also exploring compiler techniques to exploit the less strict restrictions of release consistency. Finally, we are investigating programming language and programming environment enhancements that allow the compiler to gather higher level information about the shared accesses.

## 8    Acknowledgments

We would like to thank Rohit Chandra for several useful discussions, and Jaswinder Pal Singh and Sarita Adve for their comments on the paper. We also wish to thank the reviewers for their helpful comments. This research was supported by DARPA contract N00014-87-K-0828. Daniel Lenoski is supported by Tandem Computer Incorporated. Phillip Gibbons is supported in part by NSF grant CCR-86-10181 and DARPA contract N00014-88-K-0166.

## References

[1] Sarita Adve and Mark Hill. Personal communication. March 1990.

[2] Forest Baskett, Tom Jermoluk, and Doug Solomon. The 4D-MP graphics superworkstation: Computing + graphics = 40 MIPS + 40 MFLOPS and 100,000 lighted polygons per second. In *Proceedings of the 33rd IEEE Computer Society International Conference – COMPCON 88*, pages 468–471, February 1988.

[3] W. C. Brantley, K. P. McAuliffe, and J. Weiss. RP3 processor-memory element. In *Proceedings of the 1985 International Conference on Parallel Processing*, pages 782–789, 1985.

[4] Michel Dubois, Christoph Scheurich, and Fayé Briggs. Memory access buffering in multiprocessors. In *Proceedings of the 13th Annual International Symposium on Computer Architecture*, pages 434–442, June 1986.

[5] James R. Goodman. Cache consistency and sequential consistency. Technical Report no. 61, SCI Committee, March 1989.

[6] Anoop Gupta, Milind Tambe, Dirk Kalp, Charles Forgy, and Allen Newell. Parallel implementation of OPS5 on the Encore multiprocessor: Results and analysis. *International Journal of Parallel Programming*, 17(2):95–124, 1988.

[7] Leslie Lamport. How to make a multiprocessor computer that correctly executes multiprocess programs. *IEEE Transactions on Computers*, C-28(9):241–248, September 1979.

[8] Dan Lenoski, James Laudon, Kourosh Gharachorloo, Anoop Gupta, and John Hennessy. The directory-based cache coherence protocol for the DASH multiprocessor. In *Proceedings of the 17th Annual International Symposium on Computer Architecture*, May 1990.

[9] G. F. Pfister, W. C. Brantley, D. A. George, S. L. Harvey, W. J. Kleinfelder, K. P. McAuliffe, E. A. Melton, V. A. Norton, and J. Weiss. The IBM research parallel processor prototype (RP3): Introduction and architecture. In *Proceedings of the 1985 International Conference on Parallel Processing*, pages 764–771, 1985.

[10] C. Scheurich and M. Dubois. Correct memory operation of cache-based multiprocessors. In *Proceedings of the 14th Annual International Symposium on Computer Architecture*, pages 234–243, June 1987.

[11] Christoph Scheurich. *Access Ordering and Coherence in Shared Memory Multiprocessors*. PhD thesis, University of Southern California, May 1989.

[12] G. E. Schmidt. The Butterfly parallel processor. In *Proceedings of the Second International Conference on Supercomputing*, pages 362–365, 1987.

[13] Dennis Shasha and Marc Snir. Efficient and correct execution of parallel programs that share memory. *ACM Transactions on Programming Languages and Systems*, 10(2):282–312, April 1988.

## Appendix A: Proof for SC = RCsc

In this appendix we present a proof of the equivalence between $SC$ and $RCsc$ for PL programs (with respect to $SC$). For brevity, we will use the terms $RC$ to denote $RCsc$ and PL to denote PL programs properly-labeled with respect to $SC$. We begin with a few definitions.

An *execution* of a program on an implementation defines a pair, $(T, EO)$, as follows.

- The *per-processor trace*, $T$, is a set of traces, one for each processor, showing the instructions executed by the processor during the execution. The order among instructions in the trace is adjusted to depict program order for each processor.

- The execution order, $EO$, specifies the order in which conflicting accesses are executed. (Recall from section 3 that two accesses, $u$ and $v$, *conflict* if and only if $u$ and $v$ are to the same location and one is a STORE.) $EO$ fully specifies the results of a program, since any sequential execution of the accesses in an order that extends the execution order (i.e., topological sort) will give the same result.

The *delay relation*, $D$, is an ordering constraint among instructions within a processor as imposed by some event ordering. For example, the delay relation for $RC$ enforces Condition 3.1, as well as local data and control dependences. These notions of execution order, conflicting accesses, and delay relation were developed previously in [13]. To prove various equivalences, we extend the notions presented in [13] to handle conditionals, non-atomic writes, and consistency models other than $SC$ (we are preparing a technical report on this). Although writes are not atomic, we can assume that conflicting accesses are totally ordered by $EO$ since the implementations we are considering provide cache coherence (i.e., all processors observe two writes to the same location in the same order). Also we make the common assumption that accesses are only to words of memory: each read access returns the value written by some (single) write access.

The execution order $EO$ on an implementation is considered legal if $EO \cup D$ is acyclic. The graph corresponding to $EO \cup D$ is called the *precedence graph*, $G$, of the execution. Thus a cycle in $G$ denotes an impossible execution. An instruction $x$ *reaches* an instruction $y$ in an execution if there is a (directed) path from $x$ to $y$ in the precedence graph of the execution.

We partition $EO$ into two disjoint sets, $EO_s$ and $EO_o$, where $EO_s$ defines the execution order among any two (conflicting) special accesses and $E_o$ defines the execution order among any two (conflicting) accesses where at least one is an ordinary access. Likewise, $G$ is partitioned into $G_s$ and $G_o$.

Given these preliminary definitions, we now proceed with the proof. We first assume that special accesses are not affected by ordinary accesses. This permits us to claim that $EO_{s:SC} = EO_{s:RC}$ follows if $T_{SC} = T_{RC}$. We will later describe how this restriction can be lifted. In lemma 1, we show that if the same per-processor trace can occur on both $SC$ and $RC$, then the program results are the same. This lemma is then used to prove the main theorem, which shows that $SC = RC$ for all PL programs. The difficulty in extending the lemma to the main theorem is in showing that any legal trace on $RC$ may occur on $SC$ despite any conditional branches or indirect addressing. Note that $SC \geq RC$ for any program, so it suffices to show that $RC \geq SC$.

**Lemma 1:** Consider an execution $E = (T_{RC}, EO_{RC})$ on $RC$ of a PL program. If there exists a trace on $SC$ such that $T_{SC} = T_{RC}$, then there is a corresponding execution on $SC$ with the same results (i.e., $EO_{SC} = EO_{RC}$).

**Proof:** Since the event ordering on special accesses is $SC$ for both implementations, and special accesses are not affected by ordinary accesses, $G_{s:SC} = G_{s:RC}$ is a legal precedence graph for special accesses on $SC$. We will show there exists a legal execution on $SC$, based on $G_{s:SC}$, such that $EO_{o:SC} = EO_{o:RC}$.

Let $u$ and $v$ be two conflicting accesses from $T_{SC}$, such that $u$ is an ordinary access. If $u$ and $v$ are on the same processor, then the execution order, $EO$, between the two is determined by local dependences and is enforced in the same way on $SC$ and $RC$.

If $u$ and $v$ are on different processors, then the two accesses need to be ordered through special accesses for the program to be a PL program. Access $v$ can be either an ordinary or a special access. Consider the case where $v$ is an ordinary access. For $u$ and $v$ to be ordered, there is either (a) a release $REL_u$ and an acquire $ACQ_v$

such that $REL_u$ reaches $ACQ_v$ in $G_{s:SC}$ or (b) a release $REL_v$ and an acquire $ACQ_u$ such that $REL_v$ reaches $ACQ_u$ in $G_{s:SC}$. If (a) holds, then $u$ before $v$, $uEOv$, is the only possible execution order on $SC$. The same is true on $RC$, since $vEOu$ will lead to a cycle in the precedence graph. This is because clauses (A) and (B) of Condition 3.1 are upheld. Likewise, a symmetric argument can be used if (b) holds. The same correspondence between $SC$ and $RC$ can be shown for the case where $v$ is a special access. Thus the execution order $EO$ between $u$ and $v$ is the same on $SC$ and $RC$.

Since $EO_{s:SC} = EO_{s:RC}$, and this execution order determines an $E_o$ that is the same for both $SC$ and $RC$, we have shown that $EO_{SC} = EO_{RC}$. □

Therefore, $RC \geq SC$ for a program if, for every execution of a program on $RC$, there is an execution on $SC$ such that the traces are the same.

How can the traces for a program on $SC$ and $RC$ differ? There are two possible sources for any discrepancies between traces: conditional control flow (affecting which instructions are executed) and indirect addressing (affecting the location accessed by a read or write instruction). In what follows, we consider only conditionals. Extending the argument to handle programs with indirect addressing is trivial, and omitted in this proof.

We will prove that $SC = RC$ for PL programs as follows. We must show that there exists an execution on $SC$ in which the outcome of each conditional is the same. A conditional for which we have shown this correspondence will be designated *proven*, otherwise it will be called *unproven*. Initially, all conditionals in the trace on $RC$ are *unproven*. We will construct the trace on $SC$ inductively in a series of stages, where at each stage, we show that an unproven conditional occurs the same way on $SC$. Once all conditionals are proven, the traces must be equal and we can apply lemma 1.

**Theorem 2:** $SC = RC$ for PL programs.

**Proof:** Let $P$ be a PL program. Consider any execution $E = (T_{RC}, EO_{RC})$ on $RC$. Let $G_{RC}$ be the precedence graph for $E$. By the definition of a precedence graph, any instruction that affected another instruction in $E$, e.g., affected the existence of a write access or the value returned on a read access, reaches that instruction in $G_{RC}$.

As indicated above, we proceed in a series of stages, one for each conditional. At each stage, we construct an execution on $SC$ such that some unproven conditional and all previously proven conditionals have the same outcome on $SC$ and $RC$.

We begin with stage 1. The proof for stage 1 will be shown using a series of claims. As we shall see, the proof for each remaining stage is identical to stage 1.

Since $G_{RC}$ is acyclic, there is at least one unproven conditional, $u_1$, that is not reached by any other unproven conditional. Let $p_{u_1}$ be the processor that issued $u_1$. Let $A_1$ be the set of instructions that reach $u_1$ in $G_{RC}$. Although $A_1$ is only a subtrace (not even a prefix) of the entire execution $E$, we will show that the set $A_1$, constructed in this way, can be used to prove $u_1$.

Let $A_{1s}$ be the special accesses in $A_1$. We have the following characterization of $A_{1s}$.

**Claim 1:** All special accesses program ordered prior to an access in $A_{1s}$ are themselves in $A_{1s}$. There are no special accesses within any branch of an unproven conditional, $u$, where $u$ is program ordered prior to an access in $A_{1s}$.

**Proof:** We first show that the claim holds for acquires. Any acquire program ordered prior to an access, $x$, in $A_1$ reaches $x$ and hence will itself be in $A_{1s}$. There are no acquires within any branch of an unproven conditional program ordered prior to an access in $A_{1s}$ since no access after such a conditional can complete prior to the conditional itself.

We claim that the last program ordered access in $A_1$ for each processor (other than $p_{u_1}$) is a special access. This fact can be shown by contradiction. Let $z_1$, an ordinary access, be the last program ordered access for some processor in $A_1$ (other than $p_{u_1}$). Since $z_1$ is in $A_1$, there is a path, $z_1, z_2, \ldots, u_1$, in $G_{RC}$. No access in $A_1$ is locally dependent on $z_1$ since it is the last program ordered access on its processor. Since $P$ is a PL program, a release below $z_1$ is needed to order the access ahead of $z_2$ on $SC$. However, there is no release below $z_1$ in $A_1$. Thus the only way for $z_1$ to affect $z_2$ on $RC$ would be in a competing manner that was prevented on $SC$. This can happen only if some acquire above either $z_1$ or $z_2$ were missing in $A_{1s}$, which contradicts the claim of the previous paragraph.

Claim 1 follows since program order is preserved on $RC$ for special accesses. □

Given this characterization of $A_{1s}$, we show that there is an execution on $SC$ such that special accesses are the same as in $A_1$. In other words, we show that both implementations have the same $G_s$ for $A_1$. This will be used to show that the results returned by read accesses are the same and hence the outcome of conditional $u_1$ is the same.

**Claim 2:** There is a prefix of an execution on $SC$ such that the special accesses are precisely the accesses in $A_{1s}$, and the execution order among these special accesses is identical to $EO_{s:RC}$.
**Proof:** The special accesses in $A_{1s}$ are self-contained, i.e., there are no acquires in $A_{1s}$ that are waiting on releases not in $A_{1s}$. By claim 1, there is an execution on $SC$ such that all special accesses in $A_{1s}$ occur. Since special accesses are $SC$ on both implementations, the same execution order among these special accesses is possible on both. To complete the proof, we argue that no other special access (i.e., not in $A1_s$) can be forced to occur prior to an access in $A1_s$ in every execution on $SC$ that includes $A_{1s}$. How can a special access be forced to occur on $SC$? Either the special access is program ordered prior to some access in $A_{1s}$ or it is a release satisfying an acquire that is not satisfied in $A_{1s}$. But the former case contradicts claim 1 and the latter case contradicts $A_{1s}$ being self-contained. Thus there is an execution on $SC$ and a point in this execution in which the special accesses performed are precisely the accesses in $A1_s$, and the execution order among these special accesses is identical to $EO_{s:RC}$. □

**Claim 3:** There is an execution on $SC$ in which the outcome of $u_1$ is the same as in $E$.
**Proof:** Since $A_1$ consists of all instructions that affect $u_1$ in $E$, the outcome of $u_1$ in the full execution $E$ is determined by only the accesses in $A_1$. Thus it suffices to show that (a) there is an execution $E_{SC}$ on $SC$ in which the instructions in $A_1$ occur, (b) all read accesses in $A_1$ return the same results in $E_{SC}$ as in $E$, and (c) the outcome of $u_1$ in $E_{SC}$ is determined by only the accesses in $A_1$.

The accesses in $A_1$ will occur on $SC$ since none of them are within an unproven conditional. This follows from the fact that if an access within a conditional can reach $u_1$, then so can its conditional (since $RC$ enforces control dependence).

Consider the prefix execution, $E_1$, constructed in claim 2, and let $EO_{1s}$ be the execution order among special accesses in $A_1$. Since $E_1$ is a prefix of a PL program, $EO_{1s}$ determines $EO_{\alpha:SC}$ for the accesses in $A_1$.

We claim that $EO_{1s}$ determines $EO_{\alpha:RC}$ for the accesses in $A_1$. We must show that the instructions in $E_1$ that are not in $A_1$ have no effect on the results returned by read accesses in $A_1$. Consider a write access, $w_1$, in $E_1$ that reaches a read access, $r_1$, in $A_1$ on $SC$, but does not reach it in $G_{RC}$. Since $r_1$ is in $A_1$, it cannot be reached on $G_{RC}$ by an unproven conditional. Thus any local dependence chain from $w_1$ to $r_1$, inclusive, does not include any instruction within an unproven conditional. Hence, if there is a local dependence on $SC$, then there will be one on $RC$. Moreover, if $w_1$ is ordinary, then it must be followed by a release on $SC$. Since all accesses complete on $RC$ prior to a release, $w_1$ must be in $A_1$ and reach the release in $G_{RC}$. Since $EO_{1s}$ is the execution order for both $SC$ and $RC$, $w_1$ must reach $r_1$ in $G_{RC}$. Similarly, if $w_1$ is a special access, it must reach $r_1$ in $G_{RC}$. In either case, we have a contradiction.

Therefore, the results returned by read accesses in $A_1$ on $SC$ depend only on other accesses in $A_1$. Thus we can view the traces as being the same. Hence by lemma 1, all read accesses in $A_1$ up to the last special access on $p_{u_1}$ return the same results in $E_{SC}$ as in $E$.

Finally, the outcome of conditional $u_1$ depends on the values read by $p_{u_1}$. These read accesses can be ordinary or special. Since $P$ is a PL program, an ordinary read access affecting $u_1$ returns the value of a write access, $w_1$, that is ordered by local dependence or through an acquire. A special read access affecting $u_1$ is already shown to return the correct value. Thus the outcome of $u_1$ is the same as in $E$. □

**Stage $k > 1$.** Inductively, we can assume that $k - 1$ unproven conditionals have been shown to correspond on $SC$ and $RC$, such that there is a $k^{th}$ unproven conditional, $u_k$, that is not reached by any other unproven conditional. At this stage, we add to the current subtrace all instructions that can reach $u_k$. Let $A_k$ be this new set of instructions. As before, although $A_k$ is not a complete trace on $SC$ (or even a prefix), we can argue that there is at least one execution on $SC$ such that (1) the same $G_s$ occurs on $A_k$ in both $SC$ and $RC$, and thus (2) the outcome of $u_k$ is the same as in $E$. The arguments are identical to those in claims 1–3 above, where $u_1, \ldots, u_{k-1}$ are no longer unproven conditionals.

Therefore, by induction, there is an execution on $SC$ such that the outcome of all conditionals is the same as in $E$. Since all unprovens correspond, we know that the full traces are equal. Thus there exists a valid trace $T_{SC}$ of $P$ on $SC$ such that $T_{SC} = T_{RC}$. Hence by lemma 1, there exists an execution on $SC$ such that $E_{SC} = E_{RC}$, i.e., the results are the same. This shows that $RC \geq SC$ for $P$. Since $SC \geq RC$, it follows that $RC = SC$ for $P$. □

We have assumed for the above proof that special accesses are not affected by ordinary accesses. This is used in the proof, for example, when we assume in lemma 1 that $EO_{s:SC} = EO_{s:RC}$ follows if $T_{SC} = T_{RC}$. In general, however, an ordinary access can affect a special access, e.g., it can be to the same location. Our proof can be extended to handle this general case in which special accesses are affected by ordinary accesses, as follows. Consider special read accesses, conditional branches, and accesses with indirect addressing all to be initially unproven. As above, include one new unproven at each stage, until all are proven. Since we are proving special read accesses along the way, we ensure the correspondence among special accesses between $SC$ and $RC$ at each stage (i.e., $EO_{s:SC} = EO_{s:RC}$). Therefore, theorem 2 holds for general PL programs.

Adve and Hill [1] have proved a similar equivalence between sequential consistency and their version of weak ordering.

# Lazy Release Consistency
# for Software Distributed Shared Memory

Pete Keleher, Alan L. Cox, and Willy Zwaenepoel
Department of Computer Science
Rice University

## Abstract

Relaxed memory consistency models, such as *release consistency*, were introduced in order to reduce the impact of remote memory access latency in both software and hardware distributed shared memory (DSM). However, in a software DSM, it is also important to reduce the number of messages and the amount of data exchanged for remote memory access. *Lazy release consistency* is a new algorithm for implementing release consistency that *lazily* pulls modifications across the interconnect only when necessary. Trace-driven simulation using the SPLASH benchmarks indicates that lazy release consistency reduces both the number of messages and the amount of data transferred between processors. These reductions are especially significant for programs that exhibit false sharing and make extensive use of locks.

## 1   Introduction

Over the past few years, researchers in hardware distributed shared memory (DSM) have proposed relaxed memory consistency models to reduce the *latency* associated with remote memory accesses [1, 8, 9, 10, 14]. For instance, in release consistency (RC) [9], writes to shared memory by processor $p_1$ need to be performed (become visible) at another processor $p_2$ only when a subsequent *release* of $p_1$ performs at $p_2$. This relaxation of the memory consistency model allows the DASH implementation of RC [12] to combat memory latency by pipelining writes to shared memory (see Figure 1). The processor is stalled only when executing a release, at which time it must wait for all its previous writes to perform.

In software DSMs, it is also important to reduce the *number* of messages exchanged. Sending a message in a software DSM is more expensive than in a hardware DSM, because it may involve traps into the operating system kernel, interrupts, context switches, and the execution of several layers

This work is supported in part by NSF Grant No. CDA-8619893 and Texas ATP Grant No. 0036404013. Pete Keleher was supported by a NASA Fellowship.

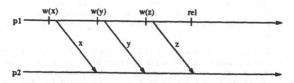

Figure 1: Pipelining Remote Memory Accesses in DASH.

of networking software. Ideally, the number of messages exchanged in a software DSM should equal the number of messages exchanged in a message passing implementation of the same application. Therefore, Munin's write-shared protocol [6], a software implementation of RC, buffers writes until a release, instead of pipelining them as in the DASH implementation. At the release, all writes going to the same destination are merged into a single message (see Figure 2).

Even Munin's write-shared protocol may send more messages than a message passing implementation of the same application. Consider the example of Figure 3, where processors $p_1$ through $p_4$ repeatedly acquire the lock $l$, write the shared variable $x$, and then release $l$. If an update policy is used in conjunction with Munin's write-shared protocol, and $x$ is present in all caches, then all of these cached copies are updated at every release. Logically, however, it suffices to update each processor's copy only when it acquires $l$. This results in a single message exchange per acquire, as in a message passing implementation. This problem is not peculiar to the use of an update policy. Similar examples can be constructed for an invalidate policy.

*Lazy release consistency* (LRC) is a new algorithm for implementing RC, aimed at reducing both the number of messages and the amount of data exchanged. Unlike *eager* algorithms such as Munin's write-shared protocol, *lazy* algorithms such as LRC do not make modifications globally visible at the time of a release. Instead, LRC guaran-

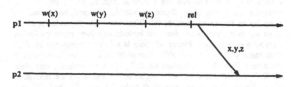

Figure 2: Merging of Remote Memory Updates in Munin.

Reprinted from. *Proc. 19th Ann. Int'l Symp. Computer Architecture*, 1992, pp. 13–21.

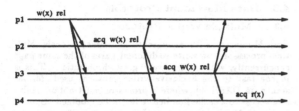

Figure 3: Repeated Updates of Cached Copies in Eager RC.

tees only that a processor that acquires a lock will see all modifications that "precede" the lock acquire. The term "preceding" in this context is to be interpreted in the transitive sense: informally, a modification precedes an acquire, if it occurs before any release such that there is a chain of release-acquire operations on the same lock, ending with the current acquire (see Section 4 for a precise definition). For instance, in Figure 3, all modifications that occur in program order before any of the releases in $p_1$ through $p_3$ precede the lock acquisition in $p_4$. With LRC, modifications are propagated at the time of an acquire. Only the modifications that "precede" the acquire are sent to the acquiring processor. The modifications can be piggybacked on the message that grants the lock, further reducing message traffic. Figure 4 shows the message traffic in LRC for the same shared data accesses as in Figure 3. $l$ and $x$ are sent in a single message at each acquire.

By not propagating modifications globally at the time of the release, and by piggybacking data movement on lock transfer messages, LRC reduces both the number of messages and the amount of data exchanged. We present the results of a simulation study, using the SPLASH benchmarks, that confirms this intuition. LRC is, however, more complex to implement than eager RC because it must keep track of the "precedes" relation. We intend to implement LRC to evaluate its runtime cost. The message and data reductions seen in our simulations seem to indicate that LRC will outperform eager RC in a software DSM environment.

The outline of the rest of this paper is as follows. In Section 2, we state the definition of RC. In Section 3, we present an eager implementation of RC based on Munin's write-shared protocol. In Section 4, we define LRC and outline its implementation. In Section 5, we describe a comparison through simulation of eager RC and LRC. We briefly discuss related work in Section 6, and we draw conclusions and explore avenues for further work in Section 7.

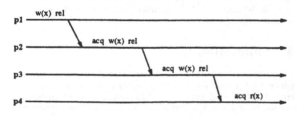

Figure 4: Message Traffic in LRC.

## 2  Release Consistency

Release consistency (RC) [9] is a form of relaxed memory consistency that allows the effects of shared memory accesses to be delayed until certain *specially labeled* accesses occur. RC requires shared memory accesses to be labeled as either *ordinary* or *special*. Within the *special* category, accesses are divided into those labeled *sync* and *nsync*, and *sync* accesses are further subdivided into *acquires* and *releases*.

**Definition 2.1** *A system is* release consistent *if:*

1. *Before an ordinary access is allowed to perform with respect to any other processor, all previous acquires must be performed.*

2. *Before a release is allowed to perform with respect to any other processor, all previous ordinary reads and writes must be performed.*

3. *Special accesses are sequentially consistent with respect to one another.*

A write is performed with respect to another processor when reads by that processor return the new write's (or a subsequent write's) value. Reads are performed with respect to another processor when a write issued by that processor can no longer affect the value returned by the read. Accesses are *performed* when they are performed with respect to all processors in the system.

*Properly labeled* programs [9] produce the same results on RC memory as they would on sequentially consistent memory [11]. Informally, a program is properly labeled if there are "enough" accesses labeled as acquires or releases, such that, for all legal interleavings of accesses, each pair of conflicting ordinary accesses is separated by a release-acquire chain. Two accesses *conflict* if they reference the same memory location, and at least one of them is a write.

RC implementations can delay the effects of shared memory accesses as long as they meet the constraints of Definition 2.1.

## 3  Eager Release Consistency

We base our eager RC algorithm on Munin's write-shared protocol [6]. A processor delays propagating its modifications to shared data until it comes to a *release*. At that time, it propagates the modifications to all other processors that cache the modified pages. For an invalidate protocol, this simply entails sending invalidations for all modified pages to the other processors that cache these pages. In order to limit the amount of data exchanged, an update protocol sends a *diff* of each modified page to other cachers. A *diff* describes the modifications made to the page, which are then merged in the other cached copies. In either case, the release blocks until acknowledgments have been received from all other cachers.

No consistency-related operations occur on an acquire. The protocol locates the processor that last executed a release on the same variable, and the resulting value is sent from the last releaser to the current acquirer.

On an access miss, a message is sent to the directory manager for the page. The directory manager forwards the request to the current owner, and the current owner sends the page to the processor that incurred the access miss.

## 4   Lazy Release Consistency

In LRC, the propagation of modifications is further postponed *until the time of the acquire*. At this time, the acquiring processor determines which modifications it needs to see according to the definition of RC. To do so, LRC uses a representation of the *happened-before-1* partial order introduced by Adve and Hill [2]. The *happened-before-1* partial order is a formalization of the "preceding" relation mentioned in Section 1.

### 4.1   The *happened-before-1* Partial Order

We summarize here the relevant aspects of the definitions of *happened-before-1* [2].

**Definition 4.1** *Shared memory accesses are partially ordered by* happened-before-1, *denoted* $\xrightarrow{hb1}$, *defined as follows:*

- *If $a_1$ and $a_2$ are accesses on the same processor, and $a_1$ occurs before $a_2$ in program order, then $a_1 \xrightarrow{hb1} a_2$.*

- *If $a_1$ is a release on processor $p_1$, and $a_2$ is an acquire on the same memory location on processor $p_2$, and $a_2$ returns the value written by $a_1$, then $a_1 \xrightarrow{hb1} a_2$.*

- *If $a_1 \xrightarrow{hb1} a_2$ and $a_2 \xrightarrow{hb1} a_3$, then $a_1 \xrightarrow{hb1} a_3$.*

RC requires that before a processor may continue past an acquire, all shared accesses that precede the acquire according to $\xrightarrow{hb1}$ must be performed at the acquiring processor. LRC guarantees that this property holds by propagating *write-notices* on the message that effects a release-acquire pair. A write-notice is an indication that a page has been modified in a particular interval, but it does not contain the actual modifications. Write-notices and actual values of modifications may be sent t different times in different messages.

### 4.2   Write-Notice Propagation

We divide the execution of each processor into distinct *intervals*, a new interval beginning with each special access executed by the processor. We define a *happens-before-1* partial order between intervals in the obvious way: an interval $i_1$ precedes an interval $i_2$ according to $\xrightarrow{hb1}$, if all accesses in $i_1$ precede all accesses in $i_2$ according to $\xrightarrow{hb1}$. An interval is said to be performed at a processor if all modifications made during that interval have been performed at that processor.

Let $V^p(i)$ be the *vector timestamp* [15] for interval $i$ of processor $p$. The number of elements in the vector $V^p(i)$ is equal to the number of processors. The entry for processor $p$ in $V^p(i)$ is equal to $i$. The entry for processor $q \neq p$ in $V^p(i)$ denotes the most recent interval of processor $q$ that has performed at $p$.

On an acquire, the acquiring processor, $p$, sends its current vector timestamp $V^p$ to the previous releaser, $q$. Processor $q$ uses this information to send $p$ the write-notices for all intervals of all processors that have performed at $q$ but have not yet performed at $p$. Releases are purely local operations in LRC, no messages are exchanged.

### 4.3   Data Movement Protocols

#### 4.3.1   Multiple Writer Protocols

Both Munin and LRC allow *multiple-writer* protocols. Multiple processors can write to different parts of the same page concurrently, without intervening synchronization. This is in contrast to the exclusive-writer protocol used, for instance, in DASH [9], where a processor must obtain exclusive access to a cache line before it can be modified. Experience with Munin [6] indicates that multiple-writer protocols perform well in software DSMs, because they can handle false sharing without generating large amounts of message traffic. Given the large page sizes in software DSMs, false sharing is an important problem. Exclusive-writer protocols may cause falsely shared pages to "ping-pong" back and forth between different processors. Multiple-writer protocols allow each processor to write into a falsely shared page without any message traffic. The modifications of the different processors are later merged using the *diffs* described in Section 3.

#### 4.3.2   Invalidate vs. Update

In the case of an invalidate protocol, the acquiring processor invalidates all pages in its cache for which it received write-notices. In the case of an update protocol, the acquiring processor updates those pages. Let $i$ be the current interval. For each page in the cache, *diffs* must be obtained from all *concurrent last modifiers*. These are all intervals $j$, such that $j \xrightarrow{hb1} i$, the page was modified in interval $j$, and there is no interval $k$, such that $j \xrightarrow{hb1} k \xrightarrow{hb1} i$, in which the modification from interval $j$ was overwritten.

#### 4.3.3   Access Misses

On an access miss, a copy of the page may have to be retrieved, as well as a number of *diffs*. The modifications summarized by the *diffs* are then merged into the page before it is accessed.

On an access miss during interval $i$, *diffs* must be obtained for all intervals $j$, such that $j \xrightarrow{hb1} i$, the missing page was modified in interval $j$, and there is no interval $k$, such that $j \xrightarrow{hb1} k \xrightarrow{hb1} i$, in which the modification from interval $j$ was overwritten.

If the processor still holds an (invalidated) copy of the page, LRC does not send the entire page over the interconnect. The write-notices contain all the information necessary to determine which *diffs* need to be applied to this copy of the page in order to bring it up-to-date. The *happened-before-1* partial order specifies the order in which the *diffs* need to be applied. This optimization reduces the amount of data sent.

## 5   Simulation

We present the results of a simulation study based on multiprocessor traces of five shared-memory application programs from the SPLASH suite [17]. We measured the number of messages and the amount of data exchanged by each program for an execution using each of four protocols: lazy update (LU), lazy invalidate (LI), eager update (EU), and eager invalidate (EI). We then relate the communication

| | Access Miss | Locks | Unlocks | Barriers |
|---|---|---|---|---|
| LI | 2m | 3 | 0 | 2(n-1) |
| LU | 2m | 3+2h | 0 | 2(n-1)+2u |
| EI | 2 or 3 | 3 | 2c | 2(n-1) + v |
| EU | 2 | 3 | 2c | 2(n-1) + 2u |

$m$ = # concurrent last modifiers for the missing page

$h$ = # other concurrent last modifiers for any local page

$c$ = # other cachers of the page

$n$ = # processors in system

$p$ = # pages in system

$u = \sum_{i=1}^{n}($ # other cachers of pages modified by $i)$

$v = \sum_{i=1}^{p}($ # excess invalidators of page $i)$

Table 1: Shared Memory Operation Message Costs

behavior to the shared memory access patterns of the application programs.

### 5.1  Methodology

A trace was generated from a 32-processor execution of each program using the Tango multiprocessor simulator [7]. These traces were then fed into our protocol simulator. We simulated page sizes from 512 to 8192 bytes.

We assume infinite caches and reliable FIFO communication channels. We do not assume any broadcast or multicast capability of the network.

### 5.2  Message Counts

The SPLASH programs use barriers and exclusive locks for synchronization. Communication occurs on barrier arrival and departure, on lock and unlock, and on an access miss. Table 1 shows the message count for each of these events under each of the protocols.

A miss costs either two or three messages for the eager protocols, depending on whether or not the directory manager has a valid copy of the page (see  ction 3). For the lazy protocols, a miss requires collecting *diffs* from the *concurrent last modifiers* of the page (see Section 4.3.2).

For a lock operation, three messages are used by all four protocols for finding and transferring the lock. In addition, in LU, the new lock holder collects all the *diffs* necessary to bring its cached pages up-to-date, causing $2h$ additional messages. No extra messages are required at this time for LI, because the invalidations are piggybacked on the lock transfer message. Also, no additional messages are required for EU and EI.

On unlocks, the eager protocols send write-notices to all cachers of locally modified pages, using $2c$ messages. The lazy protocols do not communicate on unlocks.

Barriers are implemented by sending an arrival message to the *barrier master* and waiting for the return of an exit message. Consequently, $2(n-1)$ messages are used to implement a barrier. In addition, both update protocols require $2u$ messages to send updates to all processors caching modified pages. The LI protocol requires no additional messages, because invalidations are piggybacked on the messages used for implementing the barrier. The EI protocol may require

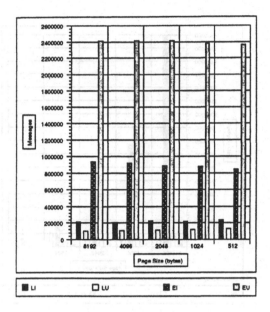

Figure 5: LocusRoute Messages.

a small number of additional messages $v$ to resolve multiple invalidations of a single page.

### 5.3  SPLASH Program Suite

#### 5.3.1  LocusRoute

LocusRoute is a VLSI cell router. The major data structure is a cost grid for the cell, a cell's cost being the number of wires already running through it. Work is allocated to processors a wire at a time. Synchronization is accomplished almost entirely through locks that protect access to a central task queue.

Data movement in LocusRoute is largely migratory [18]: locks dominate the synchronization, and data moves according to lock accesses. As page size increases, false sharing also becomes important. Both of these factors favor lazy protocols.

Figures 5 and 6 show LocusRoute's performance. The lazy protocols reduce the number of messages and the amount of data exchanged, for all page sizes.

#### 5.3.2  Cholesky Factorization

Cholesky performs the symbolic and numeric portions of a Cholesky factorization of a sparse positive definite matrix. Locks are used to control access to a global task queue and to arbitrate access when simultaneous supernodal modifications attempt to modify the same column. No barriers are used.

Data motion in Cholesky is largely migratory, as in LocusRoute. The resulting performance of Cholesky is therefore also similar to that of LocusRoute: Figures 7 and 8 show that the lazy protocols reduce the number of messages and the amount of data exchanged, for all page sizes.

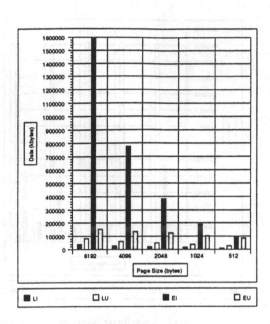

Figure 6: LocusRoute Data.

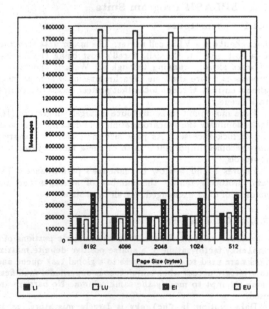

Figure 7: Cholesky Messages.

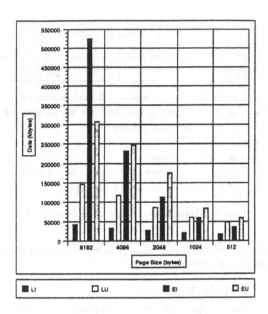

Figure 8: Cholesky Data.

### 5.3.3   MP3D

MP3D simulates rarefied hypersonic airflow over an object using a Monte Carlo algorithm. Each timestep involves several barriers, with locks used to control access to global event counters.

The message traffic for MP3D is dominated by access misses. Figures 9 and 10 show MP3D's performance. The lazy protocols exchange less data than the eager ones, because they only need to send *diffs* on an access miss and not full pages, as do the eager protocols. The update protocols exchange fewer messages, because they incur fewer access misses.

### 5.3.4   Water

Water performs an N-body molecular dynamics simulation, evaluating forces and potentials in a system of water molecules in the liquid state. At each timestep, every molecule's velocity and potential is computed from the influences of other molecules within a spherical cutoff range. Several barriers are used to synchronize each timestep, while locks are used to control access to a global running sum and to each molecule's force sum.

Of the five benchmark programs, Water has the least communication. Figures 11 and 12 show the message and data traffic for Water. While the lazy protocols use only slightly fewer messages than eager protocols for large page sizes, their data totals are significantly lower because they can often avoid bringing an entire page across the network on an access miss.

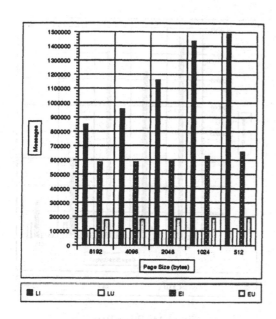

Figure 9: MP3D Messages.

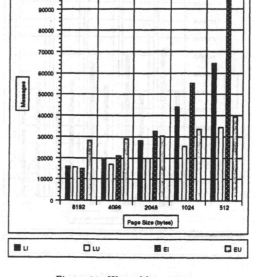

Figure 11: Water Messages.

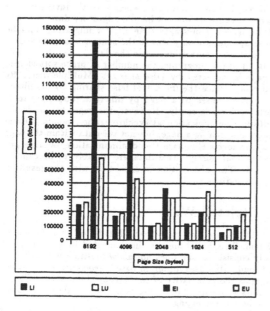

Figure 10: MP3D Data.

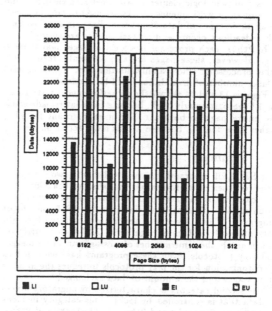

Figure 12: Water Data.

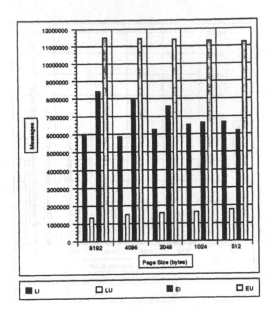

Figure 13: Pthor Messages.

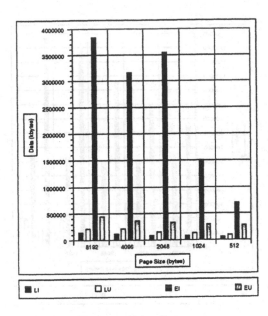

Figure 14: Pthor Data.

### 5.3.5  Pthor

Pthor is a parallel logic simulator. The major data structures represent logic elements, wires between elements, and per-processor work queues. Locks are used to protect access to all three types of data structures. Barriers are used only when deadlock occurs and all task queues are empty.

In Pthor, each processor has a set of pages that it modifies. However, these pages are also frequently read by the other processors. Under an invalidation protocol, this causes a large number of invalidations and later reloads.

Figures 13 and 14 show Pthor's performance. Data totals for EI are particularly high, because frequent reloads cause the entire page to be sent. The message count for LI is higher than for LU, because LI has more access misses.

### 5.4  Summary

The SPLASH programs can be divided into two categories based on their synchronization and sharing behavior. The first category is characterized by heavy use of barrier synchronization. This category includes the MP3D and Water programs. These programs performed poorly with invalidate protocols and large page sizes. Although barriers result in nearly the same number of messages under both eager and lazy protocols, even these programs have enough lock synchronization for the lazy protocols to reduce the number of messages and the amount of data exchanged.

The second category is characterized by migratory access to data that is controlled by locks. This category includes LocusRoute, Cholesky and Pthor. In Cholesky and Pthor, the locks protect centralized work queues, while the locks in LocusRoute protect access to individual cost array elements. The use of locks tends to cause the sharing patterns to closely follow synchronization. Since the lazy protocols

move data according to synchronization, they handle this type of synchronization much better than eager protocols.

LU performed well for both categories of programs. In contrast, EU often performed worse than the invalidate protocols, because it does not handle migratory data very well. LU sends fewer messages than EU for migratory data because updates are only sent to the next processor to acquire the lock that controls access to the data.

In all of the programs, the number of processors sharing a page is increased by false sharing. Multiple-writer RC protocols reduce the impact of false sharing by permitting ordinary accesses to a page by different processors to be performed concurrently. However, the eager protocols still perform communication at synchronization points between processors sharing a page, but not the data within the page. Lazy protocols eliminate this communication, because processors that falsely share data are unlikely to be causally related. This observation is consistent with the results of our simulations.

## 6  Related Work

Ivy [13] was the first page-based distributed shared memory system. The shared memory implemented by Ivy is sequentially consistent, and does not allow multiple writers.

Clouds [16] uses program-based *segments* rather than pages as the granularity of consistency. In addition, Clouds permits segments to be locked down at a single processor to prevent "ping-ponging".

Release consistency was introduced by Gharachorloo *et al.* [9]. It is a refinement of weak consistency, defined by Dubois and Scheurich [8]. The DASH multiprocessor takes advantage of release consistency by pipelining remote memory accesses [12]. Pipelining reduces the impact of remote memory access latency on the processor.

Munin [6] was the first software distributed shared memory system to use release consistency. Munin's implementation of release consistency merges updates at release time, rather than pipelining them, in order to reduce the number of messages transferred between processors. Munin uses multiple consistency protocols to further reduce the number of messages.

Ahamad *et al.* defined a relaxed memory model called *causal memory* [3]. Causal memory differs from RC because conflicting pairs of *ordinary* memory accesses establish causal relationships. In contrast, under RC, only *special* memory accesses establish causal relationships.

*Entry consistency*, defined by Bershad and Zekauskas [5], is another related relaxed memory model. EC differs from RC because it requires all shared data to be explicitly associated with some synchronization variable. As a result, when a processor acquires a synchronization variable, an EC implementation only needs to propagate the shared data associated with the synchronization variable. EC, however, requires the programmer to insert additional synchronization in shared memory programs, such as the SPLASH benchmarks, to execute correctly on an EC memory. Typically, RC does not require additional synchronization.

## 7    Conclusions

The performance of software DSMs is very sensitive to the number of messages and the amount of data exchanged to create the shared memory abstraction. We have described a new algorithm for implementing release consistency, *lazy release consistency*, aimed at reducing both the number of messages and the amount of data exchanged. Lazy release consistency tracks the causal dependencies between writes, acquires, and releases, allowing it to propagate writes lazily, only when they are needed.

We have used trace-driven simulation to compare lazy release consistency to an eager algorithm for implementing release consistency, based on Munin's write-shared protocol. Traces were collected from the programs in the SPLASH benchmark suite, and both update and invalidate protocols were simulated for lazy and eager RC. The simulations confirm that the number of messages and the amount of data exchanged are generally smaller for the lazy algorithm, especially for programs that exhibit false sharing and make extensive use of locks. Further work will include an implementation of lazy release consistency to assess the runtime cost of the algorithm.

## References

[1] S. Adve and M. Hill. Weak ordering: A new definition. In *Proceedings of the 17th Annual International Symposium on Computer Architecture*, pages 2–14, May 1990.

[2] S. V. Adve and M. D. Hill. A unified formalization of four shared-memory models. Technical Report CS-1051, University of Wisconsin, Madison, September 1991.

[3] M. Ahamad, P. W. Hutto, and R. John. Implementing and programming causal distributed shared memory. In *Proceedings of the 11th International Conference on Distributed Computing Systems*, pages 274–281, May 1991.

[4] J.K. Bennett, J.B. Carter, and W. Zwaenepoel. Toward large-scale shared memory multiprocessing. In M. Dubois and S. Thakkar, editors, *Scalable Shared Memory Multiprocessors*. Kluwer Academic Publishers, 1991.

[5] B.N. Bershad and M.J. Zekauskas. Midway: Shared memory parallel programming with entry consistency for distributed memory multiprocessors. Technical Report CMU-CS-91-170, Carnegie-Mellon University, September 1991.

[6] J.B. Carter, J.K. Bennett, and W. Zwaenepoel. Implementation and performance of Munin. In *Proceedings of the 13th ACM Symposium on Operating Systems Principles*, pages 152–164, October 1991.

[7] H. Davis, S. Goldschmidt, and J. L. Hennessy. Tango: A multiprocessor simulation and tracing system. Technical Report CSL-TR-90-439, Stanford University, 1990.

[8] M. Dubois and C. Scheurich. Memory access dependencies in shared-memory multiprocessors. *IEEE Transactions on Computers*, 16(6):660–673, June 1990.

[9] K. Gharachorloo, D. Lenoski, J. Laudon, P. Gibbons, A. Gupta, and J. Hennessy. Memory consistency and event ordering in scalable shared-memory multiprocessors. In *Proceedings of the 17th Annual International Symposium on Computer Architecture*, pages 15–26, Seattle, Washington, May 1990.

[10] J.R. Goodman. Cache consistency and sequential consistency. Technical Report Technical report no. 61, SCI Committee, March 1989.

[11] L. Lamport. How to make a multiprocessor computer that correctly executes multiprocess programs. *IEEE Transactions on Computers*, C-28(9):690–691, September 1979.

[12] D. Lenoski, J. Laudon, K. Gharachorloo, A. Gupta, and J. Hennessy. The directory-based cache coherence protocol for the DASH multiprocessor. In *Proceedings of the 17th Annual International Symposium on Computer Architecture*, pages 148–159, May 1990.

[13] K. Li and P. Hudak. Memory coherence in shared virtual memory systems. *ACM Transactions on Computer Systems*, 7(4):321–359, November 1989.

[14] R.J. Lipton and J.S. Sandberg. Pram: A scalable shared memory. Technical Report CS-TR-180-88, Princeton University, September 1988.

[15] F. Mattern. Virtual time and global states of distributed systems. In Michel Cosnard, Yves Robert, Patrice Quinton, and Michel Raynal, editors, *Parallel & Distributed Algorithms*, pages 215–226. Elsevier Science Publishers, Amsterdam, 1989.

[16] U. Ramachandran, M. Ahamad, and Y.A. Khalidi. Unifying synchronization and data transfer in maintaining coherence of distributed shared memory. Technical Report GIT-CS-88/23, Georgia Institute of Technology, June 1988.

[17] J.P. Singh, W.-D. Weber, and A. Gupta. Splash: Stanford parallel applications for shared-memory. Technical Report CSL-TR-91-469, Stanford University, April 1991.

[18] W.-D. Weber and A. Gupta. Analysis of cache invalidation patterns in multiprocessors. In *Proceedings of the 3th Symposium on Architectural Support for Programming Languages and Operating Systems*, pages 243–256, April 1989.

# The Midway Distributed Shared Memory System

Brian N. Bershad, Matthew J. Zekauskas, and Wayne A. Sawdon
School of Computer Science
Carnegie Mellon University
5000 Forbes Avenue
Pittsburgh, PA 15213

## Abstract

*This paper describes the motivation, design and performance of Midway, a programming system for a distributed shared memory multicomputer (DSM) such as an ATM-based cluster, a CM-5, or a Paragon. Midway supports a new memory consistency model called entry consistency. Entry consistency guarantees that shared data becomes consistent at a processor when the processor acquires a synchronization object known to guard the data. Entry consistency is weaker than other models described in the literature, such as processor consistency and release consistency, but it makes possible higher performance implementations of the underlying consistency protocols. Midway programs are written in C, and the association between synchronization objects and data must be made with explicit annotations. As a result, pure entry consistent programs can require more annotations than programs written to other models. In addition to entry consistency, Midway also supports the stronger release consistent and processor consistent models at the granularity of individual data items. Consequently, the programmer can tradeoff potentially reduced performance for the additional programming complexity required to write an entry consistent parallel program.*

This research was sponsored in part by The Defense Advanced Research Projects Agency, Information Science and Technology Office, under the title "Research on Parallel Computing", ARPA Order No. 7330, issued by DARPA/CMO under Contract MDA972-90-C-0035, by the Open Software Foundation (OSF), and by a grant from the Digital Equipment Corporation. Bershad was partially supported by a National Science Foundation Presidential Young Investigator Award. Sawdon was partially supported by a grant from the International Business Machines Corporation.

The views and conclusions contained in this document are those of the authors and should not be interpreted as representing the official policies, either expressed or implied, of DARPA, OSF, DEC, IBM, the NSF, or the U.S. government.

## 1 Introduction

Midway is a distributed shared memory (DSM) programming system supporting multiple memory consistency models within a single parallel program. Midway is intended for use on medium-scale multicomputers (fewer than 100 nodes), such as an ATM-based cluster [Rider 89], a TMC CM-5, or an Intel Paragon. In addition to supporting processor consistency and release consistency, Midway supports a new memory consistency model called entry consistency. Entry consistency guarantees that shared data becomes consistent at a processor only when the processor acquires a synchronization object that guards the data. Furthermore, the only data that is guaranteed to be consistent is that guarded by the acquired synchronization object. This allows an implementation of entry consistency to reduce the frequency of global communication by exploiting synchronization patterns between processors. Midway's implementation of entry consistency requires that the relationship between data and synchronization objects (which is implicit in the structure of a parallel program) be made explicit to the compiler and the runtime system.

Midway supports multiple consistency models within a single program to ease the task of constructing a program that runs efficiently on a DSM system. A program running under Midway may contain data that is processor consistent, release consistent, or entry consistent. Furthermore, within a single run of a program, multiple consistency models may be active at the same time. This allows the programmer to begin with a processor consistent parallel program, and then selectively relax its consistency requirements for shared data by modifying the program to use one of the weaker models.

## 1.1    Motivation

A wide range of memory consistency models exists, and each offers a different guarantee about the strength and timeliness with which updates to shared memory take effect at processors distributed throughout a network. In order of strength, these models include sequential consistency [Lamport 79], processor consistency [Goodman & Woest 88], weak consistency [Dubois et al. 86], release consistency [Gharachorloo et al. 90] and entry consistency, which is described in this paper. In order, each model can increase a processor's tolerance for latency in the memory system by relaxing the rules that determine the behavior of operations which write to shared memory. Aggressive implementations of the weaker models are capable of delivering higher performance than those of stronger ones because they better tolerate network delays and limited bandwidth [Gharachorloo et al. 91, Zucker & Baer 92].

Programmers often assume that memory is *sequentially consistent*. This means that the "result of any execution is the same as if the operations of all the processors were executed in some sequential order, and the operations of each processor appear in this sequence in the order specified by its program" [Lamport 79]. In a sequentially consistent system, one processor's update to a shared data value is reflected in every other processor's memory before the updating processor is able to issue another memory access. Unfortunately, sequentially consistent memory systems preclude many optimizations such as reordering, batching, or coalescing. These optimizations reduce the performance impact of having distributed memories with non-uniform access times [Dubois et al. 86].

Memory consistency requirements can be relaxed by taking advantage of the fact that most parallel programs already define their own higher-level consistency requirements. This is done by means of explicit synchronization operations such as lock acquisition and barrier entry. These operations impose an ordering on access to data within the program. In the absence of such operations, a multithreaded program is in effect relinquishing all control over the order and atomicity of memory operations to the underlying memory system.

These observations about explicit synchronization have led to a class of *weakly consistent* protocols [Dubois et al. 86, Scheurich & Dubois 87, Adve

& Hill 89, Gharachorloo et al. 90]. Such protocols distinguish between normal shared accesses and synchronization accesses. The only accesses that must execute in a sequentially consistent order are those relating to synchronization.[1]

A weaker model offers fewer guarantees about memory consistency, but it ensures that a "well-behaved" program executes as though it were running on a sequentially consistent memory system. The definition of "well-behaved" varies according to the model. For example, in a processor consistent system, the programmer may not assume that all memory operations are *performed* in the same order at all processors. (A load or store is globally performed when it is performed with respect to all processors. A load is performed with respect to a processor when no write by that processor can change the value returned by the load. A store is performed with respect to a processor when a load by that processor will return the value of the store.) For weak consistency, the programmer may not assume that a processor's updates are performed at other processors until the updating processor issues a synchronization operation. For release consistency, only a processor's releasing synchronization operation guarantees that its previous updates will be performed at other processors, and only a processor's acquiring synchronization operation guarantees that other processors' updates have been performed at it. (A releasing synchronization operation signals to other processors that shared data is available, while an acquiring operation signals that shared data is needed.) For entry consistency, data is only consistent on an acquiring synchronization operation, and only the data known to be guarded by the acquired object is guaranteed to be consistent.

Programs with good behavior do not assume a stronger consistency guarantee from the memory system than is actually provided. Each model's definition of good behavior places demands on the programmer to ensure that a program's access to shared data conforms to that model's consistency rules. For example, with entry consistency, a processor must not access a shared item until it has performed a synchronization operation on the item's associated synchronization object. These rules provide the memory system with in-

---

[1] In practice, synchronization accesses need only be *processor consistent* [Goodman & Woest 88], that is, writes issued from a single processor must be performed in the order issued at all processors, but writes from different processors need not be observed in the same order everywhere. The distinction between sequentially consistent and processor consistent synchronization is small, however it is easier to build a processor consistent system.

formation to allow a well-behaved program to execute as though it were running on sequentially consistent memory system. Unfortunately, the rules can add an additional dimension of complexity to the already difficult task of writing new parallel programs and porting old ones. The additional programming complexity can result in higher performance, though, because it provides greater control over communication costs.

## 1.2 Multiple models

Midway allows a programmer to navigate through a subset of the consistency models, selecting one, or several, to achieve an acceptable tradeoff between performance and programmability. A program written for Midway can use entry consistency, release consistency, or processor consistency. For all of these models, local memories on each processor cache recently used data and synchronization objects. With entry consistency, communication between processors occurs only when a processor acquires a synchronization object. Only the data guarded by the synchronization object is guaranteed to become consistent at the time of the acquire. Consequently, Midway provides an execution environment where a parallel program's performance is ultimately limited only by its internal synchronization patterns.

Although entry consistency enables the use of low-overhead consistency mechanisms, writing an entry consistent program requires more work than writing one to a stronger model. For example, every synchronization object must be identified; every use of such an object must be explicit; every shared data item must be associated with a synchronization object; and synchronization accesses should be qualified as read-only or read-write for best performance.

To make these restrictions less onerous, Midway provides a graceful migration path away from more strongly consistent models to entry consistency. A programmer begins with a processor consistent parallel program or algorithm and sets Midway's consistency model "dial" to processor consistency. The runtime system can be used to collect reference patterns for shared data so that strongly consistent code which accesses heavily shared data can be reorganized to use a weaker consistency model. With this, a programmer can quickly get an application running on the DSM, although the application may not run very quickly.

Midway implements its consistency protocols in software and has no dependencies on any specific hardware characteristic other than the ability to send messages between processors. A strictly software solution is attractive because it allows us to exploit application

specific information at the lowest levels of the system. It also ensures portability across a wide range of multi-computer architectures. The system described in this paper is operational on a cluster of MIPS R3000-based DECstations running CMU's Mach 3.0 operating system [Accetta et al. 86] over both ethernet and an ATM network.

## 1.3 Related work

Memory consistency models for DSM systems have been implemented in both hardware and software. Earlier hardware-based systems used snooping protocols where each processor monitored a shared bus to implement processor consistency. The Stanford DASH [Lenoski et al. 92] multiprocessor supports release consistency in hardware using a directory-based protocol over a dedicated low-latency interconnect.

Most software systems intended for parallel programming have implemented these same consistency models using conventional virtual memory management hardware and local area networks. Li's Ivy system [Li 86] described the first implementation of such a *page-based* DSM and was followed by several other systems [Fleisch 87, Forin et al. 89]. Munin [Carter et al. 91] is a software system which uses release consistency to support automatic data caching over a local area network. Munin is unique among weak consistency systems, in that it implements multiple consistency *protocols* which can be used on a type-specific basis. Munin uses hints from the programmer to determine the access patterns to shared data items, and then selects the best consistency protocol for each. Munin differs from Midway in that it offers multiple implementations of a single consistency model (release consistency), whereas Midway supports multiple consistency models within a single program.

Lazy release consistency [Keleher et al. 92] is a technique for implementing release consistency through causal broadcast. It has been shown through simulation to greatly reduce the number of messages required by systems such as Munin. Our work with entry consistency can be considered as an extreme variant of lazy release consistency in that Midway's explicit association between synchronization objects and data offers the runtime system additional information about causality.

## 1.4 The rest of this paper

In Section 2 we describe entry consistency. In Section 3 we describe Midway's programming interface in the context of multiple consistency models. In Section 4 we describe the important aspects of Midway's implementation and show that the infrastructure required by entry consistency can be adapted to provide each of the stronger consistency models. In Section 5 we discuss performance. In Section 6 we present our conclusions.

## 2    Entry consistency

Entry consistency takes advantage of the relationship between specific synchronization objects that protect critical sections and the shared data accessed within those critical sections. A critical section is a region of code that accesses data which may have been written by another processor. A synchronization object controls a processor's access to the code and data in the critical section. Examples of critical sections are code sequences guarded by a mutex, or phased by a barrier. In an entry consistent system, a processor's view of shared memory becomes consistent with the most recent updates *only* when it enters a critical section.

The entry consistent model matches that already used by many shared memory parallel programs, namely, the use of critical sections to guard access to shared data for which the results of an unguarded access is undefined.

### 2.1    Performing store operations

A consistency model does not define whether store operations are performed at a processor using an invalidation-based or an update-based protocol. With an invalidation-based protocol, an operation is performed at a remote processor by invalidating an entry in that processor's local cache. The processor's next access to the invalidated entry results in a cache miss and a round-trip network message to fetch the missed value. With an update-based protocol, an operation is performed at a remote processor when the stored value is deposited in that processor's cache. This allows the next access to the item to always be satisfied locally. The advantage of an invalidation-based protocol is that consistency messages can be smaller because they contain only addresses, not data. The advantage of the update-based protocol is that it greatly reduces the likelihood of a cache miss.

Midway's implementation of entry consistency uses an update-based protocol. In relatively high latency networks, where interprocessor communication is on the order of thousands of processor cycles, the effect of a cache miss on processor performance can be substantial. For example, assuming a RISC processor with a 10 *ns* cycle time, the latency of resolving a cache miss over an ATM network with a 100 *µsec* round-trip time is on the order of 10,000 instructions. Consequently, it is critical to use an update-based protocol to minimize the chance that a processor experiences a cache miss.

An advantage of entry consistency with an update-based protocol is that interprocessor communication is only necessary during the acquisition of synchronization objects. By updating only at synchronization points, and only between the synchronizing processors, new values for data guarded by a synchronization object may be coalesced and delivered to a processor all at once. By ensuring that updates are performed with respect to a processor when it enters a critical section, unexpected delays in a critical section as a result of cache misses cannot occur. Moreover, no communication is required for repeated accesses and releases of the same synchronization object on the same processor — common patterns in parallel programs [Eggers 89, Bennett et al. 90].

### 2.2    Caching synchronization objects

Entry consistency facilitates strategies which permit synchronization objects to be cached on the processor(s) where they were most recently used. For a synchronization object *s*, we define the *owner* as the processor that last acquired *s*. Only the owner of *s* may perform updates to the data guarded by *s*. The processor that owns a synchronization object may enter and exit the associated critical sections without having to communicate updates of shared memory to other processors. A processor becomes an owner of *s* by sending a message to the current owner. The current owner ensures that all updates to the data guarded by *s* are then performed at the new owner.

An unfortunate aspect of single ownership is that no more than one processor at a time can access a given shared location even if the location is only being read. To guarantee consistency, a processor must hold the appropriate synchronization object. However, that synchronization object, if used in the classical sense (such as a semaphore), only permits mutually exclusive access to the data. Consequently, straightforward use of synchronization objects to ensure consistency can limit concurrency.

We address this problem by defining two modes of access to synchronization objects: *exclusive* and *non-exclusive*. Synchronization objects continue to be owned by a single processor, but may be replicated if they are held only in non-exclusive mode. A processor must perform an exclusive access to a synchronization object $s$ in order to update any data guarded by $s$. By definition, that processor becomes the owner of $s$. Reading data guarded by $s$, though, only requires non-exclusive access to $s$.

An exclusive-mode access to a synchronization object $s$ requires that no other processor holds $s$ in non-exclusive mode. After an exclusive mode access to $s$ has been performed, any processor's next non-exclusive mode access to $s$ is performed with respect to the owner of $s$. This enables a processor to perform a sequence of non-exclusive accesses to $s$ without having to communicate with $s$'s owner each time.

## 2.3 Programming to entry consistency

Entry consistency makes several assumptions about the behavior of parallel programs and the runtime environment. First, as an instance of a weakly consistent protocol, entry consistency requires that synchronization accesses be distinguished from other accesses. Second, entry consistency requires an association between shared data and its guarding synchronization object. Third, to enable concurrent read-sharing, entry consistency requires that exclusive synchronization accesses are distinguished from non-exclusive accesses. Finally, entry consistency requires that updates are performed with respect to an acquiring processor. The last constraint affects Midway's implementation, while the first three affect its programming interface. Specifically,

- All synchronization objects should be explicitly declared as instances of one of Midway's synchronization data types, which include locks and barriers.

- All shared data must be explicitly labeled with the keyword `shared`, which is understood by the compiler.

- All shared data must be explicitly associated with at least one synchronization object. This is made by calls to the runtime system, is dynamic, and may change during the execution of a program.

Programs that include the necessary labeling information, and precede all accesses to shared data with an access to the appropriate synchronization object will observe a sequentially consistent shared memory.

## 3 Other models in Midway

A parallel program's consistency requirements can be buried within its algorithms and sharing patterns. Midway's implementation of entry consistency requires that they be made explicit. This may be difficult because it can require a complete understanding of a program or algorithm, and can be a major barrier to porting someone else's code.

From a performance standpoint, a complete transformation into entry consistency may not be necessary. In many parallel programs, most communication is of a few primary data structures. While a large number of secondary data structures may be used, they are shared, or at least modified, with low frequency. There would be only a marginal performance impact when using a stronger consistency model to manage these infrequently modified items. For example, some programs maintain a set of flags which change infrequently, such as when new data is available, or when an algorithm has terminated. This kind of data may be most easily managed as processor consistent. There also exist programs that can tolerate minor inconsistencies in their results, and underspecify their synchronization. This is done, for example by *locus*, *mp3d* and *pthor* from the Splash application suite [Singh et al. 92]. These programs can be converted to entry consistency by, for example, binding all data to a barrier, but this would oversynchronize the processors. Instead, managing the data with its initially assumed consistency model may be the best solution.

Because entry consistency may be hard to use and may not always offer a performance advantage, a Midway program may also contain data which is release or processor consistent. Entry consistent data is associated with a synchronization object. Data not associated with a synchronization object, but with a "flush interval" is maintained according to processor consistency. The flush interval controls the rate at which updates are propagated (in issue order) to other processors. An item that is neither associated with a synchronization object nor a flush interval is assumed to be release consistent. A processor's updates to release consistent data are performed at remote processors only when a release from the updating processor is necessary to satisfy another processor's acquire.

## 4 Implementation

The implementation of Midway consists of three main components: a set of keywords and function calls used to annotate a parallel program, a compiler which generates code to maintain reference information for shared data, and a runtime system to implement several consistency models.

## 4.1  Compiler and language support for Midway

Midway's concurrency primitives are based on the Mach C-Threads interface [Cooper & Draves 88]. A Midway program is written in C, and looks like many other parallel C programs that use thread management directives such as *fork* and *join*, and synchronization primitives such as *lock* and *unlock*. Shared data can be allocated either dynamically or statically, but must be tagged as shared during storage allocation. All references to shared data, however, do not need a shared qualifier, so procedures can take pointers to data which is either shared or unshared.

Midway requires a small amount of compile-time support to implement its consistency protocols. Whenever the compiler generates code to store a new value into a shared data item, it also generates code that marks the item as "dirty" in an auxiliary data structure. Other information necessary to implement entry consistency, such as the association between synchronization objects and guarded data, is specified at runtime with procedure calls into Midway's runtime system.

An alternative to relying on the compiler to generate code which marks items as dirty is to use the virtual memory system to trap writes to shared data. This is the approach taken with page-based systems such as Ivy and Munin. Although this approach allows programs to run with an unmodified compiler, it has several drawbacks that can limit its performance. First, virtual memory systems, and their underlying MMU hardware, do not have particularly fast fault handling times [Appel & Li 91], and those times are getting relatively slower, not faster [Anderson et al. 91]. Second, page-based strategies can incur a large number of write-faults in the presence of false sharing. This happens when unrelated data items on the same page are written by different processors. Third, faults which occur during a critical section increase the amount of time to execute the critical section, thereby increasing contention. Similarly, faults which occur during a barrier sequence result in processors finishing at staggered times, even though the computation may statically appear load-balanced.

## 4.2  Synchronization management

Distributed synchronization management enables processors to acquire synchronization objects not presently held in their local memories. Two types of synchronization objects are supported: locks and barriers. Locks are acquired in either exclusive or non-exclusive mode by locating the lock's owner using a distributed queueing algorithm [Forin et al. 89].

Barriers permit SIMD-style processing by synchronizing multiple processors across sequential phases of a computation. A processor delays at a barrier until all other processors reach that same barrier. Shared data accessed within a barrier must be made consistent only at the point where the barrier computation proceeds from one phase to the next. Within a phase there are no consistency guarantees for data updated during that phase (unless other synchronization primitives are used).

Midway associates a manager processor with each barrier synchronization object. Processors "cross" the barrier by sending a message to the manager and waiting for a reply. The crossing message contains the barrier name and all updates to shared data associated with the barrier that were performed by the crossing processor. The manager coalesces the updated values it receives from all processors, then releases the processors by sending the coalesced updates back to each processor. Midway also supports a terminating barrier that can be used to coalesce the final results of a program at a single processor. Upon crossing a terminating barrier, the data is coalesced at the manager, but is not flushed back to the participating processors.

## 4.3  Cache management

Distributed cache management ensures that a processor never enters a critical section without having received all updates to the shared data guarded by that synchronization object. While this condition could be satisfied by transferring all shared data guarded by the synchronization object, entry consistency requires only that updated data more recent than that contained in an acquiring processor's cache be transferred. To determine which updates are more recent than others, Midway uses Lamport's happens-before relationship [Lamport 78] to impose a partial ordering on updates to shared data with respect to synchronization accesses.

Each processor $p_i$ maintains a monotonically increasing counter $c_i$ which serves as its local clock. Whenever $p_i$ sends a message, for example to synchronize, to $p_j$, it increments $c_i$ and includes $c_i$ in the message. Upon receipt of the message, $p_j$ sets its clock $c_j$ to $max(c_j, c_i)$. Each synchronization object $s$ has an associated timestamp $t_s$ which is set to the value of $c_j$ whenever its ownership transfers to another processor $p_j$. Each shared data value $v$ guarded by $s$ has an associated timestamp $t_v$ that is logically set to the local clock value whenever $v$ is updated. When processor $p_i$ requests $s$ from $p_j$, the request contains $p_i$'s last value of $t_s$, $t_s.i$, which is the "time" that $p_i$ last observed $s$. For each shared value $v$ guarded by $s$, if $t_v > t_s.i$, then $p_i$'s cache has a stale version of $v$ and $p_j$ must transfer the new value of $v$ with $s$.

Timestamps are arranged in memory so that the runtime system can quickly convert from a shared item's address to its timestamp. Midway avoids computing a timestamp for each update, delaying until the timestamp is needed by the synchronization protocol. On store, the local timestamp field is set to zero to indicate that the associated data item has been modified. When a synchronization object $s$ is requested from a processor $p_i$, all data guarded by $s$ whose timestamp is zero will have their timestamps set to $c_i$. When a shared data item is allocated, the granularity of the timestamp (in effect, the cache line size) can be selected by the programmer according to the expected access patterns to the item. For example, a large contiguous object may be backed by many timestamps to improve the granularity of sharing and update information. Timestamp granularity can be as fine as a single byte.

Midway does not assume that processors have infinite caches. At any point, a processor may discard a shared data item as long as that processor does not presently own the synchronization object guarding the item. When next acquiring the guarding synchronization object $s$, the discarding processor indicates that it has not held $s$ for a "very long time."

## 4.4 Supporting stronger consistency models

Much of Midway's infrastructure for entry consistency can be leveraged to support processor consistency and release consistency. Supporting these other models requires that the compiler and runtime detect writes to shared data, perform updates at other processors in the order required by the model, and recover from cache misses which occur when a processor accesses a shared data item not present in its local cache. For this, Midway overloads the timestamp mechanism described earlier. The compiler emits the same code for a store to a shared address, but, at runtime, the computed timestamp is treated differently.

Data items maintained according to processor or release, but not entry, consistency, initially have the high bit in their associated timestamp set. On a store to the line, if the high bit of the timestamp field is set, then the store will be performed at all other processors independent of any *particular* synchronization operation. The modified address is recorded in a per-processor queue of pending updates and the high bit of the timestamp is cleared to ensure the item is not queued again. This strategy for queue updates allows us to use the same compiler-emitted code sequence when updating both entry consistent and non-entry consistent data. Once the non-entry consistent data has been queued, subsequent stores continue to clear the timestamp field just as if the data were entry consistent.

Associated with each cache line is a *copyset* that defines the processors holding a copy of the line in their local memories. A pending update to a line need only be performed at the processors in that line's copyset. For release consistent data, pending updates are flushed by a processor any time the processor's releasing synchronization operation is performed at another acquiring processor. Processor consistent data is flushed at these points, as well as at the periodic interval specified by the programmer. In either case, when an update is flushed by a processor, the high bit in the item's timestamp is set to catch that processor's next store to the item at that processor.

Under entry consistency, all data bound to a synchronization object is prefetched when the object is acquired. With processor consistency and release consistency, there is no associated synchronization object and no way to know which data to prefetch or when to prefetch it. Consequently, on a processor's first reference to an item, that processor will not be in the item's copyset and will not have received any prior updates. We detect this condition with a *copyset fault*, which is implemented with virtual memory page faults.

Each processor marks virtual memory pages that contain cache lines for which the processor is not in the copyset as *no-access*. Access to such a page causes a page fault, and the faulting processor fetches the faulted page from the page's *home* processor. Every page has a home, based on the page's virtual address. Before the home node returns the page's data, the faulting node is added to the page's copyset and all other members are informed of the change. Any processor but the home processor may remove itself from the copyset of a page by notifying the page's home processor.

With this strategy, all cache lines within a virtual

page are part of the same copyset. A page fault occurs only when a processor adds itself to a cache line's copyset; otherwise runtime write detection to shared data is done with compiler-emitted code, rather than with faults. Thus multiple processors may write to a page at the same time.

For all three consistency models, Midway uses update, rather than invalidate, to perform writes to other processors. This is done for two reasons. First, it guarantees that processors never experience a cache miss except on a copyset fault. Second, it enables the use of the same update machinery used for entry consistency.

## 5    Performance

In this section we look at the behavior of a simple parallel program under Midway using both entry consistency and release consistency. For our measurements, we use two metrics which we present as a function of the number of processors on which an application runs: execution time and message count. Our measurements show that a program written to entry consistency requires substantially fewer messages than one to the stronger models. This translates into improved execution time.

### 5.1    The hardware platforms

Our implementation of Midway runs on MIPS R3000-based DECstation 5000/120s and 5000/200s on top of two networks: a 10Mb/sec ethernet and a 155 Mb/sec ATM network. The operating system is Mach 3.0 with CMU's Unix⁻ server [Golub et al. 90]. The DECstation 5000/120 uses a 20Mhz R3000 with a 12.5Mhz Turbochannel (TC) bus interface. The 5000/200 uses a 25Mhz R3000 with a 25Mhz Turbochannel interface. Presently, we have only four 155Mb/sec ATM network interfaces, and we use these to connect the faster and more network capable 5000/200s through the central switch.

We present results on three configurations: *slow-ether*, which uses the slower DS5000/120s connected by ethernet; *fast-ether*, which uses the faster DS5000/200s connected by ethernet, and *fast-atm*, which is like fast-ether, except that we use the ATM network instead. The slow-ether configuration allows us to evaluate performance on more than four processors, while the fast-ATM network lets us look at the system's behavior on a faster network with faster processors. We include the fast-ether numbers to provide a common point of comparison between slow-ether and fast-ATM.

## 5.2    Matrix multiply

We present the results of a simple matrix multiply application running on several processors to provide an integrity check for Midway, to show the interaction between processor speed and network speed, and to compare the behavior of a single program under two different consistency models. *MM-ec* is a matrix multiply program which multiplies two $512 \times 512$ floating point matrices on from one to eight processors using entry consistency. A master processor writes the two input matrices $A$ and $B$, and then spawns slave processes on the other machines. The master and each slave machine acquires a non-exclusive (read) lock on all of $A$, and a non-exclusive lock on a portion of $B$. Each processor then computes its portion of the result matrix $C$, and crosses a final barrier. It returns that portion of $C$ that it has written back to the master.

The main advantage of using entry consistency for matrix multiply is that the initial message required to satisfy each slave processor's non-exclusive lock acquisition transfers the input matrices. Similarly, when a slave terminates, the message it sends indicating that it has crossed a barrier also transfers the results back to the master. In effect, the consistency model in combination with a synchronization protocol natural to the problem provides optimal clustering of data, both in terms of number of bytes transferred and number of messages generated.

To assess the importance of this clustering, we have written a version of matrix multiply to use release, rather than entry, consistency (*MM-rc*). Table 1 shows the elapsed time, speedup, time spent computing and transferring data, amount of data transferred, and the total number of messages for *MM-ec* and *MM-rc*. Since fast-ATM represents the best possible configuration, we show the results of *MM-rc* only for it. In the single-processor case, we compiled the program to run on a uniprocessor, eliminating synchronization and timestamp management overhead.

Elapsed time is the interval beginning after all processors have started and ending when the master processor terminates. This includes the time to move the input and output data sets between processors. The data transfer times shown are from the perspective of the master processor (which sources and sinks all data). The input and output data sizes are only a function of the number of processors (problem partitioning), and not the processor, network or consistency model. The number of messages is a function of the number of processors and the consistency model. The compute time is the time spent actually working on the matrices and, as shown, scales with the number

| | # Procs. | Elapsed (secs) | Speedup | Input Transfer (secs) | Compute Results (secs) | Output Transfer (secs) | Data Transferred (mbytes) | # Msgs |
|---|---|---|---|---|---|---|---|---|
| *MM-ec*: slow-ether | 1 | 282 | 1 | 0 | 0 | 0 | 0 | 0 |
| | 2 | 148.4 | 1.90 | 12.92 | 132.4 | 3.05 | 2.14 | 24 |
| | 4 | 84.9 | 3.32 | 12.08 | 66.3 | 6.51 | 4.81 | 72 |
| | 6 | 65.0 | 4.34 | 13.72 | 44.4 | 6.92 | 7.13 | 120 |
| | 8 | 58.6 | 4.81 | 17.56 | 33.2 | 7.87 | 9.36 | 168 |
| *MM-ec*: fast-ether | 1 | 164 | 1 | 0 | 0 | 0 | 0 | 0 |
| | 2 | 92.8 | 1.77 | 8.70 | 81.4 | 2.66 | 2.14 | 24 |
| | 4 | 53.3 | 3.08 | 8.50 | 40.6 | 4.17 | 4.81 | 72 |
| *MM-ec*: fast-ATM | 1 | 164 | 1 | 0 | 0 | 0 | 0 | 0 |
| | 2 | 83.5 | 1.96 | 1.53 | 81.7 | 0.31 | 2.14 | 24 |
| | 4 | 43.3 | 3.79 | 1.86 | 40.9 | 0.50 | 4.81 | 72 |
| *MM-rc*: fast-ATM | 1 | 164 | 1 | 0 | 0 | 0 | 0 | 0 |
| | 2 | 86.8 | 1.89 | 3.14 | 82.0 | 1.61 | 2.17 | 1802 |
| | 4 | 48.4 | 3.39 | 6.06 | 41.1 | 1.28 | 4.97 | 5106 |

Table 1: *Breakdown of the performance of matrix multiply using both entry consistency and release consistency.*

of processors.

Looking only at the entry consistent configurations, speedup is slightly less than linear because the communication overheads do not decrease as processors are added. The fact that speedup at 4 processors for fast-ether is worse than for slow-ether shows the impact of increasing processor performance without increasing network performance. A single DECstation 5000/200 is roughly twice as fast at matrix multiply as a DECstation 5000/120. Communication overhead on both systems is roughly the same, therefore there is less room for improvement when running on a network of 5000/200s. In contrast, speedup is much closer to linear on the fast-ATM network where communication overhead is less than 6% of total execution time (as opposed to almost 25% on the fast-ether configuration).

By point of comparison, the Munin system yielded an 8-fold speedup for an 8 processor matrix multiply using release consistency running over a 10 Mb/sec ethernet [Carter et al. 91]. The processors used there, however were substantially slower than those used in our fast-ether configuration. A single Munin processor could compute the product of two 400x400 *integer* matrices in a little over 700 seconds, almost five times slower than a DS5000/200 running on a larger (512×512) and harder (floating point) input set. From this we conclude that uniprocessor performance has reached the point where ethernet is no longer a viable network for parallel processing, even for well-structured parallel applications such as matrix multiply.

Moving to the release consistent runs, we can see the impact of Midway's implicit prefetch that comes during lock acquisition for entry consistency. Instead of transferring the entire input and output matrices in single messages, as is done with entry consistency, the release consistent implementation misses frequently as can be seen by the number of messages sent. Most of the messages correspond to the transfer of a page of data. Specifically, each message for the entry consistent run corresponds to a synchronization request, which also occurs during the release consistent run. The additional messages for the release consistent run are for data transfer. The elapsed time difference between the release and entry consistent runs is due to the overhead of having to send more messages, even though the total amount of data transferred is nearly unchanged.

## 6   Conclusions

There exist a range of memory consistency models that provide different kinds of behavior both in terms of semantics and performance. Strongly consistent memory systems simplify porting and reasoning about programs written for shared memory multiprocessors but are limited in their ability to conceal latency. Entry consistency takes into account both synchronization behavior and the relationship between synchronization objects and data. This allows the runtime system to hide the network overhead of memory references by folding all memory updates into synchronization operations.

# References

[Accetta et al. 86] Accetta, M. J., Baron, R. V., Bolosky, W., Golub, D. B., Rashid, R. F., Tevanian, Jr., A., and Young, M. W. Mach: A New Kernel Foundation for Unix Development. In *Proceedings of the Summer 1986 USENIX Conference*, pages 93–113, July 1986.

[Adve & Hill 89] Adve, S. V. and Hill, M. D. Weak Ordering – A New Definition. In *Proceedings of the 16th Annual Symposium on Computer Architecture*, pages 2–14, May 1989.

[Anderson et al. 91] Anderson, T., Levy, H., Bershad, B., and Lazowska, E. The Interaction of Architecture and Operating System Design. In *Proceedings of the Fourth Symposium on Architectural Support for Programming Languages and Operating Systems (ASPLOS IV)*, pages 108–121, April 1991.

[Appel & Li 91] Appel, W. and Li, K. Virtual Memory Primitives for User Programs. In *Proceedings of the Fourth Symposium on Architectural Support for Programming Languages and Operating Systems (ASPLOS IV)*, pages 96–107, April 1991.

[Bennett et al. 90] Bennett, J. K., Carter, J. B., and Zwaenepoel, W. Adaptive Software Cache Management for Distributed Shared Memory Architectures. In *Proceedings of the 17th Annual Symposium on Computer Architecture*, pages 125–134, May 1990.

[Carter et al. 91] Carter, J. B., Bennett, J. K., and Zwaenepoel, W. Implementation and Performance of Munin. In *Proceedings of the 13th ACM Symposium on Operating Systems Principles*, pages 152–164, October 1991.

[Cooper & Draves 88] Cooper, E. C. and Draves, R. P. C Threads. Technical Report CMU-CS-88-54, Department of Computer Science, Carnegie-Mellon University, February 1988.

[Dubois et al. 86] Dubois, M., Scheurich, C., and Briggs, F. Memory Access Buffering in Multiprocessors. In *Proceedings of the 13th Annual Symposium on Computer Architecture*, pages 434–442, June 1986.

[Eggers 89] Eggers, S. J. *Simulation Analysis of Data Sharing in Shared Memory Multiprocessors*. PhD dissertation, University of California, Berkeley, March 1989.

[Fleisch 87] Fleisch, B. D. Shared Memory in a Loosely Coupled Distributed System. In *Proceedings of the SIGCOMM87 Workshop on Frontiers in Computer Communications Technology*, August 1987.

[Forin et al. 89] Forin, A., Barrera, J., Young, M., and Rashid, R. Design, Implementation and Performance Evaluation of a Distributed Shared Memory Server for Mach. In *Proceedings of the Summer 1986 USENIX Conference*, January 1989.

[Gharachorloo et al. 90] Gharachorloo, K., Lenoski, D., Laudon, J., Gibbons, P., Gupta, A., and Hennessy, J. Memory Consistency and Event Ordering in Scalable Shared Memory Multiprocessors. In *Proceedings of the 17th Annual Symposium on Computer Architecture*, pages 15–26, May 1990.

[Gharachorloo et al. 91] Gharachorloo, K., Gupta, A., and Hennessy, J. Performance Evaluation of Memory Consistency Models for Shared Memory Multiprocessors. In *Proceedings of the Fourth Symposium on Architectural Support for Programming Languages and Operating Systems (ASPLOS IV)*, pages 245–259, April 1991.

[Golub et al. 90] Golub, D., Dean, R., Forin, A., and Rashid, R. Unix as an Application Program. In *Proceedings of the Summer 1990 USENIX Conference*, pages 87–95, June 1990.

[Goodman & Woest 88] Goodman, J. and Woest, P. The Wisconsin Multicube: A New Large-Scale Cache-Coherent Multiprocessor. In *Proceedings of the 15th Annual Symposium on Computer Architecture*, pages 422–431, Honolulu, Hawaii, June 1988.

[Keleher et al. 92] Keleher, P., Cox, A., and Zwaenepoel, W. Lazy Release Consistency for Software Distributed Shared Memory. In *Proceedings of the 19th Annual Symposium on Computer Architecture*, pages 13–21, May 1992.

[Lamport 78] Lamport, L. Time, Clocks and the Ordering of Events in a Distributed System. *Communications of the ACM*, 21(7):558–565, July 1978.

[Lamport 79] Lamport, L. How to Make a Multiprocessor Computer That Correctly Executes Multiprocess Programs. *IEEE Transactions on Computers*, C-28(9):690–691, September 1979.

[Lenoski et al. 92] Lenoski, D., Laudon, J., Gharachorloo, K., Weber, W., Gupta, A., Hennessy, J., Horowitz, M., and Lam, M. The Stanford DASH Multiprocessor. *IEEE Computer Magazine*, 25(3):63–79, March 1992.

[Li 86] Li, K. *Shared Virtual Memory on Loosely Coupled Multiprocessors*. PhD dissertation, Department of Computer Science, Yale University, September 1986.

[Rider 89] Rider, M. Protocols for ATM Access Networks. *IEEE Network*, January 1989.

[Scheurich & Dubois 87] Scheurich, C. and Dubois, M. Correct Memory Operation of Cache-Based Multiprocessors. In *Proceedings of the 14th Annual Symposium on Computer Architecture*, pages 234–243, June 1987.

[Singh et al. 92] Singh, J., Weber, W., and Gupta, A. SPLASH: Stanford Parallel Applications for Shared Memory. *Computer Architecture News*, 20(1):5–44, March 1992.

[Zucker & Baer 92] Zucker, R. N. and Baer, J.-L. A Performance Study of Memory Consistency Models. In *Proceedings of the 19th Annual Symposium on Computer Architecture*, pages 2–12, May 1992.

# Chapter 4

# Distributed Shared Memory Implementations at the Software Level

## Editors' Introduction

This chapter surveys a number of representative software-based distributed shared memory (DSM) solutions, described and analyzed in the following papers:

1. K. Li, "IVY: A Shared Virtual Memory System for Parallel Computing," *Proc. 1988 Int'l Conf. Parallel Processing*, Penn State Press, University Park, Pa., 1988, pp. 94–101.

2. J.B. Carter, J.K. Bennet, and W. Zwaenepoel, "Implementation and Performance of Munin," *Proc. 13th ACM Symp. Operating System Principles*, ACM Press, New York, N.Y., 1991, pp. 152–164.

3. B.D. Fleisch and G.J. Popek, "Mirage: A Coherent Distributed Shared Memory Design," *Proc. 14th ACM Symp. Operating System Principles*, ACM Press, New York, N.Y., 1989, pp. 211–223.

4. U. Ramachandran and M.J.A. Khalidi, "An Implementation of Distributed Shared Memory," *Software—Practice and Experience*, Vol. 21, No. 5, 1991 pp. 443–464.

5. S. Ahuja, N. Carriero, and D. Gelernter, "Linda and Friends," *Computer*, Vol. 19, No. 8, Aug. 1986, pp. 26–34.

6. H.E. Bal and A.S. Tanenbaum, "Distributed Programming with Shared Data," *Proc. 1988 Int'l Conf. Computer Languages*, IEEE CS Press, Los Alamitos, Calif., 1988, pp. 82–91.

7. S. Zhou et al., "Heterogeneous Distributed Shared Memory," *IEEE Trans. Parallel and Distributed Systems*, Vol. 3, No. 5, Sept. 1992, pp. 540–554.

8. P. Keleher et al., "TreadMarks: Distributed Shared Memory on Standard Workstations and Operating Systems," *Proc. USENIX Winter 1994 Conf.*, 1994, pp. 115–132.

9. I. Schoinas et al., "Fine-Grain Access Control for Distributed Shared Memory," *Proc. 6th Int'l Conf. Architectural Support for Programming Languages and Operating Systems*, ACM Press, New York, N.Y., 1994, pp. 297–306.

Traditional distributed systems widely employ two communication paradigms: message-passing and remote procedure calls (RPCs). Both methods have two obvious drawbacks—they are more complicated for the programmer than the shared memory paradigm, and they introduce severe problems in passing complex data structures, since the concept of passing pointers used by uniprocessors does not make sense when there is no common address space. Therefore, the idea of building a mechanism that provides the shared memory paradigm to the programmer on top of message passing seemed reasonable. The general flexibility of the software approach also enabled researchers to better tailor the consistency mechanisms to the application behavior, in their efforts to gain better performance.

The concept of DSM solutions implemented in software is somewhat similar to the hardware-implemented NUMA (nonuniform memory access) architecture and COMA (cache-only memory architecture) systems, since all data units can either have predetermined home locations, as in NUMA, or they can freely migrate between sites without restrictions, as in COMA systems. Larger grain sizes (on the order of kilobytes) are typical for software solutions, because DSM and virtual memory mechanisms are often integrated. This can be an advantage for applications that express high levels of locality, as well as a drawback for those characterized by fine-grain sharing, owing to the adverse effects of thrashing.

Software support for DSM is generally more flexible than hardware support, but in many cases it cannot compete with hardware implementations in performance. Apart from trying to introduce hardware accelerators to solve the problem, designers have concentrated on relaxing the consistency model, in order to increase performance. For some consistency models, this can put an additional burden on the programmer. Some systems also try to integrate both the message-passing and DSM paradigm. The fact that research and experiments in the area of software-implemented DSM can rely on widely available distributed programming languages and operating systems resulted in numerous solutions that have been proposed and implemented in existing systems. Therefore, Chapter 4 contains a larger number of papers, in order to provide broad insight into the variety of approaches to the problem.

The paper "IVY: A Shared Virtual Memory System for Parallel Computing," by Li, describes the design and implementation of IVY—one of the first proposed software DSM solutions, implemented as a set of user-level modules. After discussing the advantages of the shared virtual memory concept in loosely coupled multiprocessors (in comparison to message passing), the article gives some details of its implementation in the Apollo Domain on top of the modified operating system Aegis. Three IVY modules from the client interface (remote process management, memory allocation, and initialization) consist of a set of primitives that can be used by application programs. Remote operation and memory-mapping routines use operating system low-level support. IVY provides a mechanism for consistency maintenance, using an invalidation approach on 1-Kbyte pages. For experimental purposes, three algorithms are implemented: the improved centralized manager, the fixed distributed manager, and the dynamic distributed manager algorithms. Performance measurements on the system with up to eight nodes are described for six typical parallel programs, with some of them showing linear speedup in comparison with the best sequential solutions.

In the paper "Implementation and Performance of Munin," Carter Bennet, and Zwaenepoel report on the Munin DSM system, which includes two important features: type-specific coherence mechanisms and a release consistency model. Munin can be classified as a runtime system implementation, although a preprocessor that converts the program annotations, a modified linker, some library routines, and operating system support are also required. It employs different coherence protocols well suited to the expected access pattern for a shared object. The programmer is responsible for providing one of several annotations for each shared object, which selects appropriate low-level parameters of the coherence protocol for this object. The release consistency model is implemented in software with delayed update queues for efficient merging and propagating write sequences. Some support for synchronization and advanced programming capabilities are also provided. The paper describes in detail the Munin prototype implementation on an Ethernet network of 16 SUN-3 workstations based on preprocessor, linker, and runtime library routines. Evaluation using two representative programs (written for Munin, with only minor annotations) shows that their performance is less than 10 percent worse compared to their carefully hand-coded message-passing counterparts.

Another DSM system implementation on an Ethernet network, using the System V interface, is proposed by Fleisch and Popek in their paper "Mirage: A Coherent Distributed Shared Memory Design." A contribution to DSM concepts, introduced by Mirage, is the idea that the writer of the page should retain access to that page for a fixed period of time—time window $\Delta$. This tuning parameter makes it possible to avoid thrashing, and allows the inherent processor locality to be better exploited. The value of $\Delta$ is tuned statically or dynamically. This DSM system uses the model based on page segmentation. A process that creates a shared segment defines its size, name, and access protection, while the other processes locate and access the segment by name. All requests are sent to the site of the segment creation, where they are queued and sequentially processed. In Mirage, coherence maintenance is implemented at the level of the operating system kernel. Performance evaluation is based on specially constructed applications, such as the worst case example, in which two processes interchangeably perform writes to the same page. Analysis shows that the throughput increase is highly sensitive to the proper choice of the parameter Δ value.

In the paper "An Implementation of Distributed Shared Memory," Ramachandran and Khalidi describe Clouds—an operating system that incorporates software-based DSM management and implements a set of primitives either on top of Unix, or in the context of the object-based operating system kernel Ra. Therefore, it can be classified as an operating system implementation, out of kernel. Clouds has been implemented on SUN-3 workstations connected via Ethernet. The distributed shared memory consists of objects, composed of segments, that have access attributes: read-only, read-write, weak-read, or none. Fetching of segments is based on *get* and *discard* operations provided by a distributed shared memory controller (DSMC). This software module also offers P and V semaphore primitives as separate operations. The DSMC is, therefore, a part of the Clouds operating system, but implemented outside its kernel Ra. It is invoked by a DSM partition that handles segment requests from both Ra and user objects, and determines whether the request for segment should be satisfied locally, by disk partition, or remotely, by distributed shared memory controller. Both DSM and DSMC partitions are also implemented on top of Unix, with minor changes due to the operating system dependencies. Performance figures reported for the Unix version of the solution show that an average fetching time for a segment is comparable to that measured for the RPC.

An architecture-independent language concept for parallel programming is introduced in the paper "Linda and Friends," by Ahuja, Carrieto, and Gelernter. Distributed shared memory in Linda is organized as a "tuple space"—a common pool of user-defined tuples (basic storage and access units consisting of data elements) that are addressed by logical names. Linda provides two special language operators for dealing with such distributed data structures as inserting, removing, and reading tuples, and so on. The consistency problem is avoided since the tuple must be removed from the tuple space before an update, and a modified version is reinserted again. By its nature, the Linda environment offers possibilities for process decoupling, transparent communication, and dynamic scheduling. The paper concentrates in particular on the model of replication as a method of problem partitioning. Some software implementation details of the Linda concept within the S/Net kernel are also explained.

Software implementation of distributed shared memory is extensively elaborated on by Bal and Tanenbaum, in their paper "Distributed Programming with Shared Data." A brief comparative discussion of several different approaches (communication ports in CSP language, shared variables in Ada, object-oriented languages, problem-oriented memory, shared memory in Agora, tuple space in Linda, Li's shared virtual memory, and shared logical variables), which try to achieve data sharing without physically shared memory, is provided. After that, a new model of shared data objects (passive objects accessible through the set of predefined operations) is proposed. The distributed implementation is based on selective replication, migration, and an update mechanism. Different means of updating (point-to-point messages, reliable messages, and unreliable multicast messages) are considered and discussed. The paper also introduces a new language for distributed programming, Orca, based on a shared data-object model, and briefly illustrates its features.

The paper "Heterogeneous Distributed Shared Memory," by S. Zhou et al., presents Mermaid—an implementation of the Li algorithm in a heterogeneous distributed shared memory (HDSM) environment. The prototype configuration included SUN/Unix workstations and the DEC Firefly multiprocessor. The system, named Mermaid, is implemented at the user level, as a library package to be linked into the application programs. Data conversion is a vital issue in such an environment. It is simple for integers, and somewhat more complicated for floating point numbers, the numerical precision of which can be affected. For user-defined data types, conversion routines and a table for mapping data types to them must be provided by the user. Just one data type is allowed per page. Mermaid ensures the variable page size that can be suited to data access patterns. This exhaustive performance study includes various experiments, using two typical parallel applications, in order to examine the introduced overheads in comparison with homogeneous systems and the effects of page size. Since Firefly is a shared memory multiprocessor, the article also compares physical shared memory versus HDSM and concludes that the introduced overhead caused by heterogeneity is more than acceptable.

In the paper "TreadMarks: Distributed Shared Memory on Standard Workstations and Operating Systems," Keleher et al. present a sophisticated software DSM implementation that runs on commonly available Unix systems. TreadMarks is a user-level implementation that requires no modifications to the operating system kernel or any particular compiler. The authors apply the lazy release consistency model, as well as an invalidation-based protocol, that allows multiple concurrent writers to modify the page. On the first write to a shared page, DSM software makes a copy called *twin*, which later can be compared to the current copy of the page in order to make a *diff*—a record that contains all modifications to the page. Lazy release consistency does not require *diff* creation at each release (as in the Munin implementation), but allows it to be postponed, in order to obtain better performance. The paper describes experiments performed using DECstation-5000/240s connected by a 100-Mbps ATM network and a 10-Mbps Ethernet, and good speedups for five SPLASH programs. The authors conclude that the latency and bandwidth limitations should be overcome using more efficient communication interfaces, in order to narrow further the gap between software DSM systems and supercomputers.

The paper "Fine-Grain Access Control for Distributed Shared Memory," by Schoinas et al., considers the trade-offs in achieving fine granularity in DSM systems, which is essential for high performance. The first part of the paper gives the hardware and software alternatives for DSM access control. It also provides a brief taxonomy of some existing systems that implement fine-grain access control, including performance, implementation, and cost consideration. On the basis of this analysis, the authors present Blizzard, a system that supports fine-grain DSM granularity on the CM-5 in a cost-effective way. The entirely software variant, Blizzard-

S, modifies the application code by inserting a short access check before each shared memory reference. Another variant, Blizzard-E, uses the memory error correction code bits to indicate invalid states of data blocks. Blizzard-ES represents a hybrid of the former two variants. Performance analysis shows that Blizzard-S is the most efficient of the three; however, it is typically several times slower than the KSR1, a representative hardware implementation.

## Suggestions for Further Reading

1. M. Ahamad, P. Hutto, and R. John, "Implementing and Programming Causal Distributed Shared Memory," *Proc. 11th Int'l Conf. Distributed Computing Systems,* IEEE CS Press, Los Alamitos, Calif., 1991, pp. 274–281.

2. H.E. Bal, J.G. Steiner, and A.S. Tanenbaum, "Programming Languages for Distributed Computing Systems," *ACM Computing Surveys,* Vol. 21, No. 2, Sept. 1989, pp. 261–322.

3. J. Bennet, J. Carter, and W. Zwaenepoel, "Adaptive Software Cache Management for Distributed Shared Memory Architectures," *Proc. 17th Ann. Int'l Symp. Computer Architecture,* IEEE CS Press, Los Alamitos, Calif., 1990, pp. 125–134.

4. A. Black et al., "Distribution and Abstract Types in Emerald," *IEEE Trans. Software Eng.,* Vol. SE-13, No. 1, Jan. 1987, pp. 65–76.

5. M.L. Blount and M. Butrico, "DSVM6K: Distributed Shared Virtual Memory on the Risc System/6000," *Proc. COMPCON '93,* IEEE CS Press, Los Alamitos, Calif., 1993, pp. 491–499.

6. L. Borrmann and M. Herdieckerhoff, "Parallel Processing Performance in a Linda System," *Proc. 1989 Int'l Conf. Parallel Processing,* Penn State Press, University Park, Pa., 1989, pp. I-51–I-58.

7. R.H. Campbell et al., "Designing and Implementing Choices: An Object-Oriented System in C++," *Comm. ACM,* Vol. 36, No. 9, Sept. 1993, pp. 117–126.

8. J.S. Chase et al., "The Amber System: Parallel Programming on a Network of Multiprocessors," *Proc. 14th ACM Symp. Operating System Principles,* ACM Press, New York, N.Y., 1989, pp. 147–158.

9. N. Islam and R.H. Campbell, "Design Considerations for Shared Memory Multiprocessor Message System," *IEEE Trans. Parallel and Distributed Systems,* Vol. 3, No. 6, Nov. 1992, pp. 702–711.

10. D.C. Kulkarni et al., "Structuring Distributed Shared Memory with the $\pi$ Architecture," *Proc. 13th Int'l Conf. Distributed Computing Systems,* IEEE CS Press, Los Alamitos, Calif., 1993, pp. 93–100.

11. K. Li and R. Schaefer, "A Hypercube Shared Virtual Memory System," *Proc. 1989 Int'l Conf. Parallel Processing,* Penn State Press, University Park, Pa., 1989, pp. I-125–I-132.

12. R.G. Minich and D.J. Farber, "The Mether System—Distributed Shared Memory for SunOS 4.0," *Proc. 1989 Summer USENIX Conf.,* 1989, pp. 51–60, .

13. A.S. Tanenbaum, M.F. Kaashoek, and H.E. Bal, "Parallel Programming Using Shared Objects and Broadcasting," *Computer,* Vol. 25, No. 8, Aug. 1992, pp. 10–19.

14. C. Amza et al., "TreadMarks: Shared Memory Computing on Networks of Workstations," *Computer,* Vol. 29, No. 2, Feb. 1996, pp. 18–28.

# IVY: A Shared Virtual Memory System
# for Parallel Computing

Kai Li
Department of Computer Science
Princeton University
Princeton, NJ 08544

## Abstract

A *shared virtual memory* system can provide a virtual address space shared among all processors in a loosely-coupled multiprocessor. This paper shows that such a memory can solve many problems in message passing systems on loosely-coupled multiprocessors, and describes the design and implementation of a prototype shared virtual memory system, IVY, implemented on an Apollo ring network. The experiments on the prototype system show that parallel programs using a shared virtual memory yield almost linear and occasionally super-linear speedups and that it is practical to implement such a system on existing architectures.

## Introduction

Much of the work on distributed computing has focused on message passing models such as Hoare's communicating sequential processes [16] and Actor [15], perhaps because message passing matches the basic communication mechanism in loosely-coupled multiprocessors. Many people have studied shared memory models for tightly coupled multiprocessors, but few have studied that model for loosely-coupled multiprocessors. Because not enough work has been done, it has not been clear whether a message passing model is better than a shared memory model for parallel computation on loosely-coupled multiprocessors. It has also not been clear whether it is possible to design an efficient system to support the shared memory model on loosely-coupled multiprocessors.

Systems based on message passing suffer mainly in two aspects: passing complex data structures and process migrations. This paper shows that a solution to these problems is to build a *shared virtual memory*. The shared virtual memory provides a virtual address space that is shared among all processors in a loosely-coupled distributed-memory multiprocessor system. Application programs can use the shared virtual memory just as they do a traditional virtual memory, except that processes can run on different processors in parallel. The shared virtual memory keeps its memory pages coherent all the time and data can naturally *migrate* between processors on demand [23,22]. Furthermore, just as a conventional virtual memory swaps *processes*, so does the shared virtual memory. Thus the shared virtual memory provides a natural and efficient form of *process migration* between processors in a distributed system. This is quite a gain because process migration is usually very difficult to implement. In effect, process migration subsumes *remote procedure calls*.

A prototype shared virtual memory has been implemented on a network of Apollo workstations. A number of practical parallel program examples are chosen to run on the prototype system. The experimental results show that parallel programs using such a not well-tuned, user-mode shared virtual memory system yield almost linear and occasionally super-linear speedups over a uniprocessor. The success of this implementation suggests a new operating mode for loosely-coupled multiprocessor architectures in which parallel programs can exploit the total processing power and memory capabilities in a far more unified way than the traditional "message-passing" approach.

## Shared Memory vs. Message Passing

Message passing in concurrent systems is characterized by multiple threads of control. A pure message passing system usually does not have any shared global data; instead processes access ports or mailboxes to achieve interprocess communication. Parallel programs need to use primitives such as *send* and *receive* explicitly through channels, ports, or mailboxes. Although programmers can use these primitives to synchronize parallel programs, they need to be conscious of data movement between processes at all times.

*Remote procedure call* is a mechanism for language-level transfer of control and data between programs in disjoint address spaces whose primary communication medium is a narrow channel [24]. A remote procedure call mechanism allows programmers to worry less about data movement and provides clients with a fairly transparent interface so that remote procedure calls look much like local procedure calls. However, the transparency of remote procedure calls is limited because a remote procedure call mechanism actually simulates the execution in the same address space using completely different address spaces.

Since both message passing and remote procedure calls deal with multiple address spaces, they both have difficulties with passing complex data structures. In fact, the difficulty of passing complex data structures is the main drawback of message passing and remote procedure calls for parallel programming. For example, passing a list data structure by sending messages will introduce considerable complexity in programming and substantial overhead in both space and time [14]. In a remote procedure call, there is no good way to pass a pointer argument [24]. This problem becomes more severe when the data structures are fundamental to a language being implemented on a parallel machine.

In contrast, a shared memory multiprocessor has no difficulty passing pointers because processors can share a single address space. Therefore, there is no need to pack and unpack the data structures containing pointers in messages. Passing a list data structure simply requires passing a pointer.

Another problem with message passing systems is the difficulty of process migration because there are multiple address

"IVY: A Shared Virtual Memory System for Parallel Computing" by K. Li from *Proc. 1988 Int'l Conf. Parallel Processing,* Vol. II, 1988, pp. 94–101. Reprinted by permission.

spaces. When migrating a process, all the operating system resources allocated by the process have to be moved together; this is expensive [25]. In the case where a process has a few opened ports and files, the pending messages and file access control blocks need to be transferred. Furthermore, the code and the stack of the process have to be moved because there is no easy way to translate the contents of different address spaces efficiently on the fly.

In a shared memory multiprocessor system, a process migration only requires moving a process from the ready queue on the source processor to the ready queue on the destination processor because process control block, code, and stack are all in the same address space.

Some systems use a set of primitives to access a global space that is used to store shared data structures of processes [8,5]. Although programming the global space does not require data movement as much as message passing, programmers still have to explicitly use the primitives. In a primitive global-space system, passing complex data structures and process migration are as difficult as in message passing systems, since accessing the data structures and process migration are by value or by name. Furthermore, using primitives may greatly reduce the efficiency of parallel programs because a primitive operation requires at least one procedure call, which costs much more than a simple memory reference.

Both data structure passing and process migration are important for implementing parallel programming languages. Although some implementations of parallel programming languages are based on a message passing facility, implementing existing parallel languages on a shared memory multiprocessor can greatly simplify the implementations. In summary, shared memory is highly desirable for parallel computation.

## Shared Virtual Memory

A *shared virtual memory* is a single address space shared by a number of processors (Figure 1). Any processor can access any memory location in the address space directly. Memory mapping managers implement the mapping between local memories and the shared virtual memory address space. Other than mapping, their chief responsibility is to keep the address space *coherent* at all times; that is, the value returned by a read operation is always the same as the value written by the most recent write operation to the same address. In short, a shared virtual memory provides clients with the same interface as the shared memory address space on a shared-memory multiprocessor.

A shared virtual memory address space is partitioned into *pages*. Pages that are marked *read-only* can have copies residing in the physical memories of many processors at the same time. But a page marked *write* can reside in only one processor's physical memory. The memory mapping manager views its local memory as a large cache of the shared virtual memory address space for its associated processor. Like traditional virtual memory [11], the shared memory itself exists only *virtually*. A memory reference will cause a page fault when the page containing the memory location is not in a processor's current physical memory. When this happens, the memory mapping manager retrieves the page from either disk or the memory of another processor. If the faulting memory reference is the target of a write operation, then the memory mapping manager must guarantee the atomicity of the operation [23].

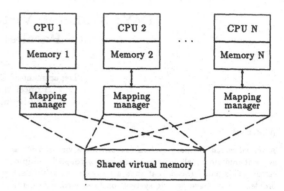

Figure 1: Shared virtual memory mapping

In a shared virtual memory system, the model of a parallel program is a set of *processes* (or threads) that share a single virtual memory address space. These processes are "lightweight"—they share the same address space and thus the cost of a process context switch, process creation, or process termination is small, say, on the order of a few procedure calls [20]. One of the key goals of the shared virtual memory, of course, is to allow processes of a program to execute on different processors in parallel. To do so, the appropriate process manager and memory allocation manager must be integrated properly with the memory mapping manager.

The performance of parallel programs on a shared virtual memory system depends mainly on two things: the number of parallel processes and the degree of data sharing (i.e. contention). Theoretically, performance improves as the number of parallel processes increases and contention decreases. Contention is less if a program exhibits *locality of references*. One of the main justifications for the traditional virtual memory is that memory references in sequential programs generally exhibit a high degree of locality [10,12]. Although memory references in parallel programs may behave differently from those in sequential ones, a single process is still a sequential program, and should exhibit a high degree of locality. Contention among parallel processes for the same piece of data depends on the algorithm, of course, but a common goal in designing parallel algorithms is to minimize such contention for optimal performance.

## Prototype Implementation

In order to answer the question of whether it is practical to build a shared virtual memory on a loosely-coupled multiprocessor and whether most parallel application programs will get speedup on such a system, a user-mode prototype system has been implemented on the Apollo Domain [1,21], an integrated system of personal workstations and server computers connected by a 12M bit/sec baseband, single token ring network. IVY is implemented on top of the modified operating system Aegis of the Domain environment. The implementation is not particularly efficient but simple and tractable.

IVY consists of 5 modules, namely, remote operation, memory mapping, process management, memory allocation, and initialization. The hierarchy of the system is shown in Figure 2. The three top modules in the hierarchy form the IVY client interface. Each consists of a set of primitives that can be used by application programs.

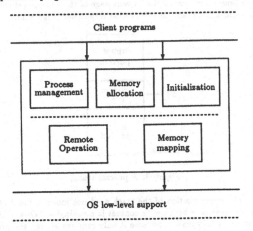

Client programs

Process management  Memory allocation  Initialization

Remote Operation  Memory mapping

OS low-level support

Figure 2: IVY hierarchy.

### Shared Virtual Memory Mapping

Memory mapping managers implement the mapping between local memories and the shared virtual memory address space. Other than mapping, their chief responsibility is to keep the address space *coherent* at all times; that is, the value returned by a read operation is always the same as the value written by the most recent write operation to the same address. The memory coherence problem is similar to that encountered in cache and multicache designs for shared memories on multiprocessors (see [27,2] for a survey), but most memory coherence techniques for multicaches do not apply, because a loosely-coupled multiprocessor has no physically shared memory and the communication cost between processors is non-trivial. [23] gives a detailed description and analysis of the algorithms for memory coherence.

Since memory coherence memory coherence of a shared virtual memory is maintained at page level, it is important to choose the right page size. On a stock loosely-coupled multiprocessor, one has to use a page size which is consistent with or the multiple of that provided in a Memory Management Unit (MMU) in order to use its protection mechanisms to detect incoherent memory references and trap them to appropriate fault handlers. These page fault handlers and their servers implement memory coherence strategy that keeps the memory space coherent at all times. Since sending large packets of data (say 1,000 bytes) in a loosely-coupled multiprocessor is not much more expensive than sending small ones (say 100 bytes) [28], relatively large page sizes are possible in a shared virtual memory. On the other hand, the larger the memory unit, the greater the chance for contention. The possibility of contention indicates the need for relatively small page sizes. Our experience with a page size of 1K bytes has been pleasant and we expect that smaller page sizes (perhaps as low as 256 bytes) will work well also, but we are not as confident about larger page sizes, due to the contention problem. The right size is clearly application dependent, however, and we simply do not have the implementation experience to say what size is best for a sufficiently broad range of parallel programs.

In IVY, each user address space is divided into two portions. The shared virtual memory address space is in the high portion and the private memory is in the low portion. For simplicity, the data structure of the page table is a vector of records and each record is a table entry. The whole table is stored in the private memory.

The memory coherence strategies implemented IVY use *invalidation* approach. In this approach, all read-only copies of a page are invalidated (changed to nil access) before a processor writes to a page. For experimental purposes, we implemented three algorithms: the improved centralized manager algorithm, the fixed distributed manager algorithm, and the dynamic distributed manager algorithm. These algorithms and other algorithms for solving the memory coherence problem have been studied in depth [23]. Briefly, The *centralized manager* algorithm is similar to the cache coherence solution [6]. The centralized manager resides on a single processor, and maintains all ownership information. When having a page fault, a processor will ask the manager for the copy of the page. The manager will then ask the owner of the page to send a copy to the requesting processor.

The *fixed distributed manager* algorithm gives every processor a predetermined set of pages to manage. The most straightforward approach is to distribute pages evenly in a fixed manner to all processors (the distributed directory map solution to the multicache coherence problem [2] is similar). With this approach there is one manager per processor, each responsible for the pages specified by the fixed mapping function $H$. When a fault occurs on page $p$, the faulting processor asks processor $H(p)$ where the true page owner is, and then proceeds as in the centralized manager algorithm.

The *dynamic distributed manager algorithm* keeps track of the ownership of all pages in each processor's local page table, using a field called *probOwner* in each page entry. The value of this field can be either the true owner or the "probable" owner of the page. The information that it contains is just a hint; it is not necessarily correct at all times, but if incorrect it will at least provide the beginning of a sequence of processors through which the true owner can be found. Initially, the *probOwner* field of every entry on all processors is set to some default processor that can be considered the initial owner of all pages. As the system runs, each processor uses the *probOwner* field to keep track of the last change of the ownership of a page. This field is updated whenever a processor receives an invalidation request, relinquishes ownership of the page, or forwards a page fault request.

The fixed distributed manager algorithm, the dynamic distributed manager algorithm, and their variations are more appropriate than others.

### Process and Process Scheduling

The process management module implements all the operations for process control, process migration, and process synchronization. The module provides clients with a set of calls for writing parallel programs.

All the processes in IVY are lightweight. The program code of a process is stored in its private memory; therefore, IVY need not have its own loader. The stack of a process is allocated from the shared memory portion. Each process has a process control block (PCB) that contains necessary information like process state, stack, context, and other process control-dependent information. The PCBs are stored in the private memory of the address space. Therefore, the PID of a process is represented as a pair—processor number and the address of its PCB.

The process scheduling mechanism is designed to be simple. Each processor has a local ready queue using a last-in-first-out policy, that is, processes do not have priorities. The process dispatcher always picks up the process in the front of the ready queue. If there is no ready process available, the dispatcher runs a system process called the null process.

The null process implements a passive load balancing algorithm. It normally waits on two low level eventcounts, one for timeout and another for new ready processes. The null process is invoked when either of them is advanced. When a timeout event occurs, the null process will run the passive load balancing algorithm. The main idea of the algorithm is to let each processor ask for work when it is idle using some hints. The eventcount for new ready processes can be advanced only when a process is migrated to the current processor, a remote resume operation is performed, or a remote notification operation results in waking up a process. Of course, when a new ready process is available, the null process will suspend itself. The dispatcher will then do another schedule.

The hint information about the number of ready processes is important for minimizing the number of rejections of migration requests. The processors in IVY keep each other up to date on their current work loads by adding a few extra bits to the messages transmitted for remote operations. Usually, a byte will be enough to transfer the information. This byte can be packed into every message at almost no extra cost.

Experiments with many parallel application programs show that the algorithm will not work well if the number of ready processes on each processor is used as the only criterion for migrating processes. A better way is to use the number of processes (including both ready and suspended) controlled by thresholds [22]. When such a number is less than the lower threshold, the processor will try to ask for work. When such a number is greater than the upper threshold, the processor will migrate processes to other processors upon requests.

### Process migration

A process in IVY is either migratable or non-migratable, indicated by a field in its PCB. Clients can modify the field by using a primitive so that a migratable process can become non-migratable or vice versa at run time. Only a ready, migratable process can migrate from one processor to another. When a process is migrated, a forwarding pointer is put into its PCB and the migrated attribute is set. The PCBs of migrated processes are used for storing forwarding pointers. The collection of non-reachable PCB's has not been implemented in IVY.

Since PCBs are stored in the private memory portion of the address space, a process migration must

- send the PCB of the process to the destination processor and put it into a PCB,

- copy the current page of the process's stack to the destination processor and transfer the ownership of the page,

- transfer the ownership of all the pages in the upper portion of the stack to the destination processor, and

- put the PCB in the ready queue on the destination processor.

The reason for moving the current page of the process's stack is to avoid a page fault in the process dispatcher (Figure 3).

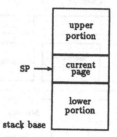

Figure 3: A process stack.

The upper portion of the stack need not move to the destination processor because its content is meaningless. Ownership transfer is inexpensive because it only requires setting the protection bits of the page frames. There is no need to do anything with the lower portion of the stack because the stack can grow without having further page faults after the current page and the upper portion of the stack become writable.

### Eventcount Implementation

In a shared virtual memory system, it is possible to implement a process synchronization mechanism based on either global memory or message passing. Eventcount [26] is the process synchronization mechanism in IVY. The main reason for choosing eventcount is that the Aegis operating system uses eventcounts as its synchronization mechanism.

An eventcount synchronization mechanism has four primitive operations:

- Init( ec ) — initializes an eventcount.

- Read( ec ) — returns the value of the eventcount.

- Await( ec, value ) — suspends the calling process itself until the value of the eventcount reaches the value specified.

- Advance( ec ) — increments the value of the eventcount by one and wakes up awaiting processes.

After an eventcount is initialized, any process can use it without knowing where it resides.

The implementation of these primitives is based on shared virtual memory. The atomic operation is implemented by pinning memory pages and using test-and-set instructions. This implementation is much cleaner than that based on message-passing; furthermore, the performance is better when there is more than one process on each processor because eventcount primitives become local operations when the eventcount data structure has been paged into the local processor.

The data structures of an eventcount usually reside together in one page. The shared virtual memory mapping mechanism can move this page on demand when an eventcount operation is performed and on a processor where there is no such eventcount data structures. If the data structures of an eventcount require more than one page, then the additional pages will be linked together. This mechanism increases the locality of the eventcount data structure. In most cases, only one page is needed for each eventcount.

### Memory Allocation

IVY has a simple memory allocation module that uses a "first fit" algorithm with one-level centralized control. The processor with which the user directly contacts will be appointed to the centralized memory manager. To reduce the memory contention, the memory allocator allocates each piece of memory to the boundary of a page.

Both allocate and free are atomic operations. IVY uses a binary lock on each processor for memory allocation purposes. At the beginning of each memory management primitive, a test-and-set operation is performed on the lock. A failed process will be put into a queue and will be awakened by an unlock operation on the lock which is done at every end of each primitive.

A more efficient approach is two-level memory management. In this approach, each processor has a local allocator maintaining a big chunk of memory allocated from the central memory allocator. This big chunk of memory serves for the local memory allocations. When there is not enough free memory left in the big chunk, the local allocator will allocate another big chunk from the central allocator. This approach has not been implemented yet, though it is expected to have better performance.

### Remote Operation

The remote operation module implements a remote request/reply mechanism that handles all the remote operations of other modules. Such a mechanism (also called simple RPC) is similar to remote procedure call facility [24,3], but it is simpler than the general one and has a few special features for implementing shared virtual memory system.

One of such features is broadcast or multicast remote operation mechanism. A broadcast or a multicast request has three reply schemes: a reply from any receiving processor, replies from all receiving processors, and no reply at all. The first option is useful for broadcasting page fault requests to locate page owners (see [23]). The second option can be used for implementing invalidation operations. The third option is for broadcasting approximate information for process scheduling.

Another feature is a forwarding request mechanism that allows a processor to forward a request to another processor. For example, processor 1 can send a request to processor 2, processor 2 forwards the request to processor 3, and so on until processor $k$ performs the operation and sends a reply back to processor 1. There are no intermediate replies involved in the operation. This mechanism is particularly useful for implementing the dynamic distributed manager algorithm.

The retransmission protocol is based on the philosophy of resending replies only when necessary. Such a design is based on two assumptions: local computation is always correct, and communication may be unreliable, but once a packet is received, its content is always correct. The protocol is reliable only when these assumptions hold. In practice, the assumptions are reasonable. Retransmission checking is done in a null process, which checks all the outgoing channels every half second when there is nothing to do.

### Programming in the IVY Environment

Programmers can use any programming language in the Apollo DOMAIN to write parallel programs as long as they can interact with the procedure calls in the Apollo DOMAIN Pascal in which IVY is implemented. Since all the languages in the Apollo DOMAIN are designed for sequential programming, the programmer has to program parallel constructs explicitly with the primitives provided by IVY.

Programmers or compilers using IVY need to decide which piece of data puts into shared virtual memory and which into private memory. Programs later do not need to know where the shared data structures are in the sense that references to these data structures are the same as to other data structures. If IVY had its own loader, explicit memory allocation would not be necessary.

Clients can use primitives provided by the process management module to create lightweight processes (or threads) for a parallel computation. The programmer can choose how to schedule processes when calling an initialization procedure at the beginning of the program. There are two options: manual scheduling and system scheduling. If system scheduling is used, the programmer only needs to create and terminate processes. But if manual scheduling is chosen, the programmer needs to tell where and when a process goes. It is the programmer's responsibility to program process synchronization. The methodology of such programming is the same as that of "conventional" concurrent programming developed since the 1960s. Although there is no parallel programming language, such a primitive environment has proven to be convenient enough to write benchmark programs.

IVY does not have any special debugging tools. Initial debugging programs can be done on a single processor. Since an IVY image file can run on any number of processors, there is no need to have a simulator. If a program follows IVY parallel programming conventions, debugging on a single processor is usually easy. After debugging on a single processor, the programmer should debug on two and then three processors. My experience indicates that if a program can run on three processors correctly, there are few bugs left.

### Experiments

Given the difficulties of finding practical parallel programs, the only reasonable way to do experiments is to select a set of application programs from different fields as a benchmark suite. All benchmarks have the following two properties:

- *reasonably fine granularity of parallelism, and*
- *side-effects in shared data structures.*

Parallel programs with rather coarse granularity can obviously perform well in the shared virtual memory system. There are parallel functional programs that do not have any side-effects in their data structures at run time. The shared virtual memory system is clearly a big win in these applications. The main goal in using the two criteria is to avoid weighing the experiments in favor of the shared virtual memory system by picking problems that suit the system well. The benchmark set in the experiments consists of six parallel programs that are written in Pascal. All of them are transformed manually from sequential algorithms into parallel ones in a straightforward way.

**Linear Equation Solver**   This program implements a parallel Jacobi algorithm for solving linear equations. The algorithm is transformed from the traditional, sequential Jacobi algorithm that solves the linear equation $Ax = b$ where $A$ is an $n$ by $n$ matrix. In each iteration, $x_i^{(k+1)}$ is obtained by

$$x_i^{(k+1)} = \left(b_i - \sum_{j=1}^{i-1} a_{ij}x_j^{(k)} - \sum_{j=i+1}^{n} a_{ij}x_j^{(k)}\right)/a_{ii}.$$

The parallel algorithm creates a number of processes to partition the problem by the number of rows of matrix $A$. All the processes are synchronized at each iteration by using an eventcount. The data structures $A, x$, and $b$ are stored linearly in the shared virtual memory, and the processes access them freely without regard to their location.

**3D PDE Solver**  This program solves three dimensional partial differential equations (PDEs) using a parallel Jacobi algorithm. The algorithm and its transformation are similar to the linear equation solver except that in the equation $Ax = b$, $A$ is a sparse matrix. Since this matrix is never updated in the program, the practical PDE solvers in scientific computing usually eliminate the matrix by coding it into programs to save space and time. In practice, matrix $A$ is large and it is read-only, coding it into program will not be in favor of the shared virtual memory performance. To be more realistic, we choose to do so. The vectors $x$ and $b$ are stored linearly in the shared virtual memory.

**Traveling Salesman Problem**  The traveling salesman problem is to find a tour that visits each city once with the minimum cost. The cities are represented as the nodes in an undirected graph. The cost of a tour is the sum of the weights of the edges on the tour. The algorithm used in the program is a simplified version of the branch-and-bound approach proposed in [13]. At each step, an 1-tree (a variation of the minimum spanning tree) of the remaining graph is computed. The sum of the cost of the subtour and the 1-tree is compared with the cost of the current least upper bound. If the cost is less than the upper bound, it will replace the upper bound and the subtour is still valid; otherwise, the subtour will be thrown away. The available branches, the graph, and the least upper bound are stored in the shared virtual memory. The program creates a process for each processor that performs the branch-and-bound algorithm on a branch obtained from the shared virtual memory. These processes run in parallel until the tour is found. Each process is not much different from the sequential one except it needs to access shared data structures mutual exclusively.

**Matrix Multiply**  This program computes $C = AB$ where $A, B$ and $C$ are square matrices. A number of processes are created to partition the problem by the number of columns of matrix $B$. All the matrices are stored in the shared virtual memory. The program assumes that matrix $A$ and $B$ are on one processor at the beginning and they will be paged to other processors on demand.

**Dot-product**  The dot-product program computes

$$S = \sum_{i=1}^{n} x_i y_i.$$

A number of processes are created to partition the problem. Each process computes a partial sum and $S$ is obtained by summing up the partial sums produced by the individual processes. Both vector $x$ and $y$ are stored in the shared virtual memory in a random manner, under the assumption that $x$ and $y$ are not fully distributed before doing the computation. The main reason

for choosing this example is to show the weak side of the shared virtual memory system; dot-product does little computation but requires a lot of data movement.

**Split-merge Sort**  This program implements a variation of the block odd-even based merge-split algorithm described in [4]. The sorted data is a vector of records that contain random strings. At the beginning, the program divides the vector into $2N$ blocks for $N$ processors, and creates $N$ processes, one for each processor. Each process sorts two blocks by using a quicksort algorithm [17]. This internal sorting is naturally done in parallel. Each process then does an odd-even block merge-split sort $2N-1$ times. The vector is stored in the shared virtual memory, and the spawned processes access it freely. Because the data movement is implicit, the parallel transformation is straightforward.

The speedup of a program is the ratio of the execution time of the program on a single processor to that on the shared virtual memory system. In order to obtain a fair speedup measurement, all the programs in the experiments partition their problems by creating a certain number of processes according to the number of processors used. As a result of such a parameterized partitioning, any program does its best for any given number of processors. Unlike message-passing systems or primitive global-space systems, IVY has almost no extra overhead when programs run on a single processor. The only additional costs are in creating processes, which takes milliseconds in total, and mutual exclusion, which takes two 68000 instructions for each locking. Since there are few locking operations in the programs above, the programs using one processor run just as fast as their sequential programs.

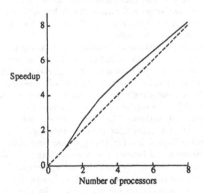

Figure 4: Super-linear speedup

The 3D PDE program, when matrix $A$ is $50^3$ by $50^3$, experienced super-linear speedup as shown in Figure 4. At first glance, the result seems impossible because the fundamental law of parallel computation says that a parallel solution utilizing $p$ processors can improve the best sequential solution by at most a factor of $p$. Since the algorithm in both programs is a straightforward transformation from the sequential Jacobi algorithm and all the processes are synchronized at each iteration, the algorithm cannot yield super-linear speedup. The reason is that the fundamental law of parallel computation assumes that every processor has an infinitely large memory, which is not true in practice. For instance, in the parallel 3-D PDE example, the data structure for the problem is greater than the size of physical memory on a single processor, so when the program is run on one processor there is a large amount of paging between the physical memory and disk.

Table 1 shows the total number of disk I/O page transfers of the first six iterations when the 3D PDE program runs on one processor and two processors. Obviously, the number of the disk I/O page transfers on two processors is substantially less than that on one processor. In the two-processor case, the program initializes its data structures only on one processor, this processor causes most disk I/O transfers because it cannot hold all the data structures in its physical memory. As the program runs, the processes start to access some portions of the data structures, causing the shared virtual memory page faults to move pages from one processor to another. When the shared virtual memory distributes the data structure into individual physical memories whose cumulative size is large enough, few disk I/O data movements will occur. On the other hand, IVY is a user-mode system implemented on top of the Aegis virtual memory system which performs an approximate LRU page replacement strategy; the pages recently moved from the processor with initialized data structures may not be replaced because these pages are also most recently referenced ones. This explains why the number of disk I/O page transfers in the two-processor case decreases gradually.

| | Disk page transfers of each iteration | | | | | |
|---|---|---|---|---|---|---|
| | 1 | 2 | 3 | 4 | 5 | 6 |
| 1 processor | 899 | 1600 | 1543 | 1515 | 1542 | 1540 |
| 2 processors | 1432 | 1072 | 466 | 156 | 101 | 105 |

Table 1: Disk page transfers

When the data structure of the problem is not larger than the physical memory on a processor (matrix $A$ is $40^3$ by $40^3$), the result of the 3D PDE is no longer super-linear, as shown in Figure 5. They are similar to what we see in the past. For example, the result is similar to that generated by similar experiments on CM*, a shared memory multiprocessor [18,9]. Indeed, the shared virtual memory system is as good as the best curve in the published experiments on CM* for the same program; but the efforts and costs of the two approaches are dramatically different. In fact, the best curve in CM* was obtained by keeping the private program code and stack in the local memory on each processor. The main reason that the performance of this program is so good in the shared virtual memory system is that the program exhibits a high degree of locality. While the shared virtual memory system pays the cost of local memory references, CM* pays the cost of remote memory references across its Kmaps.

The dot-product program did not perform well on IVY, as indicated in Figure 5. It is included here so as not to paint too bright a picture. Since this program only references each element once, the ratio of the communication cost to the computation cost in this program is large. For programs like dot-product, it is not appropriate to use a shared virtual memory system, unless the communication cost can be reduced.

Matrix multiply and traveling salesman problem perform well on IVY system. They show the good side of the shared virtual memory system. Both programs exhibit a high degree of localized computation. Since the algorithm used in the traveling salesman problem is a parallel branch-and-bound, there are

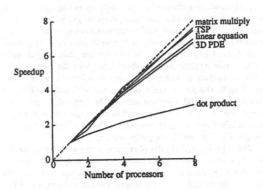

Figure 5: Speedups

anomalies [19]. It is possible that the program gets super-linear speedup or no speedup at all. In this example, it happens to have super-linear speedup.

Figure 6 shows the speedup of merge-split sort program. The curve does not look very good because even with no communication costs, the algorithm does not yield linear speedup. The program uses the best strategy for any given number of processors. For example, there is one merge-split sorting when running the program on one processor, there are 4 blocks when running the program on two processors, and so on. Using a fixed number of blocks for any number of processors would result in a better speedup, but such an approach is not reasonable.

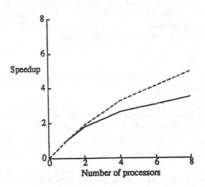

Figure 6: Speedup of merge-split sort

## Conclusion

The difficulties with passing complex data structures and process migration are the main drawbacks of the message passing model for parallel computing. Shared virtual memory on loosely-coupled multiprocessors can solve these problems. The success of implementing the prototype shared virtual memory system IVY and the experiments show that it is practical to implement such a system on existing loosely-coupled multiprocessors such as local area networks.

The implementation experience shows that, although it is possible to implement a shared virtual memory without modifying an existing system like the Aegis operating system, it is necessary to modify the existing system to get acceptable performance. IVY is a user-mode implementation, so it has a lot of overhead. A system-mode implementation ought to provide a substantial improvement. It is expected that a well-tuned system-mode implementation should improve the performance of remote operations and page moving by a factor of at least two according to the performance comparison with some well tuned systems [28,7]. I/O overlaps among the lightweight processes do not exist in IVY. An integrated heavyweight and lightweight process scheduler is highly desirable. The disk I/O overlap may also greatly improve IVY's performance.

The experimental results of running some non-trivial parallel programs on the prototype system strongly support the idea of shared virtual memory on loosely-coupled multiprocessors. The results demonstrate that the shared virtual memory can effectively exploit not only the available processors but also the combined physical memories of a multiprocessor system.

The experimental results reported in this paper are limited because there were only up to eight processors available for running the modified Aegis operating system at the time. Experiments on more processors will show more insights of shared virtual memory and behaviors of parallel programs. To answer many unanswered questions, we plan to perform more experiments on a shared virtual memory system being implemented on a large-scale multiprocessor at Princeton.

## Acknowledgement

I wish to thank John Ellis for his invaluable suggestions and helpful discussions and Nat Mishkin for his help with understanding the Aegis kernel, which made my modifications to the OS possible. I would like to thank Paul Hudak and Alan Perlis for their continual help inspiration. I also wish to thank Jeff Naughton and the referees for their helpful comments.

## References

[1] Apollo. *Apollo DOMAIN Architecture.* Apollo Computer Inc., Chelmsford, Mass., 1981.

[2] J. Archibald and J. Baer. Cache Coherence Protocols: Evaluation Using a Multiprocessor Simulation Model. *ACM Transactions on Computer Systems*, 4(4):273–298, November 1986.

[3] A.D. Birrell and B.J. Nelson. *Implementing Remote Procedure Calls.* Technical Report CSL-83-7, Xerox PARC, December 1983.

[4] D. Bitton, D.J. DeWitt, D.K. Hsaio, and J. Menon. A Taxonomy of Parallel Sorting. *ACM Computing Surveys*, 16(3):287–318, September 1984.

[5] N. Carriero and D. Gelernter. The S/Net's Linda Kernel. *ACM Transactions on Computer Systems*, 4(2):110–129, May 1986.

[6] L.M. Censier and P. Feautrier. A New Solution to Coherence Problems in Multicache Systems. *IEEE Transactions on Computers*, C-27(12):1112–1118, December 1978.

[7] David R. Cheriton. The V kernel: A Software Base for Distributed Systems. *IEEE Software*, 1(2):19–43, 1984.

[8] D.R. Cheriton and M. Stumm. The Multi-Satellite Star: Structuring Parallel Computations for A Workstation Cluster. To appear, 1988.

[9] Jarek Deminet. Experience with Multiprocessor Algorithms. *IEEE Transactions on Computers*, C-31(4), April 1982.

[10] Peter J. Denning. On Modeling Program Behavior. In *Proceedings of Spring Joint Computer Conference*, pages 937–944, AFIPS Press, 1972.

[11] Peter J. Denning. Virtual Memory. *ACM Computing Surveys*, 2(3):153–189, September 1970.

[12] Peter J. Denning. Working Sets Past and Present. *IEEE Transactions on Software Engineering*, SE-6(1):64–84, January 1980.

[13] M. Heid and R.M. Karp. The Traveling-salesman Problem and Minimum Spanning Trees. *Operation Research*, 17(12):1139–1167, December 1970.

[14] M. Herlihy and B. Liskov. A Value Transmission Method for Abstract Data Types. *ACM Transactions on Programming Languages and Systems*, 4(4):527–551, October 1982.

[15] Carl Hewitt. The Apiary Network Architecture for Knowledgeable Systems. In *Proceedings of the Lisp Conference*, pages 107–117, August 1980.

[16] C.A.R. Hoare. Communicating Sequential Processes. *Communications of the ACM*, 21(11):666–677, August 1978.

[17] C.A.R. Hoare. Quicksort. *Computer Journal*, 5(1):10–15, 1962.

[18] A. K. Jones and P. Schwarz. Experience Using Multiprocessor Systems — A Status Report. *ACM Computing Surveys*, 12(2), June 1980.

[19] T. Lai and S. Sahni. Anomalies in Parallel Branch-and-Bound Algorithms. *Communications of the ACM*, 27(6):594–602, June 1984.

[20] B. M. Lampson and D. D. Redell. Experience with Processes and Monitors in Mesa. *Communications of the ACM*, 23(2):105–117, February 1980.

[21] P.J. Leach, P.H. Levine, B.P. Douros, J.A. Hamilton, D.L. Nelson, and B.L. Stumpf. The Architecture of an Integrated Local Network. *IEEE Journal on Selected Areas in Communications*, 1983.

[22] Kai Li. *Shared Virtual Memory on Loosely-coupled Multiprocessors.* PhD thesis, Yale University, October 1986. Tech Report YALEU-RR-492.

[23] Kai Li and Paul Hudak. Memory Coherence in Shared Virtual Memory Systems. In *Proceedings of the 5th Annual ACM Symposium on Principles of Distributed Computing*, pages 229–239, August 1986. A journal version will appear in *ACM Transactions on Computer Systems*.

[24] Bruce J. Nelson. *Remote Procedure Call.* PhD thesis, Carnegie-Mellon University, May 1981.

[25] M.L. Powell and B.P. Miller. Process Migration in DEMOS/MP. In *Proceedings of the ninth Symposium on Operating Systems Principles*, pages 110–119, 1983.

[26] David P. Reed and Rajendra K. Kanodia. Synchronization with Eventcounts and Sequencers. *Communications of the ACM*, 22(2):115–123, February 1979.

[27] Alan J. Smith. Cache Memories. *ACM Computing Surveys*, 14(3):473–530, September 1982.

[28] Alfred Z. Spector. Performing Remote Operations Efficiently on a Local Computer Network. *Communications of the ACM*, 25(4):260–273, April 1982.

# Implementation and Performance of Munin

*John B. Carter, John K. Bennett, and Willy Zwaenepoel*

Computer Systems Laboratory
Rice University
Houston, Texas

## Abstract

Munin is a distributed shared memory (DSM) system that allows shared memory parallel programs to be executed efficiently on distributed memory multiprocessors. Munin is unique among existing DSM systems in its use of *multiple consistency protocols* and in its use of *release consistency*. In Munin, shared program variables are annotated with their expected access pattern, and these annotations are then used by the runtime system to choose a consistency protocol best suited to that access pattern. Release consistency allows Munin to mask network latency and reduce the number of messages required to keep memory consistent. Munin's multi-protocol release consistency is implemented in software using a *delayed update queue* that buffers and merges pending outgoing writes. A sixteen-processor prototype of Munin is currently operational. We evaluate its implementation and describe the execution of two Munin programs that achieve performance within ten percent of message passing implementations of the same programs. Munin achieves this level of performance with only minor annotations to the shared memory programs.

## 1   Introduction

A distributed shared memory (DSM) system provides the abstraction of a shared address space spanning the processors of a distributed memory multiprocessor. This abstraction simplifies the programming of distributed memory multiprocessors and allows parallel programs written for shared memory machines to be ported easily. The challenge in building a DSM system is to achieve good performance without requiring the programmer to deviate significantly from the conventional shared memory programming model. High memory latency and the high cost of sending messages make this difficult.

To meet this challenge, Munin incorporates two novel features. First, Munin employs *multiple consistency protocols*. Each shared variable declaration is annotated by its expected access pattern. Munin then chooses a consistency protocol suited to that pattern. Second, Munin is the first software DSM system that provides a *release-consistent* memory interface [19]. Roughly speaking, release consistency requires memory to be consistent only at specific synchronization points, resulting in a reduction of overhead and number of messages.

The Munin programming interface is the same as that of conventional shared memory parallel programming systems, except that it requires (i) all shared variable declarations to be annotated with their expected access pattern, and (ii) all synchronization to be visible to the runtime system. Other than that, Munin provides thread, synchronization, and data sharing facilities like those found in shared memory parallel programming systems [7].

We report on the performance of two Munin programs: Matrix Multiply and Successive Over-Relaxation (SOR). We have hand-coded the same programs on the same hardware using message passing, taking special care to ensure that the two versions of each program perform identical computations. Comparison between the Munin and the message passing versions has allowed us to assess the overhead associated with our approach. This comparison is encouraging: the performance of the Munin programs differs from that of the hand-coded message passing programs by at most ten percent, for configurations from one to sixteen processors.

This research was supported in part by the National Science Foundation under Grants CDA-8619893 and CCR-9010351, by the IBM Corporation under Research Agreement No. 20170041, and by a NASA Graduate Fellowship. Willy Zwaenepoel was on sabbatical at UT-Sydney and INRIA-Rocquencourt while a portion of this research was conducted.

The Munin prototype implementation consists of four parts: a simple preprocessor that converts the program annotations into a format suitable for use by the Munin runtime system, a modified linker that creates the shared memory segment, a collection of library routines that are linked into each Munin program, and operating system support for page fault handling and page table manipulation. This separation of functionality has resulted in a system that is largely machine- and language-independent, and we plan to port it to various other platforms and languages. The current prototype is implemented on a workstation-based distributed memory multiprocessor consisting of 16 SUN-3/60s connected by a dedicated 10 Mbps Ethernet. It makes use of a version of the V kernel [11] that allows user threads to handle page faults and to modify page tables.

A preliminary Munin design paper has been published previously [5], as well as some measurements on shared memory programs that corroborate the basic design [6]. This paper presents a refinement of the design, and then concentrates on the implementation of Munin and its performance.

## 2 Munin Overview

### 2.1 Munin Programming

Munin programmers write parallel programs using threads, as they would on a shared memory multiprocessor [7]. Munin provides library routines, CreateThread() and DestroyThread(), for this purpose. Any required user initialization is performed by a sequential user_init() routine, in which the programmer may also specify the number of threads and processors to be used. Similarly, there is an optional sequential user_done() routine that is run when the computation has finished. Munin currently does not perform any thread migration or global scheduling. User threads are run in a round robin fashion on the node on which they were created.

A Munin *shared object* corresponds to a single shared variable, although like Emerald [9], the programmer can specify that a collection of variables be treated as a single object or that a large variable be treated as a number of independent objects by the runtime system. By default, variables larger than a virtual memory page are broken into multiple page-sized objects. We use the term "object" to refer to an object as seen by the runtime system, i.e., a program variable, an 8-kilobyte (page-sized) region of a variable, or a collection of variables that share an 8-kilobyte page. Currently, Munin only supports statically allocated shared variables, although this limitation can be removed by a minor modification to the memory allocator. The programmer annotates the declaration of shared variables with a shar-

ing pattern to specify the way in which the variable is expected to be accessed. These annotations indicate to the Munin runtime system what combination of protocols to use to keep shared objects consistent (see Section 2.3).

Synchronization is supported by library routines for the manipulation of locks and barriers. These library routines include CreateLock(), AcquireLock(), ReleaseLock(), CreateBarrier(), and WaitAtBarrier(). All synchronization operations must be explicitly visible to the runtime system (i.e., must use the Munin synchronization facilities). This restriction is necessary for release consistency to operate correctly (see Section 2.2).

### 2.2 Software Release Consistency

Release consistency was introduced by the DASH system. A detailed discussion and a formal definition can be found in the papers describing DASH [19, 23]. We summarize the essential aspects of that discussion.

Release consistency requires that each shared memory access be classified either as a *synchronization* access or an *ordinary* access.[1] Furthermore, each synchronization accesses must be classified as either a *release* or an *acquire*. Intuitively, release consistency requires the system to recognize synchronization accesses as special events, enforce normal synchronization ordering requirements,[2] and guarantee that the results of all writes performed by a processor prior to a release be propagated before a remote processor acquires the lock that was released.

More formally, the following conditions are required for ensuring release consistency:

1. Before an ordinary load or store is allowed to perform with respect to any other processor, all previous acquires must be performed.

2. Before a release is allowed to perform with respect to any other processor, all previous ordinary loads and stores must be performed.

3. Before an acquire is allowed to perform with respect to any other processor, all previous releases must be performed. Before a release is allowed to perform with respect to any other processor, all previous acquires and releases must be performed.

The term "all previous accesses" refers to all accesses by the same thread that precede the current access in program order. A load is said to have "performed with

---

[1] We ignore chaotic data [19] in this presentation.

[2] For example, only one thread can acquire a lock at a time, and a thread attempting to acquire a lock must block until the acquire is successful.

respect to another processor" when a subsequent store on that processor cannot affect the value returned by the load. A store is said to have "performed with respect to another processor" when a subsequent load by that processor will return the value stored (or the value stored in a later store). A load or a store is said to have "performed" when it has performed with respect to all other processors.

Previous DSM systems [3, 10, 17, 25, 27] are based on *sequential consistency* [22]. Sequential consistency requires, roughly speaking, that each modification to a shared object become visible immediately to the other processors in the system. Release consistency postpones until the next release the time at which updates must become visible. This allows updates to be buffered until that time, and avoids having to block a thread until it is guaranteed that its current update has become visible everywhere. Furthermore, if multiple updates need to go to the same destination, they can be coalesced into a single message. The use of release consistency thus allows Munin to mask memory access latency and to reduce the number of messages required to keep memory consistent. This is important on a distributed memory multiprocessor where remote memory access latency is significant, and the cost of sending a message is high.

To implement release consistency, Munin requires that all synchronization be done through system-supplied synchronization routines. We believe this is not a major constraint, as many shared memory parallel programming environments already provide efficient synchronization packages. There is therefore little incentive for programmers to implement separate mechanisms. Unlike DASH, Munin does not require that each individual shared memory access be marked.

Gharachorloo et al. [16, 19] have shown that a large class of programs, essentially programs with "enough" synchronization, produce the same results on a release-consistent memory as on a sequentially-consistent memory. Munin's multiple consistency protocols obey the ordering requirements imposed by release consistency, so, like DASH programs, Munin programs with "enough" synchronization produce the same results under Munin as under a sequentially-consistent memory. The experience with DASH and Munin indicates that almost all shared memory parallel programs satisfy this criterion. No modifications are necessary to these programs, other than making all synchronization operations utilize the Munin synchronization facilities.

## 2.3    Multiple Consistency Protocols

Several studies of shared memory parallel programs have indicated that no single consistency protocol is best suited for all parallel programs [6, 14, 15]. Furthermore, within a single program, different shared variables are accessed in different ways and a particular variable's access pattern can change during execution [6].

Munin allows a separate consistency protocol for each shared variable, tuned to the access pattern of that particular variable. Moreover, the protocol for a variable can be changed over the course of the execution of the program. Munin uses program annotations, currently provided by the programmer, to choose a consistency protocol suited to the expected access pattern of each shared variable.

The implementation of multiple protocols is divided into two parts: high-level sharing pattern annotations and low-level protocol parameters. The high-level annotations are specified as part of a shared variable declaration. These annotations correspond to the expected sharing pattern for the variable. The current prototype supports a small collection of these annotations that closely correspond to the sharing patterns observed in our earlier study of shared memory access patterns [6]. The low-level protocol parameters control specific aspects of the individual protocols, such as whether an object may be replicated or whether to use invalidation or update to maintain consistency. In Section 2.3.1, we discuss the low-level protocol parameters that can be varied under Munin, and in Section 2.3.2 we discuss the high-level sharing patterns supported in the current Munin prototype.

### 2.3.1    Protocol Parameters

Munin's consistency protocols are derived by varying eight basic protocol parameters:

- **Invalidate or Update? (I)** This parameter specifies whether changes to an object should be propagated by invalidating or by updating remote copies.

- **Replicas allowed? (R)** This parameter specifies whether more than one copy of an object can exist in the system.

- **Delayed operations allowed? (D)** This parameter specifies whether or not the system may delay updates or invalidations when the object is modified.

- **Fixed owner? (FO)** This parameter directs Munin *not* to propagate ownership of the object. The object may be replicated on reads, but all writes must be sent to the owner, from where they may be propagated to other nodes.

- **Multiple writers allowed? (M)** This parameter specifies that multiple threads may concurrently modify the object with or without intervening synchronization.

- **Stable sharing pattern? (S)** This parameter indicates that the object has a stable access pattern, i.e., the same threads access the object in the same way during the entire execution of the program. If a different thread attempts to access the object, Munin generates a runtime error. For stable sharing patterns, Munin always sends updates to the same nodes. This allows updates to be propagated to nodes prior to these nodes requesting the data.

- **Flush changes to owner? (Fl)** This parameter directs Munin to send changes only to the object's owner and to invalidate the local copy whenever the local thread propagates changes.

- **Writable? (W)** This parameter specifies whether the shared object can be modified. If a write is attempted to a non-writable object, Munin generates a runtime error.

### 2.3.2 Sharing Annotations

Sharing annotations are added to each shared variable declaration, to guide Munin in its selection of the parameters of the protocol used to keep each object consistent. While these annotations are syntactically part of the variable's declaration, they are not programming language types, and as such they do not nest or cause compile-time errors if misused. Incorrect annotations may result in inefficient performance or in runtime errors that are detected by the Munin runtime system.

**Read-only** objects are the simplest form of shared data. Once they have been initialized, no further updates occur. Thus, the consistency protocol simply consists of replication on demand. A runtime error is generated if a thread attempts to write to a read-only object.

For **migratory** objects, a single thread performs multiple accesses to the object, including one or more writes, before another thread accesses the object [29]. Such an access pattern is typical of shared objects that are accessed only inside a critical section. The consistency protocol for migratory objects is to migrate the object to the new thread, provide it with read and write access (even if the first access is a read), and invalidate the original copy. This protocol avoids a write miss and a message to invalidate the old copy when the new thread first modifies the object.

**Write-shared** objects are concurrently written by multiple threads, without the writes being synchronized, because the programmer knows that the updates modify separate words of the object. However, because of the way that objects are laid out in memory, there may be *false sharing*. False sharing occurs when two shared variables reside in the same consistency unit, such as a cache block or a virtual memory page. In systems that do not support multiple writers to an object, the consistency unit may be exchanged between processors even though the processors are accessing different objects.

**Producer-consumer** objects are written (produced) by one thread and read (consumed) by one or more other threads. The producer-consumer consistency protocol is to *replicate* the object, and to *update*, rather than invalidate, the consumer's copies of the object when the object is modified by the producer. This eliminates read misses by the consumer threads. Release consistency allows the producer's updates to be buffered until the producer releases the lock that protects the objects. At that point, all of the changes can be passed to the consumer threads in a single message. Furthermore, producer-consumer objects have *stable* sharing relationships, so the system can determine once which nodes need to receive updates of an object, and use that information thereafter. If the sharing pattern changes unexpectedly, a runtime error is generated.

**Reduction** objects are accessed via `Fetch_and_Φ` operations. Such operations are equivalent to a lock acquisition, a read followed by a write of the object, and a lock release. An example of a reduction object is the global minimum in a parallel minimum path algorithm, which would be maintained via a `Fetch_and_min`. Reduction objects are implemented using a fixed-owner protocol.

**Result** objects are accessed in phases. They are alternately modified in parallel by multiple threads, followed by a phase in which a single thread accesses them exclusively. The problem with treating these objects as standard write-shared objects is that when the multiple threads complete execution, they unnecessarily update the other copies. Instead, updates to result objects are sent back only to the single thread that requires exclusive access.

**Conventional** objects are replicated on demand and are kept consistent by requiring a writer to be the sole owner before it can modify the object. Upon a write miss, an invalidation message is transmitted to all other replicas. The thread that generated the miss blocks until it has the only copy in the system [24]. A shared object is considered conventional if no annotation is provided by the programmer.

The combination of protocol parameter settings for each annotation is summarized in Table 1.

New sharing annotations can be added easily by modifying the preprocessor that parses the Munin program annotations. For instance, we have considered supporting an invalidation-based protocol with delayed invalidations and multiple writers, essentially invalidation-based write-shared objects, but we have chosen not to implement such a protocol until we encounter a need for it.

| Sharing | Parameter Settings | | | | | | | |
|---------|:-:|:-:|:-:|:-:|:-:|:-:|:-:|:-:|
| Annotation | I | R | D | FO | M | S | Fl | W |
| Read-only | N | Y | - | - | - | - | - | N |
| Migratory | Y | N | - | N | N | - | N | Y |
| Write-shared | N | Y | Y | N | Y | N | N | Y |
| Producer-Consumer | N | Y | Y | N | Y | Y | N | Y |
| Reduction | N | Y | N | Y | N | - | N | Y |
| Result | N | Y | Y | Y | Y | - | Y | Y |
| Conventional | Y | Y | N | N | N | - | N | Y |

**Table 1** Munin Annotations and Corresponding Protocol Parameters

## 2.4 Advanced Programming

For Matrix Multiply and Successive Over-Relaxation, the two Munin programs discussed in this paper, simply annotating each shared variable's declaration with a sharing pattern is sufficient to achieve performance comparable to a hand-coded message passing version. Munin also provides a small collection of library routines that allow the programmer to fine-tune various aspects of Munin's operation. These "hints" are optional performance optimizations.

In Munin, the programmer can specify the logical connections between shared variables and the synchronization objects that protect them [27]. Currently, this information is provided by the user using an `AssociateDataAndSynch()` call. If Munin knows which objects are protected by a particular lock, the required consistency information is included in the message that passes lock ownership. For example, if access to a particular object is protected by a particular lock, such as an object accessed only inside a critical section, Munin sends the new value of the object in the message that is used to pass lock ownership. This avoids one or more access misses when the new lock owner first accesses the protected data.

The `PhaseChange()` library routine purges the accumulated sharing relationship information (i.e., what threads are accessing what objects in a producer-consumer situation). This call is meant to support adaptive grid or sparse matrix programs in which the sharing relationships are stable for long periods of time between problem re-distribution phases. The shared matrices can be declared `producer-consumer`, which requires that the sharing behavior be stable, and `PhaseChange()` can then be invoked whenever the sharing relationships change.

`ChangeAnnotation()` modifies the expected sharing pattern of a variable and hence the protocol used to keep it consistent. This lets the system adapt to dynamic changes in the way a particular object is accessed. Since the sharing pattern of an object is an indication to the system of the consistency protocol that should be used to maintain consistency, the invocation of `ChangeAnnotation()` may require the system to perform some immediate work to bring the current state of the object up-to-date with its new sharing pattern.

`Invalidate()` deletes the local copy of an object, and migrates it elsewhere if it is the sole copy or updates remote copies with any changes that may have occurred.

`Flush()` advises Munin to flush any buffered writes immediately rather than waiting for a release.

`SingleObject()` advises Munin to treat a large (multi-page) variable as a single object rather than breaking it into smaller page-sized objects.

Finally, `PreAcquire()` advises Munin to acquire a local copy of a particular object in anticipation of future use, thus avoiding the latency caused by subsequent read misses.

## 3 Implementation

### 3.1 Overview

Munin executes a distributed directory-based cache consistency protocol [1] in software, in which each directory entry corresponds to a single object. Munin also implements locks and barriers, using a distributed queue-based synchronization protocol [20, 26].

During compilation, the sharing annotations are read by the Munin preprocessor, and an auxiliary file is created for each input file. These auxiliary files are used by the linker to create a shared data segment and a shared data description table, which are appended to the Munin executable file. The program is then linked with the Munin runtime library.

When the application program is invoked, the Munin root thread starts running. It initializes the shared data segment, creates Munin worker threads to handle consistency and synchronization functions, and registers itself with the kernel as the address space's page fault handler (as is done by Mach's external pagers [28]). It then executes the user initialization routine `user_init()`, spawns the number of remote copies of the program specified by `user_init()`, and initializes the remote shared data segments. Finally, the Munin root thread creates and runs the user root thread. The user root thread in turn creates user threads on the remote nodes.

Whenever a user thread has an access miss or executes a synchronization operation, the Munin root thread is invoked. The Munin root thread may call on one of the local Munin worker threads or a remote Munin root thread to perform the necessary operations. Afterwards, it resumes the user thread.

## 3.2 Data Object Directory

The data object directory within each Munin node maintains information about the state of the global shared memory. This directory is a hash table that maps an address in the shared address space to the entry that describes the object located at that address. The data object directory on the Munin root node is initialized from the shared data description table found in the executable file, whereas the data object directory on the other nodes is initially empty. When Munin cannot find an object directory entry in the local hash table, it requests a copy from the object's home node, which for statically defined objects is the root node. Object directory entries contain the following fields:

- **Start address** and **Size**: used as the key for looking up the object's directory entry in a hash table, given an address within the object.

- **Protocol parameter bits**: represent the protocol parameters described in Section 2.3.1.

- **Object state bits**: characterize the dynamic state of the object, e.g., whether the local copy is *valid*, *writable*, or *modified* since the last flush, and whether a *remote copy* of the object exists.

- **Copyset**: used to specify which remote processors have copies of the object that must be updated or invalidated. For a small system, such as our prototype, a bitmap of the remote processors is sufficient.[3]

- **Synchq** (optional): a pointer to the synchronization object that controls access to the object (see Section 2.4).

- **Probable owner** (optional): used as a "best guess" to reduce the overhead of determining the identity of the Munin node that currently owns the object [24]. The identity of the owner node is used by the ownership-based protocols (**migratory**, **conventional**, and **reduction**), and is also used when an object is locked in place (**reduction**) or when the changes to the object should be flushed only to its owner (**result**).

- **Home node** (optional): the node at which the object was created. It is used for a few record keeping functions and as the node of last resort if the system ever attempts to invalidate all remote copies of an object.

---

[3]This approach does not scale well to larger systems, but an earlier study of parallel programs suggests that a processor list is often quite short [29]. The common exception to this rule occurs when an object is shared by every processor, and a special All_Nodes value can be used to indicate this case.

- **Access control semaphore**: provides mutually exclusive access to the object's directory entry.

- **Links**: used for hashing and enqueueing the object's directory entry.

## 3.3 Delayed Update Queue

The *delayed update queue* (DUQ) is used to buffer pending outgoing write operations as part of Munin's software implementation of release consistency. A write to an object that allows delayed updates, as specified by the protocol parameter bits, is stored in the DUQ. The DUQ is flushed whenever a local thread releases a lock or arrives at a barrier.

Munin uses the virtual memory hardware to detect and enqueue changes to objects. Initially, and after each time that the DUQ is flushed, the shared objects handled by the DUQ are write-protected using the virtual memory hardware. When a thread first attempts to write to such an object, the resulting protection fault invokes Munin. The object's directory entry is put on the DUQ, write-protection is removed so that subsequent writes do not experience consistency overhead, and the faulting thread is resumed. If multiple writers are allowed on the object, a copy (*twin*) of the object is also made. This twin is used to determine which words within the object have been modified since the last update.

When a thread releases a lock or reaches a barrier, the modifications to the objects enqueued on the DUQ are propagated to their remote copies.[4] The set of remote copies is either immediately available in the *Copyset* in the data object directory, or it must be dynamically determined. The algorithm that we currently use to dynamically determine the *Copyset* is somewhat inefficient. We have devised, but not yet implemented, an improved algorithm that uses the owner node to collect *Copyset* information. Currently, a message indicating which objects have been modified locally is sent to all other nodes. Each node replies with a message indicating the subset of these objects for which it has a copy. If the protocol parameters indicate that the sharing relationship is stable, this determination is performed only once.

If an enqueued object does not have a twin (i.e., multiple writers are not allowed), Munin transmits updates or invalidations to nodes with remote copies, as indicated by the invalidate protocol parameter bit in the object's directory entry. If the object does have a twin, Munin performs a word-by-word comparison of the object and its twin, and run-length encodes the results of

---

[4]This is a conservative implementation of release consistency, because the updates are propagated at the time of the release, rather than being delayed until the release is performed (see Section 2.2).

this "diff" into the space allocated for the twin. Each run consists of a count of identical words, the number of differing words that follow, and the data associated with those differing words. The encoded object is sent to the nodes that require updates, where the object is decoded and the changes merged into the original object. If a Munin node with a dirty copy of an object receives an update for that object, it incorporates the changes immediately. If a Munin node with a dirty copy of an object receives an invalidation request for that object and multiple writers are allowed, any pending local updates are propagated. Otherwise, a runtime error is generated.

This approach works well when there are multiple writes to an object between DUQ flushes, which allows the expense of the copy and subsequent comparison to be amortized over a large number of write accesses. Table 2 breaks down the time to handle updates to an 8-kilobyte object through the DUQ. This includes the time to handle a fault (including resuming the thread), make a copy of the object, encode changes to the object, transmit them to a single remote node, decode them remotely, and reply to the original sender. We present the results for three different modification patterns. In the first pattern, a single word within the object has changed. In the second, every word in the object has changed. In the third, every other word has changed, which is the worst case for our run-length encoding scheme because there are a maximum number of minimum-length runs.

We considered and rejected two other approaches for implementing release consistency in software:

1. Force the thread to page fault on every write to a replicated object so that the modified words can be queued as they are accessed.

2. Have the compiler add code to log writes to replicated objects as part of the write.

| Component | One Word | All Words | Alternate Words |
|---|---|---|---|
| Handle Fault | 2.01 | 2.01 | 2.01 |
| Copy object | 1.15 | 1.15 | 1.15 |
| Encode object | 3.07 | 4.79 | 6.57 |
| Transmit object | 1.72 | 12.47 | 12.47 |
| Decode object | 3.12 | 4.86 | 6.68 |
| Reply | 2.27 | 2.27 | 2.27 |
| Total | 13.34 | 27.55 | 31.15 |

**Table 2**  Time to Handle an 8-kilobyte Object through DUQ (msec.)

The first approach works well if an object is only modified a small number of times between DUQ flushes, or if the page fault handling code can be made extremely fast. Since it is quite common for an object to be updated multiple times between DUQ flushes [6], the added overhead of handling multiple page faults makes this approach generally unacceptable. The second approach was used successfully by the Emerald system [9]. We chose not to explore this approach in the prototype because we have a relatively fast page fault handler, and we did not want to modify the compiler. This approach is an attractive alternative for systems that do not support fast page fault handling or modification of virtual memory mappings, such as the iPSC-i860 hypercube [12]. However, if the number of writes to a particular object between DUQ flushes is high, as is often the case [6], this approach will perform relatively poorly because each write to a shared object will be slowed. We intend to study this approach more closely in future system implementations.

## 3.4  Synchronization Support

Synchronization objects are accessed in a fundamentally different way than data objects [6], so Munin does *not* provide synchronization through shared memory. Rather, each Munin node interacts with the other nodes to provide a high-level synchronization service. Munin provides support for distributed locks and barriers. More elaborate synchronization objects, such as monitors and atomic integers, can be built using these basic mechanisms.

Munin employs a queue-based implementation of locks, which allows a thread to request ownership of a lock and then to block awaiting a reply without repeated queries. Munin uses a synchronization object directory, analogous to the data object directory, to maintain information about the state of the synchronization objects. For each lock, a queue identifies the user threads waiting for the lock, so a release-acquire pair can be performed with a single message exchange if the acquire is pending when the release occurs. The queue itself is distributed to improve scalability.

When a thread wants to acquire a lock, it calls `AcquireLock()`, which invokes Munin to find the lock in the synchronization object directory. If the lock is local and free, the thread immediately acquires the lock and continues executing. If the lock is not free, Munin sends a request to the probable lock owner to find the actual owner, possibly requiring the request to be forwarded multiple times. When the request arrives at the owner node, ownership is forwarded directly to the requester if the lock is free. Otherwise, the owner forwards the request to the thread at the end of the queue, which puts the requesting thread on the lock's queue. Each enqueued thread knows only the identity of the thread that follows it on the queue. When a thread performs an `Unlock()` and the associated queue is non-empty, lock ownership is forwarded directly to the thread at the head of the queue.

To wait at a barrier, a thread calls `WaitAtBarrier()`, which causes a message to be sent to the owner node, and the thread to be blocked awaiting a reply. When the Munin root thread on the owner node has received messages from the specified number of threads, it replies to the blocked threads, causing them to be resumed. For future implementations on larger systems, we envision the use of barrier trees and other more scalable schemes [21].

## 4   Performance

We have measured the performance of two Munin programs, Matrix Multiply and Successive Over-Relaxation (SOR). We have also hand-coded the same programs on the same hardware using the underlying message passing primitives. We have taken special care to ensure that the actual computational components of both versions of each program are identical. This section describes in detail the actions of the Munin runtime system during the execution of these two programs, and reports the performance of both versions of these programs. Both programs make use of the DUQ to mitigate the effects of false sharing and thus improve performance. They also exploit Munin's multiple consistency protocols to reduce the consistency maintenance overhead.

### 4.1   Matrix Multiply

The shared variables in Matrix Multiply are declared as follows:

```
shared read_only int input1[N][N];
shared read_only int input2[N][N];
shared result int output[N][N];
```

The `user_init()` routine initializes the input matrices and creates a barrier via a call to `CreateBarrier()`. After creating worker threads, the user root thread waits on the barrier by calling `WaitAtBarrier()`. Each worker thread computes a portion of the output matrix using a standard (sub)matrix multiply routine. When a worker thread completes its computation, it performs a `WaitAtBarrier()` call. After all workers reach the barrier, the program terminates. The program does not utilize any of the optimizations described in Section 2.4.

On the root node, the input matrices are mapped as read-only, based on the **read-only** annotation, and the output matrix is mapped as read-write, based on the **result** annotation. When a worker thread first accesses

an input matrix, the resulting page fault is handled by the Munin root thread on that node. It acquires a copy of the object from the root node, maps it as read-only, and resumes the faulted thread. Similarly, when a remote worker thread first writes to the output matrix, a page fault occurs. A copy of that page of the output matrix is then obtained from the root node, and the copy is mapped as read-write. Since the output matrix is a **result** object, there may be multiple writers, and updates may be delayed. Thus, Munin makes a twin, and inserts the output matrix's object descriptor in the DUQ. When a worker thread completes its computation and performs a `WaitAtBarrier()` call, Munin flushes the DUQ. Since the output matrix is a **result** object, Munin sends the modifications only to the owner (the node where the root thread is executing), and invalidates the local copy.

Table 3 gives the execution times of both the Munin and the message passing implementations for multiplying two 400 × 400 matrices. The System time represents the time spent executing Munin code on the root node, while the User time is that spent executing user code. In all cases, the performance of the Munin version was within 10% of that of the hand-coded message passing version. Program execution times for representative numbers of processors are shown. The program behaved similarly for all numbers of processors from one to sixteen.

Since different portions of the output matrix are modified concurrently by different worker threads, there is false sharing of the output matrix. Munin's provision for multiple writers reduces the adverse effects of this false sharing. As a result, the data motion exhibited by the Munin version of Matrix Multiply is nearly identical to that exhibited by the message passing version. In the Munin version, after the workers have acquired their input data, they execute independently, without communication, as in the message passing version. Furthermore, the various parts of the output matrix are sent from the node where they are computed to the root node, again as in the message passing version. The only

| # of | DM | Munin | | | % |
|---|---|---|---|---|---|
| Procs | Total | Total | System | User | Diff |
| 1 | 753.15 | — | — | — | — |
| 2 | 378.74 | 382.15 | 1.21 | 376.24 | 0.9 |
| 4 | 192.21 | 196.92 | 2.45 | 191.26 | 2.5 |
| 8 | 101.57 | 105.73 | 5.82 | 97.31 | 4.1 |
| 16 | 66.31 | 72.41 | 8.51 | 54.19 | 9.2 |

**Table 3**   Performance of Matrix Multiply(sec.)

difference between the two versions is that in Munin the appropriate parts of the input matrices are paged in, while in the message passing version they are sent during initialization. The additional overhead present in the Munin version comes from the page fault handling and the copying, encoding, and decoding of the output matrix. In a DSM system that does not support multiple writers to an object, portions of the output matrix could "ping-pong" between worker threads.

The performance of Matrix Multiply can be optimized by utilizing one of the performance optimizations discussed in Section 2.4. If Munin is told to treat the first input array as a single object rather than breaking it into smaller page-sized objects, via a call to `SingleObject()`, the entire input array is transmitted to each worker thread when the array is first accessed. Overhead is lowered by reducing the number of access misses. This improves the performance of the Munin version to within 2% of the hand-coded message passing version. Execution times reflecting this optimization are shown in Table 4.

## 4.2  Successive Over-Relaxation

SOR is used to model natural phenomena. An example of an SOR application is determining the temperature gradients over a square area, given the temperature values at the area boundaries. The basic SOR algorithm is iterative. The area is divided into a grid of points, represented by a matrix, at the desired level of granularity. Each matrix element corresponds to a grid point. During each iteration, each matrix element is updated to be the average of its four nearest neighbors. To avoid overwriting the old value of a matrix element before it is used, the program can either use a scratch array or only compute every other element per iteration (so-called "red-black" SOR). Both techniques work equally well under Munin. Our example employs the scratch array approach.

| # of |  DM  | Munin | | | % |
|------|------|-------|--------|------|------|
| Procs | Total | Total | System | User | Diff |
| 1 | 753.15 | — | — | — | — |
| 2 | 378.74 | 380.51 | 0.34 | 376.16 | 0.5 |
| 4 | 192.21 | 194.27 | 0.57 | 190.15 | 1.1 |
| 8 | 101.57 | 102.84 | 0.87 | 97.21 | 1.3 |
| 16 | 66.31 | 67.21 | 1.26 | 54.18 | 1.4 |

**Table 4**  Performance of Optimized Matrix Multiply (sec.)

SOR is parallelized by dividing the area into sections and having a worker thread compute the values for each section. Newly computed values at the section boundaries must be exchanged with adjacent sections at the end of each iteration. This exchange engenders a producer-consumer relationship between grid points at the boundaries of adjacent sections.

In the Munin version of SOR, the user root thread creates a worker thread for each section. The matrix representing the grid is annotated as

```
shared producer_consumer int matrix [...]
```

The programmer is *not* required to specify the data partitioning to the runtime system. After each iteration, worker threads synchronize by waiting at a barrier. After all workers have completed all iterations, the program terminates. The Munin version of SOR did not utilize any of the optimizations described in Section 2.4.

A detailed analysis of the execution, which exemplifies how producer-consumer sharing is currently handled by Munin, follows:

- During the first compute phase, when the new average of the neighbors is computed in the scratch array, the nodes read-fault in copies of the pages of the matrix as needed.

- During the first copy phase, when the newly computed values are copied to the matrix, nodes write-fault, enqueue the appropriate pages on the DUQ, create twins of these pages, make the originals read-write, and resume.

- When the first copy phase ends and the worker thread waits at the barrier, the sharing relationships between producer and consumer are determined as described in Section 3.3. Afterwards, any pages that have an empty *Copyset*, and are therefore private, are made locally writable, their twins are deleted, and they do not generate further access faults. In our SOR example, all non-edge elements of each section are handled in this manner.

- Since the sharing relationships of producer-consumer objects are stable, after all subsequent copy phases, updates to shared portions of the matrix (the edge elements of each section) are propagated only to those nodes that require the updated data (those nodes handling adjacent sections). At each subsequent synchronization point, the update mechanism automatically combines the elements destined for the same node into a single message.

Table 5 gives the execution times of both the Munin and the message passing implementation of 100 iterations of SOR on a 512 × 512 matrix, for representative

| # of Procs | DM Total | Munin | | | % Diff |
|---|---|---|---|---|---|
| | | Total | System | User | |
| 1 | 122.62 | — | — | — | — |
| 2 | 63.68 | 66.87 | 2.27 | 61.83 | 5.5 |
| 4 | 36.46 | 39.70 | 3.58 | 31.77 | 8.9 |
| 8 | 26.72 | 28.26 | 5.17 | 16.57 | 5.8 |
| 16 | 25.62 | 27.64 | 8.32 | 8.51 | 7.9 |

**Table 5**  Performance of SOR (sec.)

numbers of processors. In all cases, the performance of the Munin version was within 10% of that of the hand-coded message passing version. Again, the program behaved similarly for all numbers of processors from one to sixteen.

Since the matrix elements that each thread accesses overlap with the elements that its neighboring threads access, the sharing is very fine-grained and there is considerable false sharing. After the first pass, which involves an extra phase to determine the sharing relationships, the data motion in the Munin version of SOR is essentially identical to the message passing implementation. The only extra overhead comes from the fault handling and from the copying, coding, and decoding of the shared portions of the matrix.

### 4.3  Effect of Multiple Protocols

We studied the importance of having multiple protocols by comparing the performance of the multi-protocol implementation with the performance of an implementation using only **conventional** or only **write-shared** objects. **Conventional** objects result in an ownership-based write-invalidate protocol being used, similar to the one implemented in Ivy [24]. We also chose **write-shared** because it supports multiple writers and fine-grained sharing.

The execution times for the unoptimized version of Matrix Multiply (see Table 4) and SOR, for the previous problem sizes and for 16 processors, are presented in Table 6. For Matrix Multiply, the use of **result** and

| Protocol | Matrix Multiply | SOR |
|---|---|---|
| Multiple | 72.41 | 27.64 |
| Write-shared | 75.59 | 64.48 |
| Conventional | 75.85 | 67.64 |

**Table 6**  Effect of Multiple Protocols (sec.)

**read_only** sped up the time required to load the input matrices and later purge the output matrix back to the root node and resulted in a 4.4% performance improvement over **write-shared** and a 4.8% performance improvement over **conventional**. For SOR, the use of **producer-consumer** reduced the consistency overhead, by removing the phase in which sharing relationships are determined for all but the first iteration. The resulting execution time was less than half that of the implementations using only **conventional** or **write-shared**. The execution time for SOR using **write-shared** can be improved by using an better algorithm for determining the *Copyset* (see Section 3.3).

### 4.4  Summary

For Matrix Multiply, after initialization, each worker thread transmits only a single result message back to the root node, which is the same communication pattern found in a hand-coded message passing version of the program. For SOR, there is only one message exchange between adjacent sections per iteration (after the first iteration), again, just as in the message passing version.

The common problem of false sharing of large objects (or pages), which can hamper the performance of DSM systems, is relatively benign under Munin because we do *not* enforce a single-writer restriction on objects that do not require it. Thus, intertwined access regions and non-page-aligned data are less of a problem in Munin than with other DSM systems. The overhead introduced by Munin in both Matrix Multiply and SOR, other than the determination of the sharing relationships after the first iteration of SOR, comes from the expense of encoding and decoding modified objects.

By adding only minor annotations to the shared memory programs, the resulting Munin programs executed almost as efficiently as the corresponding message passing versions. In fact, during our initial testing, the performance of the Munin programs was *better* than the performance of the message passing versions. Only after careful tuning of the message passing versions were we able to generate message passing programs that resulted in the performance data presented here. This anecdote emphasizes the difficulty of writing efficient message passing programs, and serves to emphasize the value of a DSM system like Munin.

## 5  Related Work

A number of software DSM systems have been developed [3, 8, 10, 17, 25, 27]. All, except Midway [8], use sequential consistency [22]. Munin's use of release consistency only requires consistency to be enforced at specific synchronization points, with the resulting reduction in latency and number of messages exchanged.

Ivy uses a single-writer, write-invalidate protocol, with virtual memory pages as the units of consistency [25]. The large size of the consistency unit makes the system prone to false sharing. In addition, the single-writer nature of the protocol can cause a "ping-pong" behavior between multiple writers of a shared page. It is then up to the programmer or the compiler to lay out the program data structures in the shared address space such that false sharing is reduced.

Clouds performs consistency management on a per-object basis, or in Clouds terminology, on a per-segment basis [27]. Clouds allows a segment to be locked by a processor, to avoid the "ping-pong" effects that may result from false sharing. Mirage also attempts to avoid these effects by locking a page with a certain processor for a certain $\Delta$ time window [17]. Munin's use of multiple-writer protocols avoids the adverse effects of false sharing, without introducing the delays caused by locking a segment to a processor.

Orca is also an object-oriented DSM system, but its consistency management is based on an efficient reliable ordered broadcast protocol [3]. For reasons of scalability, Munin does not rely on broadcast. In Orca, both invalidate and update protocols can be used. Munin also supports a wider variety of protocols.

Unlike the designs discussed above, in Amber the programmer is responsible for the distribution of data among processors [10]. The system does not attempt to automatically move or replicate data. Good speedups are reported for SOR running on Amber. Munin automates many aspects of data distribution, and still remains efficient by asking the programmer to specify the expected access patterns for shared data variables.

Linda provides a different abstraction for distributed memory programming: all shared variables reside in a tuple space, and the only operations allowed are atomic insertion, removal, and reading of objects from the tuple space [18]. Munin stays closer to the more familiar shared memory programming model, hopefully improving its acceptance with parallel programmers.

Midway [8] proposes a DSM system with *entry consistency*, a memory consistency model weaker than release consistency. The goal of Midway is to minimize communications costs by aggressively exploiting the relationship between shared variables and the synchronization objects that protect them.

Recently, designs for hardware distributed shared memory machines have been published [2, 23]. Our work is most related to the DASH project [23], from which we adapt the concept of release consistency. Unlike Munin, though, DASH uses a write-invalidate protocol for all consistency maintenance. Munin uses the flexibility of its software implementation to also attack the problem of read misses by allowing multiple writers to a single shared object and by using update proto-

cols (producer-consumer, write-shared, result) and pre-invalidation (migratory) when appropriate. The APRIL machine takes a different approach in combatting the latency problem on distributed shared memory machines [2]. APRIL provides sequential consistency, but relies on extremely fast processor switching to overlap memory latency with computation.

A technique similar to the delayed update queue was used by the Myrias SPS multiprocessor [13]. It performed the *copy-on-write* and *diff* in hardware, but required a restricted form of parallelism to ensure correctness.

Munin's implementation of locks is similar to existing implementations on shared memory multiprocessors [20, 26].

An alternative approach for parallel processing on distributed memory machines is to have the compiler produce a message passing program starting from a sequential program, annotated by the programmer with data partitions [4, 30]. Given the static nature of compile-time analysis, these techniques appear to be restricted to numerical computations with statically defined shared memory access patterns.

# 6 Conclusions and Future Work

The objective of the Munin project is to build a DSM system in which shared memory parallel programs execute on a distributed memory machine and achieve good performance without the programmer having to make extensive modifications to the shared memory program. Munin's shared memory is different from "real" shared memory only in that it provides a release-consistent memory interface, and in that the shared variables are annotated with their expected access patterns. In the applications that we have programmed in Munin so far, the release-consistent memory interface has required no changes, while the annotations have proved to be only a minor chore. Munin programming has been easier than message passing programming. Nevertheless, we have achieved performance within 5–10 percent of message passing implementations of the same applications. We argue that this cost in performance is a small price to pay for the resulting reduction in program complexity.

Further work on Munin will continue to examine the tradeoff between performance and programming complexity. We are interested in examining whether memory consistency can be relaxed further, without necessitating more program modifications than release consistency. We are also considering more aggressive implementation techniques, such as the use of a *pending updates queue* to hold incoming updates, a dual to the delayed update queue already in use. We also wish to design higher-level interfaces to distributed shared memory in which the access patterns will be determined without user annotation. Another important issue is Munin's scalability in terms of processor speed, interconnect bandwidth, and number of processors. To explore this issue, we intend to implement Munin on suitable hardware platforms such as a Touchstone-class machine or a high-speed network of supercomputer workstations. In this vein, we are also studying hardware support for selected features of Munin.

## Acknowledgements

Dave Johnson provided important guidance during the prototype implementation and his feedback throughout the project was very useful. Peter Ostrin developed and timed the distributed memory programs reported in this paper.

The authors wish to thank the anonymous referees for their many helpful comments. Brian Bershad, Elmootazbellah Elnozahy, and Matt Zekauskas also provided many suggestions for improving the paper.

## References

[1] A. Agarwal, R. Simoni, J. Hennessy, and M. Horowitz. An evaluation of directory schemes for cache coherence. In *Proceedings of the 15th Annual International Symposium on Computer Architecture*, pages 280–289, June 1988.

[2] Anant Agarwal, Beng-Hong Lim, David Kranz, and John Kubiatowicz. APRIL: A processor architecture for multiprocessing. In *Proceedings of the 17th Annual International Symposium on Computer Architecture*, pages 104–114, May 1990.

[3] Henri E. Bal and Andrew S. Tanenbaum. Distributed programming with shared data. In *Proceedings of the IEEE CS 1988 International Conference on Computer Languages*, pages 82–91, October 1988.

[4] Vasanth Balasundaram, Geoffrey Fox, Ken Kennedy, and Uli Kremer. An interactive environment for data partitioning and distribution. In *Proceedings of the 5th Distributed Memory Computing Conference*, Charleston, South Carolina, April 1990.

[5] John K. Bennett, John B. Carter, and Willy Zwaenepoel. Munin: Distributed shared memory based on type–specific memory coherence. In *Proceedings of the 1990 Conference on the Principles and Practice of Parallel Programming*, March 1990.

[6] John K. Bennett, John B. Carter, and Willy Zwaenepoel. Adaptive software cache management for distributed shared memory architectures. In *Proceedings of the 17th Annual International Symposium on Computer Architecture*, pages 125–134, May 1990.

[7] Brian N. Bershad, Edward D. Lazowska, and Henry M. Levy. PRESTO: A system for object-oriented parallel programming. *Software—Practice and Experience*, 18(8):713–732, August 1988.

[8] Brian N. Bershad and Matthew J. Zekauskas. Shared memory parallel programming with entry consistency for distributed memory multiprocessors. Technical Report CMU-CS-91-170, Carnegie-Mellon University, September 1991.

[9] Andrew Black, Norman Hutchinson, Eric Jul, and Henry Levy. Object structure in the Emerald system. In *Proceedings of the ACM Conference on Object-Oriented Programming Systems, Languages and Applications*, pages 78–86, October 1986. Special Issue of SIGPLAN Notices, Volume 21, Number 11, November, 1986.

[10] Jeffrey S. Chase, Franz G. Amador, Edward D. Lazowska, Henry M. Levy, and Richard J. Littlefield. The Amber system: Parallel programming on a network of multiprocessors. In *Proceedings of the 12th ACM Symposium on Operating Systems Principles*, pages 147–158, December 1989.

[11] David R. Cheriton and Willy Zwaenepoel. The distributed V kernel and its performance for diskless workstations. In *Proceedings of the 9th ACM Symposium on Operating Systems Principles*, pages 129–140, October 1983.

[12] Intel Corporation. i860 64-bit Microprocessor Programmer's Manual. Santa Clara, California, 1990.

[13] Myrias Corporation. System Overview. Edmonton, Alberta, 1990.

[14] Susan J. Eggers and Randy H. Katz. A characterization of sharing in parallel programs and its application to coherency protocol evaluation. In *Proceedings of the 15th Annual International Symposium on Computer Architecture*, pages 373–383, May 1988.

[15] Susan J. Eggers and Randy H. Katz. The effect of sharing on the cache and bus performance of parallel programs. In *Proceedings of the 3rd International Conference on Architectural Support for Programming Languages and Systems*, pages 257–270, April 1989.

[16] Kourosh Gharachorloo, Anoop Gupta, and John Hennessy. Performance evaluations of memory consistency models for shared-memory multiprocessors. In *Proceedings of the 4th International Conference on Architectural Support for Programming Languages and Systems*, April 1991.

[17] Brett D. Fleisch and Gerald J. Popek. Mirage: A coherent distributed shared memory design. In *Proceedings of the 12th ACM Symposium on Operating Systems Principles*, pages 211–23, December 1989.

[18] David Gelernter. Generative communication in Linda. *ACM Transactions on Programming Languages and Systems*, 7(1):80–112, January 1985.

[19] Kourosh Gharachorloo, Daniel Lenoski, James Laudon, Phillip Gibbons, Anoop Gupta, and John Hennessy. Memory consistency and event ordering in scalable shared-memory multiprocessors. In *Proceedings of the 17th Annual International Symposium on Computer Architecture*, pages 15–26, May 1990.

[20] James R. Goodman, Mary K. Vernon, and Philip J. Woest. Efficient synchronization primitives for large-scale cache-coherent multiprocessor. In *Proceedings of the 3rd International Conference on Architectural Support for Programming Languages and Systems*, pages 64–75, April 1989.

[21] Debra Hensgen, Raphael Finkel, and Udi Manber. Two algorithms for barrier synchronization. *International Journal of Parallel Programming*, 17(1):1–17, January 1988.

[22] Leslie Lamport. How to make a multiprocessor computer that correctly executes multiprocess programs. *IEEE Transactions on Computers*, C-28(9):690–691, September 1979.

[23] Dan Lenoski, James Laudon, Kourosh Gharachorloo, Anoop Gupta, and John Hennessy. The directory-based cache coherence protocol for the DASH multiprocessor. In *Proceedings of the 17th Annual International Symposium on Computer Architecture*, pages 148–159, May 1990.

[24] Kai Li. *Shared Virtual Memory on Loosely Coupled Multiprocessors*. PhD thesis, Yale University, September 1986.

[25] Kai Li and Paul Hudak. Memory coherence in shared virtual memory systems. *ACM Transactions on Computer Systems*, 7(4):321–359, November 1989.

[26] John M. Mellor-Crummey and Michael L. Scott. Synchronization without contention. In *Proceedings of the 4th International Conference on Architectural Support for Programming Languages and Systems*, pages 269–278, April 1991.

[27] Umakishore Ramachandran, Mustaque Ahamad, and M. Yousef A. Khalidi. Coherence of distributed shared memory: Unifying synchronization and data transfer. In *Proceedings of the 1989 Conference on Parallel Processing*, pages II-160—II-169, June 1989.

[28] Richard Rashid, Avadis Tevanian, Jr. Michael Young, David Golub, Robert Baron, David Black, William Bolosky, and Jonathan Chew. Machine-independent virtual memory management for paged uniprocessor and multiprocessor architectures. *IEEE Transactions on Computers*, 37(8):896–908, August 1988.

[29] Wolf-Dietrich Weber and Anoop Gupta. Analysis of cache invalidation patterns in multiprocessors. In *Proceedings of the 3rd International Conference on Architectural Support for Programming Languages and Systems*, pages 243–256, April 1989.

[30] Hans P. Zima, Heinz J. Bast, and Michael Gerndt. Superb: A tool for semi-automatic SIMD/MIMD parallelization. *Parallel Computing*, 6:1–18, 1988.

# Mirage: A Coherent Distributed Shared Memory Design[1]

Brett D. Fleisch[2]
Gerald J. Popek

University of California
Los Angeles, CA

## Abstract

Shared memory is an effective and efficient paradigm for interprocess communication. We are concerned with software that makes use of shared memory in a single site system and its extension to a multimachine environment. Here we describe the design of a *distributed shared memory* (DSM) system called Mirage developed at UCLA. Mirage provides a form of network transparency to make network boundaries invisible for shared memory and is upward compatible with an existing interface to shared memory. We present the rationale behind our design decisions and important details of the implementation. Mirage's basic performance is examined by component timings, a worst case application, and a "representative" application. In some instances of page contention, the tuning parameter in our design improves application throughput. In other cases, thrashing is reduced and overall system performance improved using our tuning parameter.

## 1.0 Introduction

Distributed computation has evolved using message passing as its principal communication technique. The message passing approach may not be well suited for multiprocessors and tightly coupled processors that have access to shared memory. Message passing interfaces require the programmer to use conceptually different primitives and organize the programmed code differently than shared memory interfaces used in single shared memory spaces. Further, communicating large or complex data structures may be difficult or inefficient using message passing. An alternate approach is to provide *distributed shared memory* (DSM).

Mirage is a DSM system implemented in the kernel of an existing operating system. The protocol used in Mirage is different from previous work in the following ways:

1. The model is based on paged segmentation[DALE68, DENN70].

2. The writer of a page retains access to that page for a fixed period of time independent of subsequent read and write requests.

3. There may be upgrades or downgrades in the modes of pages that are distributed throughout the network.

The techniques described here were designed to reduce network traffic and sustain high performance. The overall goals of this work are: 1) to present a protocol for DSM, 2) to minimize the overheads in DSM access and show effective performance of the protocols employed, and 3) to measure the performance of Mirage applications. To accomplish 3) we examine component timings and an important worst case application. Further, we attempt to characterize average case performance with a "representative" case which could be representative of a larger class of applications. This latter case provides an evaluation of our tuning parameter discussed in Section 4.1.

We have chosen to implement Mirage in the OS kernel rather than analytically model, simulate, or implement a library layer for a variety of reasons. Some of these include the difficulty in otherwise accurately capturing: 1) the asynchronous behavior of computer systems, 2) the interactions between scheduling, interrupt processing, and the user program requests and 3) the host behavior and network loading from the use of the protocols, and the interaction of all these with applications. Most importantly, a primary motivation for a kernel implementation of Mirage was to gain insight into the performance of DSM systems.

We originally planned to test the kernel prototype using real applications that exercise the system's functionality. Therefore, to improve our prospects of obtaining useful applications for performance testing we built a distributed shared memory system that is upward compatible with the UNIX System V IPC defined interface[ATT86]. Our goal was to compare the performance of existing applications running on single site

---

[1] This research was sponsored by DARPA Contract No. F29601-87-C-0072

[2] Author's current address: Tulane University, Computer Science Dept, School of Engineering, 301G Stanley Thomas, New Orleans, LA 70118

systems to those same applications executing in a multi-site configuration. However, we were unsuccessful in locating suitable real applications of shared memory and instead studied the performance of Mirage using synthetic applications.

The work described here does not specifically examine communication failures nor site crashes. We expect reliability and fault tolerance issues to be significant areas for future research. However, our results are important since we expect many applications to be characterized by a "tight" degree of sharing among a small number of reliable, well-behaved, communicating sites.

## 2.0 The System V Interface Model and Environment

In this section we describe the System V Model of shared memory. Its selection as the basis of a DSM prototype is independent of the underlying protocol. In fact, one could develop other protocols for DSM and adopt the System V interface; conversely, one could use other interfaces for our protocol.

In Mirage, as in System V, processes access shared memory through the use of a *segment*. A segment stores shared memory data. Segments are not meant to store program text nor system state except as raw data. A process creates a shared segment by defining a segment's size, name, and access protection. Segment access protection works in a similar fashion as UNIX file access protection, but allows only read and write permissions. Other processes locate and *attach* the segment into their virtual memory address space by name. The attaching process can choose the exact virtual address range or elect to place the segment at a first-fit location in the address space. Unlike other sharing models, processes can share locations at different virtual address ranges. Once attached, the shared memory can be used like any normal locations of memory, the only difference being that changes to the underlying memory are also visible to the other processes that share the segment. When a process is finished with the segment it may be *detached*. The last detach of a segment destroys it.

Mirage provides *transparent access* where remote memory access operates in an identical manner as local memory access. The upward compatible system call interface permits site independent creation, location, and destruction of System V shared memory segments. Also, reads and writes to shared memory operate identically whether memory is being accessed locally or remotely. Mirage features *preserved semantics*, where the UNIX System V IPC semantics are preserved in the distributed environment from the local environment. Lastly, *binary compatibility* is provided. Applications written using the System V IPC interface need not be recompiled and should execute unchanged in our new environment.

Our prototyping environment consists of 3 VAX 11/750s networked together using a 10 megabit/sec Ethernet[METC76]. The VAXs run an early version of the Locus operating system[POPE81, WALK83] compatible with the UNIX System V interface specifications. We briefly highlight Locus and describe how that system led to the development of our model and the prototype.

The Locus operating system is a distributed version of UNIX that provides a superset of UNIX services. Support for the underlying network is almost entirely invisible to users and application programs. The system supports a high degree of *network transparency:* that is, it makes the network of machines appear to users and programs as a single computer, completely hiding machine boundaries during normal operation.

Locus provides a fully transparent file system and facilities for distributed processes. In a Locus network, which may consist of machines of various CPU types, both files and programs may be moved without effect on correct operation. Central to the design of the Locus architecture is the underlying distributed file system. The file system supports a number of high-reliability facilities, including a more robust filesystem facility than that of conventional UNIX systems, and support for interprocess communication. Process creation and migration are fully supported. Lastly, new distributed interprocess communication facilities based on System V messages and semaphores were added to Locus previously[FLEI86].

## 3.0 Coherence

Consistency control is a challenge in the design of distributed systems. At the outset of the design we decided that it would be unacceptable for processes to read data that has become out-of-date or *stale*. Two approaches to memory consistency control were examined: coherence and user-level synchronization. Like Li[LI86] we have chosen to maintain *coherence* at the lowest system level. A coherent implementation is one in which a write to an address in a given segment is always visible by all subsequent read operations to the same address, independent of the machine location on which the read takes place.

In contrast to coherence, synchronization has been used in parallel programs to ensure that processes observe an application-specific consistent state. Whereas coherency is defined in an application-independent way solely in terms of reads and writes to distributed data in a loosely coupled system, programs may need synchronized access to shared memory even in a single site where coherency is often not an issue. Similarly, distributed programs may desire coherency without synchronization. Therefore, in Mirage it is the responsibility of user-level processes to synchronize writes from different processes.

Coherence can be a problem in a multiprocessor environment as well as in a loosely coupled environment. In multiprocessors, data may be buffered and instructions may not be atomic. Accesses are buffered if multiple accesses can be queued before reaching their destination, such as main memory or caches. In a loosely coupled environment, consistency protocols must guarantee network delays do not affect correctness in managing data copies that may be present at various sites.

To implement coherence, fixed size pages of the segment (the same pages as the hardware memory management) are used as the basis for all intersite consistency. Although only one site in a network will have a valid writable copy of a given page at any instant, there may be many sites simultaneously possessing readable copies of the page. In general, a given page will have either one site acting as writer or multiple sites acting as readers.

There are many situations in which an implementation of shared memory coherence could perform poorly. A worst case scenario might be an alternating sequences of reads and writes to the same page issued by different sites. This situation requires that the page be written and then transferred to the reader for the last write to be visible. The page would be passed back and forth between sites in alternation. Our implementation attempts to handle such pathological cases of thrashing with tunable controls explained in Section 4.1.

## 4.0 Distributed Shared Memory Protocol Terminology

In Locus as UNIX, user processes are relatively heavyweight. Lightweight processes are used in the operating system to service network messages and provide efficient remote access.

Users organize shared memory data in *segments* which may be attached into the address space of a process with read-only or read-write protection. Segments attached read-only are useful in some applications when cross network sharing is required with the restriction that the data never be written. However, our discussion will, for the most part, focus on segments that have been attached read-write by at least some of the processes involved in sharing.

A paged segmentation scheme [DALE68, DENN70] is used where segments are partitioned into pages. Pages are the unit of distribution because of their fixed size and commonality with the underlying hardware. A Mirage process may read segment pages, write segment pages, or both. Processes at network sites act as readers or writers of a given page. Each process records whether or not its segment pages are present at the given site. In addition, the protection of each page is stored in accordance with the hardware architecture. In many architectures, as in ours, a page may be read-only or read-write. Colocated processes share the pages that are present using the standard System V IPC implementation mechanisms augmented for Locus.

There is one distinguished site associated with each segment, called the *library site*. The library site is the controller for the pages of a given segment. Requests for pages are sent to the library site, queued, and sequentially processed. Depending on the configuration there may be several different sites used as library sites for the various segments created by user programs. This case is envisioned for a network of homogeneous processors of similar power. In an alternate configuration, one distinguished library site for all segments may be appropriate for a network where a fast backbone processor performs the library's queueing discipline. This processor may be a different type of CPU than the sites that manipulate the pages of the segment. In Mirage, the site that creates the segment is configured to be the library site for that segment.

The library site's primary function is to service the incoming request queue and record which sites are storing a given page. The library distinguishes writers from readers; there may only be one writable copy of a given page in the network at any one time. While there may be multiple read copies of the page in the net simultaneously, there may not be read copies at the same time as the write copy. All pages must be "checked out" through the library. To obtain a page, the requester sends a message to the library site and the requested page is returned directly from the site which is storing it.

Another distinguished site in our model is the current *clock site* for a page. The clock site is the site that has the most recent copy of a page. For example, if there is a writer for the page on the network, its site is always chosen as clock site. On the other hand, if there are a set of readers using the page simultaneously, one of the readers is selected and its site chosen as the page's clock site. We discuss the purpose of the clock site and why it is named this way in the next section.

## 4.1 Distributed Shared Memory Protocol Overview

Segments consist of pages that may be distributed throughout the network to sites that have had page faults and requested them. Locus interrupt handlers were modified to obtain the most recent copy of a given page from another site. When a page fault or protection fault occurs, the interrupt handler checks to see if the page is a shared memory page. If it is, the page is associated with a segment, the library located, and a network message sent to the library site queueing a request for the page. The network message indicates whether a read or write copy of the page is required.

All requests for DSM pages are queued at the library. Write requests are sequentially processed. Read requests for the same page are batched together (with a prior request) and granted to all the readers at one time when the request is processed. We do not allow batched read requests to be placed in the queue ahead of any queued write requests. During a user-level interrupt fault, the faulting process awaits the library's request processing by sleeping, the standard way UNIX tasks await the completion of an I/O operation.

A goal of this protocol is to ensure coherence. In order to maintain coherence, when a process writes to a page, all readable copies of the page must be *invalidated* before the write completes. Our invalidation unmaps and discards the page for all processes at all sites. If a writable copy was outstanding instead of multiple read copies, the page with stale data must be invalidated before the write to the new page completes. These operations are potentially expensive because of the number of sites that may be involved and the frequency with which these invalidations occur.

Our method attempts to: 1) to control thrashing that might otherwise occur, 2) decrease the number of times we perform network invalidations, and 3) minimize the amount of network activity required to provide coherence. To do so, we use a clock mechanism to control when a site may be interrupted from its read/write processing to relinquish pages it is using. The clock mechanism grants the readers or the current writer a *time window* ($\Delta$) in which they are guaranteed to uninterruptably possess the page. Much like the traditional time slice used when allocating processes to a central processor, $\Delta$ is used to apportion time for the page (or the read page set) to the site(s). During the time window, processes may read or write the page; the page may also be idle during portions of $\Delta$. The time window provides a control that allows fairness between processes requesting page access, the current process using the page, and the library which attempts to invalidate the page on behalf of another request. In a sense, $\Delta$ provides some degree of control over the *processor locality*, the number of references to a given page a processor will make before another processor is allowed to reference that page.

To invalidate a given page, the library site sends an invalidation message to the clock site. Recall the clock site is chosen to be one of the readers or the current writer. When the clock site gets the invalidation message, it checks to see if the page's $\Delta$ has expired. If not, the clock site replies immediately with the amount of time the library must wait until the invalidation can be honored. The library waits until $\Delta$ expires and then re-requests page invalidation[3].

Although the library site maintains the $\Delta$ value for each outstanding page, it is useful to have two distinguished sites. Network delays can cause impreciseness in using the $\Delta$ value; it is useful to have a clock site for this reason. Also, as we discuss in Section 7, it is useful to have a clock site so that timing information is associated with the page itself and one could convert $\Delta$ (measured in real-time) to user-time, or some combination thereof, more easily. Lastly, decentralizing control from the library site to the clock site may have performance benefits in that it decreases reliance on what could be a centralized bottleneck.

When an invalidation is accepted by the clock site, typically it: 1) invalidates the local page, 2) invalidates any other outstanding readers, if the page is a read-copy and 3) distributes the page to the new writer or any new readers. Table 1 below governs the specific actions of the clock site depending on the modes of the specific request. The clock site will either be a reader or a writer. The current state is indicated in the column "Current". The column "Incoming" indicates whether the incoming request is for readable copies of the page or a writable copy of the page. The "Clock Check" column indicates whether the clock check is required. The column "Invalidation" indicates whether it is necessary to invalidate the current copy of the page.

The actual protocol contains two important optimizations unique to this work:

1.    When a reader is upgraded to a writer, a new copy of the page is not sent; a notification acknowledges the write request.

2.    When write access is removed because readers require the page, the writer retains read access.

---

[3] A scheme where the clock site queues the invalidation (defers it until $\Delta$ expires) was not implemented, but is a possibility at the cost of additional implementation complexity.

| Current | Incoming | Clock Check | Invalidation |
|---------|----------|-------------|--------------|
| Readers | Readers | No | No |
| Readers | Writer | Yes | Yes, possible upgrade if new writer is in old read set |
| Writer | Reader | Yes | Downgrade writer to reader |
| Writer | Writer | Yes | Yes |

**Table 1: Page Operations for Read and Write Requests**

The first optimization reduces network traffic by not sending a page copy to a reader becoming a writer. The second optimization is based on the belief that the probability of subsequent read or write access by an invalidated writer is high; the resulting reduction in network traffic by downgrading the writer compensates for the increase in network traffic to invalidate that page if a remote write were to occur. If there is no remote write during the downgrade period, and the downgraded site requires subsequent write access, an upgrade can occur. In total, two advisory messages are sent rather than first invalidating the page and then later, when the process needs to write, transmitting the complete page to the site. Figure 1 shows an example of a remote page fault. Figure 2 depicts invalidation of a set of readers of a given page. Note that the two optimizations described above are unique to this work.

Table 1 shows there is only one condition where the clock check can be ignored. This is the case when there are read-copies outstanding and an additional read request for the page is processed by the library. We have decentralized control from the library site to the clock site for invalidations. Thus, to assure proper invalidations the current clock site must not change when additional readers require page access because only the library and current clock site store the most recent status information (see Section 4.3). Further, the clock site must be informed of the additional reader so that the proper sites are invalidated during the next invalidation phase.

### 4.2 Tuning $\Delta$

Selecting an appropriate value for $\Delta$ is not straightforward. We expect that $\Delta$ selection will be quite heavily influenced by the degree of locality exhibited by the applications which use the DSM facility. As we show in Section 5.0, $\Delta$ can be a useful parameter in improving overall system performance as well as in improving specific application throughput in a number of cases.

The value $\Delta$ can be tuned statically or dynamically. One can either select values before applications use specific shared memory segments, or alternately when the library distributes the page to the new clock site. $\Delta$ may be selected dynamically based on factors such as page utilization and queued requests pending.

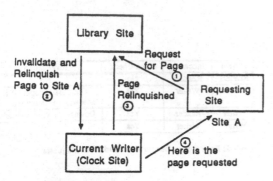

If Site A requires a writeable copy, the current writer is invalidated. If Site A requires a readable copy, the current writer is downgraded to be a reader.

**Figure 1**
**Remote Page Fault**

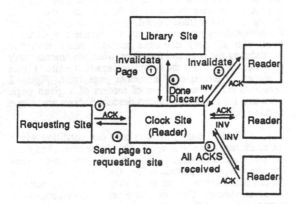

**Figure 2**
**Invalidation of Multiple Readers**

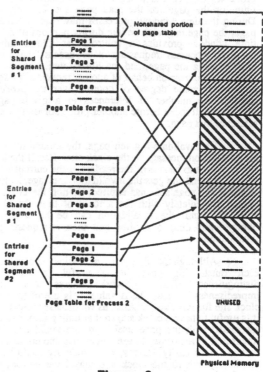

**Figure 3**
**Two Processes Sharing Segments**

### 4.3 Implementation Details

Our machine architecture deals with the segments using a *page table*. In the architecture we are using the page table is linearly structured. At a given site, for the processes sharing the same segments, and for the entries that pertain to those segment pages, each process' page table entries refer to the same resident page frames. Thus, when a process attaches a segment into its address space, a master copy of the shared segment's page table entries (PTEs) is conjoined with the current process's page table entries. The conjunction of these forms the process' virtual memory address space. Figure 3 shows two processes sharing common segments. Pages are 512 bytes in the current implementation of Mirage.

In the standard implementation of System V shared memory, segments are part of system space and are never swapped. In most machine architectures the *valid* bit indicates whether a page frame is resident or has been swapped out. For *standard* System V shared memory the PTEs are never marked *invalid*. Mirage needs to mark a page invalid to indicate that a page is not present at this network site. To do this, Mirage must locate all PTEs in *all* processes which share the page and mark them invalid - not just the current process's PTE. We discuss the design alternatives and the solution we use shortly.

Pages whose writable (or readable) copies are not present at a site are marked invalid for hardware interrupt processing to occur. We use an unused bit in the standard page table entry which indicates that an *auxiliary parallel page table* should be consulted when a page fault occurs. Table 2 shows an auxiliary parallel page table entry (auxpte). There is one shared copy of the complete table for each segment at each site. There are N entries in this table that correspond to the pages of the segment.

Generally speaking, most architectures do not have sufficient space in the architecturally provided PTEs for the data stored in the auxpte.

It should be observed that the library site and the current clock site store the most up-to-date auxpte information for a given page. While both will store the current reader mask or writer, only the clock site's install time is relied upon.

| Contents | Comment |
|----------|---------|
| reader mask | list of sites using this page |
| writer | current writer site |
| window ticks | number of ticks allocated for this page |
| install time | installation time for this page at this site |

**Table 2: Contents of an auxpte entry**

Typed page fault detection is necessary for a reasonable implementation. The machine architecture must be able to distinguish between a read page-fault and a write page-fault. Even though some architectures can distinguish between these types of faults many operating systems never use this information in their memory management code. We have modified the interrupt service routine assembly code to examine the VAX hardware bit that indicates the fault type and have passed this data to the Locus interrupt service routine.

We encountered an implementation problem when marking a page invalid at a given site. The difficulty arises in consistency between the master version of the PTE table and each of the corresponding PTEs associated with processes that have the page mapped. Although most UNIX implementations describe each page of physical memory with a table that provides the page's state, location, and number of referring processes[BACH86], we observed that system space used no such table and so this mechanism would not assist our implementation. When an incoming network message invalidates a page, the master version of the PTE table is updated by the network server process. In addition, however, it is necessary to invalidate the page in all processes which map the page.

There are two broad categories of consistency control design alternatives: *active* methods and *lazy* methods. In an active method once there is a change in the master PTE, all processes that map the page are immediately notified and updated. The active class of methods is rejected because it would be expensive and difficult to implement in a UNIX environment. Further, because the page is mapped, there is no guarantee (especially if the process executes at low priority) the process would be scheduled before the entry or other entries change again. Even with a mechanism to postpone the invalidation until the process is scheduled (a "summary" mechanism), it would be necessary to queue requests.

Another class of methods are termed *lazy* methods. This class is the one we selected to use. Whenever a process is scheduled, we determine if it is using shared memory. If it is, before the context of the new process is resumed, the appropriate master PTE entry is copied into the new process' map. For simplicity in the prototype, we remap *all* the shared memory pages of the process using a simple for-loop rather than detecting which specific ones have changed. Every time a shared memory process is scheduled, the system must remap its pages. The cost of this mapping is not a fixed cost; it is a function of the size of the segments being mapped. The measured cost of mapping one 512 byte page ranges from 106-125 microseconds; the largest segment allowed in our intersection of memory configurations for the various VAXs is 128K. We observe that Xenix System V shared memory systems use a similar remapping strategy and that processes that do not use shared memory pay no penalty.

## 5.0 Performance

In order to measure the effectiveness of Mirage we examine component timings, a worst case, and a "representative" application. These component timings provide a breakdown of the cost of each operation. The worst case application is useful because it provides an analysis of what can be expected at the extreme ranges of the performance spectrum. The representative case illustrates the effect of the time window, $\Delta$.

We considered other approaches to measuring performance. One measurement approach (taken by Li[LI86]) is to characterize the system using a suite of synthetic test programs such as matrix multiply, dot product, traveling salesman, etc. However, these programs may not be representative of the actual everyday performance these systems exhibit. Some of the programs are data size or data input sensitive in their fault rates. For example, the size of the matrix in matrix multiplication could significantly affect the page fault rate. Further, it is heavily-used applications that are representative of the performance users will likely encounter using DSM. We would like to obtain these applications from outside sources.

Perhaps a more theoretical approach to assessing performance is to examine access characteristics of shared memory by comparing it to similar shared data spaces. For example, there are strong similarities between Mirage's shared data segments and shared text segments. Because of these similarities there may be some previous performance studies that can be applied to our work. In shared C libraries Arnold[ARN86] has observed that some parts of the library execute frequently, while other parts rarely execute. The C libraries are reported to exhibit random execution patterns because many kinds of applications use its routines. However, libraries dedicated to a single purpose (akin to our segments), such as database or graphics service, are reported to have much different dynamic behavior than the C library. Taking this information into account, it would be hard to generalize access patterns to Mirage segments without carefully analyzing the programs which access segments and the types of segments in use. Mirage's general purpose nature makes it difficult to capitalize on these analyses.

## 5.1 Component Costs

We examined Mirage's performance by instrumenting the implementation to read the microsecond clock before and after kernel operations. The measured performance of a short network message (no buffer) sent round trip between two sites is 12.9 ms. This message is sent through the protocol layers and in and out of the network interface cards. When sending a network message with a 1024 byte buffer and receiving a short response message, an average of 21.5 msecs elapsed time was measured.

| Operation Time | Total Time (msec) | Time(msec) |
|---|---|---|
| Using Site Read Request* | | 2.5 |
| Read Request output transmission elapsed | | 3.2 |
| Page input reception elapsed | | 7.5 |
| TOTAL | 13.2 | |
| Server process time for request* | | 1.5 |
| Read request input reception elapsed | | 3.2 |
| Page output transmission elapsed | | 7.5 |
| Processing Time* | | 2 |
| TOTAL | 14.2 | |
| TOTAL ELAPSED TIME* | 27.5 | |

**Table 3: Component Breakdown: Time to obtain an in-memory page remotely** (*) indicates directly measured values

Table 3 depicts a breakdown of the amount of time required to obtain a checked-in page from the library site[4]. The items marked with an (*) indicate directly measured values. The other items were extrapolated from the measured cost of receiving similar messages. For example, transmitting and receiving a 1024 byte message one-way in the prototype can be extrapolated from 21.5 msecs to take roughly 15 msecs[5].

There are two significant caveats in the implementation that affect performance. First, an invalidation which is not honored must be resent later. Because of the overhead in sending and receiving this (short) invalidation message, if there is less than 12.9 msecs remaining in $\Delta$, the invalidation should be honored (or delayed and then honored) rather than requiring the requester repeat the invalidation later. So, in Mirage it may require two attempts to invalidate a page since the clock site replies with the amount of time to wait before the library should retry. Unfortunately, the current implementation does not support the queued invalidation optimization. Second, invalidations are processed sequentially rather than using a broadcast or multicast. Locus supports point-to-point communication. The Locus programmer uses network messages to communicate between sites, while the Locus system at the lowest of

----

[4]When a page is "checked-in", the library site is the clock site.

[5] Note that to handle page requests, server processes at both requesting and servicing sites allocate a PTE, map in the data to be sent or received from the appropriate frame in system space, copy it to or from the network message, and then unmap and deallocate the PTE.

----

levels, maintains a form of virtual circuit between sites to sequence network messages and maintain topology. Although providing multicasting would be a short project in some workstation environments, the effort to integrate such a facility would be substantial in our system. Considering the few sites in our experimental network, the investment did not seem warranted.

## 5.2 Worst Case Description and Analysis

In order to exercise Mirage, a worst case application was constructed. This application consists of 2 processes that execute at different sites. First, an adjacent pair of memory locations on the same page is chosen. Process 1 writes a value into the first location and waits for process 2 to write its value into the next. Process 2 waits for Process 1 to write and then writes its value into the second location. We then choose another adjacent pair of memory locations and repeat these operations.

This application is a worst case application for Mirage. Its N-site version (each process on a different site) is the most general worst case for this example. For each read or write to the specific locations, page faults occur which transfer the entire page between sites. The ratio between accesses to shared memory and the amount of system operation to support those accesses is very low. Notice that while spatial locality is high in the application, it executes in a configuration that causes significant system overhead. Such a configuration has poor processor locality because each processor retains the page for an exceedingly short duration. This program is an example of a worst case for a network virtual memory system and in that way is analogous to an application executing on a single site that is thrashing.

Figure 4 shows the modes of the page during the various steps of the program. Read copies are necessary for page faults that occur during program statements such as "if (*pint == CHECKVAL)." Figure 5 shows a timeline of the exact messages sent and received in the protocol. By running this program we can observe the system overhead because there are few application (user-level) operations between required system events. The program provides us with an intense exercise of the protocol at full speed of the host memory, processor, and network interface cards. This experiment factors into the measurements the effects of process scheduling and other operating system services.

To gauge our experiments, we executed the application on a single site. However, our initial measured throughput was surprisingly only 5 cycles/second[6]. We reinspected the program for problems and observed that once a process did its write, it remained in a while-loop waiting for the other process to execute its write. The while-loop continually read a shared variable waiting for it to change. Obviously what was happening was that the entire remaining portion of the process's scheduling quantum was being wasted busy waiting. To solve the low throughput problem a new system call *yield()* was added to our experimental version of Locus. The call was inserted in the application during all loops that inspect shared variables. We remeasured the performance of the application locally and obtained 166 cycles/second or a

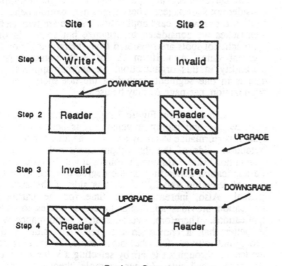

**Figure 4**
**Two Site Worst Case Application**

Back to Step 1
(Shaded Box indicates active site)

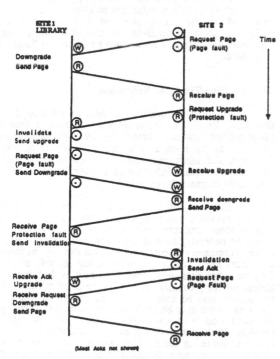

(Most Acks not shown)

**Figure 5**
**Sequence of Message Events
for Worst Case Application**

factor of 35 speedup.

With 2 sites, 9 messages are sent for one cycle of the application. Three of these message are large responses (1024 bytes of data); the other 6 are short messages. Based on the component timings, the raw communications component should be 84 msec, excluding interrupt processing CPU time. We add 12.5ms for the 5 interrupts that request remote pages. We add 9ms for the 6 input interrupts to install, invalidate, or upgrade the page. Additionally, two faults are generated locally and serviced by a library colocated with the requester. We add 3ms to service these two faults. Our total is 109 ms. This total corresponds to roughly 9 cycles/second in the distributed case. We can do no better than this bound unless interrupts could be serviced more rapidly or our message passing component times were improved. Further, these calculations assume that user-level processes are synchronized and ready for immediate execution after network messages change the underlying segment state. Scheduling overhead generally does not permit such user-level response.

Lastly, we experimented with the test&set instruction on the VAX. This preferred instruction[AGAR88] uses busy waiting and did not perform well. After a locking writer sets the bit to enter a critical section, the testing reader obtains the page remotely. When the locking writer completes, it faults on write to clear the lock bit and exit the critical section. If the locking writer requires use of the page for data access while the region is locked, the tester and the writer thrash the page; the use of $\Delta > 0$ can be helpful to the writer in this situation. However, for improved performance a user spinlock package could be constructed in which 1) a failed test&set operation does not cost a page transfer to a site where the failure occurs and 2) a successful test&set transfers the page to the site where the operation succeeded. In summary, we recommend that the test&set instruction not be used because of its poor performance and that a user-level package be substituted to perform these functions more efficiently.

### 5.3 Worst Case Measurements

We measured the performance of the application varying $\Delta$ during each of the experiments. Our experiments were run on otherwise idle processors when there was little network traffic. Figure 6 shows the throughput for the application as a function of $\Delta$. One curve depicted in Figure 6 is for a version of the application that uses yield() and one curve is for a version without yield(). Notice that at $\Delta=2$ there is nearly a 50% improvement in throughput using the yield() instruction remotely. Observe the divergence of the two curves at $\Delta<=6$, which is the system's scheduling quantum. Performance is significantly better using the yield() call at $\Delta<=6$.

We observed that with $\Delta = 2$, 2.75 sleeps of 33 msecs were added into each cycle for the yield() version of the program. This additional time adjusts the 109 ms figure to total 200 ms per cycle. Thus, 5 cycles/second is the maximum rate we could expect. Our observed performance

---

[6] A cycle consists of a write by Process 1 and by Process 2 and subsequent operations performed until Process 1 is about to write again.

is 90% of the calculated maximum at $\Delta=2$. At $\Delta=0$ we would expect roughly 8 cycles/second.

One reason for the performance degradation is that one site acts as user and library site. In order to perform these two functions, the site must context switch to perform some of the library functions and later resume the user process which is reading and writing. At the other extreme, if a third site were performing only library functions there would be a fixed cost involved in transmitting and receiving messages from a remote library. The tradeoff between context switches locally vs. remote communications costs to the library in our prototype greatly favors colocating the library and the requester. For reasonable process loads, our component costs for remote communication far exceed the system's rescheduling speed.

Lastly, we observed that the effect of an application that is thrashing on overall system performance can be ameliorated by adjusting $\Delta$. By increasing $\Delta$, although application throughput is reduced, system performance is improved for other processes. Therefore, $\Delta$ can have a more global impact on system performance even in cases where $\Delta$ does not improve specific application throughput.

## 6.0 Time Window Evaluation

We constructed a simulated application that has a higher degree of processor locality than our worst case example. This application is intended to be more representative of typical applications that execute in a DSM environment, or more specifically, an average case. Our purpose is to evaluate the utility of $\Delta$ rather than to measure performance per se. The application consists of two process that execute for-loops that decrement separate values in shared memory on the same page. The loops execute for a fixed period of time[7] until the decremented values reach zero. Each time a for-loop is executed the termination condition is tested. Thus, the for-loops exhibit read faults and write faults.

Figure 7 depicts throughput as a function of $\Delta$. The curve has two distinct portions. One side, $\Delta<600$, we call the "contention" side. The other side, $\Delta>600$ we call the "retention" side. The low throughput on the "contention" side when $\Delta<120$ is because of page conflicts between the processes that are reading and writing. When $\Delta=600$ a maximum of 115,000 read-write instructions/second are achieved. When $\Delta>600$ throughput is decreased because one of the processes retains the page for longer than it needs. Notice the decrease in throughput is more gradual in slope than the "contention" side when $\Delta<120$. Also note that the range between $(120<=\Delta<=600)$ exhibits relatively good performance. Retention is an artifact of a protocol which uses a time window, but contention is a general problem for most network virtual memory management systems.

Mirage currently uses $\Delta$s that are uniform for a particular segment. Uniform $\Delta$s are not intrinsic to the design nor the implementation. The auxpte data structure contains the per-page $\Delta$ values and the implementation

could be easily modified to use different values to tune system performance and page access. As one example, consider hot spot pages. These pages may exhibit behavior similar to our worst case application. There are two useful approaches we considered to organize hot spots. In one approach, hot spots are separated from the remainder of the segment data. A uniform $\Delta$ for each segment is a possibility in this organization. In another approach all data is in one segment, including the hot spots. In this organization, per-page $\Delta$s may be useful.

Our data from Figure 7 suggests general strategies for selecting and tuning $\Delta$ values. It is best for overall system performance to err by selecting a value for $\Delta$ on the "retention" side of the throughput curve rather than the "contention" side. Although throughput will be reduced for the application depending on the degree of error from the optimal selection, the falloff on this side of the curve is gradual. Also, increased sleep time for the particular application provides additional processor cycles to other applications. Therefore, overall system performance will be better than a choice on the "retention" side of the throughput curve. On the other hand, it is best for application throughput to err by selecting a value for $\Delta$ on the "contention" side. In our example, there are a wide range of values that give high throughput before the rapid falloff at $\Delta<120$, in this example. However, a choice on the "contention" side would more severely affect overall system performance.

As discussed in Section 4.2, the system itself could assist by increasing or decreasing page $\Delta$s dynamically. When the library sends an invalidation to the clock site, the page's $\Delta$ value can be changed before it is forwarded to the target site and installed. We are evaluating some alternatives for this dynamic tuning. Currently, the Mirage routine which performs this function is disabled.

## 7.0 Measuring Time and References

Mirage's performance is affected by how $\Delta$ is measured. Recall that $\Delta$ provides the amount of time a given process retains a shared memory page for read or write access. In Mirage $\Delta$ is measured using real-time. However, site loads can influence a real-time measure because heavy loads influence scheduling latencies. The load would decrease the effective $\Delta$.

The time window $\Delta$ could be measured using user-process time. The problem with this approach is there may be many processes sharing the page on one site. It would be necessary to sum the individual process's page usage to accurately calculate when $\Delta$ has expired. Because of process loads, if one site executes considerably slower than the other sites, user time will not provide fair time allocations for processes using the page at other sites. Of course, one may be able to factor the site's load into the user time, but it may be of limited value because knowing the exact load does not adequately describe how many processes in the scheduling queue will reference the page. If few processes in the scheduling queue access the page versus many processes in the scheduling queue requiring access to the page, a different function may be required.

---

[7] In this example loops execute for 10 seconds. This amount of time is used for easier presentation.

Lastly, Mirage provides a facility for logging all page requests at the library site. Each log entry contains the memory location, a timestamp, and the process identifier of the requester. We envision that a user-level process could analyze these reference strings as the basis for an automatic process migration facility or for later reference string analysis. Note, however, that reference strings from sites with valid page copies are not recorded.

## 8.0 Kai Li

Kai Li[LI86] experimented with a coherent shared virtual memory system on a loosely-coupled multiprocessor, the Apollo Domain system[LEAC83]. Shared data is paged between processors, some of which have copies of the virtual address space pages. The model assumes ownership of pages can vary from processor to processor either statically or dynamically. This work concentrates on consistency problems and theoretical performance based on experimentation with centralized and distributed managers to locate the page owner. The last writer to a page becomes the new owner. Unless the local processor owns the page a managing site must be inquired before a write can occur.

One problem is there are no hard performance figures because his prototype was built outside of the kernel. The implementation was approximately 4700 lines of application-level code. While results favor the use of distributed shared memory on loosely-coupled systems, a distributed implementation would have to be built in the kernel of the underlying operating system to assess performance. Further, Li's work provided measurements of numeric applications only; no non-numeric computations were measured.

In contrast to Li's work, our work is a kernel implementation. The model is based on paged segmentation which gives the user additional flexibility in memory access. A time window ($\Delta$) is employed to avoid possible thrashing and to facilitate performance tuning. Page modes may be upgraded or downgraded which is unique to this design. Lastly, our policies were selected with a time-driven and demand-driven approach in mind rather than merely a demand-driven approach.

### 8.1 Agora

The Agora system[BISI88, FORI87] supports operating system and programming language functionality for parallel programs. Of interest is the operating system functionality which implements a form of shared memory for heterogeneous distributed computers. This sharing is done at the level of objects or data structures. A data structure is stored in the memory of the machine that creates it and is replicated in all the other machines that read it. These *cache* copies are always the copies read. A master copy is stored on one machine; all writes are forwarded to this master copy. A special agent notifies other machines when the master copy is changed, but no guarantee is made as to the recency of data read. Cache copies may become out-of-date and thus Agora does not assume coherence of the underlying objects.

Agora is the first implemented mechanism for sharing memory across machines in a heterogeneous computing environment. Generally, this is difficult to do because of incompatible byte orderings or alignment requirements of different processors. There is little hope of taking a low level (unstructured) shared memory system and expecting it to work across heterogeneous machines. The only way we could expect this to work is to build higher level representations whose semantics can be understood so that data representations can be translated. This could be expensive.

Although it would be expensive to implement heterogeneity support in Mirage, our main point of disagreement with the Agora approach is that without the ability to make a positive statement about the recency of data being used, there may be little benefit for many applications. User level synchronization is an unsatisfactory substitute for coherence.

### 8.2 Distributed Shared Memory Hardware Controller

In this work [RAMA88], the authors propose a distributed shared memory controller that provides efficient access and consistency maintenance of distributed shared memory. There is no low level coherence protocol; user programs are expected to utilize process synchronization primitives for consistency maintenance. The environment for the distributed shared memory controller is the *Clouds* distributed operating system. This system is an object-oriented operating system that supports synchronization within objects, and atomicity of computation.

The described hardware device has not been implemented but simulations have been performed to illustrate its effectiveness. The authors claim that their controller is effective relative to its object oriented environment. However, the object-oriented approach may not to be the best way to structure our low level UNIX system which is not object oriented. Nor does it seem reasonable to support objects on the particular hardware we are using because of architectural inefficiencies.

### 8.3 Mach

Mach[ACCE86, FORI89] now supports a shared memory server. Memory objects are managed either by the kernel or by user programs through a message interface. Sharing of memory is provided between tasks running on the same machine or across machines. An external memory paging task handles the paging duties and is responsible for the memory object. Mach attempts to deal with multiple page sizes and some aspects of heterogeneity. Coherence is supported. A substantial difference in philosophy between our work and Mach's pertains to overall system structure. In Mach, memory is managed by processes outside of the kernel including an external pager and network server processes. In our system shared memory management is handled by the kernel in the system nucleus. Communication is direct between kernels and no external networking processes are used. Since there are fewer user level context switches than in Mach with its external system processes, our scheme should perform favorably.

## 8.4 Caching File Systems

There are a number of similarities between caching file systems and our work[NELS88, GRAY89]. For example, in Leases[GRAY89], a time-based consistency mechanism is employed. This mechanism provides a time period, or lease, in which a cache is guaranteed to possess an up-to-date file version. The lease can reduce the number of file server inquiries to verify the cached file is consistent. The file lease is similar to our page Δ, however Δ was designed to control thrashing and improve application throughput or system performance.

Caching file systems bear some similarity to our work, but operate on a different level of granularity (files). DSM systems may be more sensitive to application level programming constructs and memory subsystem performance than caching file systems whose performance will be closely related to the performance of secondary storage systems. Thus, different solutions will be required between DSM systems and caching file systems.

## 9.0 Conclusions

From our preliminary results we approach DSM with cautious optimism. Mirage's component costs in accessing a shared page are no worse than average disk access latencies. However, in a network with a larger number of sites sharing pages than ours, invalidations may become expensive. Mirage's performance can be sensitive to simple application-level programming constructs. For example, loops that wait for shared variables to change should make the yield() call so that the remainder of the process's scheduling quantum is not wasted. Additionally, we found that the use of test&set can degrade performance substantially if the process in the locked region writes to the particular page of the lock while a remote test&set reader is testing. However, our design parameters are meant to ameliorate some of these difficulties by providing latitude in tuning page access. The time window Δ is Mirage's primary mechanism for doing so.

Mirage's performance for applications with poor processor locality suggest that Δ be small or equal to zero for such cases. However, for our synthetic application which exhibits substantially improved processor locality, throughput is best optimized with a larger Δ. Furthermore, this synthetic application showed the page contention portion of the throughput curve was worse in terms of performance than page retention side of the curve. The effect of an application that is thrashing on overall system performance can be ameliorated using a Δ > 0 at the cost of reduced application throughput.

Lastly, implementing Mirage with a more modern machine architecture, faster CPU, better Ethernet interfaces, and with a more recent version of Locus would improve performance substantially. Since memory and processor speeds are rapidly improving, our fixed costs will decrease significantly. These aspects make distributed shared memory a much better performing and more attractive facility.

## 10.0 References

[ACCE86] Accetta, M., Baron, R., Bolosky, W., Golub, D., Rashid, R., Tevanian, A., Young, M., Mach: A New Kernel Foundation for UNIX Development, *Proceedings USENIX 1986 Summer Conference*, Atlanta, Georgia, 1986.

[AGAR88] Agarwal, A., Gupta, A., Memory-Reference Characteristics of Multiprocessor Applications under Mach, *Proceedings of the 1988 ACM SIGMETRICS Conference on Measurement and Modeling of Computer Systems*, Santa Fe, New Mexico, May 24-27, 1988, pp. 215-225.

[ARNO86] Arnold, J. Q., Shared Libraries on UNIX System V, *Proceedings USENIX 1986 Summer Conference*, Atlanta, Georgia, 1986, pp. 395-404.

[ATT86] AT&T. *System V Interface Definition, Issue 2*, Customer Information Center, P.O. Box 19901, Indianapolis, IN, 1986.

[BACH86] Bach, M. A., The Design of the UNIX Operating System, Prentice-Hall, Englewood Cliffs, New Jersey, 1986.

[BISI87] Bisiani, R., Forin, A., Architectural Support for Multilanguage Parallel Programming on Heterogeneous Systems, *Proceedings Second International Conference on Architectural Support for Programming Languages and Operating Systems*, Palo Alto, CA, Oct 5-8, 1987, pp. 21-30.

[DALE68] Daley, R. C., Dennis, J. B., Virtual Memory, Processes and Sharing in Multics, *CACM*, Vol. 11, No. 5, May, 1968, pp. 306-311.

[DENN70] Denning, P. J., Virtual Memory, *ACM Computing Surveys*, Vol. 2, No. 3, September, 1970, pp. 153-189.

[FLEI86] Fleisch, B. D., Distributed System V IPC in LOCUS: A Design and Implementation Retrospective, *Proceedings ACM SIGCOMM 86 Symposium on Communications Architectures and Protocols*, Stowe, Vermont, August 5-7, 1986, pp. 386-396.

[FLEI89] Fleisch, B. D., Distributed Shared Memory in a Loosely Coupled Environment, Ph.D. Dissertation, University of California, Los Angeles, July, 1989.

[FORI87] Forin, A., Bisiani, R., Correrini, F., Parallel Processing with Agora, Technical Report CMU-CS-87-183, Carnegie-Mellon University, Computer Science Department, Pittsburgh, PA, December 1987.

[FORI89] Forin, A., Barrera, J., Sanzi, R., The Shared Memory Server, *Proceedings 1989 Winter USENIX Technical Conference*, San Diego, CA, Jan-Feb, 1989, pp. 229-244.

[GRAY89] Gray, C., Cheriton, D., Leases: An Efficient Fault- Tolerant Mechanism for Distributed File Cache Consistency, to appear in *Proceedings 12th ACM Symposium on Operating Systems Principles*, Litchfield Park, AZ, December 4-6, 1989.

[LEAC83] Leach, P. J., Levine, P. H., Douros, B. P., Hamilton, J. A., Nelson, D. L., Stumpf, B. L., The Architecture of An Integrated Local Network, *IEEE Journal on Selected Areas in Communications*, Volume SAC-1, No. 5, November, 1983, pp. 842-857.

[LI86] Li, K., Hudak, P., Memory Coherence in Shared Virtual Memory Systems, *Proceedings 5th ACM SIGACT-SIGOPS Symposium of Principles of Distributed Computing*, Canada, August, 1986.

[METC76] Metcalfe, R. M., Boggs, D. R., Ethernet: Distributed Packet Switching for Local Computer Networks, *Communications of the ACM*, July, 1976, Vol. 19, No. 7, pp. 395-403.

[NELS88] Nelson, Michael N., Welch, Brent B., Ousterhout, J. K., Caching in the Sprite Network File System, *ACM Transactions on Computer Systems*, Vol. 6, No. 1, February, 1988, pp. 134-154.

[OUST88] Ousterhout, J. K., Cherenson, A. R., Douglis, F., Nelson, M. N., Welch, B. B., The Sprite Network Operating System, *Computer*, Vol. 21, No. 2, February, 1988, pp. 23-35.

[POPE81] Popek, G., Walker, B., Chow, J., Edwards, D., Kline, C., Rudisin, G. and Thiel, G., LOCUS: A Network Transparent, High Reliability Distributed System, *Proceedings of the Eighth Symposium on Operating System Principles*, Published as SIGOPS Operating Systems Review, Vol. 15, No. 5, December, 1981, pp. 169-177.

[RAMA88] Ramachandran, U., Ahamad, M., Khalidi, M., Unifying Synchronization and Data Transfer in Maintaining Coherence of Distributed Shared Memory, Technical Report GIT-ICS-88/23, June 1988.

[WALK83] Walker, B., Popek, G., English, R., Kline, C., Thiel, G., The LOCUS Distributed Operating System, *Proceedings of the Ninth Symposium on Operating System Principles*, Published as SIGOPS Operating Systems Review, Vol. 17, No. 5, October, 1983.

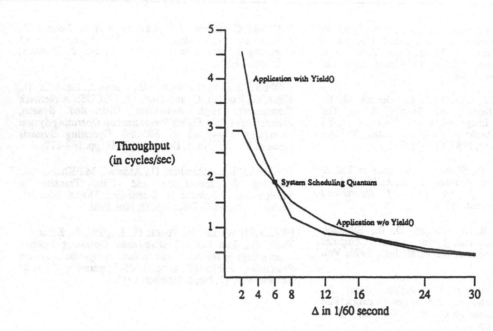

**Figure 6: Worst Case Application with two remote processes**

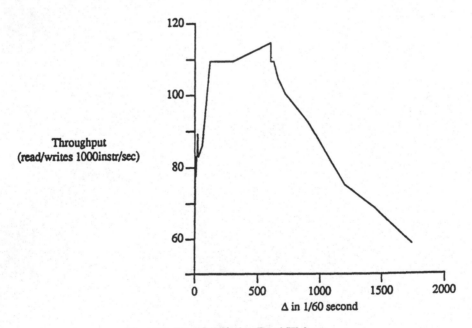

**Figure 7: Two Conflicting Read-Writers**

# An Implementation of Distributed Shared Memory

UMAKISHORE RAMACHANDRAN

*College of Computing, Georgia Institute of Technology, Atlanta, Ga 30332, U.S.A.*

AND

M. YOUSEF A. KHALIDI

*Sun Microsystems, 2550 Garcia Avenue, Mountain View, Ca 94043, U.S.A.*

## SUMMARY

**Shared memory is a simple yet powerful paradigm for structuring systems. Recently, there has been an interest in extending this paradigm to non-shared memory architectures as well. For example, the virtual address spaces for all objects in a distributed object-based system could be viewed as constituting a global *distributed shared memory*. We propose a set of primitives for managing distributed shared memory. We present an implementation of these primitives in the context of an object-based operating system as well as on top of Unix.**

KEY WORDS    Distributed shared memory    Distributed operating systems    Object-based system

## INTRODUCTION

Programming with shared memory is well-understood and despite the interest in distributed and parallel systems for reasons of availability, fault-tolerance and increased computational power, the style of programming these systems has not changed drastically. Even in non-shared memory architectures researchers have proposed a style that presents to the programmers an abstraction of a logical shared memory.[1-4] Other researchers have proposed algorithms for maintaining the consistency of such a logically shared memory in non-shared memory architectures.[5-7] The abstraction for supporting the notion of shared memory on a non-shared memory (distributed) architecture is referred to as *distributed shared memory* (DSM) in this paper.

A second motivation for DSM is the current trend in structuring distributed systems using a collection of diskless computational servers, namely workstations, and a few data servers or file servers. In such an environment the code and data for program execution has to be paged-in from the data server. There are two issues here: The first one is a scheduling decision of 'where' to execute the program, one that is best left to a higher level policy making entity. The second one is the chore of bringing in the required data and code, i.e. remote paging. If sharing is coupled with this second issue, then we see that DSM presents itself as a natural facility for combining the two.

Several other researchers have proposed software architectures based on the shared memory paradigm, in different settings:

1. Li[6] presents a variation of the Berkeley protocol for multiprocessor cache consistency[8] as a solution to maintain the consistency of distributed shared memory. Using Li's scheme, the entire memory in the distributed system is considered potentially sharable for both reads and writes. The consistency protocol maintains the coherency of memory even when accessed by processes running on different nodes.

2. In a speech recognition application, Bisiani and Forin[3] use data structures that are shared by multiple language modules that are distributed on heterogeneous machines. They show that communication through shared memory is a viable alternative to message-passing even when the environment involves co-operation between multilingual program modules and heterogeneous machines.

3. Processes in the programming language *Linda*[9, 10] communicate via a globally-shared collection of ordered tuples.

4. A logically shared bulletin-board is proposed by Birman *et al.*[11] for structuring asynchronous interactions between processes in distributed systems.

5. By integrating the mechanisms for virtual memory management and local interprocess communication, Mach[12] achieves efficient implementation of local interprocess communication. Currently, researchers at CMU are investigating the duality of shared memory and message passing in the context of network communications as well.[13]

6. Zayas[14] achieves substantial reduction in the cost of process migration by using copy-on-write techniques[15] and on-demand fetches during remote execution.

7. Cheriton[16] advocates problem-oriented shared memory as the basic concept for structuring distributed systems.

8. Emerald[2] is a distributed object-based language and system with support for object mobility.

The purpose of this paper is to present a set of mechanisms for DSM and an implementation of these mechanisms. All the resources of the system are viewed as potentially shared objects. The name space of these objects constitute a distributed shared memory. The objects are composed of segments, where a segment is a logical entity that has attributes such as read-only, and read-write. There is a concept of *ownership* and the node where a segment is created (the owner node) is responsible for guaranteeing the consistency of the segment. The *distributed shared memory controller* (DSMC) to be described next is the entity that provides the mechanisms for managing these segments.

## DISTRIBUTED SHARED MEMORY CONTROLLER

The basic operations provided by the DSMC are get and discard. The get operation is used to fetch a segment from its owner, whereas discard is used to return a segment to its owner. The DSMC provides synchronization primitives as separate operations (P and V semaphore operations), or as combined access and lock operations using the get and discard primitives.

Using the get primitive a segment may be acquired in one of four modes: read-only, read-write, weak-read or none. Read-only mode signifies non-exclusive access but guarantees that the segment will not change until the node explicitly discards the segment. Read-write mode signifies exclusive access (for the requesting process) with a guarantee that the segment will not be thrown away until the node explicitly discards the segment. When a get primitive is issued with mode read-only or read-write the local DSMC sends a request to the owner DSMC and suspends the requesting process until the segment is received. The segment is kept until an explicit discard is issued. Multiple copies of the segment may be held by several readers at the same time (mode read-only) but only one writer (mode read-write) may have access to the segment at a time. The owner node keeps a count of the number of requesters that have a copy of the segment in read-only mode.

Weak-read mode signifies non-exclusive access with no guarantee whether the segment will change or not. The owner DSMC immediately honours a weak-read request by sending a copy of the segment to the requesting DSMC. None mode signifies exclusive access with no guarantee whether the segment will be thrown away or not. When a get primitive is issued with mode none the local DSMC sends a request to the owner DSMC and suspends the requesting process until the segment is received. None mode requests are enqueued in the appropriate segment queue, if the segment is currently held in either read-only or read-write modes. If the segment is available at the owner DSMC, it responds by sending the segment to the requesting DSMC. The requesting DSMC becomes the *keeper* of the segment and the owner remembers the current keeper. If the segment is held in another node in mode none, then the owner DSMC instructs the current keeper to forward the segment to the requesting DSMC. A segment held in mode none at a keeper node may be returned to its owner by issuing a discard primitive, or it may be taken away by its owner when the keeper DSMC is instructed to forward the segment to another node.

The DSMC also provides the semaphore operations P and V that act on semaphores that are contained in semaphore segments (see the section 'Implementation on Ra' below).

## RELATED WORK

The Apollo Domain[5] system implements a single level store in an integrated local network of workstations. To ensure consistency of the replicated copies of an object a two-level approach is adopted. The lower level detects concurrency violations using a time-stamp based version number scheme for each object. It also provides primitives such as flushing the stale pages of a cached object, inquiring the current version number of an object, and sending back modified pages of a cached object. The higher level implements a variety of locks including a multiple-readers/single-writer lock using the lower level primitives.

Our work differs from Domain in that we have provided a small set of primitives, four to be exact, that combine the two levels of Domain in maintaining a single level store. The advantage with the Domain approach is the flexibility to use different synchronization mechanisms at the higher level. However, our algorithms are simpler, requiring no mechanisms such as time-stamps since the algorithms exploit the synchronization information that is inherent in computations that use the single level store concept. Our limited experience in using these primitives[4] suggests that they are adequate for several applications that can be programmed with the single level store concept. We also provide P and V primitives for applications such as resource managers that need to use the semaphore operations. Domain locks are for the entire object, whereas our locks are for segments that are part of an object thus reducing the possibility of limited concurrency due to false sharing.

Lastly, our primitives are fair since they implement a first-come–first-served queue of processes waiting for a lock at the owner node. Domain on the other hand either grants or refuses the lock request immediately and can thus lead to starvation. On the other hand our protocol can lead to deadlock if a process 'forgets' to unlock or crashes while holding locks. But we expect our primitives to be used by systems programmers and such an error is tantamount to a 'system bug'. We envision a higher level entity that detects and resolves such deadlocks when they occur.

## CLOUDS

Although the mechanisms provided by DSMC are general, we describe an implementation of these mechanisms in the context of *Clouds*, an object-based distributed operating system. Therefore, a brief description of Clouds is appropriate.

Clouds, being developed at Georgia Tech,[17] is intended to provide a unified environment over distributed hardware. Location independence for data as well as processing, atomicity of distributed computation and fault-tolerance are some of the research goals of Clouds. *Objects* and *threads* are the basic building blocks of Clouds. Objects are passive entities and specify a *distinct* and *disjoint* piece of the global virtual address space that spans the entire network. An object is the encapsulation of the *code* and *data* needed to implement the *entry points* in the object. Thus a Clouds object can be considered to be syntactically equivalent to an abstract data type in the programming language parlance. Access to entry points in the object is accomplished through a capability mechanism in software.

Threads are the only active entities in the system. A thread is a unit of activity from the user's perspective. Upon creation, a thread starts executing in an object. A thread enters an object by invoking an entry point in the object. It then executes the code in the entry point, and returns to the caller object. Binding the object invocations to the entry points in the object takes place at execution time. Figure 1 shows the model of computation in Clouds. A thread in the course of its computation traverses the virtual address spaces of the objects that it invokes.

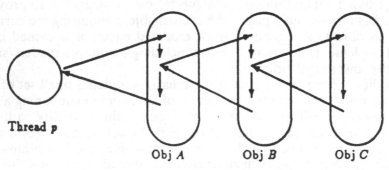

Thread *p*     Obj *A*     Obj *B*     Obj *C*

*Figure 1. Model of computation*

In a distributed object-based system, the virtual address spaces of all objects can be viewed as constituting a global distributed shared memory. Such a view is attractive from the perspective of software architecture since it suggests a uniform implementation of a system-wide memory-management mechanism.

For remote object invocation there are two choices: the first choice is to perform the computation at the node where the object resides, referred to as remote procedure call. The second choice is to make the invocation appear local by bringing in the segments required for the invocation. Although we have to support the former for immovable objects, such as an object that reads disk blocks, we believe that the latter may be a better choice for movable objects. There are two reasons to support this belief:

(i) the principle of locality,[18] which suggests that an invocation or other invocations in the same object may be repeated

(ii) the reduction in computational overhead due to the elimination of slave process management to support remote invocation at the node where the object resides.[19, 20]

## THE STRUCTURE OF CLOUDS

### Ra kernel

Ra[21, 22] is an operating system kernel designed to be the nucleus of Clouds operating system.[17] It is currently implemented on the Sun-3 architecture. Ra defines and manages three primitive abstractions: *segment*, *virtual space* and *isiba*. Segments serve as containers of data and may be viewed as uninterpreted sequences of bytes. The contents of a segment may only be accessed when the segment is *attached* to a range of virtual addresses. Segments persist until explicitly destroyed. Each segment resides in a *partition* that is responsible for providing backing store for the segment. A partition is an entity that realizes, maintains, and manipulates segments (see the next subsection).

Virtual spaces abstract the notion of an addressing domain. A Ra virtual space is a monotonically increasing range of virtual addresses with possible 'holes' in the range. A virtual space has a descriptor segment associated with it that contains a collection of windows. Each window is a data structure that maps a contiguous piece of the virtual space to a segment. Figure 2 shows the relationship between the Ra virtual space, the windows, and the segments. The segmentation scheme in the Chorus system[23] has some similarity to the Ra virtual space.

Ra isibas are an abstraction of the fundamental notion of computation or activity and can be thought of as light-weight processes. Isibas may be used as daemons within the kernel or they may be associated with a Ra virtual space to implement a user process. A Clouds thread can potentially span machine boundaries and is implemented as a collection of processes.

A Ra virtual space is a software abstraction not to be confused with the virtual address space provided by the machine architecture. The latter is assumed to be composed of three distinct regions that are called O, P and K spaces for object, process and kernel, respectively. Note that such a distinction may not exist in a

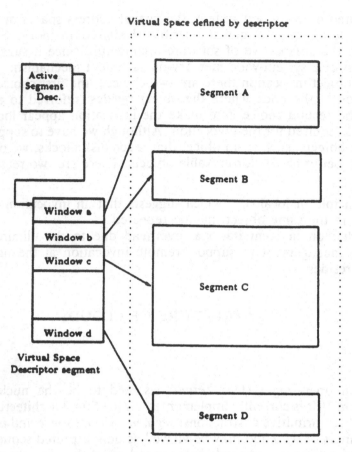

Virtual Space defined by descriptor

Active Segment Desc.

Segment A

Segment B

Window a

Window b

Window c

Segment C

Window d

Virtual Space
Descriptor segment

Segment D

*Figure 2. Ra virtual space*

given machine architecture. In that case the division is enforced based on address range 'high' and 'low' water marks.

The kernel is mapped in the K space. A process consists of an isiba and a Ra virtual space that contains the process stack for invocations. Note that a process' virtual space does not contain any code. A process' virtual space is mapped into the P space and unmapped on context switch. An object is a Ra virtual space that consists of code and data segments. The code segment of an object's virtual space has entry points that can be invoked by user processes. The object in which a process is currently executing is mapped into the O space. System objects, which we discuss in the next subsection, are mapped into the K space; but may be installed and removed dynamically.

### System objects

System objects are trusted software modules that are loaded dynamically in the K space. System objects encapsulate necessary and/or useful operating system services and resource managers that have direct access to the Ra kernel, but are none the less outside the kernel. They implement and encapsulate policy as the kernel itself does not make any policy decisions. System objects serve as intermediaries between the user objects and the kernel, and they provide system services to user objects. Examples of system objects include resource managers, user-level object support, device drivers, and partitions. Of particular concern to this paper is the partition system objects.

The Ra kernel runs on machines that provide suport for virtual memory. The Ra kernel is responsible for mapping segments into virtual memory using the memory management hardware provided by the underlying architecture. The size of a segment is a multiple of the physical page size. Ra assumed the existence of partitions that are responsible for storing segments.

Segments are maintained by partitions, and a segment is said to be controlled by a partition. Several operations are possible on segments via their controlling partition: segments may be *created* and *destroyed*. The *page-in* and *page-out* operations on segments allow the partition to co-operate with virtual memory management in order to access the contents of a segment and to update its representation on secondary storage when necessary. Finally, segments may be *activated* and *deactivated*. Activating a segment prepares the partition for further activity relating to the segment, whereas deactivating a segment informs the partition that further access to the segment is unlikely in the near future. The activate and deactivate operations are similar to *open* and *close* file operations in conventional systems.

Therefore, each partition provides, at least, the following calls for use by Ra: activate/deactivate segment, create/destroy segment and page-in/page-out portions of segments. Ra services segment requests from other system objects, such as to map a segment into a virtual space. In addition, Ra fields page faults, determines the virtual space and in turn the segment where the fault occurred, and calls the appropriate fault handler. When Ra is instructed to service a segment request (e.g. to map a segment into a virtual space), it invokes the appropriate partition to fetch the segment into physical memory. Ra then manipulates the memory management hardware to map the physical pages appropriately.

The Ra architecture assigns to the kernel the task of mapping a segment onto the memory management hardware, and hides the details of storing the segment on external storage in the partition system objects. The fact that the segment is stored on a local disk or on a remote node is hidden from the kernel.

## PROCESS AND OBJECT MIGRATION

To illustrate the use of the DSMC primitives, we consider the example of process and object migration in Clouds. Reference 4 gives more examples of the utility of these primitives in programming a variety of distributed applications.

One of the design goals of Clouds is to provide distribution of data and computation transparent to the application. To efficiently exploit the resources available in a distributed system, Clouds should be able to migrate processes and objects among nodes. Through the DSMC primitives, Ra provides the operating system with mechanisms to migrate objects and processes. Using DSMC a segment can be activated and accessed on any node in the system, barring any protection limitations imposed by the operating system. As we mentioned earlier, an object is a Ra virtual space that consists of a collection of data and code segments with entry points, and the composition of the object is specified by a descriptor segment. An object, therefore, is accessed on any node by activating the descriptor segment at the desired node. The DSMC primitives ensure that accesses to the object from different nodes are handled correctly.

Since Clouds objects are passive, process migration is performed separately from remote activations of the object. Note that a process consists of a Ra virtual space (in P space) and an isiba. To migrate a process, the operating system performs the following steps:

1. The isiba is stopped (i.e. it is removed from the run queue).
2. The kernel structure—isiba control block (ICB)—that describes the isiba is copied to a new ICB on the remote node. The local ICB structure is returned to a local free list. The ICB includes the name of the process virtual space descriptor segment, as well as the name of the segment that describes the object currently being invoked.
3. The process virtual space is deactivated. This operation can be done in the background and need not be completed before executing the following steps.
4. The same process virtual space is activated on the remote node. The object virtual space in which the process was executing is activated, if need be.
5. The new isiba is scheduled to run on the remote node.
6. The process page faults on the required segments of the process and object virtual spaces which are fetched on demand.

The migration code is organized as follows. Each node has a process_migration system object that contains a migration routine (migrate) that migrates processes away from this node, and a migration server (migration_daemon) that accepts process migration requests to the local node. Each migration_daemon has associated with it a communication segment and a semaphore. The communication segment is arranged as a circular list of ICB slots. The migration system has a simple name service mechanism that maintains tables containing the system names for the communication segment and semaphore for each ⟨host,migration_daemon⟩ pair. The semaphores used by the migration system belong to a well-known semaphore segment (semaphore_seg). To migrate a process, migrate is called giving the name of the process to migrate and destination host id:

```
migrate(SysName process, HostID host)
    ICB = stop_process(process)
    comm_seg = lookup_comm_segment(host, migration_daemon)
    semaphore = lookup_semaphore(host, migration_daemon)

    Get(comm_seg, read-write)
    copy ICB to next free slot in comm_seg
    Discard(comm_seg)
    V(semaphore_seg, semaphore)

    deactivate(ICB.process virtual space)
    return ICB to free list
    return
```

The migration_daemon at a node blocks on its semaphore. On unblocking, it reads the ICB from the next slot in its communication segment. This information is copied to a new ICB, and the process and object virtual spaces are activated. Finally, a kernel routine is called to make the ICB runnable.

```
migration_daemon()
    comm_seg = lookup_comm_segment(my_host(), migration_daemon)
    semaphore = lookup_semaphore(my_host(), migration_daemon)

    loop
      allocate(ICB)
      P(semaphore_seg, semaphore)   /* block waiting for request */
      Get(comm_seg, read-write)
      ICB := comm_seg.next_slot()
      Discard(comm_seg)

      activate(ICB.process virtual space)
      if not active(ICB.object virtual space)
        activate(ICB.object virtual space)
      schedule(ICB)
    end loop
```

Except for copying the ICB structure (around 130 bytes in the current implementation), all required portions of the process virtual space are fetched on demand only. Zayas[24] has shown that, when migrating processes, using on-demand fetching has considerable performance advantages over copying all of the process' data at the time of migration.

At any point of time, a segment is owned by one node only. *Segment migration* is the process of passing the ownership of a segment from one node to another, and is accomplished by copying the whole segment from the stable storage of the previous owner to the stable storage of the new owner.* To permanently move an object to another node, the segments that make up the object need to be migrated. Note that, in general, the segment that describes an object, as well as the segments that make up the object, can be owned by different nodes. Therefore, if a decision is made to migrate an object to one node, several nodes may have to be involved in transferring the ownerships of segments to the destination node.

Process and object migration uses the DSMC and Ra primitives without having to add additional mechanisms or communication protocols, and without a need for modifying the kernel. This feature is in contrast to other implementations of process migration such as in the V,[25] Accent[24] and DEMOS/MP[26] systems.

## IMPLEMENTATION ON Ra

### Overview

Figure 3 shows the organization of the DSMC implementation (roughly 3500 lines of C++ code[27]) on Ra. The boxes in the Figure denote system objects. The DSMC

---

*This requires deactivating the segment first and updating/invalidating location caches, if any.

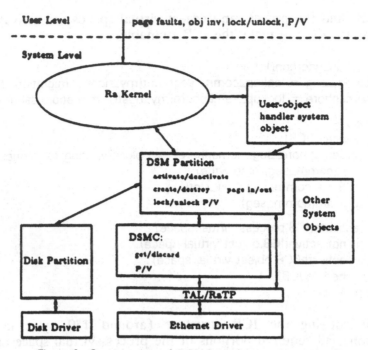

*Figure 3. Organization of DSMC implementation under Ra*

co-operates with remote DSMC's to implement the distributed shared memory primitives. The DSM partition is a Ra partition that provides the kernel with the ability to create/destroy and activate/deactivate segments, page-in/page-out portions of segments, and semaphore P/V operations. The DSM partition decides if a segment is owned by the local node or a remote node. It uses the disk partition to access local segments, and uses the DSMC to access remote segments. The disk partition maintains segments owned by the local node on the local stable storage (if any).

The DSMC algorithms require simple reliable request/response messages (possibly with message forwarding). In our implementation, we use the *transaction abstract layer* that is built on the *Ra transaction support protocol* (TAL/RaTP).[28] The TAL/RaTP protocol is similar to other transaction-oriented protocols such as VMTP.[29] However, it is much simpler than VMTP since it is tailored to our requirements.

## Handling local requests

### DSM partition

The DSM partition provides the minimum set of partition operations plus the semaphore operations. The DSM partition handles segment requests from the Ra kernel or from other system objects (Figure 3). An example of a system object that uses the DSM partition is the user-level object handler that is responsible for implementing object invocation and servicing user-visible segment operations. Such user-visible operations may include lock/unlock and P/V operations.

The DSM partition maintains the status of cached (local and remote) segments on the local node in a table called dtable (Figure 4). Each dtable entry maintains information about a block of a segment (where a block is a multiple of the physical page size). In the current implementation, a block is equal to the physical page size on the Sun-3 (8K bytes). Each valid entry in the dtable is doubly linked on a hash list. The table is hashed by the segment name, and searched with the key ⟨segment name, block#⟩. All free entries are linked on a free list. In addition, an *active segment table* (ast) contains an entry per active segment on the local node.

Each dtable entry represents one segment block and includes the following fields:

  (a) segment,block_number—these two fields identify the segment block represented by this entry
  (b) wait_lock—a lock that is used to synchronize access to this entry
  (c) phys_frame—an array of physical frame numbers that contain this block (in the current implementation, the cardinality of the array is one)
  (d) pending—a flag indicating that a read from disk is in progress, or a get with mode none has been issued to the owner DSMC
  (e) Mode—this field indicates the current mode of the block
  (f) readers—a field that indicates the number of requesters that have this block in read-only mode
  (g) owner_flag—a flag that indicates if the local node is the owner of the segment
  (h) keeper_owner—this field gives the current keeper of the segment (if owner_flag is true), or the owner of the segment (if owner_flag is false)
  (i) squeue—a list used by the owner DSMC to queue read-only and read-write requests for this block from remote DSMCs.

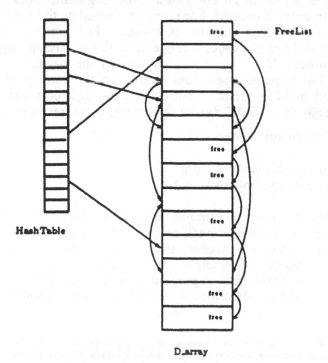

Figure 4. *Organization of* dtable

The DSM partition operations can be classified into three groups:

1. *Control operations:*

   activate(segment)
   deactivate(segment)
   create(segment)
   destroy(segment)

   The control operations search the ast for an entry describing the segment. If an entry is not found, the *location system object* is consulted for the location of the segment.* If the segment is available on a local disk partition, the corresponding control operation is invoked on the disk partition. Otherwise, the segment is owned by a remote node, and a msg_control message is sent to the DSM partition on the remote node. Note that locating the segment is the responsibility of the location system object, and that the DSMC is not involved in handling any of the control operations.

2. *Data transfer operations:*

   page_in(segment, block, physical page)
   page_in(segment, block, physical page, mode)
   page_out(segment, block)

   The page_in operation activates the segment, if necessary. The page_in operation searches the dtable for an entry describing ⟨segment, block⟩. If no such entry is found, an entry is created. For segments owned by the local node, the page_in operation on the disk partition is invoked. For remote segments, the DSM partition translates the page_in requests to the DSMC get operations with the specified mode. If no mode is indicated in the page_in call, mode none is assumed. The page_out operations locates the dtable entry describing ⟨segment, block⟩, and invokes the page_out call on the disk partition if the segment is local, or calls the DSMC discard operation, if the segment is remote.

3. *Synchronization operations*

   P(segment, semaphore_num)
   V(segment, semaphore_num)

   Semaphores are stored in *semaphore segments*. Semaphore segments have the format shown in Figure 5. Each semaphore segment consists of three parts: a descriptor structure, *n* semaphore structures, and *m* block structures. Descriptor contains the number of semaphore and block structures, a bit-map of free/used semaphore structures, and a pointer to a free list of block structures. Each semaphore structure describes a semaphore, and includes a counter and a

---

*Given the name of a segment, the location system object returns the location of the segment owner. A simple location system object broadcasts a search request for each location operation (see References 30 and 31 for more sophisticated location algorithms).

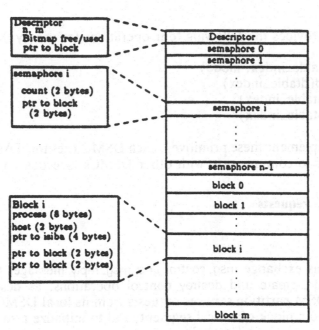

*Figure 5. Structure of a semaphore segment*

pointer to a doubly-linked list of block structures. Each block structure describes a process waiting for a semaphore. Each block contains the name of the waiting process, the host name where the process is blocked, and a pointer to the *isiba control block* (ICB) on the host where the process is blocked. Note that the hostname and ICB pointers are *hints* to the location of the blocked process because processes can migrate from one node to another. The process name field is an absolute pointer to the process and can be used by the locator system object to find the process if necessary. Processes (as well as other entities in Ra) have unique network-wide names.

Semaphore segments can be attached to a range of virtual addresses like any other segment in Ra. Therefore, they can be initialized and manipulated directly. The DSM partition maintains a table (called semtable) that describes each semaphore in use. Semtable acts as a cache of the active semaphores that are in the semaphore segments. Semtable is organized in a similar fashion as the dtable, but it is searched using the key (segment, semaphore number). Each semtable entry caches exactly one semaphore from a semaphore segment. The structure of each semtable entry is the same as the semaphor structure in semaphore segments (see Figure 5). A pool of in-memory block structures are used to cache contents of block structures from semaphore segments.

Operations on a semaphore that belongs to a local segment are performed locally by reading the segment from the disk partition, initializing a semtable entry, and then performing the operations on the semtable entry. In the current implementation, all semaphore operations are performed at the node that owns the semaphore segment. Therefore, operations on semaphores that belong to remote segments are translated into DSMC P and V operations (see the section on 'performing semaphore operations locally', below).

*DSMC*

The DSMC provides the following four operations for use by the DSM partition:

> get(dtable_index, mode)
> discard(dtable_index)
> P(semtable_index)
> V(semtable_index)

In order to implement these primitives, each DSMC uses the TAL/RaTP messages listed in Table I to communicate with other DSMCs (see below).

## Handling remote requests

### DSM partition

DSM partitions exchange msg_control and msg_reply messages to implement the activate, deactivate, create and destroy control operations, as described above. In addition, each DSM partition services requests from its local DSMC to activate local segments, to read a block of a local segment, and to initialize a semtable entry from a local semaphore segment (see below).

## DSMC

The DSMC may receive several messages from remote DSMCs. We describe the DSMC action for each message received:

1. msg_get(segment, block, mode). If there is no ast entry for this segment, the DSMC asks the DSM partition to activate the segment and to read the required block into memory. The DSMC examines the dtable entry describing the required block. Depending on the information contained in the dtable, the DSMC performs one of the following actions:

### Table I. Summary of TAL messages

| Type | From | To | Description |
|------|------|------|-------------|
| msg_control | DSM part. | DSM part. | used for control operations |
| msg_reply | DSM part. | DSM part. | reply to msg_control |
| msg_get | keeper DSMC | owner DSMC | fetches a segment block |
| msg_discard | keeper DSMC | owner DSMC | returns a segment block |
| msg_forward | owner DSMC | keeper DSMC | forwards a segment block |
| msg_segment | any DSMC | any DSMC | delivers requested segment block |
| msg_P | keeper DSMC | owner DSMC | semaphore P operation |
| msg_V | keeper DSMC | owner DSMC | semaphore V operation |
| msg_unblock | owner DSMC | keeper DSMC | continues suspended process |
| msg_error | any | any | indicates an exception |

(a) If the segment mode does not conflict with the requested mode and the block is available locally, send a msg_segment message that includes the block to the requesting DSMC.

(b) If the segment mode is none, the requested mode is also none and the segment is held at a remote node, then send a msg_forward message to the remote DSMC, instructing it to forward the block to the requester.

(c) If the segment mode and requested mode conflict (e.g. segment is held in read-only mode and requested mode is read-write, queue request until segment is available.

(d) If the segment does not exist at this node, then send a msg_error message to the requesting DSMC.

2. msg_discard(segment, block). The DSMC updates the dtable entry describing the discarded block. If there exist any pending get requests for this block that now can be satisfied, they are serviced by sending msg_segment messages to the requesting DSMCs.

3. msg_segment(segment, block). The DSMC receives a msg_segment message as a response for msg_get message. The DSMC locates the dtable entry describing the block, and resumes the suspended processes that are awaiting the arrival of the block.

4. msg_forward(segment, block, destination host). The DSMC informs the DSM partition that this block is no longer available, and then issues a msg_segment message containing the required block to the destination host.

5. msg_P(segment, semaphore_num). If there is no semtable entry for the required semaphore, the DSMC requests its local DSM partition to initialize an entry. The DSM partition may have to activate the required semaphore segment and then read the information of semaphore semaphore_num into the new semtable entry. The DSMC decrements the semaphore count, and responds with a msg_unblock message if the count is greater than or equal to zero. Otherwise, it links to the semtable entry a new block structure that describes the requesting process.

5. msg_V(segment, semaphore_num). If there is no semtable entry for the required semaphore, the DSMC requests its local DSM partition to initialize the entry. The DSMC increments the semaphore count. If the count is less than or equal to zero, the DSMC unlinks the first block structure from the semtable entry and sends a msg_unblock to resume the process described by the unlinked block structure.

7. msg_unblock(segment, semaphore_num, ptr to ICB). The DSMC resumes the execution of the waiting process identified by the msg_unblock message.

8. msg_error(segment, block, error_type). An error indication may be received if a request cannot be satisfied. The error_type field gives the reason for the failure of the request. Upon receiving an msg_error message as a response for a request, the DSMC returns an error indication to the original requester.

## Table management

As mentioned above, the DSM partition is responsible for maintaining ast, semtable and dtable structures. The size of ast is equal to the maximum number of active segments at any point of time, and ast entries can be reclaimed when the segments they represent are deactivated. Semtable acts as a cache of the information contained in semaphore segments, and its size is equal to the expected number of semaphores in use. To reclaim a semtable entry, the contents of the entry has to be written back into its semaphore segment. The size of the dtable depends on whether or not the node acts as an owner of segments. For nodes that act only as keepers, the size of the dtable is less than or equal to the number of physical pages at the node. For a node that acts as an owner, the size of the dtable is determined by the number of nodes serviced and the size of their physical memories. A dtable entry is reclaimed when the block it represents is paged-out. If the entry represents a block that is cached at a keeper node, the entry can be reclaimed when the block is returned to the owner.

### Performing semaphore operations locally

As described above, all semaphore operations in the current implementation are performed at the node that owns the semaphore segment. To exploit synchronization locality (e.g. when all processes using the same semaphore are at the same node), it should be possible to perform the semaphore operations at the local node without the intervention of the owner node on each operation.

Because semaphores reside in segments, it is possible to fetch the semaphore segment from its owner, read its contents into the local semtable, and perform the operations locally. When a decision is made to move the semaphore segment from its current node, the DSM partition must ensure that the contents of the segment is up to date by flushing any semtable entries that belong to the segment prior to sending the segment to another node. Processes blocked on a semaphore need not be migrated when the semaphore segment is moved to another node, because the semaphore segment contains the name of the host where the process is blocked (Figure 5).

The following simple modifications to the DSMC P and V primitives are required: instead of sending all semaphore operations to the owner DSMC, a check is made to see if the semaphore segment is cached locally. If it is, the operation is performed locally and the owner DSMC is not contacted. Otherwise, the semaphore operation is sent to the owner DSMC. When the owner DSMC receives a semaphore operation message (msg_P or msg_V), it checks to see whether the required semaphore segment is available locally, or is cached at a remote keeper. If the semaphore segment is available locally, the semaphore operation is performed as before at the owner node. Otherwise, the semaphore operation is forwarded to the current keeper of the semaphore segment. Note that the owner DSMC maintains at all times the location of the current keeper of each segment, and therefore can easily forward semaphore operations on segments that are cached at remote keepers.

The semaphore mechanisms presented in this section do not address the issue of where (or when) to move semaphore segments. Instead, they perform the P and V semaphore operations at the *current* location of the semaphore segment. Other system objects are responsible for deciding on where to place semaphore segments in the distributed system, and when to move them to other nodes.

**Fault tolerance**

The DSMC implementation assumes the existence of a reliable transport protocol underneath. Any failures in the network (either node or link failure) results in an 'error' indication being propagated to the system object that made the request to the DSMC. Recovering from such failures could possibly involve reconstructing the segments at a different node. Failure handling clearly involves policy issues, best left to appropriate system objects. The DSM layer concerns itself only with segment transport and gives the necessary error indication to higher level system objects for appropriate corrective action. Increased availability is provided by replicating the owners responsible for a given segment, while mechanisms for atomic commitment of writes to segments are provided via a two-phase commit system object. More details on these mechanisms for achieving fault-tolerance in a DSM environment may be found in Reference 32, and are beyond the scope of this paper.

## IMPLEMENTATION ON UNIX

The DSMC and the DSM partition have been implemented on top of Unix as well. This implementation serves three purposes:

1. The Unix environment makes it easy to test and verify the DSMC and TAL/-RaTP protocols.
2. The Unix file system is available for use as permanent store for segments. Ra executes on diskless Sun-3 workstations with backing store provided by Unix machines.
3. The strength of Unix is the rich program development environment that it provides. The strength of Clouds is the transparent management of distributed data and computation. Providing inter-operability between Unix and Clouds is one of our design goals. DSM implementation on Unix and Ra serves this purpose. System and user objects are developed on Unix and demand-paged to Ra via the DSM mechanisms.

The organization of the DSMC implementation on Unix is shown in Figure 6. TAL/RaTP runs as a user process that uses SUN's network interface tap (NIT)[33] to receive packets from the net and to route them among a set of clients and servers. The DSMC code is linked-in with the server code that uses the Unix file system to store segments and service requests from Ra DSM partitions. The DSM code is also linked-in with client code that is used to test the DSM system.

Most of the DSMC and DSM partition code that runs on Ra are re-used for the Unix implementation, and the operating system dependencies are isolated in a few C++ classes. To enable more than one Unix process to share the DSM tables, we use Unix System V shared memory regions.[33] In addition, Unix System V semaphores are used to synchronize access to the tables. In our initial implementation, we also used System V semaphores to synchronize the TAL/RaTP process and its client processes. A client process requested TAL/RaTP services by writing in a shared region of memory and blocking on a semaphore. TAL/RaTP eventually resumed the process by issuing a V operation on the semaphore.

In the current implementation, however, we switched to using Unix 4.2 BSD socket IPC primitives instead of system V semaphores because of the poor performance of

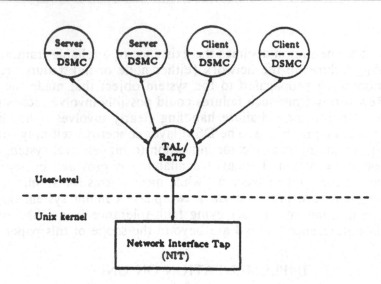

*Figure 6. Organization of DSMC implementation on Unix*

the initial implementation (see the next section). The TAL/RaTP process communicates with its client processes through shared memory and sockets. Processes communicate their requests to TAL/RaTP via socket IPC primitives. However, data blocks are passed through shared memory regions to minimize copying.

## PERFORMANCE EVALUATION

In this section, we report on the performance of the DSM implementation on Unix and Ra. The measurements are done on a configuration using Sun 3/50s for the Clouds Ra nodes, and Sun 3/60s for the Unix nodes. The machines are connected through a 10M bits/s ETHERNET. We mask out the cost of secondary storage access by caching segments in memory before measuring the costs of the DSMC primitives.

### Unix

Table II summarizes the results of the performance measurements between two Unix nodes. The Table shows that on an average fetching a segment (without forwarding) of size 8K bytes (the page size on the Sun-3) takes 43·4 ms. Van Renesse *et al.* report a transfer rate of 40 ms for 8K bytes between two user processes on

Table II. Measurements of DSMC operations on Unix

| Get or discard (8K bytes) | | | |
|---|---|---|---|
| without forwarding: | 43·4 ms | throughput: | 185 Kbytes/s |
| with forwarding: | 63·7 ms | throughput: | 126 Kbytes/s |
| V operation: | 16·5 ms | | |
| P operation: | 31·5 ms | | |
| Activate segment: | 23·3 ms | | |

different nodes using Sun RPC on a 10M bits/sec ETHERNET.[34] Our implementation uses two user processes per node and still compares favourably with the figures reported by van Renesse *et al*. A null message from one DSMC to another costs roughly 20 ms, a large portion of which is spent context switching between the kernel and TAL/RaTP, and between TAL/RaTP and DSMC. Moving TAL/RaTP into the Unix kernel would eliminate the additional context switching, and we are currently investigating such an implementation. A semaphore V operation costs only 16·5 ms since it is non-blocking, i.e. the issuing process continues without waiting for the final acknowledgment from the remote DSMC.

As mentioned in the previous section, we experimented with using socket IPC primitives and System V semaphore primitives to synchronize the TAL/RaTP process and its clients. The numbers reported in this section are from the implementation that used the socket IPC primitives. When using System V semaphores, the average cost of an 8K bytes get request is almost 20 ms more than the cost reported in Table II. We believe that the difference is due to the System V implementation of the semaphore primitives, since the two implementations differ only in the code that synchronizes the TAL/RaTP process and its clients.

**Ra**

Table III summarizes the preliminary measurements of a Ra node communicating with a Unix node using DSM. Once again the dominant cost in both segment activation/deactivation and page-in is the context switch time at the Unix end.

Ra to Ra communication times are shown in Table IV. A null round-trip message (72 bytes) time between two isibas making use of the ETHERNET driver system object takes 2·6 ms. Of this time, only 450 μs is transmission time at the sender. The remaining time is accounted by the context switch at the receiver, the reply and context switching to the sending isiba on receipt of the reply. The RaTP level null round-trip time is 7·8 ms. The unusually high round-trip time at RaTP level is because the implementation is not yet tuned for performance.

Given this null round-trip time, an 8K page transfer time of 20·3 ms at RaTP level is reasonable since RaTP breaks up an 8K message into eight packets. Note that this message could be sent in six packets, as ETHERNET allows a maximum packet size of 1526 bytes,[35] but for debugging purposes RaTP sends it in 8 packets. A Ra

Table III. Ra to Unix communication using DSM

| | |
|---|---|
| Page-in (8K) | 35·2 ms |
| Segment activation/deactivation | 25·1 ms |

Table IV. Ra to Ra communication

| DSM operations | Time |
|---|---|
| Null round trip time using ETHERNET system object | 2·60 ms |
| Null round-trip time at RaTP level | 7·80 ms |
| Transfer time at RaTP level for 8K page (one-way) | 20·30 ms |
| DSM get for 8K page | 28·23 ms |

to Ra DSM get takes 28·23 ms. Comparing the DSM and RaTP timings (Table II) it is seen that the DSM protocol has an overhead of 7·93 ms for 8K page transfer from Ra to Ra.

Although the preliminary measurements are not spectacular, the system is not tuned for performance. We are currently in the process of refining the RaTP protocol and removing some of the redundancies that exist between the ETHERNET driver and the RaTP protocol in checking for errors and time-outs. Further, we are porting the implementation to Sun SPARCstations that have a computing capacity of 15 MIPS compared to the 1·5 MIPS of Sun 3/50s. Given that most of the communication cost may be attributed to the processing overhead as opposed to data transfer on the wire, we expect the refinements and porting to faster processor to yield a significant improvement in performance.

## CONCLUSIONS AND FUTURE WORK

We have presented an architecture of a distributed shared memory system and descibed an implementation of the system in the context of the Ra kernel. We have also described and reported on the preliminary performance of an implementation of the system. Detailed algorithms for the DSMC primitives, and simulation studies comparing these primitives to RPC are presented in Reference 36. The utility of these primitives in programming distributed algorithms is illustrated in Reference 4. So far, our work has concentrated on the mechanisms of distributed shared memory. As part of our future work, we intend to gain more experience with the system and address policy issues such as when to use the RPC mechanism and when to use the DSMC primitives, where to place the semaphore segments, and how to recover from failures.

### ACKNOWLEDGEMENT

This work has been funded in part by NSF grants CCR-8619886 and MIPS-8809268, and an NSF PYI Award MIP-9058430 for U. Ramachandran. An earlier version of this paper was presented at the USENIX workshop on experiences in building distributed and multiprocessor systems, Ft. Lauderdale, Florida, October 1989.

### REFERENCES

1. B. Liskov and R. Scheifler, 'Guardians and actions: linguistic support for robust, distributed programs', *Ninth Conference on Principles of Programming Languages*, 1982, pp 7–19.
2. Eric Jul, Henry Levy, Norman Hutchinson and Andrew Black, 'Fine-grained mobility in the Emerald system', *ACM Transactions on Computer Systems*, **6**, (1), 109–133 (1988).
3. R. Bisiani and A. Forin, 'Multilanguage parallel programming of heterogeneous machines', *IEEE Trans. Computers*, **C-37**, (8), 930–945 (1988).
4. Umakishore Ramachandran and M. Yousef Amin Khalidi 'Programming with distributed shared memory', *IEEE 13th International Computer Software and Applications Conference, COMPSAC'89*, Orlando, Florida, September 1989, pp. 176–183. Also *Technical Report GIT-ICS-88/38*.
5. P. J. Leach, P. H. Levine, B. P. Douros, J. A. Hamilton, D. L. Nelson and B. J. Stumpf, 'The architecture of an integrated local network', *IEEE J. Selected Areas in Communications*, **SAC-1**, (5), 842–857 (1983).
6. Kai Li and Paul Hudak, 'Memory coherence in shared virtual memory systems', *Proceedings of the 5th ACM Symposium Principles of Distributed Computing*, ACM, August 1986, pp. 229–239.
7. Umakishore Ramachandran, Mustaque Ahamad and M. Yousef A. Khalidi, 'Coherence of distrib-

uted shared memory: unifying synchronization and data transfer', *18th International Conference on Parallel Processing*, St. Charles, Ill, August 1989.

8.  R. Katz, S. Eggers, D. A. Wood, C. Perkins and R. G. Sheldon, 'Implementing a cache consistency protocol', *Proceedings of the 12th International Symposium on Computer Architecture*, June 1985, pp. 276–283.

9.  N. Carriero and D. Gelernter, 'The S/Net's Linda kernel', *ACM Transactions on Computer Systems*, **4**, (2), 110–129 (1986).

10. D. Gelernter, 'Generative communications in Linda', *ACM Transactions on Programming Languages and Systems*, **7**, (1), 80–112 (1985).

11. K. P. Birman, T. A. Joseph, F. Schmuck and P. Stephenson, 'Programming with shared bulletin boards in asynchronous distributed systems', *Technical Report 86–772*, Cornell University, Department of Computer Science, August 1986.

12. R. Rashid, A. Tevanian, M. Young, D. Golub, R. Bar on, D. Black, W. Bolosky and J. Chew, 'Machine-independent virtual memory management for paged uniprocessor and multiprocessor architectures', *IEEE Trans. Computers*, C-37, 896–908 (1988).

13. M. Young, A. Tevanian, R. Rashid, D. Golub, J. Eppinger, J. Chew, W. Bolosky, D. Black and R. Baron, 'The duality of memory and communication in the implementation of a multiprocessor operating system', *Proceedings of the 11th Symposium on Operating Systems Principles*, November 1987, pp 63–76.

14. E. Zayas, 'Attacking the process migration bottleneck', *Proceedings of the 11th Symposium on Operating Systems Principles*, November 1987, pp. 13–24.

15. R. Rashid and G. Robertson, 'Accent: a communication oriented network operating system kernel', *Proceedings of the 8th Symposium on Operating Systems Principles*, December 1981, pp. 64–75.

16. D. R. Cheriton, 'Problem-oriented shared memory: a decentralized approach to distributed systems design', *Proceedings of the 6th International Conference on Distributed Computing Systems*, May 1986, pp. 190–197.

17. José M. Bernabéu Aubán, Phillip W. Hutto, M. Yousef A. Khalidi, Mustaque Ahamad, Willian F. Appelbe, Partha Dasgupta, Richard J. LeBlanc and Umakishore Ramachandran, 'Clouds—a distributed, object-based operating system: architecture and kernel implementation', *European UNIX Systems User Group Autumn Conference*, EUUG, October 1988, pp. 25–38.

18. P. J. Denning, 'On modeling program behavior', *Proceedings of the Spring Joint Computer Conference, Volume 40*, Arlington, VA, 1972, AFIPS Press, pp. 937–944.

19. M. Yousef A. Khalidi, 'Hardware support for distributed object-based systems', *PhD. Thesis*, School of Information and Computer Science, Georgia Institute of Technology, June 1989. *Technical Report GIT-ICS-89/19*.

20. Umakishore Ramachandran and M. Yousef A. Khalidi, 'A measurement-based study of hardware support for object invocation', *Software—Practice and Experience*, **19**, 809–828 (1989).

21. José M. Bernabéu Aubán, Phillip W. Hutto and M. Yousef A. Khalidi, 'The architecture of the Ra kernel', *Technical Report GIT-ICS-87/35*, School of Information and Computer Science, Georgia Institute of Technology, December 1987.

22. José M. Bernabéu Aubán, Phillip W. Hutto, M. Yousef A. Khalidi, Mustaque Ahamad, William F. Appelbe, Partha Dasgupta, Richard J. LeBlanc and Umakishore Ramachandran, 'The architecture of ra: a kernel for *clouds*', *Proceedings of the Twenty-Second Annual Hawaii International Conference on System Sciences*, January 1989.

23. François Armand, Frédéric Herrmann, Michel Gien and Marc Rozier, 'Chorus, a new technology for building unix systems', *European UNIX systems User Group Autumn Conference*, EUUG, October 1988, pp. 1–18.

24. E. Zayas, 'The use of copy-on-reference in a process migration system', *PhD. Thesis*, Carnegie-Mellon University, April 1987. *Technical Report CMU-CS-87-121*.

25. Marvin M. Theimer, Keith A. Lantz and David R. Cheriton, 'Preemptable remote execution facilities for the V-system', *Proceedings of the Tenth Symposium on Operating Systems Principles*, 1985, pp. 2–12.

26. Michael L. Powell and Barton P. Miller, 'Process migration in DEMOS/MP', *Proceedings of the 9th Symposium on Operating Systems Principles*, 1983, 110–119.

27. Bjarne Stroustrup, *The C++ Programming Language*, Addison-Wesley Publishing Company, 1986.

28. Christopher J. Wilkenloh, 'RaTP: a transaction support protocol for *ra*', *Master's thesis*, School of Information and Computer Science, Georgia Institute of Technology, 1989.

29. D. R. Cheriton, 'VMTP: a transport protocol for the next generation of communication systems', *Proceedings of SIGCOMM '86*, August 1986.

30. José M. Bernabéu Aubán, 'Locating resources in distributed systems', *Ph.D. thesis*, School of Information and Computer Science, Georgia Institute of Technology, December 1988.

31. Mustaque Ahamad, Mostafa H. Ammar, José M. Bernabéu Aubán and M. Yousef A. Khalidi, 'Locating resources in a distributed system using multicast communication', *Proceedings of the 13th Conference on Local Computer Networks*, October 1988. (Also available as *Technical Report GIT-ICS-87/44*).

32. Ajay Mohindra and Umakishore Ramachandran, 'Implementation of fault-tolerant transactions using distributed shared memory', *Technical Report GIT-ICS-89/41*, School of Information and Computer Science, Georgia Institute of Technology, 1989.

33. Sun Microsystems, *Unix Interface Reference Manual*, Mountain View, California, 1986.

34. Robbert van Renesse, Hans van Staveren and Andrew S. Tanenbaum, 'Performance of the world's fastest distributed operating system', *Operating Systems Review*, **22**, (4), 25–34 (1988).

35. John F. Shoch, Yogen K. Dalal, David D. Redell and Ronald C. Crane, 'Evolution of the ETHERNET Local Computer Network', *IEEE Computer*, August 1982, pp. 1–27.

36. Umakishore Ramachandran, Mustaque Ahamad and M. Yousef A. Khalidi, 'Unifying synchronization and data transfer in maintaining coherence of distributed shared memory', *Technical Report GIT-ICS-88/23*, School of Information and Computer Science, Georgia Institute of Technology, June 1988.

# Linda and Friends

Sudhir Ahuja, AT&T Bell Laboratories
Nicholas Carriero and David Gelernter, Yale University

**Linda consists of a few simple primitives that support an "uncoupled" style of parallel programming. Implementations exist on a broad spectrum of parallel machines.**

Linda consists of a few simple operators designed to support and simplify the construction of explicitly-parallel programs. Linda has been implemented on AT&T Bell Labs' S/Net multicomputer and, in a preliminary way, on an Ethernet-based MicroVAX network and an Intel iPSC hypercube. Although the implementations are new and need refinement, our early experiences with them have been revealing, and we take them as supporting our claim that Linda is a promising tool.

Parallel programming is often described as being fundamentally harder than conventional, sequential programming, but in our experience (limited so far, but growing) it isn't. Parallel programming in Linda is conceptually the same order of task as conventional programming in a sequential language. Parallelism does, though, encompass a potentially difficult problem. A conventional program consists of one executing process, of a single point in computational time-space, but a parallel program consists of many, and to the extent that we have to worry about the relationship among these points in time and space, the mood turns nasty. Linda's mission, however, is to make it largely unnecessary to think about the coupling between parallel processes. Linda's uncoupled processes, in fact, never deal with each other directly. A parallel program in Linda is a spatially and temporally unordered bag of processes, not a process

graph. To the extent that process uncoupling succeeds, the difficulty of designing, debugging, and understanding a parallel program grows additively and not multiplicatively with the variety of processes it encompasses.

When the simple operators Linda provides are injected into a host language $h$, they turn $h$ into a parallel programming language. A Linda system consists of the runtime kernel, which implements interprocess communication and process management, and a preprocessor or compiler. A Linda-based parallel language is in fact a new language, not an old one with added system calls, to the extent that the preprocessor or compiler recognizes the Linda operations, checks and rewrites them on the basis of symbol table information, and can optimize the pattern of kernel calls that result based on its knowledge of constants and loops, among other things. Most of our programming experiments so far have been conducted in C-Linda (and we use C-Linda for the examples below), but we have implemented a Fortran-Linda preprocessor as well. The kernel is language-independent. It will support $N$-Linda for any language $N$.

Associated with the Linda operators is a particular programming methodology, based on distributed data structures. (The language doesn't restrict programmers to this methodology. It merely allows the methodology, which most other languages don't.) The distributed-data-structure

Reprinted from *Computer*, Vol. 19, No. 8, Aug. 1986, pp. 26–34.

methodology in turn suggests a particular strategy for dealing with parallelism. Most models of parallelism assume that a program will be parallelized by partitioning it into a large number of simultaneous activities. This partitioning appears, however, to be relatively difficult to do, especially when we consider large multicomputers that support thousand-fold parallelism and beyond. In the Linda framework, we can get parallelism by *replicating* as well as by partitioning. We anticipate that it will frequently be simpler to stamp out many identical copies of one process than to create the same number of distinct processes. So the final ingredient in the Linda framework is a strategy for coping with parallelism by replication rather than by partitioning.

In the following we discuss first what it seems to us that parallel programmers need. We then describe Linda, some programming experiments using Linda, the current implementation, and the project now underway to go beyond the current software implementation and build a hardware Linda machine. We go on to discuss some related higher-level parallel languages that can be implemented on top of the Linda kernel, particularly the symmetric languages. We close in a blaze of speculation.

## What parallel programmers need

Many parallel algorithms are known and more are in development; many parallel machines are available and many more will be soon. But the fate of the whole effort will ultimately be decided by the extent to which working programmers can put the algorithms and the machines together. The needs of parallel programmers have not been accommodated very well to date.

**A machine-independent and (potentially) portable programming vehicle.** Designers of parallel languages generally hold that programming tools should accommodate a high-level programming model, not a particular architecture. But as parallel machines emerge commercially, there has been little effort spent on making high-level, machine-independent tools available on them. Young debutante machines are sometimes gotten-up in their own full-

blown parallel languages; more often they come dressed in only a handful of idiosyncratic system calls that support the local variant of message-passing or memory-sharing. In either case, so long as each new machine is provided with its own parallel programming system, programs for multicomputer $x$ will not only have to be re-coded, they may need to be conceptually reformulated to run on multicomputer $y$. (This is particularly true if $x$ is a shared-memory machine like a BBN Butterfly[1] or an IBM RP3[2] and $y$ is a network, like an Intel iPSC.) But users need to be able to run parallel programs on a range of architectures, particularly now, when interesting designs of unknown merit proliferate. They need to be able to communicate parallel algorithms. Methodological knowledge can't grow when sources are cluttered with local dialect. Finally, they need programming tools suited to their needs, not to the machine's.

**A programming tool that absolves them as fully as possible from dealing with spatial and temporal relationships among parallel processes.** We referred to the general problem of uncoupling above. Uncoupling has both a spatial and a temporal aspect. Spatially, each process in a parallel program will usually develop a result or a series of results that will be accepted as input by certain other processes. Uncoupling suggests that process $q$ should not be required to know or care that process $j$ accepts $q$'s data as input. Instead of requiring $q$ to execute an explicit "send this data to $j$" statement, we would rather that $q$ be permitted simply to tag its new data with a logical label (for example, "new data from $q$") and then forget about it, under the assumption that any process that wants it will come and get it. At some later point in program development, a different process may decide to deal with $q$'s data. Under the spatially-uncoupled scheme, this won't matter to $q$.

Temporal uncoupling involves similar though perhaps slightly more subtle issues. If $q$ is forced to send to $j$ explicitly, the system is constrained to have both processes loaded simultaneously (or at least to have buffer space allocated for $j$ when $q$ runs). Further, most parallel languages attach some form of synchronization constraint to send. A synchronized send operation like Ada's entry call or CSP-Occam's out-

put statement forces the system not merely to load but to run the receiving process before the sender can continue. We would rather that our parallel programs be largely free of scheduling implications like these. Not only do they constrain the system in ways that may be undesirable, but they force programmers to think in simultaneities. As far as possible, we would like programmers to be able to develop $q$'s code without having to envision other simultaneous execution loci. To achieve this, we would like $q$ to be allowed to take each new datum it develops and heave it overboard without a backwards glance. (We make this a bit more concrete below.)

**A programming tool that allows tasks to be dynamically distributed at runtime.** Generally there is more logical parallelism in a parallel algorithm than physical parallelism in a host multicomputer, which means that at runtime there are more ready tasks than idle processors. Good speedup obviously requires that tasks be evenly distributed among available processors. Many systems require that this distribution be performed statically at load time. Sometimes, finding a good static distribution is easy, notably when the program's logical structure matches the machine's physical structure. As the program's logical structure grows more irregular, the task gets harder, and when the program's computational focus develops dynamically at runtime, finding a good static mapping may be impossible. Many important applications and program structures fall into the first, easily-handled category, but many more do not. For those that don't, dynamic distribution of tasks is essential.

**A programming tool that can be implemented efficiently on existing hardware.** Obviously. Parallel language research has produced far more designs than implementations. Elegant language ideas will always be interesting regardless of the existence of good implementations, but parallel programmers, as opposed to language researchers, require implementable elegance.

## Linda

Linda centers on an idiosyncratic memory model. Where a conventional memory's storage unit is the physical byte (or

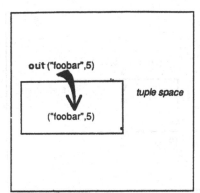

**Figure 1. out** statement: drop it in.

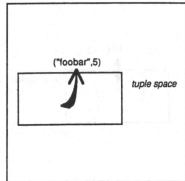

**Figure 2. in** statement: haul it out.

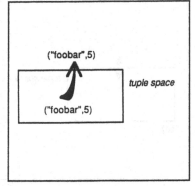

**Figure 3. read** statement: read it and leave it.

something comparable), Linda memory's storage unit is the logical tuple, or ordered set of values. Where the elements of a conventional memory are accessed by address, elements in Linda memory have no addresses. They are accessed by *logical name*, where a tuple's *name* is any selection of its values. Where a conventional memory is accessed via two operations, read and write, a Linda memory is accessed via three: read, add, and remove.

It is a consequence of the last characteristic that tuples in a Linda memory can't be altered *in situ*. To be changed, they must be physically removed, updated, and then reinserted. This makes it possible for many processes to share access to a Linda memory simultaneously; using Linda we can build distributed data structures that, unlike conventional ones, may be manipulated by many processes in parallel. Furthermore, as a consequence of the first characteristic (a Linda memory stores tuples, not bytes), Linda's shared memory is coarse-grained enough to be supported efficiently without shared-memory hardware. Shared memory has long been regarded as the most flexible and powerful way of sharing data among parallel processes, but a naive shared memory requires hardware support that is complicated, expensive to build, and suitable only for multicomputers, not for local area networks. Linda's variant of shared memory, on the other hand, runs both on the S/Net and on a MicroVAX network, neither of which provides any physically shared memory. (Of course, Linda may be im-

plemented on shared-memory multicomputers as well, as we discuss below.)

Linda's shared memory is referred to as *tuple space*, or TS. Messages in Linda are never exchanged between two processes directly. Instead, a process with data to communicate adds it to tuple space and a process that needs to receive data seeks it, likewise, in tuple space. There are four operations defined over TS: **out()**, **in()**, **read()**, and **eval()**. **out(***t***)** causes tuple *t* to be added to TS; the executing process continues immediately. **in(***s***)** causes some tuple *t* that matches template *s* to be withdrawn from TS; the values of the actuals in *t* are assigned to the formals in *s* and the executing process continues. If no matching *t* is available when **in(***s***)** executes, the executing process suspends until one is, then proceeds as before. If many matching *t*'s are available, one is chosen arbitrarily. **read(***s***)** is the same as **in(***s***)**, with actuals assigned to formals as before, except that the matched tuple remains in TS.

For example, executing
    out("P", 5, false)

causes the tuple ("P", 5, false) to be added to TS. The first component of a tuple serves as a logical name, here "P"; the remaining components are data values. Subsequent execution of
    in("P", int i, bool b)

might cause tuple ("P", 5, false) to be withdrawn from TS. **5** would be assigned to **i** and **false** to **b**. Alternatively, it might cause any other matching tuple (any other, that is, whose first component is "P" and

whose second and third components are an integer and a Boolean, respectively) to be withdrawn and assigned. Executing
    read("P", int i, bool b)

when ("P", 5, false) is available in TS may cause 5 to be assigned to *i* and false to *b*, or equivalently may cause the assignment of values from some other type consonant tuple, with the matched tuple itself remaining in TS in either case. **eval(***t***)** is the same as **out(***t***)**, except that **eval** adds an unevaluated tuple to TS. (**eval** is not primitive in Linda; it will be implemented on top of **out**. We haven't done this yet in S/Net-Linda, so we omit further mention of **eval**.) See Figures 1, 2, and 3.

The parameters to an **in()** or **read()** statement needn't all be formals. Any or all may be actuals as well. All actuals must be matched by corresponding actuals in a tuple for tuple-matching to occur. Thus the statement
    in("P", int i, 15)

may withdraw tuple ("P", 6, 15) but not tuple ("P", 6, 12). When a variable appears in a tuple without a type declarator, its value is used as an actual. The annotation **formal** may precede an already-declared variable to indicate that the programmer intends a formal parameter. Thus, if **i** and **j** have already been declared as integer variables, the following two statements are equivalent to the preceding one:
    j = 15; in("P", formal i, j)

This extended naming convention (it resembles the **select** operation in relational

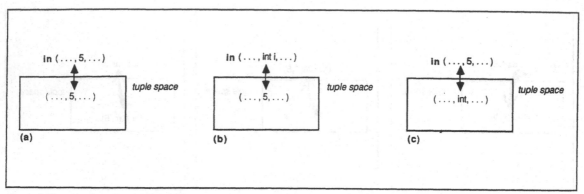

**Figure 4.** Structured naming: legal matches.

databases) is referred to as *structured naming*. Structured naming makes TS content-addressable, in the sense that processes may select among a collection of tuples that share the same first component on the basis of the values of any other component fields. Any parameter to **out()** or **eval()** except the first may likewise be a formal; a formal parameter in a tuple matches any type-consonant actual in an **in** or **read** statement's template. See Figure 4.

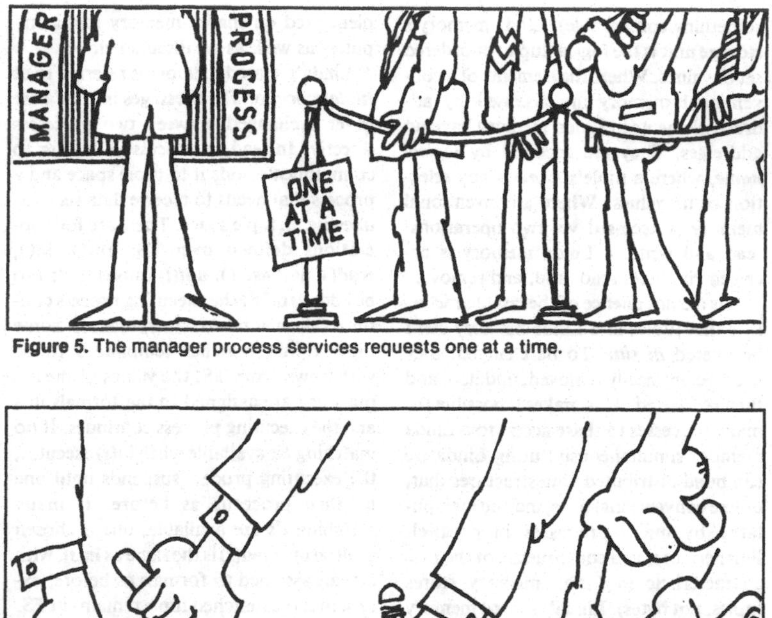

## Programming in Linda

Linda accommodates the needs for uncoupling and dynamic scheduling we listed above by relying on distributed data structures. As noted, a distributed data structure is one that may be manipulated by many parallel processes simultaneously. Distributed data structures are the natural complement to parallel program structures, but despite this natural relationship, distributed data structures are impossible in most parallel programming languages. Most parallel languages are based instead on what we call the *manager process* model of parallelism, which requires that shared data objects be encapsulated within manager processes. Operations on shared data are carried out, on request, by the manager process on the user's behalf. See Figures 5 and 6.

The manager-process model has important advantages, and manager-process programs are easy to write in Linda. What

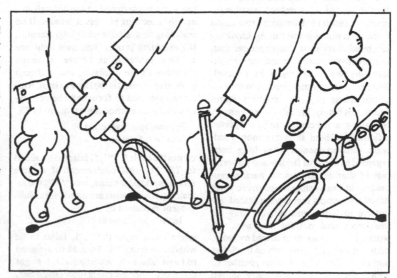

**Figure 5.** The manager process services requests one at a time.

**Figure 6.** Data are directly accessible to all parallel processes.

> The processes in a partitioned-network program are coupled, while those in a replicated-worker program are uncoupled.

is significant, though, is the number of cases in which distributed data structure programs come closer to achieving the qualities we want. They do so particularly in the context of parallel programs structured not as logical networks but as collections of identical workers. In logical-network-style parallelism (the more common variety), a program is partitioned into $n$ pieces, where $n$ is determined by the logic of the algorithm. Each of the $n$ logical pieces is implemented by a process, and each process keeps its attention demurely fixed on its own conventional, local data structures. In the replicated worker model, we don't partition our program at all; we replicate it $r$ times, where $r$ is determined by the number of processors we have available. All $r$ processes scramble simultaneously over a distributed data structure, seeking work where they can get it. There is a strong underlying sense in which the processes in a partitioned-network program are coupled, while those in a replicated-worker program are uncoupled. In the partitioned network program, each process must, in general, deal with its neighbor processes; in the replicated-worker program, workers ignore each other completely. The replicated worker model is interesting for a number of more specific reasons as well.

1. It scales transparently. Once we have developed and debugged a program with a single worker process, our program will run in the same way, only faster, with ten parallel workers or a hundred. We need be only minimally aware of parallelism in developing the program, and we can adjust the degree of parallelism in any given run to the available resources.

2. It eliminates logically-pointless context switching. Each processor runs a single process. We add processes only when we add processors. The process-managment burden per node is exactly the same when the program runs on one node as when it runs on a thousand. (This is not true, of course, in the network model. A network program always creates the same number of processes. If many processors are available, they spread out; if there are only a few, they pile up.)

3. It balances load dynamically, by default. Each worker process repeatedly searches for a task to execute, executes it, and loops. Tasks are therefore divided at runtime among the available workers.

It's important to note that most of the programs we've experimented with are not pure replicated-worker examples; they involve some partitioning as well as some replication of duties. It's also true that purely network-style programs may be written in Linda and may rely on distributed data structures. Linda programs that tend towards the replicated style seem to be the most idiomatic and interesting, though.

We illustrate with a simple example that doesn't exercise the mechanism fully, but makes some basic points. We've tested several matrix multiplication programs using S/Net-Linda. One version consists of a setup-cleanup process and at least one, but ordinarily many, worker processes. Each worker is repeatedly assigned some element of the product matrix to compute; it computes this assigned element and is assigned another, until all elements of the product matrix have been filled in. If $A$ and $B$ are the matrices to be multiplied, then specifically

1. The initialization process uses a succession of **out** statements to dump $A$'s rows and $B$'s columns into TS. When these statements have completed, TS holds

```
("A", 1, A's-first-row)
("A", 2, A's-second-row)
        .
        .
        .
("B", 1, B's-first-column)
("B", 2, B's-second-column)
        .
        .
        .
```

Indices are included as the second element of each tuple so that worker processes, using structured naming, can select the $i$th

row or $j$th column for reading. The initializer then adds the tuple

```
("Next", 1)
```

to TS and tèrminates. 1 indicates the next element to be computed.

2. Each worker process repeatedly decides on an element to compute, then computes it. To select a next element, the worker removes the "Next" tuple from TS, determines from its second field the indices of the product element to be computed next, and reinserts "Next" with an incremented second field:

```
in("Next", formal NextElem);
if(NextElem < dim * dim)
    out("Next", NextElem + 1);
i = (NextElem − 1)/dim + 1;
j = (NextElem − 1)%dim + 1;
```

The worker now proceeds to compute the product element whose index is $(i,j)$. Note that if $(i,j)$ is the last element of the product matrix, the "Next" tuple is not reinserted. When the other workers attempt to remove it, they will block. A Linda program terminates when all processes have terminated or have blocked at **in** or **read** statements.

To compute element $(i,j)$ of the product, the worker executes

```
read("A", i, formal row);
read("B", j, formal col);
out("result", i, j, DotProduct(row, col));
```

Thus each element of the product is packed in a separate tuple and dumped into TS. (Note that the first **read** statement picks out a tuple whose first element is "A" and second is the value of $i$; this tuple's third element is assigned to the formal *row*.)

3. The cleanup process reels in the product-element tuples, installs them in the result matrix *prod*, and prints *prod*:

```
for (row = 1; row < = NumRows; row++)
    for (col = 1; col < = NumCols; col++)
        in ("result", row, col, formal prod
            [row][col]);
    print prod;
```

This simple program depends entirely on distributed data structures. The input matrices are distributed data structures; all worker processes may read them simultaneously. In the manager-process model, processes would send read-requests to the appropriate manager and await its reply. The "Next" tuple is a distributed data structure; all worker processes share direct access to it. In the manager process model, again, worker processes would read and update the "Next" counter indirectly via a manager. The product matrix is a distributed data structure, which all workers participate in building simultaneously.

We discuss the performance of this program, and of another version that assigns coarser-grained tasks that compute an entire row rather than a single inner product, elsewhere.[3] Both versions show good speedup as we add processors up to the limited number available to us on our S/Net (currently eight). The version discussed above requires only two parallel workers and one control process to beat a conventional uniprocessor C program on $32 \times 32$ matrices, and continues to show linear speedup as we add workers. The coarser-grained version, with its lower communication overhead, shows speedup close to ideal linear speedup of the uniprocessor C version: our figures show close to a progressive doubling, tripling, and so on of the C program's speed as we add Linda workers.

The matrix program displays the uncoupling and dynamic-scheduling properties that we claimed above were important. Uncoupling: no worker deals directly with any other. Dynamic task scheduling: the matrix program assigns tasks to workers dynamically. But of course, in a problem as simple and regular as matrix multiplication, dynamic scheduling isn't important. We could just as well have assigned each of $n$ workers $1/n$ of the product matrix to compute. (It's interesting to note, however, that even with a problem as orderly as matrix multiplication, dynamic scheduling might be the technique of choice if we were running on a nonhomogeneous network, on which processors vary in speed and in runtime loading. We've been studying just such a network—a collection of VAXes ranging from MicroVAX I's to 8600's.)

Dynamic scheduling becomes important when tasks require varying amounts of time to complete. In the general case, moreover, new tasks may be developed dynamically as old ones are processed. Linda techniques to deal with this general problem are based on a distributed data structure called a *task bag*. Workers repeatedly draw their next assignment from the task bag, carry out the specified assignment, and drop any new tasks generated in the process back into the task bag. The program completes when the bag is empty. The scheme is easily imple-

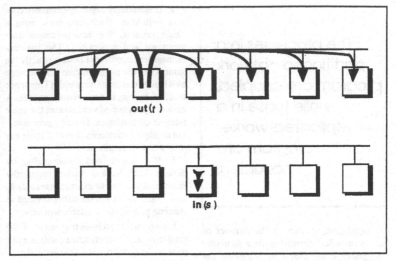

**Figure 7.** An S/Net kernel. (a) shows **out**: broadcast, while (b) shows **in**: check locally. (The inverse of this scheme is also possible.)

mented in Linda. Elements of the bag will be tuples of the form

("Task", task descriptor)

Each worker executes the following loop:

```
loop {
    /* withdraw a task from the bag: */
    in("Task", formal NextTask);
    process "NextTask";
    for (each NewTask generated in the
        process)
    /* drop the new task into the bag: */
    out("Task", NewTask);
}
```

We've experimented with programs of this sort to perform LU decomposition with pivoting and to find paths through a graph, among others. Note that, if it were necessary to process tasks in a particular order rather than in arbitrary order, we would build a task queue instead of a task bag. The technique would involve numbered tuples and structured naming.

## The S/Net's Linda kernel

Linda has often been regarded as posing a particularly difficult implementation problem. The difficulty lies in the fact that, as noted above, Linda supplies a form of logically-shared memory without assuming any physically-shared memory in the underlying hardware. The following

paragraphs summarize the way in which we implemented Linda on the S/Net (the S/Net implementation is discussed in detail elsewhere[3]); there are many other possible implementations as well.

Our implementation buys speed at the expense of communication bandwidth and local memory. The reasonableness of this trade-off was our starting point. (Possible variants are more conservative with local memory.)

Executing **out**($t$) causes tuple $t$ to be broadcast to every node in the network; every node stores a complete copy of TS. Executing **in**($s$) triggers a local search for a matching $t$. If one is found, the local kernel attempts to delete $t$ network-wide using a procedure we discuss below. If the attempt suceeds, $t$ is returned to the process that executed **in**(). (The attempt fails only if a process on some other node has simultaneously attempted to delete $t$, and has succeeded.) If the local search triggered by **in**($s$) turns up no matching tuple, all newly-arriving tuples are checked until a match occurs, at which point the matched tuple is deleted and returned as before. **read**() works in the same way as **in**(), except that no tuple-deletion need be attempted. As soon as a matching tuple is found, it is immediately returned to the reading process. See Figure 7.

The delete protocol must satisfy two requirements. First, all nodes must receive

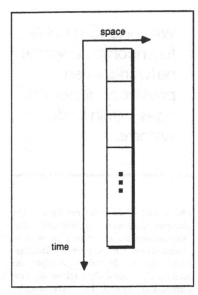

Figure 8. Execute sequentially.

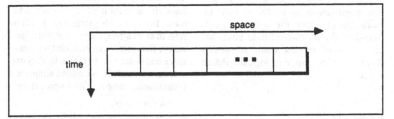

Figure 9. Execute in parallel.

the "delete" message, and second, if many processes attempt to delete simultaneously, only one must succeed. The manner in which these requirements are met will depend, of course, on the available hardware.

When some node fails to receive and buffer a broadcast message, a negative-acknowledgement signal is available on the S/Net bus. One possible delete protocol has two parts: The sending kernel rebroadcasts repeatedly until the negative-acknowlegement signal is not present. It then awaits an "ok to delete *t*" message from the node on which *t* originated. In this protocol the kernel on the tuple's origin node is responsible for allowing one process, and only one, to delete it. (We have implemented other protocols as well. Processes may use the bus as a semaphore to mediate multiple simultaneous deletes, for example, and avoid the use of a special "ok to delete" message.)

Evidence suggests that a minimal out-in transaction, from kernel entry on the out side to kernel exit on the in side, takes about 1.4 ms.

We are working on other implementations as well. The VAX-network Linda kernel (which was designed and is being

implemented by Jerry Leichter) uses a technique that is in a sense the inverse of the existing S/Net scheme. We're in the process of trying this new technique on the S/Net also. In the new protocol, out requires only a local install; in(*s*) causes template *s* to be broadcast to all nodes in the network. Whenever a node receives a template *s*, it checks *s* against all of its locally-stored tuples. If there is a match, it sends the matched tuple off to the template's node. If not, it stores the template for *x* ticks (checking all tuples newly-generated within this period against it), then throws it out. If the template's origin node hasn't received a matching tuple after *x* ticks, it rebroadcasts the template. More than one node may respond with a matching tuple to a template broadcast; when a template broadcaster receives more than one tuple, it simply installs the extras alongside its locally-generated tuples and sends them onward when they're needed. (In a more elaborate version, we can forestall the arrival of un-needed tuples by having potential senders monitor the bus, or by broadcasting an "I've got one, enough already" message at the appropriate point.) This scheme doesn't require hardware support for reliable broadcast and it doesn't require tuples to be replicated on each node, so per-node storage requirements are much lower.

The Linda kernel for the Intel iPSC hypercube, designed and implemented by Rob Bjornson, relies on point-to-point rather than broadcast communication. His scheme implements tuple space as a hash table distributed throughout the network. Each tuple is hashed on out to a unique network node and is sent there for storage. Templates are hashed and stored in the same way.

Finally, several of us (Bjornson, Carriero, Leichter, and Gelernter) have begun, in conjunction with Scientific Computing Associates, to design and implement a Linda kernel for the Encore Multimax. Nodes on the Multimax have direct access to physically shared memory. The Multimax Linda kernel should therefore be faster and simpler than the kernels described above, and in fact it is. The relationship between Linda and shared-memory multiprocessors like the Multimax is roughly similar to what holds between block-structured languages and stack architectures. The architecture strongly supports the language; the language refines the power of the architecture and makes it accessible to programmers. Of course, for all its promise, the Encore doesn't end our interest in networks like the S/Net. Shared memory seems ideal for small or medium-sized collections of processors. S/Net-like architectures, particularly the Linda machine we describe below, may well scale upwards to enormous sizes.

We have referred to Linda as a programming language, but it really isn't. It is a new machine model, in the same sense in which dataflow or graph-reduction may be regarded as machine models as much as programming methodologies. The kernels described above are software realizations of a Linda machine, but Ahuja and Venkatesh Krishnaswamy of Yale are designing a hardware Linda machine as well, based on the S/Net. The heart of the Linda machine is a box to be interposed between each processor and the S/Net bus. The box implements the Linda communication kernel in hardware, turning an ordinary bus into a tuple space. The current box is designed for the S/Net exclusively, but we are interested in general versions that will connect arbitrary nodes and communication media as well. Installation of either the software Linda kernel or the hardware Linda boxes has the effect of uniting many physically-disjoint nodes into one logically-shared space.

## Friends

Linda may be regarded as machine language for the Linda machine. We can in fact compile higher-level parallel languages into Linda. Higher-level languages may, for example, support shared variables that are directly accessible to parallel processes. If $v$ is a shared variable, the compiler might translate

    v: = expr

to

    in("v", formal v_value);
    out("v", *expr*)

and

    $f(...v,...)$

to

    read ("v", formal v_value);
    $f(...v\_value,...)$

We can support data objects like streams on top of Linda in the same general way.

The higher-level parallel languages that interest us particularly are the so-called symmetric languages. Symmetric languages are based on the proposition that, just as we can give names to arbitrary statement sequences and nest their execution in arbitrary ways, we should be able to name arbitrary horizontal combinations, or environments, and nest them in arbitrary ways.

Consider an arbitrary "execute sequentially" statement:

    s1; s2; ...; s*n*

We can represent the execution of this sequence at runtime as as in Figure 8. Each box represents the execution of one statement in the sequence. The boxes are stacked on top of each other; the evaluations of successive elements occupy disjoint intervals of time, but they may successively occupy the same space. (Thus if each *si* is a block that creates local variables, we can always reuse the previous block's storage space for the next block's variables, once evaluation of the previous block is complete.) Now suppose we transpose this structure around the time-space

axis, as in Figure 9. Again, each box represents the execution of a separate statement. In the resulting structure, which we refer to as an *alpha*, the evaluations of successive elements occupy disjoint regions of space and share one time; that is, they execute concurrently. If we added alphas to a programming language and wrote them

    s1& s2& ...& s*n*,

the resulting statement calls for the execution of all *si* in parallel.

Suppose we add one more element to the alpha's definition. In most programming languages, a local variable's scope is specified explicitly and its lifetime is inferred from its scope by the following simple rule: A variable must live for at least as long as the statements that refer to it, so that they may be assured of finding it when they look. In symmetric languages we reverse this rule and infer scope from lifetime: If a variable is guaranteed to live for at least as long as a group of statements, then those statements may refer to it because they are assured of finding it when they look. Now consider the alpha: Execution of an alpha as a whole can't be complete until each of its components has executed to completion. (The same rule holds for the standard "execute sequentially" form.) Because alpha execution isn't complete until every component has been fully evaluated, no box in the alpha representation above will disappear until they all do. It follows that, if we store a named variable instead of an executable statement inside some box, then that variable should be accessible to statements in adjacent boxes, because the variable and the statement live for the same interval of time. The statement is therefore assured of finding the variable when it looks for it. Hence, symmetric languages will use alphas to create blocks as well as to create parallel-execution streams. For example, the Pascal block

    var i: real; j: integer; **begin ... end**

becomes

    i: real& j: integer& **begin ... end**

in Symmetric Pascal.

The alpha can in fact be used as a flexible computational cupboard. We can store any assortment of named values and active processes in its slots. Symmetric languages use alphas to serve the purpose of a Pascal record, of a Simula class or Scheme closure, of a package or a module,

> We'd like to be able to encompass whole networks, even physically-dispersed ones, within Linda systems.

and in fact of an entire program or environment. All symmetric languages naturally encompass interpreted as well as compiled execution. A symmetric-language interpreter simply builds an alpha incrementally, repeatedly tacking on new elements at the end. This incrementally-growing alpha is the interpreter's environment. Because the elements of an alpha may be evaluated in parallel, the symmetric interpreter is a parallel interpreter: Each new expression the user enters is evaluated in a separate process, concurrently with all previous expressions. The values returned by all these concurrent evaluations coalesce into a single shared naming environment.

This is a mere sketch. Symmetric languages are discussed in detail elsewhere. [4] We are particularly interested in Symmetric C and Symmetric Lisp; either may be implemented on top of the runtime environment provided by the Linda kernel.

## The future

We have many future plans.

The semantics of a tuple space allow it, like a file, to exist independently of any particular process or program. A tuple space might in the abstract outlive many invocations of the same program. What we'd like, then, is for tuple spaces to be regarded as a special sort of file (or equivalently, for files to be special tuple spaces). We'd like to be able to keep tuple spaces along with files in hierarchical directories. With many tuple spaces to choose from, Linda processes must be given a way to indicate which one is the current one. Once some such mechanism has been provided, the availability of multiple tuple spaces greatly expands the system's capabilities. We can associate different protection attributes with different tuple spaces, just as we do with different files. We can use tuple spaces to support communication between user and system processes by making tuple spaces available for **out** only, **read** only, and so on. We can also allow **in** operations that remove whole tuple spaces at one blow and **outs** that add whole tuple spaces. The design and implementation of such an extension is a goal for the immediate future.

It's clear that Linda can be an interpreted command language as well as a compiled one. It would be useful to allow users to add, read, and remove tuples from active tuple spaces interactively. We've taken some preliminary steps towards implementing such a system. We'd like, too, to be able to encompass whole networks, even physically-dispersed ones, within Linda systems. We can then use Linda to write distributed network utilities like mailers and file systems. Our work on the VAX-network implementation is leading toward experiments of this sort.

Finally, we imagine, as an object of prime interest for the future, an enormous Linda machine highly optimized to support Linda primitives. We don't yet know how to build such a machine, but it's hard not to notice that very large networks with small diameters might be constructed out of multidimensional grids of S/Net-like buses. Having built such a machine, we imagine tuple space itself as the machine's main memory. (Outside of tuple space, only registers and local caches exist.) As the Linda primitives become faster and more efficient, such an architecture looks more and more like a sort of dataflow machine, but with a crucial difference. As in a dataflow machine, we can create task templates (stored in tuples), update them with new values as they become available, and mark them "enabled" when all values are filled in. General-purpose evaluator processes, much like the replicated workers discussed above, use **in** to pick out task tuples marked "enabled." But unlike the token space of a dataflow machine, a Linda machine's tuple space can store data structures as well as task descriptors. Processes are free to build whatever (distributed) data structures they want, and manipulate and side-effect them as they choose. We might even use such a Linda machine to store large databases operated upon in parallel.

Such work is for the future. We still lack a polished Linda implementation on any machine. We hope to have one soon. And clearly we can learn a great deal by continuing to refine and to experiment with Linda kernels for present-generation architecture. This is what we plan to do.□

## References

1. J. T. Deutsch and A. R. Newton, "MSplice: A Multiprocessor-based Circuit Simulator," *Proc. 1984 Int'l Conf. Parallel Processing*, Aug. 1984, pp. 207-214.

2. G. F. Pfister et al., "The IBM Research Parallel Processor (RP3): Introduction and Architecture," *Proc. 1985 Int'l Conf. Parallel Processing*, Aug. 1985.

3. N. Carriero and D. Gelernter, "The S/Net's Linda Kernel," *Proc. Symp. Operating System Principles*, Dec. 1985, and *ACM TOCS*, May 1986.

4. D. Gelernter, "Symmetric Programming Languages," Yale Univ. Dept. Comp. Sci. tech. report yaleu/dcs/ rr#253, Dec. 1984.

## Acknowledgments

Rob Bjornson, Venkatesh Krishnaswamy, and Jerry Leichter are our collaborators in the Yale Linda group. Thanks also to Erik DeBenedictis, Robert Gaglianello, Howard Katseff, and Thomas London of AT&T Bell Labs.

# Distributed Programming with Shared Data

*Henri E. Bal*     *Andrew S. Tanenbaum*

Dept. of Computer Science
Vrije Universiteit
Amsterdam, The Netherlands

### ABSTRACT

Until recently, at least one thing was clear about parallel programming: tightly coupled (shared memory) machines were programmed in a language based on shared variables and loosely coupled (distributed) systems were programmed using message passing. The explosive growth of research on distributed systems and their languages, however, has led to several new methodologies that blur this simple distinction. Operating system primitives (e.g., problem-oriented shared memory, Shared Virtual Memory, the Agora shared memory) and languages (e.g., Concurrent Prolog, Linda, Emerald) for programming distributed systems have been proposed that support the shared variable paradigm without the presence of physical shared memory. In this paper we will look at the reasons for this evolution, the resemblances and differences among these new proposals, and the key issues in their design and implementation. It turns out that many implementations are based on replication of data. We take this idea one step further, and discuss how automatic replication (initiated by the run time system) can be used as a basis for a new model, called the shared data-object model, whose semantics are similar to the shared variable model. Finally, we discuss the design of a new language for distributed programming, Orca, based on the shared data-object model.

## 1. INTRODUCTION

Parallel computers of the MIMD (Multiple Instruction Multiple Data) class are traditionally divided into two broad subcategories: tightly coupled and loosely coupled systems. In a tightly coupled system at least part of the primary memory is *shared*. All processors have direct access to this shared memory, in one machine instruction. In a loosely coupled (*distributed*) system, processors only have access to their own local memories; processors can communicate by sending messages over a communication channel, such as a point-to-point link or a local area network [1]. Tightly coupled systems have the significant advantage of fast communication through shared memory. Distributed systems, on the other hand, are much easier to build, especially if a large number of processors is required.

Initially, programming language and operating system designers strictly followed the above classification, resulting in two parallel programming paradigms: shared variables (for tightly coupled systems) and message passing (for distributed systems). Some languages and operating systems for uniprocessors or shared-memory multiprocessors support processes that communicate via message passing (e.g., MINIX [2]). More recently, the dual approach, applying the shared variable paradigm to distributed systems, has become a popular research topic. At first sight, this approach may seem to be against the grain, as the message passing paradigm much better matches the primitives provided by the distributed hardware. For sequential languages, however, we have become quite used to programming paradigms like functional, logic, and object-oriented programming, which do not directly reflect the underlying architecture either.

This research was supported in part by the Netherlands Organization for Scientific Research (N.W.O.) under grant 125-30-10.

The purpose of this paper is twofold. First, we will classify existing techniques for providing conceptual shared memory by looking at their most important similarities and differences. Analysis of the semantics shows that many proposals are not strictly like message passing nor like shared variables, but somewhere in between. In other words, there exists a *spectrum* of communication mechanisms, of which shared variables and message passing are the two extremes. Most primitives towards the shared-variable end of the spectrum use *replication* of data for an efficient distributed implementation.

The second purpose of the paper is to discuss a new model providing conceptual shared memory and a new programming language, Orca, based on this model. Unlike most other languages for distributed programming, Orca is intended for distributed application programming rather than systems programming. A major issue in its design was to keep the language as simple as possible and to exclude features that are only useful for systems programming. The simple design has been realized by using an intelligent run time system, which dynamically decides where to store data and how to replicate data.

Some theoretical work has been done in the area of simulating shared memory in distributed systems [3,4]. In these studies, a distributed system is usually regarded as a (possibly incomplete) graph, where nodes represent processors and arcs represent communication channels. These studies typically aim at minimizing the number of messages needed to read or write a simulated shared variable. In this paper, we are more interested in real-life distributed computing systems (like those advocated by V [5] and Amoeba [6]). In such systems, all processes can directly communicate with each other, although communication between processes on different processors is expensive. These systems frequently support additional communication primitives, like multicast and broadcast.

## 2. SHARED VARIABLES AND MESSAGE PASSING

Communication through shared variables probably is the oldest paradigm in parallel programming. Many operating systems for uni-processors are structured as collections of processes, executing in quasi-parallel, and communicating through shared variables. Synchronizing access to shared data has been a research topic since the early sixties. Numerous programming languages exist that use shared variables.

The semantics of the model are fairly simple, except for what happens when two processes simultaneously try to write (or read and write) the same variable. The semantics may either define simple reads and writes to be indivisible (conflicting reads or writes are serialized) or may leave the effect of simultaneous writes undefined.

The basis for message passing as a programming language construct is Hoare's classic paper on CSP [7]. A message in CSP is sent from one process (the sender) to one other process (the receiver). The sender waits until the receiver has accepted the message (*synchronous* message passing).

Many variations of message passing have been proposed [8,9]. With *asynchronous* message passing, the sender continues immediately after sending the message. Remote procedure call and rendez-vous are two-way interactions between two processes. Broadcast and multicast are interactions between one sender and many receivers [10]. Communication ports or mailboxes can be used to avoid explicit addressing of processes.

Below, we will describe the most important differences between the two extremes of our spectrum: shared variables and simple (synchronous and asynchronous) message passing. Some of the extensions to message passing mentioned above make the differences less profound.

- A message transfers information between two processes, which must both exist (be alive) when the interaction takes place. At least the sender must know the identity of the receiver. Data stored in a shared variable is accessible to any process. Processes interacting through shared variables need not even have overlapping lifetimes or know about each other's existence. They just have to know the address of the shared variable.

- An assignment to a shared variable has immediate effect. In contrast, there is a measurable delay between sending a message and its being received. For asynchronous message passing, for example, this has some ramifications for the order in which messages are received. Usually, the semantics are *order-preserving*: messages between a pair of processes are received in the same order they were sent. With more than two processes, the delay still has to be taken into account. Suppose Process $P_1$ sends a message $X$ to $P_2$ and then to $P_3$. Upon receiving $X$, $P_3$ sends a message $Y$ to $P_2$. There is no guarantee that $P_2$ will receive $X$ before $Y$.

- Message passing intuitively is more *secure* than sharing variables. Security means that one program module cannot effect the correctness of other modules (e.g., by a "wild store" through a bad pointer). The feasibility of a secure message passing language was demonstrated by NIL [11]. Shared variables can be changed by any process, so security is a bigger problem. One solution is to use *monitors*, which encapsulate data and serialize all operations on the data.

- A message exchanges information, but it also *synchronizes* processes. The receiver waits for a message to arrive; with synchronous message passing, the sender also waits for the receiver to be ready. With shared variables, two different types of synchronization are useful [8]. *Mutual exclusion* prevents simultaneous writes (or reads and writes) of the same variable; *condition synchronization* allows a process to wait for a certain condition to be true. Processes can synchronize through shared variables by using busy-waiting (polling), but this behavior is undesirable, as it wastes processor cycles. Better mechanisms are semaphores, eventcounts, and condition variables.

The message passing model has some additional implementation problems, as noted, for example, by Kai Li [12]. Passing a complex data structure to a remote process is difficult. Processes cannot easily be moved (migrated) to another processor, making efficient process management more complicated. The shared variable model does not suffer from these problems.

## 3. IN BETWEEN SHARED VARIABLES AND MESSAGE PASSING

The shared variable and message passing paradigms each have their own advantages and disadvantages. It should come as no surprise that language and operating system designers have looked at primitives that are somewhere in between these two extremes, and that share the advantages of both. In this section, we will discuss several such approaches.

In theory, a shared variable can simply be simulated on a distributed system by storing it on one processor and letting other processors read and write it with remote procedure calls. In most distributed systems, however, a remote procedure call is two to four orders of magnitude slower than reading local data. (Even Spector [13] reports an overhead of 150 microseconds for a certain class of remote references, despite a highly tuned, microcoded implementation). This difference makes a straightforward simulation unattractive.

Most systems described in this section offer primitives that have some properties of shared variables and some of message passing. The semantics are somewhere in between shared variables and message passing. Often, the data are only accessible by some of the processes and only through some specific operations. These restrictions make the primitives

more secure than regular shared variables and make an efficient implementation possible even if physical shared memory is absent.

We will discuss four key issues for every primitive:

- What are the *semantics* of the primitive?
- How are shared data *addressed*?
- How is access to shared data *synchronized*?
- How can the primitive be *implemented efficiently* without using physical shared memory?

We will first discuss proposals that are "close" to message passing; subsequent designs are increasingly similar to shared variables. The results are summarized in Figure 1 at the end of this section.

### 3.1. Communication Ports

In CSP-like languages, interacting processes must explicitly name each other. For many applications (e.g., those based on the client/server model) this is inconvenient. A solution is to send messages indirectly through a *communication port* [14]. A port or mailbox is a variable where messages can be sent to or received from.

A port can be regarded as a shared *queue* data structure, with the following operations defined on it:

```
send(msg,q);  # Append message to end of queue.
msg := receive(q);  # Wait until queue not empty;
                    # get message from head of queue.
```

The latter operation also synchronizes processes. Ports can be addressed like normal variables. The implementation is fairly straightforward; a buffer is needed to store messages sent but not yet received.

Although the semantics of ports are essentially those of asynchronous message passing, it is interesting to note that ports can be described as shared data structures with specialized access operations.

### 3.2. Ada's shared variables

Processes (tasks) in Ada* can communicate through the rendez-vous mechanism or through shared variables. Shared variables in Ada are normal variables that happen to be visible to several tasks, as defined by the Ada scope rules. In an attempt to make the language implementable on memory-disjunct architectures, special rules for shared variables were introduced (section 9.11 of the language reference manual [15]). Between synchronization points (i.e., normal rendez-vous communication), two tasks sharing a variable cannot make any assumptions about the order in which the other task performs operations on the variable. In essence, this rule permits a distributed implementation to use copies (replicas) of shared variables and to update these copies only on rendez-vous.

The semantics of Ada's shared variables are quite different from normal shared variables, as updates do not have immediate effect. Also, other features of the language design complicate a distributed implementation [16]. Introducing conceptual shared data this way does not seem like a major breakthrough in elegant language design, but it does illustrate the idea of replication.

### 3.3. The object model

Object-oriented languages are becoming increasingly popular, not only for writing sequential programs, but also for implementing parallel applications. Different languages have different definitions of the term "object," but in general an object encapsulates both *data* and *behavior*. Concurrent languages that are strongly influenced by the object-oriented programming paradigm include: ABCL/1 [17], Aeolus [18], Concurrent-Smalltalk [19], Emerald [20], Raddle [21], and Sloop [22].

An object in a concurrent object-based language can be considered as shared data that are accessible only through a set of *operations* defined by the object. These operations are invoked by sending a message to the

---

*Ada is a registered trademark of the U.S. Dept. of Defense, Ada Joint Program Office

object. Operation invocation can either be asynchronous (the invoker continues immediately after sending the message) or synchronous (the invoker waits until the operation has been completed).

Objects are usually addressed by an object *reference* (returned upon creation of the object) or by a global object name. To synchronize access to (shared) objects, several approaches are conceivable. Emerald uses a monitor-like construct to synchronize multiple operation invocations to the same object. Sloop supports *indivisible* objects, for which only one operation invocation at a time is allowed to execute. For condition synchronization, Sloop allows operations to suspend on a boolean expression, causing the invoking process to block until the expression is "true."

A key issue in a distributed implementation of objects is to locate objects on those processors that use them most frequently. Both Emerald and Sloop allow (but do not enforce) the programmer to control the locations of objects; these locations can be changed dynamically (object migration). Alternatively, the placement of objects can be left entirely to the run time system. For this purpose, Sloop dynamically maintains statistical information about the program's communication patterns. Some language implementations also support replication of immutable (read-only) objects.

The object model already presents the illusion of shared data. Access to the shared data is restricted to some well-defined operations, making the model more secure than the simple shared variable model. Synchronization can easily be integrated with the operations. In Sloop, operations are invoked by asynchronous messages, so the semantics of Sloop still resemble message passing. Emerald uses synchronous operation invocations, resulting in a model closer to shared variables.

### 3.4. Problem-oriented shared memory

Cheriton [23] has proposed a kind of shared memory that can be tailored to a specific application, the so-called problem-oriented shared memory. The shared memory can be regarded as a distributed system service, implemented on multiple processors. Data are stored (replicated) on one or more of these processors, and may also be cached on client workstations.

The semantics of the problem-oriented shared memory are tuned to the needs of the application using it. In general, the semantics are more relaxed than those of shared variables. In particular, inconsistent copies of the same data are allowed to coexist temporarily, so a "read" operation does not necessarily return the value stored by the most recent "write." There are several different approaches to deal with these *stale* data, for example to let the applications programmer worry about it, or to let the shared memory guarantee a certain degree of accurateness (e.g., a shared variable containing the "time of the day" can be kept accurate within, say, 5 seconds).

The problem-oriented shared memory is addressed also in an application specific way. Addresses are broadcast to the server processors. There is no special provision to synchronize processes (processes can synchronize using message passing).

The implementation significantly benefits from the relaxed semantics. Most important, it does not have to use complicated schemes to atomically update all copies of the same data.

### 3.5. The Agora shared memory

The Agora shared memory allows processes written in different languages and executing on different types of machines to communicate [24]. It has been implemented on closely coupled as well as loosely coupled architectures, using the Mach operating system.

The memory contains shared data structures, accessible through an (extendible) set of standard functions. These functions are available (e.g., as library routines) in all languages supported by the system. A shared data structure is organized as a set of immutable data elements, accessed indirectly through (mutable) *maps*. A map maps an index (integer or string) onto the address of a data element. To change an element of the set, a new element must be added and the map updated accordingly. Elements that are no longer accessible are automatically garbage collected.

Exclusive access to a data structure is provided by a standard function that applies a user function to a data structure. For condition synchronization, a pattern-directed mechanism is supported. For example, a process can wait until a certain element is added to a set.

The implementation is based on replication of data structures on reference. As in Cheriton's model, read operations may return stale data.

### 3.6. Tuple Space

The Tuple Space is a novel synchronization mechanism, designed by David Gelernter for his language Linda [25,26]. The Tuple Space is a global memory containing *tuples*, which are similar to records in Pascal. For example, the tuple "["Miami", 305]" consists of a string field and an integer field. Tuple Space is manipulated by three atomic operations: **out** adds a tuple to Tuple Space, **read** reads an existing tuple, and **in** reads and deletes a tuple. Note that there is no operation to *change* an existing tuple. Instead, the tuple must first be removed from Tuple Space, and later be put back.

Unlike all other conceptual shared memory systems discussed in this paper, Tuple Space is addressed *associatively* (by contents). A tuple is denoted by supplying actual or formal parameters for every field. The tuple mentioned above can be read and removed, for example, by

> **in**("Miami", 305);

or by

> **integer** areacode;
> **in**("Miami", **var** areacode);

In the latter case, the formal parameter *areacode* is assigned the value 305.

Both **read** and **in** block until a matching tuple exists in Tuple Space. If two processes simultaneously try to remove (**in**) the same tuple, only one of them will succeed and the other one will block. As tuples have to be removed before being changed, simultaneous updates are automatically synchronized.

Although the semantics of Tuple Space are significantly different from shared variables (e.g., it lacks assignment), the Tuple Space clearly gives the illusion of a shared memory. The Tuple Space has been implemented on machines with shared memory (Encore Multimax, Sequent Balance) as well as on memory-disjunct machines (iPSC hypercube, S/Net, Ethernet based network of MicroVaxes). A distributed implementation can benefit from the availability of multicast [27]. As associative addressing is potentially expensive, several compile-time optimizations have been devised to make it reasonably efficient [28].

### 3.7. Shared virtual memory

Kai Li has extended the concept of *virtual memory* to distributed systems, resulting in a *shared virtual memory* [12]. This memory is accessible by all processes and is addressed like traditional virtual memory. Li's system guarantees memory *coherence*: the value returned by a "read" always is the value stored by the last "write."

The address space is partitioned into a number of fixed-size *pages*. At any point in time, several processors may have a *read-only* copy of the same page; alternatively, a single processor may have a *read-and-write* copy.

If a process tries to write on a certain page while its processor does not have a read-and-write copy of it, a "write page-fault" occurs. The fault-handling routine tells other processors to *invalidate* their copies, fetches a copy of the page (if it did not have one yet), sets the protection mode to read-and-write, and resumes the faulting instruction.

If a process wants to read a page, but does not have a copy of it, a "read page-fault" occurs. If any processor has a read-and-write copy of the page, this processor is instructed to change the protection to read-only. A copy of the page is fetched and the faulting instruction is resumed.

Shared Virtual Memory is addressed like normal virtual memory. An implementation may support several synchronization mechanisms, such as semaphores, eventcounts, and monitors.

| technique | semantics | addressing | synchronization | implementation |
|---|---|---|---|---|
| Comm. ports | shared queues | variables | blocking receive() | straight message passing |
| Ada's shared variables | weird | variables | rendez-vous | replication, updates on rendez-vous |
| object model | shared objects | object-references | indivisible objects, blocking oper. | object migration, repl. read-only objects |
| problem-oriented shared memory | shared mem. with stale data | application-specific | through messages | replication, multicast |
| Agora shared memory | shared data struct. stale data | flat name space | pattern-directed | replication on reference |
| Tuple Space (Linda) | shared memory, no assignment | associatively | blocking read() and in() | compile-time analysis, replication, multicast |
| shared virtual memory | shared mem. | linear address space | semaphores, eventcounts, etc. | MMU, replication, multicast |
| shared logical variables | logical var. (single assignm.) | unification | suspend on unbound vars. | replication on reference |

Fig. 1. Overview of conceptual shared memory techniques

The shared virtual memory can be used to simulate true shared variables, with exactly the right semantics. The implementation uses the hardware Memory Management Unit and can benefit from the availability of multicast (e.g., to invalidate all copies of a page). Several strategies exist to deal with the problem of multiple simultaneous writes and to administrate which processors contain copies of a page [12]. The entire scheme will perform very poorly if processes on many different processors repeatedly write on the same page. Migrating these processes to the same processor is one possible cure to this problem.

### 3.8. Shared logical variables

Most concurrent logic programming languages (PARLOG [29,30], Concurrent Prolog [31,32], Flat Concurrent Prolog) use shared logical variables as communication channels. Shared logical variables have the *single-assignment* property: once they are bound to a value (or to another variable) they cannot be changed. (In "sequential" logic languages, variables may receive another value after backtracking; most concurrent logic languages eliminate backtracking, however.) Single-assignment is not a severe restriction, because a logical variable can be bound to a structure containing one or more other, unbound variables, which can be used for future communication. In fact, many communication patterns can be expressed using shared logical variables [31].

Synchronization in concurrent logic languages resembles data-flow synchronization: processes can (implicitly) wait for a variable to be bound. Shared logical variables provide a clean semantic model, resembling normal logic variables. Addressing also is the same for both types of variables (i.e., through unification).

The single-assignment property allows the model to be implemented with reasonable efficiency on a distributed system. An implementation of Flat Concurrent Prolog on a Hypercube is described in [33]. If a process tries to read a logical variable stored on a remote processor, the remote processor adds the process to a list associated with the variable. As soon as the variable gets bound (if it was not already), its value is sent to all processes on the list. These processes will keep the value for future reference. In this way, variables are automatically replicated on reference.

### 3.9. Discussion

Figure 1 summarizes the most important properties of the techniques we discussed. The systems differ widely in their semantics and addressing and synchronization mechanisms. A key issue in the implementation is *replication*. Multicast is frequently used to speed up the implementation.

Replication of data has already been used for a long time in distributed databases to increase the availability of data in the presence of processor failures. Replication introduces a severe problem: the possibility of having inconsistent copies of the same logical data. For databases, several solutions exist [34]. Typically, multiple copies of the same data are accessed when reading or writing data.

The techniques discussed in this section use replication to decrease the *access time* to shared data, rather than to increase availability. Therefore, it is unattractive to consult several processors on every access to the data. Instead, just the local copy should suffice for as many accesses as possible. With this restriction, different solutions must be found to deal with the consistency problem.

Figure 1 shows three different ways of dealing with inconsistency. Ada, the problem-oriented shared memory, and the Agora shared memory relax the semantics of the shared memory. The latter two systems allow "read" operations to return stale data. Higher level protocols must be used by the programmer to solve inconsistency problems. Ada requires copies to be updated only on rendez-vous.

The second approach (used for objects, Tuple Space, and shared logical variables) is to replicate only *immutable* data (data that cannot be changed). This significantly reduces the complexity of the problem, but it may also introduce new problems. The approach is most effective in languages using single-assignment. Such languages, however, will need a complicated distributed garbage algorithm to get rid of unaccessible data. In Linda, tuples are immutable objects. A tuple can conceptually be changed by first taking it out of Tuple Space, storing it in normal (local) variables. After changing these local data, they can be put back in a new tuple. As tuples are accessed by contents, it makes little difference that the old tuple has been replaced by a new one, instead of being modified while in Tuple Space. As a major advantage of doing the modification outside Tuple Space, updates by different processes are automatically synchronized. On the other hand, a small modification to a large tuple (like setting a bit in a 100K bitvector) will be expensive, as the tuple has to be copied twice.

The third approach to the consistency problem is exemplified by the shared virtual memory: use protocols that guarantee memory coherence. Before changing a page, all copies of the page are invalidated, so subsequent reads will never return stale data. Great care must be taken in the implementation, however, to avoid thrashing. For badly behaving programs, the system may easily spend most of its time moving and invalidating pages.

## 4. THE SHARED DATA-OBJECT MODEL

We have developed a new conceptual shared-memory model, called the *shared data-object* model. In this model, shared data are encapsulated in passive objects. The data contained by the object are only accessible through a set of *operations* defined by the object's type. Objects are instances of *abstract data types*. Unlike, say, Emerald and Sloop, we do not consider objects to be active entities; neither do we consider all entities in the system to be objects.

Parallel activity originates from the dynamic creation of multiple sequential (single-threaded) processes. When a process spawns a child process, it can pass any of its objects as **shared** parameters to the child. The children can pass the object to *their* children, and so on. In this way, the object gets distributed among some of the descendants of the process that declared the object. All these processes *share* the object and can perform the same set of operations on it, as defined by the object's type. Changes to the object made by one process are visible to other processes, so a shared data-object is a communication channel between processes. This mechanism is similar to call-by-sharing in CLU [35].

The shared data-object model has many advantages over regular shared variables. Access to shared data is only allowed through operations defined by an abstract data type. All these operations are *indivisible*. Simultaneous operation invocations of the same object have the effect as if they were executed one by one, so access to shared data is automatically synchronized. Blocking operations are used for condition synchronization of processes, as will be explained later.

### 4.1. Implementing shared data-objects in a distributed system

Shared data-objects are a simple, secure mechanism for sharing data and synchronizing access to the data. The design cannot be judged, however, without also considering the implementation. The distributed implementation we have designed is based on *selective replication* and *migration* of objects, under full control of the run time system. The compiler distinguishes between two kinds of operations:

- a "read" operation does not modify the object; it is performed on a local copy, if one exists.

- a "write" operation may read and write the object's data; it affects all copies.

For sake of clarity, we will use a simplified view of our model to describe its implementation. In particular, we will assume an object to contain a single integer and we will consider only two operations:

```
operation read(x: object): integer;
    # return current value
operation write(x: object; val: integer);
    # store new value
```

The run time system dynamically keeps track of how many times processors perform remote read and write operations on each object. If a processor frequently reads a remote object, it is profitable for it to maintain a local copy of the object. The execution time overhead of maintaining the statistics is neglectable compared with the time needed to do remote references. The space overhead is not a real concern either, considering the current state of memory technology.

A major issue in implementing replication is how to propagate changes made to the data. Two approaches are possible: invalidating all-but-one copies of the data, or updating all copies. Kai Li's Shared Virtual Memory uses invalidation. In our model, invalidation is indeed feasible, but it has some disadvantages. First, if an object is big (e.g., a 100K bitvector) it is wasteful to invalidate its copies, especially if an operation changes only a small part (e.g., 1 bit). In this case, it is far more efficient to apply the operation to all copies, hence updating all copies. Second, if an object is small (e.g., an integer), sending the new value is probably just as expensive as sending an invalidation message. Although update algorithms are more complicated than invalidation algorithms, we think it is useful to study them.

A related issue is how to synchronize simultaneous operation invocations that try to modify the same object. To serialize such invocations we appoint one replica of the object as *primary copy*, direct all "write" operations to this primary copy, and then propagate them to the secondary copies. An alternative approach would be to treat all copies as equals and use a distributed locking protocol to provide mutual exclusion. The primary copy method, however, allows one important optimization: the primary copy can be migrated to the processor that most frequently changes the object, making updates more efficient. The statistical information described above is also used for this purpose.

### 4.2. Dealing with inconsistency

The presence of multiple copies of the same data introduces the consistency problem discussed in section 3.9. As we do not want to clutter up the semantics of our model, the implementation should adequately solve this problem. In the following sections we will describe such implementations for different kinds of distributed architectures.

To deal with the consistency problem, we will first need a deeper understanding of the problem itself. Suppose we implement our model as follows. To update an object $X$, its primary copy is locked and a message containing the new value of $X$ is sent to all processors containing a secondary copy. Such a processor updates its copy and then sends an acknowledgement back. When all messages have been acknowledged, the primary copy is updated and unlocked.

During the update protocol some processors have received the new value of $X$ while others still use its old value. This is intuitively unappealing, but by itself is not the real problem. Far more important, not all processors will observe modifications to different objects in the same *order*. As a simple example, consider the program in Figure 2.

```
X,Y: shared object;  # initially 0

Process P₁:
    for i := 1 to ∞ do
        write(X, i);

Process P₂:
    repeat
        y := read(Y); x := read(X);
        if x > y then
            write(Y, x);

Process P₃:
    repeat
        y := read(Y); x := read(X);
        assert x ≥ y;
```

Fig. 2. Example program.

$P_2$ tries to keep $Y$ up-to-date with $X$; $P_3$ verifies that $X$ is greater than or equal to $Y$. Clearly, the latter condition should always be true.

Now suppose $X$ and $Y$ are replicated as shown in Figure 3. $P_1$ contains the primary copy of $X$, $P_2$ and $P_3$ have secondary copies. $P_2$ has the primary copy of $Y$, $P_3$ has a secondary copy.
The following sequence of events may happen:

1.  $X$ is incremented and becomes 1; $P_1$ sends an update message to $P_2$ and $P_3$.

2.  $P_2$ receives the update message, assigns 1 to the variable $Y$ and sends an update message of $Y$ to $P_3$.

3.  $P_3$ receives the update message from $P_2$, puts the value 1 in its copy of $Y$, and is surprised to see that $Y$ now is greater than $X$ (which still contains 0).

4.  $P_3$ receives the update message from $P_1$, and stores the value 1 in its copy of $X$.

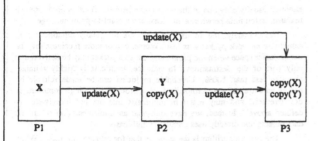

**Fig. 3.** Distribution of X and Y.

$P_3$ observes the changes to X and Y in the wrong order. The problem is caused by the arbitrary amount of time that messages may take to travel from the source to the destination and by the inability to transfer information simultaneously from one source to many destinations. Such an implementation basically provides message passing semantics disguised in shared variable syntax.

The solution to the consistency problem depends very much on the architecture of the underlying distributed system. We will discuss solutions for three different classes of architectures: systems supporting point-to-point messages, reliable multicast, and unreliable multicast respectively.

### 4.3. Implementation with point-to-point messages

One model of a distributed system is a collection of processors that communicate by sending point-to-point messages to each other. A communication path between any two processors is provided, either by the hardware or the software. Messages are delivered reliably, in the same order they were sent.

To implement consistent updating of objects in such a system, we use a *2-phase update* protocol. During the first phase, the primary copy is updated and locked, and an update message is sent to all processors containing a secondary copy. Unlike in the incorrect protocol outlined above, all secondary copies are locked (and remain locked) before being updated. A user process that tries to read a locked copy blocks until the lock is released (during the second phase). When all update messages have been acknowledged (i.e., all copies are updated and locked), the second phase begins. The primary copy is unlocked and a message is sent to all processors containing a secondary copy, instructing them to unlock their copies.

To implement the protocol, we use one *manager process* for every processor. We assume the manager process and user processes on the same processor can share part of their address space. Objects (and replicas) are stored in this shared address space. Write operations on shared objects are directed to the manager of the processor containing the primary copy; user processes can directly *read* local copies, although they may temporarily block, as described above. Each manager process contains multiple threads of control. One thread communicates with remote managers; the remaining threads are created dynamically to handle write-operations. So multiple write-operations to different objects may be in progress simultaneously; write-operations to the same object are serialized, as discussed below.

Upon receiving a request from a (possibly remote) user process W to perform an operation "write(X, Val)," the manager of X creates a new thread of control to handle the request:

```
receive write-req(X, Val) from W →
    fork handle_write(X, Val, W);
```

The process "handle_write" is defined by the following algorithm:

```
process handle_write(X, Val, W);
begin
    set write-lock on X;
    store Val in X;
    let S = set of processors having a copy of X;
    # first phase
    forall P ∈ S do
        send update-and-lock(X, Val) to manager of P;
    for i := 1 to |S| do
        receive ack;
    # second phase
    forall P ∈ S do
        send unlock(X) to manager of P
    unlock X;
    send ack to W;
end;
```

The process issuing the write request waits until it receives an acknowledgement. A manager responds as follows to messages from remote managers:

```
receive update-and-lock(X, Val) from P →
    set write-lock on local copy of X;
    store Val in local copy of X;
    send ack to P;

receive unlock(X) →
    unlock local copy of X;
```

The 2-phase update protocol guarantees that no process uses the new value of an object while other processes are still using the old value. The new value is not used until the second phase. When the second phase begins, all copies contain the new value. Simultaneous write-operations on the same object are serialized by locking the primary copy. The next write-operation may start before all secondary copies are unlocked. New requests to *update-and-lock* a secondary copy are not serviced until the *unlock* message generated by the previous write has been handled (recall that point-to-point messages are received in the order they were sent).

Deadlock is prevented by using multi-threaded managers. Setting a write-lock on a primary copy may block one thread of a manager, but not an entire manager process. Locking a secondary copy always succeeds within a finite amount of time, provided that all read-operations terminate properly.

If an object has N secondary copies it takes 3*N messages to update all these copies. Reading a remote object takes 2 messages (one request, one reply). So, objects should only be replicated on processors that read the object at least twice before it is changed again. This can be determined (or estimated) dynamically, as discussed earlier. The protocol can easily be optimized into a 1-phase update protocol if an object has only one secondary copy.

For a small object (like an integer) that is frequently changed, it may be more efficient to invalidate copies when the object is changed and to replicate it on reference. The first read-operation after a write fetches the object from a remote processor and creates a local copy. Subsequent reads use this local copy, until it is invalidated by a modification to the object.

### 4.4. Implementation with reliable multicast messages

The 2-phase update protocol adequately solves the consistency problem, although at the cost of some communication overhead. The semantics provided by the implementation closely resemble those of shared variables. If a write-operation completes at time $T_w$, read operations issued at time $T_r > T_w$ return the new value.

This strict *temporal* ordering, however, is not a necessary requirement for programming MIMD-like systems, in which processors are executing *asynchronously*. Processors in such systems are not synchronized by physical clocks. Each sequential process in an asynchronous system performs a sequence of computation steps: $C_0, C_1, \ldots, C_i, \ldots$

Within a single process, these steps are *totally* ordered; $C_n$ happens after $C_m$ if and only if $n > m$. There is no total ordering between computation steps of different processes, however, as discussed by Lamport [36]. There is only a *partial* ordering, induced by explicit interactions (like sending a message or setting and testing shared variables).

This lack of total ordering allows an implementation of shared data-objects to slightly relax the semantics without affecting the underlying programming model. Suppose Process $P_1$ executes "write(X, Val)" and Process $P_2$ executes "read(X)." If there is no precedence relation between these two actions (i.e., neither one of them comes before the other in the partial ordering), the value read by $P_2$ may be either the old value of X or the new value. Even if, physically, the write is executed before the read, the read still can return the old value. The major difference with systems that allow read-operations to return arbitrary old (stale) data is that our model supports a consistent logical ordering of events, as defined implicitly in the program. Programs like those in Figure 2 still execute as expected.

In a distributed system supporting only point-to-point messages, a consistent logical ordering is difficult to obtain, because messages sent to different destinations may arrive with arbitrary delays. Some distributed systems (e.g., broadcast-bus systems) give hardware support to send a single message to several destinations simultaneously. More precisely, we are interested in systems supporting reliable, indivisible multicasts, which have the following properties:

- A message is sent reliably from one source to a set of destinations.
- If two processors simultaneously multicast two messages (say $m_1$ and $m_2$), then either all destinations first receive $m_1$, or they all receive $m_2$ first.

With this multicast facility we can implement a simple update protocol. A "write(X, Val)" request is handled as follows by the manager of X:

```
receive write-req(X, Val) from W →
    set write-lock on X;
    store Val in X;
    let S = set of processors having a copy of X;
    multicast update(X, Val) to manager of every P ∈ S;
    unlock X;
    send write-ack(W) to manager of W;
```

After the *write-req* message has been handled, the acknowledgement is sent to the manager of W (the process that issued the request). The manager forwards it to W. This guarantees that the local copy of X on W's processor has been updated when W resumes execution. The manager can be a single-threaded process in this implementation. A manager handles all incoming *write-req*, *update*, and *write-ack* messages in the order they were sent. A manager containing a secondary copy responds as follows to messages from remote managers:

```
receive update(X, Val) →
    set write-lock on local copy of X;
    store Val in local copy of X;
    unlock local copy of X
receive write-ack(W) →
    send ack to W;
```

If a processor P reads a new value of an object X, an *update* message for X containing this value has also been sent to all other processors. Other processors may not have handled this message yet, but they certainly will do so before they handle any other messages. Any changes to shared objects initiated by P will be observed by other processors after accepting the new value of X. Problems like those in Figure 3 do not occur.

### 4.5. Implementation with unreliable multicast messages

A cost-effective way to build a distributed system is to connect a collection of micro-computers by a local area network. Such systems are easy to build and easy to extend. Many distributed operating systems have been designed with this model in mind [1].

Many LANs have hardware support for doing multicasts. An Ethernet, for example, physically sends a packet to every computer on the net,

although usually only one of them reads the packet. There is no difference in transmission time between a multicast and a point-to-point message.

Unfortunately, multicasts in a LAN are not totally reliable. Occasionally, a network packet gets lost. Worse, one or more receivers may be out of buffer space when the packet arrives, so a packet may be delivered at only part of the destinations. In practice, multicast is highly reliable, although less than 100%. Unreliable multicast can be made reliable by adding an extra software protocol. Such a protocol has a high communication overhead and may result in multicasts that are not indivisible (as defined above). Instead, we have designed an implementation of shared data-objects that directly uses unreliable multicasts.

The basic algorithm is the same as that for reliable multicast. When a shared variable X is updated, some (or all) processors containing a secondary copy of X may fail to receive the update(X,Val) message. They will continue to use the old value of X. This is not disastrous, as long as the partial (logical) ordering of events is obeyed, as described above. To guarantee a consistent ordering, processors that failed to receive the update(X,Val) message must detect this failure before handling other update messages that logically should arrive after X's message.

This is realized as follows. Update messages are multicast to *all* processors participating in the program, not just to those processors containing a secondary copy. Every processor counts the number of update messages it sends. This number is called its *mc-count*. Every processor records the *mc-count*s of all processors. These numbers are stored in a vector, called the *mc-vector* (initialized to all zeroes). For Processor P, mc-vector[P] always contains the correct value of P's *mc-count*; entries for other processors may be slightly out of date.

Whenever a processor multicasts a message, it sends its own *mc-vector* as part of the message. When a processor Q receives a multicast message from P, it increments the entry for P in its own *mc-vector* and then compares this vector with the *mc-vector* contained in the message. If an entry R in its own vector is less than the corresponding entry in the message, Q has missed a multicast message from Processor R. Q updates the entry for R in its own vector. As Q does not know which variable should have been updated by R's message, Q temporarily invalidates the local copies of all variables that have their primary copy on Processor R. It sends (reliable) point-to-point messages to the manager of R, asking for the current values of these variables. The reply messages from R also contain *mc-vector*s, and undergo the same procedure as for multicast messages. Until the copies are up-to-date again, local read operations of these copies block.

It is quite possible that lost update messages will remain undetected for a while. Suppose Processor Q misses an update message for a variable Y from Processor R and then receives an update message for X from Processor P. If P also missed R's message, the entry for R in the *mc-vector* of P and Q will agree (although they are both wrong) and the copy of X will be updated. However, as P contained the old value of Y when it updated X, the new value of X does not depend on the new value of Y, so it is consistent to update X.

If a process misses an update message for X, this failure will eventually be detected while handling subsequent messages. The assumption is that there will be subsequent messages. This assumption need not be true. For example, a process may set a shared flag-variable and wait for other processes to respond. If these other processes missed the flag's update message, the system may very well come to a grinding halt. To prevent this, dummy update messages are generated periodically, which do not update any copy, but just cause the *mc-vector*s to be checked.

The implementation outlined above has one considerable advantage: it takes a single message to update any number of copies, provided that the message is delivered at all destinations. There is a severe penalty on losing messages. As modern LANs are highly reliable, we expect this to happen infrequently. The implementation also has several disadvantages. Update messages are sent to every processor. Each message contains extra information (the *mc-vector*), which must be checked by all receiving processors. For a limited number of processors, say 32, we think this overhead is acceptable. The protocol can be integrated with the 2-phase update protocol described in Section 4.3. For example, objects that are replicated on only a few processors can be handled with the 2-phase update protocol while objects replicated on many processors are handled by the multicast protocol.

## 5. A LANGUAGE BASED ON SHARED DATA-OBJECTS

We have designed a simple, general purpose programming language called Orca, based on shared data-objects. Unlike most other parallel languages, Orca is intended for applications programming rather than for systems programming. Parallelism in Orca is based on dynamic creation of sequential processes. Processes communicate indirectly, through shared data-objects. An object can be shared by passing it as **shared** parameter to a newly created process, as discussed in Section 4.

### 5.1. Object type definitions

An object is an instance of an object type, which is essentially an abstract data type. An object type definition consists of a *specification* part and an *implementation* part. The specification part defines one or more operations on objects of the given type. For example, the declaration of an object type *IntObject* is shown in Figure 4.

```
object specification IntObject;
    operation value(): integer;   # current value
    operation assign(val: integer); # assign new value
    operation min(val: integer);
        # set value to minimum of current value
        # and "val"
    operation max(val: integer); # idem for maximum
end;
```

Fig. 4. Specification of object type IntObject.

The implementation part contains the data of the object, code to initialize the data of new instances (objects) of the type, and code implementing the operations. The code implementing an operation on an object can access the object's internal data. The implementation of object type `IntObject` is shown in Figure 5.

Objects can be created and operated on as follows:

```
myint: IntObject; # create object
...
myint$assign(83); # assign 83 to myint
...
x := myint$value();  # read value of myint
```

### 5.2. Synchronization

Access to the shared data is automatically synchronized. All operations defined in the specification part are indivisible. If two processes simultaneously invoke X$min(A) and X$min(B), the new value of X is the minimum of A, B, and the old value of X. On the other hand, a sequence of operations, such as

```
if A < X$value() then
    X$assign(A);
fi
```

is not indivisible. This rule for defining which actions are indivisible and which are not is both easy to understand and flexible: single operations are indivisible, sequences of operations are not. The set of operations can be tailored to the needs of a specific application by defining single operations to be as complex as necessary.

```
object implementation IntObject;
    X: integer;  # local data

    operation value(): integer;
    begin
        return X;
    end

    operation assign(val: integer);
    begin
        X := val;
    end

    operation min(val: integer);
    begin
        if val < X then X := val; fi;
    end

    operation max(val: integer);
    begin
        if val > X then X := val; fi;
    end
begin
    X := 0;  # initialize internal data
end;
```

Fig. 5. Implementation of object type IntObject.

For condition synchronization, *blocking* operations can be defined. A blocking operation consists of one or more *guarded commands*:

```
operation name(parameters);
begin
    guard expr₁ do statements₁ od;
    guard expr₂ do statements₂ od;
    ...
    guard exprₙ do statementsₙ od;
end;
```

The expressions must be side-effect free boolean expressions. The operation initially blocks (suspends) until at least one of the guards evaluates to "true." Next, one true guard is selected nondeterministically, and its sequence of statements is executed. As an example, a type IntQueue with a blocking operation remove_head can be implemented as outlined in Figure 6.

An invocation of remove_head suspends until the queue is not empty. If the queue is initially empty, the process waits until another process appends an element to the queue. If the queue contains only one element and several processes try to execute the statement simultaneously, only one process will succeed in calling remove_head. Other processes will suspend until more elements are appended to the queue.

### 5.3. An example program

We have used the object types discussed above to design a distributed Traveling Salesman Problem (TSP)* algorithm, based on an earlier algorithm described in [37]. The algorithm uses one process to generate partial routes for the salesman (containing only part of the cities) and any number of worker processes to further expand (search) these partial solutions. A worker systematically generates all full routes that start with the given initial route, and checks if they are better (shorter) than the current best solution. Every time a worker finds a shorter full route, it updates a variable shared by all workers, containing the length of the shortest route so far. This variable is used to cut-off partial routes that are already longer than the current shortest route, as these will never lead to an optimal solution.

---
* The Traveling Salesman Problem is the problem of finding the shortest route for a salesman to visit each of a number of cities in his territory exactly once.

```
object implementation IntQueue;
    Q: list of integer;  # internal representation

    operation append(X: integer);
    begin  # append X to the queue
        add X to end of Q;
    end

    operation remove_head(): integer;
        R: integer;
    begin
        # wait until queue not empty,
        # then get head element
        guard Q not empty do  # blocking operation
            R := first element of Q;
            remove R from Q;
            return R;
        od;
    end
begin
    Q := empty;  # initialize IntQueue object
end;
```

Fig. 6. Outline of implementation of object type IntQueue.

The basic algorithm for the worker processes is outlined in Figure 7. (Figure 7 does not show how termination of the worker processes is dealt with; this requires an extension). Conceptually, the distributed algorithm is as simple as the sequential TSP algorithm.

```
process worker(m: shared IntObject; q: shared TaskQueue);
    r: route;
begin
    do  # forever
        r := q$remove_head();
        tsp(r, m);
    od
end;

procedure tsp(r: route; minimum: shared IntObject);
begin
    if length(r) < minimum$value() then
        if "r" is a full solution then
            # r is a full route shorter than the current
            # best route, so update current best solution.
            minimum$min(length(r));
        else
            for all cities "c" not on route "r" do
                tsp(r||c, minimum);  # search extended route
            od
        fi
    fi
end;
```

Fig. 7. Algorithm for TSP worker processes.

The shared variable is implemented as an object of type IntObject (see Figure 4). As several workers may simultaneously try to decrease the value of this variable, it is updated using the indivisible min operation. The work-to-do is stored in an ordered task queue, the order being determined by one of the many heuristics that exist for the Traveling Salesman Problem, such as "nearest-city-first." The task queue is similar to the IntQueue data type of Figure 6, except that the elements are "routes" rather than integers.

## 6. CONCLUSIONS

We have classified several communication primitives for distributed programming that support the shared variable paradigm without the presence of physical shared memory. Of the many programming languages for distributed systems that are around today [9], several recent ones present a computational model based on sharing data. More significant, novel programming styles are emerging. Examples include distributed data structures and the replicated worker model of Linda [26], and incomplete messages, difference streams, and the short-circuit technique of concurrent logic programming languages [31]. These techniques achieve a much higher level of abstraction than message passing languages, at the cost of some efficiency. More research is still needed to achieve the same level of efficiency for languages based on abstract shared data.

## REFERENCES

[1] Tanenbaum, A.S. and Renesse, R. van, "Distributed Operating Systems," *Computing Surveys*, vol. 17, no. 4, pp. 419-470 (Dec. 1985).

[2] Tanenbaum, A.S., "Operating Systems: Design and Implementation," Prentice-Hall, Inc., Englewood Cliffs, NJ (1987).

[3] Upfal, E. and Wigderson, A., "How to Share Memory in a Distributed System," *Journal of the ACM*, vol. 34, no. 1, pp. 116-127 (Jan. 1987).

[4] Karlin, A.R., "Sharing Memory in Distributed Systems - Methods and Applications," STAN-CS-87-1164 (Ph.D. dissertation), Stanford University, Stanford, Calif. (Jan. 1987).

[5] Berglund, E.J., "An Introduction to the V-system," *IEEE Micro*, vol. 6, no. 4, pp. 35-52 (August 1986).

[6] Mullender, S. J. and Tanenbaum, A. S., "Design of a Capability-Based Distributed Operating System," *Computer J.*, vol. 29, no. 4, pp. 289-299 (August 1986).

[7] Hoare, C.A.R., "Communicating Sequential Processes," *Commun. ACM*, vol. 21, no. 8, pp. 666-677 (August 1978).

[8] Andrews, G.R. and Schneider, F.B., "Concepts and Notations for Concurrent Programming," *Computing Surveys*, vol. 15, no. 1, pp. 3-43 (March 1983).

[9] Bal, H.E., Steiner, J.G., and Tanenbaum, A.S., "Programming Languages for Distributed Systems," IR-147, Vrije Universiteit, Amsterdam, The Netherlands (Feb. 1988).

[10] Gehani, N.H., "Broadcasting Sequential Processes (BSP)," *IEEE Trans. Softw. Eng.*, vol. SE-10, no. 4, pp. 343-351 (July 1984).

[11] Strom, R.E. and Yemini, S., "Typestate: A Programming Language Concept for Enhancing Software Reliability," *IEEE Trans. Softw. Eng.*, vol. SE-12, no. 1, pp. 157-171 (Jan. 1986).

[12] Li, K., "Shared Virtual Memory on Loosely Coupled Multiprocessors," RR-492 (Ph.D. dissertation), Yale University, New Haven, CT (Sept. 1986).

[13] Spector, A.Z., "Performing Remote Operations Efficiently on a Local Computer Network," *Commun. ACM*, vol. 25, no. 4, pp. 246-258 (April 1982).

[14] Mao, T. William and Yeh, R.T., "Communication Port: A Language Concept for Concurrent Programming," *IEEE Trans. Softw. Eng.*, vol. SE-6, no. 2, pp. 194-204 (March 1980).

[15] U.S. Department of Defense, "Reference Manual for the Ada Programming Language," ANSI/MIL-STD-1815A (Jan. 1983).

[16] Stammers, R.A., "Ada on Distributed Hardware," pp. 35-40 in *Concurrent Languages in Distributed Systems*, ed. G.L. Reijns and E.L. Dagless, Elsevier Science Publishers (North-Holland) (1985).

[17] Shibayama, E. and Yonezawa, A., "Distributed Computing in ABCL/1," pp. 91-128 in *Object-Oriented Concurrent Programming*, ed. A. Yonezawa and M. Tokoro, M.I.T. Press, Cambridge, Mass. (1987).

[18]  Wilkes, C.T. and LeBlanc, R.J., "Rationale for the Design of Aeolus: A Systems Programming Language for an Action/Object System," *Proc. IEEE CS 1986 Int. Conf. on Computer Languages*, pp. 107-122, Miami, Florida (Oct. 1986).

[19]  Yokote, Y. and Tokoro, M., "Experience and Evolution of ConcurrentSmalltalk," *SIGPLAN Notices (Proc. Object-Oriented Programming Systems, Languages and Applications 1987)*, vol. 22, no. 12, pp. 406-415, Orlando, Florida (Dec. 1987).

[20]  Black, A., Hutchinson, N., Jul, E., Levy, H., and Carter, L., "Distribution and Abstract Types in Emerald," *IEEE Trans. Softw. Eng.*, vol. SE-13, no. 1, pp. 65-76 (Jan. 1987).

[21]  Forman, I.R., "On the Design of Large Distributed Systems," *Proc. IEEE CS 1986 Int. Conf. on Computer Languages*, pp. 84-95, Miami, Florida (Oct. 1986).

[22]  Lucco, S.E., "Parallel Programming in a Virtual Object Space," *SIGPLAN Notices (Proc. Object-Oriented Programming Systems, Languages and Applications 1987)*, vol. 22, no. 12, pp. 26-34, Orlando, Florida (Dec. 1987).

[23]  Cheriton, D.R., "Preliminary Thoughts on Problem-oriented Shared Memory: A Decentralized Approach to Distributed Systems," *Operating Systems Reviews*, vol. 19, no. 4, pp. 26-33 (Oct. 1985).

[24]  Bisiani, R. and Forin, A., "Architectural Support for Multilanguage Parallel Programming on Heterogenous Systems," *Proc. 2nd Int. Conf. on Architectural Support for Programming Languages and Operating Systems*, pp. 21-30, Palo Alto (Oct. 1987).

[25]  Gelernter, D., "Generative Communication in Linda," *ACM Trans. Program. Lang. Syst.*, vol. 7, no. 1, pp. 80-112 (Jan. 1985).

[26]  Ahuja, S., Carriero, N., and Gelernter, D., "Linda and Friends," *IEEE Computer*, vol. 19, no. 8, pp. 26-34 (August 1986).

[27]  Carriero, N. and Gelernter, D., "The S/Net's Linda Kernel," *ACM Trans. Comp. Syst.*, vol. 4, no. 2, pp. 110-129 (May 1986).

[28]  Carriero, N., "The Implementation of Tuple Space Machines," RR-567 (Ph.D. dissertation), Yale University, New Haven, CT (Dec. 1987).

[29]  Clark, K.L. and Gregory, S., "PARLOG: Parallel Programming in Logic," *ACM Trans. Program. Lang. Syst.*, vol. 8, no. 1, pp. 1-49 (Jan. 1986).

[30]  Gregory, S., "Parallel Logic Programming in PARLOG," Addison-Wesley, Wokingham, England (1987).

[31]  Shapiro, E., "Concurrent Prolog: A Progress Report," *IEEE Computer*, vol. 19, no. 8, pp. 44-58 (August 1986).

[32]  Shapiro, E., "Concurrent Prolog: Collected Papers," M.I.T. Press, Cambridge, Mass. (1987).

[33]  Taylor, S., Safra, S., and Shapiro, E., "A Parallel Implementation of Flat Concurrent Prolog," *Int. J. of Parallel Programming*, vol. 15, no. 3, pp. 245-275 (1987).

[34]  Bernstein, P.A. and Goodman, N., "Concurrency Control in Distributed Database Systems," *Computing Surveys*, vol. 13, no. 2, pp. 185-221 (June 1981).

[35]  Liskov, B., Snyder, A., Atkinson, R., and Schaffert, C., "Abstraction Mechanisms in CLU," *Commun. ACM*, vol. 20, no. 8, pp. 564-576 (August 1977).

[36]  Lamport, L., "Time, Clocks, and the Ordering of Events in a Distributed System," *Commun. ACM*, vol. 21, no. 7, pp. 558-565 (July 1978).

[37]  Bal, H.E., Renesse, R. van, and Tanenbaum, A.S., "Implementing Distributed Algorithms Using Remote Procedure Calls," *Proc. AFIPS Nat. Computer Conf.*, pp. 499-506, AFIPS Press, Chicago, Ill. (June 1987).

# Heterogeneous Distributed Shared Memory

Songnian Zhou, *Member, IEEE*, Michael Stumm, *Member, IEEE*, Kai Li, and David Wortman, *Member, IEEE*

*Abstract*—Heterogeneity in distributed systems is increasingly a fact of life, due to specialization of computing equipment. It is highly desirable to integrate heterogeneous hosts into a coherent computing environment to support distributed and parallel applications, so that the individual strengths of the different hosts can be exploited together. Distributed shared memory (DSM), a high-level, highly transparent model for interprocess communication in distributed systems, is a promising vehicle for achieving such an integration.

This paper studies the design, implementation, and performance of heterogeneous distributed shared memory (HDSM). As a practical research effort, we have developed a prototype HDSM system that integrates very different types of hosts, and have ported a number of applications to this system. Our experience shows that, despite a number of difficulties in data conversion, HDSM is indeed implementable with minimal loss in functional and performance transparency when compared to homogeneous DSM systems.

*Index Terms*—Data consistency, data sharing, distributed computer systems, distributed shared memory, heterogeneous computer systems, interprocess communication, parallel computation, performance evaluation, virtual memory systems.

## I. INTRODUCTION

**D**ISTRIBUTED shared memory (DSM) is a model for interprocess communication in distributed systems. In the DSM model, processes running on separate hosts can access a shared address space through normal load and store operations and other memory access instructions. The underlying DSM system provides its clients with a shared, coherent memory address space. Each client can access any memory location in the shared address space at any time and see the value last written by any client. The primary advantage of DSM is the simpler abstraction it provides to the application programmer, making it the focus of recent study and implementation efforts [10], [11], [15]–[18], [24], [3], [14], [25]. (See Stumm and Zhou [24] for an overview.) The abstraction is one the programmer already understands well, since the access protocol is consistent with the way sequential applications access data. The communication mechanism is entirely hidden from the application writer so that the programmer does not have to be conscious of data movement between processes, and complex data structures can be passed by reference, requiring no packing and unpacking.

In principle, the performance of applications that use DSM is expected to be worse than if they use message passing

Manuscript received July 19, 1990; revised June 19, 1991.
S. Zhou, M. Stumm, and D. Wortman are with the Computer Systems Research Institute, University of Toronto, Toronto, Ont., Canada M5S 1A4.
K. Li is with the Department of Computer Science, Princeton University, Princeton, NJ.
IEEE Log Number 9202077.

directly, since message passing is a direct extension to the underlying communication mechanism of the system, and since DSM is typically implemented as a separate layer between the application and a message passing system. However, several implementations of DSM algorithms have demonstrated that DSM can be competitive to message passing in terms of performance for many applications [5], [18], [11]. For some existing applications, we have found that DSM can result in superior performance. This is possible for two reasons. First, for many DSM algorithms, data is moved between hosts in large blocks. Therefore, if the application exhibits a reasonable degree of locality in its data accesses, communication overhead is amortized over multiple memory accesses, reducing overall communication requirements. Second, many (distributed) parallel applications execute in phases, where each compute phase is preceded by a data exchange phase. The time needed for the data exchange phase is often dictated by the throughput of existing communication bottlenecks. In contrast, DSM algorithms typically move data on demand as they are being accessed, eliminating the data exchange phase, spreading the communication load over a longer period of time, and allowing for a greater degree of concurrency. One could argue that the above methods of accessing data could be programmed using messages, in effect imitating DSM in the individual applications. Such programming for communication, however, usually represents substantial effort in addition to that for the implementation of the application itself.

The most widely known algorithm for implementing DSM is due to Li [17], [18], which is well suited for a large class of algorithms. In Li's algorithm, known as SVM, the shared address space is partitioned into pages, and copies of these pages are distributed among the hosts, following a multiple-reader/single-writer (MRSW) protocol: Pages that are marked *read-only* can be replicated and may reside in the memory of several hosts, but a page being written to can reside only in the memory of one host.

One advantage of Li's algorithm is that it can easily be integrated into the virtual memory of the host operating system.[1] If a shared memory page is held locally at a host, it can be mapped into the application's virtual address space on that host and therefore be accessed using normal machine instructions for accessing memory. An access to a page not held locally triggers a page fault, passing control to a fault handler. The fault handler then communicates with the remote hosts in order to obtain a valid copy of the page before mapping it into the application's address space. Whenever

---

[1] It is for this reason that Li called this algorithm and the concept it supports *Shared Virtual Memory* (SVM). In this paper, the more general term, DSM, will be used.

Reprinted from *IEEE Trans. Parallel and Distributed Systems*, Vol. 3, No. 5, Sept. 1992, pp. 540–554.

a page is migrated away from a host, it is removed from any local address space it has been mapped into. Similarly, whenever a host attempts to write to a page for which it does not have a local copy marked as *writable*, a page fault occurs and the local fault handler communicates with the other hosts (after having obtained a copy of the page, if necessary) to invalidate all other copies in the system, before marking the local copy as writable and allowing the faulted process to continue. This protocol is similar to the write-invalidate algorithms used for cache consistency in shared-memory multiprocessors, except that the basic unit on which operations occur is a page instead of a cache line. The DSM fault handlers communicate with DSM memory managers, one of which runs on each host. Each DSM memory manager manipulates local virtual page mapping tables according to the MRSW protocol, keeps track of the location of copies of each DSM page it manages, and passes pages to requesting page fault handlers. In this paper, we assume this protocol for supporting DSM.

For parallel and distributed application programming, distributed shared memory can hide communication complexity from the application when used on a homogeneous set of hosts. DSM in homogeneous systems achieves complete *functional transparency*, in the sense that a program written for a shared memory multiprocessor system can run on DSM without change. The fact that no physical memory is shared can be completely hidden from the applications programmer, as can the fact that, to transfer data, messages have to be passed between the hosts. On the other hand, *performance transparency* can only be achieved to a limited degree, since the physical location(s) of the data being accessed affect application performance, whereas in a uniform memory access (UMA) multiprocessor, the data access cost is not affected by its location in the shared memory. In the case of the MRSW protocol, if a page is not available on the local host when being accessed, it has to be brought in from another host, causing extra delay.

In this paper, we study how DSM can be extended to heterogeneous system environments, and to what degree the functional and performance transparency can be maintained. Heterogeneity exists in many (if not most) computing environments and is usually unavoidable because hardware and its software is often designed for a particular application domain. For example, supercomputers and multiprocessors are good at compute-intensive applications, but often poor at user interfaces and device I/O. Personal computers and workstations, on the other hand, usually have very good user interfaces. There exist many applications that require sophisticated user interfaces, dedicated I/O devices, as well as massive computing power. Examples of such applications can be found in CAD/CAM, artificial intelligence, interactive graphics, and interactive simulation. Hence, it is highly desirable to integrate heterogeneous machines into a coherent distributed system, and to share resources among them.

Heterogeneity in a distributed system comes in a number of forms. The hardware architectures of the machines may be different, including the instruction sets, the data representations, the hardware page sizes, and the number of processors on a host (i.e., uni- or multiprocessors). The operating systems, the system and application programming languages and their compilers, the types of distributed file systems, and the communications protocols may also differ.

A number of methods have been proposed to achieve heterogeneous system integration. (See Notkin *et al.* [22] for an overview.) For example, several remote procedure call (RPC) systems enable servers and application software running on hosts of different types to communicate [26], [1], [4], [12]. Such systems typically define a network standard data format for the procedure call and return messages that all hosts follow by converting between their local representations and this standard. Another method for heterogeneous system integration is to build a heterogeneous distributed file system [13], [9], [21], [2], [7]. Again, a file system access interface and data format is defined that all the hosts must follow to share files among them.

Heterogeneous distributed shared memory (HDSM) is useful for distributed and parallel applications to exploit resources available on multiple types of hosts at the same time. For instance, a CAM application controlling a manufacturing line in real time would be able to acquire data through I/O devices attached to a workstation and output results on its bit-mapped display, while doing most of the computation on compute servers. With HDSM, not only can workstations and compute servers be used simultaneously, but multiple compute servers can be used to increase the aggregate amount of computing power available to a single application. A similar effort to provide heterogeneous distributed shared memory is being undertaken by Bisiani and Forin [11] with their Agora system. However, they use a different DSM algorithm (one where the shared data is replicated on all hosts accessing the data). As discussed by Stumm and Zhou [24], we believe that the MRSW protocol performs better for a larger class of applications than the fully replicated algorithm used by Bisiani and Forin. Forin, Barrera, and Sanzi implemented a shared memory server on heterogeneous processors running the Mach operating system [11]. Their work addressed the issues of multiple VM page sizes, and the conversion of basic hardware data types, such as integer, in the context of Mach.

This paper studies the design, implementation, and performance of heterogeneous distributed shared memory. As a practical research effort, we have developed a prototype HDSM system with hosts that differ significantly. Our experience shows that, despite a number of difficulties in data conversion, HDSM can be implemented while retaining functional and performance transparency close to that of homogeneous DSM. Very good performance is obtained for a number of sample applications running on our prototype. In Section II, we discuss the problems that need to be addressed in order to achieve an HDSM system. Although some of the problems are very difficult, in Section III we show that it is possible to build an HDSM system supporting a wide range of applications, using our prototype system as an example. The performance characteristics of our system, as measured by its overhead and the performance of a number of applications running on it, are discussed in Section IV. Finally, concluding remarks are made in Section V.

## II. ISSUES RELATED TO HETEROGENEITY

Since with DSM, the components of a distributed application share memory directly, they are more tightly coupled than when data is shared through RPC or a distributed file system. For this reason, it is more difficult to extend DSM to a heterogeneous system environment. These difficulties are explained in this section. Our techniques for overcoming them will be discussed in the next section.

### A. Data Conversion

Data items may be represented differently on various types of hosts due to differences in the machine architectures, the programming languages for the applications, and their compilers. For data types as simple as integers, the order of the bytes can be different. For floating point numbers, the lengths of the mantissa and exponent fields, as well as their positions can differ. For higher level structured data types (e.g., records, arrays), the alignment and order of the components in the data structure can differ between hosts. A simple example, depicted in Table I, presents two data types, an array of four characters and an integer, first in big-endian order and then in little-endian order [6]. This example illustrates the *type dependent* differences in data representation that can arise between hosts.

Sharing data among heterogeneous hosts means that the physical representation of the data will have to be converted when the data is transferred between hosts of different types. In the most general case, data conversion will not only incur run-time overhead, but also may be impossible due to nonequivalent data content (e.g., lost bits of precision in floating point numbers, and mismatch in their ranges of representation). This may represent a potential limitation to HDSM for some systems and applications. The question that needs to be addressed is whether, for a specific set of hosts and programming languages, data conversion can be performed for all or most data types to form a *useful* HDSM system (i.e., a system that supports a large collection of realistic applications).

### B. Thread Management

As a means of supporting a shared address space, distributed shared memory usually goes hand in hand with a thread system that allows multiple threads to share the same address space. Such a combination makes programming of parallel applications particularly easy. In a heterogeneous system environment, the facilities for thread management, which includes thread creation, termination, scheduling and synchronization primitives, may all be different on different types of hosts, if they exist at all.

Migrating a thread from one host to another in a homogeneous DSM system is usually easy, since minimal context is kept for the threads. Typically, the per-thread stack is allocated in the shared address space, so the stack need not be moved explicitly. The descriptor, or Thread Control Block (TCB), constitutes a small amount of data that needs to be moved at migration time. In a heterogeneous DSM system, however, thread migration is much more difficult. The binary images of the program are different, so it is hard to identify "equivalent

TABLE I
BIG-ENDIAN AND LITTLE-ENDIAN BYTE ORDERING

| Byte | Big-Endian | | Little-Endian | |
|------|------|------------|------|------------|
| | int | char array | int | char array |
| $i$ | MSB | 'J' | LSB | 'J' |
| $i+1$ | | 'O' | | 'O' |
| $i+2$ | | 'H' | | 'H' |
| $i+3$ | LSB | 'N' | MSB | 'N' |

MSB = Most Significant Byte;    LSB = Least Significant Byte.

points of execution" in the binaries (i.e., the places in the different binary program images at which execution can be suspended and later resumed on another host of a different type such that the result of the execution is not affected). Similarly, the formats of the threads' stacks are likely to be different, due to architectural, language, and compiler differences; therefore, converting the stacks at migration time may be very difficult, if not impossible.

While it is clear that thread migration presents yet another limitation to HDSM, its significance is debatable for two reasons. First, in HDSM, threads can be created and started on remote hosts of any type, thus reducing the need for dynamic thread migration. Second, migration between hosts of the same type is still easy to achieve in HDSM, and, for many applications, this may be all that is required. For an application running on a workstation and a set of (homogeneous) compute servers, for instance, its threads can freely migrate between the compute servers to balance their load.

### C. Page Sizes

The unit of data managed and transferred by DSM is a data block, which we call a *DSM page*. In a homogeneous DSM system, a DSM page has usually the same size as a native virtual memory (VM) page, so that the memory management hardware (MMU) can be used to trigger a DSM page fault. In a heterogeneous DSM system, the hosts may have different VM page sizes, presenting both complexity in the page coherency algorithm and opportunity in control of the granularity of data sharing.

### D. Uniform File Access

A DSM system supporting an application running on a number of hosts benefits from the existence of a distributed file system that allows the threads to open files and perform I/O in a uniform way. While this is likely to be the case in a modern, homogeneous system, multiple incompatible distributed file systems may exist on heterogeneous hosts, due to the multiplicity of distributed file system protocols currently in existence. A uniform file access interface, encompassing both file names and file operations, should be provided to an HDSM application. One possibility is to choose one of the file systems as the standard and make the other(s) emulate it. It is also possible to define an independent file system structure, and make the native distributed file systems emulate it. Recent research on heterogeneous distributed file system is applicable here [7]. Since heterogeneous distributed file system is a research topic on its own, we will not address it any further in this paper.

### E. Programming Languages

The system programming languages used on the heterogeneous hosts may be different. This implies that multiple (more-or-less) equivalent implementations of an HDSM system may have to be done in the various languages. However, applications running on HDSM should not be affected by the language(s) used to implement HDSM, as long as a functionally equivalent application interface is supported by HDSM on all the hosts. If a common application programming language is available on all the hosts, then the same program would be usable on the hosts (with recompilation). Otherwise, multiple (equivalent) implementations of an application would have to be written, increasing the difficulties in using HDSM substantially.

### F. Interhost Communication

The realization of HDSM requires the existence of a common communication protocol between the different types of hosts involved. This requirement is not particular to HDSM, however, some common transport protocol must exist for the hosts to communicate in any case. The availability of the OSI and TCP/IP protocols on most systems makes the interhost communication increasingly feasible.

### III. MERMAID: A PROTOTYPE

In the preceding section, we identified a number of issues that need to be addressed in order to build an HDSM system. Instead of studying these issues in the abstract, we have taken an experimental approach by designing and building an HDSM prototype, Mermaid, and by studying its performance. We discuss our experience in this section. Although the techniques we used to resolve the issues related to heterogeneity are in the context of Mermaid, we believe that most of them are generally applicable. For the use of Mermaid, please see [19].

### A. System Overview

In selecting the types of hosts participating in Mermaid, we wanted to include machines that are sufficiently different, so that the difficult issues arising from heterogeneity can be studied. Based on suitability and availability, SunOS workstations and DEC Firefly multiprocessors were chosen. Sun-3 workstations are based on M68020 CPU's and run Sun's version of the UNIX operating system, SunOS. The system programming language is C. The Firefly, developed at DEC's System Research Center, is a small-scale multiprocessor workstation with up to 7 DEC CVAX processors [27]. Each processor has a direct-mapped 64 kilobyte cache. The caches are coherent, so that all processors within a single Firefly have a consistent view of shared memory. The operating system for the Firefly is Taos [20], an Ultrix with threads and inexpensive thread synchronization. The system programming language is

Modula-2+, an augmented version of Modula-2 [23]. Table II highlights the differences between the two types of machines.[2]

To focus on our research problems, we adopted a system architecture for Mermaid similar to that of the IVY system developed by Li [17] that uses a page-based MRSW consistency protocol, as described in Section I. It consists of three modules, as shown in Fig. 1. The *thread management module* provides operations for thread creation, termination, scheduling, as well as synchronization primitives. The *shared memory module* allocates and deallocates shared memory and handles page faults. It uses a page table for the shared address space to maintain data consistency, and performs data conversion at page transfer time, if necessary. The responsibility for managing the pages is assigned to the participating hosts in a round-robin fashion (named *fixed-distributed algorithm* by Li [18]). The above two modules are supported by the *remote operations module*, which implements a simple request-response protocol for communication between the hosts.

We chose to implement Mermaid at the user level, as a library package to be linked into application programs using DSM. Although a kernel-level implementation would be more efficient, the difference in performance is not expected to affect applications performance significantly, as evidenced by the low overhead of Mermaid which will be discussed in Section IV-A. More importantly, a user-level implementation has a number of advantages. First, it is more flexible and easier to implement; experimentation may be carried out without rebooting the hosts.

Second, several DSM packages can be provided to the applications on the same system. Our analysis of the performance of applications using different shared data algorithms showed that the correct choice of algorithm was often dictated by the memory access behavior of the application [24]. It is therefore desirable to provide multiple DSM systems employing different algorithms for applications to choose from. A user-level implementation makes this much easier.

Finally, a user-level DSM system is more portable, although some small changes to the operating system kernel are still needed for some systems. For example, Mermaid requires kernel support for setting the access permissions of memory pages from the user level, so that a memory access fault is generated if a nonresident page is accessed on a host. It was necessary to add a new system call to SunOS for this purpose (Taos provides such a call). A second change to the operating system kernel was to pass the address of the DSM page that has an access violation to its user-level fault handler. No other kernel changes were necessary for these two host types.

### B. Basic Support

*Programming Languages:* As discussed in Section II-E, it is necessary to choose languages for implementing HDSM and for implementing applications running on HDSM. While it would be simpler to use a single language to implement HDSM, interfacing HDSM to the native operating systems is

---

[2] The hardware MMU page size on a CVAX is 512 bytes, but the VM implementation on the Firefly uses two MMU pages for one VM page of 1 kilobyte. On the Sun, both the hardware MMU page and the VM page have a size of 8 kilobytes.

TABLE II
HIGHLIGHTS OF THE HETEROGENEOUS FEATURES OF THE SUN AND FIREFLY

| Attribute | Sun-3 | Firefly |
|---|---|---|
| Processor | M68020 | CVAX |
| Number of processors | 1 | 4–6 (user usable) + 1 (I/O) |
| Byte order | Little-endian | Big-endian |
| Floating point | IEEE | VAX |
| VM page size | 8 kilobytes | 1 kilobyte |
| Operating system | SunOS 3.5 | Taos |
| System language | C | Modula-2+ |
| Application language | C | Modula-2+, C |
| Thread management | unavailable | available |
| Communication protocol | TCP/IP, UDP/IP, Sun RPC | UDP/IP subsets, FF RPC |
| File system | SUN NFS | RFS |

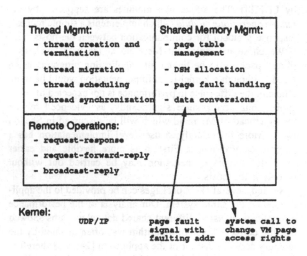

Fig. 1. Structure of the Mermaid system.

easier if the native system implementation languages are used. For Mermaid, we chose the latter approach by having a C implementation for the Sun, and a Modula-2+ implementation for the Firefly. As a result, most of the Mermaid functionalities had to be implemented twice, and, whenever changes are made to Mermaid, both implementations must be modified. Though certainly cumbersome, the modification process has been relatively straightforward.

The situation for application programs is quite different, since it is highly undesirable to force the user to implement an application in multiple languages. We therefore chose C as the common application language. We have ported to Mermaid a number of large, complex applications originally written in C for sequential machines, by only modifying the top-level logic to break the computation into parallel tasks, (without understanding the low-level algorithms employed by the application, which typically constitutes 80–95% of the code). This would have been impossible had multiple languages been required.

*Communication Substrate:* The distributed shared memory modules typically operate in a request-response mode. For instance, when a page fault occurs, the fault handler sends a page request to the manager for this page, which either supplies the page, or forward the request to the owner on another host. The most suitable protocol for the remote operations module is therefore a request-response protocol, with forwarding and multicast capabilities. Multicast is used for write invalidation.

We implemented our own presentation layer protocol in the Remote Operations module following the above requirements, and use it to support all interactions between the memory and thread management modules running on different hosts. This presentation layer protocol is implemented using UDP/IP, a simple, datagram-based transport protocol. Our implementation was complicated by the fact that fragmentation in UDP/IP is not supported on the Fireflies, We did not use the RPC packages available on the Suns and Fireflies, since they are incompatible and do not meet our requirements with respect to functionality, i.e., broadcast and forwarding. Moreover, since data conversion is performed in HDSM, we need not incur the overhead of data marshalling and demarshalling at the RPC level.

*Thread Support:* Many well established operating systems, including SunOS, do not provide direct support for multiple threads that share a common address space. Mermaid therefore provides a simple thread module at the user level on the Sun. Since all threads in a Sun address space run within a single Unix process, the suspension of one thread by the operating system scheduler (e.g., for *synchronous* I/O) makes the other threads nonexecutable as well. This has not been a problem for the Mermaid applications we ported, since parallel applications often allocate only one thread on each processor. For the Firefly, a system-level thread package is available and is used by Mermaid. Mermaid threads in an address space may be created on one host and later moved to and started on other hosts of any type. Alternatively, threads may be created and started on remote hosts directly. However, no dynamic thread migration facility is provided in the current implementation of Mermaid.

Parallel executing threads need a way to synchronize. In principle, this could be supported by using atomic instructions on shared memory locations. In practice, however, this leads to an excessive movement of (large) DSM pages between the hosts involved. We therefore implemented a separate distributed synchronization facility that provides for more efficient P and V operations and events.

### C. Data Conversion

When data is transferred from a machine of one type to a machine of another type, it must be converted before it is accessed on the destination machine. In Mermaid, the unit of data that is converted is a page, and the conversion is based on the type of data stored on the page. Our goals for data conversion were to minimize the amount of work the user has to do, to make the conversion method as general as possible, and to achieve good performance. We adopted a three-part conversion scheme for Mermaid. First, the types of data to be allocated in the shared memory are indicated in the memory allocation requests. Second, routines to convert the various types of data are automatically generated by utility software. Finally, a mechanism is built into Mermaid so that the appropriate conversion routine is invoked whenever a page is transferred. We discuss the three parts in more detail in the following sections.

*1) Typed Data Allocation:* The information about the layout of a page has to be passed to Mermaid so that appropriate conversion can be performed upon page transfer. For this purpose, we provide a special memory allocation subroutine similar to `malloc` in Unix that has an additional argument identifying the type of data being allocated, as shown in Fig. 2(b). When processing such a request, the memory management module of Mermaid records the range of the shared address space allocated for this request, and the data type, in the corresponding DSM page table entry or entries. There is no restriction as to the type or size of data that can be allocated; a structure may be larger than a page. For example, Fig. 2(a) depicts a user-defined structure, `sharedType`, that is allocated by the call in Fig. 2(b).

In principle, multiple types of data could be coallocated in the same page, but this makes keeping track of the data types complicated and the dynamic data conversion inefficient. We therefore made the restriction that a page contain data of one type only,[3] so that information with respect to only one data type needs to be kept in each HDSM page table entry, and only one conversion routine needs to be invoked (which may invoke other routines in turn, as will be discussed below). Multiple allocation requests for the same type of data may be satisfied, fully or partially, by the same page, given that there is space in the page.

Our requirement of allocating only one data type per page may result in more memory usage, since now several pages may be partially filled, rather than at most one. However, the number of pages wasted is limited by the number of distinct data types being allocated in the shared memory. For modern machines with a large main memory, this is typically not a serious problem. Also, as an optimization in our implementation, when a partially filled page is being transferred, only the part with valid data is transferred and converted (if necessary). Despite the increased memory usage,

segregating data by types may have the desirable side effect of reducing page contention for some applications, if unrelated data of different types no longer co-reside in a page.

*2) Automatic Data Conversion:* In addition to data type information, Mermaid also needs a corresponding conversion routine for each type. In Section II-A, we noted that data conversion may not be possible for some types due to differences in data content, size, or alignment. Here, we first assume that conversion is possible, and discuss a general framework for automatically generating the conversion routines. We then study the Mermaid case to expose its limitations.

*Conversion Code Generation:* In general, a hierarchy of conversion routines must be constructed that partially reflects the data type hierarchy defined in the application program. This hierarchy is partial, because only those types directly or indirectly allocated in the shared memory need conversion routines. For the basic data types defined by the language and supported by the hardware, such as `int`, `short`, `float`, and `double` in C, efficient conversion routines can be provided by the HDSM system itself.[4] For user-defined data types, a conversion routine is invoked that consists of a sequence of calls to lower level routines, mirroring the structure of the data type. If an element is of a basic type, then its HDSM routine is invoked directly. Otherwise, a routine composed for the element is invoked. Ultimately every data type is composed of basic types. Fig. 2(c) gives an example of the conversion code for user-defined, nested data types.

We have constructed a fully automatic conversion routine generator that processes the compiler output for a program and produces all the necessary conversion routines.[5] The conversion routines generated are structural, in that they only specify the names of the lower level routines and the order in which they should be invoked; the same source code may therefore be used on all machines, independent of which machine the routines are generated on. The machine-dependent basic conversion routines provided by HDSM ensure that the conversion is correct on each machine. A number of simple optimizations are made in our current implementation. For example, a single routine is called for an array of data elements, as shown in Fig. 2(c) for the structure `embeddedType`.

In addition to the conversion routines, the generator also generates a table matching the data types that are directly specified in the memory allocation routines to their corresponding conversion routines. This table is used by Mermaid at page transfer time to invoke the appropriate conversion routine.

*Feasibility of Conversion:* We now address the issue of the feasibility of data conversion. Three problems are involved: 1) the conversion of basic data types, 2) the handling of a data item crossing a page boundary, and 3) the handling of different ordering of fields in a record.

On both the Sun and the Firefly, the ASCII standard is used for characters (`char` in C); hence, no character conversion is needed. Conversion of integers (either the four-byte `int` or the two-byte `short`) is a matter of proper byte swapping.

---

[3] Note that the data type need not be a basic type provided by the programming language, but can be an application defined compound type.

[4] These are implemented as inline code for efficiency reasons.

[5] It was necessary to work with the compiler output since we were unable to obtain access to the source code or internal documentation for the C compilers on both machines.

```
struct embeddedType {
    double d;                      /* an 8-byte double precision floating number */
    char c[8];                     /* an array of eight ASCII characters */
};

struct sharedType {
    int *p;                        /* a (4-byte) pointer to an integer */
    float b;                       /* a 4-byte single precision floating number */
    struct embeddedType e[16];     /* an array of 16 records declared above */
};
```

(a)

```
ptr = (struct sharedType *) DSM_Alloc((sizeof(struct sharedType) * n, "sharedType");
```

(b)

```
conv_embeddedType(dst, src, numrecords)
  struct embeddedType dst[], src[];
  int numrecords;
{
  register struct embeddedType *dstp = dst, *srcp = src, *srcend = &src[numrecords-1];

  for (; srcp <= srcend; srcp++, dstp++) {
    conv_float64(dstp->d,srcp->d);
    conv_chars(dstp->c,srcp->c, 8);
  }
}

conv_sharedType(dst, src, numrecords)
  struct sharedType dst[], src[];
  int numrecords;
{
  register struct sharedType *dstp = dst, *srcp = src, *srcend = &src[numrecords-1];

  for (; srcp <= srcend; srcp++, dstp++) {
    conv_pointer(dstp->p,srcp->p);
    conv_float32(dstp->b,srcp->b);
    conv_embeddedType(dstp->e,srcp->e,16);
  }
}
```

(c)

Fig. 2. An example of data conversion. (a) Sample data structure with embedded substructure. (b) Sample allocation statement for the second structure in (a). (c) Data conversion routines generated for the structures in (a).

Conversion of floating point numbers is somewhat more complicated. While both the VAX and the IEEE formats of single precision floating point numbers (float in C) use 23 bits to represent a 24 bit mantissa, 7 bits to represent the exponent, and 1 bit for the sign, their layout is quite different. In the IEEE format, the bits in the mantissa are stored contiguously, while in the VAX format they are partitioned across bits 0–6 and 16–31. The bias used to represent the exponents differ by one in the two formats. Despite these differences, equivalent conversion is achievable, except for the following special cases. The IEEE format used on the Sun supports unnormalized numbers and special cases, such as infinity and NAN's (not a number), which are not supported by the VAX format on the Firefly. These cases can be detected with two additional comparison operations. The positions and lengths of the exponent and mantissa fields may be different (such is the case with IEEE and VAX), requiring bit manipulation operations.

The VAX and IEEE formats for representing double precision floating point numbers differ more significantly. The IEEE format uses an 11-bit exponent and a 52-bit mantissa, whereas the VAX uses an 8-bit exponent and a 55-bit mantissa. Therefore, the smaller exponent field and the smaller mantissa field of the two representations dictate the range of (floating point) numbers that can be correctly represented on both types of machines.

For pointers, conversion is necessary if the shared address space starts at different virtual addresses on different host types. The HDSM system on each host may obtain the starting address of the shared memory for each host type at initialization time by communicating with each other, without application intervention. Converting a pointer is then a simple matter of adding an offset to the value of the pointer. This is the scheme used in Mermaid.

In Mermaid, all the corresponding basic data types have the same sizes, but their alignment requirements may be different. For the double type, for instance, Sun requires only even-byte alignment, whereas Firefly (VAX) requires quad-byte alignment. Thus the size of a compound structure and the alignment of the elements in it may be different on the two machines. Our automatic conversion generator detects this problem and automatically generates a revised structure definition with dummy elements inserted to force data structure elements of interest to have the same alignment on both machines. The application program is then recompiled on both machines with the revised data structure definition and correct alignment of corresponding elements is achieved. This process will result in some wasted storage on the machine with the less strict alignment requirements but it is essential for the operation of HDSM.

In general, it is also possible for a data item to cross a page boundary. If the item is a compound structure, and none of its basic data items crosses the page boundary, then the partial structure on the page to be converted may be copied to a temporary buffer (with the missing part of the structure filled with some default values taken from a template), where the conversion may be performed in-place using the appropriate routine. The partial structure is then copied back to the appropriate location in the page. If, on the other hand, a basic data item crosses a page boundary, then the conversion will need the parts on both (neighboring) pages. One of these pages may be resident on another host, making it necessary for it to be transferred. For certain data types, page-based data conversion may not be possible. Consider, for example, an integer with its first two bytes at the end of one page, and its last two bytes at the beginning of the following page. If byte swapping is necessary in converting an integer, then transferring one of the two pages between hosts with different byte orders can result in the loss of half of the integer, since the two pages held by their owner(s) may end up having the *same* two bytes of the integer. Such a problem does not arise in Mermaid, since we ensure, by forced alignment, that no basic data items cross page boundaries.

A similar problem arises if compilers on different machines ordered the space allocated for the fields of a structure differently. Even if no basic data item crosses a page boundary, the same field in a structure may be located on different pages, depending on the type of machine(s) holding the data. Again, neighboring pages would be needed for conversion, and it is possible to lose some of the data items during conversion. For the C compilers on the Sun and the Firefly, this problem does not exist.

The union structure in C allows various formats for a compound data type. Unfortunately, C does not require a tag field to indicate the format being used, thus making automatic conversion of union structures impossible. In Mermaid, we require the user to add a tag field at the beginning of a union structure, and to set its value to indicate the interpretation of the rest of the structure. Such a requirement would not be necessary in more sensibly designed languages, such as Pascal and Modula-2.

*3) Dynamic Conversion Mechanism:* Once the conversion routines are generated as described above, they can be compiled and linked with the user program on each type of machine, without additional effort from the user. Upon page transfer, the remote machine type is checked, and, if different from the local one, the appropriate conversion routine is invoked. The conversion mechanism in Mermaid uses the data type information stored in the HDSM page table entries, and the table matching the data types to their corresponding conversion routines produced by the code generator described in Section III-C1.

In our current implementation, conversion is always done by the receiving machine. This is desirable for some cases, such as when a master thread distributes input data to multiple worker threads, because the conversion can be performed by the workers in parallel, rather than by the master sequentially. For other cases, such as when the master collects results from the workers, it is better to have the sending machine perform the conversion. Our primary motivation for the current scheme is simplicity and transparency. Since only two types of machine are involved, data is always converted from the foreign format to the native format, rather than using an intermediate, network standard format as in some RPC systems [9].

*4) Limitations: A Summary:* The data conversion problem is complex. Our experience indicates that our solution is sufficient for many practical applications in the context of Mermaid, and we believe that it is similar in complexity to the solution used by existing heterogeneous RPC schemes [26]. However, as pointed out above, our solution does have a number of limitations:

1) Some functional transparency is sacrificed by requiring the programmer to specify the type of data being allocated. This is usually only a small annoyance.

2) Floating point numbers can lose precision when being converted. Since an application does not have direct control over how many times a page is migrated between hosts of different types and hence converted, the numerical accuracy of results may become questionable. However, we do not consider this to be a practical problem for many environments; for example, in an environment consisting of workstations and computation servers, data is typically transferred once to the computation servers and then transferred back again at the end of the computation. The initial (floating point) data and final results are not likely to be in the extreme ranges, or nonnumbers. During the computation phase, data pages may be transferred among the (homogeneous) compute servers without conversion.

3) Entire pages are converted even though only a small portion of a page may be accessed before it is transferred away. However, we have found that the cost of page conversion to be small compared to the overall migration cost (to be discussed in Section IV-A). Applications that access only a few data items of a page between page migrations will perform poorly in both the homogeneous and heterogeneous cases when using a page-based MRSW algorithm. A DSM system based on the MRSW algorithm performs poorly with this type of access behavior in both the homogeneous and the heterogeneous cases.

4) An additional tag field is required in union structures in languages such as C and Modula-2; the value of the tag must be set by the application to indicate the interpretation of data in the structure.

5) The order of the fields within compound structures must be the same on each host.

6) A memory page may contain data of only one type, which may be a compound type containing multiple data items of other types.

Of the above limitations, the first three are "hard" in that they are limitations to our design. The fourth limitation is particular to the C language. The fifth is not a problem in any of the systems we know of, including the Sun and the Firefly. The last limitation is not necessary, but is desirable for efficiency.

### D. Page Sizes

In a heterogeneous system with machines supporting different VM page sizes, choosing a size for the DSM page becomes an important issue. We may use the largest VM page size for DSM pages. Since VM page sizes are most likely powers of 2, multiple small VM pages fit exactly in one DSM page; hence, they can be treated as a group on page faults. The potential drawback of such a *largest page size* algorithm is that more data than necessary may be moved between hosts with smaller VM page sizes. In severe cases, *page thrashing* may occur, when data items in the same DSM page are being updated by multiple hosts at the same time, causing large numbers of page transfers among the hosts without much progress in the execution of the application. While page thrashing may occur with any DSM page size, it is more likely with larger DSM page sizes, due to increased *false sharing*, where nonoverlapping regions in the same page are shared and updated by threads on different hosts, causing repeated page transfers. False sharing should be contrasted to real sharing, in which a number of data items are shared and updated by multiple hosts. While performance degradation due to real sharing is hard to avoid, performance degradation due to false sharing can often be reduced by using smaller DSM pages.[6]

One way to reduce data contention is to use the smallest VM page size for the DSM pages. If a page fault occurs on a host with a larger page size, multiple DSM pages are moved to fill that (larger) page. If a fault occurs on a host with a small (DSM) page and no host with a large page size is sharing the data, then only this small (DSM) page needs to be obtained. We call this the *smallest page size* algorithm.[7]

Typically, if page thrashing does not occur, more DSM page faults occur on hosts with small VM page sizes, resulting in more fault handling overhead and (small) page transfers. Although intermediate DSM page sizes are possible, the above two algorithms represent the two extremes of the page size algorithms. We have implemented both algorithms in Mermaid, and the performance comparison between them will be discussed in Section IV-C2.

---

[6]False sharing can also be reduced by rearranging memory layout, so that data that would be falsely shared if placed on the same page is assigned to different pages.

[7]The actual algorithm must differentiate between many cases depending on the type of page fault (read or write), the page sizes of the requesting and the owner hosts, and how the page is currently being shared (what type of hosts have read/write accesses).

### IV. PERFORMANCE EVALUATION

We have performed a number of experiments on our prototype Mermaid system in order to study the impacts of heterogeneity on the performance of distributed shared memory systems. Along the way, some performance aspects of distributed shared memory in general are also studied. In the following, we first discuss a number of overhead measurements, followed by the response time measurements of three Mermaid applications. We then assess the performance impact of DSM page size algorithms and page thrashing. All measurements were performed on Sun3/60 workstations and Fireflies. The measured hosts were idle during the experiments; except for the activities being studied. The results we observed were very stable (except for the page thrashing cases to be discussed in Section IV-C2). The Mermaid prototype is not fine-tuned to achieve optimal performance, since our goal is not to push the performance of HDSM to its limit, but to assess its practical value in terms of its performance and ability in supporting applications.

### A. Overhead Assessment

Compared to physical shared memory, distributed shared memory has a number of additional overheads. Since data is no longer physically shared, DSM pages need to be moved between hosts upon page faults, typically over a slow, bit-serial network, such as the Ethernet. In a user-level implementation, the access rights of the DSM pages have to be set, and DSM page faults have to be passed to the user level. The allocation of shared memory, thread scheduling, and thread synchronization also introduce overhead, but they are relatively small compared to the communication overheads. Finally, for heterogeneous systems, the costs of data conversion and the page size algorithm must be added.

The basic costs of handling a page fault in Mermaid are shown in Table III. Included are the invocation of the user-level handler, the identification of page fault type (read or write), the HDSM page table processing, and the request message transmission time.[8] The delay in transferring the page over the network is not included. The values of a few milliseconds are considered to be quite small. The costs on the Fireflies are higher, due to the higher overhead of the page fault handling mechanism for access violation (about 4.5 ms or higher). The operating system kernel, the "nub," of Taos version 72.4 on the Fireflies, considers access violation fault to be a rare case.

Table IV shows the costs of transferring 8 kilobyte and 1 kilobyte pages between hosts. The higher cost when the Firefly is involved is partially due to user level message fragmentation and reassembly processing. The costs for 8 kilobyte transfers are only about three times that of 1 kilobyte transfers, due to the fixed portion of the cost of the message transport. Hence, in the absence of page thrashing, larger DSM pages incur fewer page faults and lower data transfer overhead.

---

[8]To collect the data for this and subsequent overhead measurements, the Mermaid system was slightly modified so that a large number of the same operation (e.g., 100 000) are performed in a sequence, and the total elapsed time measured.

TABLE III
COSTS OF PAGE FAULT HANDLING (ms)

|       | Sun  | Firefly |
|-------|------|---------|
| Read  | 1.98 | 6.80    |
| Write | 2.04 | 6.70    |

TABLE IV
COSTS OF TRANSFERRING A PAGE (ms)

| to<br>from | Sun | Firefly | Sun | Firefly |
|------------|-----|---------|-----|---------|
| Sun        | 18  | 27      | 5.1 | 7.6     |
| Firefly    | 25  | 33      | 7.3 | 6.7     |
| page size  | 8 kilobyte | | 1 kilobyte | |

TABLE V
COSTS OF DATA CONVERSIONS (ms)

| page<br>data type | 8 kilobyte page | | 1 kilobyte | |
|------|------|---------|------|---------|
|      | Sun  | Firefly | Sun  | Firefly |
| int  | 5.01 | 7.75    | 0.63 | 1.00    |
| short | 6.53 | 10.0   | 0.82 | 1.15    |
| float | 9.72 | 13.9   | 1.22 | 1.68    |
| double | 11.6 | 29.0  | 1.46 | 3.63    |
| user structure | 6.61 | 21.6 | 0.67 | 2.15 |

The measured costs of converting a page of integers, shorts, floating point numbers (single and double precision), and the user-defined structure of Fig. 2(a) on a Sun3/60 and a Firefly are shown in Table V. In all of the cases except that of double on Fireflies, the conversion costs are substantially lower than those of page transfer. The cost of converting an 1 kilobyte page is approximately 1/8 of that for an 8 kilobyte page. It is interesting to note that the overhead for converting the user-defined structure with an embedded structure is not much larger than that for the basic types. We also measured several other user data structures and found their conversion costs to be comparable.

To consider the combined effects of the overhead costs discussed above, we show the end-to-end page fault delays for different types of hosts in Table VI. Three different scenarios are considered, depending on the locations of the host on which the thread triggering the page fault resides (Requester), the host acting as the manager for the page (Manager), and the host currently having ownership of the page (Owner). While the Requester and the Owner are always different (otherwise there would not be a page fault in the first place), the Requester and the Manager, or the Manager and the Owner may be the same host. The cost for (integer) data conversion is included when the Requester and Owner hosts are of different types. The measurements are based on the largest page size algorithm, so the values are for 8 kilobyte pages only. The costs for read and write page faults were found to be very similar. The HDSM page fault delay is comparable to that of a VM page fault involving a disk seek. The costs of page faults involving both the Sun and the Firefly are very comparable to the homogeneous case of Firefly, but higher than that of Sun, partly due to user-level message fragmentation and reassembly. As with traditional VM, if the HDSM fault rate is not excessive, the application's performance under distributed shared memory may be close to that under physical shared memory.

### B. Evaluation of Application Performance

*1) Three Sample Applications:* While the cost measurements above are useful in assessing the performance penalty of distributed shared memory, the most direct measure of DSM performance is the execution times of applications. One of the

applications we implemented on Mermaid is a parallel version of matrix multiplication (MM) in which the computation of the rows in the result matrix is performed by a number of threads running simultaneously, each on a separate processor. The result matrix is divided into a number of groups of adjacent rows equal to the number of threads, and assigned to the threads. The result matrix is write-shared among the threads, whereas the two argument matrices are only read-shared, and can hence be replicated. At the end of the computation, pieces of the result matrix are transferred (implicitly) to the master thread, which creates and coordinates the activities of the slave threads, but performs no multiplication itself. Except where noted, the experiments discussed below use $512 \times 512$ matrices of double[9] numbers.

Another application we converted to run under Mermaid is a program that detects flaws in printed circuit boards (PCB). Two digital images (front- and back-lit) of a sample PCB are taken by a camera, digitized, and then transferred to a workstation to be stored as large matrices. The software then checks the geometric features on the board, such as conductors, wire holes, and spacing between them. If design rule violations are found, they are high-lighted in a third image, which is displayed on the workstation, so that a human decision may be made to rectify the problem. The amount of computation involved in the rule checking is substantial: on a Firefly, it takes about 11 min to process a 2 cm × 32 cm area using a sequential version of the software. Obviously, speeding up the execution would make the feedback on the manufacturing line more timely, reducing the number of boards that may have to be discarded. A suitable computing environment for on-line PCB inspection is a workstation with bit-mapped display, coupled with compute servers on which the checking software runs in parallel. We therefore used Mermaid as a prototype for such a system. Our version of the PCB software has a master thread that runs on a Sun, divides the board area into stripes, and creates threads on the Fireflies to check them.[10] All data including the raw and processed images, and the data structures containing the design rules and the flaw statistics are allocated in the DSM space, and are properly converted when transferred between the Sun master and the Firefly slave threads. For our measurements, an area of 2 cm × 32 cm is used.

A third application we used to study Mermaid performance is a partial differential equation solver that uses the Successive

---

[9] 64-bit, double precision floating point numbers.

[10] Small overlaps of the stripes are necessary so that features on the borders are checked properly.

TABLE VI
END-TO-END PAGE FAULT DELAYS FOR 8 KB PAGES (ms)

| | Sun→Sun | | Ffly→Sun | | Sun→Ffly | | Ffly→Ffly | |
|---|---|---|---|---|---|---|---|---|
| | R | W | R | W | R | W | R | W |
| R/M→O | 26.4 | 26.7 | 47.7 | 48.3 | 56.3 | 47.8 | 46.5 | 46.4 |
| R→M/O | 29.6 | 27.9 | 50.9 | 51.6 | 58.6 | 59.4 | 49.6 | 49.1 |
| R→M→O | 31.7 | 31.3 | 54.7 | 55.5 | 61.9 | 61.3 | 54.4 | 53.6 |

R = Requester host;  M = Manager host;  O = Page Owner R/M:
R/M: Requester and Manager are on the same host.
M/O: Manager and Owner are on the same host.

Over-Relaxation method (SOR). Data is represented as a large two-dimensional matrix. With the boundary values fixed, the internal values are then iteratively updated to be the average of the values of their four neighbors, until they converge. While this application is again based on large matrices (so we can partition the computation along with the data by assigning groups of adjacent rows of the matrix to the threads on various Fireflies), its data access behavior is quite different from the above two applications. The threads update values in their regions asynchronously with each other. The entries in the matrix are updated many times, and, for each iteration, the neighboring entries in the neighboring rows are needed. Thus, page sharing occurs in every iteration, and the number of iterations generally grows with the size of the matrix. Furthermore, to reach a decision on global convergence, the local convergence condition of each thread needs to be recorded in a shared array, and is checked by all threads. Given the simple model of data sharing used in Mermaid, it is interesting to see if page thrashing can be avoided, and good speedup can be achieved. For the experiments described below, a matrix of 128 × 816 of `double` numbers is used.

*2) Physical Versus Distributed Shared Memory:* Since the Firefly is a multiprocessor, we are able to compare the performance of physical shared memory to that of distributed shared memory. The same number of threads are either allocated to the processors on the same Firefly or to multiple Fireflies, (with one thread on each). The speedups of MM for both cases are shown in Table VII, for up to a maximum number of four threads. The slightly worse performance for the distributed case is due mainly to the cost of transferring pages between the machines. As also observed with the PCB and SOR applications, the penalty for running in a distributed system depends on the costs of data distribution and replication and the costs of data consistency and less so on the costs of data conversion. The distribution and replication costs are determined by the underlying communication and data conversion costs, whereas data conversion costs also depend on the applications' data access behaviors.

*3) Heterogeneous Versus Homogeneous Shared Memory:* To assess the effect of heterogeneity, we measured the response times of the three sample applications with a number of threads running on one or multiple Fireflies, and the master thread running on a Sun3/60. This is a representative configuration of heterogeneous distributed shared memory that takes advantages of both the user-friendly programming environment on a workstation, and the computing power of the background server hosts. Compared to the similar case in which both

TABLE VII
SPEEDUPS OF MATRIX MULTIPLICATION WHEN
EXECUTED ON ONE OR MULTIPLE FIREFLIES

| | number of processors | | | |
|---|---|---|---|---|
| | 1 | 2 | 3 | 4 |
| physical shared memory | 1.00 | 1.98 | 3.00 | 3.97 |
| distributed shared memory | 0.97 | 1.91 | 2.87 | 3.32 |

the master and the slave threads run on Fireflies, very little performance difference is observed. In the first case, pages of the matrices are moved from the Sun to the Fireflies and the result matrix is then moved back to the Sun after the computation; all data movements are accompanied by appropriate data conversions. No data conversion is needed for the homogeneous case. This is further evidence that data conversion does not add significant overhead to HDSM.

*4) Application Performance with HDSM:* The speedup curves of the MM, PCB, and SOR applications running on Mermaid are shown in Figs. 3, 4, and 5. The speedups are computed with respect to a sequential execution on a Firefly. For all the data points, the master thread is located on a separate Sun3/60. One to four Fireflies are used, and the numbers of threads allocated to each are approximately balanced. Better performance was observed using the largest page size algorithm for MM and PCB, while for SOR the smallest page size algorithm produced the best results (to be discussed further in Section IV-C2). For MM, performance improvements are observed as more and more threads are added to the computation, up to 18, the maximum number of Firefly processors available, for a maximum speedup of 12.

For PCB, there are two additional limitations to speedup: First, the volume of data to be transferred is very high (about 5 megabytes for each image), incurring substantial synchronous delays to remote worker threads as parts of the images are faulted in from the master. Second, the overlapping areas of the images must be processed by two threads, and represent extra computation, which grows as more threads are used. Despite these limitations, good speedup (up to 10 using 14 threads on four Fireflies) were still observed. Hence, the checking can now be completed in 65 s on four Fireflies, instead of 11 min in the sequential case. In some cases, super-linear speedup was observed. This is due to a reduction in the VM working set, as the data is partitioned among more and more processors where CPU caching becomes more effective. This observation is analogous to one made by Li with respect to main memory and VM paging [17].

The performance of SOR is comparable to that of MM,

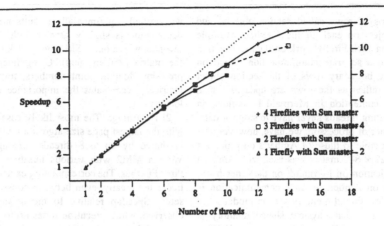

Fig. 3.   Matrix multiplication with master on Sun and slaves on one to four Fireflies.

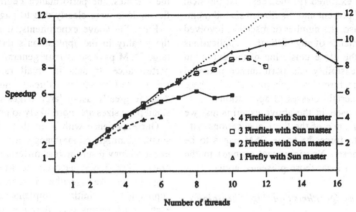

Fig. 4.   PCB with master on Sun and slaves on one to four Fireflies.

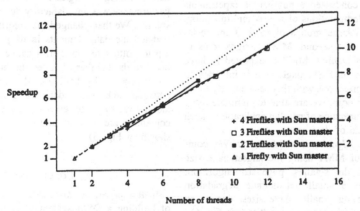

Fig. 5.   SOR with master on Sun and slaves on one to four Fireflies.

despite the large numbers of iterations made by the threads, causing many page faults on the pages that are shared by threads running on different Fireflies. Thrashing does not usually happen, since an iteration for each thread takes 150 ms or more, whereas a fault on an 1 kilobyte page only takes approximately 15 ms.

The same application has been studied in the Amber system at the University of Washington [8]. In Amber, an object-oriented approach is used for parallel application support. For the SOR application, the Amber implementation partitions the matrix into groups of rows called section objects, and stores one section object on each of the Fireflies. Multiple computation threads on each Firefly work on the local section object in parallel, and a separate communication thread on each Firefly sends the boundary rows of the section object to the neighboring Fireflies as the rows are updated. Thus, the potential of data contention in Mermaid is avoided in Amber, and the computing threads never have to stop for data. With the limited number of processors we have, however, our results are very comparable to those of Amber's on problems of similar sizes. (A 122 × 842 matrix was used with Amber.) Programming an application on Mermaid, on the other hand, is much simpler than on Amber, because communication is completely hidden in the shared memory system model.

It is interesting to note that physical shared memory is treated as a special case of distributed shared memory in Mermaid; the two types of memory are fully integrated throughout the heterogeneous system base, and the performance potential of such a system is well explored (in the sense that physical shared memory is used if present and distributed shared memory is used otherwise). Also, the number of machines involved does not affect the performance of any of the three applications much, as evidenced by the close clustering of the curves in Figs. 3, 4, and 5. The feasibility and performance potential of HDSM systems are therefore clearly demonstrated by these experiments, at least for certain classes of applications.

Besides the data sizes used in the above experiments, we also measured the performance of the three applications with several other data sizes to force the same DSM pages to be shared among multiple hosts. No significant changes to the speedup values were found from those presented above.

### C. Effects of the Page Size Algorithms and Page Thrashing

To assess the effects of page thrashing due to data contention among threads, and to study the relationship between page size and thrashing, we conducted a number of experiments using two different implementations of matrix multiplication. The first, MM1, assigns large groups of rows of the result matrix to each thread,[11] the second, MM2, assigns rows to threads in a round-robin fashion. MM2 is expected to have more data contention on its DSM pages and is intended to represent the class of applications with this behavior. By using matrix multiplication for both, we are able to eliminate other factors affecting the performance of parallel applications, such as scalability and the size of data sets.

*1) Effects of Page Size Algorithms and Locality:* We compared the performance of MM1 using the largest page size algorithm to that using the smallest page size algorithm, and found that there is a small but definite degradation in performance when using smaller page sizes, due to an increased number of page faults on the Fireflies (see Fig. 6).

Since MM2 divides the result matrix into rows for the slave threads (4 kilobyte, or 512 `double` floats each), and since the smallest page size algorithm operates on 1 kilobyte pages, we expected the degradation of MM2 over MM1 using this smallest page size algorithm to be very small, which

[11] MM1 is the implementation of MM being used so far.

we verified experimentally (results not presented here). The degradation is slightly greater with 256 × 256 matrices of integers, where one DSM page of 1 kilobyte holds one row of the matrix (256 integers). Using integers instead of double precision floating point numbers, together with the smaller matrices, accentuates the importance of communication and locality.

*2) Thrashing:* The most likely case for thrashing is MM2 with the largest page size algorithm, where an 8 kilobyte page is shared by up to 8 threads running on several Fireflies. We ran MM2 with various numbers of threads on two or three Fireflies. The corresponding execution times we observed fluctuated greatly, even between consecutive runs of identical setup. Speedup relative to the sequential case was rarely observed, while execution times up to 10 times of that of the sequential case were measured. Examination of the detailed statistics of the numbers of page faults and transfers revealed that a large number of pages were being transferred between the Fireflies; the performance degradation and unpredictable fluctuations were clearly due to page thrashing.

From the above experiments, it may be concluded that if the locality in the application's data accesses is very good, large DSM page sizes may generate less overhead and better performance. If data in small ranges of the DSM space are updated by separate threads, however, performance may degrade greatly using large pages due to false sharing, and small page sizes are more likely to provide stable performance.

Our experience with a number of applications shows that small, seemingly minor changes to an implementation of an application may result in very different data sharing patterns and drastically different performance. MM1 versus MM2, using the largest page size algorithm, is such an example. For the SOR application, we initially implemented the algorithm so that each thread, during each iteration, updated the data elements in its portion of the matrix from top to bottom, thus sharing data with neighboring threads in every iteration. The resulting performance was unsatisfactory due to the frequent read–write sharing. We then changed the algorithm such that each thread updated the data elements in its portion of the matrix from top to bottom to top. Performance is improved substantially because the number of times the boundary rows are worked on is reduced by half, and the amount of computation in between such shared data zones is doubled. Consequently, data movement between machines and the possibility of data contention are reduced, and better speedups are observed (as shown in Fig. 5).

## V. Concluding Remarks

In this paper, we discussed the main issues and solutions of building a DSM system on a network of heterogeneous machines. As a practical research effort, we designed and implemented an HDSM system, Mermaid, for a network of Sun workstations and Firefly multiprocessors, and we ported a number of applications to Mermaid. We conclude that heterogeneous DSM is indeed feasible. From a functional point of view, we showed that little transparency need be lost due to heterogeneity. The most important problem is data

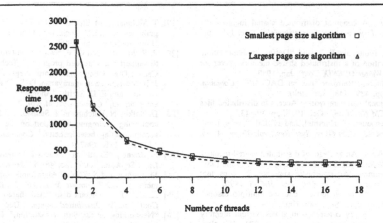

Fig. 6.  Response times of MM1 using the largest (smallest) page size algorithms.

conversion. Our solution requires that the user specify the type of data being allocated in the HDSM space, which is usually natural to the programmer. For different representations of floating point numbers, equivalent data conversion may be impossible for extreme values. However, with the increasing use of the IEEE floating point standard, this may be considered to be a passing problem. We were able to easily integrate our HDSM system into the physical shared memory system on the Firefly, allowing the programmer to exploit both physical and distributed shared memory using one and the same mechanism.

From a performance point of view, we again showed that little transparency is lost due to heterogeneity; that is, our heterogeneous DSM implementation performs comparably to an equivalent homogeneous DSM system. Overall, we have found that the cost of data conversion does not substantially increase the cost of paging across the network. Other aspects of heterogeneity, such as accommodating different page sizes and user-level processing of messages, also do not contribute significantly to the DSM overhead. The presence of multiple VM page sizes on different types of machines presents applications with the opportunity of selecting the DSM page size according to their data access patterns; we noticed substantial performance gains in using suitable DSM page sizes.

Our measured performance results corroborate the results of other researchers in that distributed shared memory can be competitive to the direct use of message passing, for a reasonably large class of applications. In some cases, they actually outperform their message passing counterparts, even though the shared memory system is implemented in a layer on top of a message passing system.

Although our prototype Mermaid system integrates only two types of hosts, we believe that the techniques we developed to accommodate heterogeneity are easily extensible to more than two types of hosts, without significant additional overhead. For conversion of user-defined data types, the same conversion routines can be used on all machines since the routines only contain structural information. However, for the basic types, separate conversion routines need to be written for each (ordered) pair of machines, with a total of $N \times (N-1)$ routines for each basic data type allocated in the HDSM space.

For the implementor of the HDSM system, this is a one-time only effort and is transparent to the application programmer. In contrast, defining a network standard data format would decrease the conversion coding effort, but increase the run-time conversion overhead.

### ACKNOWLEDGMENT

T. McInnerny was responsible for most of the Mermaid implementation work, and conducted the measurements reported in this paper. M. Lalovic and S. Fink separately implemented two versions of the data conversion routine generator software. A. Yip performed an initial porting of the PCB software to Mermaid running on Suns. The SOR application is based on a parallel implementation for a Firefly by R. Unrau. Comments by the anonymous referees helped us to improve the presentation of this paper. Partial support for this work was generously provided by the Information Technology Research Center of Ontario and Digital Equipment Corporation.

### REFERENCES

[1] "Network computing systems reference manual," Tech. rep., Apollo Computer Inc., Chelmsford, MA, 1987.

[2] E. Balkovich, S. Lerman, and R. P. Parmelee, "Computing in higher education: The Athena experience," *Commun. ACM*, vol. 28, no. 11, pp. 1214–1224, 1985.

[3] J. Bennet, J. Carter, and W. Zwaenepoel, "Munin: Distributed shared memory based on type-specific memory coherence," in *Proc. PPoPP*, Mar. 1990, pp. 168–176.

[4] B. N. Bershad, D. T. Ching, E. D. Lazowska, H. Sanislo, and M. Schwartz, "A remote procedure call facility for interconnecting heterogeneous computer systems," *IEEE Trans. Software Eng.*, vol. SE-13, no. 8, pp. 880–894, 1987.

[5] D. R. Cheriton, "Preliminary thoughts on problem-oriented shared memory: A decentralized approach to distributed systems," *ACM Oper. Syst. Rev.*, vol. 19, no. 4, Oct. 1985.

[6] D. Cohen, "On holy wars and a plea for peace," *IEEE Comput. Mag.*, vol. 14, no. 10, 1981.

[7] C. Pinkerton *et al.*, "A heterogeneous distributed file system," in *Proc. Tenth IEEE Int. Conf. Distributed Comput. Syst.*, 1990.

[8] J. Chase *et al.*, "The Amber system: Parallel programming on a network of multiprocessors," in *Proc. Twelfth ACM Symp. Oper. Syst. Principles*, 1989.

[9] R. Sandberg *et al.*, "Design and implementation of the Sun network filesystem," in *Proc. 1985 Summer USENIX Conf.*, 1985.

[10] B. D. Fleisch, "Mirage: A coherent distributed shared memory design," in *Proc. 12th ACM Symp. Oper. Syst. Principles*, Dec. 1989, pp. 211–223,

[11] A. Forin, J. Barrera, M. Young, and R. Rashid, "Design, implementation, and performance evaluation of a distributed shared memory server for Mach," in *Proc. 1989 Winter USENIX Conf.*, Jan. 1989.

[12] K. Geihs and U. Holberg, "Retrospective on DACNOS," *Commun. ACM*, vol. 33, no. 2, pp. 439–448, Apr. 1990.

[13] D. P. Geller, "The national software works: Access to distributed files and tools," in *Proc. ACM Nat. Conf.*, Oct. 1977, pp. 39–43,

[14] M. Kaashoek, A. Tanenbaum, S. Hummel, and H. Bal, "An efficient reliable broadcast protocol," *ACM Oper. Syst. Rev.*, vol. 23, no. 4, pp. 5–19, Oct. 1989.

[15] R.E. Kessler and M. Livny, "An analysis of distributed shared memory algorithms," in *Proc. 9th Int. Conf. Distributed Comput. Syst.*, June 1989.

[16] O. Krieger and M. Stumm, "An optimistic approach for consistent replicated data for mulitcomputers," in *Proc. 1990 HICSS*, 1990.

[17] K. Li, "Shared virtual memory on loosely coupled multiprocessors," Ph.D. dissertation, Dep. Comput. Sci., Yale Univ. 1986.

[18] K. Li and P. Hudak, "Memory coherence in shared virtual memory systems," *ACM Trans. Comput. Syst.*, vol. 7, no. 4, pp. 321–359, Nov. 1989.

[19] T. McInnerny, M. Stumm, and S. Zhou, "Mermaid user's guide and programmer's manual," Tech. rep., Computer Systems Research Institute, Univ. Toronto, Sept. 1990.

[20] P. R. McJones and G. F. Swart, "Evolving the UNIX system interface to support multithreaded programs," Tech. Rep. 21, Systems Research Center, Digital Equipment Corp., Sept. 1987.

[21] J. H. Moris, M. Satyanarayanan, D. S. H. Rosenthal M. H. Conner, J. H. Howard, and F. D. Smith, "Andrew: A distributed personal computing environment," *Commun. ACM*, vol. 29, no. 3, pp. 184–201, 1986.

[22] D. Notkin, N. Hutchinson, J. Sanislo, and M. Schwartz, "Heterogeneous computing environments: Report on the ACM SIGOPS workshop on accommodating heterogeneity," *Commun. ACM*, vol. 30, no. 2, pp. 142–162, Feb. 1987.

[23] P. Rovner, "Extending Modula-2 to build large integrated systems," *IEEE Software*, vol. 6, pp. 46–57, Nov. 1986.

[24] M. Stumm and S. Zhou, "Algorithms implementing distributed shared memory," *IEEE Comput. Mag.*, vol. 23, no. 5, May 1990.

[25] ———, "Fault tolerant distributed shared memory," in *Proc. IEEE Int. Conf. Parallel Distributed Comput.*, Dec 1990.

[26] "Networking on the Sun workstation," Tech. rep., Sun Microsystems Inc., Mt. View CA, 1985.

[27] C. P. Thacker, L. C. Stewart, and E. H. Satterthwaite, "Firefly: A multiprocessor workstation," *IEEE Trans. Comput.*, vol. 37, no. 8, pp. 909–920, Aug. 1988.

# TreadMarks: Distributed Shared Memory on Standard Workstations and Operating Systems

*Pete Keleher, Alan L. Cox, Sandhya Dwarkadas and Willy Zwaenepoel*

Department of Computer Science
Rice University
Houston, TX 77251-1892

## Abstract

TreadMarks is a *distributed shared memory* (DSM) system for standard Unix systems such as SunOS and Ultrix. This paper presents a performance evaluation of TreadMarks running on Ultrix using DECstation-5000/240's that are connected by a 100-Mbps switch-based ATM LAN and a 10-Mbps Ethernet. Our objective is to determine the efficiency of a user-level DSM implementation on commercially available workstations and operating systems.

We achieved good speedups on the 8-processor ATM network for Jacobi (7.4), TSP (7.2), Quicksort (6.3), and ILINK (5.7). For a slightly modified version of Water from the SPLASH benchmark suite, we achieved only moderate speedups (4.0) due to the high communication and synchronization rate. Speedups decline on the 10-Mbps Ethernet (5.5 for Jacobi, 6.5 for TSP, 4.2 for Quicksort, 5.1 for ILINK, and 2.1 for Water), reflecting the bandwidth limitations of the Ethernet. These results support the contention that, with suitable networking technology, DSM is a viable technique for parallel computation on clusters of workstations.

To achieve these speedups, TreadMarks goes to great lengths to reduce the amount of communication performed to maintain memory consistency. It uses a lazy implementation of release consistency, and it allows multiple concurrent writers to modify a page, reducing the impact of false sharing. Great care was taken to minimize communication overhead. In particular, on the ATM network, we used a standard low-level protocol, AAL3/4, bypassing the TCP/IP protocol stack. Unix communication overhead, however, remains the main obstacle in the way of better performance for programs like Water. Compared to the Unix communication overhead, memory management cost (both kernel and user level) is small and wire time is negligible.

## 1  Introduction

With increasing frequency, networks of workstations are being used as parallel computers. High-speed general-purpose networks and very powerful workstation processors have narrowed the performance gap between workstation clusters and supercomputers. Furthermore, the workstation approach provides a relatively low-cost, low-risk entry into the parallel computing arena. Many organizations already have an installed workstation base, no special hardware is required to use this facility as a parallel computer, and the resulting system can be easily maintained, extended and upgraded. We expect that the workstation cluster approach to parallel computing will gain further popularity, as advances in networking continue to improve its cost/performance ratio.

This research was supported in part by the National Science Foundation under Grants CCR-9116343, CCR-9211004, CDA-9222911, and CDA-9310073, by the Texas Advanced Technology Program under Grant 003604014, and by a NASA Graduate Fellowship.

"TreadMarks: Distributed Shared Memory on Standard Workstations and Operating Systems" by P. Keleher, et al. from *USENIX Winter 1994 Conf.*, pp. 115–132. Reprinted by permission of the author.

Various software systems have been proposed and built to support parallel computation on workstation networks, e.g., tuple spaces [2], distributed shared memory [18], and message passing [23]. TreadMarks is a *distributed shared memory* (DSM) system [18]. DSM enables processes on different machines to share memory, even though the machines physically do not share memory (see Figure 1). This approach is attractive since most programmers find it easier to use than a message passing paradigm, which requires them to explicitly partition data and manage communication. With a global address space, the programmer can focus on algorithmic development rather than on managing partitioned data sets and communicating values.

Many DSM implementations have been reported in the literature (see [20] for an overview). Unfortunately, none of these implementations are widely available. Many run on in-house research platforms, rather than on generally available operating systems, or require kernel modifications that make them unappealing. Early DSM systems also suffered from performance problems. These early designs implemented the shared memory abstraction by imitating consistency protocols used by hardware shared memory multiprocessors. Given the large consistency units in DSM (virtual memory pages), false sharing was a serious problem for many applications.

TreadMarks overcomes most of these problems: it is an efficient DSM system that runs on commonly available Unix systems. This paper reports on an implementation on Ultrix using 8 DECStation-5000/240s, connected both by a 100-Mbps point-to-point ATM LAN and by a 10-Mbps Ethernet. The system has also been implemented on SunOS using SPARCstation-1's and -2's connected by a 10-Mbps Ethernet. The implementation is done at the *user* level, without modification to the operating system kernel. Furthermore, we do not rely on any particular compiler. Instead, our implementation relies on (user-level) memory management techniques to detect accesses and updates to shared data. In order to address the performance problems with earlier DSM systems, the TreadMarks implementation focuses on reducing the amount of communication necessary to keep the distributed memories consistent. It uses a lazy implementation [14] of release consistency [13] and multiple-writer protocols to reduce the impact of false sharing [8].

On the 100-Mbps ATM LAN, good speedups were achieved for Jacobi, TSP, Quicksort, and ILINK (a program from the genetic LINKAGE package [16]). TreadMarks achieved only a moderate speedup for a slightly modified version of the Water program from the SPLASH benchmark suite [22], because of the high synchronization and communication rates. We present a detailed decomposition of the overheads. For the applications measured, the software communication overhead is the bottleneck in achieving high performance for finer grained applications like Water. This is the case even when using a low-level adaptation layer protocol (AAL3/4) on the ATM network, bypassing the TCP/IP protocol stack. The communication overhead dominates the memory management and consistency overhead. On a 100-Mbps ATM LAN, the "wire" time is all but negligible.

The outline of the rest of this paper is as follows. Section 2 focuses on the principal design decisions: release consistency, lazy release consistency, multiple-writer protocols, and lazy diff creation. Section 3

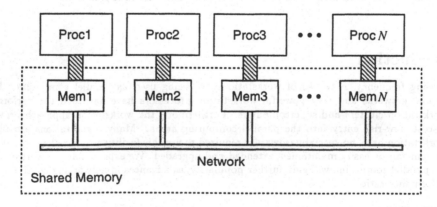

**Figure 1** Distributed Shared Memory

describes the implementation of these concepts, and also includes a discussion of the Unix aspects of the implementation. The resulting performance is discussed in Section 4, and compared against earlier work using eager release consistency in Section 5. We discuss related work in Section 6, and conclude in Section 7.

# 2   Design

TreadMarks' design focuses on reducing the amount of communication necessary to maintain memory consistency. To this end, it presents a *release consistent* memory model [13] to the user. Release consistency requires less communication than conventional, sequentially consistent [15] shared memory, but provides a very similar programming interface. The *lazy* implementation of release consistency in TreadMarks further reduces the number of messages and the amount of data compared to earlier, eager implementations [8]. False sharing is another source of frequent communication in DSM systems. TreadMarks uses *multiple-writer* protocols to address this problem. Multiple-writer protocols require the creation of *diffs*, data structures that record updates to parts of a page. With lazy release consistency, diff creation can often be postponed or avoided, a technique we refer to as *lazy diff creation*.

## 2.1   Release Consistency

Release consistency (RC) [13] is a *relaxed* memory consistency model that permits a processor to delay making its changes to shared data visible to other processors until certain synchronization accesses occur. Shared memory accesses are categorized either as *ordinary* or as *synchronization* accesses, with the latter category further divided into *acquire* and *release* accesses. Acquires and releases roughly correspond to synchronization operations on a lock, but other synchronization mechanisms can be implemented on top of this model as well. For instance, arrival at a barrier can be modeled as a release, and departure from a barrier as an acquire. Essentially, RC requires ordinary shared memory updates by a processor $p$ to become visible at another processor $q$, only when a subsequent release by $p$ becomes visible at $q$.

In contrast, in *sequentially consistent* (SC) memory [15], the conventional model implemented by most snoopy-cache, bus-based multiprocessors, modifications to shared memory must become visible to other processors immediately [15]. Programs written for SC memory produce the same results on an RC memory, provided that (i) all synchronization operations use system-supplied primitives, and (ii) there is a release-acquire pair between conflicting ordinary accesses to the same memory location on different processors [13]. In practice, most shared memory programs require little or no modifications to meet these requirements.

Although execution on an RC memory produces the same results as on a SC memory for the overwhelming majority of the programs, RC can be implemented more efficiently than SC. In the latter, the requirement that shared memory updates become visible immediately implies communication on each write to a shared data item for which other cached copies exist. No such requirement exists under RC. The propagation of the modifications can be postponed until the next synchronization operation takes effect.

## 2.2   Lazy Release Consistency

In *lazy release consistency* (LRC) [14], the propagation of modifications is postponed *until the time of the acquire*. At this time, the acquiring processor determines which modifications it needs to see according to the definition of RC.

To do so, LRC divides the execution of each process into *intervals*, each denoted by an *interval index*. Every time a process executes a release or an acquire, a new interval begins and the interval index is incremented. Intervals of different processes are partially ordered [1]: (i) intervals on a single processor are totally ordered by program order, and (ii) an interval on processor $p$ precedes an interval on processor $q$ if the interval of $q$ begins with the acquire corresponding to the release that concluded the interval of $p$. This partial order can be represented concisely by assigning a *vector timestamp* to each interval. A vector timestamp contains an entry for each processor. The entry for processor $p$ in the vector timestamp of interval $i$ of processor $p$ is equal to $i$. The entry for processor $q \neq p$ denotes the most recent interval of processor $q$ that precedes the current interval of processor $p$ according to the partial order. A processor computes a new vector timestamp at an acquire according to the pair-wise maximum of its previous vector timestamp and the releaser's vector timestamp.

RC requires that before a processor $p$ may continue past an acquire, the updates of all intervals with a smaller vector timestamp than $p$'s current vector timestamp must be visible at $p$. Therefore, at an acquire, $p$ sends its current vector timestamp to the previous releaser, $q$. Processor $q$ then piggybacks on the release-acquire message to $p$, *write notices* for all intervals named in $q$'s current vector timestamp but not in the vector timestamp it received from $p$.

A write notice is an indication that a page has been modified in a particular interval, but it does *not* contain the actual modifications. The timing of the actual data movement depends on whether an invalidate, an update, or a hybrid protocol is used (see [9]). TreadMarks currently uses an invalidate protocol: the arrival of a write notice for a page causes the processor to invalidate its copy of that page. A subsequent access to that page causes an access miss, at which time the modifications are propagated to the local copy.

Alternative implementations of RC generally cause more communication than LRC. For example, the DASH shared-memory multiprocessor [17] implements RC in hardware, buffering writes to avoid blocking the processor until the write has been performed with respect to main memory and remote caches. A subsequent release is not allowed to perform (i.e., the corresponding lock cannot be granted to another processor) until all outstanding shared writes are acknowledged. While this strategy masks latency, LRC sends far fewer messages, an important consideration in a software implementation on a general-purpose network because of the high per message cost. In an *eager* software implementation of RC [8], a processor propagates its modifications of shared data when it executes a release. This approach also leads to more communication, because it requires a message to be sent to all processors that cache the modified data, while LRC propagates the data only to the next acquirer.

## 2.3 Multiple-Writer Protocols

False sharing was a serious problem for early DSM systems. It occurs when two or more processors access different variables within a page, with at least one of the accesses being a write. Under the common single-writer protocols, false sharing leads to unnecessary communication. A write to any variable of a page causes the entire page to become invalid on all other processors that cache the page. A subsequent access on any of these processors incurs an access miss and causes the modified copy to be brought in over the network, although the original copy of the page would have sufficed, since the write was to a variable different from the one that was accessed locally. This problem occurs in snoopy-cache multiprocessors as well, but it is more prevalent in software DSM because the consistency protocol operates on pages rather than smaller cache blocks.

To address this problem, Munin introduced a *multiple-writer* protocol [8]. With multiple-writer protocols two or more processors can simultaneously modify their local copy of a shared page. Their modifications are merged at the next synchronization operation in accordance with the definition of RC, thereby reducing the effect of false sharing.

## 2.4 Lazy Diff Creation

In order to capture the modifications to a shared page, it is initially write-protected. At the first write, a protection violation occurs. The DSM software makes a copy of the page (a *twin*), and removes the write protection so that further writes to the page can occur without any DSM intervention. The twin and the current copy can later be compared to create a *diff*, a runlength encoded record of the modifications to the page.

In TreadMarks, diffs are only created when a processor requests the modifications to a page or a write notice from another processor arrives for that page. In the latter case, it is essential to make a diff in order to distinguish the modifications made by the different processors. This *lazy* diff creation is distinct from Munin's implementation of multiple-writer protocols, where at each release a diff is created for each modified page and propagated to all other copies of the page. The lazy implementation of RC used by TreadMarks allows diff creation to be postponed until the modifications are requested. Lazy diff creation results in a decrease in the number of diffs created (see Section 5) and an attendant improvement in performance.

# 3   Implementation

## 3.1   Data Structures

Figure 2 gives an overview of the data structures used. The principal data structures are the *PageArray*, with one entry for each shared page, the *ProcArray*, with one entry for each processor, a set of *interval records* (containing mainly the vector timestamp for that interval), a set of *write notice records*, and a *diff pool*. Each entry in the *PageArray* contains:

1. The current state: no access, read-only access, or read-write access.

2. An *approximate copyset* specifying the set of processors that are believed to currently cache this page.

3. For each page, an array indexed by processor of head and tail pointers to a linked list of *write notice records* corresponding to write notices received from that processor for this page. If the diff corresponding to the write notice has been received, then a pointer to this diff is present in the write notice record. This list is maintained in order of decreasing interval indices.

Each entry in *ProcArray* contains a pointer to the head and the tail of a doubly linked list of *interval records*, representing the intervals of that processor that the local processor knows about. This list is also maintained in order of decreasing interval indices. Each of these interval records contains a pointer to a list of write notice records for that interval, and each write notice record contains a pointer to its interval record.

## 3.2   Interval and Diff Creation

Logically, a new interval begins at each release and acquire. In practice, interval creation can be postponed until we communicate with another process, avoiding overhead if a lock is reacquired by the same processor. When a lock is released to another processor, or at arrival at a barrier, a new interval is created containing

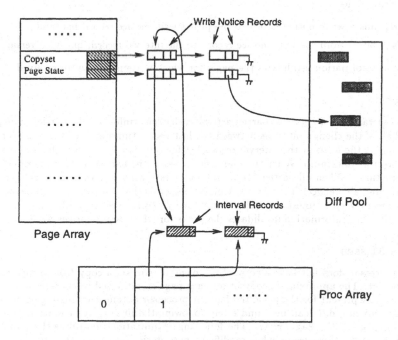

**Figure 2**   Overview of TreadMarks Data Structures

a write notice for each page that was twinned since the last remote synchronization operation. With lazy diff creation these pages remain writable until a diff request or a write notice arrives for that page. At that time, the actual diff is created, the page is read protected, and the twin is discarded. A subsequent write results in a write notice for the next interval.

## 3.3 Locks

All locks have a statically assigned manager. Lock management is assigned in a round-robin fashion among the processors. The manager records which processor has most recently requested the lock. All lock acquire requests are directed to the manager, and, if necessary, forwarded to the processor that last requested the lock.

The lock acquire request contains the current vector timestamp of the acquiring processor. The lock request arrives at the processor that either holds the lock or did the last release on it, possibly after forwarding by the lock manager. When the lock is released, the releaser "informs" the acquirer of all intervals between the vector timestamp in the acquirer's lock request message, and the releaser's current vector timestamp. The message contains the following information for each of these intervals:

1. The processor id.

2. The vector timestamp.

3. All write-notices. The write notice in the message is a fixed 16-bit entry containing the page number.

All of this information can easily be derived by following the pointers from the *ProcArray* to the appropriate interval records and from there to the appropriate write notice records.

After receiving this message, the acquirer "incorporates" this information into its data structures. For each interval in the message,

1. the acquirer appends an interval record to the interval record list for that processor, and

2. for each write notice

   (a) it prepends a write notice record to the page's write notice record list, and

   (b) adds pointers from the write notice record to the interval record, and vice versa.

Incorporating this information invalidates the pages for which write notices were received.

## 3.4 Barriers

Barriers have a centralized manager. At barrier arrival, each client "informs" the barrier manager of its vector timestamp and all of the client's intervals between the last vector timestamp of the manager that the client is aware of (found at the head of the interval record list for the *ProcArray* entry for the manager) and the client's current vector timestamp. When the manager arrives at the barrier, it "incorporates" these intervals into its data structures. When all barrier arrival messages have been received, the manager then "informs" all clients of all intervals between their vector timestamp, as received in their barrier arrival message, and the manager's current vector timestamp. The clients then "incorporate" this information as before. As for locks, incorporating this information invalidates the pages for which write notices were received.

## 3.5 Access Misses

If the faulting processor does not have a copy of the page, it requests a copy from a member of the page's approximate copyset. The approximate copyset for each page is initialized to contain processor 0.

If write notices are present for the page, the faulting processor obtains the missing diffs and applies them to the page. The missing diffs can be found easily following the linked list of write notices starting from the entry for this page in the **PageArray**. The following optimization minimizes the number of messages necessary to get the diffs. If processor $p$ has modified a page during interval $i$, then $p$ must have all the diffs of all intervals (including those from processors other than $p$) that have a smaller vector timestamp than $i$. It therefore suffices to look at the largest interval of each processor for which we have a write notice but no diff. Of that subset of the processors, a message needs to be sent only to those processors for which the vector timestamp of their most recent interval is not dominated by the vector timestamp of another processor's most recent interval.

After the set of necessary diffs and the set of processors to query have been determined, the faulting processor sends out requests for the diffs in parallel, including the processor id, the page number and the interval index of the requested diffs. When all necessary diffs have been received, they are applied in increasing vector timestamp order.

### 3.6   Garbage Collection

Garbage collection is necessary to reclaim the space used by write notice records, interval records, and diffs. During garbage collection, each processor validates its copy of every page that it has modified. All other pages, all interval records, all write notice records and all diffs are discarded. In addition, each processor updates the copyset for every page. If, after garbage collection, a processor accesses a page for which it does not have a copy, it requests a copy from a processor in the copyset.

The processors execute a barrier-like protocol, in which processors request and apply all diffs created by other processors for the pages they have modified themselves. Garbage collection is triggered when the amount of free space for consistency information drops below a threshold. An attempt is made to make garbage collection coincide with a barrier, since many of the operations are similar.

### 3.7   Unix Aspects

TreadMarks relies on Unix and its standard libraries to accomplish remote process creation, interprocessor communication, and memory management. In this section, we briefly describe the implementation of each of these services.

TreadMarks interprocessor communication can be accomplished either through UDP/IP on an Ethernet or an ATM LAN, or through the AAL3/4 protocol on the ATM LAN. AAL3/4 is a connection-oriented, unreliable message protocol specified by the ATM standard. Since neither protocol guarantees reliable delivery, TreadMarks uses operation-specific, user-level protocols on top of UDP/IP and AAL3/4 to insure delivery.

To minimize latency in handling incoming asynchronous requests, TreadMarks uses a `SIGIO` signal handler. Message arrival at any socket used to receive request messages generates a `SIGIO` signal. Since AAL3/4 is a connection-oriented protocol, there is a socket corresponding to each of the other processors. To determine which socket holds the incoming request, the handler for AAL3/4 performs a `select` system call. The handler for UDP/IP avoids the `select` system call by multiplexing all of the other processors over a single receive socket. After the handler receives the message, it performs the request and returns.

To implement the consistency protocol, TreadMarks uses the `mprotect` system call to control access to shared pages. Any attempt to perform a restricted access on a shared page generates a `SIGSEGV` signal. The `SIGSEGV` signal handler examines the local *PageArray* to determine the page's state. If the local copy is read-only, the handler allocates a page from the pool of free pages and performs a `bcopy` to create a *twin*. Finally, the handler upgrades the access rights to the original page and returns. If the local page is invalid, the handler executes the access miss procedure.

## 4   Performance

### 4.1   Experimental Environment

Our experimental environment consists of 8 DECstation-5000/240's running Ultrix V4.3. Each machine has a Fore ATM interface that is connected to a Fore ATM switch. The connection between the interface boards and the switch operates at 100-Mbps; the switch has an aggregate throughput of 1.2-Gbps. The interface board does programmed I/O into transmit and receive FIFOs, and requires fragmentation and reassembly of ATM cells by software. Interrupts are raised at the end of a message or a (nearly) full receive FIFO. All of the machines are also connected by a 10-Mbps Ethernet. Unless otherwise noted, the performance numbers describe 8-processor executions on the ATM LAN using the low-level adaptation layer protocol AAL3/4.

## 4.2  Basic Operation Costs

The minimum roundtrip time using send and receive for the smallest possible message is 500 $\mu$seconds. The minimum time to send the smallest possible message through a socket is 80 $\mu$seconds, and the minimum time to receive this message is 80 $\mu$seconds. The remaining 180 $\mu$seconds are divided between wire time, interrupt processing and resuming the processor that blocked in receive. Using a signal handler to receive the message at both processors, the roundtrip time increases to 670 $\mu$seconds.

The minimum time to remotely acquire a free lock is 827 $\mu$seconds if the manager was the last processor to hold the lock, and 1149 $\mu$seconds otherwise. In both cases, the reply message from the last processor to hold the lock does not contain any write notices (or diffs). The time to acquire a lock increases in proportion to the number of write notices that must be included in the reply message. The minimum time to perform an 8 processor barrier is 2186 $\mu$seconds. A remote page fault, to obtain a 4096 byte page from another processor takes 2792 $\mu$seconds.

## 4.3  Applications

We used five programs in this study: Water, Jacobi, TSP, Quicksort, and ILINK. Water, obtained from SPLASH [22], is a molecular dynamics simulation. We made one simple modification to the original program to reduce the number of lock accesses. We simulated 343 molecules for 5 steps. Jacobi implements a form of Successive Over-Relaxation (SOR) with a grid of 2000 by 1000 elements. TSP uses a branch-and-bound algorithm to solve the traveling salesman problem for a 19-city tour. Quicksort sorts an array of 256K integers, using a bubblesort to sort subarrays of less than 1K elements. ILINK, from the LINKAGE package [16], performs genetic linkage analysis (see [10] for more details). ILINK's input consists of data on 12 families with autosomal dominant nonsyndromic cleft lip and palate (CLP).

## 4.4  Results

Figure 3 presents speedups for the five applications. The speedups were calculated using uniprocessor times obtained by running the applications without TreadMarks. Figure 4 provides execution statistics for each of the five applications when using 8 processors.

The speedup for Water is limited by the high communication (798 Kbytes/second and 2238 messages/second) and synchronization rate (582 lock accesses/second). There are many short messages (the average message size is 356 bytes), resulting in a large communication overhead. Each molecule is protected by a lock that is accessed frequently by a majority of the processors. In addition, the program uses barriers for synchronization.

Jacobi exclusively uses barriers for synchronization. Jacobi's computation to communication ratio is an order of magnitude larger than that of Water. In addition, most communication occurs at the barriers and between neighbors. On the ATM network, this communication can occur in parallel. The above two effects compound, resulting in near-linear speedup for Jacobi.

TSP is an application that exclusively uses locks for synchronization. Like Jacobi, TSP has a very high computation to communication ratio, resulting in near-linear speedup. While the number of messages per second is slightly larger than for Jacobi, TSP transmits only a quarter of the amount of data transmitted by Jacobi.

Quicksort also uses locks for synchronization. Quicksort's synchronization rate is close to that of Jacobi's. It, however, sends over twice as many messages and data per second, resulting in slightly lower, although good, speedups. The number of kilobytes per second transmitted by Quicksort is similar to that transmitted by Water, but it sends 3 times fewer messages and the number of synchronization operations is an order of magnitude lower than for Water. As a result, speedup for Quicksort is higher than for Water.

ILINK achieves less than linear speedup on TreadMarks because of a load balancing problem inherent to the nature of the algorithm [10]. It is not possible to predict in advance whether the set of iterations distributed to the processors will result in the same amount of work on each processor, without significant

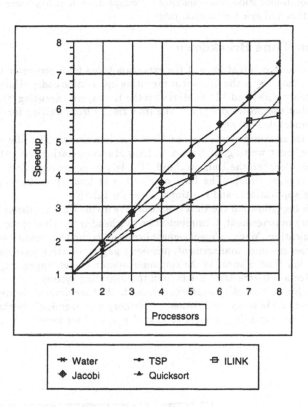

**Figure 3**   Speedups Obtained on TreadMarks

|                | Water              | Jacobi                | TSP           | Quicksort          | ILINK |
|----------------|--------------------|-----------------------|---------------|--------------------|-------|
| Input          | 343 mols<br>5 steps | 2000x1000<br>floats  | 19-city tour  | 256000<br>integers | CLP   |
| Time (secs)    | 15.0               | 32.0                  | 43.8          | 13.1               | 1113  |
| Barriers/sec   | 2.5                | 6.3                   | 0             | 0.4                | 0.4   |
| Locks/sec      | 582.4              | 0                     | 16.1          | 53.9               | 0     |
| Msgs/sec       | 2238               | 334                   | 404           | 703                | 456   |
| Kbytes/sec     | 798                | 415                   | 121           | 788                | 164   |

**Figure 4**   Execution Statistics for an 8-Processor Run on TreadMarks

computation and communication. Consequently, speedups are somewhat lower than one would expect based on the communication and synchronization rates.

## 4.5 Execution Time Breakdown

Figure 5 shows a percentage breakdown of the execution times for 8-processor versions of all 5 applications. The "Computation" category is the time spent executing application code; "Unix" is the time spent executing Unix kernel and library code; and "TreadMarks" is the time spent executing TreadMarks code. "Idle Time" refers to the time that the processor is idle. Idle time results from waiting for locks and barriers, as well as from remote communication latency.

The largest overhead components are the Unix and idle times. The idle time reflects to some extent the amount of time spent waiting for Unix and TreadMarks operations on other nodes. The TreadMarks overhead is much smaller than the Unix overhead. The largest percentage TreadMarks overhead is for Water (2.9% of overall execution time). The Unix overhead is at least three times as large as the TreadMarks overhead for all the applications, and is 9 times larger for ILINK.

Figure 6 shows a breakdown of the Unix overhead. We divide Unix overhead into two categories: communication and memory management. Communication overhead is the time spent executing *kernel* operations to support communication. Memory management overhead is the time spent executing *kernel* operations to support the *user-level* memory management, primarily page protection changes. In all cases, at least 80% of the kernel execution time is spent in the communication routines, suggesting that cheap communication is the primary service a software DSM needs from the operating system.

Figure 7 shows a breakdown of TreadMarks overhead. We have divided the overhead into three categories: memory management, consistency, and "other". "Memory management" overhead is the time spent at the *user-level* detecting and capturing changes to shared pages. This includes twin and diff creation and diff

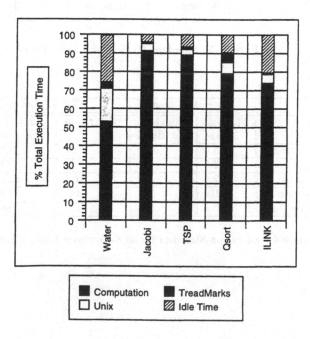

**Figure 5**   TreadMarks Execution Time Breakdown

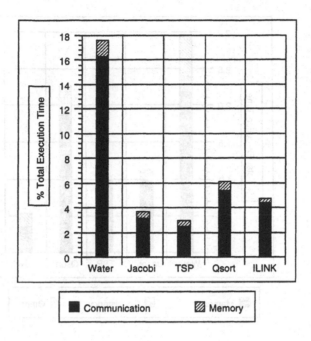

**Figure 6**  Unix Overhead Breakdown

application. "Consistency" is the time spent propagating and handling consistency information. "Other" consists primarily of time spend handling communication and synchronization. TreadMarks overhead is dominated by the memory management operations. Maintaining the rather complex partial ordering between intervals adds only a small amount to the execution time.

## 4.6  Effect of Network and Communication Protocol

We ran Water, the application the highest communication overhead on two other communication substrates: UDP over the ATM network, and UDP over an Ethernet. Figure 8 shows the total 8-processor execution times for all three different communication substrates and a breakdown into computation, Unix overhead, TreadMarks overhead, and idle time.

Overall execution time increases from 15.0 seconds on ATM-AAL3/4 to 17.5 seconds on ATM-UDP and to 27.5 seconds on Ethernet-UDP. Computation time and TreadMarks overhead remain constant, Unix overhead increases slightly, but the idle time increases from 3.9 seconds on AAL3/4 to 5.0 seconds on ATM/UDP, and to 14.4 seconds over the Ethernet. The increase from ATM-AAL3/4 to ATM-UDP is due to increased protocol overhead in processing network packets. For the Ethernet, however, it is largely due to network saturation.

## 4.7  Summary

TreadMarks achieves good speedups for Jacobi, TSP, Quicksort, and ILINK on the 100 Mbit/sec ATM LAN. For a slightly modified version of the Water program from the Splash benchmark suite, TreadMarks achieved only a moderate speedup, because of the large number of small messages.

The overhead of the DSM is dominated by the communication primitives. Since wire time is negligible on the ATM LAN for our applications, the greatest potential to improve overall performance is reducing

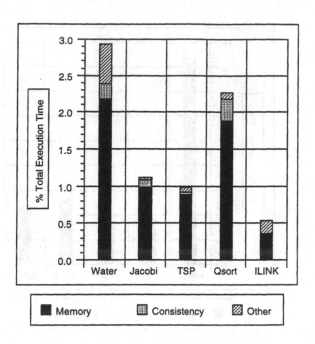

**Figure 7**   TreadMarks Overhead Breakdown

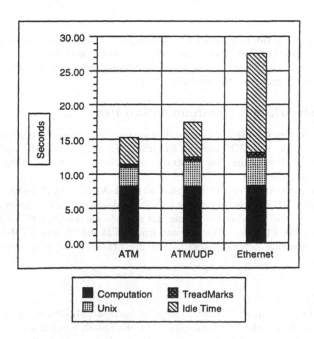

**Figure 8**   Execution Time for Water

the *software* communication overhead. Although the use of the lightweight AAL3/4 protocol reduces the total send and receive time, these are only a part of the overall communication overhead. Lower-overhead user-level communications interfaces or a kernel-level implementation would improve performance.

A kernel implementation of the memory management would have little effect on overall performance. In the worst case (Water), TreadMarks spent less than 2.2% of its time detecting and capturing changes to shared pages. Most of this time is spent copying the page and constructing the diff. Less than 0.8% of the time is spent in the kernel generating the signal or performing the mprotect.

## 5    Lazy vs. Eager Release Consistency

### 5.1    Eager Release Consistency: Design and Implementation

We implemented an *eager* version of RC (ERC) to assess the performance differences between ERC and LRC. At the time of a release, ERC creates diffs of modified pages, and distributes each diff to all processors that cache the corresponding page. Our implementation of ERC uses an update protocol. Eager invalidate protocols have been shown to result in inferior performance for DSM systems [14]. We are thus comparing LRC against the best protocol available for ERC. With an eager invalidate protocol, the diffs cause a large number of invalidations, which trigger a large number of access misses. In order to satisfy these access misses, a copy of the entire page must be sent over the network. In contrast, lazy invalidate protocols only move the diffs, because they maintain enough consistency information to reconstruct valid pages from the local (out-of-date) copy and the diffs.

### 5.2    Performance

Figures 9 to 12 compare the speedups, the message and data rates, and the rate of diff creation between the eager and lazy version of the five applications. In order to arrive at a fair comparison of the message and the data rate, we normalize these quantities by the average execution time of ERC and LRC.

LRC performs better than ERC for Water and Quicksort, because the LRC sends fewer messages and a smaller amount of data. In Water, in particular, ERC sends a large number of updates at each release, because all processors have copies of most of the shared data.

Jacobi performs slightly better under LRC than under ERC. Although communication requirements are similar in both cases, Figure 12 shows that the lazy diff creation of LRC generates 25% fewer diffs than ERC, thereby decreasing the overhead. For ILINK, performance is comparable under both schemes.

For TSP, ERC results in better performance than LRC. TSP is implemented using a branch-and-bound algorithm that uses a *current minimum* to prune searching. The performance on LRC suffers from the fact that TSP is not a *properly labeled* [13] program. Although updates to the current minimum tour length are synchronized, read accesses are not. Since LRC updates cached values only on an *acquire*, a processor may read an old value of the current minimum. The execution remains correct, but the work performed by the processor may be redundant since a better tour has already been found elsewhere. With ERC, this is less likely to occur since ERC updates cached copies of the minimum when the lock protecting the minimum is released. By propagating the bound earlier, ERC reduces the amount of redundant work performed, leading to a better speedup. Adding synchronization around the read accesses would deteriorate performance, given the very large number of such accesses.

## 6    Related Work

Among the many proposed relaxed memory consistency models, we have chosen release consistency [13], because it requires little or no change to existing shared memory programs. An interesting alternative is *entry consistency* (EC) [4]. EC differs from RC in that it requires all shared data to be explicitly associated with some synchronization variable. On a lock acquisition EC only propagates the shared data associated with that lock. EC, however, requires the programmer to insert additional synchronization in shared memory programs to execute correctly on an EC memory. Typically, RC does not require additional synchronization.

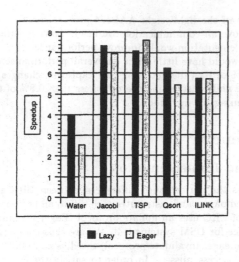

**Figure 9** Comparison of Lazy and
Eager Speedups

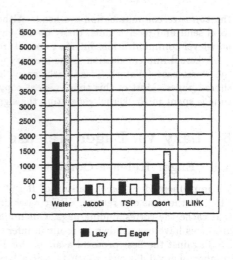

**Figure 10** Message Rate (messages/sec)

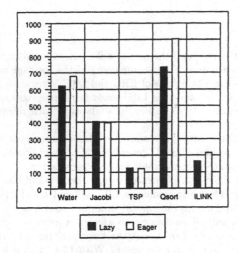

**Figure 11** Data Rate (kbytes/sec)

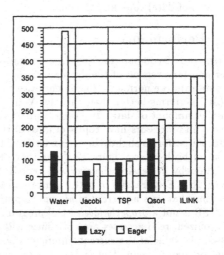

**Figure 12** Diff Creation Rate (diffs/sec)

In terms of comparisons with other systems, we restrict ourselves to implementations on comparable processor and networking technology. Differences in processor and network speed and their ratio lead to different tradeoffs [9], and makes comparisons with older systems [3, 8, 11, 12, 18, 21] difficult. We have however borrowed from Munin [8] the concept of multiple-writer protocols. Munin also implements eager release consistency, which moves more messages and data than lazy release consistency.

Bryant et al. [7] implemented SSVM (Structured Shared Virtual Memory) on a star network of IBM RS-6000s running Mach 2.5. Two different implementation strategies were followed: one using the Mach external pager interface [24], and one using the Mach exception interface [5]. They report that the latter implementation—which is very similar to ours—is more efficient, because of the inability of Mach's external pager interface to asynchronously update a page in the user's address space. Also, the time to update a page in a user's address space is higher for the external pager interface than for the exception interface (1.2 vs. 0.7 milliseconds) because the need for a data_request - data_provided message transaction when using the external pager interface. The overhead of a page fault (without the actual page transfer) is approximately 1 milliseconds, half of which is attributed to process switching overhead in the exception-based implementation. The time to transfer a page (11 milliseconds) dominates all other overheads in the remote page fault time.

Bershad et al. [4] use a different strategy to implement EC in the Midway DSM system, running on DECStation-500/200s connected by an ATM LAN and running Mach 3.0. Instead of relying on the VM system to detect shared memory updates, they modify the compiler to update a software dirty bit. Our results show that, at least in Ultrix and we suspect in Mach as well, the software communication overhead dominates the memory management overhead.

DSVM6K [6] is a sequentially consistent DSM system running on IBM RS/6000s connected by 220-Mbps fiber optic links and a nonblocking crossbar switch. The system is implemented inside the AIX v3 kernel and uses a low-overhead protocol for communication over the fiber optic links (IMCS). A remote page fault takes 1.75 milliseconds when using IMCS, and is estimated to take 3.25 milliseconds when using TCP/IP. The breakdown of the 1.75 milliseconds page fault time is: 1.05 milliseconds for DSVM6K overhead, 0.47 milliseconds for IMCS overhead and 0.23 milliseconds of wire time. Shiva [19] is an implementation of sequentially consistent DSM on an Intel IPSC/2. Shiva is implemented outside the kernel. A remote page fault takes 3.82 milliseconds, and the authors estimate that time could be reduced by 23 percent by a kernel implementation. In comparison, our page fault times are 2.8 milliseconds using AAL3/4. While these numbers are hard to compare because of differences in processor and networking hardware, our results highlight the cost of the software communication overhead. Either an in-kernel implementation or fast out-of-kernel communication interfaces need to be provided in order to build an efficient DSM system.

# 7    Conclusions

Good performance has been achieved for DSM systems built on various research operating systems. However, in order to use DSM as a platform for parallel computation on clusters of workstations, efficient user-level implementations must be available on commercial operating systems. It is with this goal in mind that we set out to conduct the experiment described in this paper.

We implemented a DSM system at the user level on DECstation-5000/240's connected to a 100-Mbps ATM LAN and a 10-Mbps Ethernet. We focused our implementation efforts on reducing the cost of communication, using techniques such as lazy release consistency, multiple-writer protocols, and lazy diff creation. On the ATM network, we avoided the overhead of UDP/IP by using the low-level AAL3/4 protocol.

On the ATM network, we achieved good speedups for Jacobi, TSP, Quicksort, and ILINK, and moderate speedups for a slightly modified version of Water. Latency and bandwidth limitations reduced the speedups by varying amounts on the Ethernet. We conclude that user-level DSM is a viable technique for parallel computation on clusters of workstations connected by suitable networking technology.

In order to achieve better DSM performance for more fine-grained programs like Water, the software communication overhead needs to be reduced through lower-overhead communication interfaces and implementations.

# References

[1] S. Adve and M. Hill. Weak ordering: A new definition. In *Proceedings of the 17th Annual International Symposium on Computer Architecture*, pages 2–14, May 1990.

[2] S. Ahuja, N. Carreiro, and D. Gelernter. Linda and friends. *IEEE Computer*, 19(8):26–34, August 1986.

[3] H.E. Bal, M.F. Kaashoek, and A.S. Tanenbaum. A distributed implementation of the shared data-object model. *Distributed Systems and Multiprocessor Workshop*, pages 1–19, 1989.

[4] B.N. Bershad, M.J. Zekauskas, and W.A. Sawdon. The Midway distributed shared memory system. In *Proceedings of the '93 CompCon Conference*, pages 528–537, February 1993.

[5] D. Black, D. Golub, R. Rashid, A. Tevanian, and M. Young. The Mach exception handling facility. *SigPlan Notices*, 24(1):45–56, May 1988.

[6] M.L. Blount and M. Butrico. DSVM6K: Distributed shared virtual memory on the Risc System/6000. In *Proceedings of the '93 CompCon Conference*, pages 491–500, February 1993.

[7] R. Bryant, P. Carini, H.-Y. Chang, and B. Rosenburg. Supporting structured shared virtual memory under Mach. In *Proceedings of the 2nd Mach Usenix Symposium*, November 1991.

[8] J.B. Carter, J.K. Bennett, and W. Zwaenepoel. Implementation and performance of Munin. In *Proceedings of the 13th ACM Symposium on Operating Systems Principles*, pages 152–164, October 1991.

[9] S. Dwarkadas, P. Keleher, A.L. Cox, and W. Zwaenepoel. Evaluation of release consistent software distributed shared memory on emerging network technology. In *Proceedings of the 20th Annual International Symposium on Computer Architecture*, pages 244–255, May 1993.

[10] S. Dwarkadas, A. A. Schäffer, R. W. Cottingham Jr., A. L. Cox, P. Keleher, and W. Zwaenepoel. Parallelization of general linkage analysis problems. To appear in Journal of Human Heredity, 1993.

[11] B. Fleisch and G. Popek. Mirage: A coherent distributed shared memory design. In *Proceedings of the 12th ACM Symposium on Operating Systems Principles*, pages 211–223, December 1989.

[12] A. Forin, J. Barrera, and R. Sanzi. The shared memory server. In *Proceedings of the 1989 Winter Usenix Conference*, pages 229–243, December 1989.

[13] K. Gharachorloo, D. Lenoski, J. Laudon, P. Gibbons, A. Gupta, and J. Hennessy. Memory consistency and event ordering in scalable shared-memory multiprocessors. In *Proceedings of the 17th Annual International Symposium on Computer Architecture*, pages 15–26, May 1990.

[14] P. Keleher, A. L. Cox, and W. Zwaenepoel. Lazy release consistency for software distributed shared memory. In *Proceedings of the 19th Annual International Symposium on Computer Architecture*, pages 13–21, May 1992.

[15] L. Lamport. How to make a multiprocessor computer that correctly executes multiprocess programs. *IEEE Transactions on Computers*, C-28(9):690–691, September 1979.

[16] G.M. Lathrop, J.M. Lalouel, C. Julier, and J. Ott. Strategies for multilocus linkage analysis in humans. *Proceedings of National Academy of Science*, 81:3443–3446, June 1984.

[17] D. Lenoski, J. Laudon, K. Gharachorloo, A. Gupta, and J. Hennessy. The directory-based cache coherence protocol for the DASH multiprocessor. In *Proceedings of the 17th Annual International Symposium on Computer Architecture*, pages 148–159, May 1990.

[18] K. Li and P. Hudak. Memory coherence in shared virtual memory systems. *ACM Transactions on Computer Systems*, 7(4):321–359, November 1989.

[19] K. Li and R. Schaefer. A hypercube shared virtual memory system. *1989 International Conference on Parallel Processing*, 1:125–131, 1989.

[20] B. Nitzberg and V. Lo. Distributed shared memory: A survey of issues and algorithms. *IEEE Computer*, 24(8):52–60, August 1991.

[21] U. Ramachandran and M.Y.A. Khalidi. An implementation of distributed shared memory. *Software: Practice and Experience*, 21(5):443–464, May 1991.

[22] J.P. Singh, W.-D. Weber, and A. Gupta. SPLASH: Stanford parallel applications for shared-memory. Technical Report CSL-TR-91-469, Stanford University, April 1991.

[23] V. Sunderam. PVM: A framework for parallel distributed computing. *Concurrency:Practice and Experience*, 2(4):315–339, December 1990.

[24] M. Young, A. Tevanian, R. Rashid, D. Golub, J. Eppinger, J. Chew, W. Bolosky, D. Black, and R. Baron. The duality of memory and communication in the implementation of a multiprocessor operating system. In *Proceedings of the 11th ACM Symposium on Operating Systems Principles*, pages 63–76, October 1987.

# Fine-grain Access Control for Distributed Shared Memory*

Ioannis Schoinas, Babak Falsafi, Alvin R. Lebeck,
Steven K. Reinhardt, James R. Larus, David A. Wood

Computer Sciences Department
University of Wisconsin–Madison
1210 West Dayton Street
Madison, WI 53706 USA
wwt@cs.wisc.edu

## Abstract

This paper discusses implementations of fine-grain memory access control, which selectively restricts reads and writes to cache-block-sized memory regions. Fine-grain access control forms the basis of efficient cache-coherent shared memory. This paper focuses on low-cost implementations that require little or no additional hardware. These techniques permit efficient implementation of shared memory on a wide range of parallel systems, thereby providing shared-memory codes with a portability previously limited to message passing.

This paper categorizes techniques based on where access control is enforced and where access conflicts are handled. We incorporated three techniques that require no additional hardware into Blizzard, a system that supports distributed shared memory on the CM-5. The first adds a software lookup before each shared-memory reference by modifying the program's executable. The second uses the memory's error correcting code (ECC) as cache-block valid bits. The third is a hybrid. The software technique ranged from slightly faster to two times slower than the ECC approach. Blizzard's performance is roughly comparable to a hardware shared-memory machine. These results argue that clusters of workstations or personal computers with networks comparable to the CM-5's will be able to support the same shared-memory interfaces as supercomputers.

---

*This work is supported in part by NSF PYI/NYI Awards CCR-9157366 and CCR-9357779, NSF Grants CCR-9101035 and MIP-9225097, an AT&T Ph.D. Fellowship, and donations from Digital Equipment Corporation, Thinking Machines Corporation, and Xerox Corporation. Our Thinking Machines CM-5 was purchased through NSF Institutional Infrastructure Grant No. CDA-9024618 with matching funding from the Univ. of Wisconsin Graduate School.

## 1   Introduction

Parallel computing is becoming widely available with the emergence of networks of workstations as the parallel "minicomputers" of the future [1]. Unfortunately, current systems directly support only message-passing communication. Shared memory is limited to page-based systems, such as TreadMarks [17], which are not sequentially consistent and which can perform poorly in the presence of fine-grain data sharing [11].

These systems lack *fine-grain access control*, a key feature of hardware shared-memory machines. Access control is the ability to selectively restrict reads and writes to memory regions. At each memory reference, the system must perform a *lookup* to determine whether the referenced data is in local memory, in an appropriate state. If local data does not satisfy the reference, the system must invoke a protocol *action* to bring the desired data to the local node. We refer to the combination of performing a lookup on a memory reference and conditionally invoking an action as *access control*. Access control *granularity* is the smallest amount of data that can be independently controlled (also referred to as the *block size*). Access control is fine-grain if its granularity is similar to a hardware cache block (32–128 bytes).

Current shared-memory machines achieve high performance by using hardware-intensive implementations of fine-grain access control. However, this additional hardware would impose an impossible burden in the cost-conscious workstation and personal computer market. Efficient shared memory on clusters of these machines requires low- or no-cost methods of fine-grain access control. This paper explores this design space by identifying where the lookup and action can be performed, fitting existing and proposed systems into this space, and illustrating performance trade-offs with a simulation model. The paper then focuses on three techniques suitable for existing hardware. We used these techniques to implement three variants of Blizzard, a system that uses the Tempest interface [32] to support distributed shared memory on a Thinking Machines CM-5. The first variant, Blizzard-S, adds a fast lookup before each shared-memory reference [22] by modifying the program's executable [21]. The second, Blizzard-E, employs the memory's error-correcting code (ECC) bits as block valid bits [30]. The third, Blizzard-ES, combines the two techniques.

Blizzard's performance—running six programs written for hardware cache-coherent shared-memory machines—is consistent with our simulation results. Blizzard-S's (software) performance ranged from slightly faster than Blizzard-E to twice as slow, depending on a program's shared-memory communication behavior. To calibrate Blizzard's absolute performance, we compared it against a Kendall Square Research KSR-1 shared-memory machine. For one program, Blizzard-E outperforms the KSR-1; for three others, it is within a factor of 2.4–3.6; and two applications ran 6–7 times faster on the KSR-1.

These results show that clusters of workstations or personal computers can efficiently support shared memory when equipped with networks and network interfaces comparable to the CM-5's [23]. Blizzard also demonstrates the portability provided by the Tempest interface. Tempest allows clusters to support the same shared-memory abstraction as supercomputers, just as MPI and PVM support a common interface for coarse-grain message passing.

The paper is organized as follows. Section 2 examines alternative implementations of fine-grain access control. In particular, Section 2.5 presents a simulation of the effect of varying access control overheads. Section 3 describes Blizzard. Finally, Section 4 concludes the paper.

## 2  Access Control Alternatives

Fine-grain access control performs a lookup at each memory reference and, based on the result of the lookup, conditionally invokes an action. The referenced location can be in one of three states: *ReadWrite*, *ReadOnly*, or *Invalid*. Program loads and stores have the following semantics:

> **load**(*address*) =
> if (lookup(*address*) $\notin$ {*ReadOnly*, *ReadWrite*})
>   invoke-action(*address*)
> perform-load(*address*)

> **store**(*address*) =
> if (lookup(*address*) $\neq$ *ReadWrite*)
>   invoke-action(*address*)
> perform-store(*address*)

| Lookup | Action | | |
|---|---|---|---|
| | Dedicated Hardware | Primary Processor | Auxiliary Processor |
| Software | | Orca (object) Blizzard-S | |
| TLB | | IVY (page) | |
| Cache | Alewife[1] KSR-1 | Alewife[1] | |
| Memory | S3.mp | Blizzard-E | FLASH |
| Snoop | DASH | | Typhoon |

[1]Location of action depends on protocol state.

Table 1: Taxonomy of shared-memory systems.

Fine-grain access control can be implemented in many ways. The lookup and action can be performed in either software, hardware, or a combination of the two. These alternatives have different performance, cost, and design characteristics. This section classifies access control techniques based on where the lookup is performed and where the action is executed. Table 1 shows the design space and places current and proposed shared-memory systems within it.

The following sections explore this taxonomy in more detail. Section 2.3 discusses the lookup and action overheads of the systems in Table 1. Section 2.4 discusses how the tradeoffs in the taxonomy affect a wide range of shared-memory machines. Section 2.5 presents a simulation study of the effect of varying access control overheads.

### 2.1  Where is the Lookup Performed?

Either software or hardware can perform an access check. A software lookup avoids the expense and design cost of hardware, but incurs a fixed overhead at each lookup. Hardware typically incurs no overhead when the lookup does not invoke an action. Lookup hardware can be placed at almost any level of the memory hierarchy—TLB, cache controller, memory controller, or a separate snooping controller. However, for economic and performance reasons, most hardware approaches avoid changes to commodity microprocessors.

**Software.** The code in a software lookup checks a main-memory data structure to determine the state of a block before a reference. As described in Section 3.2, careful coding and liberal use of memory makes this lookup reasonably fast. Our current implementation adds 15 instructions before each shared-memory load or store. Static analysis can detect and potentially eliminate redundant tests. However, the asynchrony in parallel programs makes it difficult to predict whether a cache block will remain accessible between two instructions.

Either a compiler or a program executable editing tool [21] can insert software tests. We use the latter approach in Blizzard so every compiler need not reimplement test analysis and code generation. Compiler-inserted lookups, however, can exploit application-level information. Orca [2], for example, provides access control on program objects instead of blocks.

**TLB.** Standard address translation hardware provides access control, though at memory page granularity. Nevertheless, it forms the basis of several distributed-shared-memory systems—for example, IVY [26], Munin [4], and TreadMarks [17]. Though unimplemented by current commodity processors, additional, per-block access bits in a TLB entry could provide fine-grain access control. The "lock bits" in some IBM RISC machines, including the 801 [7] and RS/6000 [29], provide access control on 128-byte blocks, but they do not support the three-state model described above.

**Cache controller.** The MIT Alewife [6] and Kendall Square Research KSR-1 [18] shared-memory systems use custom cache controllers to implement access control. In addition to detecting misses in hardware cache(s), these controllers determine when to invoke a protocol action. On Alewife, a local directory is consulted on misses to local physical addresses to determine if a protocol action is required. Misses to remote physical addresses always invoke an action. Due to the KSR-1's COMA architecture, any reference that misses in both levels of cache requires protocol action. A trend toward on-chip second-level cache controllers [15] may make modified cache controllers incompatible with future commodity processors.

**Memory controller.** If the system can guarantee that the processor's hardware caches never contain *Invalid* blocks and that *ReadOnly* blocks are cached in a read-only state, the memory controller can perform the lookup on hardware cache misses. This approach is used by Blizzard-E, Sun's S3.mp [28], and Stanford's FLASH [20].

As described in Section 3.3, Blizzard-E uses the CM-5's memory error-correcting code (ECC) to implement a cache-block valid bit. While effective, this approach has several shortcomings. *ReadOnly* access is enforced with page-level protection, so stores may incur an unnecessary protection trap. Also, modifying ECC values is an awkward and privileged operation. The Nimbus NIM6133, an MBUS memory controller co-designed by Nimbus Technology, Thinking Machines, and some of the authors [27], addressed these problems. The NIM6133 supports Blizzard-like

systems by storing a 4-bit access control tag with each 32-byte cache block. The controller encodes state tags in unassigned ECC values, which requires no additional DRAM. On a block write, the controller converts the 4-bit tag to a unary 1-of-16 encoding. For each 64-bit doubleword in the block, it appends the unary tag, computes the ECC on the resulting 80-bit value, and stores the 64 data bits plus ECC (but not the tag). On a read, the controller concatenates 16 zeros to each 64-bit doubleword. The ECC single-bit error correction then recovers the unary tag value. Because the tag is stored redundantly on each doubleword in the block, double-bit error detection is maintained. Tag manipulations are unprivileged and the controller supports a *ReadOnly* state.

S3.mp has a custom memory controller that performs a hardware lookup at every bus request. FLASH's programmable processor in the memory controller performs the lookup in software. It keeps state information in regular memory and caches it on the controller.

Custom controllers are possible with most current processors. However, future processors may integrate on-chip memory controllers (as do the TI MicroSPARC and HP PA7100LC).

**Bus snooping.** When a processor supports a bus-based coherence scheme, a separate bus-snooping agent can perform a lookup similar to that performed by a memory controller. Stanford DASH [24] and Wisconsin Typhoon [32] employ this approach. On DASH, as on Alewife, local misses may require protocol action based on local directory state and remote misses always invoke an action. Typhoon looks up access control state for all physical addresses in a reverse-translation cache with per-block access bits that is backed by main-memory page tables.

## 2.2 Where is the Action Taken?

When a lookup detects a conflict, it must invoke an action dictated by a coherence protocol to obtain an accessible copy of a block. As with the lookup itself, hardware, software, or a combination of the two can perform this action. The protocol action software can execute either on the same CPU as the application (the "primary" processor) or on a separate, auxiliary processor.

**Hardware.** The DASH, KSR-1, and S3.mp systems implement actions in dedicated hardware, which provides high performance for a single protocol. While custom hardware performs an action quickly, research has shown that no single protocol is optimal for all applications [16] or even for all data structures within an application [3, 12]. High design costs and resource constraints also make custom hardware unattractive. Hybrid hardware/software

| System | Lookup | | | | Action | | Remote miss time (approx.) |
|---|---|---|---|---|---|---|---|
| | Bytes/ Block | Where Performed | No Action | Action Needed | Where Executed | Action Invocation | |
| Alewife | 8 | cache | 0 | 1 / ~10 | hardware prim. proc. | 0 13 | 30 |
| KSR-1 | 128 | cache | 0 | ~10 | hardware | 0 | 200 |
| DASH | 16 | snoop | 0 | 10 / ~20 | hardware | 0 | 100 |
| FLASH | 128 | memory | 0 | 4 / ~14 | aux. proc. | 0 | ~100 |
| Typhoon | 32 | memory | 0 | 3 | aux. proc. | 2 | 100 |
| Blizzard-S | 32 | software | 18 | 18 | prim. proc. | 25 | 6000 |
| Blizzard-E   r,w[1] | 32 | memory | 0 | ~10 | prim. proc. | 250 | 6000 |
| w[1] | 32 | software (OS) | 230 | 230 | | | |
| Blizzard-ES r | 32 | memory | 0 | ~10 | prim. proc. | 250 | 6000 |
| w | 32 | software | 18 | 18 | | 25 | |
| Munin | 4K | TLB | 0 | ~50 | prim. proc. | 2.01 ms | ?? |
| TreadMarks | 4K | TLB | 0 | ~50 | prim. proc. | 2600 | 110,000 |

[1]Lookup cost for writes depends on whether there are *ReadOnly* blocks on the page (see Section 3.3).

Table 2: Overheads of fine-grain access control for various systems (in processor cycles).

protocols—e.g., Alewife's LimitLESS [6] and $Dir_1SW$ [13]—implement the expected common cases in hardware and trap to system software to handle complex, infrequent events.

**Primary processor.** Performing actions on the main CPU provides protocol flexibility and avoids the additional cost of custom hardware or an additional CPU. Blizzard uses this approach, as do page-based DSM systems such as IVY and Munin. However, as the next section discusses, interrupting an application to run an action can add considerable overhead. Alewife addressed this problem with a modified processor that supports rapid context switches.

**Auxiliary processor.** FLASH and Typhoon achieve both high performance and protocol flexibility by executing actions on an auxiliary processor dedicated to that purpose. This approach avoids a context switch on the primary processor and may be crucial if the primary processor cannot recover from late arriving exceptions caused by an access control lookup in the lower levels of the memory hierarchy. In addition, an auxiliary processor can provide rapid invocation of action code, tight coupling with the network interface, special registers (e.g., Typhoon's home node and protocol state pointer registers), and special operations (e.g., FLASH's bit field instructions). Of course, the design effort increases as the processor is more extensively customized.

## 2.3  Performance

Table 2 summarizes the access control overheads and remote miss times for existing and proposed distributed-shared-memory systems [4, 5, 17, 20, 25, 32, 33]. Values marked with '~' are estimated.

The left side of Table 2 lists the overhead of testing a shared memory reference for accessibility. Software lookups incur a fixed overhead, while the overhead of hardware lookups depends on whether or not action is required. Hardware typically avoids overhead when no action is needed by overlapping the lookup and local data access. When action is required (e.g., a remote miss), the data cannot be used so the lookup counts as overhead. Alewife, DASH, and FLASH have two numbers in the "Action Needed" column because misses to remote physical addresses immediately invoke an action but misses to local addresses require an access to local directory state. For Munin and TreadMarks, this column reflects the overhead of a TLB miss and page-table walk to detect a page fault.

Table 2 also lists action invocation overheads. This overhead reflects the time required from when an access conflict is detected to the start of the protocol action (e.g., for software actions, the execution of the first instruction). Dedicated hardware incurs no overhead since the lookup and action mechanisms are tightly coupled. FLASH also has no overhead because the auxiliary processor is already running lookup code, so the overhead of invoking software is reflected in the "Action Needed" column. Typhoon's overhead is very low because, like FLASH, its auxiliary processor is customized for fast dispatch.

Systems that perform lookup in hardware and execute actions on the primary processor incur much higher invocation overheads. A noticeable exception to this rule is Alewife. Its custom support for fast context switching can invoke actions in 13 cycles. By contrast, TreadMarks requires 2600 cycles on a DEC-Station 5000/240 running Ultrix 4.3 [17]. Of course, the overhead is the fault of Ultrix 4.3, not TreadMarks. With careful kernel coding (on a different processor), Blizzard-E's invocation overhead is 250 cycles, including 50 cycles that are added to every

CM-5 trap by a workaround for a hardware bug.

The final column of Table 2 presents typical round-trip miss times for these systems. These times are affected by access control overheads and other factors, such as network overheads and latencies. The systems in the first group of Table 2 provide low-latency interconnects that are closely coupled to the dedicated hardware or auxiliary processors. At the other extreme, TreadMarks communicates through Unix sockets using heavy-weight protocols. Its send time for a minimum size message is 3200 cycles (80 $\mu$s) [17]. Blizzard benefits from the CM-5's low-latency network and user-level network interface. Blizzard's performance would be better if the network supported larger packets (as, for example, the CM-5E). To efficiently communicate, packets must hold at least a virtual address, program counter, and a memory block (40 bytes total on Blizzard). Our CM-5 limits packets to 20 bytes, which requires block data messages to be split into multiple packets. Our implementation buffers only packets that arrive out-of-order, which eliminates buffering for roughly 80% of all packets.

## 2.4 Discussion

Both the cost of implementing access control and its speed increase as the lookup occurs higher in the memory hierarchy and as more hardware resources (e.g., an auxiliary processor) are dedicated to protocol actions. Because of the wide range of possible implementation techniques, a designer can trade-off cost and performance in a family of systems.

In the high-end supercomputer market, implementations will emphasize performance over cost. These systems will provide hardware support for both the access control test and protocol action. An auxiliary processor in the memory system, as in FLASH and Typhoon, minimizes invocation and action overhead while still exploiting commodity (primary) processors. However, this approach requires either a complex ASIC or full-custom chip design, which significantly increases design time and manufacturing cost.

In mid-range implementations targeted toward clusters of high-performance workstations, the cost and complexity of additional hardware is more important because workstations must compete on uniprocessor cost/performance. For these systems, simple hardware support for the test—as in the Nimbus memory controller—may be cost-effective.

The low end of parallel systems—networks of personal computers—will not tolerate additional hardware for access control. For these systems, implementations must rely on software access control, like that described in Section 3.2.

These tradeoffs would change dramatically if access control was integrated into commodity processors. For example, combining an RS/6000-like TLB with Alewife's context switching support would permit fast access control and actions at low hardware cost. Unfortunately, modifying a processor chip is prohibitively expensive for most, if not all, parallel system designers. Even the relatively cost-insensitive supercomputer manufacturers are resorting to commodity microprocessors [19] because of the massive investment to produce competitive processors. Commodity processor manufacturers are unlikely to consider this hardware until fine-grain distributed shared memory is widespread. The solutions described in this paper and employed by Blizzard provide acceptable performance on existing hardware to break this chicken and egg problem.

## 2.5 Access Control Overheads

This section describes a simulation that studies the effect of varying the overhead of access control and action invocation on the performance of a fine-grain distributed shared-memory system. Our simulator is a modified version of the Wisconsin Wind Tunnel [31] modeling a machine similar to the CM-5. The target nodes contain a single-issue SPARC processor that runs the application, executes protocol action handlers on access faults, and handles incoming messages via interrupts. As on the CM-5, the processor has a 64 Kbyte direct-mapped cache with a 32-byte line size. Instruction cycle times are accurately modeled, but we assume a perfect instruction cache. Local cache misses take 29 cycles. Misses in the fully-associative 64-entry TLB take 25 cycles. Message data is sent and received using single-cycle 32-bit stores and loads to a memory-mapped network interface. Message interrupts incur a 100-cycle overhead before the interrupt handler starts. Fine-grain access control is maintained at 32-byte granularity. The applications run under the full-map, write-invalidate Stache coherence protocol with 32-byte blocks [32].

In the simulations of two programs shown in Figure 1, we varied the overhead of lookups and the overhead of invoking an action handler. The "ideal" case is an upper bound on performance. It models a system in which access fault handlers and message processing run on a separate, infinitely-fast processor. In particular, the protocol software runs in zero time without polluting the processor's cache. However, to make the simulation repeatable, message sends are charged one cycle. The ideal case is 2.2–2.8× faster than a realistic system running protocol software on the application processor with hardware access control that reduces lookup overhead to zero and invocation overhead near zero. The simulations show that lookup overhead has a far larger effect on system performance than invocation overhead. For example, in

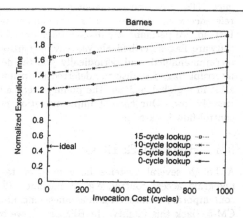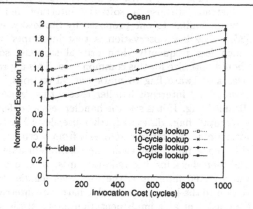

Figure 1: Simulation of fine-grain access control overheads.

*Barnes*, increasing the invocation overhead from 0 to 1000 cycles decreases performance less than increasing the lookup overhead from 0 to 5 cycles.

## 3   Access Control in Blizzard

Blizzard is our system that implements the Tempest interface on a Thinking Machines CM-5. Tempest is a communication and memory management interface [32] that can be supported on on a wide range of systems, ranging from multi-million-dollar supercomputers to low-cost clusters of workstations. Tempest provides four basic mechanisms necessary for both fine-grain shared memory and message passing [32]: active messages, bulk data transfer, virtual memory management, and fine-grain access control. This section presents an overview of Blizzard, with a focus on alternative implementations of fine-grain access control. Although we implemented these techniques for Tempest, they could also be used in other distributed-shared-memory systems.

Blizzard consists of a modified version of the CM-5 operating system and a user-level library. A shared-memory program is executed by compiling it with a standard compiler (e.g., *gcc*), linking it with the Blizzard library and a Tempest-compliant user-level protocol (e.g., Stache [32]), and running it on a CM-5 with the modified OS.

The next section describes our modifications to the CM-5 operating system. We then describe the three implementations of fine-grain access control: Blizzard-S, Blizzard-E, and Blizzard-ES.

### 3.1   Kernel Support for Blizzard

The Thinking Machines CM-5 [14] is a distributed-memory message-passing multiprocessor. Each processing node consists of a 33 MHz SPARC microprocessor with a 64 KB direct-mapped unified cache and

a memory management unit, up to 128 MB of memory, a custom network interface chip, and optional custom vector units.

Blizzard uses a variant of the "executive interface" extensions developed for the Wisconsin Wind Tunnel [30]. These extensions provide protected user-level memory-management support, including the ability to create, manipulate, and execute within subordinate contexts. The executive interface also provides support for fine-grain access control using a memory tag abstraction. Although the executive interface provides the required functionality, there are several important differences discussed below.

First, the executive interface is optimized for switching contexts on all faults, which incurs a moderately-high overhead due to SPARC register window spills, etc. Tempest handles faults in the same address space and runs most handlers to completion. This change allowed a much faster implementation, in which exceptions (including user-level message interrupts) are handled on the same stack. Exceptions effectively look like involuntary procedure calls, with condition codes and other volatile state passed as arguments. In the common case, this interface eliminates all unnecessary stack changes and register window spills and restores. Furthermore, handlers can usually resume a faulting thread without entering the kernel. A kernel trap is only required in the relatively rare cases when the handler must re-enable hardware message interrupts or the SPARC PC and NPC are not sequential.

Second, Tempest requires that active message handlers and access fault handlers execute atomically. However, we use the CM-5's user-level message interrupt capability to implement our active message model. To preserve atomicity, we need to disable user-level interrupts while running in a handler. Unfortunately, the CM-5 does not provide user-level access to the interrupt mask, so it requires expensive kernel traps to both disable and re-enable interrupts.

Instead, we use a software interrupt masking scheme similar to one proposed by Stodolsky, et al. [35]. The key observation is that interrupts occur much less frequently than critical sections, so we should optimize for this common case. This approach uses a software flag to mark critical sections. The lowest-level interrupt handler checks this "software-disable" flag. If it is set, the handler sets a "deferred-interrupt" flag, disables further user-level hardware interrupts, and returns. On exit from a critical section, code must first clear the software-disable flag and then check for deferred interrupts. After processing deferred interrupts, the user-level handler traps back into the kernel to re-enable hardware interrupts. Stodolsky, et al.'s implementation uses a static variable to store the flags. To minimize overhead, our scheme uses a global register.

## 3.2    Blizzard-S: Software

Blizzard-S implements fine-grain access control entirely in software, using a variant of the Fast-Cache simulation system [22]. Fast-Cache rewrites an existing executable file [21] to insert a state table lookup before every shared-memory reference. The lookup table is indexed by the virtual address and contains two bits for each 32-byte block (the size is a compile-time constant). The state and reference type (i.e., load or store) determine the handler. When the current state requires no action (i.e., a load to a ReadWrite block) Blizzard-S invokes a special NULL handler which immediately resumes execution. Otherwise, it invokes a user handler through a stub that saves processor state. With the table lookup and null handlers, Blizzard-S avoids modifying the SPARC condition codes, which are expensive to save and restore from user code. Although Blizzard-S reserves address space for a maximum sized lookup table, it allocates the table on demand, so memory overhead is proportional to the data set size.

The lookup code uses two global registers left unused by programs conforming to the SPARC application binary interface (ABI). These registers are temporaries used to calculate the effective address, index into the lookup table, and invoke the handler. The current implementation adds 15 instructions (18 cycles in the absence of cache and TLB misses) before all load and store instructions that cannot be determined by inspection to be a stack reference. Simple optimizations, such as scavenging free registers and recognizing redundant tests could lower the average overhead, but these were not completed in time for inclusion in this paper.

To avoid inconsistency, interrupts cannot be processed between a lookup and its corresponding reference. Disabling and re-enabling interrupts on every reference would increase the critical lookup overhead. Instead, we permanently disable interrupts with the software flag described above, leaving hardware interrupts enabled, and periodically poll the deferred-interrupt flag. Because the deferred-interrupt flag is a bit in a global register, the polling overhead is extremely low. Our current implementation polls on control-flow back-edges.

## 3.3    Blizzard-E: ECC

Although several systems have memory tags and fine-grain access control, e.g., J-machine [10], most contemporary commercial machines—including the CM-5—lack this facility. In Blizzard-E, we synthesized the *Invalid* state on the CM-5 by forcing uncorrectable errors in the memory's error correcting code (ECC) via a diagnostic mode [30, 31]. Running the SPARC cache in write-back mode causes all cache misses to appear as cache block fills. A fill causes an uncorrectable ECC error and generates a precise exception, which the kernel vectors to the user-level handler. The Wisconsin Wind Tunnel [31] and Tapeworm II [36] both use this ECC technique to simulate memory systems.

This technique causes no loss of reliability. First, uncorrectable ECC faults are treated in the normal way (e.g., panic) unless a program specified a handler for a page. Second, the ECC is only forced "bad" when a block's state is Invalid, and hence the block contains no useful data. Third, the Tempest library and kernel maintain a user-space *access bit vector* that verifies that a fault should have occurred. The final possibility is that a double-bit error changes to a single-bit error, which the hardware automatically corrects. This is effectively solved by writing bad ECC in at least two double-words in a memory block, so at least two single bit errors must occur.

Unfortunately, the ECC technique provides only an *Invalid* state. Differentiating *ReadOnly* and *ReadWrite* is more complex. Blizzard-E uses the MMU to enforce read-only protection. If any block on a page is *ReadOnly*, the page's protection is set read-only. On a write-protection fault, the kernel checks the access bit vector. If the block is *ReadOnly*, the fault is vectored to the user-space Blizzard-E handler. If the block is *ReadWrite*, the kernel completes the write and resumes the application. Despite careful coding, this path through the kernel still requires ~230 cycles.

Protection is maintained in two ways. First, this check is only performed if the user has installed an access bit vector for the page. This ensures that write faults are only processed in this fashion on Blizzard-E's shared-data pages. Second, the kernel uses the SPARC MMU's "no fault" mode to both

| Benchmark | Brief Description | Input |
|-----------|------------------|-------|
| Appbt | Computational fluid dynamics | $32^3$, 10 iters |
| Barnes | Barnes-Hut N-body simulation | 8192 bodies |
| Mp3d | Hypersonic flow simulation | 24000 mols, 50 iters |
| Ocean | Hydrodynamic simulation | 386 x 386, 8 days |
| Tomcatv | Parallel version of SPEC benchmark | $1026^2$, 50 iters |
| Water | Water molecule simulation | 256 mols, 10 iters |

Table 3: Benchmark descriptions.

| Application | Blizzard-E | Blizzard-S | Blizzard-ES | Blizzard-P | KSR-1 |
|-------------|-----------|-----------|-------------|-----------|-------|
| Appbt | 137 (1.00) | 177 (1.29) | 142 (1.04) | 732 (5.35) | 38 (0.28) |
| Barnes | 48 (1.00) | 60 (1.27) | 51 (1.07) | 288 (6.05) | 7 (0.14) |
| Mp3d | 134 (1.00) | 132 (0.98) | 147 (1.09) | 716 (5.33) | 24 (0.18) |
| Ocean | 81 (1.00) | 111 (1.37) | 82 (1.01) | 380 (4.67) | 34 (0.42) |
| Tomcatv | 78 (1.00) | 162 (2.08) | 87 (1.11) | 478 (6.12) | 94 (1.20) |
| Water | 57 (1.00) | 83 (1.47) | 62 (1.09) | 99 (1.74) | 16 (0.28) |

Table 4: Execution time in CPU seconds and (in parentheses) relative to Blizzard-E.

read the access bit vector and perform the store, allowing it to safely perform these operations with traps disabled.

## 3.4  Blizzard-ES: Hybrid

We also implemented a hybrid version of Blizzard that combines ECC and software checks. It uses ECC to detect the *Invalid* state for load instructions, but uses executable rewriting to perform tests before store instructions. This version—Blizzard-ES—eliminates the overhead of a software test for load instructions and the overhead introduced for stores to *ReadWrite* blocks on read-only pages in Blizzard-E.

## 3.5  Blizzard Performance

We examined the overall performance of Blizzard for six shared-memory benchmarks, summarized in Table 3. These benchmarks—four from the SPLASH suite [34]—were written for hardware shared-memory systems. Page-granularity DSM systems generally perform poorly on these codes because of their fine-grain communication and write sharing [9].

We ran these benchmarks on five 32-node systems: Blizzard-E, Blizzard-S, Blizzard-ES, Blizzard-P, and a Kendall Square KSR-1. The first three Blizzard systems use a full-map invalidation protocol implemented in user-level software (Stache) [32] with a 128-byte block size. Blizzard-P is a sequentially-consistent, page-granularity version of Blizzard. The

KSR-1 is a parallel processor with extensive hardware support for shared memory. Table 4 summarizes the performance of these systems. It contains both the measured times of these programs and the execution time relative to that of Blizzard-E.

Blizzard-E usually ran faster than Blizzard-S (27%–108%), although for *Mp3d*, Blizzard-S is 2% faster. Blizzard-E's performance is generally better for computation-bound codes, such as *Tomcatv*, in which remote misses are relatively rare. Blizzard-S performs well for programs, such as *Mp3d* and *Barnes*, that have frequent, irregular communication and many remote misses. Surprisingly, Blizzard-ES is always worse than Blizzard-E. This indicates that writes to cache blocks on read-only pages are infrequent and that synthesizing Tempest's four memory states by a combination of valid bits and page-level protection is viable. Blizzard-P predictably performs worse than the fine-grain shared-memory systems (74% to 512% slower than Blizzard-E) because of severe false-sharing in these codes. Relaxed consistency models would certainly help, but we have not implemented them.

To provide a reference point to gauge the absolute performance of Blizzard, we executed the benchmarks on a commercial shared-memory machine, the KSR-1.[1] The KSR-1 ranges from almost 7 times faster to 20% slower than Blizzard-E. These results

---

[1] KSR operating system version R1.2.1.3 (release) and C compiler version 1.2.1.3-1.0.2.

are encouraging given the KSR-1's extensive hardware support for shared memory and relative performance of the processors. The KSR-1 uses a custom dual-issue processor running at 20 MHz, while the CM-5 uses a 33 MHz SPARC. Uniprocessor measurements indicate that the CM-5 has slightly higher performance for integer codes, but much lower floating-point performance. (We currently do not support the CM-5 vector units.)

The variation in KSR-1 performance can be explained by the ratio of computation to communication in each program. *Appbt*, *Ocean*, and *Water* are dominated by computation. On these benchmarks, Blizzard-E's performance is within a factor of four of the KSR-1, which is consistent with the difference in floating point performance. *Tomcatv* is also compute-bound and should behave similarly; we were unable to determine why it performs poorly on the KSR-1. Most of *Tomcatv*'s computation is on large, private arrays, and it is possible that the KSR-1 suffers expensive, unnecessary remote misses on these arrays due to cache conflicts. *Mp3d* incurs a large number of misses due to poor locality [8]. The high miss ratio explains both Blizzard-E's poor performance relative to the KSR-1and Blizzard-S's ability to outperform Blizzard-E. *Barnes* also has frequent, irregular communication that incurs a high penalty on Blizzard.

## 4   Summary and Conclusions

This paper examines implementations of fine-grain memory access control, a crucial mechanism for efficient shared memory. It presents a taxonomy of alternatives for fine-grain access control. Previous shared-memory systems used or proposed hardware-intensive techniques for access control. Although these techniques provide high performance, the cost of additional hardware precludes shared memory from low-cost clusters of workstations and personal computers.

This paper describes several alternatives for fine-grain access control that require no additional hardware, but provide good performance. We implemented three in Blizzard, our system that supports fine-grain distributed shared memory on the Thinking Machines CM-5. Blizzard-S relies entirely on software and modifies an application's executable to insert a fast (15 instruction) access check before each load or store. Blizzard-E uses the CM-5's memory error correcting code (ECC) to mark invalid cache-block-sized regions of memory. Blizzard-ES is a hybrid that combines both techniques. The relative performance of these techniques depends on an application's shared-memory communication, but on six programs, Blizzard-S ran from 2% faster to 108% slower than Blizzard-E.

We believe that the CM-5's network interface and network performance is similar to facilities that will be available soon for commodity workstations and networks, so Blizzard's performance is indicative of how these techniques will perform on widely-available hardware in the near future. We ran six applications, written for hardware shared-memory machines, and compared their performance on Blizzard and the KSR-1. The results are very encouraging. Blizzard outperforms the KSR-1 for one program. For three others Blizzard is within a factor of 2.4–3.6 times. Only two of the six applications run more than four times faster on the KSR-1, and none more than seven times faster, despite its hardware shared-memory support and faster floating-point performance.

While Blizzard on the CM-5 will not supplant shared-memory machines, these results show that programmers need not eschew shared memory in order to run on a wide variety of systems. A portable interface—such as Tempest—can provide the same shared-memory abstraction on a cluster of personal computers as on a supercomputer. The software approach of Blizzard-S provides an acceptable common denominator for widely-available low-cost workstations. Higher performance, at a higher price, can be achieved by tightly-coupled parallel supercomputers, either current machines like the KSR-1 and KSR-2 or future machines that may resemble Typhoon or FLASH. The widespread availability of shared-memory alternatives will hopefully motivate manufacturers to develop midrange systems using Blizzard-E-like technology (e.g., the Nimbus NIM6133).

### Acknowledgments

This work was performed as part of the Wisconsin Wind Tunnel project, which is co-lead by Profs. Mark Hill, James Larus, and David Wood and funded by the National Science Foundation. We would like to thank Mark Hill, Anne Rogers, and Todd Austin for helpful comments on this research and earlier drafts of this paper. We would especially like to thank the Universities of Washington and Michigan for allowing us access to their KSR-1s.

## References

[1] Tom Anderson, David Culler, and David Patterson. A Case for Networks of Workstations: NOW. Technical report, Computer Science Division (EECS), University of California at Berkeley, July 1994.

[2] Henri E. Bal, Andrew S. Tanenbaum, and M. Frans Kaashoek. Orca: A Language for Distributed Programming. *ACM SIGPLAN Notices*, 25(5):17–24, May 1990.

[3] John K. Bennett, John B. Carter, and Willy Zwaenepoel. Munin: Distributed Shared Memory Based on Type-Specific Memory Coherence. In *Second ACM SIGPLAN*

*Symposium on Principles & Practice of Parallel Programming (PPOPP)*, pages 168–176, February 1990.

[4] John B. Carter, John K. Bennett, and Willy Zwaenepoel. Implementation and Performance of Munin. In *Proceedings of the Thirteenth ACM Symposium on Operating System Principles (SOSP)*, pages 152–164, October 1991.

[5] David Chaiken and John Kubiatowicz. Personal Communication, March 1994.

[6] David Chaiken, John Kubiatowicz, and Anant Agarwal. LimitLESS Directories: A Scalable Cache Coherence Scheme. In *Proceedings of the Fourth International Conference on Architectural Support for Programming Languages and Operating Systems (ASPLOS IV)*, pages 224–234, April 1991.

[7] Albert Chang and Mark F. Mergen. 801 Storage: Architecture and Programming. *ACM Transactions on Computer Systems*, 6(1):28–50, February 1988.

[8] David R. Cheriton, Hendrik A. Goosen, and Philip Machanick. Restructuring a Parallel Simulation to Improve Cache Behavior in a Shared-Memory Multiprocessor: A First Experience. In *International Symposium on Shared Memory Multiprocessing*, pages 109–118, April 1991.

[9] Alan L. Cox, Sandhya Dwarkadas, Pete Keleher, Honghui Lu, Ramakrishnan Rajamony, and Willy Zwaenepoel. Software Versus Hardware Shared-Memory Implementation: A Case Study. In *Proceedings of the 21st Annual International Symposium on Computer Architecture*, pages 106–117, April 1994.

[10] William J. Dally and D. Scott Wills. Universal Mechanism for Concurrency. In *PARLE '89: Parallel Architectures and Languages Europe*. Springer-Verlag, June 1989.

[11] Susan J. Eggers and Randy H. Katz. The Effect of Sharing on the Cache and Bus Performance of Parallel Programs. In *Proceedings of the Third International Conference on Architectural Support for Programming Languages and Operating Systems (ASPLOS III)*, pages 257–270, 1989.

[12] Babak Falsafi, Alvin Lebeck, Steven Reinhardt, Ioannis Schoinas, Mark D. Hill, James Larus, Anne Rogers, and David Wood. Application-Specific Protocols for User-Level Shared Memory. In *Proceedings of Supercomputing 94*, November 1994. To appear.

[13] Mark D. Hill, James R. Larus, Steven K. Reinhardt, and David A. Wood. Cooperative Shared Memory: Software and Hardware for Scalable Multiprocessors. *ACM Transactions on Computer Systems*, 11(4):300–318, November 1993. Earlier version appeared in ASPLOS V, Oct. 1992.

[14] W. Daniel Hillis and Lewis W. Tucker. The CM-5 Connection Machine: A Scalable Supercomputer. *Communications of the ACM*, 36(11):31–40, November 1993.

[15] Peter Yan-Tek Hsu. Designing the TFP Microprocessor. *IEEE Micro*, 14(2):23–33, April 1994.

[16] Anna R. Karlin, Mark S. Manasse, Larry Rudolph, and Daniel D. Sleator. Competitive Snoopy Caching. *Algorithmica*, (3):79–119, 1988.

[17] Pete Keleher, Sandhya Dwarkadas, Alan Cox, and Willy Zwaenepoel. TreadMarks: Distributed Shared Memory on Standard Workstations and Operating Systems. Technical Report 93-214, Department of Computer Science, Rice University, November 1993.

[18] Kendall Square Research. Kendall Square Research Technical Summary, 1992.

[19] R. E. Kessler and J. L. Schwarzmeier. CRAY T3D: A New Dimension for Cray Research. In *Proceedings of COMPCON 93*, pages 176–182, San Francisco, California, Spring 1993.

[20] Jeffrey Kuskin et al. The Stanford FLASH Multiprocessor. In *Proceedings of the 21st Annual International Symposium on Computer Architecture*, pages 302–313, April 1994.

[21] James R. Larus and Thomas Ball. Rewriting Executable Files to Measure Program Behavior. *Software Practice & Experience*, 24(2):197–218, February 1994.

[22] Alvin R. Lebeck and David A. Wood. Fast-Cache: A New Abstraction for Memory System Simulation. Technical Report 1211, Computer Sciences Department, University of Wisconsin–Madison, January 1994.

[23] Charles E. Leiserson et al. The Network Architecture of the Connection Machine CM-5. In *Proceedings of the Fifth ACM Symposium on Parallel Algorithms and Architectures (SPAA)*, July 1992.

[24] Daniel Lenoski, James Laudon, Kourosh Gharachorloo, Wolf-Dietrich Weber, Anoop Gupta, John Hennessy, Mark Horowitz, and Monica Lam. The Stanford DASH Multiprocessor. *IEEE Computer*, 25(3):63–79, March 1992.

[25] Daniel Lenoski, James Laudon, Truman Joe, David Nakahira, Luis Stevens, Anoop Gupta, and John Hennessy. The DASH Prototype: Logic Overhead and Performance. *IEEE Transactions on Parallel and Distributed Systems*, 4(1):41–61, January 1993.

[26] Kai Li and Paul Hudak. Memory Coherence in Shared Virtual Memory Systems. *ACM Transactions on Computer Systems*, 7(4):321–359, November 1989.

[27] NIMBUS Technology. NIM 6133 Memory Controller Specification. Technical report, NIMBUS Technology, 1993.

[28] A. Nowatzyk, M. Monger, M. Parkin, E. Kelly, M. Borwne, G. Aybay, and D. Lee. S3.mp: A Multiprocessor in a Matchbox. In *Proc. PASA*, 1993.

[29] R. R. Oehler and R. D. Groves. IBM RISC System/6000 processor architecture. *IBM Journal of Research and Development*, 34(1):32–36, January 1990.

[30] Steven K. Reinhardt, Babak Falsafi, and David A. Wood. Kernel Support for the Wisconsin Wind Tunnel. In *Proceedings of the Usenix Symposium on Microkernels and Other Kernel Architectures*, September 1993.

[31] Steven K. Reinhardt, Mark D. Hill, James R. Larus, Alvin R. Lebeck, James C. Lewis, and David A. Wood. The Wisconsin Wind Tunnel: Virtual Prototyping of Parallel Computers. In *Proceedings of the 1993 ACM Sigmetrics Conference on Measurement and Modeling of Computer Systems*, pages 48–60, May 1993.

[32] Steven K. Reinhardt, James R. Larus, and David A. Wood. Tempest and Typhoon: User-Level Shared Memory. In *Proceedings of the 21st Annual International Symposium on Computer Architecture*, pages 325–337, April 1994.

[33] Rafael H. Saavedra, R. Stockton Gaines, and Michael J. Carlton. Micro Benchmark Analysis of the KSR1. In *Proceedings of Supercomputing 93*, pages 202–213, November 1993.

[34] Jaswinder Pal Singh, Wolf-Dietrich Weber, and Anoop Gupta. SPLASH: Stanford Parallel Applications for Shared Memory. *Computer Architecture News*, 20(1):5–44, March 1992.

[35] Daniel Stodolsky, J. Brad Chen, and Brian Bershad. Fast Interrupt Priority Management in Operating Systems. In *Second USENIX Symposium on Microkernels and Other Kernel Archtitectures*, pages 105–110, September 1993. San Diego, CA.

[36] Richard Uhlig, David Nagle, Trevor Mudge, and Stuart Sechrest. Tapeworm II: A New Method for Measuring OS Effects on Memory Architecture Performance. In *Proceedings of the Sixth International Conference on Architectural Support for Programming Languages and Operating Systems (ASPLOS VI)*, October 1994. To appear.

# Chapter 5

# Distributed Shared Memory Implementations at the Hardware Level

## Editors' Introduction

Chapter 5 presents an overview of representative distributed shared memory (DSM) hardware solutions. It consists of the following papers:

1. G. Delp et al., "Memory as a Network Abstraction," *IEEE Network Magazine*, Vol. 5, No. 4, July 1991, pp. 34–41.

2. D. Lenoski et al., "The Stanford Dash Multiprocessor," *Computer*, Vol. 25, No. 3, Mar. 1992, pp. 63–79.

3. D.V. James, "The Scalable Coherent Interface: Scaling to High-Performance Systems," *Proc. COMPCON '94: Digest of Papers*, IEEE CS Press, Los Alamitos, Calif., 1994, pp. 64–71.

4. S. Frank, H. Burkhardt III, and J. Rothnie, "The KSR1: Bridging the Gap between Shared Memory and MPPs," *Proc. COMPCON '93*, IEEE CS Press, Los Alamitos, Calif., 1993, pp. 285–294.

5. E. Hagersten, A. Landin, and S. Haridi, "DDM—A Cache-Only Memory Architecture," *Computer*, Vol. 25, No. 9, Sept. 1992, pp. 44–54.

6. C. Maples and L. Wittie, "Merlin: A Superglue for Multicomputer Systems," *Proc. COMPCON '90*, IEEE CS Press, Los Alamitos, Calif., 1990, pp. 73–81.

7. A. Grujić, M. Tomašević, and V. Milutinović, "A Simulation Analysis of Hardware-Implemented DSM Approaches," *Proc. IEEE Region 10's 9th Ann. Int'l Conf.*, 1994, pp. 386–390.

The problem of maintaining the consistency of global shared virtual space in DSM systems is very similar to the cache coherence problem in shared memory multiprocessors. In addition, private caches are inevitably implemented in all modern computer systems, including DSM, as one of the basic memory and network latency-reducing techniques. Therefore, it is quite natural that hardware DSM approaches are, in fact, extended cache coherence protocols adapted to the DSM environment. These solutions are predominantly based on directory schemes with potential for scalability, which is ultimately important for the building of large-scale systems. The snooping principle is occasionally used in systems with an appropriate type of network (bus, ring).

Hardware DSM approaches offer significant advantages, as they are completely transparent to the user, providing direct support for the shared memory programming model. Avoiding any software layer, these solutions can be much faster than the software DSM approaches. Since hardware implementations typically use smaller units of sharing (for example, cache blocks), they are successful in eliminating false sharing and thrashing effects. This approach is especially superior for applications that express a high level of fine-grain sharing. The aforementioned advantages obviously are achieved at the expense of increased system hardware complexity.

The presentation of DSM systems in Chapter 5 is based on their classification into three groups: CC-NUMA (cache coherent nonuniform memory access) architecture, COMA (cache-only memory architecture), and RMS (reflective memory system) architecture. In a CC-NUMA system, the shared virtual address space is distributed across local memory modules of clusters, which can be accessed both by the local processors and by processors from other clusters in the system, although with quite different access latencies. Dash and SCI (Scalable Coherent Interface) belong to CC-NUMA. COMA provides the dynamic partitioning of data in the form of distributed memories, organized as large second-level caches (attraction memories). In COMA systems, there is no physical memory home location predetermined for a particular data item. The Data Diffusion Machine (DDM; see below) and KSR1 are typical COMA representatives. Reflective memory systems immediately propagate every write operation to all sharing sites, using a broadcast or multicast mechanism, while read is always performed from the local memory. Because of the property of "reflection," this kind of memory is also sometimes called "mirror memory." Merlin is a representative of reflective memory systems.

The paper "Memory as a Network Abstraction," by Delp et al., describes Memnet, one of the first hardware-based DSM systems. The motivation for this research is to provide the abstraction of shared virtual memory directly to application, instead of using the operating system services to pass the data through the network. Since each data item has a predetermined home location, this system can be conditionally classified as CC-NUMA. The basic Memnet system consists of nodes connected by a token ring, while the global address space is divided into 32-byte chunks. The Memnet interface device (and memory controller) of each node stores the state information for the overall address space in two tag tables, and implements an MRSW (multiple reader/single writer) snooping consistency protocol in hardware. The authors discuss the overall performance of this approach, together with system considerations and error recovery. The paper also describes some other closely related DSM approaches, such as Mether—a software implementation of Memnet on SUN workstations under the SunOS 4.0 operating system, CapNet—a DSM implementation for high-speed, packet-switched WAN environment, and UPWARDS—a software complement to the CapNet approach.

Lenoski et al. provide a clear overview of all relevant issues and details of an important DSM system in their paper "The Stanford Dash Multiprocessor." The goal of the project was to design a scalable, high-performance architecture. The paper describes the Dash system organization, which consists of common-bus clusters with two-level caches and local memory, linked by a pair of wormhole-routed meshes. Cache coherence is maintained using a distributed directory and an invalidation-based hardware protocol. To enhance performance, Dash provides support for memory latency-reducing and hiding techniques such as release consistency, prefetching, and update and deliver operations, as well as an efficient synchronization mechanism. The authors briefly mention system software support—a new parallel language Jade and the operating system DashOS. The paper also contains some performance measures, obtained both on the simulator and the prototype. Finally, a comparative overview of the related work in the field of DSM is given.

In the paper "The Scalable Coherent Interface: Scaling to High-Performance Systems," James presents the coherence issues of the SCI standard specification, also intended for large-scale, high-performance systems. The scheme is based on distributed directories with entries in the form of doubly linked sharing lists. The SCI scheme ensures the scalability in terms of the amount of directory storage. This approach employs a simple packet-based, split request/response protocol. The paper proposes some enhancements to the basic concept—request combining within interconnect and converting sharing lists to trees. It also discusses the problem of deadlock avoidance and the exploitation of a weakly consistent memory model by SCI. Also, it briefly touches on synchronization issues. The paper points out that distributed directories can be updated concurrently, reducing the latencies to logarithmic rather than linear dependence on the number of nodes. In summary, the proposed SCI coherence maintenance is compared to other relevant approaches and the scalability of SCI is emphasized.

The Data Diffusion Machine, a typical representative of cache-only memory-type architectures, is described in the paper "DDM—A Cache-Only Memory Architecture," by Hagersten, Landin, and Haridi. The DDM distributed memory system consists of huge local caches (called *attraction memories*). There is no static data distribution across the attraction memories and data are allowed to migrate dynamically and freely in response to program demands, in the form of *items* (equivalent to cache lines). Large systems can be built from bus-based clusters interconnected by a multilevel hierarchy of buses. Consequently, an extension of snooping protocols (of the invalidation type) is employed, to maintain the coherence on buses, while directories between levels are used to store the state information for items in the attraction memories below it. The authors explain in detail the coherence protocols for the case of a single-bus DDM, as well as for the hierarchical multilevel DDM. Special attention is devoted to deadlock avoidance, replacement strategy applied when the attraction memory runs out of space, and minimization of memory overhead. The paper also presents the results of simulations, showing that COMA principles work well for programs originally written for UMA (Unified Memory Access) architectures.

Another example of the COMA approach is described by Frank, Burkhardt, and Rothnie in their paper "The KSR1: Bridging the Gap between Shared Memory and MPPs." The KSR1—one of the rare commercially available DSM systems—is based on the ALLCACHE virtual memory system, which consists of hierarchically grouped, large local caches. Hardware ALLCACHE engines automatically manage the dynamic migration and replication of data in local caches according to program demands, while preserving the sequentially consistent shared address space. Besides the ease of programming typical of a shared memory system, the KSR1 is characterized by high performance and scalability, owing to exploiting locality of references. It also provides other features, such as prefetch and poststore instructions, that can help the programmer optimize the locality of reference, and achieve efficient fine-grain data sharing for diverse applications. The authors claim that KSR1 is able to deliver very high computing and I/O power with linear scalability.

An example of reflective memory DSM implementation with support for heterogeneous multicomputer processing is presented by Maples and Wittie in their paper "Merlin: A Superglue for Multicomputer Systems." All memory references in Merlin are satisfied in physically local memories without delay. Any part of local memory can be dynamically declared as shared, and appropriately mapped into a global virtual address space. Coherence of global shared space is based on the principle of reflective memory. Each write operation to a location within a shared region in local memory is accompanied by sending word updates to local memories of all nodes in which the same region of the shared virtual space is mapped. Therefore, this anticipatory mechanism with relaxed consistency drastically reduces the latency of shared references. The paper also presents the complete hardware support for the management of global virtual memory and control of data flow through the network. Finally, the provisions for synchronization (locks, semaphores, phased synchronization) are discussed.

An evaluation study of the most important systems mentioned in Chapter 5 is presented in the paper "A Simulation Analysis of Hardware-Implemented DSM Approaches," by Grujić, Tomašević, and Milutinović. Two NUMA approaches (Dash and SCI) and two COMA approaches (KSR1 and DDM) are comparatively evaluated by means of simulations using synthetic address traces. The analysis compares approaches, rather than implementations. For this purpose, a hierarchical two-level cluster-based system with a uniform bus-based cluster structure on the first level is assumed. The DSM mechanisms of four approaches are simulated on the second level. The comparison is carried out for a large variety and broad range of system-oriented, application-oriented, and technology-oriented parameters. The results show the somewhat better efficiency of the COMA protocols (because of dynamic migration of responsibility for shared data) and the large impact of the available interconnection network bandwidth on system scalability (an almost linear speedup is achieved with ring-based systems).

## Suggestions for Further Reading

1. R. Bisiani, A. Nowatzyk, and M. Ravishankar, "Coherent Shared Memory on a Distributed Memory Machine," *Proc. 1989 Int'l Conf. Parallel Processing*, University Park, Pa., 1989, pp. I-133–I-141.

2. D. Gustavson, "The Scalable Coherent Interface and Related Standards Projects," *IEEE Micro*, Feb. 1992, pp. 10–22.

3. M.C. Tam and D. Farber, "CapNet—An Approach to Ultra High Speed Network," *Proc. IEEE Int'l Conf. Communications '90*, IEEE Press, Piscataway, N.J., 1990, pp. 323.1.1–323.1.7.

4. M. Thapar, B. Delagi, and J.M. Flynn, "Linked List Cache Coherence for Scalable Shared Memory Multiprocessors," *Proc. 7th Int'l Parallel Processing Symp.*, CRC Press, Boca Raton, Fla., 1993, pp. 34–43.

5. D. Windheiser et al., "KSR1 Multiprocessor: Analysis of Latency Hiding Techniques in a Sparse Solver," *Proc. 1993 Int'l Parallel Processing Symp.*, CRC Press, Boca Raton, Fla., 1993, pp. 454–461.

6. V. Milutinović et al., "A Board Which Turns a Personal Computer into a Distributed Shared Memory Node Based on the Reflective Memory Approach," Technical Report TI-RTI-95-038, School of Electrical Engineering, Univ. Belgrade, Belgrade, Serbia, Yugoslavia, Dec. 1995.

# Memory As A Network Abstraction

Gary S. Delp
David J. Farber
Ronald G. Minnich
Jonathan M. Smith
Ming-Chit Tam

Computer systems are extremely complex, and one technique that has proven effective at managing this complexity is the idea of modularity. Activities are decomposed into a collection of cooperating *modules*, each of which provides an abstraction to the other modules through some interface. In the area of networking, the modularization is refined along functional lines and called *layering*. Layering is an intellectual technique that allows the various behaviors and complexities of different protocols to be decomposed into pieces, called layers, each of which takes a step towards the translation of application data into "bits on a wire," or reverses this translation. Layering can be a useful technique for matching one type of abstraction to another. For example, in systems using distributed file systems, a file system abstraction is mapped to the low-level message-based Ethernet abstraction via a series of layers. The layers, in turn, map:

- A file system operation to a remote procedure call request
- A remote procedure call request to a host-independent packet (essentially converting it to a string of characters)
- A packet to one or more messages
- A message to one or more network packets, via a multiplexed Input/Output (I/O) interface (e.g., an Ethernet card)

At each layer the abstraction changes, with some attendant processing of the data in the packet (in current protocol implementations this overhead is a large percentage of the total overhead), copying or fragmentation of that data to smaller units, and encapsulation of that data in a larger packet.

Some idea of the amount of copying overhead can be seen from the fact that current protocol stacks are more memory-bandwidth constrained than processor constrained, due to the number of copies that must be performed. Even with fast processors, Interprocess Communication (IPC) over fast communications networks has often achieved only a small fraction of the bandwidth of which the network is capable.

A problem with layering is that it can conceal some set of initial assumptions that may no longer be valid. For example, in the distributed file system case, much effort has been expended on avoiding network overhead. The effort has been put into caching local copies of a file; or making the Remote Procedure Call (RPC) more efficient; or minimizing the path length from the RPC code to the Ethernet interface. The basic assumption, that a message-based hardware interface, that is multiplexed and accessed only, be the operating system, has not changed.

David Farber suggested a fundamentally different approach to the problem of IPC over fast networks. He argued that the essence of the problem was the network abstraction, that is, what model the hardware network interface provided to the computer. Current network interfaces are based on the I/O abstraction, which requires the host processor to direct the input and output of each message on the network. No data may flow through the interface directly to an application; rather, the operating system must become involved in every step of the process. The nature of this interface forces the computer to perform expensive processing to transform the data into a form acceptable to computations.

Farber argued that the network should provide the abstraction of computer memory, directly to the application, with no operating system intervention required to effect the movement of data. This abstraction had been successfully applied to secondary storage, such as drums and disks, with the idea of *virtual memory*. The idea seemed ripe for exploration with the advent of high-speed local networks and switches that enable fast packet-switched Wide Area Networks (WANs).

Gary Delp performed the explorations, starting in 1985, that resulted in Memnet in 1988. Memnet demonstrated that the memory abstraction was effective when implemented entirely in hardware and would provide good performance. It connected a number of computers using a parallel 200 Mb/s insertion-modification token ring, and is described below. The success of Memnet led to a number of further efforts, that are discussed here. Ron Minnich had worked with the Memnet system and wanted to preserve its applications interface while exploring a variety of optimizations. His Mether system [1] was originally intended to be a software Memnet that used broadcast Ethernet. The system has evolved from a software Memnet to a unique DSM in its own right, with new mechanisms for allowing applications to specify the type of service they require from the Distributed Shared Memory (DSM) on a memory-fetch basis, as well as mechanisms for supporting synchronization based on the memory operation. The result is minimized messages and easier synchronization, which imply better performance in high-latency settings. The changes from the original version of Mether to the current Mether 3.0 are the result of extensive applications experience. Ming-Chit (Ivan) Tam has investigated the extension of DSM to high-speed packet-switched WANs with his CapNet system, which augments the switching fabric with support for memory operations. The CapNet research has implications for the design of future high-speed interconnection networks. The CapNet design is discussed below. Jonathan Smith's University of Pennsylvania Wide Area Distributed System (UPWARDS) attempts to extend optimizations used elsewhere in the memory hierarchy into the network.

## Related Work

There has been a spate of DSM studies and implementations recently; many of which are discussed in a survey by Tam, Smith, and Farber [2]. Other than Memnet, all of these have been implemented as software systems and, for the most

Reprinted from *IEEE Network Magazine*, Vol. 5, No. 4, July 1991, pp. 34–41.

part, have been focused on extending shared memory properties to distributed systems. There are essentially two varieties. Page-oriented systems have used the assistance provided by existing memory-management hardware to shuttle requests for fixed-size chunks of data (pages) to be shuttled around a Local Area Network (LAN). Object-oriented systems have attempted to minimize the unnecessary transfer of data (due to mismatch between the units of shared data and page sizes) by defining objects that encapsulate the shared state and manage its consistency. The difficulty with the object-oriented approach is the inability of applications (e.g., existing binaries) to use it transparently. Such approaches as well, often require rewriting in a specialized language, such as Bal's ORCA [3]. Another problem with the object-oriented approach is that it must still, at some point, have access to a network system; if the system is software-based, it will not be able to make effective use of the network. The use of a system such as ORCA does not have any implications, pro or con, about the use of a Memnet-like network to effect communications.

While the Memnet consistency control mechanism is similar to the cache management used by several other systems, such as Li's IVY, it is important to remember that Memnet represents a network abstraction, not an operating system extension.

### Organization

In *Memnet*, we discuss motivating the abstraction and focusing on the performance and lessons learned from the implementation of the system. Mether 3.0 is discussed in *Mether*. CapNet follows, where we argue that message count is the crucial performance measure in a high-speed WAN setting. CapNet demonstrates a scheme that minimizes the number of messages necessary to maintain consistent shared memory. *UPWARDS* is an attempt to provide extremely high-performance IPC, based on DSM, and attempts to include multimedia in the abstraction. *Conclusions and Open Questions* concludes the article, points out a number of difficulties with distributed shared memory, and provides our expectations for future developments.

## Memnet

### Memnet Programming Model

In the programming model of the Memnet system all of the processors have equal and fast access to a large amount of memory (see Figure 1). While this abstraction is convenient for the programmer, if the system were implemented in this simple manner the system response time would suffer from memory contention and transmission latency. As additional hosts are added to the network, the potential required memory bandwidth will increase linearly in the number of hosts.

A solution for the memory contention that works in the large majority of cases is for each host to cache the memory that it is currently using. With a cache of the appropriate size, the number of references that must be satisfied by the central resource can be reduced dramatically. Caching memory is a relatively simple task. Keeping multiple copies of the same memory location consistent with each other is a more difficult matter. Consistency protocols used for tightly coupled multiprocessors do not scale well.

Bus-based systems suffer from decreased transmission bandwidth as the length of the bus is increased. The Memnet system uses a token-ring interconnect system to avoid the bandwidth decrease coincident with bus extension. Memory access latency may increase as the physical distribution of hosts increases, but the bandwidth of the access media does not decrease, as is the case with a bus-based system that needs to allow access control signals to propagate to the ends of the bus

and echo back for each bit. Figure 2 gives a macro view of a Memnet system.

In the system, each computing node has a Memnet device as a memory controller on its local bus. These devices are interconnected with a dedicated, parallel, high-speed token ring. The interface from the node to the ring is through a dual ported memory. Each computing node references this memory as real memory on its local bus, with the Memnet interface hardware managing a local cache of recently used data. The interfaces communicate between themselves using the token ring. To keep ring contention from limiting the average access speed to memory, network use is reduced by the caching of data at each node. A multiplexed, distributed interrupt channel is provided to distribute control information.

The Memnet token-ring interface uses hardware state machines to manage the ring traffic. The data consistency information on each interface can be affected only by ring traffic. The host cannot access the ring directly. All ring traffic is generated by the interface, not the local host, and is interpreted by the interface with minimal impact on the local bus. The only impact that the ring traffic has is the possibility of some Memnet memory references being delayed due to concurrent network and local node accesses to the Memnet device.

A ring is used for two reasons. First, the token ring provides an absolute upper bound on the time of network access. Second, because the packets that traverse the ring arrive at each interface in the same order, the tags used to manage the consistency protocol are themselves kept consistent.

The ring is a token, insertion, modification ring. The default action of the interface is to echo what is received on its input port onto its output port. The latency at each interface is long enough to modify the output as appropriate. When an interface wishes to use the ring, it waits for a token, assembles and transmits a ring packet, then releases the token. Each interface has a hardware state machine watching the input port. As packets arrive on the input, they are examined for effects on local memory and requests that this interface can satisfy. If the incoming packet is a packet that this interface generated, this interface does not echo this packet to the output, thereby removing the packet from the ring. If the incoming packet is a request that this interface can satisfy, the filler in the incoming packet is replaced with data supplied by this interface. All of this communication with the ring takes place without any intervention from the local host.

The address space of the Memnet environment is divided into 32 byte *chunks*. The word chunk is used to describe this division to avoid some of the connotations of the terms *page* or *cache frame*. A discussion of the choice of chunk size is part of the analysis contained in [4].

The entire address space of the Memnet environment is mapped onto the local address space of each node. Each Memnet interface has two tag tables that are used to maintain consistency information for each chunk in the entire Memnet space and manage the resources of the local interface. The tags used in the first of the two tables include: VALID, EXCLUSIVE, RESERVED, CLEAN, INTERRUPT, and Cached Location. These tags are maintained on *each* interface for *all* of the chunks in the *entire* Memnet address space. The second tag table is associated with the local chunk cache, and contains an entry for each location in the cache. These tags include CLEAN, INUSE, and Chunk Contained (a backward pointer).

The consistency protocol run by the interfaces is a single writer/multiple reader protocol. The operation is similar to *snooping caches*, however, there are two major differences. First, while the multicomputers that use snooping cache techniques have all of the processors on a single bus, the Memnet scheme allows systems with the physical range of a LAN. Second, the snooping systems rely on some separate main memory

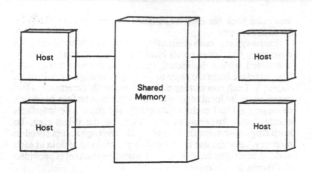

*Fig. 1. Programmer's view of Memnet.*

to which all of the caches have access. In the Memnet environment, the *main memory* is distributed among the interfaces.

Traffic is kept to a minimum on the ring through the use of large chunk caches on each interface. With effective caching, most of the node accesses to the Memnet address space will be satisfied by the data cached at the local interface, and will not generate any ring traffic. If the ring traffic is minimized, the average time an interface must wait for a token to satisfy a cache miss is also minimized. Behavior of the Memnet environment under varying hit/miss ratios, chunk sizes, and number of nodes has been projected in [4].

## Overall Performance

The Memnet system provides a very fast channel into and out of the domain of the processor. The processor ↔ memory interconnect is one that has been greatly optimized; it is no surprise that communications that use the characteristics and processor interface of memory are fast. In a 10 node system [4], a one-way communication action has the time domain overhead of <20 bus memory accesses. The projected communications overhead for a 100 node system, assuming availability of the network, is in the neighborhood of 125 memory access times. If memory is being used in the ratio of 1 Memnet access for every 99 local memory accesses, the access times only degrade to 20 and 150 local memory access times (for 10 and 100 node systems).

The average memory access times for the 99:1 and 999:1 cases are affected only slightly by an increase in the number of nodes in the system. In both of these cases, the *network* (miss) accesses are resolved in less time than it would take 200 local bus cycles, even for a network of 100 nodes. To put this figure in perspective, the network transaction, including transit latency, is approximately equivalent to executing less than 40 lines of "C" code. By comparison, a typical context switch code in an operating system is at minimum over 100 lines. Thus, it is usually cheaper to wait for the chunk to return than to switch to another process while waiting for the returned chunk.

It has been argued that using nodes that have very little or no local memory, whose entire system memory is made up of Memnet memory, will offer the most seamless interface between local processes and the distributed system within which they operate. It is clear that some local storage will be required on each node, but the fact that nodes with mostly Memnet memory do not need to distinguish between memory that is shared and memory that must be copied to be shared means that many management and communication tasks can be performed more simply and efficiently. The potential of lightweight task migration and distributed *virtual* memory, as well as the simplicity issues, all argue toward systems with mostly active, global memory.

## System Considerations and Error Recovery

Many of the systems aspects of the use of the Memnet scheme have yet to be fully explored. Many of the problems and opportunities of the Memnet scheme are the same as for a shared memory multicomputer such as the Sequent, the Alliant, or the TC2000. The requirements of the shared memory schemes of System 5 and 4.3bsd, and Linda system [5] of content addressable shared data spaces, are directly supported by the Memnet system. The multiprocessor process fork and join primitives for manipulating control flow find support in the atomic memory operations and multiplexed signaling portions of Memnet. The physical extent of the Memnet system, however, adds a degree of bus bandwidth and physical distribution not found in single bus, single location systems. These advantages can be exploited as Memnet systems become available for experimentation.

The degree of risk sharing between nodes is more evident with a physically distributed system than with a single system, but system size considerations are similar. The Memnet interfaces are interconnected with a token ring. Errors on the ring, for the most part, can be detected by the transmitting interface. The consistency protocol is not idempotent, so if packets are corrupted, the data in the corresponding chunk is probably not recoverable. The reliability of the memory system is arguably at the same level as the reliability of a disk subsystem. Schemes for handling disk block errors exist; schemes for handling network memory errors will be developed. For applications requiring the degree of reliability that justifies the expense, checkpointed systems [6] can easily be implemented in a Memnet compatible system.

The conclusions that one reaches related to system reliability are not absolute, however, it is important to remember that ring reliability is well understood. These interfaces rarely miss packets. Of the packets missed, even rarer are those missed without notification. A two or three pass ring protocol that was closer to being idempotent could be devised, but performance in the general case would suffer greatly. Realistic reliability calculations need to be performed on the basis of experience, but it seems that this reliability factor, rather than the raw performance factor, will be the factor that limits the practical size of single memory sharing rings. This is not to say that the potential size of virtual systems implemented in the Memnet manner is limited, just that the degree of risk shared on a distributed system must be contained.

There are a myriad of possible modifications that can be made to the basic Memnet architecture in the interests of error prevention, detection, and recovery. The work that has been done in ring robustness and fault tolerant computing applies equally to the Memnet architecture. The design choices made

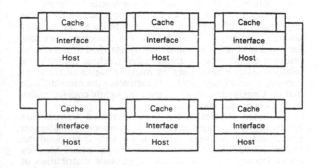

*Fig. 2. Macro view of a Memnet system.*

from the host of possibilities will, to a large extent, be economic and engineering choices.

### Memnet Conclusions

The goal of initial Memnet work was to explore the viability of using shared memory in support of distributed systems, and demonstrate that a fundamental change in the network abstraction (from I/O to memory) would result in an improved interface, both in performance and usability. It demonstrated that the memory abstraction, when implemented in hardware, can provide access to the full network bandwidth directly to the application, completely bypassing the operating system and providing up to a factor of 1,000 speedup of distributed system interaction.

We can therefore conclude that, for local area distributed systems, shared memory support of communications makes sense immediately. Moving to other environments requires that we consider changes needed in order to support growth in network size, speed of nodes, and complexity of interconnection.

We need to consider for example, how to extend the memory model to a wide area, with unreliable connections and no true broadcast. Memnet depends on the broadcast properties of token rings for its consistency protocol. It assumes a very high degree of reliability in message transmission (i.e., no drops). In a wide area system, reliable broadcast will not be available, but unreliable multicast may be. Point-to-point messages will be much less reliable. We have concluded from this fact that in a wide area environment we should explore a relaxation of the consistency properties that a Memnet-like system provides. The range of network primitive operations (which, on Memnet, consist of physical read, physical write, read-modify-write, and signal) should be extended to allow distributed management of the network resources. The way in which consistency ought to be relaxed, and the nature of the extended network primitive operations, form the focus of the work embodied by Mether, described in *Mether*.

It is not practical to model the nation's network as a large, flat address space, as we have already learned in the transition from the flat host-name address space to the Domain Name System, that is hierarchical. In Memnet follow-on systems, flat address spaces should give way to more sophisticated addressing schemes. A candidate scheme is described later, in *CapNet*.

There are many other research areas. Graceful degradation under network and node failure needs to be incorporated into the designs. In addition, new expressive tools (languages) need to be developed so the users of these distributed resources can describe interesting problems in finite time.

## Mether

Mether is a DSM implemented on Sun™ workstations under the SunOS™ 4.0 operating system. It is distributed since pages of memory are not all at one workstation, but rather move around the network in a demand-paged fashion. User programs access the data in a way indistinguishable from other memory.

Mether design began in March 1988. Experience with Memnet pointed towards experiments with a DSM in a wholly different network environment: one with a higher latency, lower bandwidth, and software-based page fault managers. Mether had several goals which were:

---

™Sun and SunOS are trademarks of Sun Microsystems Inc.

- To function as a *reality check* on the idea of DSM. Memnet had fulfilled its function in demonstrating that a DSM was practical. The next question was: Was Memnet a one-of-kind system or a specific instance of a general case? We felt that if Mether was a success then the latter was true.

- To better determine what should be the applications interface to a DSM. Memnet had certain properties, such as memory interrupts and strong consistency, that might have been necessities, or implementation decisions for one particular DSM.

- To build a system that was useful in and of itself. We believed that a DSM running on conventional workstations (e.g., Suns) using conventional networking protocols (e.g., Transmission Control Protocol/Internet Program—TCP/IP) would be useful.

The first implementation of Mether, V0, was operational in November, 1988 [1]. This version was essentially a software Memnet, supporting strong consistency and replicated read-only pages, and was thus similar to systems such as Li's IVY, and Bisiani and Forin's Mach based-DSM. Processes map in a set of pages that are distinguished by being sharable over a network. A page could be moved from one processor to another at any time. If a process accessed a page and was not present on the processor it was fetched over the network.

In using Mether V0, a number of issues became clear once a measurement study was done:

- Many shared-memory programs attempt to synchronize using memory variables as locks or semaphores, and in doing so, saturate the network with packets. Since they were synchronizing using the *value* of the memory variable, we sought to use this fact to our advantage.

- Synchronization traffic also affected the Mether communications servers, resulting in queued packets.

- Long queues of packets and blocked communications servers increased the latency of the shared memory.

- Programs trying to synchronize spend most of their execution time in loops examining unchanged variables, which increases host load.

- On workstations, packet delivery is unreliable. Even point-to-point messages can be easily dropped or misordered. Protocols had to be designed to tolerate such unreliability.

Several resolutions of these problems are possible. Synchronization mechanisms can be added as an out-of-band subsystem, as in IVY's use of RPC. However, for aesthetic reasons, we wanted synchronization to be supported as an integral part of the DSM. The shared memory model used by our DSMs needed to be extended and changed.

It might be seen as contradictory to advocate *dilution* of the shared memory model as a network interface. But this is not so; the abstraction has not changed, but rather the implementation for a specific setting. Also, as we are finding, many applications do not require the high degree of consistency provided by Memnet; they can make effective use of a more relaxed consistency model.

For this reason we were willing to have Mether depart from an emulation of the shared memory model where differences can provide a performance improvement in the face of high latency and poor operating system performance.

As testing of applications (ported from machines such as the Cray-2) progressed, the shared-memory model was adapted accordingly. In many cases processes need only examine a few variables in a page. Consistent memory is not always needed. Even the demand-driven nature so basic to the DSM model is not always desirable. We describe these changes in further detail below; none detract from the utility of memory as a network abstraction.

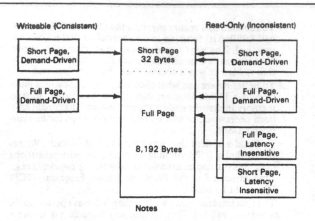

Notes

1. The choice of the read-only space or the writeable space is chosen when the application maps the Mether address space in.
2. The consistent space can only be demand-driven.
3. The choice of full or short page, demand or data driven, is determined by two address bits in the Mether address space.
4. If further applications demand it, we may opt for four different page sizes – one more bit of address space.

*Fig. 3. The Mether address space.*

## Inconsistent Memory

Mether V3 allows a process to access memory as consistent or inconsistent. A process indicates its desired access by mapping the memory read-only or writeable. There is one consistent copy of a page; for reasons described [7], we move the consistent copy of a page around, rather than the write capabilities for a page.

When a process gets an inconsistent copy of a page, the process holding a consistent copy may continue to write to it. Over time, a read-only copy will become out of date, or inconsistent. There are four ways in which an update may occur:

- A process may request the consistent copy, causing an up-to-date copy of the page to be transmitted over the network; at which time all the Mether servers having a copy of the page will refresh their copy.
- The process holding the consistent copy can cause a new version of the copy to be sent out over the network via a system call in a manner described below.
- As part of the page management policy, the local inconsistent copy will be discarded when it has been present for more than (currently) 5 s. Thus there is an absolute bound on how out-of-date a copy may be.
- The process holding the inconsistent copy can purge its copy; the next time it accesses the page a new copy will be fetched over the network.

The first three mechanism constitute a passive update. The last mechanism is an active update.

## Short Pages

Another capability added to Mether was support for *short pages*. Short pages are only 32 bytes long. They are actually the first 32 bytes of a full-sized page. A typical use is to store important state variables in the first 32 bytes of the page. The process can access these variables with extremely low overhead since few packets must be transmitted upon a fault, and determine whether to access the full (8,192 byte) page. The low overhead comes from the fact that page faults cause only 32 bytes as opposed to 8,192 bytes to transit the network. The address space for short pages completely overlays the address space for full pages, which is how the short pages can share variables with full pages. Table I shows the relationship of short pages to long pages in the address space.

## User Driven Page Propagation

Because pages can become out of date in the Mether model, there must be a way to propagate new copies of a page. Since the servers do not always know when propagation should occur, Mether supports user driven propagation.

First, processes can cause local, read-only copies of a page to be discarded, so the next reference causes a new copy of the page to be fetched over the network. Second, on those systems that support some form of broadcast or multicast, a writer can cause its copy to be broadcast to all holders of the inconsistent copy. This latter case is called *network refresh*.

## Latency Insensitive Address Space

Mether 3.0 provides an address space that is *latency insensitive*. When a reference in this space results in a page fault, Mether will use a high-latency communications channel to send out the request for the page. Pending references in the latency-insensitive address space may be resolved by a network refresh. The latency insensitive address space is used to support *data driven page faults*. This provides a base for experimentation assuming high latency environments.

## Data Driven Page Faults

An even greater departure from the standard DSM is the support Mether provides for data driven page faults. In the shared-memory systems described above, a page fault always results in a request over the network for a page.

In a data driven page fault, one process takes an action that causes another process's page fault to be satisfied. Thus, one process takes an action that causes another process's memory cycle to complete.

Data driven page faults are accomplished when a process blocks a memory read request to the latency insensitive address space. The request may be satisfied by some other process performing a network refresh of the page. Thus, one process's memory read request has been directly satisfied by an action taken by some other process. A synchronization has been performed at the memory request level, using behavior of processes at the operating system level.

The rules for paging pages in and out, mapping them into a process's address space, and locking them into one process's address space are more complex than for simple DSMs. These rules are shown in Table I. In this table *superset* refers to the containing page (i.e., the 8,192 byte page in the current implementation); *subset* refers to the contained page (i.e., the short page). Note that we may later have more than two lengths of pages.

Figure 3 shows how different virtual addresses in the Mether address space reference a single page.

## Summary

Mether V3 implements a DSM with extended semantics for memory operations, specifically short pages, a latency insensitive address space, network refresh, and data driven page requests [8]. Mether has supported a variety of applications for almost three years. Mether has demonstrated that:

- Memnet was not a one of a kind system, but a specific instance of a general case

**Table I. Rules for Subspace Operations**

| Operation | Rule For Subsets | Rule For Supersets |
|---|---|---|
| Mapping A Page In | All Subsets Must Be Present | Supersets Need Not Be Present |
| Pagein From the Network | All Subsets Paged In | No Supersets Paged In |
| Pageout | All Subsets Paged Out | All Supersets Left Paged In But Unmapped |
| Lock | All Subsets Must Be Present; If All Are Present, All Are Locked; Otherwise The Lock Fails and Any Nonpresent Subsets Are Marked Wanted | No Supersets Locked But Must Be Present; All Are Unmapped; Supersets Not Present Are Marked Wanted |
| Page Fault | All Subsets Must Be Present | Supersets Need Not Be Present |
| Purge | All Consistent Subsets Are Purged | Supersets Are Not Affected |

- The Memnet model of strongly consistent memory had to be extended and changed for a high-latency environment
- A DSM running on conventional workstations under a standard Unix operating system is useful
- Applications can make effective use of an inconsistent address space with other Mether properties

# CapNet—A DSM for WANs

One of the key questions that arose in the Memnet research was the applicability of the shared memory abstraction to the WAN environment. There are a number of crucial differences between WANs and LANs that might frustrate the abstraction:

- WANs have much larger latency (the round-trip time required to send data and receive a response)
- WANs cannot effectively support broadcast
- WANs have traditionally been bandwidth constrained

DSM remains useful as a system abstraction for writing distributed applications involving information sharing. One application example is support of distributed databases, as proposed by Hsu and Tam at Harvard. Coupled with the evidence from Mether, that applications could operate with relaxed consistency, extending DSM to the wide area environment is both technically interesting and desirable.

## CapNet Issues

Issues addressed by CapNet include those that are issues in any DSM, such as memory coherency, and some that are specific to the WAN environment. Most DSMs, as pointed to in [2], use a single writer/multiple readers serialization protocol. Our research has suggested new notions of memory coherency that would allow users to improve concurrency by exploiting characteristics of applications; Zwaenepoel of Rice and Hutto of Georgia Tech have addressed reexamination of memory coherence policies as well. We will concentrate on issues specific to a WAN-based DSM, and assume a single writer/multiple readers protocol. However, the schemes are independent of the coherency protocols used.

Wide area DSMs are built on a point-to-point switching network in which broadcasting is inherently expensive. Hence a directory of page locations must be maintained by some *page manager*. Requests for a page go to the page manager, who forwards the requests to the owner. An owner is the host that made the last modification to the page, and therefore has the most current version. The page manager designates the requesting host as the new owner before it forwards a write request to the current owner. The current owner is the host whose write request has just been forwarded. An owner honors a read request by sending the page and updating its *copyset*, the set of hosts with read copies. Set membership is used to multicast invalidation information (and avoid broadcast) when a write request is honored by the page manager. This scheme (in terms of delay) requires a round trip to the page manager and owner before a request can be honored. In a WAN, in which latency is high, the number of request/response round trips detailed above may imply a very long response time. Higher performance could be achieved if we could optimize the protocol or architecture to remove these delays. We set ourselves the goal of the requests reaching the owner directly, without reference to an intermediary directory service. Our scheme is described next.

## Page Location Scheme of CapNet

The scheme proposed in CapNet [9] is to integrate the network and the operating system software. This is done by augmenting the packet switches with information necessary for locating pages. By distributing the page table into the network switches, the network can route a page request to the owner directly. Under our scheme, a memory request is routed according to its virtual address, which is shared by the participants in an area of DSM. Each switch has its own version of the page table. Each page table entry contains an identifier for an outgoing hop leading to the owner of the page (this table resembles a routing table). Entries in the page table are updated as pages are transferred to satisfy write requests. Therefore, the current location of a page is always accurate and maintained by the network fabric. A host requesting a shared page may generate a page request. The request is sent to the network, the network locates the page and transfers it to the requester. The whole process takes only two messages and no broadcasting is required. Address information in the network is self-maintaining. It is possible that there is more than one outstanding request for a page. These requests can be held in a First In, First Out (FIFO) queue appended to the page. When the page is transferred, the queue of requests is transferred with it.

If a page request is issued when the requested page is in transit, the request may either *chase* the page to its new owner or be directed to the switch closest to the previous owner and redirected to the new owner. This will depend on whether the path of the second request intersects with the one of the first request, and if so, whether the page table of the switch at the intersection has already been altered.

Putting the entire page table in the switches may pose some problems, due to the extent of the address spaces that might be envisioned, as well as the number of participants. Fast memory, especially fast Content-Addressable Memories (CAMs) are quite expensive. We have devised a hybrid approach, that preserves much of the latency reduction of the original scheme, and does so with reduced memory requirements. The basic *hybridization* comes from distributing lookup entries across the switching nodes. To the degree that we can map entries to switches near their points of frequent use, we will succeed. Locations for pages that are infrequently referenced can be kept in a page manager. It is possible to partition the virtual address space by some scheme and designate a host as the manager for the pages in each of these partitions. The scheme we suggest is using the page manager's identifier as part of the virtual address.

The page manager of a group of pages that exhibit geographic locality can be migrated as the referencing (and hence the locality) changes, reducing the average propagation delay in comparison to using a page manager that has a fixed location.

# UPWARDS

UPWARDS is an attempt to develop software that can provide access to the bandwidth available in future high-speed WANs. The target environment for UPWARDS is the AURORA testbed, which is described in a summary published in the September 1990 *IEEE Computer Magazine*. Briefly, four sites (University of Pennsylvania in Philadelphia; IBM Research in Hawthorne, NY; Bell Communications Research (Bellcore) in Morristown, NJ; and Massachusetts Institute of Technology (MIT) in Cambridge) will be connected by a number of OC12 links. These links operate at 622 Mb/s, which is about 80 Mbyte/s. Such speeds will place a considerable burden on the operating system software of connected computers, as they represent very large fractions of the bus bandwidths of even the fastest workstations.

UPWARDS is exploring a number of technologies in an attempt to offer a significant fraction of the available bandwidth to computations.

First, UPWARDS uses distributed shared memory, as the number of instructions necessary for passing state between processes is minimized. This is because, independent of any communications scheme used, shared memory communicates using machine instructions. Traditional approaches to interprocess communications build abstract instructions such as READ and WRITE out of many simple machine instructions. Thus, shared memory communications should place a smaller burden on the machines that employ it. Evidence from MEMNET argues for the feasibility, and many DSMs have been built in the LAN environment [2].

Second, UPWARDS uses lightweight processes, as high context switch overheads are intolerable at Gb/s speeds. For example, an operating system that requires 5 ms per context switch, and has two processes, A and B, can easily accumulate 1.25 Mbytes of information. To see this, assume A is receiving data and is context-switched out, and B is context-switched in. This takes 5 ms, and assuming no work is accomplished, B is then switched out and A is context-switched in, for another 5 ms. During these 10 ms, $10^7$ b, or 1.25 Mbytes of data have arrived.

Third, UPWARDS makes heavy use of caches and cache preloading, in an attempt to address the issue of latency. Caches are portions of fast local memory containing data that has been obtained from slower memory areas. If the correct data are in the cache (i.e., the cache has a high "hit rate") the illusion of a single memory of low cost, large size, and fast access can be achieved. In the case of memory implemented using a network, a cache must be employed to defeat the latency imposed by propagation delays. We believe that caches must also be preloaded, anticipating future requests in an attempt to reduce observed latency with the application of large bandwidths.

We are developing special hardware assists [10] in order to support the memory-oriented abstraction for networks. These assists are in the form of host interfaces that connect the network fabric into the computer's bus.

We see the high throughput, cache management, and lightweight processes of UPWARDS as ideal for a number of applications of our network. One of particular interest is that of multiparty multimedia interaction. Each of the four research sites in the AURORA network has an experimental teleconferencing facility provided by Bellcore, called a *Video Wall*. The Video Wall consists of a pair of wide screen television displays, a pair of television cameras, and high-quality audio equipment. The displays and cameras operate using National Television Standards Committee (NTSC) video, which requires about 150 Mb/s uncompressed. In order to bring the full capabilities of the computer to bear in teleconferencing, we are developing video interfaces to the RS/6000 Microchannel Architecture, so the images on the screen can be processed, controlled, and augmented by computer. Ideally, one should be able to comprise a presentation using voice, images, data displays, and full-motion video, in order to share a multimedia environment with other participants in the teleconference. Processing the large amounts of shared state inherent in such a system should provide a challenging driving application for UPWARDS.

# Conclusions and Open Questions

From the initial idea of memory as a network abstraction came the Memnet DSM, which treated the network as an extended processor bus, and due to the nature of its components, was able to exhibit very good performance in a LAN environment.

Minnich originally constructed the Mether software as an attempt to preserve the Memnet interface, and much of the early design effort was spent on building software that could easily be implemented in silicon. However, experience with a number of applications led to the conclusion that DSMs that supported strongly consistent memory can exhibit poor performance, for reasons that are implementation-*independent*. Thus, there are common issues that can be addressed between Memnet and Mether.

The current version of Mether, Mether 3.0, addresses these common issues by using short pages of 32 bytes (as opposed to the 8,192 byte pages of the host operating system) for synchronization data, and relaxing consistency constraints, where possible. Thus, by moving the Memnet design from a specialized LAN fabric and custom operating system, the Mether system is able to attack variable latency, host load, and program performance. Lessons learned from Mether can guide the design of future hardware DSMs.

The CapNet design extends the Memnet scheme in another direction, that of WANs. As discussed above, the most difficult issue is the latency, or delay in message propagation, between nodes. Latency wreaks havoc on the performance of page-management schemes designed for broadcast LANs. CapNet addresses the latency by augmenting packet switches in the network with a directory system used for page location. The effect is a significant reduction in the number of messages required for page table management, and thus a significant improvement in response time. A hybrid scheme can be used to reduce the memory requirements of each switch node. Thus, CapNet suggests an extremely attractive hardware architecture for a high-performance WAN DSM.

The UPWARDS system is, in a sense, the software complement to the CAPNET research. It focuses on software resource management schemes and service primitives with which processes can communicate efficiently. It is specifically targeted at high-speed, e.g., Gb rate, WANs.

The growth of these systems from the original Memnet design and implementation suggests that this approach has merit that transcends any particular instance. What was originally a hardware DSM on a specialized LAN has been extended to constructions using WANs and implementing DSM with software. Other research has shown that memory techniques such as caching and prefetching can be used to control the traffic generated by a computer [11]. After 25 years of research, memory management is one of the best understood areas of computer science. We are trying to bring this understanding, and the power it implies, to bear on the problems of computer networking.

## Open Questions

Some of the open questions remaining are:

- How large does it make sense to let these networks grow? Memnet gave indications that dependent on the style of usage of a DSM, a network of either 30 or 300 is the reasonable upper bound. Additional characterization will need to be done before this question can be answered, but one possibility was suggested by Mether's relaxed consistency scheme.

- What lessons from virtual memory can be directly transferred to DSM systems? What new schemes will be necessary to support the virtual memory model of data access?

- What form should error prevention, detection, and recovery schemes take? How can these forms be generalized so the solution is a general solution, rather than an individual solution for each instance of a DSM application?

- How can networks of heterogeneous machines be interconnect? Issues of data alignment can affect homogeneous processor complexes. Can this be done without huge performance penalties?

- Can models of security be preserved?

- What new problems will this system solve? The introduction of a new resource with new capabilities generally enables new classes of solutions. What form those solutions will take is an open question.

## References

[1]   R. Minnich and D. Farber, "The Mether System: A Distributed Shared Memory For SunOS 4.0," *Usenix-Summer 89*, Usenix, 1989.

[2]   M.-C. Tam, J. M. Smith, and D. J. Farber, "A Taxonomy-Based Comparison of Several Distributed Shared Memory Systems," *ACM Operating Sys. Review*, vol. 24, no. 3, pp. 40–67, July 1990.

[3]   H. Bal, J. G. Steiner, and A. Tanenbaum, "Experience With Distributed Programming in ORCA," *Proc. IEEE CS Int'l. Conf. on Computer Languages*, pp. 79–89, Mar. 1990.

[4]   G. S. Delp, "The Architecture and Implementation of Memnet: A High-Speed Shared Memory Computer Communication Network," *Ph. D. Thesis, Dept. of Electrical Engineering*, University of Delaware, Apr. 1988.

[5]   L. Borrmann, and M. Herdieckerhoff, "Parallel Processing Performance in a Linda System," *ICPP*, 1989.

[6]   P. A. Bernstein, "Sequoia: A Fault-Tolerant Tightly Coupled Multiprocessor For Transaction Processing," *Computer*, vol. 21, no. 2, pp. 37–45, Feb. 1988.

[7]   R. G. Minnich and D. J. Farber, "Reducing Host Load, Network Load, and Latency in a Distributed Shared Memory," *Proc. of the Tenth IEEE Distributed Computing Sys. Conf.*, 1990.

[8]   R. G. Minnich, "Mether: A Memory System for Network Multiprocessors," *Ph. D. Thesis*, University of Pennsylvania, 1990.

[9]   I. M.-C. Tam and D. J. Farber, "CapNet—An Alternative Approach to Ultra High Speed Networks," *Proc. Int'l. Commun. Conf.*, 1990.

[10]  C. Brendan, S. Traw, and J. M. Smith, "A High-Performance Host Interface For ATM Networks," *Proc. SIGCOMM Conf.*, Sept. 1991.

[11]  J. Smith and D. Farber, "Traffic Characteristics of a Distributed Memory System," *Comp. Networks and ISDN Sys.*, 1991.

## Biography

**Gary S. Delp** received his Ph.D. degree in electrical engineering from the University of Delaware for his work on Memnet in 1988. His A.B. degree from Oberlin College and MFA degree from Memphis State University were earned for work in technical theater and design in 1977 and 1979, respectively.

Mr. Delp is a research staff member of the IBM Research Division currently on assignment at Application Business Systems in Rochester, Minnesota. His current research interests include high-speed network interfaces, latency negation systems, and VLSI design automation.

He is a member of ACM, IEEE, and HKN.

**David J. Farber** is Professor of computer and information science and electrical engineering at the University of Pennsylvania where he is leading research in ultra high-speed networking.

He was formerly with the University of Delaware, the University of California in Irvine, Scientific Data Systems, the Rand Corporation, and Bell Telephone Laboratories. Twenty years ago, he was a founder of and is currently Vice President of Caine, Farber, and Gordon, Inc.—a leading supplier of software engineering tools.

Mr. Farber currently serves on the Computer Science and Telecommunications Board (CSTB) of the National Research Council, chairs the NSF/DARPA/CNRI Gigabit Testbed Initiatives Co-ordination Committee, and is an editor of the Prentice Hall *Series in Innovative Computing*. He is a member of the ACM, Sigma Xi, and a senior member of the IEEE.

**Ronald G. Minnich** received his B.S. and M.S. degrees in electrical engineering from the University of Delaware, and his Ph.D. degree from the University of Pennsylvania in computer science. Mr. Minnich is a research staff member at the Supercomputing Research Center in Bowie, Maryland, working in the Systems and Architecture group. His current research interests include operating systems, distributed computing environments, programming environments for reprogrammable hardware engines such as Splash, and parallel processing.

His most recent work includes the Trigger symbolic debugger for Splash, a caching file system for Unix systems, and the Mether system.

**Jonathan M. Smith** completed his graduate study and research at Columbia University in New York, receiving his Ph.D. degree in computer science in 1989. He is an Assistant Professor in the Department of Computer and Information Science at the University of Pennsylvania, Philadelphia. Mr. Smith is a member of the Distributed Systems Laboratory at Pennsylvania.

Mr. Smith was a summer engineer at Boeing Aerospace in 1980, a member of technical staff at Bell Telephone Laboratories from 1981 to 1984, and in 1984 became a member of technical staff at Bell Communications Research (Bellcore), which was formed at the AT&T divestiture. He assumed his present post at the University of Pennsylvania in September 1989.

His current research interests include high-speed networks, operating systems, parallel processing, network security, and cryptology. Mr. Smith is a member of ACM, IEEE, ASEE, and Sigma Xi.

**Ming-Chit (Ivan) Tam** received his M.S. degree from Imperial College, London, England. He is a Ph.D. degree candidate at the University Pennsylvania's Computer and Information Science Department. Mr. Tam's current research interests include call repacking for virtual circuits over very high speed networks and support mechanisms for Distributed Share Memories over WANs.

# The Stanford Dash Multiprocessor

**Daniel Lenoski, James Laudon, Kourosh Gharachorloo,**

**Wolf-Dietrich Weber, Anoop Gupta, John Hennessy,**

**Mark Horowitz, and Monica S. Lam**
Stanford University

**Directory-based cache coherence gives Dash the ease-of-use of shared-memory architectures while maintaining the scalability of message-passing machines.**

T he Computer Systems Laboratory at Stanford University is developing a shared-memory multiprocessor called Dash (an abbreviation for Directory Architecture for Shared Memory). The fundamental premise behind the architecture is that it is possible to build a scalable high-performance machine with a single address space and coherent caches.

The Dash architecture is scalable in that it achieves linear or near-linear performance growth as the number of processors increases from a few to a few thousand. This performance results from distributing the memory among processing nodes and using a network with scalable bandwidth to connect the nodes. The architecture allows shared data to be cached, thereby significantly reducing the latency of memory accesses and yielding higher processor utilization and higher overall performance. A distributed directory-based protocol provides cache coherence without compromising scalability.

The Dash prototype system is the first operational machine to include a scalable cache-coherence mechanism. The prototype incorporates up to 64 high-performance RISC microprocessors to yield performance up to 1.6 billion instructions per second and 600 million scalar floating point operations per second. The design of the prototype has provided deeper insight into the architectural and implementation challenges that arise in a large-scale machine with a single address space. The prototype will also serve as a platform for studying real applications and software on a large parallel system.

This article begins by describing the overall goals for Dash, the major features of the architecture, and the methods for achieving scalability. Next, we describe the directory-based coherence protocol in detail. We then provide an overview of the prototype machine and the corresponding software support, followed by some

Reprinted from *Computer*, Vol. 25, No. 3, Mar. 1992, pp. 63–79.

preliminary performance numbers. The article concludes with a discussion of related work and the current status of the Dash hardware and software.

## Dash project overview

The overall goal of the Dash project is to investigate highly parallel architectures. For these architectures to achieve widespread use, they must run a variety of applications efficiently without imposing excessive programming difficulty. To achieve both high performance and wide applicability, we believe a parallel architecture must provide scalability to support hundreds to thousands of processors, high-performance individual processors, and a single shared address space.

The gap between the computing power of microprocessors and that of the largest supercomputers is shrinking, while the price/performance advantage of microprocessors is increasing. This clearly points to using microprocessors as the compute engines in a multiprocessor. The challenge lies in building a machine that can scale up its performance while maintaining the initial price/performance advantage of the individual processors. Scalability allows a parallel architecture to leverage commodity microprocessors and small-scale multiprocessors to build larger scale machines. These larger machines offer substantially higher performance, which provides the impetus for programmers to port their sequential applications to parallel architectures instead of waiting for the next higher performance uniprocessor.

High-performance processors are important to achieve both high total system performance and general applicability. Using the fastest microprocessors reduces the impact of limited or uneven parallelism inherent in some applications. It also allows a wider set of applications to exhibit acceptable performance with less effort from the programmer.

A single address space enhances the programmability of a parallel machine by reducing the problems of data partitioning and dynamic load distribution, two of the toughest problems in programming parallel machines. The shared address space also improves support for automatically parallelizing compilers, standard operating systems, multipro-

gramming, and incremental tuning of parallel applications — features that make a single-address-space machine much easier to use than a message-passing machine.

Caching of memory, including shared writable data, allows multiprocessors with a single address space to achieve high performance through reduced memory latency. Unfortunately, caching shared data introduces the problem of cache coherence (see the sidebar and accompanying figure).

While hardware support for cache coherence has its costs, it also offers many benefits. Without hardware support, the responsibility for coherence falls to the user or the compiler. Exposing the issue of coherence to the user would lead to a complex programming model, where users might well avoid caching to ease the programming bur-

den. Handling the coherence problem in the compiler is attractive, but currently cannot be done in a way that is competitive with hardware. With hardware-supported cache coherence, the compiler can aggressively optimize programs to reduce latency without having to rely purely on a conservative static dependence analysis.

The major problem with existing cache-coherent shared-address machines is that they have not demonstrated the ability to scale effectively beyond a few high-performance processors. To date, only message-passing machines have shown this ability. We believe that using a directory-based coherence mechanism will permit single-address-space machines to scale as well as message-passing machines, while providing a more flexible and general programming model.

## Dash system organization

Most existing multiprocessors with cache coherence rely on snooping to maintain coherence. Unfortunately, snooping schemes distribute the information about which processors are caching which data items among the caches. Thus, straightforward snooping schemes require that all caches see every memory request from every processor. This inherently limits the scalability of these machines because the common bus and the individual processor caches eventually saturate. With today's high-performance RISC processors this saturation can occur with just a few processors.

Directory structures avoid the scalability problems of snoopy schemes by removing the need to broadcast every memory request to all processor caches. The directory maintains pointers to the processor caches holding a copy of each memory block. Only the caches with copies can be affected by an access to the memory block, and only those caches need be notified of the access. Thus, the processor caches and interconnect will not saturate due to coherence requests. Furthermore, directory-based coherence is not dependent on any specific interconnection network like the bus used by most snooping schemes. The same scalable, low-latency networks such as Omega networks or $k$-nary $n$-cubes used by non-cache-coherent and

# Cache coherence

Cache-coherence problems can arise in shared-memory multiprocessors when more than one processor cache holds a copy of a data item (a). Upon a write, these copies must be updated or invalidated (b). Most systems use invalidation since this allows the writing processor to gain exclusive access to the cache line and complete further writes into the cache line without generating external traffic (c). This further complicates coherence since this dirty cache must respond instead of memory on subsequent accesses by other processors (d).

Small-scale multiprocessors frequently use a snoopy cache-coherence protocol,[1] which relies on all caches monitoring the common bus that connects the processors to memory. This monitoring allows caches to independently determine when to invalidate cache lines (b), and when to intervene because they contain the most up-to-date copy of a given location (d). Snoopy schemes do not scale to a large number of processors because the common bus or individual processor caches eventually saturate, since they must process every memory request from every processor.

The directory relieves the processor caches from snooping on memory requests by keeping track of which caches hold each memory block. A simple directory structure first proposed by Censier and Feautrier[2] has one directory entry per block of memory (e). Each entry contains one presence bit per processor cache. In addition, a state bit indicates whether the block is uncached, shared in multiple caches, or held exclusively by one cache (that is, whether the block is dirty). Using the state and presence bits, the memory can tell which caches need to be invalidated when a location is written (b). Likewise, the directory indicates whether memory's copy of the block is up to date or which cache holds the most recent copy (d). If the memory and directory are partitioned into independent units and connected to the processors by a scalable interconnect, the memory system can provide scalable memory bandwidth.

## References

1. J. Archibald and J.-L. Baer, "Cache Coherence Protocols: Evaluation Using a Multiprocessor Simulation Model," *ACM Trans. Computer Systems*, Vol. 4, No. 4, Nov. 1986, pp. 273-298.

2. L. Censier and P. Feautrier, "A New Solution to Coherence Problems in Multicache Systems," *IEEE Trans. Computers*, Vol. C-27, No. 12, Dec. 1978, pp. 1,112-1,118.

message-passing machines can be employed.

The concept of directory-based cache coherence is not new. It was first proposed in the late 1970s. However, the original directory structures were not scalable because they used a centralized directory that quickly became a bottleneck. The Dash architecture overcomes this limitation by partitioning and distributing the directory and main memory, and by using a new coherence protocol that can suitably exploit distributed directories. In addition, Dash provides several other mechanisms to reduce and hide the latency of memory operations.

Figure 1 shows Dash's high-level organization. The architecture consists of a number of processing nodes connected through directory controllers to a low-latency interconnection network. Each processing node, or *cluster*, consists of a small number of high-performance processors and a portion of the shared memory interconnected by a bus. Multiprocessing within the cluster can be viewed either as increasing the power of each processing node or as reducing the cost of the directory and network interface by amortizing it over a larger number of processors.

Distributing memory with the processors is essential because it allows the system to exploit locality. All private data and code references, along with some of the shared references, can be made local to the cluster. These references avoid the longer latency of remote references and reduce the bandwidth demands on the global interconnect. Except for the directory memory, the resulting system

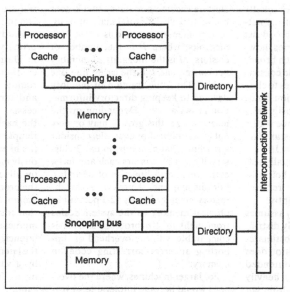

**Figure 1. The Dash architecture consists of a set of clusters connected by a general interconnection network. Directory memory contains pointers to the clusters currently caching each memory line.**

architecture is similar to many scalable message-passing machines. While not optimized to do so, Dash could emulate such machines with reasonable efficiency.

## Scalability of the Dash approach

We have outlined why we believe a single-address-space machine with cache coherence holds the most promise for delivering scalable performance to a wide range of applications. Here, we address the more detailed issues in scaling such a directory-based system. The three primary issues are ensuring that the system provides scalable memory bandwidth, that the costs scale reasonably, and that mechanisms are provided to deal with large memory latencies.

Scalability in a multiprocessor requires the total memory bandwidth to scale linearly with the number of processors. Dash provides scalable bandwidth to data objects residing in local memory by distributing the physical memory among the clusters. For data accesses that must be serviced remotely, Dash uses a scalable interconnection network. Support

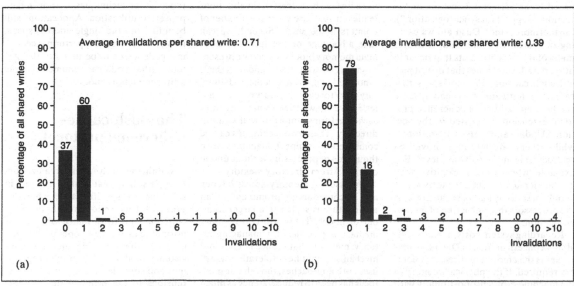

(a)    (b)

**Figure 2. Cache invalidation patterns for MP3D (a) and PThor (b). MP3D uses a particle-based simulation technique to determine the structure of shock waves caused by objects flying at high speed in the upper atmosphere. PThor is a parallel logic simulator based on the Chandy-Misra algorithm.**

of coherent caches could potentially compromise the scalability of the network by requiring frequent broadcast messages. The use of directories, however, removes the need for such broadcasts and the coherence traffic consists only of point-to-point messages to clusters that are caching that location. Since these clusters must have originally fetched the data, the coherence traffic will be within some small constant factor of the original data traffic. In fact, since each cached block is usually referenced several times before being invalidated, caching normally reduces overall global traffic significantly.

This discussion of scalability assumes that the accesses are uniformly distributed across the machine. Unfortunately, the uniform access assumption does not always hold for highly contended synchronization objects and for heavily shared data objects. The resulting *hot spots* — concentrated accesses to data from the memory of a single cluster over a short duration of time — can significantly reduce the memory and network throughput. The reduction occurs because the distribution of resources is not exploited as it is under uniform access patterns.

To address hot spots, Dash relies on a combination of hardware and software techniques. For example, Dash provides special extensions to the directory-based protocol to handle synchronization references such as queue-based locks (discussed further in the section, "Support for synchronization"). Furthermore, since Dash allows caching of shared writable data, it avoids many of the data hot spots that occur in other parallel machines that do not permit such caching. For hot spots that cannot be mitigated by caching, some can be removed by the coherence protocol extensions discussed in the section, "Update and deliver operations," while others can only be removed by restructuring at the software level. For example, when using a primitive such as a barrier, it is possible for software to avoid hot spots by gathering and releasing processors through a tree of memory locations.

Regarding system costs, a major scalability concern unique to Dash-like machines is the amount of directory memory required. If the physical memory in the machine grows proportionally with the number of processing nodes, then using a bit-vector to keep track of all

clusters caching a memory block does not scale well. The total amount of directory memory needed is $P^2 \times M/L$ megabits, where $P$ is the number of clusters, $M$ is the megabits of memory per cluster, and $L$ is the cache-line size in bits. Thus, the fraction of memory devoted to keeping directory information grows as $P/L$. Depending on the machine size, this growth may or may not be tolerable. For example, consider a machine that contains up to 32 clusters of eight processors each and has a cache (memory) line size of 32 bytes. For this machine, the overhead for directory memory is only 12.5 percent of physical memory as the system scales from eight to 256 processors. This is comparable with the overhead of supporting an error-correcting code on memory.

For larger machines, where the overhead would become intolerable, several alternatives exist. First, we can take advantage of the fact that at any given time a memory block is usually cached by a very small number of processors. For example, Figure 2 shows the number of invalidations generated by two applications run on a simulated 32-processor machine. These graphs show that most writes cause invalidations to only a few caches. (We have obtained similar results for a large number of applications.) Consequently, it is possible to replace the complete directory bit-vector by a small number of pointers and to use a limited broadcast of invalidations in the unusual case when the number of pointers is too small. Second, we can take advantage of the fact that most main memory blocks will not be present in any processor's cache, and thus there is no need to provide a dedicated directory entry for every memory block. Studies[1,2] have shown that a small directory cache performs almost as well as a full directory. These two techniques can be combined to support machines with thousands of processors without undue overhead from directory memory.

The issue of memory access latency also becomes more prominent as an architecture is scaled to a larger number of nodes. There are two complementary approaches for managing latency: methods that reduce latency and mechanisms that help tolerate it. Dash uses both approaches, though our main focus has been to reduce latency as much as possible. Although latency tolerating techniques are important, they often

require additional application parallelism to be effective.

Hardware-coherent caches provide the primary latency reduction mechanism in Dash. Caching shared data significantly reduces the average latency for remote accesses because of the spatial and temporal locality of memory accesses. For references not satisfied by the cache, the coherence protocol attempts to minimize latency, as shown in the next section. Furthermore, as previously mentioned, we can reduce latency by allocating data to memory close to the processors that use it. While average memory latency is reduced, references that correspond to interprocessor communication cannot avoid the inherent latencies of a large machine. In Dash, the latency for these accesses is addressed by a variety of latency hiding mechanisms. These mechanisms range from support of a relaxed memory consistency model to support of nonblocking prefetch operations. These operations are detailed in the sections on "Memory consistency" and "Prefetch operations."

We also expect software to play a critical role in achieving good performance on a highly parallel machine. Obviously, applications need to exhibit good parallelism to exploit the rich computational resources of a large machine. In addition, applications, compilers, and operating systems need to exploit cache and memory locality together with latency hiding techniques to achieve high processor utilization. Applications still benefit from the single address space, however, because only performance-critical code needs to be tuned to the system. Other code can assume a simple uniform memory model.

## The Dash cache-coherence protocol

Within the Dash system organization, there is still a great deal of freedom in selecting the specific cache-coherence protocol. This section explains the basic coherence protocol that Dash uses for normal read and write operations, then outlines the resulting memory consistency model visible to the programmer and compiler. Finally, it details extensions to the protocol that support latency hiding and efficient synchronization.

**Memory hierarchy.** Dash implements an invalidation-based cache-coherence protocol. A memory location may be in one of three states:

- *uncached* — not cached by any cluster;
- *shared* — in an unmodified state in the caches of one or more clusters; or
- *dirty* — modified in a single cache of some cluster.

The directory keeps the summary information for each memory block, specifying its state and the clusters that are caching it.

The Dash memory system can be logically broken into four levels of hierarchy, as illustrated in Figure 3. The first level is the processor's cache. This cache is designed to match the processor speed and support snooping from the bus. A request that cannot be serviced by the processor's cache is sent to the second level in the hierarchy, the *local cluster*. This level includes the other processors' caches within the requesting processor's cluster. If the data is locally cached, the request can be serviced within the cluster. Otherwise, the request is sent to the *home cluster* level. The home level consists of the cluster that contains the directory and physical memory for a given memory address. For many accesses (for example, most private data references), the local and home cluster are the same, and the hierarchy collapses to three levels. In general, however, a request will travel through the interconnection network to the home cluster. The home cluster can usually satisfy the request immediately, but if the directory entry is in a dirty state, or in shared state when the requesting processor requests exclusive access, the fourth level must also be accessed. The *remote cluster* level for a memory block consists of the clusters marked by the directory as holding a copy of the block.

To illustrate the directory protocol, first consider how a processor read traverses the memory hierarchy:

- *Processor level* — If the requested location is present in the processor's cache, the cache simply supplies the data. Otherwise, the request goes to the local cluster level.
- *Local cluster level* — If the data resides within one of the other caches within the local cluster, the data is sup-

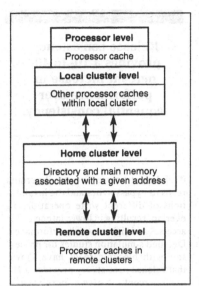

**Figure 3. Memory hierarchy of Dash.**

plied by that cache and no state change is required at the directory level. If the request must be sent beyond the local cluster level, it goes first to the home cluster corresponding to that address.

- *Home cluster level* — The home cluster examines the directory state of the memory location while simultaneously fetching the block from main memory. If the block is clean, the data is sent to the requester and the directory is updated to show sharing by the requester. If the location is dirty, the request is forwarded to the remote cluster indicated by the directory.
- *Remote cluster level* — The dirty cluster replies with a shared copy of the data, which is sent directly to the requester. In addition, a sharing write-back message is sent to the home level to update main memory and change the directory state to indicate that the requesting and remote cluster now have shared copies of the data. Having the dirty cluster respond directly to the requester, as opposed to routing it through the home, reduces the latency seen by the requesting processor.

Now consider the sequence of operations that occurs when a location is written:

- *Processor level* — If the location is dirty in the writing processor's cache, the write can complete immediately. Otherwise, a read-exclusive request is

issued on the local cluster's bus to obtain exclusive ownership of the line and retrieve the remaining portion of the cache line.

- *Local cluster level* — If one of the caches within the cluster already owns the cache line, then the read-exclusive request is serviced at the local level by a cache-to-cache transfer. This allows processors within a cluster to alternately modify the same memory block without any intercluster interaction. If no local cache owns the block, then a read-exclusive request is sent to the home cluster.
- *Home cluster level* — The home cluster can immediately satisfy an ownership request for a location that is in the uncached or shared state. In addition, if a block is in the shared state, then all cached copies must be invalidated. The directory indicates the clusters that have the block cached. Invalidation requests are sent to these clusters while the home concurrently sends an exclusive data reply to the requesting cluster. If the directory indicates that the block is dirty, then the read-exclusive request must be forwarded to the dirty cluster, as in the case of a read.
- *Remote cluster level* — If the directory had indicated that the memory block was shared, then the remote clusters receive an invalidation request to eliminate their shared copy. Upon receiving the invalidation, the remote clusters send an acknowledgment to the requesting cluster. If the directory had indicated a dirty state, then the dirty cluster receives a read-exclusive request. As in the case of the read, the remote cluster responds directly to the requesting cluster and sends a dirty-transfer message to the home indicating that the requesting cluster now holds the block exclusively.

When the writing cluster receives all the invalidation acknowledgments or the reply from the home or dirty cluster, it is guaranteed that all copies of the old data have been purged from the system. If the processor delays completing the write until all acknowledgments are received, then the new write value will become available to all other processors at the same time. However, invalidations involve round-trip messages to multiple clusters, resulting in potentially long delays. Higher processor utilization can be obtained by allowing the write to proceed immediately after the ownership reply is received from the home. Unfortunately, this may lead to inconsistencies with the memory model assumed by the programmer. The next section describes how Dash relaxes the constraints on memory request ordering, while still providing a reasonable programming model to the user.

**Memory consistency.** The memory consistency model supported by an architecture directly affects the amount of buffering and pipelining that can take place among memory requests. In addition, it has a direct effect on the complexity of the programming model presented to the user. The goal in Dash is to provide substantial freedom in the ordering among memory requests, while still providing a reasonable programming model to the user.

At one end of the consistency spectrum is the *sequential consistency* model,[3] which requires execution of the parallel program to appear as an interleaving of the execution of the parallel processes on a sequential machine. Sequential consistency can be guaranteed by requiring a processor to complete one memory request before it issues the next request.[4] Sequential consistency, while conceptually appealing, imposes a large performance penalty on memory accesses. For many applications, such a model is too strict, and one can make do with a weaker notion of consistency.

As an example, consider the case of a processor updating a data structure within a critical section. If updating the structure requires several writes, each write in a sequentially consistent system will stall the processor until all other cached copies of that location have been invalidated. But these stalls are unnecessary as the programmer has already made sure that no other process can rely on the consistency of that data structure until the critical section is exited. If the synchronization points can be identified, then the memory need only be consistent at those points. In particular, Dash supports the use of the *release consistency* model,[5] which only requires the operations to have completed before a critical section is released (that is, a lock is unlocked).

Such a scheme has two advantages. First, it provides the user with a reasonable programming model, since the programmer is assured that when the critical section is exited, all other processors will have a consistent view of the mod-

ified data structure. Second, it permits reads to bypass writes and the invalidations of different write operations to overlap, resulting in lower latencies for accesses and higher overall performance. Detailed simulation studies for processors with blocking reads have shown that release consistency provides a 10- to 40-percent increase in performance over sequential consistency.[5] The disadvantage of the model is that the programmer or compiler must identify all synchronization accesses.

The Dash prototype supports the release consistency model in hardware. Since we use commercial microprocessors, the processor stalls on read operations until the read data is returned from the cache or lower levels of the memory hierarchy. Write operations, however, are nonblocking. There is a write buffer between the first- and second-level caches. The write buffer queues up the write requests and issues them in order. Furthermore, the servicing of write requests is overlapped. As soon as the cache receives the ownership and data for the requested cache line, the write data is removed from the write buffer and written into the cache line. The next write request can be serviced while the invalidation acknowledgments for the previous write operations filter in. Thus, parallelism exists at two levels: the processor executes other instructions and accesses its first-level cache while write operations are pending, and invalidations of multiple write operations are overlapped.

The Dash prototype also provides fence operations that stall the processor or write-buffer until previous operations complete. These fence operations allow software to emulate more stringent consistency models.

**Memory access optimizations.** The use of release consistency helps hide the latency of write operations. However,

since the processor stalls on read operations, it sees the entire duration of all read accesses. For applications that exhibit poor cache behavior or extensive read/write sharing, this can lead to significant delays while the processor waits for remote cache misses to be filled. To help with these problems Dash provides a variety of prefetch and pipelining operations.

*Prefetch operations.* A prefetch operation is an explicit nonblocking request to fetch data before the actual memory operation is issued. Hopefully, by the time the process needs the data, its value has been brought closer to the processor, hiding the latency of the regular blocking read. In addition, nonblocking prefetch allows the pipelining of read misses when multiple cache blocks are prefetched. As a simple example of its use, a process wanting to access a row of a matrix stored in another cluster's memory can do so efficiently by first issuing prefetch reads for all cache blocks corresponding to that row.

Dash's prefetch operations are nonbinding and software controlled. The processor issues explicit prefetch operations that bring a shared or exclusive copy of the memory block into the processor's cache. Not binding the value at the time of the prefetch is important in that issuing the prefetch does not affect the consistency model or force the compiler to do a conservative static dependency analysis. The coherence protocol keeps the prefetched cache line coherent. If another processor happens to write to the location before the prefetching processor accesses the data, the data will simply be invalidated. The prefetch will be rendered ineffective, but the program will execute correctly. Support for an exclusive prefetch operation aids cases where the block is first read and then updated. By first issuing the exclusive prefetch, the processor avoids first obtaining a shared copy and then having to rerequest an exclusive copy of the block. Studies have shown that, for certain applications, the addition of a small number of prefetch instructions can increase processor utilization by more than a factor of two.[6]

*Update and deliver operations.* In some applications, it may not be possible for the consumer process to issue a prefetch early enough to effectively hide the latency of memory. Likewise, if multiple consumers need the same item of data, the communication traffic can be reduced if data is multicast to all the consumers simultaneously. Therefore, Dash provides operations that allow the producer to send data directly to consumers. There are two ways for the producing processor to specify the consuming processors. The *update-write* operation sends the new data directly to all processors that have cached the data, while the *deliver* operation sends the data to specified clusters.

The *update-write* primitive updates the value of all existing copies of a data word. Using this primitive, a processor does not need to first acquire an exclusive copy of the cache line, which would result in invalidating all other copies. Rather, data is directly written into the home memory and all other caches holding a copy of the line. These semantics are particularly useful for event synchronization, such as the release event for a barrier.

The *deliver* instruction explicitly specifies the destination clusters of the transfer. To use this primitive, the producer first writes into its cache using normal, invalidating write operations. The producer then issues a deliver instruction, giving the destination clusters as a bit vector. A copy of the cache line is then sent to the specified clusters, and the directory is updated to indicate that the various clusters now share the data. This operation is useful in cases when the producer makes multiple writes to a block before the consumers will want it or when the consumers are unlikely to be caching the item at the time of the write.

**Support for synchronization.** The access patterns to locations used for synchronization are often different from those for other shared data. For example, whenever a highly contended lock is released, waiting nodes rush to grab the lock. In the case of barriers, many processors must be synchronized and then released. Such activity often causes hot spots in the memory system. Consequently, synchronization variables often warrant special treatment. In addition to update writes, Dash provides two extensions to the coherence protocol that directly support synchronization objects. The first is queue-based locks, and the second is fetch-and-increment operations.

Most cache-coherent architectures handle locks by providing an atomic

test&set instruction and a cached test-and-test&set scheme for spin waiting. Ideally, these spin locks should meet the following criteria:

- minimum amount of traffic generated while waiting,
- low latency release of a waiting processor, and
- low latency acquisition of a free lock.

Cached test&set schemes are moderately successful in satisfying these criteria for low-contention locks, but fail for high-contention locks. For example, assume there are $N$ processors spinning on a lock value in their caches. When the lock is released, all $N$ cache values are invalidated, and $N$ reads are generated to the memory system. Depending on the timing, it is possible that all $N$ processors come back to do the test&set on the location once they realize the lock is free, resulting in further invalidations and rereads. Such a scenario produces unnecessary traffic and increases the latency in acquiring and releasing a lock.

The *queue-based locks* in Dash address this problem by using the directory to indicate which processors are spinning on the lock. When the lock is released, one of the waiting clusters is chosen at random and is granted the lock. The grant request invalidates only that cluster's caches and allows one processor within that cluster to acquire the lock with a local operation. This scheme lowers both the traffic and the latency involved in releasing a processor waiting on a lock. Informing only one cluster of the release also eliminates unnecessary traffic and latency that would be incurred if all waiting processors were allowed to contend. A time-out mechanism on the lock grant allows the grant to be sent to another cluster if the spinning process has been swapped out or migrated. The queued-on-lock-bit primitive described in Goodman et al.[7] is similar to Dash's queue-based locks, but uses pointers in the processor caches to maintain the list of the waiting processors.

The *fetch-and-increment* and *fetch-and-decrement* primitives provide atomic increment and decrement operations on uncached memory locations. The value returned by the operations is the value before the increment or decrement. These operations have low serialization and are useful for implementing several

synchronization primitives such as barriers, distributed loops, and work queues. The serialization of these operations is small because they are done directly at the memory site. The low serialization provided by the fetch-and-increment operation is especially important when many processors want to increment a location, as happens when getting the next index in a distributed loop. The benefits of the proposed operations become apparent when contrasted with the alternative of using a normal variable protected by a lock to achieve the atomic increment and decrement. The alternative results in significantly more traffic, longer latency, and increased serialization.

# The Dash implementation

A hardware prototype of the Dash architecture is currently under construction. While we have developed a detailed software simulator of the system, we feel that a hardware implementation is needed to fully understand the issues in the design of scalable cache-coherent machines, to verify the feasibility of such designs, and to provide a platform for studying real applications and software running on a large ensemble of processors.

To focus our effort on the novel aspects of the design and to speed the completion of a usable system, the base cluster hardware used in the prototype is a commercially available bus-based multiprocessor. While there are some constraints imposed by the given hardware, the prototype satisfies our primary goals of scalable memory bandwidth and high performance. The prototype includes most of Dash's architectural features since many of them can only be fully evaluated on the actual hardware. The system also includes dedicated performance monitoring logic to aid in the evaluation.

**Dash prototype cluster.** The prototype system uses a Silicon Graphics Power Station 4D/340 as the base cluster. The 4D/340 system consists of four Mips R3000 processors and R3010 floating-point coprocessors running at 33 megahertz. Each R3000/R3010 combination can reach execution rates up to 25 VAX MIPS and 10 Mflops. Each

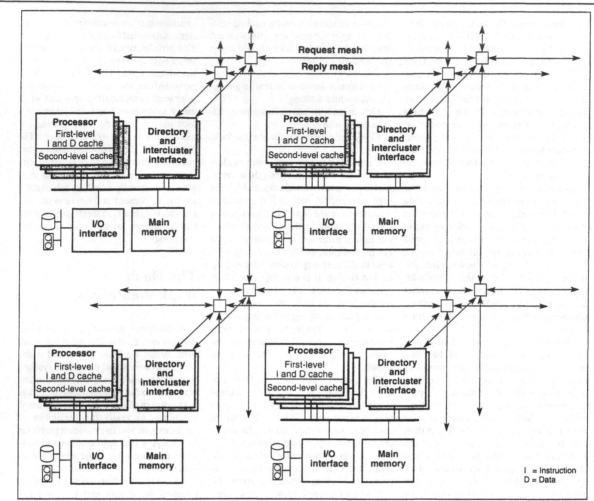

**Figure 4. Block diagram of a 2 × 2 Dash system.**

CPU contains a 64-kilobyte instruction cache and a 64-Kbyte write-through data cache. The 64-Kbyte data cache interfaces to a 256-Kbyte second-level write-back cache. The interface consists of a read buffer and a four-word-deep write buffer. Both the first- and second-level caches are direct-mapped and support 16-byte lines. The first level caches run synchronously to their associated 33-MHz processors while the second level caches run synchronous to the 16-MHz memory bus.

The second-level processor caches are responsible for bus snooping and maintaining coherence among the caches in the cluster. Coherence is maintained using an Illinois, or MESI (modified, exclusive, shared, invalid), protocol. The main advantage of using the Illinois protocol in Dash is the cache-to-cache transfers specified in it. While they do little

to reduce the latency for misses serviced by local memory, local cache-to-cache transfers can greatly reduce the penalty for remote memory misses. The set of processor caches acts as a cluster cache for remote memory. The memory bus (MPbus) of the 4D/340 is a synchronous bus and consists of separate 32-bit address and 64-bit data buses. The MPbus is pipelined and supports memory-to-cache and cache-to-cache transfers of 16 bytes every four bus clocks with a latency of six bus clocks. This results in a maximum bandwidth of 64 Mbytes per second. While the MPbus is pipelined, it is not a split-transaction bus.

To use the 4D/340 in Dash, we have had to make minor modifications to the existing system boards and design a pair of new boards to support the directory memory and intercluster interface. The main modification to the existing boards

is to add a bus retry signal that is used when a request requires service from a remote cluster. The central bus arbiter has also been modified to accept a mask from the directory. The mask holds off a processor's retry until the remote request has been serviced. This effectively creates a split-transaction bus protocol for requests requiring remote service. The new directory controller boards contain the directory memory, the intercluster coherence state machines and buffers, and a local section of the global interconnection network. The interconnection network consists of a pair of wormhole routed meshes, each with 16-bit wide channels. One mesh is dedicated to the request messages while the other handles replies. Figure 4 shows a block diagram of four clusters connected to form a 2 × 2 Dash system. Such a system could scale to support hundreds

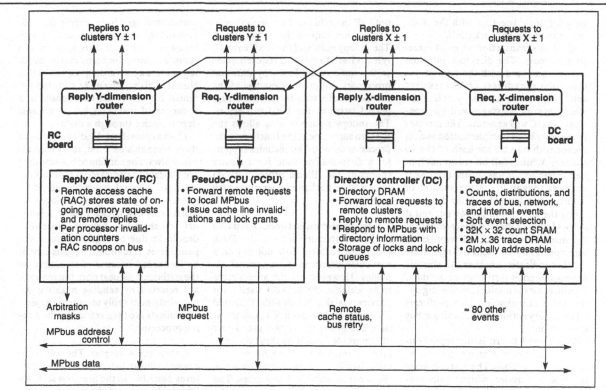

**Figure 5. Block diagram of directory boards.**

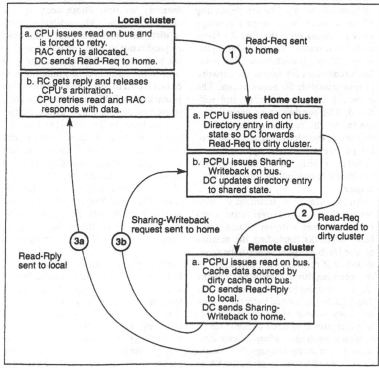

**Figure 6. Flow of a read request to remote memory that is dirty in a remote cluster.**

of processors, but the prototype will be limited to a maximum configuration of 16 clusters. This limit was dictated primarily by the physical memory addressability (256 Mbytes) of the 4D/340 system, but still allows for systems up to 64 processors that are capable of 1.6 GIPS and 600 scalar Mflops.

**Dash directory logic.** The directory logic implements the directory-based coherence protocol and connects the clusters within the system. Figure 5 shows a block diagram of the directory boards. The directory logic is split between the two logic boards along the lines of the logic used for outbound and inbound portions of intercluster transactions.

The directory controller (DC) board contains three major sections. The first is the directory controller itself, which includes the directory memory associated with the cachable main memory contained within the cluster. The DC logic initiates all outbound network requests and replies. The second section is the performance monitor, which can count and trace a variety of intra- and intercluster events. The third major section is the request and reply outbound network logic together with the $X$-dimension of the network itself.

Each bus transaction accesses directory memory. The directory information is combined with the type of bus operation, the address, and the result of snooping on the caches to determine what network messages and bus controls the DC will generate. The directory memory itself is implemented as a bit vector with one bit for each of the 16 clusters. While a full-bit vector has limited scalability, it was chosen because it requires roughly the same amount of memory as a limited pointer directory given the size of the prototype, and it allows for more direct measurements of the machine's caching behavior. Each directory entry contains a single state bit that indicates whether the clusters have a shared or dirty copy of the data. The directory is implemented using dynamic RAM technology, but performs all necessary actions within a single bus transaction.

The second board is the reply controller (RC) board, which also contains three major sections. The first section is the reply controller, which tracks outstanding requests made by the local processors and receives and buffers replies from remote clusters using the remote access cache (RAC). The second section is the pseudo-CPU (PCPU), which buffers incoming requests and issues them to the cluster bus. The PCPU mimics a CPU on this bus on behalf of remote processors except that responses from the bus are sent out by the directory controller. The final section is the inbound network logic and the $Y$-dimension of the mesh routing networks.

The reply controller stores the state of ongoing requests in the remote access cache. The RAC's primary role is the coordination of replies to intercluster transactions. This ranges from the simple buffering of reply data between the network and bus to the accumulation of invalidation acknowledgments and the enforcement of release consistency. The RAC is organized as a 128-Kbyte direct-mapped snoopy cache with 16-byte cache lines.

One port of the RAC services the inbound reply network while the other snoops on bus transactions. The RAC is lockup-free in that it can handle several outstanding remote requests from each of the local processors. RAC entries are allocated when a local processor initiates a remote request, and they persist until all intercluster transactions relative to that request have completed. The snoopy nature of the RAC naturally lends itself to merging requests made to the same cache block by different processors and takes advantage of the cache-to-cache transfer protocol supported between the local processors. The snoopy structure also allows the RAC to supplement the function of the processor caches. This includes support for a dirty-sharing state for a cluster (normally the Illinois protocol would force a write-back) and operations such as prefetch.

**Interconnection network.** As stated in the architecture section, the Dash coherence protocol does not rely on a particular interconnection network topology. However, for the architecture to be scalable, the network itself must provide scalable bandwidth. It should also provide low-latency communication. The prototype system uses a pair of *wormhole* routed meshes to implement the interconnection network. One mesh handles request messages while the other is dedicated to replies. The networks are based on variants of the mesh routing chips developed at the California Institute of Technology, where the data paths have been extended from 8 to 16 bits. Wormhole routing allows a cluster to forward a message after receiving only the first flit (flow unit) of the packet, greatly reducing the latency through each node. The average latency for each hop in the network is approximately 50 nanoseconds. The networks are asynchronous and self-timed. The bandwidth of each link is limited by the round-trip delay of the request-acknowledge signals. The prototype transfers flits at approximately 30 MHz, resulting in a total bandwidth of 120 Mbytes/second in and out of each cluster.

An important constraint on the network is that it must deliver request and reply messages without deadlocking. Most networks, including the meshes used in Dash, are guaranteed to be deadlock-free if messages are consumed at the receiving cluster. Unfortunately, the Dash prototype cannot guarantee this due, first, to the limited buffering on the directory boards and also to the fact that a cluster may need to generate an outgoing message before it can consume an incoming message. For example, to service a read request, the home cluster must generate a reply message containing the data. Similarly, to process a request for a dirty location in a remote cluster, the home cluster needs to generate a forwarding request to that cluster. This requirement adds the potential for deadlocks that consist of a sequence of messages having circular dependencies through a node.

Dash avoids these deadlocks through three mechanisms. First, reply messages can always be consumed because they are allocated a dedicated reply buffer in the RAC. Second, the independent request and reply meshes eliminate request-reply deadlocks. Finally, a back-off mechanism breaks potential deadlocks due to request-request dependencies. If inbound requests cannot be forwarded because of blockages on the outbound request port, the requests are rejected by sending negative acknowledgment reply messages. Rejected requests are then retried by the issuing processor.

**Coherence examples.** The following examples illustrate how the various structures described in the previous sections interact to carry out the coherence protocol. For a more detailed discussion of the protocol, see Lenoski et al.[8]

Figure 6 shows a simple read of a memory location whose home is in a remote cluster and whose directory state is dirty in another cluster. The read request is not satisfied on the local cluster bus, so a Read-Req (message 1) is sent to the home. At this time the processor is told to retry, and its arbitration is masked. A RAC entry is allocated to track this message and assign ownership of the reply. The PCPU at the home receives the Read-Req and issues a cache read on the bus. The directory memory is accessed and indicates that the cache block is dirty in another cluster. The directory controller in the home forwards the Read-Req (message 2) to the dirty remote cluster. The PCPU in the dirty cluster issues the read on the dirty cluster's bus and the dirty processor's cache responds. The DC in the dirty cluster sends a Read-Rply (message 3a) to the local cluster and a Sharing-Write-back (message 3b) request to the home to update the directory and main memory. The RC in the local cluster receives the reply into the RAC, releases the requesting CPU for arbitration, and then sources the data onto the bus when the processor retries the read. In parallel,

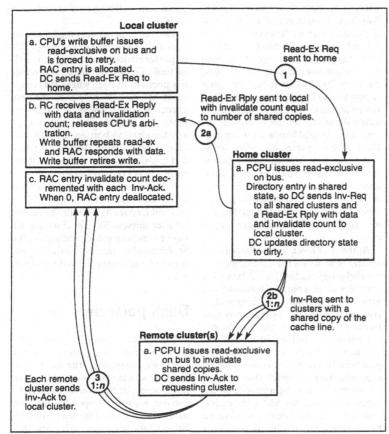

**Local cluster**

a. CPU's write buffer issues read-exclusive on bus and is forced to retry.
RAC entry is allocated.
DC sends Read-Ex Req to home.

b. RC receives Read-Ex Reply with data and invalidation count; releases CPU's arbitration.
Write buffer repeats read-ex and RAC responds with data.
Write buffer retires write.

c. RAC entry invalidate count decremented with each Inv-Ack. When 0, RAC entry deallocated.

Read-Ex Req sent to home

**1**

Read-Ex Rply sent to local with invalidate count equal to number of shared copies.

**2a**

**Home cluster**

a. PCPU issues read-exclusive on bus.
Directory entry in shared state, so DC sends Inv-Req to all shared clusters and a Read-Ex Rply with data and invalidate count to local cluster.
DC updates directory state to dirty.

**2b
1:n**

Inv-Req sent to clusters with a shared copy of the cache line.

**Remote cluster(s)**

a. PCPU issues read-exclusive on bus to invalidate shared copies.
DC sends Inv-Ack to requesting cluster.

Each remote cluster sends Inv-Ack to local cluster.

**3
1:n**

**Figure 7. Flow of a read-exclusive request to remote memory that is shared in remote clusters.**

the Sharing-Writeback request is received by the home PCPU, which issues it onto the bus. The sharing writeback updates the directory to a shared state indicating that the local and dirty clusters now have a read-only copy of the memory block.

Figure 7 shows the corresponding sequence for a store operation that requires remote service. The invalidation-based protocol requires the processor (actually the write buffer) to acquire exclusive ownership of the cache block before completing the store. Thus, if a store is made to a block that the processor does not have cached, or only has cached in a shared state, the processor issues a read-exclusive request on the local bus. In this case, no other cache holds the block dirty in the local cluster so a Read-Ex Req (message 1) is sent to the home cluster. As before, a RAC entry is allocated in the local cluster. At the home, the PCPU issues the read-exclusive request to the bus. The directory indicates that the line is in the shared state. This results in the DC sending a Read-Ex Rply (message 2a) to the local cluster and invalidation requests (Inv-Req, messages 2b) to the sharing clusters. The home cluster owns the block, so it can immediately update the directory to the dirty state indicating that the local cluster now holds an exclusive copy of the memory line. The

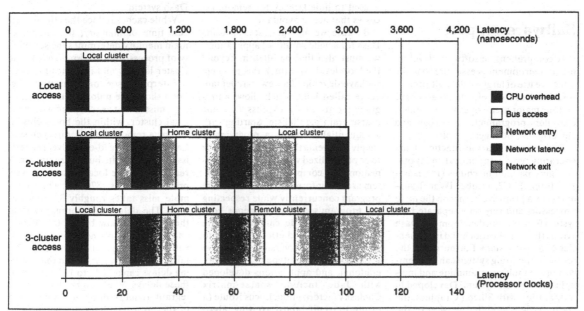

**Figure 8. Latency of read requests on a 64-processor Dash prototype without contention.**

Read-Ex Rply message is received in the local cluster by the RC, which can then satisfy the read-exclusive request. To assure consistency at release points, however, the RAC entry persists even after the write-buffer's request is satisfied. The RAC entry is only deallocated when it receives the number of invalidate acknowledgments (Inv-Ack, message 3) equal to an invalidation count sent in the original reply message. The RC maintains per-processor RAC allocation counters to allow the hardware to stall releasing synchronization operations until all earlier writes issued by the given processor have completed systemwide.

An important feature of the coherence protocol is its forwarding strategy. If a cluster cannot reply directly to a given request, it forwards responsibility for the request to a cluster that should be able to respond. This technique minimizes the latency for a request, as it always forwards the request to where the data is thought to be and allows a reply to be sent directly to the requesting cluster. This technique also minimizes the serialization of requests since no cluster resources are blocked while intercluster messages are being sent. Forwarding allows the directory controller to work on multiple requests concurrently (that is, makes it multithreaded) without having to retain any additional state about forwarded requests.

## Software support

A comprehensive software development environment is essential to make effective use of large-scale multiprocessors. For Dash, our efforts have focused on four major areas: operating systems, compilers, programming languages, and performance debugging tools.

Dash supports a full-function Unix operating system. In contrast, many other highly parallel machines (for example, Intel iPSC2, Ncube, iWarp) support only a primitive kernel on the node processors and rely on a separate host system for program development. Dash avoids the complications and inefficiencies of a host system. Furthermore, the resident operating system can efficiently support multiprogramming and multiple users on the system. Developed in cooperation with Silicon Graphics, the Dash OS is a modified version of the existing operating system on the 4D/340 (Irix, a variation of Unix System V.3). Since Irix was already multithreaded and worked with multiple processors, many of our changes have been made to accommodate the hierarchical nature of Dash, where processors, main memory, and I/O devices are all partitioned across the clusters. We have also adapted the Irix kernel to provide access to the special hardware features of Dash such as prefetch, update write, and queue-based locks. Currently, the modified OS is running on a four-cluster Dash system, and we are exploring several new algorithms for process scheduling and memory allocation that will exploit the Dash memory hierarchy.

At the user level, we are working on several tools to aid the development of parallel programs for Dash. At the most primitive level, a parallel macro library provides structured access to the underlying hardware and operating-system functions. This library permits the development and porting of parallel applications to Dash using standard languages and tools. We are also developing a parallelizing compiler that extracts parallelism from programs written for sequential machines and tries to improve data locality. Locality is enhanced by increasing cache utilization through *blocking* and by reducing remote accesses through *static partitioning* of computation and data. Finally, *prefetching* is used to hide latency for remote accesses that are unavoidable.

Because we are interested in using Dash for a wide variety of applications, we must also find parallelism beyond the loop level. To attack this problem we have developed a new parallel language called Jade, which allows a programmer to easily express dynamic coarse-grain parallelism. Starting with a sequential program, a programmer simply augments those sections of code to be parallelized with side-effect information. The compiler and runtime system use this information to execute the program concurrently while respecting the program's data dependence constraints. Using Jade can significantly reduce the time and effort required to develop a parallel version of a serial application. A prototype of Jade is operational, and applications developed with Jade include sparse-matrix Cholesky factorization, Locus Route (a printed-circuit-board routing algorithm), and MDG (a water simulation code).

To complement our compiler and language efforts, we are developing a suite of performance monitoring and analysis tools. Our high-level tools can identify portions of code where the concurrency is smallest or where the most execution time is spent. The high-level tools also provide information about synchronization bottlenecks and load-balancing problems. Our low-level tools will couple with the built-in hardware monitors in Dash. As an example, they will be able to identify portions of code where most cache misses are occurring and will frequently provide the reasons for such misses. We expect such noninvasive monitoring and profiling tools to be invaluable in pinpointing critical regions for optimization to the programmer.

## Dash performance

This section presents performance data from the Dash prototype system. First, we summarize the latency for memory accesses serviced by the three lower levels of the memory hierarchy. Second, we present speedup for three parallel applications running on a simulation of the prototype using one to 64 processors. Finally, we present the actual speedups for these applications measured on the initial 16-processor Dash system.

While caches reduce the effective access time of memory, the latency of main memory determines the sensitivity of processor utilization to cache and cluster locality and indicates the costs of interprocessor communication. Figure 8 shows the unloaded latencies for read misses that are satisfied within the local cluster, within the home cluster, and by a remote (that is, dirty) cluster. Latencies for read-exclusive requests issued by the write buffer are similar. A read miss to the local cluster takes 29 processor clocks (870 ns), while a remote miss takes roughly 3.5 times as long. The delays arise primarily from the relatively slow bus in the 3D/340 and from our implementation's conservative technology and packaging. Detailed simulation has shown that queuing delays can add 20 to 120 percent to these delays. While higher levels of integration could reduce the absolute time of the prototype latencies, we believe

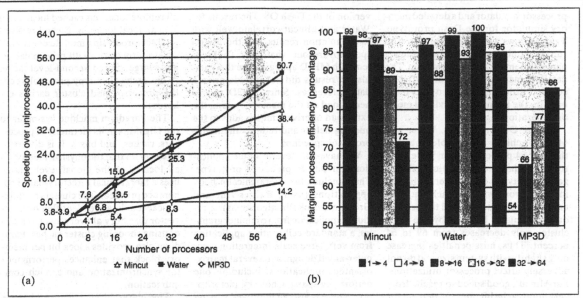

**Figure 9. Speedup of three parallel applications on a simulation of the Dash prototype with one to 64 processors: (a) overall application speedup; (b) marginal efficiency of additional clusters.**

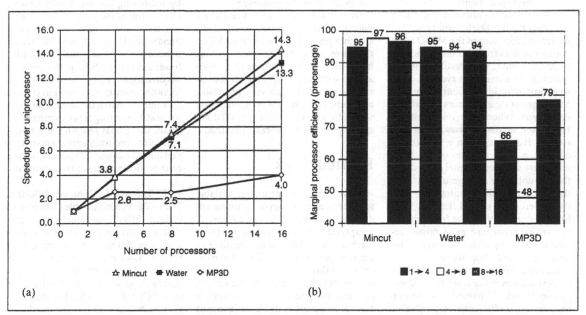

**Figure 10. Speedup of three parallel applications on the actual Dash prototype hardware with one to 16 processors: (a) overall application speedup; (b) marginal efficiency of additional clusters.**

the increasing clock rate of microprocessors implies that the latencies measured in processor clocks will remain similar.

Applications for large-scale multiprocessors must utilize locality to realize good cache hit rates, minimize remote accesses, and achieve high processor utilization. Figure 9 shows the speedup and processor efficiency for three appli-

cations on simulated Dash systems consisting of one to 64 processors (that is, one to 16 clusters). The line graph shows overall application speedup, while the bar chart shows the marginal efficiency of additional clusters. The marginal efficiency is defined as the average processor utilization, assuming processors were 100 percent utilized at the previous data point. The three applications

simulated are Water, Mincut, and MP3D. Water is a molecular-dynamics code that computes the energy of a system of water molecules. Mincut uses parallel simulated annealing to solve a graph-partitioning problem. MP3D models a wind tunnel in the upper atmosphere, using a discrete particle-based simulation.

The applications were simulated using a combination of the Tango multiprocessor simulator and a detailed memory simulator for the Dash prototype. Tango allows a parallel application to run on a uniprocessor and generates a parallel memory-reference stream. The detailed memory simulator is tightly coupled with Tango and provides feedback on the latency of individual memory operations.

On the Dash simulator, Water and Mincut achieve reasonable speedup through 64 processors. For Water, the reason is that the application exhibits good locality. As the number of clusters increases from two to 16, cache hit rates are relatively constant, and the percent of cache misses handled by the local cluster only decreases from 69 to 64 percent. Thus, miss penalties increase only slightly with system size and do not adversely affect processor utilizations. For Mincut, good speedup results from very good cache hit rates (98 percent for shared references). The speedup falls off for 64 processors due to lock contention in the application.

MP3D obviously does not exhibit good speedup on the Dash prototype. This particular encoding of the MP3D application requires frequent interprocessor communication, thus resulting in frequent cache misses. On average, about 4 percent of the instructions executed in MP3D generate a read miss for a shared data item. When only one cluster is being used, all these misses are serviced locally. However, when we go to two clusters, a large fraction of the cache misses are serviced remotely. This more than doubles the average miss latency, thus nullifying the potential gain from the added processors. Likewise, when four clusters are used, the full benefit is not realized because most misses are now serviced by a remote dirty cache, requiring a three-hop access.

Reasonable speedup is finally achieved when going from 16 to 32 and 64 processors (77 percent and 86 percent marginal efficiency, respectively), but overall speedup is limited to 14.2. Even on MP3D, however, caching is beneficial. A 64-processor system with the timing of Dash, but without the caching of shared data, achieves only a 4.1 speedup over the cached uniprocessor. For Water and Mincut the improvements from caching are even larger.

Figure 10 shows the speedup for the three applications on the real Dash hardware using one to 16 processors. The applications were run under an early

version of the Dash OS. The results for Water and Mincut correlate well with the simulation results, but the MP3D speedups are somewhat lower. The problem with MP3D appears to be that simulation results did not include private data references. Since MP3D puts a heavy load on the memory system, the extra load of private misses adds to the queuing delays and reduces the multiprocessor speedups.

We have run several other applications on our 16-processor prototype. These include two hierarchical *n*-body applications (using Barnes-Hut and Greengard-Rokhlin algorithms), a radiosity application from computer graphics, a standard-cell routing application from very large scale integration computer-aided design, and several matrix-oriented applications, including one performing sparse Cholesky factorization. There is also an improved version of the MP3D application that exhibits better locality and achieves almost linear speedup on the prototype.

Over this initial set of 10 parallel applications, the harmonic mean of the speedup on 16 processors in 10.5 Furthermore, if old MP3D is left out, the harmonic mean rises to over 12.8. Overall, our experience with the 16-processor machine has been very promising and indicates that many applications should be able to achieve over 40 times speedup on the 64-processor system.

## Related work

There are other proposed scalable architectures that support a single address space with coherent caches. A comprehensive comparison of these machines with Dash is not possible at this time, because of the limited experience with this class of machines and the lack of details on many of the critical machine parameters. Nevertheless, a general comparison illustrates some of the design trade-offs that are possible.

**Encore GigaMax and Stanford Paradigm.** The Encore GigaMax architecture[9] and the Stanford Paradigm project[10] both use a hierarchy-of-buses approach to achieve scalability. At the top level, the Encore GigaMax is composed of several clusters on a global bus. Each cluster consists of several processor modules, main memory, and a cluster cache. The cluster cache holds a copy of

all remote locations cached locally and also all local locations cached remotely. Each processing module consists of several processors with private caches and a large, shared, second-level cache. A hierarchical snoopy protocol keeps the processor and cluster caches coherent.

The Paradigm machine is similar to the GigaMax in its hierarchy of processors, caches, and buses. It is different, however, in that the physical memory is all located at the global level, and it uses a hierarchical directory-based coherence protocol. The clusters containing cached data are identified by a bit-vector directory at every level, instead of using snooping cluster caches. Paradigm also provides a lock bit per memory block that enhances performance for synchronization and explicit communication.

The hierarchical structure of these machines is appealing in that they can theoretically be extended indefinitely by increasing the depth of the hierarchy. Unfortunately, the higher levels of the tree cannot grow indefinitely in bandwidth. If a single global bus is used, it becomes a critical link. If multiple buses are used at the top, the protocols become significantly more complex. Unless an application's communication requirements match the bus hierarchy or its traffic-sharing requirements are small, the global bus will be a bottleneck. Both requirements are restrictive and limit the classes of applications that can be efficiently run on these machines.

**IEEE Scalable Coherent Interface.** The IEEE P1596 Scalable Coherent Interface (SCI) is an interface standard that also strives to provide a scalable system model based on distributed directory-based cache coherence.[11] It differs from Dash in that it is an interface standard, not a complete system design. SCI only specifies the interfaces that each processing node should implement, leaving open the actual node design and exact interconnection network. SCI's role as an interface standard gives it somewhat different goals from those of Dash, but systems based on SCI are likely to have a system organization similar to Dash.

The major difference between SCI and Dash lies in how and where the directory information is maintained. In SCI, the directory is a distributed sharing list maintained by the processor caches themselves. For example, if processors A, B, and C are caching some location, then the cache entries storing this location include pointers that form a doubly linked list. At main memory, only a pointer to the processor at the head of the linked list is maintained. In contrast, Dash places all the directory information with main memory.

The main advantage of the SCI scheme is that the amount of directory pointer storage grows naturally as new processing nodes are added to the system. Dash-type systems generally require more directory memory than SCI systems and must use a limited directory scheme to scale to a large configuration. On the other hand, SCI directories would typically use the same static RAM technology as the processor caches while the Dash directories are implemented in main memory DRAM technology. This difference tends to offset the potential storage efficiency gains of the SCI scheme.

The primary disadvantage of the SCI scheme is that the distribution of individual directory entries increases the latency and complexity of the memory references, since additional directory-update messages must be sent between processor caches. For example, on a write to a shared block cached by $N$ processors (including the writing processor), the writer must perform the following actions:

- detach itself from the sharing list,
- interrogate memory to determine the head of the sharing list,
- acquire head status from the current head, and
- serially purge the other processor caches by issuing invalidation requests and receiving replies that indicate the next processor in the list.

Altogether, this amounts to $2N + 6$ messages and, more importantly, $N + 1$ serial directory lookups. In contrast, Dash can locate all sharing processors in a single directory lookup, and invalidation messages are serialized only by the network transmission rate.

The SCI working committee has proposed several extensions to the base protocol to reduce latency and support additional functions. In particular, the committee has proposed the addition of directory pointers that allow sharing lists to become sharing trees, support for request forwarding, use of a clean cached state, and support for queue-

based locks. While these extensions reduce the differences between the two protocols, they also significantly increase the complexity of SCI.

**MIT Alewife.** The Alewife machine[12] is similar to Dash in that it uses main memory directories and connects the processing nodes with mesh network. There are three main differences between the two machines:

- Alewife does not have a notion of clusters — each node is a single processor.
- Alewife uses software to handle directory pointer overflow.
- Alewife uses multicontext processors as its primary latency-hiding mechanism.

The size of clusters (one processor, four processors, or more) is dictated primarily by the engineering trade-offs between the overhead of hardware for each node (memory, network interface, and directory) and the bandwidth available within and between clusters. Techniques for scaling directories efficiently are a more critical issue. Whether hardware techniques, such as proposed in O'Krafka and Newton[2] and Gupta et al.,[1] or the software techniques of Alewife will be more effective remains an open question, though we expect the practical differences to be small. Multiple contexts constitute a mechanism that helps hide memory latency, but one that clearly requires additional application parallelism to be effective. Overall, while we believe that support for multiple contexts is useful and can complement other techniques, we do not feel that its role will be larger than other latency-hiding mechanisms such as release consistency and nonbinding prefetch.[13]

W e have described the design and implementation decisions for Dash, a multiprocessor that combines the programmability of single-address-space machines with the scalability of message-passing machines. The key means to this scalability are a directory-based cache-coherence protocol, distributed memories and directories, and a scalable interconnection network. The design focuses on reducing memory latency to keep processor performance high, though it also provides latency-hiding techniques such as prefetch and release consistency to mit-

igate the effects of unavoidable system delays.

At the time of this writing, the $2 \times 2$ Dash prototype is stable. It is accessible on the Internet and used daily for research into parallel applications, tools, operating systems, and directory-based architectures. As indicated in the performance section, results from this initial configuration are very promising. Work on extending the $2 \times 2$ cluster system to the larger $4 \times 4$ (64-processor) system is ongoing. All major hardware components are on hand and being debugged. By the time this article is in print, we expect to have an initial version of the Unix kernel and parallel applications running on the larger machine. ∎

## Acknowledgments

This research was supported by DARPA contracts N00014-87-K-0828 and N00039-91-C-0138. In addition, Daniel Lenoski is supported by Tandem Computers, James Laudon and Wolf-Dietrich Weber are supported by IBM, and Kourosh Gharachorloo is supported by Texas Instruments. Anoop Gupta is partly supported by a National Science Foundation Presidential Young Investigator Award.

We also thank Silicon Graphics for their technical and logistical support and Valid Logic Systems for their grant of computer-aided engineering tools.

## References

1. A. Gupta, W.-D. Weber, and T. Mowry, "Reducing Memory and Traffic Requirements for Scalable Directory-Based Cache Coherence Schemes," *Proc. 1990 Int'l Conf. Parallel Processing*, IEEE Computer Society Press, Los Alamitos, Calif., Order No. 2101, pp. 312-321.

2. B.W. O'Krafka and A.R. Newton, "An Empirical Evaluation of Two Memory-Efficient Directory Methods," *Proc. 17th Int'l Symp. Computer Architecture*, IEEE CS Press, Los Alamitos, Calif., Order No. 2047, 1990, pp. 138-147.

3. L. Lamport, "How to Make a Multiprocessor Computer That Correctly Executes Multiprocess Programs," *IEEE Trans. Computers*, Sept. 1979, Vol. C-28, No. 9, pp. 241-248.

4. C. Scheurich and M. Dubois, "Dependency and Hazard Resolution in Multiprocessors," *Proc. 14th Int'l Symp. Computer Architecture*, IEEE CS Press, Los Alamitos, Calif., Order No. 776, 1987, pp. 234-243.

5.  K. Gharachorloo, A. Gupta, and J. Hennessy, "Performance Evaluation of Memory Consistency Models for Shared-Memory Multiprocessors," *Proc. Fourth Int'l Conf. Architectural Support for Programming Languages and Operating Systems*, ACM, New York, 1991, pp. 245-257.

6.  T. Mowry and A. Gupta, "Tolerating Latency Through Software in Shared-Memory Multiprocessors," *J. Parallel and Distributed Computing*, Vol. 12, No. 6, June 1991, pp. 87-106.

7.  J.R. Goodman, M.K. Vernon, and P.J. Woest, "Efficient Synchronization Primitives for Large-Scale Cache-Coherent Multiprocessors," *Proc. Third Int'l Conf. Architectural Support for Programming Languages and Operating Systems*, IEEE CS Press, Los Alamitos, Calif., Order No. 1936, 1989, pp. 64-73.

8.  D. Lenoski et al., "The Directory-Based Cache Coherence Protocol for the Dash Multiprocessor," *Proc. 17th Int'l Symp. Computer Architecture*, IEEE CS Press, Los Alamitos, Calif., Order No. 2047, 1990, pp. 148-159.

9.  A.W. Wilson, Jr., "Hierarchical Cache/Bus Architecture for Shared Memory Multiprocessors," *Proc. 14th Int'l Symp. Computer Architecture*, IEEE CS Press, Los Alamitos, Calif., Order No. 776, 1987, pp. 244-252.

10. D.R. Cheriton, H.A. Goosen, and P.D. Boyle, "Paradigm: A Highly Scalable Shared-Memory Multicomputer Architecture." *Computer*, Vol. 24, No. 2, Feb. 1991, pp. 33-46.

11. D.V. James et al., "Distributed-Directory Scheme: Scalable Coherent Interface," *Computer*, Vol. 23, No. 6, June 1990, pp. 74-77.

12. A. Agarwal et al., "Limitless Directories: A Scalable Cache Coherence Scheme," *Proc. Fourth Int'l Conf. Architectural Support for Programming Languages and Operating Systems*, ACM, New York, 1991, pp. 224-234.

13. A. Gupta et al., "Comparative Evaluation of Latency Reducing and Tolerating Techniques," *Proc. 18th Int'l Symp. Computer Architecture*, IEEE CS Press, Los Alamitos, Calif., Order No. 2146, 1991, pp. 254-263.

# The Scalable Coherent Interface: Scaling to High-Performance Systems

David V. James

Apple Computer, Cupertino, CA

## Abstract

*With the ANSI/IEEE Std 1596-1992 Scalable Coherent Interface (SCI), a few or many processors can share cached data in a coherent fashion (i.e. their caches are transparent to software). Scalability constrains the protocols to rely on simple request-response protocols, rather than the eavesdrop or 3-party transactions assumed by (unscalable) bus-based systems.*

*The linear nature of the base SCI protocols limits their performance when data is being actively shared by large numbers of processors. To meet these needs, the IEEE P1596.2 working group is currently defining a compatible set of extensions based on distributed binary trees.*

*Scalability includes optionality: simple and/or specialized noncoherent systems are not affected by the costs of coherence protocols.*

## 1: Introduction

### 1.1: Scalability

A scalable architecture remains stable over a wide range of design parameters, such as cost, performance, distance, or time. Unfortunately, the term "scalable" has become an industry buzz-word; it's included in marketing literature but has had minimal impact on product designs.

Scalable systems eliminate the need to redesign components to meet minor or dramatic changes in product requirements. Although scalability reduces development costs, it conflicts with the tenure requirements for college professors (which are based on publication counts), the size of research grants (which are based on Ph.D. thesis counts), and organizations within large companies (which need to justify distinct product developments).

As the IEEE Std 1596-1992 Scalable Coherent Interface (SCI), we had the charter and organizational support to develop a scalable system interconnect. The scalability objective avoided initial charter conflicts with the concurrently active Futurebus+ working group. The consensus-driven standards development process released researchers and designers from their normal organizational pressures.

Our operational definition for scalability was "never having to say you're sorry." We desired to avoid the "Daddy, why did you ..." telephone questions from our children taking their first graduate-school courses. Thus, the lifetime of a scalable system was defined as 10-20 years, a design lifetime which exceeded the maturation time of our young children.

### 1.2: Constraining requirements

Within any scalable system design, there is usually an overriding objective that cannot be compromised. For example, on the Serial Bus P1394 working group [Serial], the objective was low cost.

Within the SCI standard [SciStd], *high performance* was our primary objective. We believed the highest-performance systems would not be uniprocessors, but would be constructed from large numbers of multiprocessors sharing distributed memory and using caches to hide latency.

We assumed that, for software convenience, these multiprocessors would be tightly coupled: memory can be shared and the caches are transparent to software. Tightly-coupled multiprocessors mandated the development of cache coherence protocols for massively-parallel-processor (MPP) configurations.

We felt that MPP systems would be based on the workstation of today and (perhaps) the video-game components of tomorrow. Thus, the SCI protocols should be cost-effective for noncoherent uniprocessor and small coherent multiprocessor systems as well as for MPPs.

### 1.3: Eavesdrop protocols

Traditional cache-coherence protocols are based on *eavesdropping* bus transactions. When a data value is read from memory, other processors eavesdrop and (if necessary) provide the most up-to-date copy. When a data value is stored into CPU_C's cache, the read-exclusive transaction (a read with an intent to modify) is broadcast. Other processors are required to invalidate stale copies and (if memory has a stale copy) may also be required to provide the new data, as illustrated in figure 1.

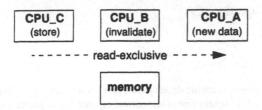

**Figure 1: Eavesdrop coherence protocols**

Eavesdrop-based protocols are cost-effective on unified-response buses, since the coherence checks can be performed while the data is fetched from memory. Eavesdropping is harder on high-speed split-response buses, where the transaction-issue rates are larger, since they are no longer constrained by memory-access-time latencies.

### 1.4: Directory protocols

Since each processor can consume a significant fraction of interconnect-link bandwidth, any MPP system would have multiple concurrently active data paths, as illustrated in figure 2. Fully-connected cross-bar topologies scale poorly (from a cost perspective), so the interconnect was assumed to be more generally switch based.

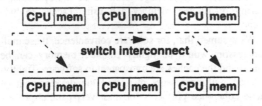

**Figure 2: Switch-based systems**

Eavesdropping is not possible within switch-based systems, since concurrently active transactions cannot be observed by all. Recent research [Caches] has therefore focussed on the development of directory-based protocols.

Central-directory coherence protocols supplement each line of memory with a tag, where the tag identifies all processors with cached copies. The memory and cache lines are typically the same size, between 32 and 256 bytes. When data is written, memory is responsible for updating or invalidating the previously shared (and now stale) copies.

Central directories have scaling limitations, because the size of the total system is limited by the size of the memory-line tag. Some systems[DashDir][DashSys] propose to use multicast or broadcast transactions when their directories overflow. Other systems[Limit] propose using memory-resident software to handle overflow, eliminating the need to support these special transactions.

Central-directory schemes serialize read and write transactions at memory. SCI avoids tag-storage overflow and memory bottlenecks by distributing the directories: the memory tags contains state and a pointer to the first processor; the cache tags contain state and pointers to other processors.

## 2: Transaction-set constraints

### 2.1: Basic SCI transactions

To simplify the design of high-performance switches, communication between SCI components uses a simple request/response transaction protocol. A transaction consists of request and response subactions. The request subaction transfers an address and command; the response subaction returns status.

For a write transaction, data is included within the request packet. For a read transaction, data is included within the response packet. For a compound transaction (such as fetch&add), data is included within the request and response packets.

Each subaction consists of a send and an echo packet. Information (including commands, status, and data) is transferred within the send packet; flow control information (busy retry) is returned within the echo packet, as illustrated in figure 3.

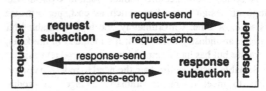

**Figure 3: Request/response transactions**

These are similar to the phases observed on a split-response backplane: the echo is a packetized equivalent of a busy-retry backplane signal.

Most of the noncoherent and all of the coherent transactions have these components. We avoided using special coherence transactions (such as multicast or three-way transactions), since these would have complicated the design (thereby reducing the performance) of the interconnect.

## 2.2: Coherent SCI transactions

For read and write transactions, the coherence protocols add a few bits in the request-send packet and a few bytes in the response-send packet. Since alignment constraints fix the size of send packets, the coherence protocols have no impact on the basic packet sizes.

However, an extended request is needed to support cache-to-cache transactions, since two addresses are involved (the memory address of the data and the routing address of the cache). The additional information is contained within an extension to the normal packet header.

Coherence bits within packets are typically ignored by the interconnect and have no impact on the design of basic SCI switches. Thus, the coherence protocols are scalable in the sense that the same switch components can be used within coherent and noncoherent SCI systems.

## 3: Distributed directory structures

### 3.1: Linear sharing lists

To support a (nearly) arbitrary number of processors, the SCI coherence protocols are based on distributed directories[SciDir]. By distributing the directories among the caching processors, the potential capacity of the directory grows as additional caches are added and directory updates need not be serialized at the memory controller.

The base coherence protocols are based on linear lists; the extended coherence protocols provide compatible support for binary trees. Linear lists are scalable, in the sense that thousands of processors can share read-only data. Thus, instructions and (mostly) read-only data can be efficiently shared by large numbers of processors.

Memory provides tags, so that each memory line has associated state and (if the data is shared) identifies the cache at the head of the sharing list. The caches also have tags, which identify the previous and next elements within the sharing list, as illustrated in figure 4. The doubly-linked structure simplifies sharing-list deletions (which are caused by cache-line replacements).

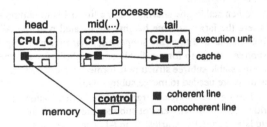

**Figure 4:  Linear-list directories**

Although illustrated separately, a single SCI component may contain processor(s) and memory. However, from the perspective of the coherence protocols, these are logically separate components. Note that each memory-line address may have a distinct sharing list, and these sharing lists change dynamically depending on the processor's load/store behavior.

### 3.2: Sharing-list updates

Updates of the sharing list involve additions (new entries are always prepended to the head), deletions (caused by cache-line replacement), and purges (the sharing list collapses to a single entry). Additions occur when the data is shared by a new processor; purges occur when shared data is modified. Except for the special case of pairwise-sharing, all modifications are performed by the sharing-list head, which purges the remaining sharing-list entries.

The sharing-list update protocols are similar to those used by software to doubly-linked data structures, subject to the following constraints:

1) Concurrent updates. Sharing-list additions, deletions, and purges may be performed concurrently—precedence rules and compare&swap-like updates ensure list integrity (central semaphores are not used).

2) Recoverable faults. The update sequences support data recovery after an arbitrary number of transmission faults—exclusive data are copied before being purged.

3) Forward progress. Forward progress is ensured (i.e. each cache eventually gets a copy)—new caches are prepended to the head, and deletions from the tail have precedence.

### 3.3: Pairwise sharing

The linear-list structures are efficient if shared data is infrequently written, or if frequently-written data is shared by only a few processors. As an option, one of these cases, pairwise-sharing, can be optimized. The pairwise-sharing option is intended to support producer/consumer applications, where exactly two caches are sharing data.

When implemented, the pairwise-sharing option maintains the sharing-list structure, rather than purging the other sharing-list entry, when data is modified. The tail entry, as well as the head entry, is allowed to modify the data.

Thus, pairwise sharing allows processors to perform cache-to-cache transfers when fetching recently modified data. This minimizes access latencies and avoids a potential memory bottleneck.

## 4: Logarithmic extensions

The base SCI coherence protocols are limited, in that sharing-list additions and deletions are serialized, at the memory and the sharing-list head respectively. Simulations indicate this is sufficient when frequently-written data is shared by a small number (10's) of processors [ExtJohn].

Although linear lists are a cost-effective solution for many applications, our scalability objectives also mandated a solution for (nearly) arbitrary applications on large multiprocessor systems. Thus, we are developing compatible extensions [ExtStd] to the base coherence protocols. The compatible extensions use combining and binary tree structures to reduce latencies from linear to logarithmic.

Sharing-list structures are created dynamically and may be destroyed immediately after creation. We therefore focussed on minimizing the latencies of sharing-list creation, utilization, and destruction, as described in the following sections.

### 4.1: Sharing list creation

Within some tightly-coupled shared-memory applications, data is concurrently accessed by large numbers of processors, typically when a synchronization point has been reached. If these read requests were serialized at the memory controller, access-time latencies would be linear.

To achieve logarithmic latencies, the read requests may be (optionally) combined within the interconnect. We assume that combining only occurs under heavy loading conditions, when queuing delays provide the time to compare request-transaction addresses for packets queued within switch components. Although combining rarely occurs, Guri Sohi noted that it occurs when it is most needed.

For example, consider how three requests (to the same memory address) may be combined during transit. Two requests (req B and req C) can be combined into one, which generates a modified request (req B-C) and an immediate response (res C). In a similar fashion, the combined request (req C-B) can be combined with another request (req A), as illustrated in figure 5.

Since combining is most useful at the "hottest" spots, we expect to see the initial implementation on the front-end of the memory controller (to improve the effective memory-access bandwidth). Depending on performance benchmarking results, combining hardware may eventually migrate into SCI switches as well.

We use coherent combining to reduce the latency of sharing-list creation; combining only returns list-pointer information (and not data, which is returned later). We expect this to be much simpler than other approaches

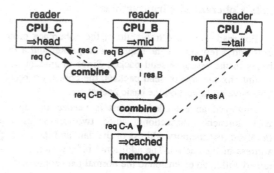

**Figure 5: Combining within the interconnect**

[NYU] which leave residual state within the interconnect, for modifying the responses when they return.

Because basic SCI nodes are accustomed to receiving responses without data, no complications are introduced by the data-not-returned nature of the combining mechanism. Thus, the basic coherent nodes function correctly when connected with a combining interconnect.

### 4.2: Converting sharing lists to trees

After the linear sharing list (or portions thereof) is available, a merge process converts the linear-list structure into a binary-tree structure. The latencies of the merge (and following) processes are $O(\log(n))$, where n is the number of sharing-list entries, a pragmatic limit of most "scalable" protocols.

The merge process is distributed and performed concurrently by the sharing caches[ExtJohn]. Data distribution (for fetch&add, as well as load accesses) is performed during the merging process. Multiple steps are involved, one for each level of the binary tree which is created. However, some of these merge-steps can be overlapped in time.

Under ideal conditions, the first step of the merge process generates a list of 1-high sub-trees, the second generates a list of 2-high sub-trees, etc. The process continues until the sharing list has reached a stable state, as illustrated in figure 6.

When stable, the sharing list is a linear list of subtrees, where the larger subtree heights are located near the tail. Incremental additions are supported; adjacent equal-height subtrees merge to form a single one-height-larger subtree, until a stable subtree structure is formed. Up to three transactions are needed to merge subtree pairs.

During the subtree-merge process, a distributed algorithm selects which pairs of subtrees are merged. To avoid update conflicts, entries 2-and-1 can't be merged if 1-and-0 are being merged. To generate balanced trees,

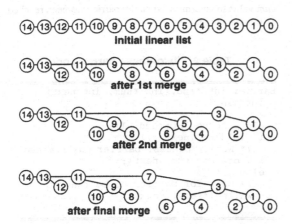

**Figure 6:   Creating binary-tree structures**

entries 3-and-2 should be merged if entries 1-and-0 are being merged.

Note that the usual software algorithms for creating balanced trees could not be used, because the process must be distributed and only localized information can be used.

The specification of the distributed merge-selection protocol is an active topic of working-group discussion. The goal is to label alternate equal-height subtrees with 0 and 1 labels, allowing combining between 0 and 1 subtree entries. Distinct label assignments are hard, because the sharing-list entries are "nearly" identical and their list positions are unknown.

Two label-assignment solutions have been proposed: one uses a (pseudo) random number to generate 0/1 labels; an alternative generates these from the system-unique 16-bit node identifiers, which are normally used to route SCI packets.

### 4.3: Utilization of sharing trees

Once formed, the sharing tree may be used to quickly invalidate other sharing-tree entries or to efficiently distribute data updates. The Store instruction is executed on the processor at the head of the sharing tree and invalidates other sharing-tree entries. If not the sharing-tree head, the processor leaves the tree and becomes the head of a (slightly modified) sharing-tree before the Store instruction is executed.

As a performance optimization, a special StoreInto instruction can also be used. The StoreInto instruction updates other copies and leaves the sharing-tree structures intact. If not the sharing-tree head, the processor updates the sharing-tree head and the data is then distributed to other sharing-tree entries.

Data updates and invalidates are performed in a similar fashion. Initiation transactions distribute information to other sharing-tree entries; confirmation transactions are returned when the initiation transactions have been processed by lower levels of the tree, as illustrated in figure 7.

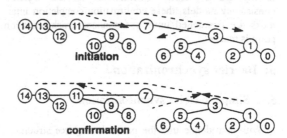

**Figure 7:   Write-through and purges**

For the Store instruction, the sharing tree is purged and the entries delete themselves during the confirmation phase. For the StoreInto instruction, data is distributed within the initiation-phase transactions and the sharing tree remains intact.

### 4.4: Deadlock avoidance

The initiation and confirmation transactions are special, in that they are forwarded through sharing-tree entries. The processing of input requests generates queued output requests. If a full output-request queue inhibits processing of incoming requests a system deadlocks could be generated.

To avoid these system deadlocks, the size of the outgoing request-queue must be sufficient to hold the number of cache-line entries within the node. Implementations are not expected to provide duplicate storage for large output queues. Instead, cache nodes are expected to implement their output-request queues as an localized linked-list of cache-line entries.

### 4.5: Weak ordering

The coherence protocols allow the sharing-list head to proceed beyond a write operation before the remaining sharing-list entries have been invalidated. Stores into the same cache line by other processors require changes in the sharing-list structure and are deferred until the confirmation phase completes. This means that the SCI protocol can fully exploit the potential parallelism of a weakly ordered memory model.

We have divorced the details of the processor's memory-consistency model from the details of the SCI coherence protocols. Depending on the processor's memory-consistency model, some or all of following load and/or store instructions may be stalled while the invalidations are being performed.

For the strongest consistency models, these confirmation-completion interlocks delay the execution of the following memory-access instruction. For the weakest consistency models, these confirmation-completion interlocks are postponed until a dependent synchronization point is reached.

## 5: Barrier synchronization

### 5.1: Simple barrier synchronization

With confidence that the basic sharing-tree structures handled many of the coherent sharing applications, we proceeded to examine "worst-case" scenarios. In particular, we considered synchronization of multiprocessors at barrier points within code (barrier synchronization).

For a design model, we assumed that barrier synchronization involved multiple processes, each of which calls a Barrier() routine, as illustrated in table 1, when its task completes. For n processors, the value of *next* is n larger than the value used on the previous barrier.

**Table 1:   Simple barrier-synchronization code**

```
Barrier(int *sum, int next) {
  int old;

  FetchAdd(sum, 1);
  /* Wait for barrier to be reached */
  while (*sum != next);
}
```

Analysis of this algorithm found potential performance problems. In typical applications, the *FetchAdd()* and *while()* accesses will occur concurrently. Sharing-tree thrashing can occur: each *FetchAdd()* operation destroys the existing sharing-tree structure; each *while()* access rebuilds a portion of the final sharing-tree structure. In addition to generation of unnecessary interconnect traffic, thrashing increases barrier-synchronization delays.

### 5.2: Two-phase barriers

To improve barrier-synchronization performance, we assume that different addresses (not in the same cache line) are used during the *accumulate* and *notify* phases of barrier synchronization. Processes increment the *add* value before the barrier has been reached and then poll the

*sum* value to determine when the barrier has been reached, as illustrated in table 2.

**Table 2:   Two-phase barrier code**

```
Barrier(int *add, int *sum, int next) {
  int old;

  old = Accumulate(add, 1);
  if (old == (next-1))
    /* Notify others, barrier was reached */
    StoreInto(sum, next);
  else
    /* Wait for barrier to be reached */
    while (*sum != next);
}
```

This code avoids the thrashing problem; the sharing tree for the sum location is unaffected by the arithmetic operations performed on the add value.

To improve the performance of repetitive barrier synchronization operations, a StoreInto instruction distributes the sum value. The sum value is written into the sharing list head and then distributed to other sharing-tree entries. By using StoreInto, rather than Store, the sharing tree structure is perserved for use during the notify phase of following barrier-synchronization operations.

### 5.3: Accumulate vs. FetchAdd

To improve performance, we have replaced the *FetchAdd()* operation with an *Accumulate()*. Accumulate differs from FetchAdd in that a NULL (zero) value (rather than the previous data value) may be returned for intermediate (but never the final) Accumulate calculations.

This distinction allows Accumulate operations to be combined within a stateless interconnect. When combined, an immediate NULL response is returned.

## 6: C code specification

The detailed SCI transport and coherence specifications are defined by executable C code [Code]; a multi-threaded execution environment is also provided. The original intent of the C code was to avoid ambiguous interpretations of the specification.

We soon found that the C code provided yet another form of scalability—the same specification could be used for clarity, for simulation purposes, or to verify hardware implementations. While creating the technical specification, bugs were often found and eliminated while running performance simulations.

## 7: Surprises

Designing for scalability has its share of surprises. Finding the scalable solution is hard, but, when compared with traditional solutions, it is often good for non-scalable implementations as well.

Our high-performance "backplane" objective forced us to use point-to-point signaling techniques. To our surprise, these techniques provided us with media independence as well.

Support of (nearly) arbitrary large switches forced us to use directory-based coherence protocols. Surprisingly, we found these techniques yielded superior pairwise-sharing performance, reduced sensitivities to tag-lookup-delay, and fault tolerance capabilities.

Supporting large numbers of processors forced us to distribute our coherence directories. We discovered that distributed directories could be updated concurrently, reducing latencies to $O(\log(n))$ rather than $O(n)$.

The most pleasant surprise came from observing the consensus process within the SCI working group. Because difficult problems have only a few (sometimes only one) scalable solutions, the requirements for scalability makes it easier to select which solutions should be used!

## 8: Summary

The coherence protocols defined within the base ANSI/IEEE Std 1596-1992 Scalable Coherent Interface specification and the P1596.2 Coherence Extensions are scalable in many ways.

When compared to unified-response backplane buses, packet-based split-response request/response protocols are scalable—they can be implemented on a wide variety of transport media and distances.

When compared to eavesdrop protocols, directory-based coherence protocols are scalable—they eliminate the need for specialized broadcast and eavesdrop capabilities.

When compared to central directories, distributed directories are scalable—large sharing lists can be supported with fixed-size memory tags.

When compared to linear sharing lists, sharing trees are scalable—large sharing lists can be efficiently created, utilized, and purged with logarithmic (rather than linear) latencies.

When compared to FetchAdd, Accumulate is scalable—separate Accumulate operations can be readily combined within the interconnect.

SCI options are scalable as well. An implementation may elect to use only the noncoherent portions of the SCI protocols. Coherent implementations may elect to use the base coherence protocols (with their linear-list constraints) or the coherence extensions (with their binary-tree improvements).

Options are designed to interoperate, so that hybrid configurations perform correctly, although their performance typically degrades to that of the lesser implementation.

Although the cache-tag update algorithms may appear to be complex, SCI's directory-based protocols are relatively insensitive to response-time delays. Thus, the protocols can be implemented in firmware, hardware, or (most likely) a cost-effective combination of the two.

## 9: Acknowledgments

Special thanks to Dave Gustavson (the SCI Chair), whose hard work and integrity has been a role model for us all. Guri Sohi proposed coherent combining and the concept of sharing trees. Ross Johnson was the P1596.2 (SCI Coherence Extensions) Chair and defined their sub-tree-merge, coehrent fetch&add, and cache-line replacement protocols. Stein Gjessing (the current P1596.2 Chair) and Jim Goodman provided academic insights and graduate-student assistance throughout the SCI development. Ernst Kristiansen and Mike Chastain's experiences with commercial systems helped us focus on practical solutions to real-world problems. A large number of unnamed volunteers also contributed to the P1596.2 development.

The Sponsor of the IEEE P1596.2 Working Group, the Microcomputer Standards Committee, had the courage to sponsor leading-edge, as well as pragmatic, standards developments. Their sponsorship of the SCI standard provided the catalyst for bringing together scientists and engineers from the international university and industry communities.

## 10: References

[Serial] P1394, SerialBus.[1]

[SciStd] ANSI/IEEE Std 1596-1992, Scalable Coherent Interface (SCI).[2]

[Caches] Michael Dubois and Shreekant Thakkar (editors), "Cache Architectures in Tightly Coupled Multiprocessors," *Computer*, June 1990, Volume 23, No 6.(special issue).

[DashDir] Daniel Lenoski, et. al., "The Directory Based Cache-Coherence Protocol for the DASH Multiprocessor," Proceedings of the 17th International Symposium on Computer Architecture, May 1990, 148-159.

[DashSys] Daniel Lenoski, et. al., "The Stanford Dash Multiprocessor," *Computer*, March 1992, Volume 25, No 3, pp. 63-80.

---

[1]P1394 is an authorized standards project that is unapproved at the time of this document's publication. The latest version of this document is available from the IEEE Computer Society.

[2]IEEE publications are available from the Institute of Electrical and Electronics Engineers, Inc., Service Center, 445 Hoes Lane, P.O. Box 1331, Piscataway, NJ 08855-1331, 800-678-4333.

[Limit] D. Chaiken, J. Kubiatowicz, and A. Agarwal, "Limit-LESS directories: a scalable cache coherence scheme", presented at the Fourth International Conference on Architectural Support for Programming Languages and Operating Systems, Santa Clara, CA, April 8-11, 1991.

[SciDir] David V. James, Anthony T. Laundrie, Stein Gjessing, and Gurinday S. Sohi, "Scalable Coherent Interface," *IEEE Computer*, June 1990, Volume 23, No 6, 74-77.

[ExtJohn] Ross Evan Johnson, "Extending the Scalable Coherent Interface for Large-Scale Shared-Memory Multiprocessors," PhD Thesis, Computer Sciences Department, University of Wisconsin-Madison, February 1993. Computer Sciences Technical Report #1136.

[ExtStd] IEEE Working Group P1596.2 Draft .31, Sept. 1993[3].

[NYU] Gottlieb, A. et. al., "The NYU Ultracomputer — Designing an MIMD Shared Memory Parallel Computer," *IEEE Trans. on Computers*, Feb ruary 1983, Volume C-32, No 2, 175-189.

[Code] ANSI X3.159–1989, Programming Language—C.[4]

[3]For most recent copy and information on future meetings, contact the Working Group Chair: Stein Gjessing, Department of Informatics, University of Oslo, Pob. 1080 Blindern, 0316 Oslo, NORWAY. Email (preferred): gjessing@ifi.uio.no. Phone: +47 22 85 24 44, Fax: +47 22 85 24 01.

[4]ANSI publications are available from the American National Standards Institute, Sales Department, 11 West 42nd St., 13th Floor, New York, NY 10036, 212-642-4900.

# The KSR1: Bridging the Gap Between Shared Memory and MPPs

Steven Frank, Henry Burkhardt III and Dr. James Rothnie

steve@ksr.com

Kendall Square Research Corporation
170 Tracer Lane, Waltham, MA 02154

## Abstract

*Historically, shared memory and virtual memory have been the main line programming model from an applications and computer science perspective for two reasons: shared memory is a flexible and high performance means of communicating between processors, tasks or threads and; shared memory provides high programming efficiency through use of conventional memory management methods.*

*The KSR1™ bridges the gap between the historical shared memory model and MPPs by delivering the shared memory programming model and all of its benefits, in a scalable, highly parallel architecture. The KSR1 runs a broad range of mainstream applications, ranging from numerically intensive computation, to on-line transaction processing (OLTP) and database management and inquiry. The use of shared memory enables a standards based open environment. The KSR1's shared memory programming model is made possible by a new architectural technique called ALLCACHE™ memory.*

## Virtual Memory: The Precursor of the KSR1 Architecture

The most fundamental influence on the KSR1 architecture was the development of virtual memory and its ability to present a single address space model to the programmer and to automatically exploit locality.

The property of locality is a program's preference for a subset of its address space over a given period of time. Exploiting locality in the construction of computers (for example, short interconnections on or between chips), as well as exploiting locality in program behavior, has been a primary factor in enhancing computer performance. To understand the relevance of locality and single address space to parallel computing, one must go back in history 30 years when the magnitude and complexity of storage management on uniprocessors caused programming difficulties similar to those experienced today on MPPs.

Three decades ago, storage management via overlay structures was an integral part of the job of writing a program. Of necessity, programmers attacked the task with a static analysis of the memory requirements of a single program.

Advances in programming practice and system architectures, however, gradually rendered static storage management impractical. The goals of machine independence and re-use of modular program elements, and the use of very complex algorithms characterized by data structures of widely varying size and shape were inconsistent with static, programmer-controlled storage management. In addition, the introduction of system environments in which computers were organized for simultaneous use by several programs made it impossible for the author of a single program to predict accurately the time-varying storage requirements of the entire system.

These factors led the designers of the Atlas Computer at the University of Manchester in the UK, to an elegant solution to the problems of storage management through the invention of virtual memory. Their invention has profoundly influenced the course of computing. [1]

Simply stated, virtual memory moves the responsibility of managing memory from the application to the computer hardware and systems software, by applying the notion that the "address" is a concept distinct from the physical location of its corresponding data. Programming is simplified, because applications are written with one simple and powerful abstraction – a single address space (see Figure 1). Virtual memory provides excellent performance by dynamically exploiting "the property of locality, which is exhibited to varying degrees by all practical programs. [2]

Virtual memory is fundamental to the architecture and programming of all modern mainframes, mini-computers and workstations. Cache memory [3], a more recent invention, is based on the ideas of virtual memory and locality, and cache is now present on all computers from mainframes to PCs (both RISC and CISC processors). The concept of single level store [4], or mapping files directly into the single address space, is also a direct descendant of the concepts of virtual memory. Modern computer systems depend on locality to extract maximum performance, from single mainframes to networks of workstations paging across a LAN, to fileservers.

Reprinted from *Proc. COMPCON '93: Digest of Papers*, pp. 285–294.

**Figure 1** Before the advent of virtual memory primary (main memory) and secondary storage were managed explicitly by the program. With virtual memory a combination of hardware and system software manage the primary store transparently to user programs.

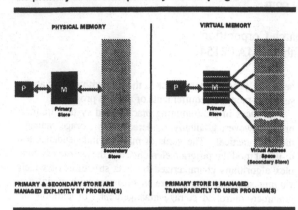

## Virtual Memory and MPPs

These parallel processing architectures reprise these early storage management issues with a new twist. All of the MPP systems that have been introduced have distributed memories. That is, the physical memory comprises a set of memory units, each connected to a unique processor. The processor-memory pairs are interconnected by a network. Distributed memories have been universal among massively parallel machines because they provide the only known means of implementing completely scalable access to memory — access whose bandwidth increases in direct proportion to the number of processors.

In these MPP systems, the task of managing the movement of codes and data among these distributed memory units belongs to the programmer. The job is similar in style to the task of managing the migration of data back and forth between primary and secondary storage prior to the introduction of virtual memory but it is much more complex. As before, programmers need to be concerned about exactly what will fit where and what to remove to make room for something new. Now, however, there are thousands of memory units to deal with instead of just two or three. Parallel systems of this type are "multi-computers" — sets of network connected independent computers. [5]

KSR1 ALLCACHE extends the concept of virtual memory to highly parallel processing for the first time, thus providing all the benefits of virtual memory, including high performance, ease of programming and scalability.

## Prior research - multiprocessors

The first research multiprocessor was C.mmp. [6] It consisted of 16 processors with an optional cache, connected through a crossbar to 16 shared memory modules. The cache was designed and prototyped, but never used because of cache coherence problems.

The problem of cache coherence on a multiprocessor was first implemented in 1981 by Synapse for greater than four processors. [7] The Synapse architecture consisted of as many as 28 processors and four memory modules on a shared bus. The basic innovation of Synapse was to introduce the concept of ownership, distributed directories and bus monitoring (later dubbed "snooping") as a way to solve the cache coherence problem. Coherence algorithms, based on the concept of ownership, reduced bus traffic significantly. But, as a rule, bus-based multiprocessors proved to be scalable only to a maximum of 20 to 30 processors on a single bus. Encore Computer Corp. and Sequent Computer Systems have developed similar bus-based multiprocessors.

## Software implementations of shared memory

The major phyla of highly parallel computers today may be differentiated by their basic computational models: shared memory versus message passing systems. Multicomputers are typically programmed using a message passing model, rather than shared memory. Several multicomputer architectures have been proposed and built on the basis of the message passing model, including the Cosmic Cube [8], IPSC and the J Machine. [9] In addition, a number of research projects have designed and prototyped a shared virtual memory software layer on a multicomputer, including Ivy [10] and Mether [11]. Although the programming model was improved, these various efforts brought a number of significant problems to the surface. Four particular difficulties with these approaches have emerged:

- Software-based implementations of shared memory are two to three orders of magnitude lower in performance than hardware implementations.

- Searching and directory functions are much slower when managed at the software level.

- Sequential consistency is extremely difficult to achieve in software alone, and sequential consistency is a key to faster porting of programs as this is the model assumed by most programmers.

- The grain size in all the software-based implementations of shared memory has been the complete page. The granularity should be smaller to avoid false sharing and provide fast cache-refill times for data movement.

## "No-Cache" architectures

Two of the key concepts of scalability are the distributed and hierarchical organization of the multiprocessor. The Cm* was the first computer of this type. [12] The basic building block of Cm* was a processor-memory pair called a computer module (Cm). The local memory associated with each processor formed the shared memory for the system. The Cedar project was similar in concept to Cm*. NYU Ultracomputer, RP3 and the BBN Butterfly were other non-hierarchical, distributed memory multiprocessors. None of these architectures fully exploited locality of reference.

In all these systems, because addresses had fixed physical locations, the programmer was compelled to copy data to local addresses to optimize performance. Coherency also had to be managed explicitly within the program.

All these systems adopted shared memory as a syntactic convention, mapping a portion of each processing cell's local memory into a global address space. However, non-local accesses invariably had a longer latency than local references, and these systems had no way to adjust automatically to the addressing pattern of a program. Such adjustments were left, instead, to the application programmer.

In essence, these machines were similar in programming style and performance to message passers: blocks of data had to be copied from global space to a processor's local space, manipulated there and then written back. Management of the contents of the local memory and the maintenance of coherence between data in local memory and data in global space were relegated back to the application programmer [13] as well. Effectively this is the same style of data movement as used in a message passing MPP with all the same drawbacks.

## Other "Some-Cache" architectures

The Alewife [14] and Dash [15] research projects share a common goal with the KSR1: development of a scalable, shared memory multiprocessor. Both research projects depend primarily on caching to achieve scalability, but have scalability limitations similar to "some-cache" and "no-cache" architectures.

Alewife and Dash are "some-cache" architectures that have a fixed home for addresses. In addition to the caches (whose constituent addresses change dynamically), both Alewife and Dash employ ordinary memory modules (whose constituent addresses are fixed). These modules provide a "home" storage location for all addresses. The location of an address's home is determined statically from the address, not dynamically according to program behavior. Local cache misses are resolved by referencing the home memory module. Since the size of the caches is small, compared to the size of ordinary memory, these research projects do not exploit locality of reference and behavior similarly to "No-Cache" architectures.

## The KSR1 memory system

ALLCACHE memory system [16] provides programmers with a uniform $2^{64}$ byte[1] address space for instructions and data. This space is called System Virtual Address space (SVA). The contents of SVA locations are physically stored in a distributed fashion.

ALLCACHE implements a sequentially consistent shared address space programming model because such consistency is the strongest requirement for shared-memory coherence, and this form of implementation guarantees that a program will behave in the most intuitive manner to the programmer: e.g., the result of program execution on a multiprocessor is equivalent to the execution of the program on a single processor with multi-tasking. In this context, the formal definition of "sequential consistency" is: [17]

> "A system is sequentially consistent if the result of any execution is the same as if the operations of all the processors were executed in some sequential order, and the operations of each individual processor appear in this sequence in the order specified by its program."

Note that any ordering scheme other than a sequentially consistent programming model inherently requires both the explicit specification of the sharing and a legal time order of access.

ALLCACHE physically comprises a set of memory arrays called local caches, each capable of storing 32 MBytes. There is one local cache for each processor in the system. Hardware mechanisms (the ALLCACHE Engine described below) cause SVA addresses and their contents to materialize in the local cache of a processor when the address is referenced by that processor. The address and data remain at that local cache until the space is required for something else.

As its name suggests, the ALLCACHE behavior is like that of familiar caches: data moves to the point of reference on demand. However, unlike the typical cache architecture (called "SOMECACHE" memory), the source for the data which materializes in a local cache is not main memory but rather another local cache. In fact, all of the memory in the machine consists of large, communicating, local caches — the main memory of the machine is identical to the collection of local caches. See Figure 2.

---

[1.] The KSR1 implements a $2^{40}$ byte (1 terabyte) address space utilizing 64 bit pointers. Future generations will implement the full $2^{64}$ byte address space of the ALLCACHE memory architecture.

**Figure 2     ALLCACHE Memory System: Data moves to the point of reference on demand. There is no fixed physical location for an "address" within ALLCACHE memory.**

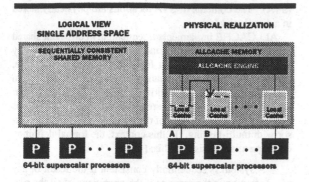

The address and data that materialize in local cache B in response to a reference by processor B may continue to reside simultaneously in other local caches. Consistency is maintained by distinguishing the type of reference made by processor B:

1) If the data will be modified by B, the local cache will receive the one and only instance of an address and its data.

2) If the data will be read but not modified by B, the local cache will receive a copy of the address and its data.

When processor B first references the address X, ALLCACHE examines that processor's local cache to see if the requested location is already stored there. If processor B's local cache contains address X, the processor request is satisfied without any request to the ALLCACHE Engine. If not, the ALLCACHE Engine hardware locates another local cache (e.g., local cache A) where the address and data exist.

If the processor request being serviced is a read request (for example, to load the value into a register) then the ALLCACHE Engine will copy the address and data from local cache A into local cache B. The amount of data copied will be 128 bytes, called a subpage.[2] At the end of this operation the subpage will reside at both A and B. If the processor request is a write request (for example, to store the contents of a register into this location) then the ALLCACHE Engine will remove the copy of the subpage from local cache A as well as from any other local caches where it may exist before copying it into local cache B. Thus the ALLCACHE Engine is responsible for finding and copying subpages stored in local caches and for maintaining consistency by eliminating old copies when new contents are stored.

In order to maintain consistency, the ALLCACHE Engine records state information about the subpages it has stored. These states are specific to the physical instance of a subpage within a particular local cache. Four states are required to describe the basic operation of the ALLCACHE Engine:[3]

• Exclusive (owner): This is the only valid copy of the subpage in the set of local caches.

• Copy: Two or more valid copies of the subpage exist among the set of local caches.

• Non-exclusive (owner): When multiple copies exist, one copy is always flagged as the non-exclusive owner.

• Invalid: Memory is currently allocated for this subpage at this local cache but the contents are not valid and will not be used.

None of these states are explicitly visible to the programmer. They are used as internal bookkeeping by the ALLCACHE Engine.

The ALLCACHE Engine manages a directory that determines which one or more local caches contain an instance of each subpage. This directory is physically stored in a distributed and compressed form but its logical function is illustrated in Figure 3. The directory is logically a matrix consisting of a row for each subpage and a column for each local cache. Each entry in the matrix is either empty, to indicate that the corresponding subpage is not present in the local cache, or it contains a "state" designator. A non-empty state designator means that a spot for a copy of this subpage is currently allocated in the corresponding local cache, and the state value indicates what operations the memory system is allowed to perform on the particular copy. This matrix is a very sparse representation of the mapping, because nearly all elements will be empty. The ALLCACHE Engine implementation actually stores this matrix by column and compresses out all of the empty elements.

---

[2] ALLCACHE stores data in units of pages and subpages. Pages contain 16 KB ($2^{14}$ bytes), divided into 128 subpages of 128 ($2^7$) bytes. The unit of allocation in local caches is a page, and each page of SVA space is either entirely represented in the system or not represented at all. The unit of transfer and sharing between local caches is a subpage. Each local cache has room for 2,048 ($2^{11}$) pages or a total of 32 MByte ($2^{25}$ bytes). When a processor references an address not found in its local cache, ALLCACHE memory first makes room for it there by allocating a page. The contents of the newly allocated page are filled as needed, one subpage at a time.

[3] Additional states, including, Atomic states are actually used in the implementation of ALLCACHE.

**Figure 3    ALLCACHE Physically distributed directory**

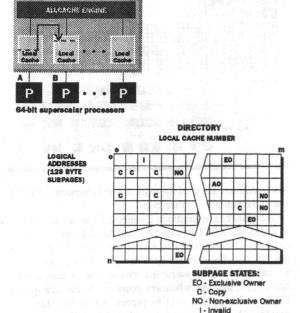

The ALLCACHE Engine manipulates the directory in response to load and store instructions from processors. For a load instruction, if a copy exists in the requesting processor's local cache, the load request can be satisfied without any interaction at all with the ALLCACHE Engine. If a copy does not exist in the local cache, the local cache sends a request packet to the ALLCACHE Engine. The ALLCACHE Engine then delivers a response packet containing a copy from any other local cache which has a valid copy, as illustrated in Figure 4. For example, Processor B issues a request for a copy to the ALLCACHE Engine. The ALLCACHE Engine routes the request to a local cache in which a copy exists (for instance, the local cache associated with Processor A). Local cache A responds to the ALLCACHE Engine, which in turn passes the copy back to the local cache of the requesting processor and automatically updates the ALLCACHE directory and the local cache directory to indicate that a copy of the subpage now exists in the local cache associated with Processor B. Had the subpage been in Exclusive (owner) state within some local cache (C, for example) at the time of the reference, the ALLCACHE Engine would create the requested copy and change the owner's state to Non-exclusive (owner).

Note that the program that issues the load or store has no knowledge of the respective physical locations of the local caches. The ALLCACHE Engine transparently manages the routing, based on the subpage address and the directory. Memory allocation is handled by the respective local caches.

**Figure 4    ALLCACHE Engine directory operation, Local Cache load miss**

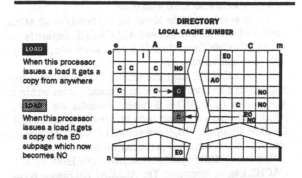

For a store instruction, if a subpage exists in the local cache in Exclusive (owner) state at the time of the request, the store can be satisfied locally without any interaction with the ALLCACHE Engine. If the requestor's local cache state is empty or invalid, the ALLCACHE Engine will move the subpage from the Exclusive (owner) to the requestor in Exclusive (owner) state (see Figure 5). In cases where multiple copies are involved, the effect is for the ALLCACHE Engine to move the ownership to the requestor's local cache in exclusive owner state and to invalidate all other copies. The ALLCACHE Engine moves ownership to the requestor and invalidates all other copies (to make the new ownership exclusive) in a single operation.

**Figure 5    ALLCACHE Engine directory operation, Local Cache store miss**

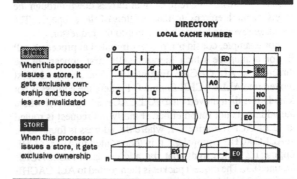

## Scalability: Hierarchical Organization of the ALLCACHE Engine

The KSR1 architecture exploits locality of reference by organizing a number of ALLCACHE Engines in a hierarchy. At the lowest and most heavily populated level of this hierarchy are ALLCACHE Group:0s (AG:0s), each of which is the combination of ALLCACHE Engine:0s and the complete set of local caches associated with them.

At the next level of the hierarchy, the family of all AG:0s, combined with their associated ALLCACHE Engine:1s, are the ALLCACHE Group:1s (AG:1s) and so on, to a potentially unlimited number of levels.

An ALLCACHE Engine:0 includes the directory which maps from addresses into the set of local caches within its group. An ALLCACHE Engine:1 includes the directory which maps from addresses into its constituent set of ALL-CACHE Group:0s. Higher level ALLCACHE Groups are hierarchically constructed in the same manner.

The initial KSR1 system implements two levels of ALL-CACHE Engine hierarchy. The ALLCACHE Engine is constructed with a fat-tree [18] topology, so that the bandwidth increases at each level of ALLCACHE Engine. For the KSR1, ALLCACHE Engine:0 has a bandwidth of 1 GB/sec and ALLCACHE Engine:1 has a bandwidth of 1, 2 or 4 GB/sec. For example a KSR1-1088 consists of 34 ALLCACHE Group:0s, each consisting of 32 processors and their associated local caches. As we shall see, due to locality of reference, the effective ALLCACHE Engine bandwidth is asymptotic to the aggregate ALLCACHE Engine:0 bandwidth of 34 GB/sec.

The hierarchical ALLCACHE Engine handles simultaneous independent requests and simultaneous requests to the same address in parallel.

Figure 6 illustrates the path of a request and response through the hierarchy of ALLCACHE Engines. A request initiated at a processor will move up through the levels of the hierarchy until it reaches an ALLCACHE Group which contains a directory entry in the appropriate state for the desired subpage address. The request then moves down through the levels of the hierarchy to the location of the subpage. The response reverses this path to return to the requestor.

For example, consider a request initiated at processor cell B, for a subpage which hierarchically first appears in the directory at ALLCACHE Engine:2.1. The request is first moved into ALLCACHE Engine:0.1 where the address is not found. It is then moved on to ALLCACHE Engine:1.1 where the address is not found either. Finally the request is routed to ALLCACHE Engine:2.1, where the address is found to be in ALLCACHE Group:1.2. It is then routed to ALLCACHE Engine:1.2 which finds that the address is in ALLCACHE Engine:0.3. The request packet is then routed to ALLCACHE Engine:0.3 which routes it to the local cache at processor A.

**Figure 6    Hierarchical Organization of the ALLCACHE Engine – Search Path Through the Hierarchy**

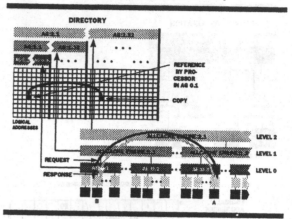

**Figure 6    Hierarchical Organization of the ALLCACHE Engine – Search Path Through the Hierarchy**

The maximum length of the request path is proportional to the log of the number of processors.

A crucial characteristic of the hierarchical structure is that it allows the KSR1 to exploit hierarchical locality of reference. The hierarchical structure of the ALLCACHE Engine exploits this characteristic by moving referenced subpages to a local cache and by satisfying data references from nearby copies of a subpage whenever possible. In the example in Figure 7, the first reference by processor B to the subpage in processor A needs to travel through ALLCACHE Engine:2.1 to find the designated subpage. The second reference to the same subpage by processor C finds the data closer as does a subsequent reference to the same subpage by processor D.

**Figure 7    Hierarchical Organization of the ALLCACHE Engine — Exploits Hierarchical Locality of Reference**

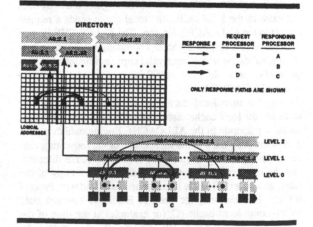

## Locality- The Key to Scalability

While the fat-tree topology of the KSR1 ensures maximization of bandwidth, the inherent ability of the ALLCACHE memory system to exploit locality of reference achieves the second major goal of scalability — reduction of the bandwidth requirement itself.

Locality is the key to the achievement of a scalable interconnect bandwidth in which the bandwidth requirement itself scales more slowly than the delivered bandwidth. Three reasons may be cited: [19]

- Because communication speeds are fundamentally limited by the speed of light, communications should be kept as close as possible to the processor.

- Communication time is also affected by the number of switches through which messages or data must pass. Thus path lengths should be minimized.

- Communication should stay within as small a subsystem as possible to avoid congestion.

The ALLCACHE Engine exploits locality – both the usual serial locality of reference and its image in parallel programs, parallel locality.

Locality of reference refers to a property of a program in which near future memory references are likely to reference memory locations nearby the addresses of recent past references. The most important memory architecture innovations of the last thirty years, virtual memory and cache memories, are designed to exploit this program behavior. The phenomenon is so pronounced in most programs that even small caches with a few tens of kilobytes of memory will exhibit high hit rates.

Parallel locality refers to a related property of parallel programs. The best predictor of future memory references by a thread of a parallel program is that thread's own recent memory reference pattern – in other words, the usual serial locality of reference applies to the serial pieces of a parallel program. But the next best predictor of future memory references is the recent memory reference pattern of related threads. This phenomenon of common reference patterns for related threads is called parallel locality.

Both serial locality of reference and parallel locality are exploited by the ALLCACHE memory system. A KSR1 has a large cache, 32 MByte, designed to exploit serial locality of reference. The hierarchical structure of the ALLCACHE Engine, combined with the scheduling algorithms of KSR OS™, provide the means to exploit parallel locality. The KSR scheduler will allocate a set of related threads to execute in the same ALLCACHE Engine:0 whenever possible. Thus, each thread of a parallel program gains a benefit from the parallel memory referencing activity of related threads: an address not found in a thread's local cache is likely to be found in the same branch of the ALLCACHE hierarchy no matter how many other branches there may be. Communication will then stay within as small a subsystem as possible, avoiding congestion. Although a fat-tree can deliver scalable bandwidth, ALLCACHE does not require that the bisection bandwidth scale in linear fashion to keep step with the number of processors.

Both types of locality are usually present in programs to a substantial extent without any effort on the part of the programmer. Programmers can increase locality by careful design of data structures and processing flow, much as they do in writing certain programs for virtual memory machines. KSR compilers and the KSR OS use a number of techniques to automatically increase locality.

Another way to look at this phenomenon is as a hierarchy of "working sets." For each processor, the addresses most likely to require reference lie in the closest and smallest working set, which is realized in the local cache of that processor. The next most likely addresses to be referenced lie in the ALLCACHE Group:0 (AG:0) working set, which is realized as the aggregate of the local caches of the AG:0.

Taken together, the local caches of all processors in a given ALLCACHE Group, e.g., "AG:N," form an AG:N cache, which holds the working set for that "AG:N." Processors with an AG:N share addresses without any communication outside their own ALLCACHE Group. Thus the hierarchical nature of the ALLCACHE Engines and ALLCACHE Groups allows the distributed local caches to form, collectively, a hierarchy of caches corresponding to the hierarchy of AGs. The KSR1 implements two levels of ALLCACHE Groups:

| Level of Hierarchy | Working Set Size |
| --- | --- |
| Local Cache | 32 MByte |
| AG:0 Cache | 1 GByte |
| AG:1 Cache | 34 GByte |

Figure 8 provides an illustration of the hierarchical organization of the ALLCACHE Engine.

**Figure 8    Hierarchical Organization of ALLCACHE Engine exploits hierarchical locality of reference by implementing a hierarchy of working sets (caches).**

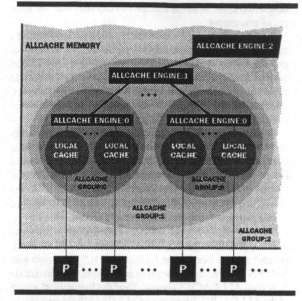

## Optimizing Locality of Reference

Locality of reference is present in programs to a substantial extent, usually without any conscious effort on the part of the programmer. Programmers can increase locality of reference by optimizing memory-reference patterns with this property in mind. KSR compilers use a number of techniques to increase locality of reference automatically.

The KSR1 also incorporates a number of features designed to assist programmers in their efforts to optimize locality of reference on a customized basis. Each is described below:

### Event Monitor Unit (EMU)

Each KSR1 processor contains an event monitor unit (EMU) designed to log various types of local memory events and intervals. The job of the EMU is to count events and elapsed time related to memory system activities that are not otherwise directly visible to the processor.

The types of events that are logged include local cache hits/misses and how far in the hierarchy a request had to travel to be satisfied. The EMU also accumulates the number of processor cycles involved in such events. These counters can be read at the appropriate points in the application code, to help characterize loop nests or other sections of code. Since the events to be logged are counted by hardware, the measure-

ment overhead is extremely low. Because the events are monitored on an individual-processor basis, an extremely clear picture can be created to facilitate the customized parallelization of applications and the optimizing of locality of reference.

### Prefetch

Prefetch is an instruction that allows memory activity to go on in parallel with computation, by planning for data needs in advance rather than stalling the processor to wait for needed data. The prefetch instruction requests the memory system to move a subpage into the local cache of the requesting processor, thus allowing the memory system to fetch data before it is needed. The processor that issues the prefetch instruction does not need to wait for this operation to be completed; it continues executing until it needs to load or store the prefetched address. If the prefetch is issued far enough in advance, the desired address will have already arrived in the local cache, and minimum latency will be incurred in accessing it. KSR1 compilers automatically insert prefetches in certain types of code sequences. Programmers may also request prefetches explicitly by means of an intrinsic function.

### Poststore

Any program that executes a store can use the poststore instruction to ask the memory system to broadcast the new value to other local caches that may need it. Local caches in which the corresponding page is allocated already (and in which the subpage state is, necessarily, invalid) take a read-only copy of the subpage. Poststore instructions allow a processor to broadcast data needed by one or more other processors at the earliest possible time the data is available, and before the other processors have to request the data.

Like prefetch, poststore is controlled by the processor that writes the data. Programmers can explicitly request poststores with an intrinsic function.

## KSR1 System

ALLCACHE forms the foundation which enables the KSR1 to provide the high performance and easy of programming of a conventional shared memory combined with scalability and low cost of parallel processing. The KSR1 provides a balanced scalability across computation, memory and I/O as illustrated in Table 1.

**Table 1    KSR1 Balanced Scalability**

| PROCESSOR CONFIGURA-TIONS | PEAK MIPS | PEAK MFLOPS | MEMORY (MBYTES) | MAX. DISK CAPACITY (GBYTES) | MAX. I/O CAPACITY MBYTES/ SEC |
|---|---|---|---|---|---|
| KSR1-8 | 320 | 320 | 256 | 210 | 210 |
| KSR1-16 | 640 | 640 | 512 | 450 | 450 |
| KSR1-32 | 1,280 | 1,280 | 1,024 | 450 | 450 |
| KSR1-64 | 2,560 | 2,560 | 2,048 | 900 | 900 |
| KSR1-128 | 5,120 | 5,120 | 4,096 | 1,800 | 1,800 |
| KSR1-256 | 10,240 | 10,240 | 8,192 | 3,600 | 3,600 |
| KSR1-512 | 20,480 | 20,480 | 16,384 | 7,200 | 7,200 |
| KSR1-1088 | 43,520 | 43,520 | 34,816 | 15,300 | 15,300 |

**Figure 9    Scalable I/O Bandwidth Combined with Standards**

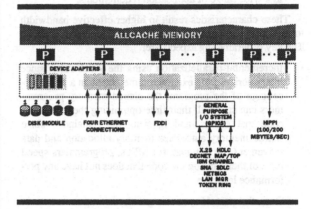

Each KSR1 ALLCACHE Processor, Router and Directory cell (APRD) consists of a 64-bit superscalar processor, a 32 Mbyte local cache memory and a portion of the ALLCACHE Engine:0. The ALLCACHE Engine:1 consists of ALL-CACHE Router Directory cells (ARD).

The KSR1 processor employs 64-bit address, 64-bit integer, and 64-bit floating point data types, and it can perform IEEE standard 64-bit floating point operations at a peak rate of 40 mflops. The processor executes two instructions per cycle: one integer or floating point execute and one memory reference or branch.

Each processor supports 30 Mbytes/sec I/O transfers to external sources and users data. A KSR1-32 configured with 32 APRD cells thus achieves an aggregate I/O rate of 450 Mbytes/sec. A KSR1-1088 with up to 510 I/O channels has an aggregate I/O capacity of 15,300 Mbytes/sec. Figure 9 shows connections between KSR1 systems and external devices. The KSR1 supports several types of direct I/O adaptors including Multiple Channel Disk, Multiple Channel Ethernet, Multiple Channel FDDI and Single Channel HiPPI. The VME Channel Controller provides an open interface for other networking and customer specific requirements.

The Multiple Channel Disk adaptor provides five differential SCSI channels to support disk array (RAID) mass storage subsystems. The KSR OS implements disk striping across multiple adaptors.

A companion paper [20] discusses KSR OS system software.

## Shared Memory Model Plus ALLCACHE Mean Higher Performance

By building on the well understood shared memory and virtual memory programming models, ALLCACHE enables the KSR1 to provide a conventional shared memory programming model. A standards based programming environment facilitates porting existing applications and writing new ones. An even greater benefit of the ALLCACHE implementation of the shared memory model is its superior scalability and performance over mainframes, and message passing MPPs.

The performance advantages of ALLCACHE and shared memory can be characterized by its machine and programming aspects. Breit, etal [21] discuss these advantages with respect to examples from numerically intensive computing and Reiner, etal [22] discusses these advantages with respect to database management and inquiry. The key machine dependent aspects are:

- Memory allocation and data movement are handled automatically by the ALLCACHE Engine and incur no processor overhead. In contrast, for MPPs, memory allocation and data movement are handled explicitly by the programmer and are executed on the processor, incurring overhead to the application.

- Dynamic memory allocation and data movement of ALLCACHE requires less bandwidth and aggregate storage than MPPs – by dynamically optimizing locality.

- Hardware based parallel directory, routing and coherency management of the ALLCACHE Engine (as opposed to these functions executed on a conventional processor) achieve higher efficiency data sharing.

- ALLCACHE Engine supports efficient movement and sharing of fine granularity of data, which is well matched to a wide range of application requirements.

These characteristics result in higher effective bandwidth to a processor and between processors at the application level. The key programming aspects are:

- Incremental parallelization using the 90/10 rule: since the majority of the execution time occurs in a small percentage of the program, the shared memory programmers can spend all their time optimizing the part of the code that counts, and ignoring the remainder, since shared memory automates memory allocation and data movement. In contrast, for MPPs, programmers spend most of their time on the code that does not have any performance leverage.

- Over the past 15 years, algorithmic improvements in many fields have proceeded at a rate equal to machine improvements. [23] Shared memory's ease of programming allows programmers to implement the latest, most computationally efficient algorithm.

- For many new applications the ultimate Amdahls Law is the elapsed time for the program to execute the first time. The conventional programming environment enabled by shared memory provides the shortest route to solution.

Although the shared memory programming model is well known for its ease of programming, the most significant advantage of the Kendall Square implementation of a scalable shared memory model is higher performance.

## References

1. Kilburn, T., Edwards, D.B.G., Lanigan, M.J., and Sumner, F.H. "One-level Storage System," IRE Transactions, EC-11, Vol.2, pps. 223-235, April, 1962.

2. Denning, Peter J. "On Modeling Program Behavior," Arlington, VA: AFIPS Press: Proceedings, Spring Joint Computer Conference, Vol. 40, pps. 937-944, 1972.

3. Smith, Alan J. Cache Memories ACM Computing Surveys, 14 (3): 473-530, September 1982.

4. Organic, E.I., "The Multics System: An Examination of Its Structure," Cambridge, MA: MIT Press, 1972.

5. Bell, C. Gordon. "Multis: A New Class of Multiprocessor Computers," Science, Vol. 228, pps. 462-467, 26 April 1985.

6. Wulf, William A. and Bell, C. Gordon. "C.mmp-A multi-miniprocessor," Proceedings, AFIPS 1972 Fall Joint Computer Conference, 41, pp. 765-777, 1972.

7. Frank, Steven J. "Tightly Coupled Multiprocessor System Speeds Memory Access Times," Electronics, pps. 164-169, 1984.

8. Seitz, Charles L. "The Cosmic Cube," Communications of the ACM, 28-1, pps. 22-33, January, 1985.

9. Dally, William L. "The J-Machine: A Fine-Grain Concurrent Computer," MIT VLSI Memo 89-532, May, 1989.

10. Li, Kai and Hudak, Paul. "Memory Coherence in Shared Virtual Memory Systems," Proceedings of the 5th Annual ACM Symposium on Principles of Distributed Computing, pps. 229-239, August, 1986.

11. Minnich, Ronald G. and Farber, David J. "The Mether System: Distributed Shared Memory for SunOS 4.0," (private communication).

12. Swan, R., Fuller, S., and Siewiorek, D. "Cm*- A modular, multi-microprocessor," Proceedings AFIPS 1977 Fall Joint Computer Conference, 46, pps. 637-644, 1977.

13. Picano, S., Brooks, E., and Hoag, J. "Programming Costs of Explicit Memory Localization on a Large Scale Shared Memory Multiprocessor," Albuquerque, NM: Proceedings of Supercomputing '91, pps. 36-45, November 1991.

14. Chaiken, David, Kubiatowicz, John and Agarwal, Anant. "LimitLESS Directories: A Scalable Cache Coherence Scheme," Proceedings of the 4th International Conference on Architectural Support for Programming Languages and Operating Systems, pps. 224-234, April 1991.

15. Lenoski, Daniel, Laudon, James, Gharachorloo, Kourosh, Wolf-Dietrich Weber, Gupta, Anoop, and Hennessy, John. "Overview and Status of the Stanford DASH Multiprocessor," Proceedings of International Symposium on Shared Memory Multiprocessing, pps. 102-108, April, 1991.

16. Kendall Square Research Corporation, "Technical Summary," 1992.

17. Lamport, Leslie: "How to Make a Multiprocessor Computer That Correctly Executes Multiprocess Programs," IEEE Transactions on Computers, C-28, No. 9 (September 1979), pps. 690-691.

18. Leiserson, Charles E. "Fat-Trees: Universal Networks for Hardware-Efficient Supercomputing," IEEE Transactions on Computers, Vol. C-34, No. 10, pps. 892-901, October, 1985.

19. Leiserson, Charles E. "VLSI Theory and Parallel Supercomputing," Pasadena, CA: Proceedings of the 1989 Decennial Caltech Conference, March, 1989.

20. Burke, E. "An Overview of System Software for the KSR1," Compcon '93 Proceedings.

21. Breit, S., Pangali, C. and Zirl, D. "Technical Applications on the KSR1: High Performance and Ease of Use," Compcon '93 Proceedings.

22. Reiner, D., Miller J. and Wheat, D. "The Kendall Square Query Decomposer," Compcon '93 Proceedings.

23. "Grand Challenges: High Performance Computing and Communications: The FY 1992 U.S. Research and Development Program," Committee on Physical, Mathematical, and Engineering Sciences, 1991.

# DDM — A Cache-Only Memory Architecture

Erik Hagersten, Anders Landin, and Seif Haridi
Swedish Institute of Computer Science

**A new architecture has the programming paradigm of shared-memory architectures but no physically shared memory. Caches attached to the processors contain all the system memory.**

**M**ultiprocessors providing a shared memory view to the programmer are typically implemented as such — with a shared memory. We introduce an architecture with large caches to reduce latency and network load. Because all system memory resides in the caches, a minimum number of network accesses are needed. Still, it presents a shared-memory view to the programmer.

**Single bus.** Shared-memory systems based on a single bus have some tens of processors, each one with a local cache, and typically suffer from bus saturation. A cache-coherence protocol in each cache snoops the traffic on the common bus and prevents inconsistencies in cache contents.[1] Computers manufactured by Sequent and Encore use this kind of architecture. Because it provides a uniform access time to the whole shared memory, it is called a uniform memory architecture (UMA). The contention for the common memory and the common bus limits the scalability of UMAs.

**Distributed.** Computers such as the BBN Butterfly and the IBM RP3 use an architecture with distributed shared memory, known as a nonuniform memory architecture (NUMA). Each processor node contains a portion of the shared memory, so access times to different parts of the shared address space can vary. NUMAs often have networks other than a single bus, and the network delay can vary to different nodes. The earlier NUMAs did not have coherent caches and left the problem of maintaining coherence to the programmer. Today, researchers are striving toward coherent NUMAs with directory-based cache-coherence protocols.[2] By statically partitioning the work and data, programmers can optimize programs for NUMAs. A partitioning that enables processors to make most of their accesses to their part of the shared memory achieves a better scalability than is possible in UMAs.

**Cache-only.** In a cache-only memory architecture (COMA), the memory organization is similar to that of a NUMA in that each processor holds a portion of the address space. However, the partitioning of data among the memories does not have to be static, since all distributed memories are organized like large (second-level) caches. The task of such a memory is twofold. Besides being a large cache for the processor, it may also contain some data from the shared address space that the processor never has accessed — in other words, it is a cache and a virtual part of

Reprinted from *Computer*, Vol. 25, No. 9, Sept. 1992, pp. 44–54.

the shared memory. We call this intermediate form of memory *attraction memory*. A coherence protocol attracts the data used by a processor to its attraction memory. Comparable to a cache line, the coherence unit moved around by the protocol is called an *item*. On a memory reference, a virtual address is translated into an item identifier. The item identifier space is logically the same as the physical address space of typical machines, but there is no permanent mapping between an item identifier and a physical memory location. Instead, an item identifier corresponds to a location in an attraction memory, whose tag matches the item identifier. Actually, there are cases where multiple locations of different attraction memories could match.

A COMA provides a programming model identical to that of shared-memory architectures, but it does not require static distribution of execution and memory usage to run efficiently. Running an optimized NUMA program on a COMA results in a NUMA-like behavior, since the work spaces of the different processors migrate to their attraction memories. However, a UMA version of the same program would have a similar behavior, because the data are attracted to the using processor regardless of the address. A COMA also adapts to and performs well for programs with a more dynamic or semidynamic scheduling. The work space migrates according to its usage throughout the computation. Programs can be optimized for a COMA to take this property into account to achieve a better locality.

A COMA allows for dynamic data use without duplicating much memory, compared with an architecture in which a cached datum also occupies space in the shared memory. To avoid increasing the memory cost, the attraction memories should be implemented with ordinary memory components. Therefore, we view the COMA approach as a second-level, or higher level, cache technique. The accessing time to the attraction memory of a COMA is comparable to that to the memory of a cache-coherent NUMA. Figure 1 compares COMAs to other shared-memory architectures.

**A new COMA.** This article describes the basic ideas behind a new COMA. The architecture, called the Data Diffusion Machine (DDM),[3] relies on a hier-

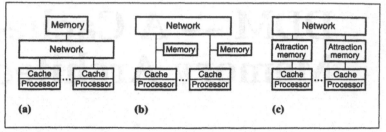

**Figure 1. Shared-memory architectures compared with COMAs: (a) uniform memory architecture (UMA), (b) nonuniform memory architecture (NUMA), and (c) cache-only memory architecture (COMA).**

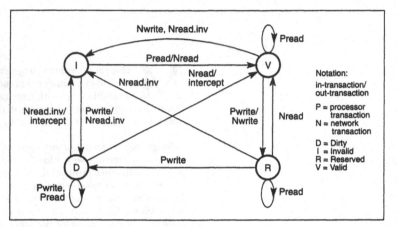

**Figure 2. An example of a protocol similar to the write-once protocol.**

archical network structure. We introduce the key ideas behind DDM by describing a small machine and its protocol. We also describe a large machine with hundreds of processors, overview the ongoing prototype project, and provide simulated performance figures.

## Cache-coherence strategies

The problem of maintaining coherence among read-write data shared by different caches has been studied extensively. Either software or hardware can maintain coherence. We believe hardware coherence is needed in a COMA for efficiency, since the item must be small to prevent performance degradation by false sharing. (In false sharing, two processors accessing different parts of the same item conflict with each other, even though they do

not share any data.) We measured a speedup of 50 percent when false sharing was removed from the wind tunnel application, MP3D-Diff, reported in the "Simulated performance" section. Hardware-based schemes maintain coherence without involving software and can be implemented more efficiently. Examples of hardware-based protocols are snooping-cache protocols and directory-based protocols.

Snooping-cache protocols have a distributed implementation. Each cache is responsible for snooping traffic on the bus and taking actions to avoid an incoherence. An example of such a protocol is the write-once protocol introduced by Goodman and discussed by Stenström.[1] As Figure 2 shows, in that protocol, each cache line can be in one of four states: Invalid, Valid, Reserved, or Dirty. Many caches can have the same cache line in the state Valid at the same time, and may read it locally. When writing to a cache line in Valid, the line changes state to Reserved, and a write is sent on the common bus to the common memory. All other caches with lines in Valid snoop the write and invalidate their copies. At this point there is only one cached copy of the cache line containing the newly written value. The common memory now also contains the new value. If a cache already has the cache line in Reserved, it can perform a write locally without any transactions on the common bus. Its value now differs from that in the memory, and its state is therefore changed to Dirty. Any read requests from other caches to that cache line must now be intercepted to provide the new value (marked by "intercept" in Figure 2).

Snooping caches rely on broadcasting and are not suited for general interconnection networks: Unrestricted broadcasting would drastically reduce the available bandwidth, thereby obviating the advantage of general networks. Instead, directory-based schemes send messages directly between nodes.[1] A read request is sent to main memory, without any snooping. The main memory knows if the cache line is cached — and in which cache or caches — and whether it has been modified. If the line has been modified, the read request is passed on to the cache with a copy, which provides a copy for the requesting cache. On a write to a shared cache line, a write request sent to the main memory causes invalidation messages to all caches with copies to be sent. The caches respond with acknowledge messages. To achieve sequential consistency, all acknowledgments must be received before the write is performed.

The cache-coherence protocol for a COMA can adopt techniques used in other cache-coherence protocols and extend them with the functionality for finding a datum on a cache read miss and for handling replacement. A directory-based protocol could have a part of the directory information, the *directory home*, statically distributed in a NUMA fashion, while the data would be allowed to move freely. Retrieving the data on a read miss would then require one extra indirect access to the directory home to find where the item current-

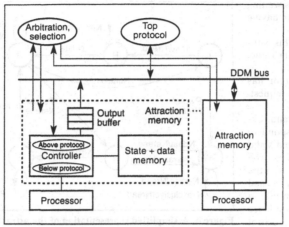

**Figure 3. The architecture of a single-bus DDM. Below the attraction memories are the processors. On top of the bus are arbitration and selection.**

ly resides. The access time, including this extra indirection, would be identical to that required for reading a dirty cache line not in a NUMA's home node. The directory home can also make sure that the last copy of an item is not lost.

Instead of the above strategy, DDM is based on a hierarchical snooping bus architecture and uses a hierarchical search algorithm for finding an item. The directory information in DDM is dynamically distributed in the hierarchy.

## A minimal COMA

We introduce DDM by looking at the smallest instance of the architecture, which could be a COMA on its own or a subsystem of a larger COMA. A single bus connects the attraction memories of the minimal DDM. The distribution and coherence of data among the attraction memories are controlled by the snooping protocol *memory above*, and the interface between the processor and the attraction memory is defined by the protocol *memory below*. The protocol views a cache line of an attraction memory, here called an item, as one unit. The attraction memory stores one small state field per item. Figure 3 shows the node architecture in the single-bus DDM.

DDM uses an asynchronous split-transaction bus: The bus is released between a requesting transaction and its reply, for example, between a read re-

quest and its data reply. The delay between the request and its reply can be of arbitrary length, and there might be a large number of outstanding requests. The reply transaction will eventually appear on the bus as a different transaction. Unlike other buses, the DDM bus has a selection mechanism to make sure that at most one node is selected to service a request. This guarantees that each transaction on the bus does not produce more than one new transaction for the bus, a requirement necessary for deadlock avoidance.

**Single-bus DDM protocol.**
We developed a new protocol, similar in many ways to the snooping-cache protocol, limiting broadcast requirements to a smaller subsystem and adding support for replacement.[4] The write coherence part of the protocol is the write-invalidate type: To keep data coherent, all copies of the item except the one to be updated are erased on a write. In a COMA with a small item size, the alternative approach, write update, could also be attractive: On a write, the new value is multicast to all "caches" with a shared copy of the item.

The protocol also handles the attraction of data (read) and replacement when a set in an attraction memory gets full. The snooping protocol defines a new state and a new transaction to send as a function of the transaction appearing on the bus, and the present state of the item in the attraction memory:

Protocol: old state × transaction → new state × new transaction

An item can be in one of seven states (the subsystem is the attraction memory):

- *Invalid.* This subsystem does not contain the item.
- *Exclusive.* This subsystem and no other contains the item.
- *Shared.* This subsystem and possibly other subsystems contain the item.
- *Reading.* This subsystem is waiting for a data value after having issued a read.

- *Waiting.* This subsystem is waiting to become Exclusive after having issued an erase.
- *Reading-and-Waiting.* This subsystem is waiting for a data value, later to become Exclusive.
- *Answering.* This subsystem has promised to answer a read request.

The first three states — Invalid, Exclusive, and Shared — correspond to the states Invalid, Reserved, and Valid in Goodman's write-once protocol. The state Dirty in that protocol — with the meaning that this is the only cached copy and its value differs from that in the memory — has no correspondence in a COMA. New states in the protocol are the transient states Reading, Waiting, Reading-and-Waiting, and Answering. Transient states are required because of the split-transaction bus and the need to remember outstanding requests.

The bus carries the following transactions:

- *Erase.* Erase all copies of this item.
- *Exclusive.* Acknowledge an erase request.
- *Read.* Read a copy of the item.
- *Data.* Carry the data in reply to an earlier read request.
- *Inject.* Carry the only copy of an item and look for a subsystem to move into — caused by a replacement.
- *Out.* Carry the item on its way out of the subsystem — caused by a replacement. It will terminate when another copy of the item is found.

A processor writing an item in Exclusive state or reading an item in Exclusive or Shared state proceeds without interruption. As Figure 4 shows, a read attempt of an item in Invalid will result in a Read request and a new state, Reading. The bus selection mechanism will select one attraction memory to service the request, eventually putting a Data transaction on the bus. The requesting attraction memory, now in Reading, will grab the Data transaction, change to Shared, and continue.

Processors are allowed to write only to items in Exclusive state. If the item is in Shared, all other copies have to be erased and an acknowledgment received before the writing is allowed. The attraction memory sends an Erase transaction and waits for the Exclusive ac-

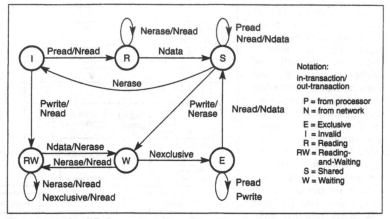

**Figure 4. A simplified representation of the attraction memory protocol not including replacement.**

knowledgment in the new state, Waiting. Many simultaneous attempts to write the same item will result in many attraction memories in Waiting, all with an outstanding Erase transaction in their output buffers. The first Erase to reach the bus is the winner of the write race.

All other transactions bound for the same item are removed from the small output buffers. Therefore, the buffers also have to snoop transactions. The output buffers can be limited to a depth of three, and deadlock can still be avoided with a special arbitration algorithm. The losing attraction memories in Waiting change state to Reading-and-Waiting, while one of them puts a read request in its output buffer. Eventually the top protocol of the bus replies with an Exclusive acknowledgment, telling the only attraction memory left in Waiting that it may now proceed. Writing to an item in the Invalid state results in a Read request and a new state, Reading-and-Waiting. Upon the Data reply, the state changes to Waiting and an Erase request is sent.

**Replacement.** Like ordinary caches, the attraction memory will run out of space, forcing some items to make room for more recently accessed ones. If the set where an item is supposed to reside is full, one item in the set is selected to be replaced. For example, the oldest item in Shared, of which there might be other copies, may be selected. Replacing an item in Shared generates an Out transaction. The space used by the item can now be reclaimed. If an Out transaction sees an attraction memory in

Shared, Reading, Waiting, or Reading-and-Waiting, it does nothing; otherwise it is converted to an Inject transaction by the top protocol. An Inject transaction can also be produced by replacing an item in Exclusive. The inject transaction is the last copy of an item trying to find a new home in a new attraction memory. In the single-bus implementation, it will do so first by choosing an empty space (Invalid state), and second by replacing an item in Shared state — in other words, it will decrease the amount of sharing. If the item identifier space, which corresponds to the physical address space of conventional architectures, is not made larger than the sum of the attraction memory sizes, it is possible to devise a simple scheme that guarantees a physical location for each item.

Often a program uses only a portion of a computer's physical address space. This is especially true of operating systems with a facility for eager reclaiming of unused work space. In DDM, the unused item space can be used to increase the degree of sharing by purging the unused items. The operating system might even change the degree of sharing dynamically.

## The hierarchical DDM

So far, we have presented a cache-coherent single-bus multiprocessor without physically shared memory. Instead, the resources form huge second-level caches called attraction memories, minimizing the number of accesses to the

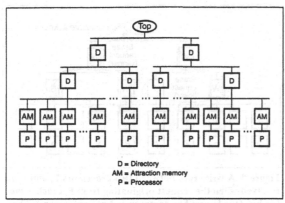

Figure 5. A hierarchical DDM with three levels.

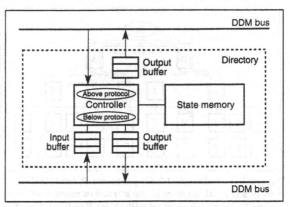

Figure 6. The architecture of a directory.

only shared resource left: the shared bus. Data can reside in any or many of the attraction memories. Data are automatically moved where needed.

To make the single-bus DDM a subsystem of a large hierarchical DDM, we replace the top with a directory, which interfaces between the bus and a higher level bus of the same type. Figure 5 shows the hierarchy.

The directory is a set-associative state memory that keeps information for all the items in the attraction memories below it, but contains no data. The directory can answer these questions: "Is this item below me?" and "Does this item exist outside my subsystem?" From the bus above, the directory's snooping protocol *directory above* behaves very much like the *memory above* protocol. From the bus below, its *directory below* protocol behaves like the *top protocol* for items in the Exclusive state. This makes operations on items local to a bus identical to those of the single-bus DDM. The directory passes through only transactions from below that cannot be completed inside its subsystem or transactions from above that need to be serviced by its subsystem. In that sense, the directory acts as a filter.

As Figure 6 shows, the directory has a small output buffer above it to store transactions waiting to be sent on the higher bus. Transactions for the lower bus are stored in another output buffer below, and transactions from the lower bus are stored in an input buffer. A directory reads from the input buffer when it has the time and space to do a lookup in its status memory. This is not part of the atomic snooping action of the bus.

The hierarchical DDM and its protocol have several similarities with architectures proposed by Wilson[5] and Goodman and Woest.[6] DDM is, however, different in its use of transient states in the protocol, its lack of physically shared memory, and its network (higher level caches) that stores only state information and no data.

**Multilevel read.** If the subsystems connected to the bus cannot satisfy a read request, the next higher directory retransmits the request on the next higher bus. The directory also changes the item's state to Reading, marking the outstanding request. Eventually, the request reaches a level in the hierarchy where a directory containing a copy of the item is selected to answer the request. The selected directory changes the item's state to Answering, marking an outstanding request from above, and retransmits the Read request on its lower bus. As Figure 7 shows, the transient states Reading and Answering in the directories mark the request's path through the hierarchy, like an unwound red read thread that shows the way through a maze, appearing in red in Figure 7.

A flow-control mechanism in the protocol prevents deadlock if too many processors try to unwind a read thread to the same set in a directory. When the request finally reaches an attraction memory with a copy of the item, its data reply simply follows the read thread back to the requesting node, changing all the states along the path to Shared.

Combined reads and broadcasts are simple to implement in DDM. If a Read request finds the read thread unwound

for the requested item (Reading or Answering state), it simply terminates and waits for the Data reply that eventually will follow that path on its way back.

**Multilevel write.** An Erase from below to a directory with the item in Exclusive state results in an Exclusive acknowledgment being sent below. An Erase that cannot get its acknowledgment from the directory will work its way up the hierarchy, changing the directories' states to Waiting to mark the outstanding request. All subsystems of a bus carrying an Erase transaction will get their copies erased. The propagation of the Erase ends when it reaches a directory in Exclusive (or the top), and the acknowledgment is sent back along the path marked Waiting, changing the states to Exclusive.

A write race between any two processors in the hierarchical DDM has a solution similar to that of a single-bus DDM. The two Erase requests are propagated up the hierarchy. The first Erase transaction to reach the lowest bus common to both processors is the winner, as shown in Figure 8. The losing attraction memory (in Reading-and-Waiting) will restart a new write action automatically upon receipt of the erase.

**Replacement in the hierarchical DDM.** Replacement of a Shared item in the hierarchical DDM results in an Out transaction propagating up the hierarchy and terminating when it finds a subsystem in any of the following states: Shared, Reading, Waiting, or Answering. If the last copy of an item marked Shared is replaced, an Out transaction

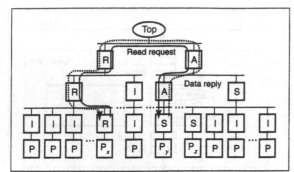

**Figure 7. A read request from processor P$_x$ has found its way to a copy of the item in the attraction memory of processor P$_y$. Its path is marked with states Reading (R) and Answering (A), which will guide the data reply back to P$_x$. (I indicates processors in the Invalid state, S processors in the Shared state.)**

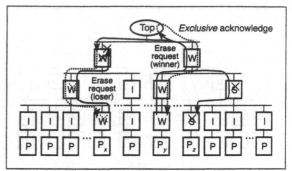

**Figure 8. A write race between two processors P$_x$ and P$_y$ is resolved when the request originating from P$_y$ reaches the top bus (the lowest bus common to both processors). The top can now send the acknowledgment, Exclusive, which follows the path marked with W's (processors in the Waiting state) back to the winning processor P$_y$. The Waiting states are changed to Exclusive by the acknowledgment. The Erase transaction will erase the data in P$_x$ and P$_z$, forcing P$_x$ to redo its write attempt.**

that fails to terminate will reach a directory in Exclusive and turn into an Inject transaction. Replacing an item in Exclusive generates an Inject transaction that tries to find an empty space in a neighboring attraction memory. Inject transactions first try to find an empty space in the attraction memories of the local DDM bus, as in the single-bus DDM. Unlike in a single-bus DDM, an Inject failing to find an empty space on the local DDM bus will turn to a special bus, its home bus, determined by the item identifier. On the home bus, the Inject will force itself into an attraction memory, possibly by throwing out a foreigner or a Shared item. The item home space is equally divided between the bottommost buses, and therefore space is guaranteed on the home bus.

The preferred location in DDM is different from memory location in NUMAs in that an item seeks a home only at replacement after failing to find space elsewhere. When the item is not in its home place, other items can use its place. The home also differs from the NUMA approach in being a bus: Any attraction memory on that bus will do. The details of the directory protocols are available elsewhere.[4]

**Replacement in a directory.** Baer and Wang studied the multilevel inclusion property,[7] which has the following implications for our system: A directory at level $i + 1$ has to be a superset of the

directories, or attraction memories, at level $i$. In other words, the size of a directory and its associativity (number of ways) must be $B_i$ times that of the underlying level $i$, where $B_i$ is the branch factor of the underlying level $i$, and size means the number of items:

Size: $Dir_{i+1} = B_i * Dir_i$
Associativity: $Dir_{i+1} = B_i * Dir_i$

Even if implementable, higher level memories would become expensive and slow if those properties were fulfilled for a large hierarchical system. However, the effects of the multilevel inclusion property are limited in DDM. It stores only state information in its directories and does not replicate data in the higher levels. Yet another way to limit the effect is to use "imperfect directories" with smaller sets (lower number of ways) than what is required for multilevel inclusion and to give the directories the ability to perform replacement, that is, to move all copies of an item out of their subsystem. We can keep the probability of replacement at a reasonable level by increasing the associativity moderately higher up in the hierarchy. A higher degree of sharing also helps to keep that probability low. A shared item occupies space in many attraction memories, but only one space in the directories above them. The implementation of directory replacement requires one extra state and two extra transactions.[4]

**Other protocols.** Our protocol gives the programmer a *sequentially consistent* system. It fulfills the strongest memory access model, but performance is degraded because the processor has to wait for the acknowledgment before it can perform the write. However, the acknowledgment is sent by the topmost node of the subsystem in which all copies of the item reside, instead of by each individual attraction memory with a copy. This not only reduces the remote delay, it also cuts down the number of system transactions. The writer might actually receive the acknowledgment before all copies are erased. Nevertheless, sequential consistency can be guaranteed.[8] The hierarchical structure can also efficiently support looser forms of consistency providing higher performance. We have designed a processor-consistent protocol[8] and a protocol combining processor consistency with an adaptive write update strategy.

## Increasing the bandwidth

Although most memory accesses tend to be localized in the machine, the hierarchy's higher levels may nevertheless demand a higher bandwidth than the lower systems, creating a bottleneck. To take the load off the higher levels, we can use a smaller branch factor at the

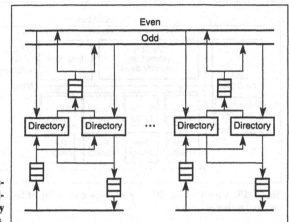

**Figure 9. Increasing the bandwidth of a bus by splitting buses.**

top of the hierarchy than lower down. This solution, however, increases the levels in the hierarchy, resulting in a longer remote access delay and an increased memory overhead. Instead, we can widen the higher levels of the hierarchy to produce a fat tree.[9] We split a directory into two directories half the original directory's size. The two directories deal with different address domains (even and odd). The communica-tion with other directories is also split, which doubles the bandwidth. We can perform a split any number of times and at any level of the hierarchy. Figure 9 shows that regardless of the number of splits, the architecture is still hierarchi-cal to each specific address.

Yet another solution is a heteroge-neous network: We use the hierarchy with its advantages as far as possible and tie several hierarchies together at their tops by a general network with a directory-based protocol. This scheme requires some changes in the protocol to achieve the same consistency model.

## The DDM prototype project

A prototype DDM design is near com-pletion at the Swedish Institute of Com-puter Science. The hardware implemen-tation of the processor and attraction memory is based on the system TP881V by Tadpole Technology, UK. Each such system has up to four Motorola MC88100 20-MHz processors, each one with two MC88200 16-Kbyte caches and memory management units; 8 or 32 Mbytes of DRAM; and interfaces for the SCSI bus, Ethernet, and terminals, all con-nected by the Motorola Mbus as shown in Figure 10.

We are developing a DDM node con-troller board to host a single-ported state memory. As Figure 10 shows, it will interface the TP881V node with the first-level DDM bus. The node control-ler snoops accesses between the proces-sor caches and the memory of the TP881V according to the memory-below protocol, and also snoops the DDM bus according to the memory-above protocol. We have integrated the copy-back protocol of multiple proces-sor caches into the protocol mechanisms. The node controller thus changes the memory's behavior into that of an at-traction memory. Read accesses to the attraction memory take eight cycles per cache line, which is one more than in the original TP881V system. Write accesses to the attraction memory take 12 cycles compared with 10 cycles for the original system. A read/write mix of 3/1 to the attraction memory results in an access time to the attraction memory on the average 16 percent slower than that to the original TP881V memory.

As Table 1 shows, a remote read to a node on the same DDM bus takes 55 cycles at best, most of which are spent making Mbus transactions (a total of four accesses). Read accesses climbing one step up and down the hierarchy add about 45 extra cycles. Write accesses to shared state take at best 40 cycles for one level and 50 cycles for two levels.

The DDM bus is pipelined in four phases: transaction code, snoop, selec-tion, and data. We designed our initial

## Related activities

At the Swedish Institute of Computer Science, we are developing an operat-ing system for the DDM prototype. This work is based on the Mach operating system from Carnegie Mellon University, which we modified to support DDM efficiently. Related activities involve a hardware prefetching scheme that dy-namically prefetches items to the attraction memory; this is especially useful when a process is started or migrated. We are also experimenting with alter-native protocols.[1]

A DDM emulator is currently under development at the University of Bristol.[2] The emulator runs on the Meiko transputer platform and models an architec-ture with a tree-shaped link-based structure, with transputers as directories. The transputers' four links permit a branch factor of three at each level. The transputers at the leaves execute the application. All references to global data are intercepted and handled in a DDM manner by software. The emulator's DDM protocol has a different representation suited for a link-based architec-ture structured like a tree, rather than for a bus-based architecture. The im-plementation has certain similarities to directory-based systems.

### References

1. E. Hagersten, *Towards a Scalable Cache-Only Memory Architecture*, PhD thesis, SICS Dissertation Series 08, Swedish Institute of Computer Science, Kista, Sweden, 1992.

2. S. Raina and D.H.D. Warren, "Traffic Patterns in a Scalable Multiprocessor Through Transputer Emulation," *Proc. Hawaii Int'l Conf. System Sciences*, Vol. I, IEEE-CS Press, Los Alamitos, Calif., Order No. 2420, 1992, pp. 267-276.

bus conservatively, since pushing the bus speed is not a primary goal of this research. The prototype DDM bus operates at 20 MHz, with a 32-bit data bus and a 32-bit address bus. It provides a moderate bandwidth of about 80 Mbytes per second, which is enough for connecting up to eight nodes — that is, 32 processors. Still, the bandwidth has not been the limiting factor in our simulation studies. We can increase bus bandwidth many times by using other structures. The slotted ring bus proposed by Barosso and Dubois[10] has a bandwidth one order of magnitude higher.

For translations to item identifiers, DDM uses the normal procedures for translating virtual addresses to physical addresses, as implemented in standard memory management units. This means that an operating system has knowledge of physical pages.

Any attraction memory node can have a connected disk. Upon a page-in, the node first attracts all the data of an item page as being temporarily locked to its attraction memory. If the items of that page were not present in the machine earlier, they are "born" at this time through the protocol. Then the node copies (by direct memory access) the page from the disk to the attraction memory, unlocking the data at the same time. Page-out reverses the process, copying a dirty page back to the disk. The operating system can purge the items of unused pages for more sharing.

## Memory overhead

It might seem that an implementation of DDM would require far more memory than alternative architectures. Extra memory is required for storing state bits and address keys for the set-associative attraction memories, as well as for the directories. We have calculated the extra bits needed if all items reside in only one copy (worst case). We assume an item size of 16 bytes — the cache line size of the Motorola MC88200.

A 32-processor DDM — that is, a one-level DDM with a maximum of eight two-way set-associative attraction memories — needs four bits of address tag per item, regardless of the attraction memory size. As we said earlier, the item space is not larger than the sum of the sizes of the attraction memories, so the size of each attraction memory is

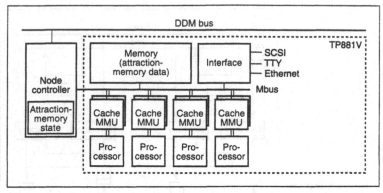

**Figure 10. A node of the DDM prototype consisting of four processors sharing one attraction memory.**

one eighth of the item space. Because each set in the attraction memory is divided two ways, 16 items can reside in the same set. In addition to the four bits needed to tell items apart, each item needs four bits of state. Thus, an item size of 128 bits gives an overhead of $(4+4)/128 = 6$ percent.

Adding another layer with eight eight-way set-associative directories brings the maximum number of processors to 256. The size of the directories is the sum of the sizes of the attraction memories in their subsystems. A directory entry consists of six bits for the address tag and four bits of state per item, using a calculation similar to the one above. The overhead in the attraction memories is larger than in the previous example because of the larger item space: seven bits of address tag and four bits of state. The total overhead per item is $(6+4+7+4)/128 = 16$ percent. A larger item size would, of course, decrease these overheads.

To minimize the memory overhead, we can use a different interpretation of the implicit state for different parts of the item space. In our initial implementation of DDM, the absence of an entry in a directory is interpreted as Invalid. The replacement algorithm introduces a home bus for an item. If an item is most often found in its home bus and nowhere else, the absence of an entry in a directory could instead be interpreted

**Table 1. Remote delay in a two-level DDM (best cases).**

| CPU Access | State in Attraction Memory | Delay, One Level (cycles) | Delay, Two Levels (cycles) |
|---|---|---|---|
| Read | Invalid | 55 | 100 |
| Write | Shared | 40 | 50 |
| Write | Invalid | 80 | 130 |

as Exclusive for items in its home subsystem, and as Invalid for items from outside. This would drastically reduce a directory's size. The technique would be practical only to a limited extent. Too small directories restrict the number of items moving out of their subsystems and thus limit sharing and migration, resulting in drawbacks similar to those of NUMAs.

Item space is slightly smaller than the sum of the attraction memories because of sharing in the system. This introduces a memory overhead not taken into account in the above calculations. However, in a COMA a "cached" item occupies only one space, while in other shared-memory architectures it requires two spaces: one in the cache and one in the shared memory.

## Simulated performance

We used an execution-driven simulation environment that lets us study large programs running on many processors in a reasonable amount of time. We parameterized the DDM simulation model with data from our ongoing prototype project. The model accurately describes DDM behavior, including the compromises introduced by taking an existing commercial product as a starting point. The model also describes parts of the virtual memory handling system. We used two-way 1-Mbyte attraction memories and a protocol similar to the one described here, providing sequential consistency.

For a representation of applications from engineering and symbolic computing, we studied parallel execution of the Stanford Parallel Applications for Shared Memory (Splash),[11] the OR-parallel Prolog system Muse, and a matrix multiplication program. All programs were originally written for UMA architectures (Sequent Symmetry or Encore Multimax computers) and use static or dynamic scheduler algorithms. They adapt well to a COMA without any changes. All programs take on the order of one CPU minute to run sequentially, without any simulations,

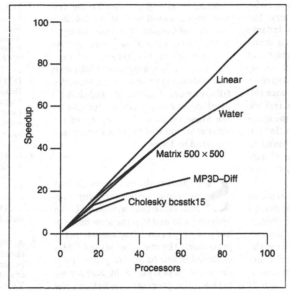

**Figure 11. Speedup curves for some of the reported programs.**

on a Sun Sparcstation. The speedups reported in Figure 11 and Table 2 are relative to the execution of a single DDM node with one processor, assuming a 100 percent hit rate in the attraction memory.

The Splash-Water program simulates the movements of water molecules. Its execution time is $O(m^2)$, where $m$ is the number of molecules. Therefore, it is often simulated with a small working set. We used 192 molecules and a working set of 320 Kbytes. Each of the 96 processors in Figure 11 handles only two molecules. Most of the locality in the small working set can be exploited on the processor cache, and only about 44 percent of the transactions reaching the attraction memory will hit. A real-size working set would still have the same good locality and would benefit more from the large attraction memories to maintain the speedup. We tested this hypothesis with a single run with 384 molecules, as shown in Table 2.

The Splash-MP3D program is a wind tunnel simulator with which a good speedup is harder to achieve because of a high invalidation frequency resulting in a poor hit rate. The program is often run with the memory filled with data

**Table 2. Statistics from DDM simulations. Hit rate statistics are for data only, except with Muse, where we used a unified I + D cache. The remote access rate is the percentage of the data accesses issued by a processor that create remote coherence traffic. An increased working set results in less load on the buses for Water and Cholesky.**

| | Water | | MP3D | MP3D-Diff | Cholesky | | Matrix | Muse |
|---|---|---|---|---|---|---|---|---|
| Input data | 192 molecules | 384 molecules | 75,000 particles | 75,000 particles | m14 (small) | m15 (large) | 500×500 | Pundit |
| Cold start included? | yes | yes | no | no | yes | yes | yes | no |
| DDM topology | 2×8×4 | 2×8×4 | 2×8×2 | 2×8×2 | 2×8×2 | 2×8×2 | 8×4 | 4×4 |
| Hit rate (data) percent | | | | | | | | |
| D cache | 99 | 99 | 86 | 92 | 96 | 89 | 92 | 98.5 |
| Attraction memory | 44 | 65 | 40 | 88 | 6 | 74 | 98 | 91 |
| Remote access rate | 0.6 | 0.4 | 8.4 | 1.0 | 3.8 | 2.8 | 0.16 | 0.20 |
| Bus utilization percent | | | | | | | | |
| Mbus | 31 | 26 | 86 | 54 | 70 | 60 | 55 | — |
| Lower DDM bus | 39 | 30 | 88 | 24 | 80 | 66 | — | — |
| Top DDM bus | 25 | 20 | 66 | 13 | 70 | 49 | 4 | — |
| Speedup per number of processors | 52/64 | 53/64 | 6/32 | 19/32 | 10/32 | 17/32 | 29/32 | —/16 |

structures representing particles, divided equally among the processors. The three-dimensional space is divided into space cells represented by data structures. MP3D runs in time phases and moves each particle once each phase. Moving a particle involves updating its state and also the state of the space cell where the molecule currently resides. All processors must write to all the space cells, resulting in a poor locality. In fact, 95 percent of the misses we found in DDM were due to this write-invalidate effect. We simulated 75,000 particles, a working set of 4 Mbytes.

MP3D-Diff is a rewritten version of the program that achieves a better hit rate. Particle distribution over processors is based on their current location in space. In other words, all particles in the same space cells are handled by the same processor. Updating of both particle state and space cell state is local to the processor. When a particle moves across a processor border, a new processor handles its data — the particle data diffuse to the new processor's attraction memory. The rewritten program has some 30 extra lines and requires a COMA to run well. In a COMA the particle data that occupy the major part of the physical memory are allowed to move freely among the attraction memories.

Splash-Cholesky factorizes a sparsely positive definite matrix. The matrix is divided into supernodes in a global task queue to be picked up by any worker — the scheduling is dynamic. We used the large input matrix bcsstk15 (m15), which occupies 800 Kbytes unfactored and 7.7 Mbytes factored. The nature of the Cholesky algorithm limits the available parallelism, which depends on the size of the input matrix. For comparison, Table 2 presents a run with the smaller matrix bcsstk14 (m14) of 420 Kbytes unfactored and 1.4 Mbytes factored.

The matrix multiplication program performs plain matrix multiplication on a $500 \times 500$ matrix using a blocked algorithm. The working set is about 3 Mbytes.

Muse is an OR-parallel Prolog system implemented in C at the Swedish Institute of Computer Science. Its input is the large natural language system Pundit from Unisys Paoli Research Center. An active working set of 2 Mbytes is touched during the execution. Muse distributes work dynamically and shows a good locality on a COMA. Because we ran Muse on an earlier version of the simulator, some of the statistics are not reported in Table 2.

Simulation shows that the COMA principle works well for programs originally written for UMA architectures and that the slow buses of our prototype can accommodate many processors. The overhead of the COMA explored in our hardware prototype is limited to 16 percent in the access time between the processor caches and the attraction memory. Memory overhead is 6 to 16 percent for 32 to 256 processors. ∎

## Acknowledgments

The Swedish Institute of Computer Science is a nonprofit research foundation sponsored by the Swedish National Board for Technical Development (NUTEK), Swedish Telecom, Ericsson Group, ASEA Brown Boveri, IBM Sweden, Nobel Tech System AB, and the Swedish Defence Materiel Administration (FMV). Part of the work on DDM is being carried out within the ESPRIT project 2741 PEPMA.

We thank our many colleagues involved in or associated with the project, especially David H.D. Warren of the University of Bristol, who is a coinventor of DDM. Mikael Löfgren of the Swedish Institute of Computer Science wrote the DDM simulator, basing his work on "Abstract Execution," which was provided to us by James Larus of the University of Wisconsin.

## References

1. P. Stenström, "A Survey of Cache Coherence for Multiprocessors," *Computer*, Vol. 23, No. 6, June 1990, pp. 12-24.

2. D. Lenoski et al., "The Directory-Based Cache Coherence Protocol for the DASH Multiprocessor," *Proc. 17th Ann. Int'l Symp. Computer Architecture*, IEEE-CS Press, Los Alamitos, Calif., Order No. 2047, 1990, pp. 148-159.

3. D.H.D. Warren and S. Haridi, "Data Diffusion Machine—A Scalable Shared Virtual Memory Multiprocessor," *Int'l Conf. Fifth Generation Computer Systems*, ICOT, Ohmsha. Ltd., Tokyo, 1988, pp. 943-952.

4. E. Hagersten, S. Haridi, and D.H.D. Warren, "The Cache-Coherence Protocol of the Data Diffusion Machine," in *Cache and Interconnect Architectures in Multiprocessors*, M. Dubois and S. Thakkar, eds., Kluwer Academic, Norwell, Mass., 1990, pp. 165-188.

5. A. Wilson, "Hierarchical Cache/Bus Architecture for Shared Memory Multiprocessor," Tech. Report ETR 86-006, Encore Computer Corp., Marlborough, Mass., 1986.

6. J.R. Goodman and P.J. Woest, "The Wisconsin Multicube: A New Large-Scale Cache-Coherent Multiprocessor," *Proc. 15th Int'l Symp. Computer Architecture*, IEEE-CS Press, Los Alamitos, Calif., Order No. 861, 1988, pp. 422-431.

7. J.-L. Baer and W.-H. Wang, "On the Inclusion Properties for Multi-Level Cache Hierarchies," *Proc. 15th Ann. Int'l Symp. Computer Architecture*, IEEE-CS Press, Los Alamitos, Calif., Order No. 861, 1988, pp. 73-80.

8. A. Landin, E. Hagersten, and S. Haridi, "Race-Free Interconnection Networks and Multiprocessor Consistency," *Proc. 18th Ann. Int'l Symp. Computer Architecture*, IEEE-CS Press, Los Alamitos, Calif., Order No. 2146, 1991, pp. 106-115.

9. C.E. Leiserson, "Fat Trees: Universal Networks for Hardware-Efficient Supercomputing," *IEEE Trans. Computers*, Vol. 34, No. 10, Oct. 1985, pp. 892-901.

10. L. Barroso and M. Dubois, "Cache Coherence on a Slotted Ring," *Proc. Int'l Conf. Parallel Processing*, IEEE-CS Press, Los Alamitos, Calif., Order No. 2355, 1991, pp. 230-237.

11. J.S. Singh, W.-D. Weber, and A. Gupta, *Splash: Stanford Parallel Applications for Shared Memory*, Tech. Report, CSL-TR-91-469, Computer Systems Laboratory, Stanford Univ., Stanford, Calif., 1991.

# MERLIN:
# A SUPERGLUE FOR MULTICOMPUTER SYSTEMS

*Creve Maples* *

Sandia National Laboratories
Albuquerque, NM 87185

and

*Larry Wittie* +

Computer Science, SUNY
Stony Brook NY 11794-4400

## ABSTRACT

Merlin is a memory based, interconnection system designed
to provide very high-performance capability in a distributed
multicomputer environment. By using dynamically mapped
reflective memory operations, the system creates a virtual
memory environment which permits users to utilize both
local and shared memory techniques. This mapped virtual
memory approach permits selected information to be shared
at high speeds and with relatively low latency. There is no
software involvement in the actual sharing of information
and the system automatically overlaps computation and
communication, to the extent possible, on a word-by-word
basis. Memory-to-memory mapping allows Merlin to
provide a uniform programming environment which is
independent of interconnection topology, processing
elements, and languages.

## 1. Introduction

As physical limitations (such as the speed of light) make it
progressively more difficult to construct faster and faster
supercomputer uniprocessors, interest has begun to focus
more heavily on the potential of parallel processing in
solving the computational challenges of tomorrow. The
rapid advances in microprocessor technology (with 100
MIP processors anticipated within a few years) make the
idea of multi-micro systems particularly attractive, both in
terms of performance and cost.

Attempts to develop multi-micro architectures have thus far
focused primarily on either of two approaches - tightly
coupled, shared memory systems, or loosely coupled,
message passing systems. Shared memory systems must
deal with the difficult problem of memory contention. This
problem has been architecturally addressed in several ways:
memory interleaving (e.g. Cray X-MP, etc.); memory

interconnection networks (e.g. NYU Ultracomputer [1],
IBM RP3 [2], etc.); and distributed caching (e.g. Sequent,
Encore, Alliant, etc.). Combinations of these techniques
have also been used to further minimize shared memory
contention problems (e.g. Cedar's use of caching and networking [3], IBM 3090's use of interleaving and caching).

Communication, and attendant latency, has been a primary
limiting factor in the utilization of message based machines
such as the Cosmic Cube [4], N-Cube, Intel iPSC, etc. It
should be noted, however, that performance limitations
faced by such architectures are not simply due to the
communication bandwidth of the system. The software
overhead involved in handling messages (e.g. operating
system calls, message formatting, transmission protocols,
interrupt handling, moving information into and out of
buffers, etc.) is frequently the dominating factor in determining system latency [5]. Indeed message based architectures are often only recommended for problems with low
interprocessor communication requirements [6].

Some hybrid architectures have attempted to combine the
two approaches. The BBN Butterfly, for example, offers a
global address space but the physical memories are separate
and locally attached to each processor [7]. A delay
therefore occurs when a processor addresses any nonlocal
memory location. The design of the Denelcor HEP [8]
attempted to hide such latency by overlapping the memory
access time with the execution of other instruction streams.

Operational shared memory systems have thus far only
been able to successfully support a few hundred processors, at most. Message passing systems with thousands of
processing elements, are, however, currently available.
Because of the relative advantages of each approach,
agreement as to which is 'better' (i.e. easier to program,

*This work was performed at Sandia National Laboratories and
supported by the U.S. Department of Energy under contract
number DE-AC04-76DP00789.

+This work has been supported in part by National Science
Foundation grants for CER DCS83-19966, research CCR87-
13865, equipment CCR87-05079; by National Aeronautics And
Space Administration grant NAG-1-249; and by Office of Naval
Research grant N00014-88-K-0383.

more general, offers the highest performance, etc.) still remain largely unresolved.

Current research in multicomputer systems is primarily focused on extensions of these two basic architectural approaches. At Stanford, for example, research is underway to develop a shared memory system (DASH) utilizing distributed, directoried caching [9]. The Nectar Project at CMU [10] is developing an efficient message based system to support a hetrogenous processing environment which features low-latency, high bandwidth communication and which is scalable. MERLIN (MEmory Routed, Logical Interconnection Network), however, provides a different perspective of processor-memory space.

## 2. Conceptual and Programming Model

A MERLIN environment pictures the world as consisting a collection of processing elements (not necessarily identical), each of which is independent and has its own local memory. It also assumes the existence of a large, separate (virtual) memory space to which each processor is connected. In SIMD operation, each processor behaves completely independently, and has no effect on the operation of any other processor in the system.

If a user desires to run a problem in parallel, a set of cooperating tasks are loaded onto a selected set of processors (typically allocated by the operating system). During the execution of the problem, various tasks may need to share or exchange information. Some information may need to be shared globally, for example, while other data may only need to be shared with a subset of the processors. To accomplish this sharing, a processor may request that the system allocate a shared virtual memory region, of the appropriate size, and map the processor's corresponding local memory region into this virtual space.

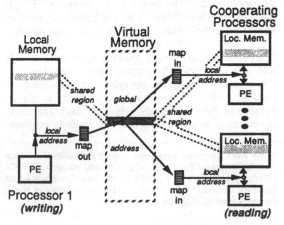

**Figure 1** - Programmer's model of shared memory operation in a Merlin system.

Once a global virtual region is allocated, it can, from a programming perspective, be treated as if it were a physically shared memory. While write operations to all other locations are stored locally, writes to a shared region *appear* to be stored in virtual memory. Other processors desiring access to this region (read, write, or read-write) simply have the operating system map an appropriately sized region of their local address space into the desired global virtual region.

The programmer's model of the operation of shared virtual memory is illustrated in Figure 1. In this example, the address of every store operation to processor 1's memory is used as an index to a local (output) mapping table. If an entry is found in the table, the address has been defined as a virtual address, and the table entry is used to translate the address to it's global virtual equivalent. From a programming perspective, the information associated with this address is then stored in global virtual space (see, however, the section on Architecture for what actually occurs). In this conceptual model, the reverse mapping processes would occur when other processors attempt to read a shared address.

It is clear from figure 1 that many different types of shared regions could exist either between cooperative processes working on a single task, or between processes working independently on other tasks in the system. The limitation would simply be on the amount of global virtual address space available. In a multitask environment, a particular process does not have to be executing, or even resident, to utilize shared memory. As long as the shared region exists information can be updated and messages received without active involvement of a process.

Note also that as long as the cooperating processes have agreed on how the shared information is being stored in global virtual memory (e.g. IEEE floating point, 32-bit integer, etc.) the processors on which they execute do not have to be identical (instruction set, cycle time, architecture, etc.). Conceptually, the global memory itself serves as a buffer which permits various components of the system to operate at different speeds.

Thus, in this programming model, a set of processes could elect, at one extreme, to share all data memory and execute in a global memory environment (e.g. Cray X/MP). Tasks operating in such an environment would typically require the use of locks, semaphores, etc., to handle synchronization issues. It is assumed that the virtual memory system will provide support for such traditional synchronization control mechanisms This does not necessarily imply, however, that such capabilities would also exist for a processor's local memory (see also the Synchronization section).

In the opposite extreme, a task could be established which viewed the world as consisting only of local memory processors interconnected by, for example, a hypercube-type of nearest neighbor communication system. For this situation, a separate shared memory region could be created for each processor which spanned only the logically nearest neighbors. Thus when a processor wished to 'send a message' to its neighbors, the information would simply be copied into the shared region. This is not necessarily the most efficient way to accomplish this task on a Merlin system, but it would serve to execute the model, potentially including support for hypercube message routines to permit such code to be run directly.

## 2.1 Comparison with Models of Other Multicomputer Systems.

Note that the physical communication network in a Merlin environment plays no role in logically programming a hypercube, or any other type of interconnection topology which might be useful to a problem. Indeed one could easily add a global memory region to the previous hypercube example or create other regions for specific purposes (e.g. the logical equivalent of a doubly rooted binary tree for searching).

The use of memory based interconnections eliminate the software involvement and overhead which exists in message passing systems. After a shared region is defined, there is no further software involvement in its use (e.g. system calls, subroutine calls, etc.). Since all shared memory operations involve individual "word packets" (data and address), there are no message protocols involved and no optimal message sizes.

By using local memory as much as possible for storage operations (instruction and data) and utilizing shared memory only in user defined areas, Merlin can reduce memory access conflicts which occur in actual shared memory systems (e.g. Cray X/MP). It's operation is also conceptually different than cached based, shared memory architectures. Such systems operate on a *'demand'* basis. If information required by a program does not reside in it's cache, the data must be located in the system and moved into the local cache (with appropriate action being taken to preserve cache coherence in the event that other copies of the same data are also in use). Merlin is an *'anticipatory'* system. By asserting that a region is shared, one is implicitly stating that processes attached to this region will, at some point, require access to the information it contains. Armed with this program supplied, preknowledge, Merlin attempts to reflect any change to information in the region, word-by-word, as fast as it becomes available. In this manner it is anticipating the requirement for the information and may be able to supply it before the actual need exists.

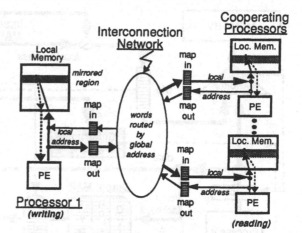

**Figure 2** - Memory routing and reflective memory operation in a Merlin system.

## 3. System Architecture

Developing a conceptual programming model and designing an architecture to realize it, are very different problems. The reality of architectural design, even at a high level, make practical trade-offs inevitable. These, in turn, impact the programming model, usually negatively. Clearly in the conceptual model described previously, a major problem would exist in the implementation of the global memory system. Such a memory would have all the problems of any shared memory system - access conflicts (even though the conceptual model reduced the frequency of shared memory access), potentially high memory latency, physical size limitations - which can significantly reduce the overall performance of the system.

Although useful as a programming concept, the global memory does not need to actually exist. In fact by eliminating it, most of the problems associated with shared memory can be avoided. The global shared memory, illustrated in figure 1, in reality serves as a communication system between sets of processes. It should therefore be possible to replace it with an interconnection network, as shown if figure 2. Such a network would have to transmit "word packets", as opposed to messages or DMA transfers, in order to support the operation of the conceptual model.

## 3.1 Reflective Memory Operation

Rather than storing shared information in a separate global memory, it can be stored in the physical memory of each processor. As shown in figure 2, this space already exists, by definition. In order to maintain the programming model of a shared memory, any change to a shared location must be *reflected* to all logically equivalent locations in the

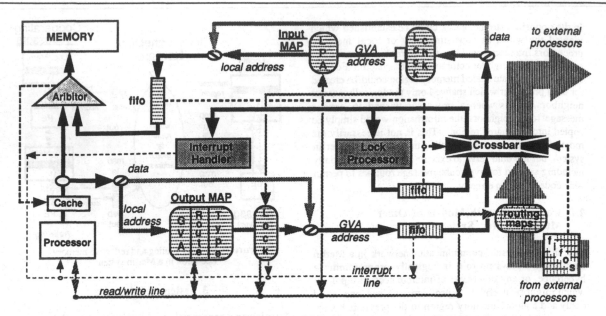

**Figure 3** - Conceptual layout of single processor interface to global virtual memory system. Illustrates reflective memory mapping, flow control, routing, and virtual memory management (locks, interrupts, etc.)

memory of processors which share this space. Shared regions are thus *duplicated* (as long as they are active) in the physical memory of all associated processors.

This use of reflected or mirrored memory considerably simplifies the architectural design, removes some potential bottlenecks, and generally enhances system performance. As illustrated in figure 2, all write operations to shared regions (solid lines) are both stored locally (as would normally occur) and broadcast, by the interconnection network, to the logically equivalent shared location in the memory of every participating processor. All read operations (dashed lines) occur locally from the processor's own memory (or cache). A simple, non-mapped, reflective memory system, of fixed size, developed by Gould, demonstrated efficient, high performance operation [11].

Replicating shared regions in each processor's memory may appear costly but it is mitigated by three factors: 1) the shared regions and their size is completely controlled by each user program; 2) maintaining multiple copies of the regions increases system performance and scalability (there are no delays or contention problems on shared read operations); and 3) technologically, memory chips will continue to get denser and cheaper. Note that both message based and shared memory architectures (which use distributed caching) maintain multiple copies of data.

A serious problem for all these architectures is latency reduction - if a process requires data which is not available locally, but is available elsewhere, how long is the delay

until it is received? In a message based system, this would be the time necessary for the sender to transmit the information to the requester, and may also include the time necessary to notify the sender that the information is needed. In a distributed cache system, the need for the data would be signalled by a cache miss. A correct copy of the information would then be located in the system and the transferred into the requestor's cache In a Merlin system, a request for information is unnecessary. Since the need for the information has been pre-established, if it is available anywhere it will either be present in the processor's local memory or it is already en route.

By dealing with individual "word packets", Merlin further reduces latency by automatically overlapping computation and communication to the fullest extent possible. Every word written to a shared region is broadcast as it is being locally stored. Since the transmission of shared data is completely independent of the local processor, it occurs in parallel with the processor's continuing computations (which may, for example, be the computation of the next shared quantity). Neither writing nor reading shared data slows down the operation of a processor, since both operations actually occur normally in the processor's own memory (see also Section 4, on Synchronization).

### 3.2 Management of Global Virtual Memory

The functional operation of a Merlin network, and the management of the virtual memory system, has been discussed elsewhere [12]. Figure 3 gives a schematic picture of data and control flow in a single processor Merlin interface. In this conceptual representation, the processing element (PE), its memory, and cache (if present) are shown on the left. To interface the PE to a Merlin environment, it's memory bus is "T'd" so that a duplicate copy of all store operations is sent to an independent Merlin communication card.

The communication card has two parts: a processor interface and an interface to the interconnection network. The first part translates local physical addresses (LPA), which are associated with shared regions, into global virtual addresses (GVA), and vice versa. A copy of the PE's memory stores are separated into address and data lines. A masked portion of the LPA is used as the index into a hardware table called the Output Map. Entries in the map are made by the PE when a mapped region is established. If no entry is present for a LPA, no further action is taken and the address (with it's associated data) are ignored.

If an entry is present, the LPA index is replaced with the entry in the table to create the appropriate GVA. Note that this type of remapping operation is very standard and can be carried out efficiently and at high speeds. When the PE initially enters a GVA into the table, it also stores some additional information. These include local routing information and, optionally, data type information. The routing information is used locally to determine the output lines on the communication card to which the global word packet will be routed (see discussion in following section).

The GVA is then used as an index into a second map table to determine if the corresponding global virtual page has been locked. If a lock is found, the global write is terminated and an interrupt is generated back to the PE (note that the PE can also read the lock table to determine status directly).

Assuming no lock is present, the GVA, with associated routing and type information, is combined with the original data to form a global 'word packet'. By current design specs, the packet would be about 128-bits long, consisting of 32-bits of virtual address, 64 bits of data, and at least 32-bits of associated data. The additional data would include such information as the ID of PE, hopcount, data type information, and various status bits. The routing information is also associated with, but not part of, the 'word packet', since it will be lost in the next stage. The global word packet then moves to a FIFO buffer for transmission to other PEs in the next stage of operation.

Receiving global information from other processors is essentially the reverse of the above procedure, albeit somewhat simpler. When a word packet, involving data shared by the processor, is received, communication interface routes the information to the input channel of the communication card. As shown in figure 3, the packet is split into address and data lines and the GVA is used as an index into a lock table. If the global page is unlocked, or if the writer has the key, the GVA is passed to the Input Map.

Again the GVA is used as an index into a translation table. If there is no corresponding entry in the table the write is killed, even though it was specifically routed here and passed through the lock check. This is an important since it gives each PE absolute control of it's own environment and security. Only the local PE can place (or remove) entries in it's associated Input Map. Thus no outside operation can access the PE's local memory without prior approval of the PE (by establishing a shared region).

If an entry is present, the GVA is replaced with the corresponding LPA from the table and the address and data lines are merged. The address replacement guarantees that an external store operation is completely confined to the local memory region allocated by the PE. The local address and data is then sent to a FIFO to be stored in the local memory as rapidly as possible.

The manner in which the local memory is physically accessed is, of course, determined by the individual PE architecture. If the memory is dual ported, for example, the external writes would simply access a second port. Alternatively, an arbitration circuit might be necessary to permit the external writes to occur when the memory bus was available (see also Section 3.4, Flow Control). If the PE is a cache based architecture, it would also be necessary to invalidate any cache lines containing the same address.

## 3.3 Interconnection System

The second stage of a processor's communication card is actually a node in the interconnection system. It should again be stressed that, in order to conform to the conceptual model, the nature of the interconnection (e.g. single bus, multiple bus, point-to-point mesh, etc.) is immaterial to the programming. Although performance may vary, a program written for a Merlin environment will execute on any other Merlin system, even if the interconnection network is totally different

With this caveat, the interconnection system selected for the prototype study is an N-dimensional mesh. Initially this will be a 2-dimensional toroidal mesh so that each PE will be directly connected to four others. Each connections is designed as unidirectional, point-to-point interconnect, so that each communication node would have four external input and four external output channels, coupled in pairs to neighboring processors. The fact that the connectivity may be varied relativity independently of the rest of the system (e.g. to support more traffic or a larger system) is a significant advantage of the Merlin design.

The interconnection channels are illustrated by the large arrows at the right side of figure 3. Each input channel has associated with it a FIFO (for buffering) and a routing map. The routing maps are tables, indexed by GVAs, which contain a bit mask defining the local routing path for the corresponding GVA. Assume, for example, there are six exit channels (two internal and 4 external channels, as shown). Each entry in the routing table would then be 6 bits long, with each bit corresponding to a exit channel. An entry of 001111 would therefore indicate that the global word packet should be broadcast on all four of the external channels.

Note that the path of a global data word is determined by its GVA and the entry in the routing table of each node through which it passes. It is not carried with the data. The path or virtual circuit between any two processors sharing the same virtual address space is therefore established by the system at the time the shared region is created. Under normal circumstances (baring system problems), these paths remain fixed for the life of the shared region. The paths are created by the PEs entering the necessary routing information in the routing table corresponding to the appropriate incoming channel.

In order to be able to maintain a weak form of data consistency, it is important that the interconnection system guarantee that *the order in which information is stored by any processor will be the order in which it is received by all participating processors.*

Other processors can easily be added to an established shared region by simply creating a path from the nearest PE which already contains the region. Similarly, failed or otherwise occupied processors can simply be routed around without user involvement. This capability also has important debugging applications. A shared region may be mapped into a previously uninvolved PE for debugging purposes. If selected carefully, the presence of this debugging PE will not change the characteristics of the system under study, and can be used to perform realtime analysis of shared memory activity.

### 3.4  Flow Control

There are three units which govern the dynamics of information flow in the system: the crossbar switches (one per PE); FIFO buffers (~7 per PE), and the PEs themselves.

The crossbar, shown in figure 3, is designed as a round robin, multipass switch. Essentially this means that each of N input channels is guaranteed access to the switch every Nth cycle. Within each cycle, however, any output channels not needed by the primary requester will be utilized to satisfy the requests of other active channels. The

only requirement is that no input channel will be permitted switch access unless all of it's output needs can be met simultaneously (i.e. no partial firing).

Because of the dynamics of the switch and the system itself, it is obvious that buffers must be available on each communication channel to facilitate flow control and to handle transient hot spots. Figure 3 shows a number of FIFO buffers in the layout of each PE's communication card. Essentially there is a separate buffer on each input line to the crossbar switch and one to buffer external writes to the PE's local memory. In a system connected as a 2-D toroidal mesh, there would be 7 buffers associated with each PE. The optimal size of these buffers are currently being investigated by simulations, but is probably on the order of 1K words each.

Although the FIFO buffers should be able to smooth out normal dynamics of the system and handle transients, it is possible that more serious hot spots could develop (due perhaps to inappropriate routing) or that the system could be over driven by a particular program. Figure 3 illustrates that every FIFO is equipped with a status line signalling a half full condition. All but one of these lines are connected to the crossbar switch's control logic. In the case of the two internal, output channels (to the Input Map and Lock Processor) these status lines will inhibit the crossbar's control unit from permitting access to these channels until the half full signal is removed.

The FIFOs associated with externally connected channels operate a little differently. When the FIFO of any channel signals the crossbar switch, the switch immediately sends an inhibit signal on the external line connected to the same PE which is transmitting to the half full buffer. This signal is stripped off by the transmitting processor's receiver (not shown) and immediately sent to the crossbar control unit on that PE. This signal inhibits the sender's crossbar from transmitting more data over the congested channel until further notice (i.e. it's FIFO is less than half full).

The system, thus far, has gracefully handled the heavy loading, filling FIFOs, temporarily closing communication channels, and generally allowing the problem to propogate, from node to node, to buffers downstream, and ultimately to the source(s). No PE has actually yet been effected, and, if the activity is transitory (i.e. burst), equilibrium will automatically be reestablished without any PE involvement.

At some point, if the heavy traffic continues, a crossbar switch somewhere in the network will be forced to block the input line from it's local, transmitting PE (see figure 3). When this happens, the FIFO associated with this line will begin to fill. When it reaches half full it will send an interrupt to the local PE itself. This interrupt signal will cause a context switch to the operating system, which will stop the active process from further transmissions. The PE's operating system may respond to such an interrupt in a variety of ways: wait until the condition has resolved itself (i.e. the interrupt goes away); execute a different task; investigate the problem (via communication with other PE's over an independent ethernet connection); notify (if the software exists) the transmitting task; notify the user; or, in bad situations, move processes to different PEs or attempt to reroute the virtual circuit. The system managment issues in such situations are the subject of continuing research.

Simulations of deliberately over driven systems have shown that the hot spots tend to occur at the interface to a PE's memory (i.e. a memory bandwidth limitation) and not within the network. This simply implys that, under worst case conditions, one PE is capable of writing information faster than another PE can absorb it. While it is hoped that such situations will be avoided by users, it is important to understand that they are not necessarily bad.

It is not unusual in multiprocessing systems, both message based and shared memory, for a PE to be temporarily blocked while access to information is being acquired. In a Merlin system, even if a PE is interrupted, the transmission of data and it's storage in memory is occurring in parallel, as rapidly as possible, throughout the network. To look at the problem differently, if a user rapidly generates large amounts of shared data, the performance of the system may be limited by the memory bandwidths of the PEs. A Merlin system would transfer data to all the processes at memory bandwidth speeds, which, given the basic problem definition, is as efficiently as it can be executed.

## 4. Synchronization

Synchronization is basically an algorithmic problem, not an architectural one. It is also true that a particular parallel architecture can make synchronization difficult and thereby significantly slow down the performance of the system. The need for synchronization, however, is a result of the approach taken to solve the problem. The requirement for frequent synchronization will adversely effect the perform-ance of a problem on any parallel architecture. Merlin offers a number of methods of dealing with synchronization requirements, ranging from self-synchronized messages, to global memory locks, to semaphores, to test-and-set oper-ations, to the technique of phased synchronization.

### 4.1 Locks, Semaphores, etc.

Since global virtual memory does not exist, it's size is only limited by the size of the address lines in the network. In the Merlin prototype currently under design, this is 32-bits, with provisions for expansion. To facilitate inter-system

communication and global memory management, the operating system reserves, at boot time, several pages of the global virtual address space for each PE in the network.

One such region is utilized for OS to OS communication. At start up time the system creates virtual circuits (routing paths) between each PE and the reserved OS page of every other PE (i.e. it creates a spanning tree rooted on each PE and covering all nodes). In a similar fashion, other dedicated regions are established on each PE to handle interprocessor interrupts, memory locks, and fetch and add operations.

Figure 3 shows a special routing circuit on each commun-ication card for handling such operations. This consists of an interrupt handler, a lock processor, and a fifo-buffered return channel to the crossbar switch. One PE can interrupt another, for example, by writing to the GVA reserved for that PE's interrupt region   This write is routed to the interrupt handler on the selected PE, which in turn actually interrupts the processor (and also supplies the ID of the interrupting PE, and a 64 bit status word).

Memory locks are handled in a somewhat similar fashion. If a region requires a lock, a request to establish one must be made to the system, and a lock address (and lockmaster) is allocated. To acquire a lock, a PE simply writes to the appropriate global virtual lock address. The lock handler on the lockmaster processes the request and returns the result to the sender. If the request is granted, a write is first initiated to the global region involved (and hence to all PEs sharing this region). Special status bits are set in this write which are intercepted by the lock checker (figure 3) on each associated PE. The lock checker recognizes this write as a 'lock set', marks the region locked (for both input and output), and stores the 'key' or ID of the lock owner. The local PE is not involved in any of these operations.

Each lock processor is also designed to support a primitive fetch-and-add type of capability within it's own special memory. A fetch-and-add location is requested and assigned by the system. A variable can then be stored in the location. Writes to this location by any PE will cause the lock processor to return the current value of the variable to the PE, and add the value written to the variable. This is carried out in one cycle and useful for such functions as queue management, etc.

### 4.2 Phased Synchronization

Phased synchronization is an method of handling inter-dependent parallel operations in an quasi-asynchronous, overlapped fashion. The approach is often quite successful in eliminating synchronization barriers and other bottle-necks to efficient parallel operation [13]. A limited type of

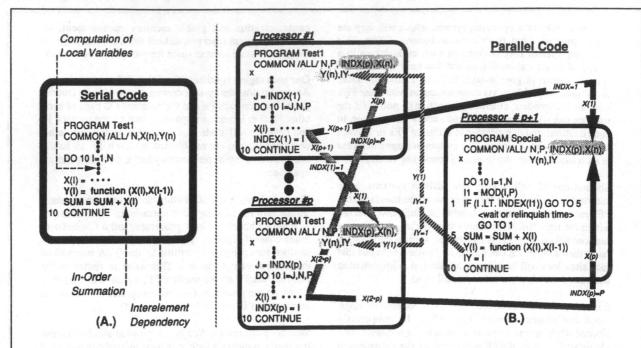

**Figure 4** - (A.) An example of serial fortran code with a barrier sum and interelement loop dependencies;
(B.) A parallel decomposition of the code using phased synchronization.

phased synchronization was supported in hardware on the Alliant Computer FX/8 [14]. In this case, interdependent loop computations were identified by the compiler and the associated memory references tagged. Processors could then execute independent loop segments until a tagged, or dependent location was encountered. The process was then halted until the necessary value was stored by another processor.

The approach taken by Alliant, while serving as an example, was restrictive and not scalable. Generally speaking, for phased synchronization to be practical it is necessary that the supporting architecture be capable of frequently broadcasting small amounts of information throughout the system with minimal overhead and latency. This can be illustrated by the simple example in figure 4.

Figure 4A shows a small serial fortran code with a loop containing an interelement dependency (y(i+1) cannot be computed until x(i) is calculated) and requiring the computation of an in-order summation (perhaps for reproducibility due to possible round-off errors). Such a program would typically not be amenable to parallel processing. Figure 4B, however, illustrates how the problem can be run in parallel by utilizing a phased synchronization approach.

The program is first separated into independent and dependent phases. The dependent code, shown on the right

in figure 4B, contains the essentially serial portion of the computation. The remaining independent code is, by construction, now parallelizable. The 'N' executions of the loop is now spread over 'P' processors as shown. In order share the results of the parallel computation, a shared common block called 'ALL' is created, containing the arrays X and Y where the computational results are stored. In this example the region ALL is defined as a globally shared region prior to the execution of the programs. Figure 4B illustrates how computational results are then simultaneously transmitted and stored, word-at-a-time, in the local memories of the processors.

The dependent computation can not, however, proceed until the necessary information is available from other processors (not unlike a macroscopic form of data flow). To provide this information, an array named 'INDX' was created and added to the globally shared region. Each entry in this array corresponds to a value for the loop index 'I' in each of the P processors. Note that the processors store the current value of this index *after* computing each value of X(I). As shown in figure 4B, the processor executing the dependent code is continually receiving values of X and INDX from the parallel computations.

Since the dependent code needs to execute the loop sequentially, it is necessary to test to verify the presence of the next X value in its local memory or to wait for its arrival. This process is thus executing in a phased manner, synchronizing at each step with the parallel computation. Even though the dependent process can not begin execution until after X(1) is available and cannot end until X(N) is received, most of the serial computation is overlapped with the parallel computation and executed concurrently

This approach requires no formal locks or messages (in the traditional sense), is extremely efficient, and can easily be adapted to handle a wide variety of other situations in which parallel processing is difficult [13] (e.g. conditional branches, load balancing, queuing, etc.). Phased synchronization operates on the principal that if processes can determine, from moment to moment, the status of information in the system, dependent computations can often be safely overlapped with other computations, thus breaking many traditional parallel processing barriers.

## 5. Summary

Merlin provides a very high performance 'anticipatory' (as opposed to a 'demand') approach to sharing memory in multicomputer environments. It provides a programming model which supports both local and dynamically created shared memory. The system eliminates all software involvement in the actual sharing of information, and yet permits shared memory regions to be created between between any set of cooperating processes. Communication latency between processors is minimized, and essentially eliminated, due to the automatic instruction-level overlap of communication and computation.

The Merlin approach can also be used, in the future, to support heterogeneous multicomputer systems (e.g. micros, mainframes, vector, systolic, database, AI, etc.). It would permit processors either to be utilized independently or, as needed, to be welded together into cohesive subsystems.

The programming flexibility of the system, it's utilization of high-level languages (including mixed language support), and the topology-independent nature of it's operation, should provide users with a versatile, high-performance system that can be logically programmed to match individual application requirements. The ability of a system to rapidly and efficiently disseminate single words of information, permit the use of phased synchronization techniques which, in turn, open up new approaches to parallel problem decomposition in a multiprocessor environment.

Investigations into system design issues are continuing. Simulations are being used to examine routing algorithms and to study network traffic patterns and behavior under heavy loading. Operating system and language extensions, to support the operation of global virtual memory, are also being developed, together with parallel debugging tools.

## REFERENCES

[1.]  J. Edler, A. Gottlieb, C. P. Kruskal, K. P. McAuliffe, L. Randolh, M. Snir, P. J. Teller and J. Wilson, "Issues Related to MIMD Shared-Memory Computers: The NYU Ultracomputer Approach", *IEEE Proc. 12th Intl. Symposium on Computer Arch.*, Boston, MA, June 1985, 126-135.

[2.]  G. F. Pfister, W. C. Brantley and D. A. George, "The IBM Research Parallel Processor Prototype (RP3): Introduction and Architecture", *Proc. 1985 Int. Conf., on Parallel Processing*, 1985, 764-771

[3.]  D. J. Kuck, E. S. Davidson, D. H. Lawrie and Ahmed H. Sameh, "Parallel Supercomputing Today and the Cedar Project", *Science*, 231, (28 Feb, 1986), 967-974.

[4.]  C. L. Seitz, "The Cosmic Cube", *Commun. Assoc. Computing Mach.*, 28, 1985, 22-33.

[5.]  L.-Felipe, E. Hunter, M. J. Karels and D. A. Mosher, "User-Process Communication Performance in Networks of Computers", *IEEE Transactions on Software Engineering 14*, 1, (January 1988), 38-53.

[6.]  Geoffrey C. Fox, "Concurrent Processing for Scientific Calculations", *COMPCON 84*, San Francisco, CA, February, 1984, 70-73.

[7.]  W. Crowther, J. Goodhue, E. Starr, R. Thomas, W. Milliken and T. Blackadar, "Performance Measurements on a 128-Node Butterfly Parallel Processor", *Proc. of the Int. Conf. on Parallel Processing*, August, 1985, 531-540.

[8.]  B. J. Smith, "A Pipelined Shared Resource MIMD Computer", *Proc. 1978 Int. Conf. on Parallel Processing*, 1978, 6-8

[9.]  A. Agarwal, R. Simoni, J. Hennessy, and M. Horowitz, "An Evaluation of Directory Schemes for Cache Coherence", *15th Intl. Symposium on Computer Architecture*, 1988.

[10]  E. A. Arnould, J. Bitz, E. C. Copper, H. T. Kung, R. D. Sansom and P. A. Steenkiste, "The Design of Nectar: A Network Backplane for Hetrogeneous Multicomputers", *Proc. 3rd Int. Conf. Arch. Support for Prog. Lang. and Op. Sys. (ASPLOS III)*, Boston, MA, April, 1989.

[11.]  Christopher Wilks, "SCI-Clone/32 - A Distributed Real Time Simulation System", *Computing in High Energy Physics*, edited by Hertzberger and Hoogland, North-Holland Press, 1986, 416-422.

[12.]  Larry D. Wittie and Creve Maples, "Merlin: Massively Parallel Hetrogeneous Computing" *Proc. 1989 Int. Conf. on Parallel Processing*, St. Charles, Illinois, August 1989, 142-150.

[13.]  Creve Maples, "Phased Synchronization and Parallel Computing", to be published.

[14.]  Robert Perron and Craig Monday, "Architecture of the Alliant FX/8", *Digest of Papers for COMPCON '86*, March, 1986, 390-393.

# A Simulation Study of Hardware-Oriented DSM Approaches

Aleksandra Grujić

Milo Tomašević

Veljko Milutinović

*Department of Computer Engineering*
*School of Electrical Engineering*
*University of Belgrade*
*POB 816*
*11000 Belgrade, Serbia*
*Yugoslavia*

## Abstract

*Representative hardware implementations of the distributed shared memory (DSM) concept are comparatively evaluated in this study—two NUMA (Dash and SCI) and two COMA (KSR1 and DDM) architectures. Analysis was oriented towards the comparison of approaches, rather than their implementations. For that purpose, a hierarchical two-level cluster-based system with a uniform bus-based cluster structure on the first level is assumed. The DSM mechanisms of four approaches were simulated on the second level. The simulation methodology based on the synthetic address traces was applied. The comparison was carried out for a large variety and a broad range of system-oriented, application-oriented, and technology-oriented parameters. The results have shown somewhat better efficiency of COMA protocols (because of dynamic migration of responsibility for shared data) and the large impact of available interconnection network bandwidth on system scalability (an almost linear speedup is achieved with ring-based systems).*

## 1. Introduction

Distributed shared memory systems (DSM) represent a successful hybrid of two parallel computer classes: shared memory multiprocessors and distributed computer systems [1]. They provide the shared memory abstraction on the top of message passing in distributed computer systems and combine the advantages of both approaches. In that way, physically distributed memory becomes logically shared. The widely used programming model of shared memory is known as a simple, general, and efficient one. In addition, programs using this paradigm are highly portable. On the other side, by applying the concept of distributed computing, very powerful and cost-effective systems characterized by good scalability are easily achievable. Because of that, the concept of distributed shared memory is recognized as one of the most attractive solutions for building large-scale, high-performance multiprocessor systems.

DSM systems vary greatly in regard to their architectures, algorithms, and approaches for implementation of DSM mechanism. Among them we focused our attention on hardware implementation of the DSM concept, since the inherent performance of this approach is most promising. The best way for the full comprehension of the issues in this field is an extensive evaluation analysis of the selected examples.

## 2. Problem Statement

DSM is currently a very active research area, with significant prospective benefits for the future. The DSM mechanism can be implemented in software or in hardware. Involvement of software layers usually increases the latencies to shared address space considerably, and, therefore, hardware-oriented approaches are preferred, since they can be much faster. Hardware implementations are also more frequently found in commercial systems. Because of that, hardware-oriented DSM approaches deserve special attention.

These techniques are founded on the well studied principles of coherence maintenance in private caches in shared-memory multiprocessor systems, since the granularity of sharing is usually of cache block size.

This research was partially supported by FNS/FTRS, Belgrade, Serbia, Yugoslavia and IFACT, Belgrade, Serbia, Yugoslavia. The research problem was defined by Encore Computer Systems, Fort Lauderdale, Florida. Questions by fax (+381) 11-762215 or email milutino@pegasus.ch or
fon.uucp!etfbg!earn_007@moumee.calstatela.edu or
earn_007%etfbg%fon.uucp@moumee.calstatela.edu

Reprinted from *Proc. IEEE Region 10's 9th Ann. Int'l Conf.*, 1994, pp. 386–390.

This fine-grain sharing ensures shorter latencies in transferring data, and prevents the adverse effects of false sharing. A prevalent number of DSM systems of this kind complies to NUMA type of system architecture. It is characterized by physically separate cluster memory modules, scalable interconnection network, and directory-based coherence. Shared address space is statically distributed among local memory modules (home property). A new type of DSM architecture was recently proposed—COMA architecture, in which cluster memory modules are implemented as large caches (called attraction memories). In this manner, data items are allowed to replicate and migrate fully dynamically upon program demands.

Since these types of architectures are recognized as the two most promising directions for scalable, high-performance systems with hardware DSM support, their further examination is quite justified (see [2]). To this end, we have chosen two representative approaches from each class in order to evaluate them. From the NUMA class, we have selected the Stanford's Dash [3] as a prominent research system and an SCI-based system [4] as an example of a possible commercial system. On the other side, following a similar principle, the DDM [5] research multiprocessor and the KSR1 [6] commercial massively parallel processing system were chosen.

Therefore, the intention of this study is the comparative evaluation of the suggested systems by means of simulation analysis [7]. The main prerequisite for this analysis is to establish the conditions for fair comparison between systems that widely differ in a number of issues. With this provision, simulation analysis has to quantify the performance and scalability of the approaches for a broad range of values of relevant parameters.

## 3. Evaluation Methodology

The goal of this evaluation study is to provide the precise and reliable comparative quantitative measures of the potential performance and scalability for the selected HW oriented DSM systems. Earlier evaluation studies of DSM architectures and algorithms used either analytical [8,9] or simulation means [2,10]. In this study, the simulation methodology is adopted as very convenient, since it allows considerable flexibility in changing the values of parameters of interest. Four functional simulators (one per each DSM system) were built using the DARPA standard N.2 package [11].

### 3.1 The underlying system architecture

Since the primary goal is to evaluate the concepts, we

made an effort to assume the common architectures in all the cases and to disregard the implementation dependent differences as much as possible. Only the details that are inherent to a specific approach were made different in order to preserve the characteristics of the approach itself. For the purpose of fair comparison, certain modifications had to be made to the original system architectures in order to adapt them to a common basis. Therefore, so called "-like" systems were evaluated, even if they are sometimes referred to with the original names in the text, for the sake of brevity.

A two level hierarchical system structure is assumed. The system consists of variable number of clusters connected by means of an interconnection network: ring for the KSR and SCI, bus in the DDM, and mesh in the Dash. Each cluster is composed of up to four processors with local caches, the cluster bus, and the network interface. Local cluster memory (or equivalent attraction memory) is also assumed.

Processors are RICS-like with one instruction per cycle (except for loads and stores). Only a data cache is assumed. Cost of local cache hits is one cycle, and cache misses fetch the entire cache block. Cache coherence is maintained according to the approach-specific protocol. A synchronous split transaction cluster bus with round robin arbitration policy is assumed. Physical main memory is equally distributed across clusters. Specific values of system- and technology-oriented parameters are given in Table 1.

### 3.2 The Workload Model

We have adopted the well-proven synthetic workload model used in [12], somewhat revised and adapted for this purpose. The model treats the private data stream in a probabilistic manner, while shared space is represented with a number of cache size blocks with specific addresses. Temporal locality of shared references is reflected by organizing them in the form of a least recently used (LRU) stack. The list of workload parameters with their values is presented in Table 2.

In our model, each cluster is the home node for equal amount of shared blocks, preassigned at the initialization time. In SCI- and Dash-like systems, this static distribution of home property is preserved throughout the entire simulation. However, in the KSR- and DDM-like systems, shared blocks change its owner dynamically over the time according to its current use by some processor in the system. Since each cluster is the home for N shared blocks (total shared address space divided by the number of clusters) in the beginning, we included the ability of rearranging the LRU stack in the way that first N addresses from the top of the stack are home addresses

Table 1. The list of system-oriented and technology-oriented parameters.

| Parameter | Min. | Typ. | Max. |
|---|---|---|---|
| CPU clock cycle [ns] | 10 | 30 | 30 |
| cache read time [ns] | 20 | 30 | 30 |
| cache write time [ns] | 20 | 30 | 30 |
| ring clock cycle [ns] | 1 | 2 | 2 |
| DDM bus clock cycle [ns] | 10 | 30 | 30 |
| mesh clock cycle [ns] | 10 | 33 | 33 |
| number of clusters | 4 | 8 | 32 |
| number of processor per cluster | 1 | 4 | 4 |
| cache block size [words] | 4 | 4 | 16 |
| word length [bytes] | 4 | 4 | 4 |

Table 2. The list of workload parameters.

| Parameter | Min. | Typ. | Max. |
|---|---|---|---|
| Max number of processor cycles between two memory references (uniform distribution) | 5 | 7 | 9 |
| Locality parameter | 2 | 4 | 6 |
| Probability of shared reference | 0.05 | 0.1 | 0.15 |
| Write probability | 0.2 | 0.3 | 0.4 |
| Number of shared blocks | 256 | 1024 | 2048 |
| Cache hit ratio for private data | 0.98 | 0.98 | 0.98 |

for that cluster, in order to be able to simulate the locality in distribution of the application. If chosen, rearranging of the LRU stack is made at initialization time instead of the usual random distribution of shared blocks.

### 3.3 Performance indicators

Our basic performance measures are processor utilization and overall system power (calculated as the sum of processor utilizations), since these figures directly express the amount of work that can be done in a specific period of time. Another important performance indicator is average latency of shared memory references, from issuing the processor request for memory access until the access is completed. This average cost generally consists of two parts: local component (access latency inside the cluster) and network component (traversing delay of requests and

data over network, which also includes the waiting time to access the network). A lot of other relevant statistics is also provided.

## 4. Results of the Analysis

Only a limited number of the most important results is presented in this chapter. In this simulation analysis, special attention was devoted to the wide diversity of conditions under which we performed the comparison to make the picture as complete as possible. Three groups of parameters were regarded as the most relevant: system-oriented, application-oriented, and technology-oriented parameters.

### 4.1 Impact of system-oriented parameters

In order to evaluate performance and scalability, the number of clusters in the system is varied and the impact on performance indicators is observed. This effect can be clearly recognized from Figure 1, which presents the processor utilization for the compared approaches. It shows that for very small system sizes, the performance of all the systems is quite comparable. Increasing the number of clusters makes that the processor utilization decreases in all cases, as can be expected. However, the differences among them are evident. While the performance of other contenders shows a graceful degradation, an abrupt decline of the DDM performance can be noticed even in the medium-scale system, which implies much lower scalability of the DDM. The KSR1 and the SCI attain almost linear speed up, as well as the Dash, although at a somewhat lower level of performance. On the contrary, the DDM system power saturates at a low level relatively quickly, and even decreases for higher number of clusters. Evidently, there is a maximum system power that can be achieved under the assumed conditions, and the adding of new clusters is useless (and even counterproductive).

References to distributed shared memory are the main cause for performance differences among them.

The mean time cost for a shared memory reference (Table 3) is very illustrative of that. The local component is an indicative measure for the efficiency of the coherence protocol itself implemented on a common cluster structure. Results pointed out that COMA seems to be more efficient than NUMA. When regarding the delay inside the cluster, KSR1 shows the shortest latency, except for the large system sizes where DDM latency is somewhat shorter. This can be explained by the fact that this latency includes the time to acquire the cluster bus, and DDM internal bus utilization is much lower, since the saturation of the DDM system bus causes the lower rate of memory references. Average cluster delay per shared memory reference in NUMA systems is higher, because of the involvement of "home" clusters in the management of remote memory references. Lower mean latency of the KSR1 compared to the SCI is attributed to the fact that remote miss is satisfied in only the rarely occurred cases, while the missed request in the SCI is sent to the home cluster in the first place, and that it can be forwarded to the current head of the list (which may require an additional ring pass).

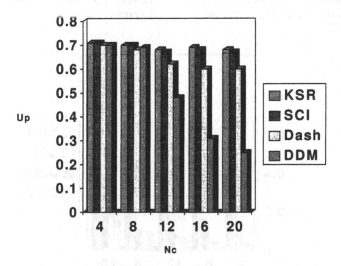

Figure 1. Impact of system size on processor utilization. Up = processor utilization; Nc = number of clusters.

Table 3. Impact of system size on average shared memory latency.

| | | Number of clusters | | | | |
|---|---|---|---|---|---|---|
| | | 4 | 8 | 12 | 16 | 20 |
| Average memory latency [ns] | KSR | 104 | 156 | 197 | 230 | 261 |
| | SCI | 108 | 167 | 218 | 261 | 302 |
| | DASH | 146 | 265 | 364 | 452 | 511 |
| | DDM | 129 | 255 | 949 | 2166 | 3480 |
| Average network latency [ns] | KSR | 1 | 4 | 7 | 11 | 16 |
| | SCI | 2 | 7 | 13 | 21 | 29 |
| | DASH | 35 | 91 | 136 | 182 | 209 |
| | DASH | 22 | 98 | 763 | 1963 | 3256 |
| Average local latency [ns] | KSR1 | 103 | 152 | 190 | 219 | 245 |
| | SCI | 106 | 160 | 205 | 240 | 273 |
| | DASH | 111 | 174 | 228 | 270 | 302 |
| | DDM | 107 | 157 | 186 | 203 | 224 |

While the efficiency of protocols is not much different, network delays among these implementations vary greatly, and can be considered as the predominant factor for the distances in their scalability. Figure 2 shows the consumed percentage of the total bandwidth of system network that interconnects the clusters (ring in the KSR1 and the SCI, mesh in Dash, and the DDM bus in the DDM). The drastically higher utilization of the DDM bus was expected, since it is much slower than the fast point-to-point links. Even for 12 clusters the DDM system bus bandwidth is almost fully utilized, while the ring utilization is less than 20 percent even for

20 clusters. The slower bus transfer is not the main reason for lower performance (ring traversals between distant nodes can also accumulate a reasonable delay, and mesh delay between two clusters is of the similar amount). The severe contention on the bus when a larger number of clusters compete for obtaining this shared source is even more responsible for the performance degradation and the significantly higher delays. This suggests that depth of bus hierarchy should be increased for large systems, and that the number of clusters per level is lower than in a ring-based hierarchy.

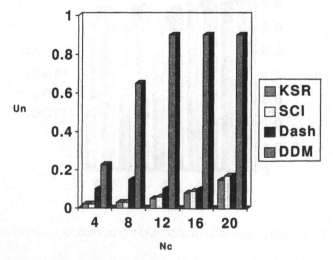

Figure 2. Network utilization for various system sizes. Un = network utilization; Nc = number of clusters.

Constant decreasing of hit ratio for all four approaches was noticed, as a consequence of an increased contention for the same amount of shared address space. Therefore, the probability of invalidation for a particular block is higher, and it is less likely that shared data will be found in local cache. Nearly equal results are the consequence of the same applied coherence policy—invalidation. Percentage of cache misses satisfied locally also decreases with the number of cluster. The probability of local data supply is somewhat higher in the Dash than in other systems because of the existence of write back messages that update the memory copy of the home cluster during supplies from remote dirty copies induced by some read request of some other cluster. It is also interesting to analyze the probability that an outgoing request for data will be satisfied by the home cluster or a non-home cluster (head in SCI or remote dirty in Dash). The collected statistics show that SCI and Dash significantly differ in that sense. The ratio of home to head supply in SCI drastically reduces with system size, while the ratio of home to remote dirty supply only moderately decreases in Dash, as a consequence of more frequent updating of home copies by write-back actions.

### 4.2 Impact of application-oriented parameters

The performance of a DSM system depends heavily on the typical memory reference characteristics of the application. One of the most preferred characteristics exhibited in memory accessing is the property of locality. The next experiment examined the impact of temporal locality by varying the value of the corresponding workload parameter—lower (L1), default (B), and higher temporal locality (Lh).

The results for system power in the system with 8 clusters are presented in Figure 3, that shows the beneficial effects of a better temporal locality for all compared approaches. Shorter period between two accesses to the same shared block increases the probability that the already fetched data are still in the cache (not invalidated by some other processor in the meantime). This is clearly reflected on cache hit values, shown in Figure 4, which indicates the increased data reusability in the local cache. Average memory reference cost decreased accordingly (especially the local component), since the read miss penalty is amortized over more accesses. The largest gain is experienced in DDM, since the contention for DDM system bus was greatly relieved and the amount of network component of mean access latency was almost halved. This component of access latency is also relatively more decreased in Dash, as it can be seen from Figure 5, which presents the ratio of network component and the mean memory access time.

Besides usual spatial and temporal locality recognized in the uniprocessor applications, an even more influential type of locality is relevant for the multiprocessor environment—processor locality, which can cut down the amount of coherence overhead in the system. Although the adopted workload model is not suitable to simulate different processor locality, we tried to measure this effect by appropriate distribution of shared blocks before execution by localized initialization of the LRU stack. Therefore, although the processor can access any shared block from the entire address space, references are very likely to be localized in its own working set, at least in the beginning. Two variants were compared: B—default (with random initialization), and W—with localized initialization, for the system of 8 clusters.

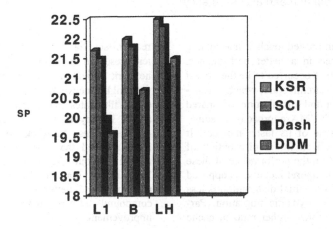

Figure 3. Impact of temporal locality parameter on system power. SP = system power.

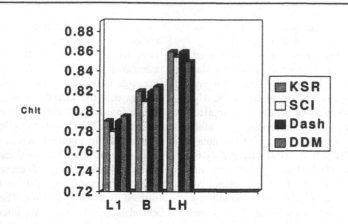

Figure 4. Efficiency of caching. Chit = hit ratio in private caches.

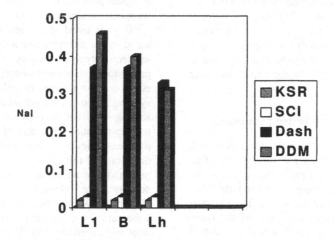

Figure 5. Impact of the temporal locality parameter on the network component of memory access time. Nal = network component of mean access latency.

It is evident that the improved locality in accessing shared references resulted in a better performance. The gain in system power is occurred to be the largest in Dash, a typical NUMA architecture, which is especially sensitive to the initial distribution of shared data. The SCI—another NUMA approach—is somewhat less affected, because of its faster network. It was shown that the localized initial distribution of data was more influential on the performance of these two approaches than the temporal locality, as opposed to COMA approaches where initial distribution is less significant, because of the dynamic migration. Particularly important is the much higher ratio of cache read misses that are satisfied locally, inside the cluster, presented in Figure 6. This leads to the reduced network utilization, especially important for systems with higher network latencies (Dash and DDM). Figure 7 illustrates the shortening of average memory access latency achieved by an improved locality in private caches. Network component was relatively more reduced than the local component, since the number of out-of-cluster messages was cut down. Experiments that combined both localized initial placement and better temporal locality have shown compound effects with a further performance improvement.

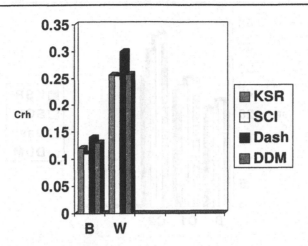

Figure 6. Ratio of local cache read misses that are satisfied inside the cluster. Crh = cluster read hit.

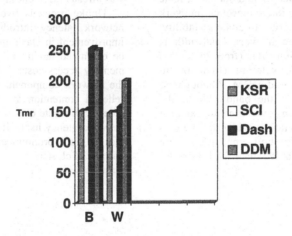

Figure 7. Shared memory access latency. Tmr = average shared memory reference costs.

### 4.3 Impact of technology-oriented parameters

Current and future trends in the field of computer engineering are characterized by permanent advances in the computer technology. Having this fact in mind, one of the very important elements is the potential of the current concepts and system architectures to take the advantage of the advanced technology in years to come.

Processor technology is one of the fastest growing and improving technologies, and that led us to examine the benefits that can be obtained by faster processors. First, the sole effect of different CPU speeds is examined, and three values are assumed for the CPU cycle time: B (30ns, default), Cl (20ns), C2 (10ns).

The results presented in Figure 8 indicate that all approaches benefited from using faster processors, but not to the same extent. While KSR1 and the SCI (and even Dash) achieved an almost liner speedup, performance movement in DDM is less rapid and tends to saturate. The reason again can be found in the limited bandwidth of DDM that cannot keep up with the increased traffic due to a larger number of references from faster processors. An interesting fact that average memory latencies are higher as CPU cycle time shortens can be explained by more severe contention on the cluster bus and increased waiting for bus access. Thus, local component of memory latency is responsible for this behavior for all systems, as well as the network component in DDM and Dash.

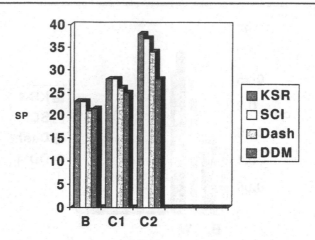

Figure 8. Impact of processor speed on system power. SP = system power.

All previous experiments pointed out the extreme importance of the large interconnection network bandwidth of the DSM in order to attain scalability. Because of that, increased network bandwidth is simulated by halving the ring cycle (from 2ns to 1ns) and shortening the network cycle time (from 30ns to 20ns and 10ns) for Dash and DDM. Although no troubles were spotted with the bandwidth of the KSR1 and the SCI systems, we tried to examine what happens if the bandwidth is widened. The performance improvements for both approaches were found to be really neglectable, since the bandwidth was already wide enough.

Unlike previous two approaches, decreasing the network latency introduced a visible performance improvement in Dash and especially DDM. This can he explained having in mind the values for average memory access costs from Table 4. It is evident that the network component is significantly reduced. The relieved contention and shorter waiting on network access contribute even more to this decrease than the network latency itself. It can be expected that this effect is more pronounced in systems with a higher number of clusters.

Table 4. Impact of network cycle on average shared memory latency.

|  |  | Network cycle [ns] | | |
|---|---|---|---|---|
|  |  | 10 | 20 | 30 |
| Average memory latency [ns] | DASH | 202 | 227 | 265 |
|  | DDM | 162 | 189 | 255 |
| Average network latency [ns] | DASH | 22 | 48 | 92 |
|  | DDM | 13 | 37 | 98 |
| Average local latency [ns] | DASH | 180 | 179 | 173 |
|  | DDM | 149 | 152 | 157 |

## 5. Conclusion

Under the stated conditions, the analysis confirmed that the DSM concept is a viable solution for the building of powerful and high performance multiprocessor systems. A local, intercluster component of an average shared memory access latency in COMA approaches indicated that dynamic migration of ownership has a beneficial effect an the efficiency of DSM algorithm. However, it was pointed out that the interconnection network bandwidth and latencies play the dominant role in determining the system scalability. Although only two-level systems are simulated, it can be concluded that ring-based systems achieve an almost linear speed up for the examined configurations, showing good scalability. On the other side of the spectrum, bus-based systems practically limit the number of clusters per one level, thus an increased depth of hierarchy is needed. The performance of the evaluated approaches is especially susceptible to memory referencing characteristics. However, an improved locality in accessing the shared references results in lower network utilization and better performance. It was also demonstrated that the evaluated approaches can take the advantages of the emerging faster technologies.

## 6. References

[1] Nitzberg, B. and V. Lo, "Distributed Shared Memory: A Survey of Issues and Algorithms," *Computer*, Vol. 24, No. 8, Aug. 1991, pp. 52–60.

[2] Stenstrom, P., T. Joe, and A. Gupta, "Comparative Performance Evaluation of Cache Coherent NUMA and COMA Architectures," *Proc. 19th Int'l Conf. Computer Architecture*, ACM Press, New York, N.Y., 1992, pp. 80–91.

[3] Lenoski, D. et al., "The Stanford Dash Multiprocessor," *Computer*, Mar. 1992, pp. 63–79.

[4] Gustavson, D., "The Scalable Coherent Interface and Related Standards Projects," *IEEE Micro*, Feb, 1992, pp. 10–22.

[5] Hagersten, E., A. Landin, and S. Haridi, "DDM—A Cache Only Architecture," *Computer*, Sept 1992, pp. 44–54.

[6] "KSR1 Technical Summary," Kendall Square Research Corp., Waltham, Mass., 1992.

[7] Tomašević, M. and V. Milutinović, (eds.) *Cache Coherence Problem in Shared Memory Multiprocessors: Hardware Solutions*, IEEE Computer Society Press, Los Alamitos, Calif., 1993.

[8] Hagersten, E. and S. Haridi, "A Quantitative Comparison of Efficiency for Large Shared Memory Architecture," Technical Report, SICS, Apr. 1993.

[9] Stumm, M. and S. Zhou, "Algorithms Implementing Distributed Shared Memory," *Computer*, May 1990, pp. 54–64.

[10] Kessler, R.E. and M. Livny, "An Analysis of Distributed Shared Memory Algorithms," *Proc. 9th Int'l Conf. Distributed Computing Systems*, IEEE Computer Society Press, Los Alamitos, Calif., 1989, pp. 498–505.

[11] "N.2 Tutorial," TDT Corporation, Cleveland Heights, Ohio, 1992.

[12] Archibald J. and J.-L. Baer, "Cache Coherence Protocols: Evaluation Using a Multiprocessor Simulation Model," *ACM Trans. Computer Systems*, Vol. 4, No. 4, Nov. 1986, pp. 273–298.

# Chapter 6

# Distributed Shared Memory Hardware/Software Hybrid Approach

## Editors' Introduction

Chapter 6 is devoted to a set of distributed shared memory (DSM) solutions that take advantage of combining both hardware and software techniques for DSM management. It includes the following papers:

1. R. Bisiani and M. Ravishankar, "PLUS: A Distributed Shared-Memory System," *Proc. 17th Ann. Int'l Symp. Computer Architecture*, IEEE CS Press, Los Alamitos, Calif., 1990, pp. 115–124.

2. D. Chaiken, J. Kubiatowicz, and A. Agarwal, "Software-Extended Coherent Shared Memory: Performance and Cost," *Proc. 21st Ann. Int'l Symp. Computer Architecture*, IEEE CS Press, Los Alamitos, Calif., 1994, pp. 314–324.

3. A.W. Wilson, Jr., R.P. LaRowe, Jr., and M.J. Teller, "Hardware Assist for Distributed Shared Memory," *Proc. 13th Int'l Conf. Distributed Computing Systems,* IEEE CS Press, Los Alamitos, Calif., 1993, pp. 246–255.

4. J. Kuskin, et al., "The Stanford FLASH Multiprocessor," *Proc. 21st Ann. Int'l Symp. Computer Architecture*, IEEE CS Press, Los Alamitos, Calif., 1994, pp. 302–313.

Early research projects such as Memnet and IVY, with the goal to explore the innovative concept of DSM, typically involved entirely hardware or software implementations. However, as usually happens in design choices that consider the hardware/software trade-offs, neither of the two approaches has all the advantages. While being completely transparent to the programmer and very successful in reducing the memory access latency, high-performance hardware solutions may result in complex and high-cost implementations. On the other hand, the increasing complexity of new algorithms can be handled efficiently in software implementations with their improved flexibility in suiting the actual environment and access patterns, at some expense to performance.

The ideas about using a combination of hardware and software in implementing DSM were generated as natural solutions to the problems in building pure hardware- and pure software-oriented systems. Some level of software support can be used in order to manage the high complexity of originally hardware-oriented solutions. Alternatively, the efficiency of software solutions can be increased by using appropriate low-cost hardware accelerators, with the goal of improving the performance of the most critical operations. In some hardware-implemented systems (such as Dash), the programmer's notion of specific application behavior can be supported by some sophisticated software mechanisms such as prefetching. On the other hand, an integrated approach to some originally software-oriented solutions (such as Linda) resulted in the building of coprocessors (for example, the Linda Machine) that can partly replace the pure software implementation. Although some of these solutions could be regarded as hybrid DSM systems, since they use the other approach to some extent, the set of systems presented in Chapter 6 includes those that use the combination of hardware and software features as a basic principle.

Bisiani and Ravishankar, in their paper "PLUS: A Distributed Shared-Memory System," propose an architecture intended for efficient execution of a single multithreaded process. After a discussion about strong and weak ordering, they conclude that the weak ordering model combined with specific synchronization operations *(fence, issue, verify)* can improve the performance of their PLUS system. Shared virtual address space consists of pages that can be replicated and migrated under software control. Consistency in each node is maintained by a hardware coherence manager that is based on a nondemand, write-update mechanism, triggered directly by the memory reference. Page replication and migration can be adapted to the access pattern by the programmer, if it is known in advance, or it can be handled by hardware that counts the number of references from each processor to each page. Further optimization is achieved by minimizing the update paths through the nodes by means of copy-list ordering by the operating system kernel. The PLUS system also provides several interlocked, delayed operations intended for efficient synchronization. A performance evaluation study, based on a simulation analysis, has shown the viability of the concept of replicated data using a write-update mechanism.

The paper "Software-Extended Coherent Shared Memory: Performance and Cost," by Chaiken and Agarwal describes a way to maintain the consistent memory view of Alewife—a large-scale distributed shared memory multiprocessor developed at MIT. Its strongly consistent DSM mechanism is based on a hardware-oriented directory coherence scheme with a limited number of pointers in each directory entry, counting on fewer incidences of sharing in most cases. Exceptionally, when the number of hardware pointers is not sufficient, additional pointers are emulated in software. In that relatively infrequent case, an interrupt is generated and the full-map directory entry is emulated. A spectrum of protocols with different number of pointers is considered and two implementations of protocol extension software are discussed: flexible C interface and fast assembly language handlers. The results of performance evaluation for different numbers of pointers are presented for various applications. Finally, some viable extensions to the basic concept are also suggested.

Another effort to apply both hardware and software methods in order to increase the performance of a DSM system is presented in the paper "Hardware Assist for Distributed Shared Memory," by Wilson, LaRowe, and Teller. After spotting the drawbacks of existing software DSM approaches (page bouncing, lower speed, and so on) the authors compare the invalidate and update-based coherence mechanisms using a simple model. It is found that, according to the simulation results, data transfer requirements are reduced with update protocols. Consequently, the authors advocate the addition of a hardware-assisted update protocol to software-based distributed shared memory. This hybrid principle is applied in the Galactica Net system, a multiprocessor that consists of mesh-connected nodes with local memories. Page replication and optional invalidation strategy are achieved through the operating system routines. On the other hand, a special hardware logic provides distributing and multicasting of the updates to the "update-shared" pages. Provisions for the implementation of a competitive algorithm (combined invalidates and updates) are also supplied in this system.

An interesting solution that combines hardware and software methods is reported in the paper "The Stanford FLASH Multiprocessor," by Kuskin et al. The basic idea is to implement the coherence protocol in software, but to remove the burden of its execution from the main processor of the node by adding dedicated hardware—a specific protocol processor. The authors have adopted the protocol used in the Dash multiprocessor, where it was implemented in hardware, and applied it with some modifications, using a custom node controller called MAGIC (Memory and General Interconnection Controller). MAGIC consists of a memory controller, an I/O controller, a network interface, and a programmable protocol processor, having a 64-bit superscalar core. The programmable processor makes FLASH very flexible and convenient for experimenting with various protocols. The authors also implement the message-passing protocol, as well as the DSM protocol, all in the system-level simulator. Preliminary performance measurements show that the sustained rate at which MAGIC can supply data depends on the memory system, and that the flexible protocol processing is not the limiting factor in MAGIC's performance.

## Suggestions for Further Reading

1. A. Agarwal, B. Lim, D. Kranz, and J. Kubiatowicz, "APRIL: A Processor Architecture for Multiprocessing," *Proc. 17th Ann. Int'l Symp. Computer Architecture*, IEEE CS Press, Los Alamitos, Calif., 1990, pp. 104–114.
2. S. Ahuja, et al., "Matching Language and Hardware for Parallel Computation in

the Linda Machine," *IEEE Trans. Computers*, Vol. 37, No. 8, Aug. 1988, pp. 921–929.

3. R. Chandra, et al., "Performance Evaluation of Hybrid Hardware and Software Distributed Shared Memory Protocols," Technical Report No. CSL-TR-93-597, Computer Systems Laboratory, Stanford University, Stanford, Calif., December 1993.

4. A. Wilson, et al., "Lynx/Galactica Net: A Distributed, Cache Coherent Multiprocessing System," *Proc. 25th Ann. Hawaii Int'l Conf. System Sciences*, IEEE CS Press, Los Alamitos, Calif., 1992, pp. 416–426.

# PLUS:
# A Distributed Shared-Memory System

Roberto Bisiani and Mosur Ravishankar
School of Computer Science
Carnegie Mellon University
Pittsburgh, PA 15213

**Abstract.**
PLUS is a multiprocessor architecture tailored to the fast execution of a single multithreaded process; its goal is to accelerate the execution of CPU-bound applications. PLUS supports shared memory and efficient synchronization. Memory access latency is reduced by non-demand replication of pages with hardware-supported coherence between replicated pages. The architecture has been simulated in detail and the paper presents some of the key measurements that have been used to substantiate our architectural decisions. The current implementation of PLUS is also described.

## 1. Introduction.

Shared memory is one of the most popular parallel processing models because of the ready availability of bus-based shared-memory systems. Bus-based systems are relatively easy to build, but, because of their limited bus-bandwidth, do not perform well with fast processors, large number of processors, or algorithms that have a poor cache hit-ratio. In fact, most shared memory systems are limited to 10-20 processors or to slow processors and their main application is executing a non-parallel multi-user Unix load. On the other hand, the system we are building, called PLUS, is aimed at efficiently executing a single multithreaded process by using distributed memories, hardware supported memory coherence and synchronization mechanisms.

In order to maintain reasonable memory performance with a large number of fast processors it is necessary to distribute the memory among the processors and connect them with a scalable communication mechanism. The implementation of such a physically distributed, but logically shared, memory system is difficult, because communication latency hinders fast access to remote memories. The operations that cause performance degradation are *remote memory access* and *synchronization*.

This research is sponsored by the Defense Advanced Research Projects Agency, DoD, through ARPA Order 5167, and monitored by the Space and Naval Warfare Systems Command under contract N00039-85-C-0163. Views and conclusions contained in this document are those of the authors and should not be interpreted as representing official policies, either expressed or implied, of the Defense Advanced Research Projects Agency or of the United States Government. Part of the implementation is sponsored by AppleComputer, Inc.

Caching is the key to implementing fast remote memory access. Usually, caching is performed by hardware on demand, together with a protocol that guarantees memory coherence. In order to be effective in a medium/large system, this requires a substantial amount of fast and expensive hardware. PLUS relies on software-controlled, non-demand caching of data among multiple memories, and a simple protocol implemented in hardware to insure memory coherence. This mechanism is described in Section 2.

The latency of synchronization operations often cannot be reduced by caching, because these operations require exclusive access to synchronization variables. Systems that use caching with invalidation must ensure no other cache has a copy of the synchronization variable before performing the synchronization. PLUS makes it possible to hide the elapsed time between the start of a synchronization operation and its completion by providing separate mechanisms for each. This mechanism and its uses are described in Section 3.

This paper is mainly concerned with architectural issues, see [4] for a description of the software environment.

Although PLUS is aimed at the execution of a single, multithreaded program, some of the ideas proposed in this paper can be applied to a general-purpose, multiuser system.

## 2. Memory Access.

Memory access protocols can be described according to the kind of ordering they enforce and the caching mechanisms they use. We will touch on these questions in general before we describe PLUS's protocol.

### 2.1 Strong and Weak Ordering.

Most programmers take for granted that the result of a sequence of write operations performed by a processor will be immediately observable by any other processor exactly in the same order as it was performed. On a bus-based system, all write operations can be easily made visible to all the processors either by immediately announcing them on the bus (as in a write-through protocol) or by announcing them only when necessary (as with copy-back protocols). These systems are

Reprinted from *Proc. 17th Ann. Int'l Symp. Computer Architecture.*, 1990, pp. 115–124.

*sequentially consistent* [16] and *strongly ordered* [8], and let programmers use ordinary read/write memory operations to implement synchronization operations.

When there are multiple physical memory units and there is no global communication medium, enforcing strong ordering requires time consuming protocols. Fortunately, a weaker form of ordering, in which actions performed by one processor do not immediately have to become visible to all the other processors, is usually sufficient.

Typically, a parallel program alternates between a long sequence of normal read and write operations on shared data structures and synchronization operations (e.g. P and V). Enforcing strong ordering among normal read and write operations is not necessary, if the programmer understands that a synchronization operation should be used whenever two concurrent computations have to obey a specific order in accessing the shared data. A memory system with these characteristics is said to implement *weak ordering*. See [18, 8] for a formal definition.

When a system implements a weak-ordering model, programmers must *explicitly* flag synchronization operations for the system to implement them correctly. For example, a buffer shared between a producer and a consumer process is usually associated with a flag that is set when the buffer is full and cleared when it is empty. In a weakly ordered system, if the flag and buffer are allocated in separate memory modules and only normal read and write operations are used, it is possible for the consumer to observe the flag as full *before* the writes to the buffer have completed. For a weakly ordered system to work correctly, operations on the flag must be strongly ordered. We believe most programs will port to a weakly ordered system without any change. For example, we have examined the code of the Mach operating system kernel and found that a synchronization had been implemented as a normal access only in one case.

In general, a computation only needs to insure the ordering of *some* of its actions in relation to a *few* other selected computations. This is very hard to express and very hard to implement in the general case, but possible in some special cases. For example, if the data that are accessed in a critical region are all stored in a cache line, the QOSB, Test_and_Set and Unset operations proposed for the Wisconsin Multicube [12] guarantee correct behavior without strict ordering. This is due to the fact that these operations return the cache line upon successful locking, the semaphore is part of the line *and* a cache line is guaranteed to be coherent by the caching protocol.

Another form of weak ordering, called *release consistency*, has been proposed for the DASH multiprocessor [10]. Under this model only certain kinds of synchronization operations enforce a specific ordering, allowing for more flexibility than in the weak-ordering model.

PLUS provides three ways of improving the performance of synchronization operations. First, an explicit *fence* operation (see Section 2.3) is available to implement strong ordering of synchronization operations when necessary (as opposed to the more restrictive approach of always enforcing strong ordering at synchronization time). Second, PLUS splits an atomic read-modify-write operation into an *issue* primitive and a *verify* primitive that reads the result; the execution of the operation can proceed concurrently with other computation. Finally, in contrast to other RISC systems, the set of read-modify-write operations comprises rather complicated operations.

## 2.2 Caching Mechanisms.

In order to obtain good performance, a bus-based system has to maintain multiple copies of read/write data and minimize the number of write operations. In pursuing these goals, snooping protocols have evolved from simple write-through to the increasingly sophisticated write-once [11], write-invalidate [15] and write-update [17] protocols.

For example, the DRAGON [17] protocol achieves very good performance, because it keeps multiple copies of shared data even if the data are being written by more than one processor, thus avoiding the ping-ponging of shared data. As a consequence, it has far fewer write misses (fewer by a factor of six, compared to a simple *write-through-with-invalidate* protocol, for one of the applications evaluated in [1]). The DRAGON protocol broadcasts an update only if other caches indicate (with a bus signal) that the line is shared, as opposed to simpler protocols that either blindly broadcast every write or blindly invalidate all copies on the first write.

Protocols that use fewer write operations are beneficial in centralized-memory bus systems, because they use less memory and bus bandwidth. In a distributed-memory non-bus-based system both memory and communication bandwidth grow with the number of processors, so it is not always necessary for a protocol to minimize the frequency of writes.

Moreover, since latency in moving data is much larger in distributed-memory systems than in bus-based systems, using a protocol that does not invalidate other copies, but instead updates them, is very useful in minimizing the cost of cache misses.

PLUS uses a write-update protocol in which all writes to shared data are propagated to all the copies. The latency of write operations does not stall the processor, because multicast operations to update the copies are carried out independently by dedicated hardware.

## 2.3 PLUS's Coherence and Caching Mechanism.

PLUS caching mechanism is an extension of the mechanisms described in [2,3]. Each PLUS node (see Figure 2-1) contains one processor with its cache, some local memory and a memory-coherence manager that is linked to other nodes through a fast interconnection network. The local memory is used both as main memory and as a cache for data in other nodes' memories. Note that any data in the local memory may also be cached in the processor cache. In order to avoid confusion, we use the terminology *replicated data* to mean data stored in more than one node's local memory, and *cached data* to mean data stored in the processor cache.

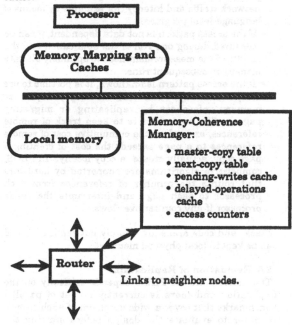

**Figure 2-1: A PLUS Node.**

PLUS uses a non-demand, write-update coherence protocol for the replicated data. The unit of replication is a page (whose size is dictated by the memory management system of the off-the-shelf CPU, 4 Kbytes in the current implementation). However, the unit of memory access and coherence maintenance is one (32-bit) word. Pages are replicated at the request of software, but the coherence manager hardware is aware of this replication and automatically keeps copies coherent. The rest of this Section describes the replicated memory structure and the implementation of coherent read and write operations.

A virtual page corresponds to a list of physical pages replicated on different nodes. The first item of this list is called the *master* copy. (An unreplicated page *only* has the master copy). A node maps each virtual page to the most convenient physical copy, i.e. the closest copy. The global address of a physical page is a *<node-id, page-id>* pair and is generated directly by the memory-mapping mechanism of the processor.

The operating system kernel orders the copy-list to minimize the network path length through all the nodes in the list. On each node, the replication structure is made visible to the coherence manager via the *master* and *nextcopy* tables, which are maintained by the operating system. For each locally replicated physical page, the master table identifies the global physical page address of the master copy, and the next-copy table identifies the successor, if any, of the local copy along the copy-list.

Read operations are implemented as follows. The *node-id* field of the translated physical address determines which node is addressed, and the page-id field specifies the page within that node. If the local node is indicated, the local memory is read. Otherwise, the coherence manager sends a read request to its counterpart in the specified remote node, waits for the response, and passes the returned data to the processor.

Write operations are more complicated, because they must take effect on every copy. Writes are always performed first on the master copy and then propagated down the ordered copy-list. This insures that all copies eventually contain the same data when all writes issued by all processors have completed. (This property is called *general coherence* [18]). The coherence manager handles writes as described below.

If the physical address indicates a remote node, the coherence manager sends a write request to that node (note that the remote node might not be the master). Otherwise, it checks the master table to determine the master-copy location. If the master copy is local, it carries out the write on the local memory, and sends an *update* request to the next copy, if any (determined by looking up the next-copy table). If the master copy is not local, it sends a write request to the node that has the master copy.

A coherence manager, that receives a write request, also goes through the process of making sure the write begins at the master copy. A coherence manager, that receives an update request, updates its memory and sends another update request to the next copy, if any. Finally, the last copy in the copy-list returns an acknowledge to the processor that originated the write operation, thus completing that operation. General coherence is guaranteed since copies of a given location are always written in the same order.

Write operations do not block the issuing processor while they propagate through the copies and a processor can issue several writes before blocking. However, reading a location that is currently being written blocks until the write completes. This is achieved by remembering the address of incomplete write operations in the pending-writes cache of the coherence manager and guarantees strong ordering within a single processor independently of replication (in the absence of concurrent writes by other processors). There is no such guarantee with respect to another processor. In particular, actions by one processor may be observed out of order by other processors.

When strong ordering is necessary between processors, e.g. for correct synchronization, a processor must use a *fence* operation, which causes the coherence manager to block any subsequent write by the processor, until all its earlier ones have completed (this is implemented by waiting until the pending-writes cache is empty). The processor can then proceed with the synchronization operation. A similar technique was proposed for the RP3 [6] multiprocessor. Three kinds of fence operations have been described in [10]: *write-fences* that block all subsequent writes, *full fences* that block all subsequent reads and writes, *immediate fences* that block only the next operation. PLUS implements explicit write fences that wait for all previous writes. A more aggressive implementation could use immediate fences. PLUS *does not* enforce full fences as part of synchronization operations, as in DASH. Instead, the user can explicitly issue the fence operation when appropriate (see Section 3-1).

Note that contents of a processor's local memory can be cached in the processor's primary cache. In order for writes to eventually propagate to all copies, all writes by a processor must be visible to its coherence manager. Hence, replicated pages must be cached with a write-through policy. At the remote site, a snooping protocol on the node bus ensures coherency between memory and cache whenever the coherence manager carries out a write or update operation.

### 2.4 Memory Mapping.

Since PLUS executes one multithreaded process at a time, all nodes use the same virtual memory space and, because of replication, different nodes might map the same virtual page to different physical copies.

Although the page tables could be fully shared, it is more efficient if each node maintains its own page tables. These tables do not have to contain all the possible mappings but only those that are actively used by the node. If a node accesses a page that is not mapped by the local page tables, the exception handler checks in a centralized table if the mapping is legal and then updates the local tables. This *lazy evaluation* of page tables limits the amount of interference caused by dynamic memory allocation and requires less memory than if the tables were fully replicated.

Software is responsible for page placement and replication policies, but the hardware helps in performing them. Deleting a copy is akin to removing a page in a paging operating system, since all the nodes that have a copy of the page must update their address translation tables and flush their TLBs. Replicating a page can be done almost entirely as a background activity: first the new entry is added to the copy-list at a convenient point, and then the hardware copies the data from the previous copy. (Note that the copy operation can be overlapped with writes to the same page by any

processor in the system, without destroying the page integrity.) When the new page has been fully written, each node can update the address translation tables to use the new copy. Page migration is achieved simply by creating a copy and then deleting the old one.

Page replication and migration can be used in three ways, possibly at the same time:

- If the access pattern is known to the programmer it is possible to request a memory layout that minimizes network traffic and latency (for example by means of language-level pragmas).
- If the access pattern is not data dependent, it can be measured during one run of the application and the results of the measurement used to optimally allocate memory in subsequent runs.
- If the access pattern is unknown, it is possible to use competitive algorithms [5] that try to optimize memory references by replicating or migrating pages. The basic idea is to keep track of remote references, and, when the cumulative cost of remote references to a page exceeds the cost of creating a page copy, actually create a copy locally. In PLUS, competitive algorithms are supported by hardware that counts the number of references from each processor to each page and interrupts the node processor if any counter overflows.

Stack and code areas are usually not replicated, and can be kept in local physical memory.

### 2.5 Evaluation of Replication.

The performance of PLUS depends critically on the application and there is currently no set of parallel benchmarks that cover a wide spectrum of applications. In order to evaluate the design before starting the implementation, we have used a few applications that we knew very well and that stress the characteristics of the architecture. These include a production system applications, a shortest-path program, and a speech recognition system. We also carried out some experiments with synthetic loads as reported in [2]. We built a PLUS simulator that is driven by an application program in C language. A library package provides functions to create simulated shared memory and to allocate it on the nodes specified by the user. When the program reads or writes data allocated in shared memory, the simulator emulates the actions of the coherence manager and the network. Caching, coherence management, routing and memory access are simulated and instrumented in detail. From the instruction stream, the simulator also computes an approximate estimate of execution time between simulated shared memory references. Unfortunately, such a detailed simulation cannot be performed for systems larger than about 100 processors, because of the time and memory space needed.

The Single Point Shortest Path problem is a good example that requires many synchronization operations.

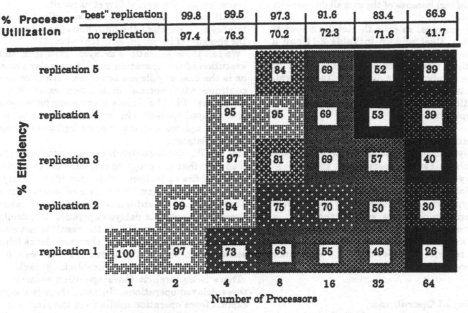

| % Processor Utilization | "best" replication | 99.8 | 99.5 | 97.3 | 91.6 | 83.4 | 66.9 |
|---|---|---|---|---|---|---|---|
| | no replication | 97.4 | 76.3 | 70.2 | 72.3 | 71.6 | 41.7 |

**Figure 2-1:** Effect of Replication on Total % Efficiency (graph) and % Processor Utilization (top table) for the Single Point Shortest Path Application.

The problem involves finding the minimum cost to traverse a graph from one vertex to any other vertex. Both sequential and concurrent algorithms for this problem work by propagating the distance cost from one vertex and updating it until no more updates are possible.

| Number of Copies | Reads Local/Remote | Writes Local/Remote | Ratio Total/ Update |
|---|---|---|---|
| 1 | 1.25 | 3.40 | 6.18 |
| 2 | 1.70 | 1.18 | 2.91 |
| 3 | 1.84 | 0.70 | 2.24 |
| 4 | 2.14 | 0.45 | 1.89 |
| 5 | 2.32 | 0.36 | 1.68 |

**Table 2-1** Effect of Replication on Messages.

The basic step in a concurrent implementation consists in choosing a vertex from a queue of vertices to be examined and computing the cost of moving to each of its neighbors. If the new cost is better than the cost stored at the vertex, the cost is updated and the vertex is queued for further expansion. When there are no more vertices to expand, the algorithm terminates. Each step requires three kinds of synchronization operations: extracting a vertex from the queue, locking a vertex in order to update its cost atomically, and inserting a vertex into the queue. Each step takes about 20 μs of processing time (not including synchronization), on a 20 MHz Motorola 88000 and requires an average of eight synchronization operations.

Our implementation uses multiple queues since, owing to queue bandwidth limitation, a single queue introduces serialization and requires long remote accesses. The vertices are evenly distributed among the nodes and there is one queue associated with each node. If a processor extracted work only from its queue, some processors would remain idle for part of the time, especially if the ratio of number of vertices to the number of processors is low. For a better load balance each processor must extract work from other queues when its local queue is empty. The shared memory model and the ability to replicate data are very helpful in this case. We have replicated the queues and vertices on more than one processor and found a substantial performance increase due to better load balancing. Figure 2-1 shows the efficiency of the algorithm and the *utilization*, i.e. ratio of average useful processor time to elapsed time for different levels of replication. With no replication, the utilization decreases substantially when more than 2 processors are used; while with replication it remains high until the number of processors exceeds 32. When more than 32 processors are used, most processors are idle waiting for work, since the problem is not large enough to occupy all processors.

Table 2-1 shows how the ratio of local to remote operations changes with replication in the 16-processor case of Figure 2-1. An increase in replication causes a drop in the number of remote reads and an increase in the number of remote writes and updates. Such a tradeoff is usually beneficial because of the overall decrease in remote read latency.

As replication increases, so does the total number of network messages (last column in Table 2-1) and a larger percentage of them is used to update copies. In this application there were no bad consequences, because the network was only lightly loaded. In general, however, uncontrolled replication can result in the system getting flooded with update requests, slowing down useful computation.

### 3. Synchronization.

Caching is only marginally useful in improving the latency of synchronization operations, since these operations always involve competitive and exclusive accesses to a variable.

For example, synchronization operations can severely degrade the performance of a system that uses a snooping coherence protocol. Constructs such as *test-and-test-and-set* were invented to minimize the overhead caused by the interference between the coherence protocol and the synchronization operations.

### 3.1 PLUS's Delayed Operations.

PLUS provides several variants of interlocked read-modify-write memory operations. Like writes, these operations take effect at all copies of the addressed location, beginning with the master and propagating down the copy-list. However, the master, in addition to executing the operation atomically and forwarding update requests to the next copy, also returns the old contents of memory to the originating node. Since this result always has to come from the master copy, there can be a substantial delay between the initiation of the operation and the availability of its result.

PLUS allows the user or the compiler to hide this latency by separating the initiation of an operation from the checking of its result, as described in [2].

We call these operations *delayed operations*, since the execution of the operation overlaps regular processing, as is the case of delayed branches. The processor can continue with normal instruction execution in the meantime. PLUS also lets a processor have more than one delayed operation in progress at any time (8 in the current implementation), thereby further reducing their average latency.

In PLUS, synchronization instructions return an identifier that the program can later use to retrieve the result of the operation. This identifier is simply the address of a location in the delayed-operations cache. This location is automatically allocated when the processor executes a delayed operation and deallocated when it reads the result. If the result is not available when the processor reads it, the read blocks (since the software can inspect the status of these locations, it is also possible to implement a non-blocking read).

There is no implicit fence operation associated with these delayed operations. Instead, there is a separate, explicit fence operation available to the programmer. It is the responsibility of the programmer or the compiler to use these primitives to implement synchronization correctly. This scheme leaves substantial room for speed improvement through code scheduling and selective use of the fence operation. (For instance, there is usually no need to issue a fence before a P operation).

The delayed operations available in the current implementation of PLUS are described in Table 3-1. The cost of a delayed operation comprises three components: the time taken by the processor to issue the operation, the

| Operation | Description | Execution cycles by the coherence manager |
|---|---|---|
| xchng | Return current value and write 30-bit unsigned word. | 39 |
| cond-xchng | Return current value of memory. If top bit set, write 30-bit unsigned word. | 39 |
| fetch-and-add | Return current value of memory. Increment memory by given signed word. | 39 |
| fetch-and-set | Return the current value and set top bit. | 39 |
| queue | (Addressed location contains offset in addressed page to tail of queue.) Return current word at tail. If top bit of tail clear, write given word there, set top bit, and increment the offset (modulo maximum queue size) to next word in queue. | 52 |
| dequeue | (Addressed location contains offset in addressed page to head of queue.) Return current word at head. If top bit of head set, clear it and increment the offset (modulo maximum queue size) to next word in queue. | 52 |
| min-xchng | Return current value, store given value if smaller than the original value. | 52 |
| delayed-read | Return current value, no modification | 39 |

**Table 3-1:** PLUS's Delayed Operations.

time taken by the coherence manager to execute the operation and obtain the result (the processor is not involved in this), and the time taken by the processor to read the result. The first step takes approximately 25 cycles (each cycle in the current PLUS implementation takes 40ns). The time to perform the second step can be divided into communication time and processing time. The round trip communication time between two adjacent nodes is about 24 cycles; if the nodes are not adjacent each extra hop adds 4 cycles (these numbers were measured on the router used in the current implementation). The processing time depends on the operation; an estimate based on the detailed hardware design is shown in Table 3-1. The last step, the processor reading the result, takes about 10 cycles, assuming the result is available. As a comparison, the cost of a remote (blocking) read is about 32 cycles plus the round-trip network delay.

Appendix) we see that, although a single kind of primitive is used (fetch-and-add), it must be used three times to correctly perform a queuing operation. As we saw before, there is a substantial delay until the result of each synchronization operation is available. If we execute a number of synchronization primitives in short succession, the issuing processor will be idle most of the time, and hiding this latency will be hard.

Performance can be improved if more powerful primitives such as the queue and dequeue operations in Table 3-1 are used. These primitives reduce the total number of read-modify-write operations compared to queues implemented with simpler primitives. We believe that a reasonable set of complicated synchronization operations is a better choice for distributed-memory systems. We evaluated different sets of synchronization operations by writing various algorithms and measuring their performance on our simulator. The

```
/* lock variable "lock" initialized to 0, i.e. busy,
    variables QP and DQP contain offsets within page to tail and head of queue,
    QP and DQP initialized to 0 and all queue words initially empty (top bit clear) */

LOCK:  if(fadd(lock, 1) != 0) {    /* lock unavailable, queue myself for obtaining lock */
        while (queue(QP, myID) & 0x80000000); /* spin if queue is full, unlikely */
        wait();                     /* go to sleep until someone wakes me up and gives me the lock */
    }                               /* my thread has lock */
   - - - - - - - - - - - - - - - - - - - - - - - - - - - - - - -
UNLOCK:  if (fadd(lock, -1) > 1) (/* some other thread waiting for lock, pop its ID from queue */
        while (! ((k = dequeue(DQP)) & 0x80000000)); /* loop if queue is empty */
        wake_up(k &= 0x7fffffff);  /* k == ID of next process in queue, wake it up; */
    }                               /* thread k now has lock */
```

Table 3-2: Lock with Queue.

## 3.2 Complex is Better.
It is often argued that simpler operations are better: the implementation is simpler and faster and the user has an easier time mastering them. In principle, many existing primitives like test-and-set and fetch-and-add are, alone, sufficient to implement all synchronization operations. (See [12] for a summary of state-of-the-art synchronization primitives). However, we should keep in mind that speed is the main concern in synchronization and not ease of use. Hardware synchronization primitives should not be used directly by users and should be either encapsulated in higher level constructs or directly generated and optimized by a compiler.

If we look at the implementation of queue operations with a fetch-and-add (see the paper by Gottlieb et.al.[13],

synchronization operations available in PLUS are part of the delayed operations, which are listed in Table 3-1. These operations allow the implementation of many common synchronization data structures, such as semaphores, queues, lists barriers and high-contention locks. For example, Table 3-2 shows the code for implementing a lock in such a way that contenders, failing to acquire the lock, can queue themselves up for obtaining it, without flooding the system with unsuccessful attempts. In terms of operations over the network, this mechanism has the same complexity as Goodman's QOSB mechanism, but is not bound to a particular cache implementation.

Delayed operations are also used for purposes other than synchronization:
  • The *min-xchng* operation is useful in load balancing algorithms that need a global

approximation of the minimum or maximum value of some variable.

- The *delayed-read* operation is like an ordinary read, except that it proceeds asynchronously and the result can be retrieved later. Since several such operations can be in progress simultaneously, this is useful for hiding the latency of remote read operations. However, it needs careful, handcrafted code or a clever optimizing compiler. We do not currently have such a compiler.

### 3.3 Software Pipelining and Context Switching.
Delayed synchronization allows two latency-avoidance

able to make good use of delayed synchronization in many cases.

Context switching is an extremely attractive way of hiding latency and a few systems based on fast context switching have been built [14] or proposed [19]. The usefulness of context switching depends mostly on the ratio between the context switch time and the time between context switches. If a context switch were to cost only a few processor cycles, it would solve all latency problems, and could be used whenever remote memory is accessed. Unfortunately, this is not possible with off-the-shelf processors.

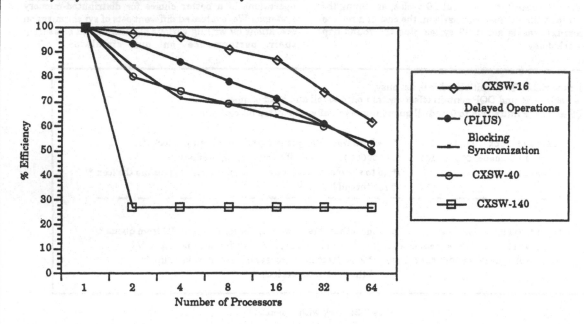

**Figure 3-1:** Efficiency of the Beam Search Application
with Different Synchronization Costs.

techniques: software pipelining and context switching.

Software pipelining is typically implemented by the compiler but, in some cases, it can be exploited directly by the programmer. For example, we programmed a primitive that returns a pointer to a free element in a queue with very little latency, because it eagerly asks for a new element every time the user consumes the previous element (the first time it is called, it retrieves two elements). In another case we have been able to issue a number of lock requests in advance, so that part of the latency was absorbed by the computation.

Although we do not have a compiler that takes advantage of delayed synchronization, we have been

### 3.4 Evaluation of Delayed Operations.
We show the performance of a beam search algorithm that searches a Hidden Markov Model representation of the speech process (a directed graph) and returns the most likely sequence of words. Beam search requires a very fine-grain parallel decomposition and a substantial amount of synchronization. Typically, a processor must dequeue one vertex from the list of vertices to be processed, lock all the vertices that follow it and finally queue a new vertex. This inner loop can be coded in about 70 RISC instructions and requires about 10 memory references per iteration, which cause about 3 cache misses if the cache line contains four words. (The

algorithm has spatial locality but almost no temporal locality.)

Queue operations on a central queue cause too much serialization, owing to bandwidth limitation at the queue. As with the shortest-path problem, the queue is split into local queues, one at each processor, to avoid this bottleneck. In this case, because of the highly data-dependent behavior of beam search, it is likely that some queues will become empty before others and some processors will remain idle and create a load imbalance. This load imbalance can be overcome by sharing a queue among a number of processors instead of keeping them all disjoint.

Figure 3-1 compares the performance with different context switching overheads and with delayed operations. The *blocking synchronization* curve has been computed by running a program that waits for synchronization primitives to return a result before proceeding. The *delayed operations* curve has been computed by explicitly programming the pipelining of synchronization operations:

• the next vertex is dequeued in parallel with the processing of the current state;

• the locking of all next vertices is performed in parallel.

The programming burden of these changes was easily hidden in two macros, so the code is not very different from the blocking-synchronization case. The context-switch curves were computed by simulating a context switch every time a synchronization operation was issued. The cost of the context switch was set to 16, 40 and 140 processor cycles (the curves in Figure 3-1 are labeled with this cost).

As expected, very fast context switching has the best performance but delayed operations are more effective than a context switching mechanism with a 40-cycle overhead. To put things in perspective, a state-of-the-art RISC processor might need to save and restore about 15 registers. If this operation can be performed entirely in cache, a context switch would cost about 40 cycles (including the instructions necessary to decide which is the new context). If the processor misses in cache, it would cost about 140 cycles because of the bus and memory latency (we are assuming a four-word line fetch takes 15 cycles). Future commercial processors might include wide busses between registers and local memory. In this case the save/restore operation could be completed in fewer cycles and the performance of the top curve of Figure 3-1 might become possible.

The results in Figure 3-1 are more pessimistic than those reported by Weber and Gupta in [19]. This is probably due to two factors. First, our application has a very short inner loop. Second, our assumptions about network delay and interface overhead (sending and receiving a message) are more conservative than theirs.

### 4. Related Work.

PLUS represents a specific trade-off in the space of distributed-memory architectures that range from large-granularity LAN-based machines, to message-passing machines, to hierarchical-bus machines to full-fledged directory-based shared-memory machines.

Operating system researchers have devised techniques to implement shared memory across distributed systems, for example by means of shared memory servers [9]. The problem with these solutions is that, regardless of network and processor speed, they result in large software overhead because the basic mechanism is paging. Faster networks will improve the performance of these systems to the point where the physical transfer of a page will take a negligible amount of time but the software overhead (a few milliseconds on one-Vax-MIP machines) will remain. Of course the usability of such systems depends heavily on the application.

Intelligent message coprocessors that relieve the main processor of the task of sending a message are now common in message passing machines. Nevertheless, the overhead to send and receive a message is still larger than 10 µseconds for state-of-the-art systems. Most of this overhead is again due to software. PLUS also uses hardware to interface processor and network, but the hardware does not require any software interface, e.g. a send function, because it is triggered directly by a memory reference.

Multiple-bus systems like the Wisconsin Multicube and Encore's extension of the Multimax, which employ an extended form of snoopy caching, and directory-based systems like DASH and the proposed SCI standard are all true shared-memory systems, and all employ sophisticated caches and cache-coherence protocols. PLUS relies on software-controlled non-demand replication of pages to achieve the same goals without the high hardware cost. We believe that in many single-user applications PLUS will perform as well as any of these machines.

### 5. Current Implementation.

The current implementation of PLUS uses a general purpose Motorola 88000 processor (25 MHz) with 32 Kbytes of cache and 8 or 32 Mbytes of main memory at each node. The memory is organized in two interleaved banks to sustain the burst bandwidth needed for cache line accesses. Global memory mapping, coherence management and atomic operations are performed by a hardware module that is implemented with Xilinx PLD's and PAL's. (It is possible to implement this module in a single ASIC device.) In this implementation, each node can have up to 8 writes and 8 delayed operations in progress. The interconnection network uses a mesh router designed at Caltech [7]. Each router has five pairs of I/O links: one for the processor and one for each of its mesh neighbors. Links operate at 20 Mbyte/second in each direction. SCSI devices, audio peripherals and host computers can be attached to each node. The implementation of PLUS is at an advanced stage. A one-node prototype has been running since November 1989, and we expect to have a working multinode system in the Summer of 1990.

## Acknowledgments.

Some ideas were originated by discussions with Lawrence Butcher and Andreas Nowatzyk. Raj Reddy and Duane Adams have been, as always, instrumental to the survival of this project. We are also extremely grateful to George White of Apple Computer, Inc. for his support. The first prototype was built with the help of John Figueroa of On Target Associates.

## References

1. Agarwal, A., Simoni, R., Hennessy, J., and Horowitz, M. An Evaluation of Directory Schemes for Cache Coherence. In *15th Int. Symp. on Comp. Arch.*, IEEE, May 1988, pp. 280-289.

2. Bisiani, R., Nowatzyk, A., and Ravishankar, M. Coherent Shared Memory on a Message Passing Machine. Tech. Rept. CMU-CS-88-204. School of Computer Science, Carnegie Mellon University, December, 1988.

3. Bisiani, R. and Forin, A. Multilanguage Parallel Programming of Heterogeneous Machines. *IEEE Trans. on Comp.* 37, 8 (August 1988), 930-945.

4. Bisiani, R. and Ravishankar, M. Shared-Memory Programming on the PLUS Distributed-Memory System. In *The Fifth Distributed Memory Computing Conference*, IEEE, Charleston, SC, April 1990.

5. Black, D.L., Gupta, A., and Weber, W. Competitive Management of Distributed Shared Memory. In *Compcon '89*, IEEE, Spring 1989.

6. Brantley, W.C., McAuliffe, K.P., and Weiss, J. RP3 Processor-Memory Element. In *1985 International Conference on Parallel Processing*, IEEE Computer Society, 1985, pp. 782-789.

7. Dally, W.J. and Seitz, C.L. Deadlock-Free Message Routing in Multiprocessor Interconnection Networks. *IEEE Trans. on Computers C-36*, 5 (May 1987), 547-553.

8. Dubois, M., Scheurich, C., and Briggs, F. Memory Access Buffering in Multiprocessors. In *13th Int. Symp. on Comp. Arch.*, IEEE, June 1986, pp. 434,442.

9. Forin, A., Barrera, J., and Sanzi, R. The Shared Memory Server. In *Intl. Winter USENIX Conference*, USENIX Association, San Diego, CA, February 1989, pp. 229-244.

10. Gharachorloo, K., Lenoski, D., Laudon, J., Gupta, A., and Hennessy, J. Memory Consistency and Event Ordering in Scalable Shared-Memory Multiprocessors. Tech. Rept. CSL-TR-89-405. Computer Systems Laboratory, Stanford University, November, 1989.

11. Goodman, J.R. Using Cache Memory to Reduce Processor Memory Traffic. In *10th Int. Symp. on Comp. Arch.*, IEEE, June 1983, pp. 124-131.

12. Goodman, J.R., Vernon, M.K., and Woest, P.J. Efficient Synchronization Primitives for Large-scale Coherent Multiprocessors. In *3rd ASPLOS*, IEEE, Boston, April 1989, pp. 64-73.

13. Gottlieb, A. The NYU Ultracomputer - Designing an MIMD Shared Memory Parallel Computer. *IEEE Trans. on Computers C-32*, 2 (February 1983), 175-189.

14. Jordan, H.F. Performance Measurements on HEP - a Pipelined MIMD Computer. In *10th Int. Symp. on Comp. Arch.*, IEEE Computer Society, June 1983, pp. 207-212.

15. Katz, R.H., Eggers, S.J., Wood, D.A., Perkins, C.L., and Sheldon, R.G. Implementing a Cache Consistency Protocol. In *12th Int. Symp. on Comp. Arch.*, IEEE, Boston, June 1985, pp. 276-283.

16. Lamport, L. Solved Problems, Unsolved Problems and Non-Problems in Concurrency. *Operating Systems Review 19*, 4 (October 1985), 34-44.

17. McCreight, E. The Dragon Computer System: An Early Overview. Tech. Rept. Xerox Corp., September, 1984.

18. Scheurich, C.E. *Access Ordering and Coherence in Shared-memory Multiprocessors*, Ph.D. dissertation, Also published as Tech, Rep. No. CENG 89-19, Computer Engineering - University of Southern Califirnia, May 1989.

19. Weber, W. and Gupta, A. Exploring the Benefits of Multiple Hardware Contexts in a Multiprocessor Architecture: Preliminary Results. In *16th Int. Symp. on Comp. Arch.*, IEEE, June 1989, pp. 273-280.

# Software-Extended Coherent Shared Memory: Performance and Cost

David Chaiken and Anant Agarwal
Laboratory for Computer Science
Massachusetts Institute of Technology
Cambridge, MA 02139

## Abstract

*This paper evaluates the tradeoffs involved in the design of the software-extended memory system of Alewife, a multiprocessor architecture that implements coherent shared memory through a combination of hardware and software mechanisms. For each block of memory, Alewife implements between zero and five coherence directory pointers in hardware and allows software to handle requests when the pointers are exhausted. The software includes a flexible coherence interface that facilitates protocol software implementation. This interface is indispensable for conducting experiments and has proven important for implementing enhancements to the basic system.*

*Simulations of a number of applications running on a complete system (with up to 256 processors) demonstrate that the hybrid architecture with five pointers achieves between 71% and 100% of full-map directory performance at a constant cost per processing element. Our experience in designing the software protocol interfaces and experiments with a variety of system configurations lead to a detailed understanding of the interaction of the hardware and software components of the system. The results show that a small amount of shared memory hardware provides adequate performance: One-pointer systems reach between 42% and 100% of full-map performance on our parallel benchmarks. A software-only directory architecture with no hardware pointers has lower performance but minimal cost.*

## 1 Introduction

Implementing shared memory for a large-scale multiprocessor requires balancing the performance of the system as a whole with the complexity and cost of its hardware and software components. Shared memory itself helps control the complexity of the application software written for a machine, but it requires an efficient design to achieve this goal. The Alewife architecture[3] uses a combination of hardware and software to provide shared memory at a constant cost per processing node, without sacrificing performance. Following the integrated systems approach, the architecture uses hardware to implement common memory accesses and uses software to extend the hardware by handling potentially complex scenarios.

The primary contribution of this paper is the demonstration of a complete software-extended shared memory system that allows measurement of the performance of its software components. This system proves that the software extension approach is a viable

alternative for implementing a shared memory system, in terms of both cost and performance. Rather than advocating a specific machine configuration, the paper seeks to examine the performance versus cost tradeoffs inherent in implementing software-extended shared memory.

At the heart of a shared memory design lies the problem of providing fast average access time while ensuring a coherent memory model. Directory-based cache coherence protocols provide an efficient implementation of coherent shared memory for large systems. These protocols allow each processing node to take advantage of typical memory access patterns by caching frequently used data, even when the data may be shared by other nodes. A directory is a structure that helps enforce the coherence of cached data by maintaining pointers to the locations of cached copies of each memory block. When one node modifies a block of data, the memory system uses the information stored in the directory to enforce a coherent view of the data. Typically, directories are not monolithic structures but are distributed to the processing nodes along with a system's shared memory.

A promising design strategy, central to the Alewife architecture, uses a combination of hardware and software to implement a cost-efficient directory[9]. Since most data blocks in a shared memory system are shared by a small number of processing nodes[2, 32, 8], the hardware can implement a small set of pointers, and provide mechanisms to allow the system's software to extend the directory when the set of pointers is insufficient for enforcing coherence. This software-extension technique catalyzes the balance between a system's performance and cost.

LimitLESS directories, a scheme proposed in [9], is a software-extended coherence protocol that permits a tradeoff between the cost and the performance of a shared memory system. LimitLESS, which stands for a *Limited* directory, *Locally Extended* through *Software Support*, implements a small number of pointers in a hardware directory (zero through five in Alewife), so that the hardware can track a few copies of any memory block. When these pointers are exhausted, the memory system hardware interrupts a local processor, thereby requesting it to maintain correct shared memory behavior by extending the hardware directory with software.

Another set of software-extended protocols (termed $Dir_1SW$) were proposed in [14] and [34]. These protocols use only one hardware pointer, rely on software to broadcast invalidates, and use hardware to accumulate the acknowledgments. In addition, they allow the programmer or compiler to insert Check-In/Check-Out (CICO) directives into programs to minimize the number of software traps.

Reprinted from *Proc. 21st Ann. Int'l Symp. Computer Architecture.*, 1994, pp. 314–324.

All software-extended memory systems require a battery of architectural mechanisms to permit a designer to make the cost versus performance tradeoff. First, the shared memory hardware must be able to invoke extension software on the processor, and the processor must have complete access to the memory and network hardware[9, 19, 34]. Second, the hardware must guarantee forward progress in the face of protocol thrashing scenarios and high-availability interrupts[20].

Each processing node must also provide support for location-independent addressing, which is a fundamental requirement of shared memory. Hardware support for location-independent addressing permits the software to issue an address that refers to an object without knowledge of where it is resident. This hardware support includes an associative matching mechanism to detect if the object is cached, a mechanism to translate the object address and identify its home location if it is not cached, and a mechanism to issue a message to fetch the object from a remote location if it is not in local memory.

Since these mechanisms comprise the bulk of the complexity of a software-extended system, it is important to note that the benefits of these mechanisms extend far beyond the implementation of shared memory[17]. Alternative approaches to implementing shared memory proposed in [26, 30, 21] use hardware mechanisms that allocate directory pointers dynamically. These schemes do not require the mechanisms listed above, but they lack the flexibility of protocol and application software design.

A number of systems rely primarily on software to implement the mechanisms required to support shared memory [10, 23, 11, 6, 5, 4]. These systems implement coherent shared memory at low cost; however, providing location-independent addressing in software forces the granularity of data sharing to be much larger than in software-extended systems. In contrast, this paper proposes a *software-only directory architecture*, which implements location-independent addressing in hardware but relies on software to handle all inter-node memory accesses. This software-extended scheme is a low-cost alternative that allows threads to share small blocks of data.

Unlike previous studies of software-extended schemes, this paper analyzes a complete system, whose hardware is in the final stages of fabrication, and whose software is fully functional. Detailed simulations of the system lead to several conclusions about the implementation of software-extended shared memory: The minimum amount of shared memory hardware that is required to provide adequate performance is a single directory pointer (that also serves as an acknowledgment counter) per memory block. Beyond this level of hardware support, the cost and mapping of a system's DRAM become more important factors than performance. In addition, processor caches should include more associativity than a simple direct-mapped cache. Alewife uses a victim cache[16, 20] to provide the required extra associativity.

The paper extends previous work in the performance analysis of software-extended coherence protocols [9, 34] to a much wider spectrum, ranging from zero hardware pointers (the software-only directory architecture) to a full-map protocol, through the use of controlled experiments using a synthetic benchmark and a set of application programs. By studying the behavior of real software protocol handlers, this paper confirms results presented in [9] on the similarity in performance of LimitLESS$_1$ (one hardware pointer), LimitLESS$_2$, LimitLESS$_4$, and full-map protocols. We also con-

firm the findings in [34] that the performance of suitably tuned one-pointer protocols is competitive with that of multiple-pointer protocols.

In order to study the software side of hybrid shared memory systems, this paper investigates two different software systems that use the same hardware to achieve different goals. One system, written in C, incorporates a flexible coherence interface that facilitates protocol software implementation. This interface proved indispensable for conducting experiments over the whole spectrum of software-extended protocols. Our continuing research relies on the flexibility of this interface for implementing enhancements to the basic system. The other system, which is written in assembly-language, is a highly optimized and specialized implementation. While the specialized system supports only a narrow range of functionality, it shows the potential benefits of well-tuned software.

This paper presents case studies that examine how application performance varies over the spectrum of software-extended protocols. Before reaching these case studies, Section 2 gives an overview of the cost versus performance tradeoff that a software-extended memory system exploits and describes a notation for such systems. The paper's experimental methodology is then described in Section 3. Section 4 analyzes how the implementation of a software-extended protocol affects application performance; Section 5 examines the converse: how application characteristics determine protocol performance. Section 6 presents the case studies of application performance, and Section 7 suggests enhancements to improve programmability and performance. Finally, Section 8 discusses the impact of this study on the design of software-extended coherent memory systems.

## 2  A spectrum of protocols

The number of directory pointers that are implemented in hardware is an important design decision involved in building a software-extended shared memory system. More hardware pointers mean fewer situations in which a system must rely on software to enforce coherence, thereby increasing performance. Having fewer hardware pointers means a lower implementation cost, at the expense of reduced performance. This tradeoff suggests a whole spectrum of protocols, ranging from 0 pointers to $n$ pointers, where $n$ is the number of nodes in the system.

### 2.1  The $n$ pointer protocol

The full-map protocol[7], which is implemented in the DASH multiprocessor[21], uses $n$ pointers for every block of memory in the system and requires no software extension. Although this protocol permits an efficient implementation that uses only one bit for each pointer, the sheer number of pointers makes it extremely expensive for systems with large numbers of nodes. Despite the cost of the full-map protocol, it serves as a good performance goal for the software-extended schemes.

### 2.2  $2 \leftrightarrow (n-1)$ pointer protocols

There is a range of protocols that use a software-extended coherence scheme to implement shared memory. It is this range of protocols that allows the designer to trade hardware cost and system performance. From the point of view of implementation complexity, the protocols that implement between 2 and $n-1$ pointers in hardware are homogeneous. Of course, the $n-1$ pointer protocol would be even more expensive to implement than the full-map protocol, but it still requires exactly the same hardware and software mechanisms as the protocols at the other end of the spectrum.

The protocol extension software needs to service only two kinds of messages: read and write requests. It handles read requests by allocating an extended directory entry (if necessary), emptying all of the hardware pointers into the software structure, and recording a pointer to the node that caused the directory overflow. Subsequent requests may be handled by the hardware until the next overflow occurs. For all of these protocols, the hardware returns the appropriate data to requesting nodes; the software only needs to record requests that overflow the hardware directory.

To handle write requests after an overflow, the software transmits invalidation messages to every node with a pointer in the hardware directory or in the software directory extension. The software then returns the hardware directory to a mode that collects one acknowledgment message for each transmitted invalidation.

### 2.3   Zero-pointer protocols

Since the software-only directory[28] has no directory memory, it requires substantially different software than the $2 \leftrightarrow (n-1)$ range of protocols. This software must implement all coherence protocol state transitions for inter-node accesses.

While other implementations are possible, our version of the zero-pointer protocol uses one extra bit per memory block to optimize the performance of purely intra-node accesses: the bit indicates whether the associated memory block has been accessed at any time by a remote node. When the bit is clear (the default value), all memory accesses from the local processor are serviced without software traps, just as in a uniprocessor. When an inter-node request arrives, the bit is set and the extension software flushes the block from the local cache. Once the bit is set, all subsequent accesses — including intra-node requests — are handled by software extension.

### 2.4   One-pointer protocols

The one-pointer protocols are a hybrid of the protocols discussed above. This paper studies three variations of this class of protocols. All three use the same software routine to transmit data invalidations sequentially, but they differ in the way that they collect the messages that acknowledge receipt of the invalidations. The first variation handles the acknowledgments completely in software, requiring a trap from the hardware upon the receipt of each message. During the invalidation/acknowledgment process, the hardware pointer is unused.

The second protocol handles all but the last of a sequence of acknowledgments in hardware. If a node transmits 64 invalidations, then the hardware will process the first 63 invalidations. This variation uses the hardware pointer to store a count of the number of acknowledgments that are still outstanding. During this process, the hardware will also transmit busy messages to requesting nodes, eliminating the livelock problem. Upon receiving the $64^{th}$

acknowledgment, the hardware invokes the software, which takes care of transmitting data to the requesting node.

The third protocol handles all acknowledgment messages in hardware. This protocol actually requires storage for two hardware pointers: one pointer to store the requesting node's identifier and another to count acknowledgments. Although a designer would always choose to implement a two-pointer protocol over this variation of the one-pointer protocol, it still provides a useful baseline for measuring the performance of the other two variations.

### 2.5   A notation for the spectrum

We now introduce a notation that allows us to articulate clearly the differences between various implementations and facilitates a precise cost comparison.

Our notation is derived from a nomenclature for directory-based coherence protocols introduced in [2]. In the previous notation, a protocol was represented as $Dir_i X$, where $i$ represented the number of explicit copies tracked, and $X$ was $B$ or $NB$ depending on whether or not the protocol issued broadcasts. Notice that this nomenclature does not distinguish between the functionality implemented in the software and in the hardware. Our notation attempts to capture the spectrum of features of software-extended protocols that have evolved over the past several years, and previously termed LimitLESS$_1$, LimitLESS$_4$, and others in [9], and $Dir_1 SW$, $Dir_1 SW+$, and others in [14, 34].

For both hardware and software, our notation divides the mechanisms into two classes: those that dictate directory actions upon receipt of processor requests, and those that dictate directory actions for acknowledgments.

Accordingly, our notation specifies a protocol as: $Dir_i H_X S_{Y,A}$, where $i$ is the number of explicit pointers recorded by the system — in hardware or in software — for a given block of data.

The parameter $X$ is the number of pointers recorded in a hardware directory when a software extension exists. $X$ is $NB$ if the number of hardware pointers is $i$ and no more than $i$ shared copies are allowed, and is $B$ if the number of hardware pointers is $i$ and broadcasts are used when more than $i$ shared copies exist. Thus the full-map protocol in DASH [21] is termed $Dir_n H_{NB} S_-$.

The parameter $Y$ is $NB$ if the hardware-software combination records $i$ explicit pointers and allows no more than $i$ copies. $Y$ is $B$ if the software resorts to a broadcast when more than $i$ copies exist.

The $A$ parameter is $ACK$ if a software trap is invoked on *every* acknowledgment. A missing $A$ field implies that the hardware keeps an updated count of acknowledgments received. Finally, the $A$ parameter is $LACK$ if a software trap is invoked only on the *last* acknowledgment.

According to this notation, the LimitLESS$_1$ protocol defined in [9] is termed $Dir_n H_1 S_{NB}$, denoting that it records $n$ pointers, of which only one is in hardware. The hardware handles all acknowledgments and the software issues invalidations to shared copies when a write request occurs after an overflow. This paper deals with three variants of the one-pointer protocols defined above. In our notation, the three one-pointer protocols are $Dir_n H_1 S_{NB,ACK}$, $Dir_n H_1 S_{NB,LACK}$, and $Dir_n H_1 S_{NB}$, respectively.

The set of software-extended protocols introduced in [14]

and [34] can also be expressed in terms of our notation. The $Dir_1SW$ protocol maintains one pointer in hardware, resorts to software broadcasts when more than one copy exists, and counts acknowledgments in hardware. In addition, their protocol traps into software on the last acknowledgment[33]. In our notation, this protocol is represented as $Dir_1H_1S_{B,LACK}$. This protocol is different from the $Dir_nH_1S_{NB,LACK}$ protocol in that $Dir_1H_1S_{B,LACK}$ maintains only one explicit pointer, while $Dir_nH_1S_{NB,LACK}$ maintains one pointer in hardware and extends the directory to $n$ pointers in software. An important consequence of this difference is that the $Dir_nH_1S_{NB,LACK}$ potentially traps on read requests, while $Dir_1H_1S_{B,LACK}$ does not. Unlike $Dir_nH_1S_{NB,LACK}$, $Dir_1H_1S_{B,LACK}$ must issue broadcasts on write requests to memory blocks that are cached by multiple nodes.

# 3    Methodology

This section first describes the MIT Alewife machine, which provides a proof of concept for software-extended memory systems and a platform for experimenting with many aspects of multiprocessor design and programming. While the machine supports an interesting range of protocols, it does not implement the full spectrum of software-extended schemes that this paper evaluates. Only a simulation system can provide the range of protocols, the deterministic behavior, and the non-intrusive observation functions that are required for analyzing the spectrum of software-extended protocols. The second half of this section describes the simulation system used to do the experiments discussed in the remainder of the paper.

## 3.1    The Alewife Machine

Alewife is a large-scale multiprocessor with distributed shared memory. Figure 1 shows an enlarged view of a node in the Alewife machine. Each node consists of a 33 MHz Sparcle processor[1], 64K bytes of direct-mapped cache, 4 Mbytes of globally-shared main memory, and a floating-point coprocessor. The nodes communicate via messages through a network[29] with a mesh topology. A single-chip communications and memory management (CMMU) on each node holds the cache tags and implements the memory coherence protocol by synthesizing messages to other nodes. All of the node components, with the exception of the CMMU, have been fabricated and tested. The CMMU is in fabrication.

In order to provide a platform for shared memory research, Alewife supports dynamic reconfiguration of coherence protocols on a block-by-block basis. The machine supports $Dir_nH_0S_{NB,ACK}$, $Dir_nH_2S_{NB}$, $Dir_nH_3S_{NB}$, $Dir_nH_4S_{NB}$, $Dir_nH_5S_{NB}$, $Dir_5H_5S_B$ and a variety of other protocols. The node diagram in Figure 1 illustrates a memory block with two hardware pointers and an associated software-extended directory structure ($Dir_nH_2S_{NB}$). The current default boot sequence configures every block of shared memory with a $Dir_nH_5S_{NB}$ protocol, which uses all of the available hardware pointers.

In addition to the standard hardware pointers, Alewife implements a special one-bit pointer for the node that is local to the directory. Several simulations show that this extra pointer improves performance by only about 2%. Its main benefit lies in reducing the complexity of the protocol hardware and software by

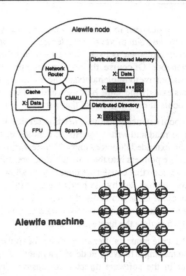

Figure 1: Alewife node, with a $Dir_nH_2S_{NB}$ memory block.

eliminating the possibility that a node will cause its local hardware directory to overflow. For the results presented in this paper, all of the protocols (except $Dir_nH_0S_{NB,ACK}$) use the one-bit pointer in addition to the normal hardware pointers.

## 3.2    NWO: the Alewife simulator

NWO is a multi-purpose simulator that provides a deterministic debugging and test environment for the Alewife machine. The simulator performs a cycle-by-cycle simulation of all of the components in Alewife. NWO is binary compatible with Alewife's hardware: programs that run on the simulator will be able to run on the actual machine *without recompilation*. The CMMU protocol state-transition tables are automatically compiled from the hardware specification into a simulator executable format, so that NWO incorporates the hardware protocol directly. NWO models the Alewife data paths accurately enough that it is used to drive the transistor-level simulations of the CMMU. Although Alewife does not support one-pointer protocols or protocols with more than five hardware pointers, NWO has been extended to support a complete spectrum of software-extended protocols, from $Dir_nH_0S_{NB,ACK}$ to $Dir_nH_{NB}S_-$.

There are two inaccuracies in the simulation. First, NWO does not model the Sparcle or FPU pipelines, even though it does model many of the pipelined data paths within the CMMU. Second, NWO models communication contention at the CMMU network transmit and receive queues, but does not model contention within the network switches.

The initial implementation of NWO targeted SPARC and MIPS-based workstations; we have also developed a version of the simulator that runs on Thinking Machines' CM-5 multiprocessors. In the latter implementation, each CM-5 node simulates the processor, memory, and network hardware of one or more Alewife nodes. The CM-5 port of our simulator has proved invaluable, especially for running simulations of 64 and 256 node Alewife systems.

# 4  Software interfaces

Two different versions of the protocol extension software have been written for the Alewife machine. One version incorporates a flexible coherence interface that allows rapid protocol implementation in the C programming language. The other version is a set of protocol handlers that are implemented in assembly language and are carefully tuned to take full advantage of the features of the Alewife architecture.

## 4.1  Protocol software implementations

The C version of the Alewife protocol extension software implements the whole range of software-extended protocols within a flexible framework. A single set of C routines implements all of the protocols from $Dir_nH_2S_{NB}$ to $Dir_nH_{NB}S_-$. Other modules linked into the same kernel support $Dir_nH_0S_{NB,ACK}$, $Dir_nH_1S_{NB}$, $Dir_nH_1S_{NB,LACK}$, and $Dir_nH_1S_{NB,ACK}$.

The flexible interface facilitates the construction of all of these protocols by providing C macros for hardware directory manipulation, protocol message transmission, a free-listing memory manager, and hash table administration. The interface eliminates the need for the protocol designer to understand many of the details of the Alewife hardware implementation. For example, the protocol interface sets up an environment that lets the protocol designer treat every protocol event as if it were generated by an asynchronous inter-node request.

In addition, the framework hides other implementation details such as atomic protocol transitions and livelock situations. The framework ensures the atomicity of protocol transitions by guaranteeing that asynchronous messages in a CMMU internal queue are processed before handling synchronous events. Livelock situations can occur when protocol software-extension requests occur so frequently that user code cannot make forward progress. The framework solves this problem by using a timer interrupt to implement a watchdog that detects possible livelock, temporarily shuts off asynchronous events, and allows the user code to run unmolested. In practice, such conditions happen only for $Dir_nH_0S_{NB,ACK}$ and $Dir_nH_1S_{NB,ACK}$, when they handle acknowledgments in software. The framework provides a very simple interface that allows these protocols to invoke the watchdog directly.

During the course of the study reported in this paper, the flexible coherence interface proved itself to be an indispensable tool for rapidly prototyping a complete set of protocols. The framework is currently being used to implement some of the enhancements to the basic protocols that are described in Section 7.

Unfortunately, flexibility comes at the cost of performance. All of the mechanisms that protect the protocol designer from the details of the Alewife hardware implementation increase the time that it takes to handle protocol requests in software. An assembly-language version of the Alewife protocol extension handlers helps investigate the performance versus flexibility tradeoff by optimizing the performance of the software. Since this approach requires a large programming effort, this version only implements $Dir_nH_5S_{NB}$.

The code for this optimized version is hand-tuned to keep instruction counts to a minimum. To reduce memory management time, it uses a special free-list of extended directory structures that are initialized when the kernel boots the machine. The assembly-language version also takes advantage of a feature of Alewife's directory that eliminates the need for a hash table lookup.

## 4.2  Comparing the implementations

The primary difference between the performance of the two implementations of the protocol extension software is the amount of time that it takes to process a protocol request. Table 1 gives the average number of cycles required to process $Dir_nH_5S_{NB}$ read and write requests for both of the implementations. These software handling latencies were measured by running the WORKER benchmark (described in the next section) on a 16 node system. The latencies are relatively independent of the number of nodes that read each memory block. In most cases, the hand-tuned version of the software reduces the latency of protocol request handlers by about a factor of two.

| Readers Per Block | C Read Request | Assembly Read Request | C Write Request | Assembly Write Request |
|---|---|---|---|---|
| 8 | 436 | 162 | 726 | 375 |
| 12 | 397 | 141 | 714 | 393 |
| 16 | 386 | 138 | 797 | 420 |

Table 1: Average software extension latencies for C and for assembly language, in execution cycles.

These latencies may be understood better by analyzing the number of cycles spent on each activity required to extend a protocol in software. Table 2 accounts for all of the cycles spent in a read and a write request from both versions of the protocol software. These counts come from cycle-by-cycle traces of read and write requests with eight readers and one writer per memory block. In order to select a representative individual from each sample, we choose a median request of each type (as opposed to the average, which we use above to summarize aggregate behavior).

The dispatch and trap return activities are standard sequences of code that invoke hardware exception and interrupt handlers and allow them to return to user code, respectively. (The dispatch activity does not include the three cycles that Sparcle takes to flush its pipeline and to load the first trap instruction.) In the assembly-language version, these sequences are streamlined to invoke the protocol software as quickly as possible. The C implementation of the software requires an extra protocol-specific dispatch in order to set up the C environment and hide the details of the Alewife hardware. For the types of protocol requests that occur when running the WORKER benchmark, this extra overhead does not significantly impact performance. The extra code in the C version that supports the non-Alewife protocols implemented only in the simulator also impacted performance minimally.

The difference between the performance of the C and assembly-language protocol handlers lies in the flexibility of the C interface. The assembly-language version avoided most of the expense of memory management and hash table administration by implementing a special-purpose solution to the directory structure allocation and lookup problem. This solution relies heavily on the format

| Activity | C Read Request | Assembly Read Request | C Write Request | Assembly Write Request |
|---|---|---|---|---|
| trap dispatch | 11 | 11 | 9 | 11 |
| system message dispatch | 14 | 15 | 14 | 15 |
| protocol-specific dispatch | 10 | N/A | 10 | N/A |
| decode and modify hardware directory | 22 | 17 | 52 | 40 |
| save state for function calls | 24 | N/A | 17 | N/A |
| memory management | 60 | 65 | 28 | 11 |
| hash table administration | 80 | N/A | 74 | N/A |
| store pointers into extended directory | 235 | 74 | 99 | 45 |
| invalidation lookup and transmit | N/A | N/A | 419 | 251 |
| support for non-Alewife protocols | 10 | N/A | 6 | N/A |
| trap return | 14 | 11 | 9 | 11 |
| total (median latency) | 480 | 193 | 737 | 384 |

Table 2: Breakdown of execution cycles measured from median-latency read and write requests. Each memory block has 8 readers and 1 writer. N/A stands for not applicable.

of Alewife's coherence directory and is not robust in the context of a system that runs a large number of different applications over a long period of time. However, it does place a minimum bound on the time required to perform these tasks. As the Alewife system evolves, critical pieces of the protocol extension software that are implemented under the flexible interface will be hand-tuned to realize the best of both worlds.

# 5   Worker sets and performance

A *worker set* is defined to be the set of nodes that simultaneously access a unit of data. The software-extension approach is predicated on the observation that, for a large class of applications, most worker sets are relatively small. Small worker sets are handled in hardware by a limited directory structure. Memory blocks with large worker sets must be handled in software, at the expense of longer memory access latency and processor cycles that are spent on protocol handlers rather than on user code.

This section uses a synthetic benchmark to investigate the relationship between an application's worker sets and the performance of software-extended coherence protocols. The benchmark, called WORKER, uses a data structure that creates memory blocks with an exact worker set size. WORKER consists of an initialization phase that builds the worker set data structure and a number of iterations that perform repeated memory accesses to the structure.

The nodes begin each iteration by reading the appropriate slots in the worker set structure. After the reads, they execute a barrier and then perform the writes to the structure. Finally, the nodes execute a barrier and continue with the next iteration. Every read request causes a cache miss and every write request causes a directory protocol to send exactly one invalidation message to each reader. This completely deterministic memory access pattern provides a controlled experiment for comparing the performance of different protocols.

In order to analyze the relationship between worker set sizes and the performance of software-extended shared memory, we perform

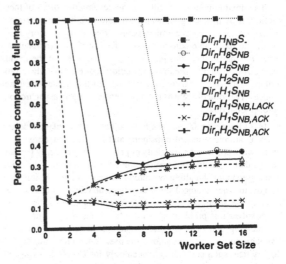

Figure 2: Protocol performance and worker set size.

simulations of WORKER running on a range of protocols. The simulations are restricted to a relatively small system because the benchmark is both regular and completely distributed, so the results would not be qualitatively different for a larger number of nodes.

Figure 2 presents the results of a series of 16 node simulations. The horizontal axis gives the size of the worker sets generated by the benchmark. The vertical axis measures the ratio of the run-time of each protocol and the run-time of a full-map protocol ($Dir_nH_{NB}S_-$) running the same benchmark configuration.

The solid curves in Figure 2 indicate the performance of some of the protocols that are implemented in the actual Alewife machine. As expected, the more hardware pointers, the better the performance of the software-extended system. The performance of $Dir_nH_5S_{NB}$ is particularly easy to interpret: its performance is exactly the same as the full-map protocol up to a worker set size of 4, because the worker sets fit entirely within the hardware directory. For small worker set sizes, software is never invoked. The performance of $Dir_n H_5 S_{NB}$ drops as the worker set size grows, due to the expense of handling memory requests in software.

At the other end of the performance scale, the $Dir_n H_0 S_{NB,ACK}$ protocol performs significantly worse than the other protocols, for all worker set sizes. Since WORKER is a shared memory stress test and exaggerates the differences between the protocols, Figure 2 shows the worst possible performance of the software-only directory. The measurements in the next section, which experiment with more realistic applications, yield a more optimistic outlook for the zero and one-pointer protocols.

The dashed curves correspond to one-pointer protocols that run only in the simulation environment. These three protocols differ only in the way that they handle acknowledgment messages (see Section 2.4). For all non-trivial worker set sizes, the protocol that traps on every acknowledgment message ($Dir_n H_1 S_{NB,ACK}$) performs significantly worse than the protocols that can count acknowledgments in hardware. $Dir_n H_1 S_{NB}$, which never traps on acknowledgment messages, has very similar performance to the $Dir_n H_2 S_{NB}$ protocol, except when running with size 1 worker sets. Since this version of $Dir_n H_1 S_{NB}$ requires the same amount of directory storage as $Dir_n H_2 S_{NB}$, the similarity in performance is not surprising.

Of the three different one-pointer protocols, the protocol that traps only on the last acknowledgment message in a sequence ($Dir_n H_1 S_{NB,LACK}$) makes the most cost-efficient use of the hardware pointers. This efficiency comes at a slight performance cost. For the WORKER benchmark, this protocol performs between 0% and 50% worse than $Dir_n H_1 S_{NB}$. When the worker set size is 4 nodes, $Dir_n H_1 S_{NB,LACK}$ actually performs slightly better than $Dir_n H_1 S_{NB}$. This anomaly is due to a memory-usage optimization that attempts to reduce the size of the software-extended directory when handling small worker sets. The optimization, implemented in the $Dir_n H_1 S_{NB,LACK}$, $Dir_n H_1 S_{NB,ACK}$ and $Dir_n H_0 S_{NB,ACK}$ protocols, improves the run-time performance of all three protocols for worker set sizes of 4 or less.

# 6  Application case studies

This section presents more practical case-studies of several programs and investigates how the performance of applications depends on memory access patterns, the coherence protocol, and other machine parameters.

The names and characteristics of the applications we analyze are given by Table 3. They are written in C, Mul-T[18] (a parallel dialect of LISP), and Semi-C[15] (a language akin to C with support for fine-grain parallelism). Each application (except MP3D) is studied with a problem size that realizes more than 50% processor utilization on a simulated 64 node machine with a full-map directory. All performance results use protocols implemented with the flexible coherence interface described in Section 4.

Figure 4 presents the basic performance data for the applications running on 64 nodes. The horizontal axis shows the number of directory pointers implemented in hardware, thereby measuring the cost of the system. The vertical axis shows the speedup of the mul-

| Name | Language | Size | Sequential |
|---|---|---|---|
| TSP | Mul-T | 10 city tour | 1.1 sec |
| AQ | Semi-C | *see text* | 0.9 sec |
| SMGRID | Mul-T | 129 × 129 | 3.0 sec |
| EVOLVE | Mul-T | 12 dimensions | 1.3 sec |
| MP3D | C | 10,000 particles | 0.6 sec |
| WATER | C | 64 molecules | 2.6 sec |

Table 3: Characteristics of applications. Sequential time assumes a clock speed of 33MHz.

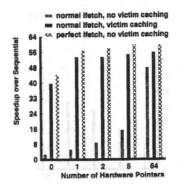

Figure 3: TSP: detailed 64 node performance analysis.

tiprocessor execution over a sequential run without multiprocessor overhead. The software-only directory is always on the left and the full-map directory on the right. All of the figures in this section show $Dir_n H_1 S_{NB,ACK}$ performance for the one-pointer protocol.

The most important observation is that the performance of $Dir_n H_5 S_{NB}$ is always between 71% and 100% of the performance of $Dir_n H_{NB} S_-$. Thus, the data in Figure 4 provides strong evidence that the software extension approach is a viable alternative for implementing a shared memory system. The rest of this section seeks to provide a more detailed understanding of the performance of software-extended systems.

**Traveling Salesman Problem**   TSP solves the traveling salesman problem using a branch-and-bound graph search. The application is written in Mul-T and uses the `future` construct to specify parallelism. In order to ensure that the amount of work performed by the application is deterministic, we seed the best path value with the optimal path. Given the characteristics of the application's memory access pattern, one would expect TSP to perform well with a software-extended protocol: the application has very few large worker sets. In fact, most – but not all – of the worker sets are small sets of nodes that concurrently access partial tours.

Figure 3 presents detailed performance data for TSP running on a 64 node machine. Contrary to our expectations, TSP suffers severe performance degradation when running with the software-extended protocols. The gray bars in the figure show that the five-pointer protocol performs more that 3 times worse than the full-map protocol. This performance decrease is due to instruction/data thrashing in Alewife's combined, direct-map caches: When we profiled the address reference pattern of the application, we found

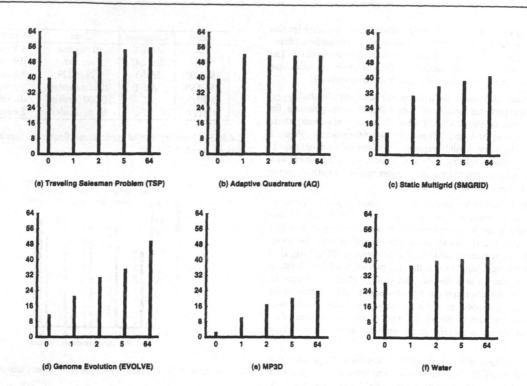

Figure 4: Application speedups over sequential, running on 64 nodes. Horizontal axis shows number of hardware pointers. Vertical axis shows speedup over sequential execution.

that two memory blocks that were shared by *every* node in the system were constantly replaced in the cache by commonly run instructions.

In order to confirm this observation, we invoked a simulator option that allows one-cycle access to every instruction without using the cache. This option, called *perfect ifetch*, eliminates the effects of instructions on the memory system. The hashed bars in Figure 3 confirm that instruction/data thrashing was a serious problem in the initial runs. Absent the effects of instructions, all of the protocols except the software-only directory realize performance equivalent (within experimental error) to a full-map protocol.

While perfect instruction fetching is not possible in real systems, there are various methods for relieving instruction/data thrashing by increasing the associativity of the cache system. Alewife's approach to the problem is to implement a version of victim caching[16], which uses the transaction store[20] to provide a small number of buffers for storing blocks that are evicted from the cache. The black bars in Figures 4(a) and 3 show the performance for TSP on a system with victim caching enabled. The few extra buffers improve the performance of the full-map protocol by 16%, and allow all of the protocols with hardware pointers to perform about as well as full-map. For this reason, the studies of all of the other applications in this section enable victim-caching by default.

It is interesting to note that $Dir_nH_0S_{NB,ACK}$ with victim caching achieves almost 70% of the performance of $Dir_nH_{NB}S_{-}$. This low-cost alternative seems viable for applications with limited amounts of sharing.

Thus far, we have compared the performance of the protocols under an environment where the full-map protocol achieves close to maximum speedup. On an application that requires only 1 second to run, the system with victim caching achieves a speedup of about 55 for the 5 pointer protocol. In order to investigate the effects of running an application with suboptimal speedups, we ran the same problem size on a 256 node machine with victim caching enabled. Figure 5 shows the results, which indicate a speedup of 142 for full-map and 134 for five-pointers. We consider these speedups remarkable for this problem size and note that the software-extended system performs only 6% worse than full-map in this configuration. The difference in performance is due primarily to the increased contribution of the transient effects over distributing data to 256 nodes at the beginning of the run.

**Adaptive Quadrature**  AQ performs numerical integration of bivariate functions using adaptive quadrature. The core of the algorithm is a function that integrates the range under a curve by recursively calling itself to integrate sub-ranges of that range. The function used for this study is $x^4y^4$, which is integrated over the square $((0,0), (2,2))$ with an error tolerance of 0.005.

Since all of the communication in the application is producer-consumer, we expect this application to perform equally well for all protocols that implement at least one directory pointer in hardware. Figure 4(b) confirms this expectation by showing the performance of the application running on 64 nodes. Again, $Dir_nH_0S_{NB,ACK}$ performs respectably due to the favorable memory access patterns

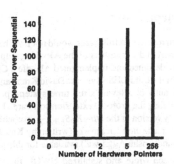

Figure 5: TSP running on 256 nodes.

in the application.

**Static Multigrid**  SMGRID uses the multigrid method to solve elliptical partial differential equations[13]. The algorithm consists of performing a series of Jacobi-style iterations on multiple grids of varying granularities. The speedup over sequential is limited by the fact that only a subset of nodes work during the relaxation on the upper levels of the pyramid of grids. Furthermore, data is more widely shared in this application than in either TSP or AQ. The consequences of these two factors appear in Figure 4(c): the absolute speedups are lower than either of the previous applications, even though the sequential time is three times longer.

The larger worker set sizes of multigrid cause the performance of the different protocols to separate. $Dir_n H_0 S_{NB,ACK}$ performs more than three times worse than the full-map protocol. The others range from 25% worse in the case of $Dir_n H_1 S_{NB,ACK}$ to 6% worse in the case of $Dir_n H_5 S_{NB}$.

**Genome Evolution**  EVOLVE is a graph traversal algorithm for simulating the evolution of genomes, which is reduced to the problem of traversing a hypercube and finding local and global maxima. The application searches for a path from the initial conditions to a local fitness maximum.

Of all of the applications in Figure 4, EVOLVE causes $Dir_n H_5 S_{NB}$ to exhibit the worst performance degradation compared to $Dir_n H_{NB} S_-$: the worker sets of EVOLVE seriously challenge a software-extended system. Figure 6 shows the number of worker sets of each size at the end of a 64 node run. Note that the vertical axis is logarithmically scaled: there are almost 10,000 one-node worker sets, while there are 25 worker sets of size 64. The significant number of nontrivial worker sets implies that there should be a sharp difference between protocols with different numbers of pointers. The large worker sets sizes impact the 0 and 1 pointer protocols most severely. Thus, EVOLVE provides a good example of a program that can benefit from a system's hardware directory pointers.

**MP3D**  The MP3D application is part of the SPLASH parallel benchmark suite [31]. For our simulations, we use a problem size of 10,000 particles, turn the locking option off, and augment the standard p4 macros with Alewife's parallel C library[25]. Since this application is notorious for exhibiting low speedups [22], the results in Figure 4(e) are encouraging: $Dir_n H_{NB} S_-$ achieves a speedup of

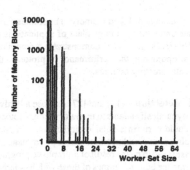

Figure 6: Histogram of worker set sizes for EVOLVE, running on 64 nodes.

24 and $Dir_n H_5 S_{NB}$ realizes a speedup of 20. These speedups are for a relatively small problem size, and we expect absolute speedups to increase with problem size.

The software-only directory exhibits the worst performance (only 11% of the speedup of full-map) on MP3D. Thus, MP3D provides another example of an application that can benefit from at least a small number of hardware directory pointers.

**Water**  The Water application, also from the SPLASH application suite, is run with 64 molecules. In addition to the p4 macros, this version of Water uses Alewife's parallel C library for barriers and reductions. Figure 4(f) shows that all of the software-extended protocols provide good speedups for this tiny problem size. Once again, the software-only directory offers almost 70% of the performance of the full-map directory.

## 7  Enhancement opportunities

This paper uses a basic definition of software-extended coherent shared memory in order to analyze the viability of the approach. The $Dir_i H_X S_{Y,A}$ notation itself implies a straightforward software directory extension. While this definition allows for a relatively simple analysis technique, the true power of the software-extension approach lies in deviating from the basic implementation. The generality of the flexible coherence interface described in Section 4 provides a platform for experimenting with schemes that enhance the performance and the functionality of the base protocols.

[9] suggests several extensions to the basic software such as a FIFO lock data type. To date, the protocol extension software has been used to implement a FIFO lock data type, stack overflow exceptions, and a fast barrier implementation. These enhancements are aimed at providing efficient functions that improve the programmability of the machine. [9] also indicates that LimitLESS software could be enhanced to improve the performance of normal shared memory variables, such as variables with large worker sets. The following types of extensions give examples of current research:

**Program and compiler annotations**  Program annotations allow a programmer to give the system information about the way that an application interacts with shared memory. [14] and [34] propose and evaluate this method for improving the performance of software-extended shared memory. The studies show that given appropriate annotations, a large class of applications can perform well on $Dir_1H_1S_{B,LACK}$. [24] demonstrates a compiler annotation scheme for optimizing the performance of protocols that dynamically allocate directory pointers.

**Dynamic detection** [12] and [27] propose a hardware mechanism that dynamically adapts to migratory data. Protocol extension software could perform similar optimizations. In addition, there are some classes of data that create severe performance bottlenecks. These classes tend to be the result of a simplistic programming style or a performance bug. Examples of these widely-shared data structures include synchronization objects, work queues, and frequently-written global objects. Preliminary results from our experiments show that protocol extension software may improve performance for this type of data by dynamically selecting sequential or parallel invalidation procedures.

**Profile, detect, and optimize** Some types of data do not create serious performance bottlenecks, but can benefit from optimization. An example of this class of data is widely-shared, read-only data. During the development phase of an application, enhanced protocol software could be used in a profiling mode to detect the existence of read-only data. The system could use the information to optimize the production version of the application.

**Data specific** Some types of data might be hard to optimize automatically, either dynamically or statically. In this case, a user could select special coherence types from a library, or even write an application-specific protocol under the flexible coherence interface.

## 8 Conclusions

The software extension approach offers a cost-efficient method for implementing scalable, coherent, high-performance shared-memory. Experience with the design of such a system shows that a minimum of one directory pointer and an acknowledgment counter should be implemented in hardware. Since all of the protocols that implement small numbers of hardware directory pointers have similar performance, factors such as the cost and mapping of each node's DRAM will dominate performance considerations when building a software-extended system.

The hardware components of a software-extended system must be tuned carefully to achieve high performance. Since the software-extended approach increases the penalty of cache misses, thrashing situations cause particular concern. Adding extra associativity to the processor side of the memory system, by implementing victim caches or by building set-associative caches, can dramatically decrease the effects of thrashing on the system as a whole.

Experiments with the implementation of protocol software indicate that such systems should include a flexible coherence interface that facilitates the implementation of specialized protocols. Such protocols could enhance the basic protocol software to improve both the programmability of machines and the performance of shared memory.

## Acknowledgments

The research reported in this paper would not have happened without the support of the members of the Alewife group at MIT. John Kubiatowicz designed and implemented Alewife's CMMU, which is the heart of the LimitLESS system. David Kranz and Beng-Hong Lim wrote much of Alewife's run-time system, parts of NWO, and helped debug the protocol extension software. John Piscitello wrote an early version of the $Dir_NH_0S_{NB,ACK}$ protocol. Beng-Hong Lim's efforts made the benchmarks (written by Kirk Johnson, Dan Nussbaum, and Anshu Aggarwal) available for this paper.

Kirk Johnson wrote and stabilized NWOP, the CM-5 version of NWO. We would like to thank Alan Mainwaring, Dave Douglas, and Thinking Machines Corporation for their generosity and assistance in porting our simulation system to the CM-5. Additional thanks to Thinking Machines Corporation (especially the folks who maintain the in-house machines) for allowing us to use many late-night CM-5 cycles during the results-generation phase of this research.

Dana Henry, Kirk Johnson, Steve Keckler, Michael Noakes, and the anonymous referees gave helpful comments during the production of this paper.

This research has been supported by NSF grant # MIP-9012773, ARPA grant #N00014-91-J-1698, and a NSF Presidential Young Investigator Award.

## References

[1] Anant Agarwal, John Kubiatowicz, David Kranz, Beng-Hong Lim, Donald Yeung, Godfrey D'Souza, and Mike Parkin. Sparcle: An Evolutionary Processor Design for Multiprocessors. *IEEE Micro*, 13(3):48–61, June 1993.

[2] Anant Agarwal, Richard Simoni, John Hennessy, and Mark Horowitz. An Evaluation of Directory Schemes for Cache Coherence. In *Proceedings of the 15th International Symposium on Computer Architecture*, pages 280–289, New York, June 1988. IEEE.

[3] A. Agarwal *et al.* The MIT Alewife Machine: A Large-Scale Distributed-Memory Multiprocessor. In *Proceedings of Workshop on Scalable Shared Memory Multiprocessors*. Kluwer Academic Publishers, 1991.

[4] Henri E. Bal and M. Frans Kaashoek. Object Distribution in Orca using Compile-Time and Run-Time Techniques. In *Proceedings of the Conference on Object-Oriented Programming Systems, Languages, and Applications (OOPSLA '93).*, September 1993.

[5] Brian N. Bershad, Matthew J. Zekauskas, and Wayne A. Sawdon. The Midway Distributed Shared Memory System. In *Proceedings of the 38th IEEE Computer Society International Conference (COMPCON'93)*, pages 528–537. IEEE, February 1993.

[6] John B. Carter, John K. Bennett, and Willy Zwaenepoel. Implementation and Performance of MUNIN. In *Proceedings of the 13th ACM Symposium on Operating Systems Principles*, pages 152–164, October 1991.

[7] Lucien M. Censier and Paul Feautrier. A New Solution to Coherence Problems in Multicache Systems. *IEEE Transactions on Computers*, C-27(12):1112–1118, December 1978.

[8] David Chaiken, Craig Fields, Kiyoshi Kurihara, and Anant Agarwal. Directory-Based Cache-Coherence in Large-Scale Multiprocessors. *IEEE Computer*, 23(6):41–58, June 1990.

[9] David Chaiken, John Kubiatowicz, and Anant Agarwal. LimitLESS Directories: A Scalable Cache Coherence Scheme. In *Fourth International Conference on Architectural Support for Programming Languages and Operating Systems (ASPLOS IV)*, pages 224–234. ACM, April 1991.

[10] David R. Cheriton, Gert A. Slavenberg, and Patrick D. Boyle. Software-Controlled Caches in the VMP Multiprocessor. In *Proceedings of the 13th Annual Symposium on Computer Architecture*, pages 367–374, New York, June 1986. IEEE.

[11] A. Cox and R. Fowler. The Implementation of a Coherent Memory Abstraction on a NUMA Multiprocessor: Experiences with PLATINUM. In *Proceedings of the 12th ACM Symposium on Operating Systems Principles*, pages 32–44, December 1989. Also as a Univ. Rochester TR-263, May 1989.

[12] Alan L. Cox and Robert J. Fowler. Adaptive Cache Coherence for Detecting Migratory Shared Data. In *Proceedings of the 20th Annual Symposium on Computer Architecture 1993*, New York, May 1993. ACM.

[13] W. Hackbusch, editor. *Multigrid Methods and Applications*. Springer-Verlag, Berlin, 1985.

[14] Mark D. Hill, James R. Larus, Steven K. Reinhardt, and David A. Wood. Cooperative Shared Memory: Software and Hardware for Scalable Multiprocessors. In *Fifth International Conference on Architectural Support for Programming Languages and Operating Systems (ASPLOS V)*, pages 262–273, Boston, October 1992. ACM.

[15] Kirk Johnson. Semi-C Reference Manual. ALEWIFE Memo No. 20, Laboratory for Computer Science, Massachusetts Institute of Technology, August 1991.

[16] N.P. Jouppi. Improving Direct-Mapped Cache Performance by the Addition of a Small Fully-Associative Cache and Prefetch Buffers. In *Proceedings, International Symposium on Computer Architecture '90*, pages 364–373, June 1990.

[17] David Kranz, Kirk Johnson, Anant Agarwal, John Kubiatowicz, and Beng-Hong Lim. Integrating Message-Passing and Shared-Memory: Early Experience. In *Practice and Principles of Parallel Programming (PPoPP) 1993*, pages 54–63, San Diego, CA, May 1993. ACM. Also as MIT/LCS TM-478, January 1993.

[18] David A. Kranz, R. Halstead, and E. Mohr. Mul-T: A High-Performance Parallel Lisp. In *Proceedings of SIGPLAN '89, Symposium on Programming Languages Design and Implementation*, June 1989.

[19] John Kubiatowicz and Anant Agarwal. Anatomy of a Message in the Alewife Multiprocessor. In *Proceedings of the International Supercomputing Conference (ISC) 1993*, Tokyo, Japan, July 1993. IEEE. Also as MIT/LCS TM, December 1992.

[20] John Kubiatowicz, David Chaiken, and Anant Agarwal. Closing the Window of Vulnerability in Multiphase Memory Transactions. In *Fifth International Conference on Architectural Support for Programming Languages and Operating Systems (ASPLOS V)*, pages 274–284, Boston, October 1992. ACM.

[21] D. Lenoski, J. Laudon, K. Gharachorloo, W. Weber, A. Gupta, J. Hennessy, M. Horowitz, and M. Lam. The Stanford Dash Multiprocessor. *IEEE Computer*, 25(3):63–79, March 1992.

[22] D. Lenoski, J. Laudon, T. Joe, D. Nakahira, L. Stevens, A. Gupta, and J. Hennessy. The DASH Prototype: Logic Overhead and Performance. *IEEE Transactions on Parallel and Distributed Systems*, 4(1):41–60, January 1993.

[23] Kai Li. IVY: A Shared Virtual Memory System for Parallel Computing. In *International Conference on Parallel Computing*, pages 94–101, 1988.

[24] David J. Lilja and Pen-Chung Yew. Improving Memory Utilization in Cache Coherence Directories. *IEEE Transactions on Parallel and Distributed Systems*, 4(10):1130–1146, October 1993.

[25] Beng-Hong Lim. Functions for Parallel C on the Alewife System. ALEWIFE Memo No. 37, Laboratory for Computer Science, Massachusetts Institute of Technology, November 1993.

[26] Brian W. O'Krafka and A. Richard Newton. An Empirical Evaluation of Two Memory-Efficient Directory Methods. In *Proceedings 17th Annual International Symposium on Computer Architecture*, pages 138–147, New York, June 1990. IEEE.

[27] Per Stenström, Mats Brorsson, and Lars Sandberg. An Adaptive Cache Coherence Protocol Optimized for Migratory Sharing. In *Proceedings of the 20th Annual Symposium on Computer Architecture 1993*, New York, May 1993. ACM.

[28] John D. Piscitello. A Software Cache Coherence Protocol for Alewife. Master's thesis, MIT, Department of Electrical Engineering and Computer Science, May 1993.

[29] Charles L. Seitz. Concurrent VLSI Architectures. *IEEE Transactions on Computers*, C-33(12):1247–1265, December 1984.

[30] Richard Simoni and Mark Horowitz. Dynamic Pointer Allocation for Scalable Cache Coherence Directories. In *Proceedings International Symposium on Shared Memory Multiprocessing*, Japan, April 1991. IPS Press.

[31] J.P. Singh, W.-D. Weber, and A. Gupta. SPLASH: Stanford Parallel Applications for Shared-Memory. Technical Report CSL-TR-92-526, Stanford University, June 1992.

[32] Wolf-Dietrich Weber and Anoop Gupta. Analysis of Cache Invalidation Patterns in Multiprocessors. In *Third International Conference on Architectural Support for Programming Languages and Operating Systems (ASPLOS III)*, April 1989.

[33] David A. Wood. Private Communication, October 1993.

[34] David A. Wood, Satish Chandra, Babak Falsafi, Mark D. Hill, James R. Larus, Alvin R. Lebeck, James C. Lewis, Shubhendu S. Mukherjee, Subbarao Palacharla, and Steven K. Reinhardt. Mechanisms for Cooperative Shared Memory. In *In Proceedings of the 20th Annual International Symposium on Computer Architecture 1993*, pages 156–167, San Diego, CA, May 1993. ACM.

# Hardware Assist for Distributed Shared Memory *

Andrew W. Wilson Jr.
Richard P. LaRowe Jr.
Marc J. Teller

Center for High Performance Computing
Worcester Polytechnic Institute

## Abstract

*The use of software implemented distributed memory (SDSM) to provide shared memory programming environments on networks of workstations and message-passing parallel computers has become quite popular. However, the memory reference patterns of many shared memory programs lead to poor performance on such systems. This paper proposes hardware assist to improve the performance of SDSM systems faced with the problematic reference patterns. An example of such a system is described. Operating system software in Mach is used to provide inter-node sharing in the example system, but is assisted through hardware support for maintaining update-based coherence of replicated pages. Simulations driven by hardware-collected parallel reference traces are used to provide an indication of the expected performance of the system.*

## 1: Introduction

Many believe that the shared memory programming paradigm is the easiest for constructing parallel applications. The shared memory model is similar to that used for developing conventional sequential programs, and shared memory can be used for both fine and coarse grain inter-process communication. This combination of familiarity and flexibility makes the shared memory model highly attractive.

Efficiently supporting the shared memory paradigm on large-scale parallel processors has proven to be quite a challenge. Numerous research projects have focused on building scalable multiprocessors with hardware-implemented shared memory (e.g., Stanford's Paradigm [11] and DASH [25], the Wisconsin Multicube [19], Carnegie-Mellon's PLUS [7], MIT's Alewife [3], the Swedish Institute of Computer Science DDM [20], SUNY Stony Brook's SESAME [32] and Encore's Gigamax [28]). These machines employ sophisticated caching strategies in addition to an assortment of clever performance optimizations to help reduce and/or hide the average shared memory reference costs. Other research groups have focused

* This research has been sponsored by the Defense Advanced Research Projects Agency (DoD), DARPA contract numbers DACA 76-89-C-0003 and DAAL 01-92-K-0261.

on ways to use operating system software to support a shared memory environment on message-passing parallel computers and even networks of workstations (e.g., Rice's Munin [6], Carnegie-Mellon's Mach [17], Li's Ivy [23], and Georgia Tech's Clouds [25]). As one might expect, the primary drawback of an exclusively hardware-based approach is cost and complexity. Purely software-based approaches, on the other hand, have potential performance problems as their primary drawback.

In order to address the cost and complexity problem associated with pure hardware-based implementations, several of the projects mentioned above have proposed some level of software support for managing shared data caching. Employing software to handle some of the more complicated aspects of the protocols can be an effective way to reduce hardware development cost. In this paper, we propose looking at the problem from the opposite viewpoint. Rather than build a hardware-based system and try to employ software to reduce cost, we consider what level of hardware support could be used to improve the performance of a software-based implementation.

Our goal is to support a shared memory environment with higher performance than purely software-based strategies at a cost much lower than that of a strictly hardware-based approach. This goal is achieved by employing hardware only for the most performance-critical operations. We believe that the hardware accelerator that we propose is significantly simpler and cheaper to build than strictly hardware-based shared memory multiprocessors currently being developed, yet can provide nearly the same level of performance as those architectures in a more distributed environment.

In the next section of this paper, we review the basic concepts behind software implemented distributed shared memory and point out the most serious performance problem associated with these systems. In Section 3, we develop a simple analytic model that captures the key parameters determining when an update based coherence protocol is preferable to an invalidation based protocol. The model is used in Section 4 to argue for hardware support of update based coherence protocols for implementing shared memory primarily in operating system

Reprinted from *Proc. 13th Int'l Conf. Distributed Computing Systems.*, 1993, pp. 246–255.

software. In Section 5, we present an overview of the Galactica Net architecture currently being developed at the Center for High Performance Computing. Internode sharing in Galactica Net is implemented in the Mach operating system. However, each Galactica Net node includes a special hardware module designed specifically to support update based coherence protocols, which the operating system uses to improve memory system performance. Preliminary performance results obtained through trace-driven simulation are presented to demonstrate the potential of this approach. Finally, in Section 6, we summarize and conclude the paper.

## 2: Software distributed shared memory

A number of projects have demonstrated that operating system software can be used to provide the abstraction of a globally shared memory without special hardware support (e.g., [6][17][23][25]). In the literature, these systems are typically referred to as distributed shared memory (DSM), distributed virtual memory (DVM), shared virtual memory (SVM), or network virtual memory (NVM) systems. To avoid confusion with the use of the term "distributed memory" to describe the physical memory organization of some multiprocessors, we shall refer to them as software distributed shared memory systems, or SDSM systems.

The basic strategy for implementing an SDSM system is to exploit the virtual memory subsystem of the operating system to treat local memories as cache space for some global virtual memory. Coherence of shared data pages can be ensured by employing a directory-based invalidation protocol implemented in OS software. Shared pages that are cached in the main memories of multiple nodes are write-inhibited, ensuring that any attempt to modify them will result in page faults. The fault handler responds by causing the invalidation of the copies in all other nodes and then allows the write to proceed. If some other process (on some other node) attempts to reference the page, another page fault occurs. The page fault handler creates a local copy of the page, and once again inhibits write access to the page by any process. Since there is never more than a single writable copy of a page, data coherence is assured.

This basic strategy for implementing SDSM systems has been widely implemented. Similar mechanisms have also been successfully applied to NUMA memory management systems to improve memory performance (e.g., [8][10][22]). However, some fairly common application memory reference patterns can cause the performance of an invalidation based SDSM system to degrade considerably.

"Page bouncing" is a term often used to describe the behavior that can occur with an invalidation based SDSM system when data is actively read/write shared at a fine granularity. For example, consider a simple producer/consumer scenario where the producer processes regularly add data items to a shared queue, and consumer processes remove items from that queue for consumption. Each time a producer adds an item to the queue, a sequence of writes occur that trigger the invalidation of the other processes' copies of the page containing the queue. Meanwhile, the consumers are attempting to remove items from the queue, which also involves modifying the queue data structure. Thus, the consumers are also causing page invalidations. The resulting behavior is characterized by frequent page faults resulting in the frequent invalidation and replication of the same shared page. In essence, the single writable copy of the page is bouncing from processor to processor, severely degrading performance. This can be a problem even if there is very little contention when accessing the queue.

Frequent page migration (bouncing) is a problem in SDSM systems because of the large size of memory pages, which are the fundamental unit of coherence. When an invalidation based protocol is employed to maintain cache coherence, modification of just a few bytes of data requires the transfer of an entire coherence unit. In an update based coherence protocol, on the other hand, individual writes to shared data are propagated to every copy of the data. Since update based protocols are not based on the idea of invalidating entire coherence units when writes occur, entire pages are rarely transferred and page bouncing does not occur. This is the reason studies comparing cache coherence protocols for bus-based multiprocessors (e.g., [2][15]) have found that update based coherence protocols become more desirable as cache line sizes (the coherence unit) increase.[1] In the case of SDSM systems, where the unit of coherence is much larger than found in hardware based caching systems, the performance difference between invalidate and update based coherence protocols is even more dramatic. The data presented in Section 4 will make this point clear.

The Munin SDSM system developed at Rice University by Carter, Bennett, and Zwaenepoel addresses the page bouncing problem by exploiting release consistency to support update based coherence in addition to the standard invalidation based strategy [5]. Despite the fact that they implement update based coherence mechanisms entirely in software, they report good performance [9]. In the next section of this paper, we develop a very simple model designed to determine the constraints that must be met in

---

1. These same studies have shown that when cache line sizes are small, invalidate based protocols sometimes perform better. This is because a process may update a line multiple times between references by another processor. If there are enough updates between references by another processor, the cost of sending the updates will exceed the cost of transferring the entire line with an invalidation based protocol.

order to successfully employ update based coherence mechanisms. Then in Section 4, we use that model to build a case for supporting update based coherence with hardware assistance, to further improve the performance of SDSM systems.

## 3: Invalidate versus update based coherence

In this section, we develop a simple model comparing invalidate and update based coherence mechanisms in terms of latency and data transfer requirements. The goal is to derive an easy way to determine whether update or invalidate coherence protocols are preferable in a given situation. Two key parameters to the model are $U$, the number of updates delivered with an update based protocol (note that a single write resulting in an update delivered to $n$ nodes is counted $n$ times), and $I$, the number of misses resulting from references to pages that have been invalidated with an invalidation based protocol (we will refer to these as invalidation misses). In Section 4, we apply values for these parameters obtained through simulation.

It is easy to see that the number of updates delivered with an update based protocol will always be as great as the number of invalidation misses encountered with an invalidation based protocol (assuming the same reference patterns and no cache or page replacement). Mathematically, $U \geq I$. In our model, we let $U = dI$. The $d$ value captures the interprocess write reference granularity of an application, and for a particular coherence granularity, is determined entirely by the workload. It is related to, though not the same as, Eggers and Katz's average write run length [14].

Let $B_U$ be the total number of coherence bytes transferred (including data and overhead bytes that must be sent to ensure coherence) with an update based protocol, and $B_I$ be the total number of coherence bytes transferred with an invalidation based protocol. To simplify matters, we will ignore the messages that must be sent to invalidate pages with the invalidate protocol, and count only the traffic resulting from invalidation misses. (Note that this simplification favors the invalidation based protocol.) We define $b_U$ and $b_I$ to be the number of bytes that must be transferred to handle the delivery of a single update and process an invalidation miss, respectively. We also define $r$ to be the ratio of $b_U$ to $b_I$ (i.e., $r = b_U/b_I$). We can derive simple expressions for $B_U$ and $B_I$:

$$B_U = U \times b_U \tag{1}$$

$$B_U = dI \times rb_I \tag{2}$$

$$B_I = I \times b_I \tag{3}$$

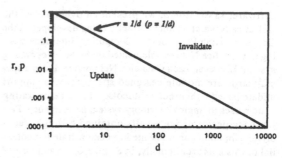

**Figure 1.    Update versus invalidate with respect to r, p, and d**

Equations (2) and (3) can be combined to give an expression indicating when $B_U$ will be less than $B_I$. In terms of data transfer requirements, the update based strategy is the preferred coherence protocol when:

$$d < \frac{1}{r} \tag{4}$$

For page-granularity caching, $b_I$ is generally significantly greater than $b_U$. For example, in the Galactica Net system we describe in Section 5, $b_I$ is 8202 bytes and $b_U$ (for a four-byte update) is 14 bytes, for an $r$ value of approximately 0.0017. Thus, for $d$ values less than about 580, update-based coherence is preferable for Galactica Net in terms of data transfer requirements. In Figure 1, $r = 1/d$ is plotted for $d$ values ranging from 0 to 10,000 (the figure also refers to $p$, which is discussed shortly). The area above the line (note the logarithmic axes) represents the region where an invalidation based protocol would be preferred, while the area below the line represents the region where an update based protocol is preferable.

The latency involved in handling coherence operations is an important concern for SDSM systems, since software is involved in most coherence operations. Our simple model can be applied to latency as well. Let $T_U$ and $T_I$ represent the total time taken to process coherence operations with the update and invalidate protocols, respectively. We let $t_U$ be the time required to process the delivery of a single update, and $t_I$ be the time required to process a single invalidation miss. As with the data transfer equations, we capture the key ratio with a single variable $p = t_U/t_I$. A simple set of expressions for the latency costs similar to those derived for bandwidth can easily be derived.

Since both $p$ and $r$ must be less than $1/d$ for an update based protocol to be preferred, the plot of Figure 1 applies to $p$ (latency requirements) as well as $r$ (data transfer requirements). The plot shows that the higher the value of $d$, the more efficient (in terms of latency and data transfer requirements) update processing must be in order

| Program | Lang. | Length | %Writes | Description |
|---|---|---|---|---|
| ecas | C | 32.8 | 11.3 | Event-driven architecture simulator |
| hart | Ada | 33.5 | 1.4 | Synthetic real-time benchmark |
| locus | C | 33.4 | 3.2 | VLSI standard cell router |
| mp3d | C | 33.3 | 15.5 | Fluid flow simulation |
| mstracer | C | 33.4 | 10.0 | Ray-tracing spheres |
| notoy | Ada | 33.5 | 16.2 | DoD real time battle management simulation |
| piletracer | C | 33.4 | 11.1 | Ray-tracing spheres |
| qsort | C | 32.9 | 9.9 | Quicksort implementation |

**TABLE 1.    Trace characteristics**

for update based protocols to perform better than invalidation based strategies.

## 4:  A case for hardware-assisted updates

To apply the model developed in Section 3, we need to determine appropriate input parameter values. Values for $r$ and $p$ are architecture dependent and, for a given coherence granularity, $d$ is workload dependent. We use trace-driven simulation to determine realistic $d$ values.

The address traces used in our simulations were generated in real time using one Encore Multimax multiprocessor to collect traces from a second Multimax [33]. Eight NS32332 processors were traced simultaneously. Each processor's trace is stored in a separate file, and includes both instruction and data references from both user and supervisor space. Synchronization references are specially marked and sequenced in the traces, so that simulations can ensure that execution proceeds through the synchronization points in some correct order. Key characteristics of the traces (source programming language, millions of references, percent of references that are writes, and a short description of the application) are presented in Table 1. In order to derive $d$ values from the traces of Table 1, we simulated invalidation and update based coherence protocols for 8192-byte pages. In both cases, the size of main memory was large enough to avoid page replacement. In Table 2, we report the number of invalidation misses for the invalidate case, the number of updates delivered for the update case, and the $d$ values for the eight simulation

| Program | Invalidation Misses | Updates Delivered | $d=UD/IM$ |
|---|---|---|---|
| ecas | 1590245 | 11133504 | 7.001 |
| hart | 29914 | 1241332 | 41.497 |
| locus | 34011 | 1084033 | 31.873 |
| mp3d | 370981 | 4470306 | 12.050 |
| mstracer | 55140 | 8050342 | 145.998 |
| notoy | 36859 | 11566166 | 313.795 |
| piletracer | 52558 | 11635671 | 221.387 |
| qsort | 1076808 | 19910114 | 18.490 |

**TABLE 2.    Basic simulation results**

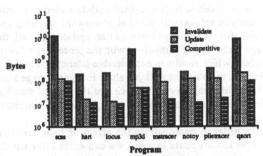

**Figure 2.    Coherence traffic for 8k invalidate, update, and competitive protocols**

experiments. The $d$ values range from 7 to 314. Referring back to Equation (4) and Figure 1 in the previous section, we see that with a $d$ value of 314, an update based coherence protocol performs best (in terms of data transfer requirements) as long as $r$ is less than approximately 0.0032. Since, as discussed in Section 3, $r$ values of only 0.0017 are easily achieved, update based coherence would be best for all of the listed applications in terms of data transfer requirements.

To further emphasize the difference in data transfer requirements between the update and invalidate protocols, the total number of coherence bytes transferred in the simulations is plotted in Figure 2. The Figure 2 data include message overhead of 10 bytes for both page and update transfers. The data clearly show that the data transfer traffic for update based coherence is significantly less than for the invalidate protocol in all eight cases (note the logarithmic y–axis). Also shown in Figure 2 are data from a combination update/invalidate protocol based on the competitive strategy proposed by Karlin, et al. [21]. The Galactica Net implementation of the competitive strategy is described in Section 5.

In terms of data transfer requirements, our simple model and the data presented in Table 2 and Figure 2 clearly support the use of an update based coherence protocol.  Of course, latency concerns also play a role in the update versus invalidate protocol decision.[2] Ideally, the protocol that minimizes data transfer requirements is also the protocol that minimizes latency. This means that when $1/r$ is greater than $d$, $1/p$ should be greater than $d$.

---

2. We present the results of coherence data transfer measurements rather than latency results, since in some sense data transfer rates are more fundamental to a particular protocol. Latency results, on the other hand, are dependent on the efficiency of the underlying communication protocols, a system's ability to exploit weak consistency optimizations through prefetching and instruction re-ordering, and the performance of the operating system code. Thus, generating simulation models which fairly compare latency would be difficult. In Section 5, we present overall performance results of Galactica Net.

It is possible to implement update-based protocols entirely in software. In the straight-forward operating system software implementation of an update protocol, the page fault handler is involved with the processing of every update, which results in considerable latency and makes it difficult to achieve small $p$ values for typical page sizes (2-8 kilobytes). In order to achieve the desired small $p$ values using this implementation approach, an extremely (unrealistically) fast fault handler is essential.

In order to demonstrate the effect of fault handling overhead on update latency, we can extend our simple model by explicitly including the fault handling components of $t_U$ and $t_I$. We define a parameter $f$ which is the fraction of time spent on fault handling processing an invalidation miss. That is, fault handling time is equal to $ft_I$. Assuming that the fault handling overhead is roughly the same for both update faults and invalidation miss faults, we can write $t_I = ft_I + t_{SI}$ and $t_U = ft_I + t_{SU}$, where $t_{SI}$ and $t_{SU}$ are the additional processing times for invalidate miss and update faults, respectively. By replacing for $t_U$ in the second equation, we get $pt_I = ft_I + t_{SU}$, which simplifies to $p = f + t_{SU}/t_I$. Since $t_{SU}/t_I$ is nonnegative, $p \geq f$, and update based coherency will be slower than invalidation based strategies unless either $d$ or $p$ is very small. Since reasonably fast fault handlers will still result in $f$ values greater than 0.05, $d$ values smaller than 20 would be required in order for the update based strategy to perform better than the invalidation based approach.

Small $p$ values can be achieved by employing weaker memory consistency models [4][13][18]. The Munin system employs release consistency and a clever update-combining strategy to amortize the fault and update delivery overhead over approximately $d$ memory updates [9]. Thus the equation for $t_U$ becomes $t_U = (ft_I + t_{SU})/d$, which implies $p = (f + t_{SU}/t_I)/d$. However, even if $t_{SU}$ is zero, $p = f/d$ and the performance improvement of the update based strategy compared to that of an invalidation based approach (in terms of latency) is limited to $f$.

When $d$ is small, both software approaches experience frequent page faults which significantly reduce performance. While our simplified analysis shows that a software update protocol with weak consistency experiences less latency than an invalidation based protocol, eliminating the fault handling costs and reducing $t_{SU}$ through update hardware can reduce latency much further. For programs with relatively small $d$ values, hardware-supported updates can achieve a significantly larger portion of the potential performance gains of update based coherence protocols.

The idea is to provide the mechanism for the operating software to place a shared page in update mode. Write references to update mode pages are detected by hardware that monitors processor references and are propagated to nodes designated by directory tables initialized by the operating system. Since update propagation is handled in hardware, very small $p$ values can be attained. For example, the Galactica Net system described in the next section has typical $p$ values well under 0.003. These small $p$ values make it possible to use update based coherence to achieve very good performance with an SDSM system.

Note that we do not claim that hardware assisted updates are a replacement for the performance optimizations that have been proposed for SDSM system, but an enhancement. For example, weaker memory consistency models can still be employed, as can update combining (implemented in the hardware accelerator) and the use of multiple coherence protocols. In fact, all of these optimizations are planned for the Galactica Net prototype currently under development. Furthermore, Galactica Net can serve as a platform for existing software-based systems that support other desired functionality (e.g., object-oriented programming support).

## 5: Galactica Net

In this section, we describe Galactica Net, a system currently being developed at the Center for High Performance Computing. Galactica Net uses SDSM techniques in combination with hardware support for processing updates to provide a large-scale shared memory computing environment. We note that the Galactica Net idea of hardware supported updates can be applied to other multicomputer implementations in addition to the one described here. In the first subsection, we describe the hardware components of Galactica Net. In Section 5.2, operating system issues are discussed. Preliminary performance results are presented in the final subsection. More detailed descriptions of Galactica Net and performance experiments can be found in [29][30][31].

### 5.1: Galactica Net hardware

A complete Galactica Net system is shown in Figure 3. Each node in the prototype system will consist of a Lynx multiprocessor (containing four Motorola 88110 processors with 256 kbyte secondary caches and 256 Mbytes of dynamic RAM), a Galactica Interface Module (GIM) and a Mesh Router Chip (MRC). The GIM implements the update based protocol used to keep shared memory pages coherent. An efficient multicasting scheme and a high-speed scalable network combine to make an extremely high performance system.

The Galactica Net protocol is implemented on a two-dimensional mesh which uses a variation of the Cal Tech router chip [12][16]. For distances less than a few dozen centimeters, direct electrical connections are used, but for

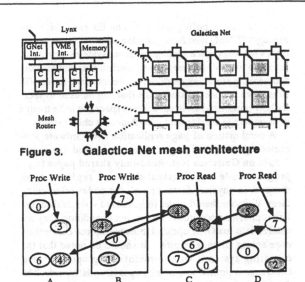

**Figure 3.    Galactica Net mesh architecture**

**Figure 4.    Snap shot of memory state**

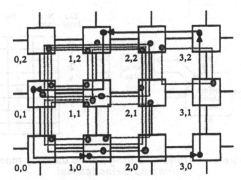

**Figure 5.    Virtual ring mechanism for distributing updates**

longer distances, fiber-optic links are required. The planned fiber optic links are capable of supporting bandwidths in the Gigabits per second range, providing support for future high-performance parallel processor nodes. The use of a mesh network can result in traffic and latency independent of the number of nodes for access patterns exhibiting spatial locality.

In the Galactica Net scheme, all processor requests go to local memory. Writes to memory locations whose contents are shared with processes in other nodes are also sent to those nodes. Local memory can be in one of three states: *Private*, *Read-Only shared*, and *Update shared*. Figure 4 shows a snap shot of the memory state on a four node system. The numbers indicate virtual addresses, which may have different physical locations in each node. Data which only reside in one node are placed in private state, and can be read or written without creating any traffic over Galactica Net, as illustrated by locations 2 and 3 in the figure. Read-only memory locations are copied into all nodes referencing them, as illustrated by location 7, but once resident create no additional global traffic. Pages that are referenced by multiple nodes and modified by at least one of them are placed in update state, as illustrated by location 4.

In order to keep the cost of Galactica Net's hardware assist mechanism low, each processor's MMU and the operating system are used to control the global memory state. Thus regions of memory are placed into update mode on a page size (e.g., 8 kbyte) granularity. While using a full page as the unit of cache coherence can result

in false sharing and hence unnecessary updates, smaller coherence unit sizes would require a large increase in hardware cost. Our use of the memory management system's pages as the coherence unit greatly reduces the cost and hardware complexity of Galactica Net.

Writes to globally shared memory are picked off by the GIM for transmission as updates on Galactica Net. An update intercept unit watches the local bus and picks off any writes which need to be sent to Galactica Net. The writes have their page addresses re-mapped between nodes to allow for different page placement in each node. The mapping unit is implemented as a static table which requires about 0.5 Mbyte of static RAM.

Updates must be multicast to all nodes which have copies of the page being updated. In Galactica Net, multicasting is done by linking all physical pages which correspond to a shared, writable virtual page in a virtual ring imposed on the mesh network. Figure 5 illustrates a set of virtual rings mapped onto a twelve node mesh network. The use of a ring approach provides built-in notification of update completion, which facilitates write ordering.

The virtual ring mechanism is implemented by adding an update routing table (the same mapping table referred to above) to each node, as illustrated in Figure 6a. This table is a simple lookup table addressed by a page index supplied with the update. The table contains a new page index for use in addressing the update routing table in the next node on the sharing ring, and X and Y offsets to that node, as indicated in Figure 6b. Because of the virtual ring approach, only one "next index" is needed per entry. In the prototype version of Galactica Net, the routing table index will actually be the page address in the local node's physical memory, allowing updates to be sent directly to local memory without additional address mapping. Since ring indices are local to each node, the amount of shared memory addressable in a Galactica Net system scales with the number of nodes.

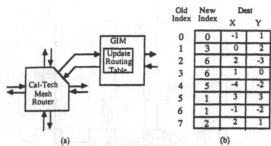

| Old Index | New Index | Dest X | Y |
|-----------|-----------|--------|-----|
| 0 | 0 | -1 | 1 |
| 1 | 3 | 0 | 2 |
| 2 | 6 | 2 | -3 |
| 3 | 6 | 1 | 0 |
| 4 | 5 | -4 | -2 |
| 5 | 1 | 3 | 3 |
| 6 | 1 | -1 | -2 |
| 7 | 2 | 2 | 1 |

(a)                                        (b)

**Figure 6.     Update routing tables used by mesh connected Galactica Net**

In order to obtain maximum performance, the Galactica Net prototype utilizes a weak consistency model.[3] Weak consistency allows processing to continue while updates are propagating to other nodes, thus hiding a large portion of the update latency [31]. The GIM provides support for internode synchronization, to simplify the task of programming in a weakly-consistent environment. As an additional performance optimization, multiple updates can be combined through hardware buffering mechanisms, resulting in more efficient utilization of the interconnection network.

While the prototype Galactica Net implementation uses a specific shared bus multiprocessor and a mesh interconnection network, there is nothing about the Galactica Net hardware update protocol which limits it to those systems. For instance, the virtual ring concept could be applied to any interconnection network to provide its processors with hardware assisted shared memory using the Galactica Net update protocol. Node architectures other than shared bus multiprocessors, such as uniprocessor workstations, are readily incorporated into Galactica Net as well. Thus the Galactica Net hardware assist protocol has wide applicability to distributed systems.

### 5.2: Operating system support

The operating system used to support SDSM on Galactica Net is a Mach [1] 3.0 µKernel with an OSF/1 server. The design of the Mach virtual memory management system [26] makes it ideally suited for this purpose, since the distribution of memory objects across the nodes of a distributed system is a natural extension to Mach.

The Galactica Net SDSM implementation will be realized using the External Memory Manager Interface that has been designed for Mach. This moves memory management "policy" into a user space multi-threaded task, providing the mechanism required to experimentally evaluate alternative policy options. The External Memory Manager (EMM) interfaces with the µKernel virtual memory (VM) and device management subsystems to provide access to local VM management mechanisms and network and backing store device drivers. The interface to the VM subsystem includes system calls that can be used to specify how portions of a virtual address space are to be treated with respect to sharing and inheritance by child threads.

A combination of page replication and hardware-supported update-based page coherence is used to support SDSM on Galactica Net. Read-only shared pages (e.g., program code and constant data) are replicated, on demand, in physical frames on all the nodes referencing them. Writable shared pages (e.g., shared volatile data) are also replicated upon initial access, but in addition, they are entered into the GIM update tables to enforce data coherence across all page copies.   It should be noted that the operating system's role in maintaining update-based coherence is limited to placing pages in update-mode. The GIM hardware takes care of all update propagation. Alternatively, the operating system may choose to keep shared writable pages coherent using a software-implemented invalidation based protocol, as is done in other SDSM systems. A competitive algorithm for choosing between invalidate and update based coherence protocols [21] may be employed to make this decision (see the discussion of invalidation hints at the end of this subsection).

Page replication is triggered by the page fault that occurs on the first access to a non-mapped (or non-resident) page. The page fault handler decodes the fault and passes this information to the VM subsystem which, in turn, forwards a request to the EMM. The EMM determines if the requested page is for local use only (i.e., private) or if it is shared. Next, the page is either provided from backing store (for a writable private page) or replicated from the nearest node containing a copy (for a read-only or writable shared page). If the page is shared writable, the VM subsystem installs it in the GIM update tables. The VM subsystem maintains complete page usage information, including a directory of all nodes sharing pages and current state information. This metadata is used to control page replication and coherence policies. The EMM Interface will be extended to provide access to these data structures for the External Memory Manager.

There are three different scenarios in which two nodes might share a page. The first is transparent and due to load balancing, where threads of the same task are run on different nodes in order to balance the system load. The second case is when two separate tasks share data through use of the VM subsystem capabilities, and the third case is when two tasks share data through memory mapped files. Though the implementation details differ, the basic strategy for implementing the sharing is similar for all three

---

3. Sequential consistency can also be supported by the Galactica Net protocols, with some increase in memory reference latency. This is discussed thoroughly in [31].

cases. For example, consider the case in which two tasks share a page. The first task (T0) allocates a page to be shared with a second task (T1) that is running on a different node. Task T0, which can modify the page, sends task T1 a message with a port representing the shared data object. Task T1 then allocates virtual space for the shared page via the port and a call to the local VM subsystem. When T1 first references the shared page a fault occurs and a copy of the page is block transferred from T0 to T1. Both task VM subsystems mark the page as shared and establish entries in the GIM update tables (thereby joining or forming a virtual sharing ring), so that the two copies of the page are kept coherent with the hardware-supported update mechanism.   If T0 and T1 share the page read-only (i.e., no task can modify the page), then there is no need to establish a virtual sharing ring for that page. In the case of more than two tasks sharing a page, the External Memory Managers must ensure that all copies of the page are linked together in a virtual sharing ring through the GIMs, so that memory updates are properly propagated to all page copies.

In order to support the competitive invalidate versus update coherence protocol proposed by Karlin, et al, the GIM implements per-page update counters and an invalidation hint mechanism. The invalidation hint (which comes to the operating system in the form of an interrupt) indicates that the number of remote updates to a page has exceeded a preset limit without a local modification to the page. If there have been no local references to the page and it is not tagged as wired-down (i.e., not pageable), then the operating system can invalidate the local copy of the page and remove the node from the page's sharing ring. This can dramatically reduce the number of updates delivered to stale page copies, significantly reducing communication bandwidth requirements. The data presented in Figure 2 of Section 4 demonstrate the potential of this strategy. Of course, the next time a local thread references the page a fault will occur and the VM subsystem will have to acquire a fresh copy of the page from some other node.

## 5.3: Performance

Galactica Net's use of a multicasting update protocol for shared, writable pages raises a number of performance issues not seen with other DSM architectures. For example, update protocols produce frequent, short transfers which can be inefficient to transport on some types of networks. This section uses simulation with hardware- and software- collected parallel address traces to investigate the actual behavior of the Galactica Net protocol. The hardware-collected traces used were described in Section 3. In addition, we consider the performance of three software-collected address traces; PDE (a partial dif-

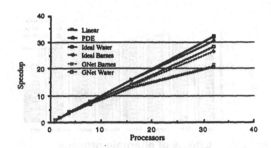

**Figure 7.    Speedup of selected benchmarks on Galactica Net**

ferential equation solver) and Barnes and Water from Stanford's SPLASH application suite [27] The software-collected address traces allow us to conduct simulations with varying numbers of processors.

The use of a weak consistency model (such as release consistency) with Galactica Net allows update propagation to be overlapped with additional computing. Ideally, the entire cost of the updates can be hidden, giving performance near that of an ideal memory system. To see how close Galactica Net can actually come to the ideal, a simulation model of Galactica Net was constructed and used to measure the projected performance for three benchmark traces. The simulations included behavior level models of the mesh routers, Galactica Net interface, and Lynx based nodes.

Speedup curves for the three benchmarks are shown in Figure 7. The PDE benchmark, which exhibits good spatial locality (each process only communicates with two "nearest neighbors"), yields nearly linear speedup. Water and Barnes track their performance on an ideal memory system through 16 processors. At 32 processors, several links approach saturation, resulting in a drop in speedup. Note that the data sets used by the Water and Barnes executions traced are rather small; larger data sets would result in improved performance. Further note that no attempt was made to optimize process placement for Water or Barnes. Also, update concatenation hardware which we have been investigating, can significantly reduce link traffic and improve speedups.

Using the hardware-collected traces, we compared the performance of two, four, and eight node Galactica Net systems with that of a hypothetical two-Lynx multiprocessor with zero cost internode communication. Since the applications and operating system where originally developed for, and traced on, a uniform access, shared bus multiprocessor, many of the traces exhibit a fairly fine grain of sharing. For example, both ECAS and Quicksort schedule small units of work off of a common work queue with the result that most global data is accessed by all processors. In addition, the OS migrates processes more frequently

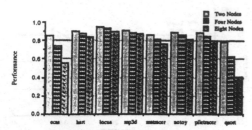

**Figure 8.** **Effects of alternate process distributions on Galactica Net**

than is appropriate for a distributed memory machine. Thus, these traces represent a worst case workload for a distributed memory multiprocessor.

The graph of Figure 8 shows the results of this experiment. Since eight-processor traces are used, the two node Galactica Net system has four active processors per node, the four node system has two, and the eight node system has one active processor per node. The simulated Lynx backplane utilization was sufficiently low in all cases that its contribution to performance was relatively constant regardless of the number of active processors on each node. Thus, the degradation in performance as the number of nodes increases fairly accurately reflects the cost of maintaining data coherence using Galactica Net's update-based coherence protocol with hardware support. For most benchmarks, the performance of Galactica Net was within 20% of ideal, and some within 10%. Some of the drop in performance from ideal is due to the latency of page transfers, which in the simulations disabled a sharing ring for its duration, thus halting several processors. Methods to overlap transfers and updates are under investigation, which will result in even better performance. In the case of ECAS and Quicksort, the fine grain of cooperation resulted in frequent synchronization and short write run lengths (as indicated by the low $d$ values in Table 2), which produced heavy link traffic and depressed the more distributed cases. These two applications perform poorly even on ideal shared memory machines.

## 6: Summary and conclusions

Developing strategies for supporting large-scale shared memory computing environments is an active research topic. Numerous projects have focused on designs for hardware-support shared memory, while others have worked to provide this support through operating system software. In this paper, we propose an alternative approach based on a software implementation of shared memory exploiting special hardware support for update based coherence. Our vision is to provide simple accelerators that can be plugged into traditional computing nodes to support update-based coherent shared memory.

A simple model is developed in Section 3 that identifies the conditions under which an update based coherence strategy will offer improved performance relative to an invalidation based approach. Using this model, we show in Section 4 that for page granularity caching, an update based coherence is preferable (in terms of data transfer requirements) to an invalidation based strategy for all of the applications in our experimental workload. We then argue that with hardware support for update based coherence, the update based strategy would be preferable to an invalidation based strategy in terms of latency as well. Though update based coherence can be effectively implemented entirely in software, the performance improvement possible with such an approach is fundamentally limited by the cost of page fault processing.

We argue that the addition of the hardware assisted update protocol to a software based distributed shared memory system can allow such a system to obtain good performance with a much wider set of applications than possible with a strictly invalidation based SDSM system. Specifically, those shared memory applications exhibiting fine-grained read/write sharing of data can have both network latency and bandwidth requirements dramatically reduced through hardware implemented updates. Results of trace driven simulation experiments indicate that typical applications written for tightly coupled shared memory multiprocessors can perform very well on the proposed hybrid system.

Galactica Net, the implementation of hardware assisted DSM described in the paper, is currently being developed by the authors at the Center for High Performance Computing. We expect to have a fully functional prototype system in 1993.

## References

[1] M. Accetta, R. Baron, W. Bolosky, D. Golub, R. Rashid, A. Tevanian, and M. Young. Mach: A new kernel foundation for Unix Development. In *Proceedings of the 1986 Summer Usenix*, July, 1986.

[2] J. Archibald and J.-L. Baer. Cache coherence protocols: Evaluation using a multiprocessor simulation model. *ACM Transactions on Computer Systems*, 4(4):273-298, November 1986.

[3] A. Agarwal, D. Chaiken, G. D'Souza, K. Johnson, D. Kranz, J. Kubiatowicz, B.-H. Lim, G. Maa, D. Nussbaum, M. Parkin, and D. Yeung. The MIT Alewife Machine: A Large-Scale Distributed-Memory Multiprocessor. MIT Laboratory for Computer Science Technical Report MIT/LCS/TM-454.b, November, 1991.

[4] S. Adve and M. Hill. Weak ordering - a new definition. In *Proceedings of the 17th Annual International Symposium on Computer Architecture*, pages 2-14, May 1990.

[5] J. K. Bennett, J. B. Carter, and W. Zwaenepoel. Adaptive software cache management for distributed shared memory architectures. In *Proceedings of the 17th Annual Interna-*

*tional Symposium on Computer Architecture*, pages 125-1135, May 1990.

[6] J. K. Bennett, J. B. Carter, and W. Zwaenepoel. Munin: Distributed shared memory based on type-specific memory coherence. In *Proceedings of the Second Symposium on Principles and Practice of Parallel Programming*, pages 168-175, March 1990.

[7] R. Bisiani and M Ravishankar. PLUS : A distributed shared-memory system. In *Proceedings of the 17th Annual International Symposium on Computer Architecture*, June 1990.

[8] W. Bolosky, M. Scott, and R. Fitzgerald. Simple but effective techniques for NUMA memory management. In *Proceedings of the Twelfth ACM Symposium on Operating Systems Principles*, December 1989.

[9] J. Carter, J. Bennett, W. Zwaenepoel. Implementation and Performance of Munin. In *Proceedings of the Thirteenth ACM Symposium on Operating Systems Principles*, October, 1991.

[10] A.L. Cox and R.J. Fowler. The implementation of a coherent memory abstraction on a NUMA multiprocessor: Experiences with Platinum. In *Proceedings of the Twelfth ACM Symposium on Operating Systems Principles*, pages 32-43, December 1989.

[11] D. Cheriton, H. Goosen, and P. Boyle. Paradigm: A Highly scalable shared-memory multicomputer architecture. IEEE Computer, 24(2):33-46, February, 1991.

[12] W. Dally and C. Seitz. The Torus Routing Chip. *Distributed Computing*. 1(4):187-196, Springer-Verlag, October, 1986.

[13] M. Dubois and C. Scheurich. Memory access dependencies in shared-memory multiprocessors. *IEEE Transactions on Software Engineering*, 16(6):660-673, June 1990.

[14] S. Eggers and R. Katz. A characterization of sharing in parallel programs and its application to coherency protocol evaluation. In *Proceedings of the 15th Annual International Symposium on Computer Architecture*, pages 373-383, May 1988.

[15] S. Eggers and R. Katz. Evaluating the performance of four snooping cache coherency protocols. In *Proceedings of the 16th Annual International Symposium on Computer Architecture*, pages 2-15, May 1989.

[16] Flaig, C. M., VLSI Mesh Routing Systems, Technical Report 5241:TR:87, California Institute of Technology, May, 1987.

[17] A. Forin, J. Barrera, M. Young, and R. Rashid. Design, Implementation, and Performance Evaluation of a Distributed Shared Memory Server for Mach. In *Proceedings of the Winter USENIX Conference*, January, 1989.

[18] K. Gharachorloo, D. Lenoski, J. Laudon, P. Gibbons, A. Gupta, and J. Hennessey. Memory consistency and event ordering in scalable shared-memory multiprocessors. In *Proceedings of the 17th Annual International Symposium on Computer Architecture*, pages 15-26, May 1990.

[19] J.R. Goodman and P.J. Woest. The Wisconsin Multicube: A new large-scale cache-coherent multiprocessor. In *Proceedings of the 15th Annual International Symposium on Computer Architecture*, pages 422-431, Honolulu, HI, 1988.

[20] E. Hagersten, A. Landin, and S. Haridi. DDM — A Cache-Only Memory Architecture. *IEEE Computer*, 25(9):44-54, September, 1992.

[21] A. Karlin, M. Manasse, L. Rudolph, and D. Sleator. Competitive snoopy caching. *Algorithmica*, 3(1):79-119, January 1988.

[22] R. P. LaRowe Jr. and C. S. Ellis. Experimental comparison of memory management policies for NUMA multiprocessors. *ACM Transactions on Computer Systems*, 9(4):319-363, November 1991.

[23] K. Li and P. Hudak. Memory coherence in shared virtual memory systems. *ACM Transactions on Computer Systems*, 7(4):229-359, November, 1989.

[24] Hennessey. The directory-based cache coherence protocol for the DASH multiprocessor. In *Proceedings of the 17th Annual International Symposium on Computer Architecture*, pages 148-159, May 1990.

[25] U. Ramachandran, M. Ahamad, and M. Y. A. Khalidi. Coherence of distributed shared memory: Unifying synchronization and data transfer. In *Proceedings of the 1989 International Conference on Parallel Processing*, pages II-160-II169, August 1989.

[26] R. Rashid, A. Trevanian, M. Young, D. Golub, R. Baron, D. Black, W. Bolosky, and J. Crew. Machine-independent virtual memory management for paged uniprocessor and multiprocessor architectures. *IEEE Transactions on Computers*, 37(8):896-908, August 1988.

[27] J. P. Singh, W.-D. Weber, and A. Gupta. SPLASH: Stanford parallel applications for shared memory. *Computer Architecture News*, 20(1):5-44, March, 1992.

[28] A. W. Wilson Jr. Hierarchical cache/bus architecture for shared memory multiprocessors. In *Proceedings of the 14th Annual International Symposium on Computer Architecture*, June 1987.

[29] A. Wilson Jr., M. Teller, T. Probert, D. Le, and R. LaRowe Jr. Lynx/Galactica Net: A distributed, cache coherent multiprocessing system. In *Proceedings of the 25th Hawaii International Conference on System Sciences*, pages 416-426, January, 1992.

[30] A. W. Wilson Jr. and R. P. LaRowe Jr. Galactica Net architecture specification. Center for High Performance Computing Technical Report 92-003R, 1992.

[31] A. W. Wilson Jr. and R. P. LaRowe Jr. Hiding shared memory reference latency on the Galactica Net distributed shared memory architecture. *Journal of Parallel and Distributed Computing*, 15(4):351-367, August 1992.

[32] Wittie, L. D., G. Hermannsson, and A. Li. Eager Sharing for Efficient Massive Parallelism. SUNY Stony Brook TR #92/01.

[33] B. Vashaw. Address Trace Collections and Trace Driven Simulation of Bus Based, Shared Memory Multiprocessors. Ph.D. thesis, Carnegie-Mellon University, May, 1992.

# The Stanford FLASH Multiprocessor

Jeffrey Kuskin, David Ofelt, Mark Heinrich, John Heinlein,
Richard Simoni, Kourosh Gharachorloo, John Chapin, David Nakahira, Joel Baxter,
Mark Horowitz, Anoop Gupta, Mendel Rosenblum, and John Hennessy

Computer Systems Laboratory
Stanford University
Stanford, CA 94305

## Abstract

The FLASH multiprocessor efficiently integrates support for cache-coherent shared memory and high-performance message passing, while minimizing both hardware and software overhead. Each node in FLASH contains a microprocessor, a portion of the machine's global memory, a port to the interconnection network, an I/O interface, and a custom node controller called MAGIC. The MAGIC chip handles all communication both within the node and among nodes, using hardwired data paths for efficient data movement and a programmable processor optimized for executing protocol operations. The use of the protocol processor makes FLASH very flexible — it can support a variety of different communication mechanisms — and simplifies the design and implementation.

This paper presents the architecture of FLASH and MAGIC, and discusses the base cache-coherence and message-passing protocols. Latency and occupancy numbers, which are derived from our system-level simulator and our Verilog code, are given for several common protocol operations. The paper also describes our software strategy and FLASH's current status.

## 1 Introduction

The two architectural techniques for communicating data among processors in a scalable multiprocessor are message passing and distributed shared memory (DSM). Despite significant differences in how programmers view these two architectural models, the underlying hardware mechanisms used to implement these approaches have been converging. Current DSM and message-passing multiprocessors consist of processing nodes interconnected with a high-bandwidth network. Each node contains a node processor, a portion of the physically distributed memory, and a node controller that connects the processor, memory, and network together. The principal difference between message-passing and DSM machines is in the protocol implemented by the node controller for transferring data both within and among nodes.

Perhaps more surprising than the similarity of the overall structure of these types of machines is the commonality in functions performed by the node controller. In both cases, the primary performance-critical function of the node controller is the movement of data at high bandwidth and low latency among the processor, memory, and network. In addition to these existing similarities, the architectural trends for both styles of machine favor further convergence in both the hardware and software mechanisms used to implement the communication abstractions. Message-passing machines are moving to efficient support of short messages and a uniform address space, features normally associated with DSM machines. Similarly, DSM machines are starting to provide support for message-like block transfers (e.g., the Cray T3D), a feature normally associated with message-passing machines.

The efficient integration and support of both cache-coherent shared memory and low-overhead user-level message passing is the primary goal of the FLASH (FLexible Architecture for SHared memory) multiprocessor. Efficiency involves both low hardware overhead and high performance. A major problem of current cache-coherent DSM machines (such as the earlier DASH machine [LLG+92]) is their high hardware overhead, while a major criticism of current message-passing machines is their high software overhead for user-level message passing. FLASH integrates and streamlines the hardware primitives needed to provide low-cost and high-performance support for global cache coherence and message passing. We aim to achieve this support without compromising the protection model or the ability of an operating system to control resource usage. The latter point is important since we want FLASH to operate well in a general-purpose multiprogrammed environment with many users sharing the machine as well as in a traditional supercomputer environment.

To accomplish these goals we are designing a custom node controller. This controller, called MAGIC (Memory And General Interconnect Controller), is a highly integrated chip that implements all data transfers both within

Reprinted from *Proc. 21st Ann. Int'l Symp. Computer Architecture.*, 1994, pp. 302–313.

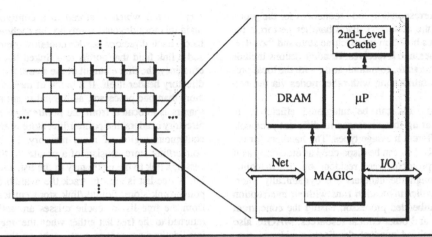

**Figure 2.1. FLASH system architecture.**

the node and between the node and the network. To deliver high performance, the MAGIC chip contains a specialized data path optimized to move data between the memory, network, processor, and I/O ports in a pipelined fashion without redundant copying. To provide the flexible control needed to support a variety of DSM and message-passing protocols, the MAGIC chip contains an embedded processor that controls the data path and implements the protocol. The separate data path allows the processor to update the protocol data structures (e.g., the directory for cache coherence) in parallel with the associated data transfers.

This paper describes the FLASH design and rationale. Section 2 gives an overview of FLASH. Section 3 briefly describes two example protocols, one for cache-coherent shared memory and one for message passing. Section 4 presents the microarchitecture of the MAGIC chip. Section 5 briefly presents our system software strategy and Section 6 presents our implementation strategy and current status. Section 7 discusses related work and we conclude in Section 8.

## 2 FLASH Architecture Overview

FLASH is a single-address-space machine consisting of a large number of processing nodes connected by a low-latency, high-bandwidth interconnection network. Every node is identical (see Figure 2.1), containing a high-performance off-the-shelf microprocessor with its caches, a portion of the machine's distributed main memory, and the MAGIC node controller chip. The MAGIC chip forms the heart of the node, integrating the memory controller, I/O controller, network interface, and a programmable protocol processor. This integration allows for low hardware overhead while supporting both cache-coherence and message-passing protocols in a scalable and cohesive fashion.[1]

The MAGIC architecture is designed to offer both flexibility and high performance. First, MAGIC includes a programmable protocol processor for flexibility. Second, MAGIC's central location within the node ensures that it sees all processor, network, and I/O transactions, allowing it to control all node resources and support a variety of protocols. Third, to avoid limiting the node design to any specific protocol and to accommodate protocols with varying memory requirements, the node contains no dedicated protocol storage; instead, both the protocol code and protocol data reside in a reserved portion of the node's main memory. However, to provide high-speed access to frequently-used protocol code and data, MAGIC contains on-chip instruction and data caches. Finally, MAGIC separates data movement logic from protocol state manipulation logic. The hardwired data movement logic achieves low latency and high bandwidth by supporting highly-pipelined data transfers without extra copying within the chip. The protocol processor employs a hardware dispatch table to help service requests quickly, and a coarse-level pipeline to reduce protocol processor occupancy. This separation and specialization of data transfer and control logic ensures that MAGIC does not become a latency or bandwidth bottleneck.

FLASH nodes communicate by sending intra- and inter-node commands, which we refer to as *messages*. To implement a protocol on FLASH, one must define what kinds of messages will be exchanged (the *message types*),

---

1. Our decision to use only one compute processor per node rather than multiple processors was driven mainly by pragmatic concerns. Using only one processor considerably simplifies the node design, and given the high bandwidth requirements of modern processors, it was not clear that we could support multiple processors productively. However, nothing in our approach precludes the use of multiple processors per node.

and write the corresponding code sequences for the protocol processor (the *handlers*). Each handler performs the necessary actions based on the machine state and the information in the message it receives. Handler actions include updating machine state, communicating with the local processor, and communicating with other nodes via the network.

Multiple protocols can be integrated efficiently in FLASH by ensuring that messages in different protocols are assigned different message types. The handlers for the various protocols then can be dispatched as efficiently as if only a single protocol were resident on the machine. Moreover, although the handlers are dynamically interleaved, each handler invocation runs without interruption on MAGIC's embedded processor, easing the concurrent sharing of state and other critical resources. MAGIC also provides protocol-independent deadlock avoidance support, allowing multiple protocols to coexist without deadlocking the machine or having other negative interactions.

Since FLASH is designed to scale to thousands of processing nodes, a comprehensive protection and fault containment strategy is needed to assure acceptable system availability. At the user level, the virtual memory system provides protection against application software errors. However, system-level errors such as operating system bugs and hardware faults require a separate fault detection and containment mechanism. The hardware and operating system cooperate to identify, isolate, and contain these faults. MAGIC provides a hardware-based "firewall" mechanism that can be used to prevent certain operations (memory writes, for example) from occurring on unauthorized addresses. Error-detection codes ensure data integrity: ECC protects main memory and CRCs protect network traffic. Errors are reported to the operating system, which is responsible for taking suitable action.

## 3 FLASH Protocols

This section presents a base cache-coherence protocol and a base block-transfer protocol we have designed for FLASH. We use the term "base" to emphasize that these two protocols are simply the ones we chose to implement first; Section 3.3 discusses protocol extensions and alternatives.

### 3.1 Cache Coherence Protocol

The base cache-coherence protocol is directory-based and has two components: a scalable directory data structure, and a set of handlers. For a scalable directory structure, FLASH uses *dynamic pointer allocation* [Simoni92], illustrated in Figure 3.1. In this scheme, each cache line-sized block — 128 bytes in the prototype — of main memory is associated with an 8-byte state word called a *direc-*

*tory header*, which is stored in a contiguous section of main memory devoted solely to the cache-coherence protocol. Each directory header contains some boolean flags and a link field that points to a linked list of sharers. For efficiency, the first element of the sharer list is stored in the directory header itself. If a block of memory is cached by more than one processor, additional memory for its list of sharers is allocated from the *pointer/link store*. Like the directory headers, the pointer/link store is also a physically contiguous region of main memory. Each entry in the pointer/link store consists of a pointer to the sharing processor, a link to the next entry in the list, and an end-of-list bit. A free list is used to track the available entries in the pointer/link store. Pointer/link store entries are allocated from the free list as cache misses are satisfied, and are returned to the free list either when the line is written and invalidations are sent to each cache on the list of sharers, or when a processor notifies the directory that it is no longer caching a block[2].

A significant advantage of dynamic pointer allocation is that the directory storage requirements are scalable. The amount of memory needed for the directory headers is proportional to the local memory per node, and scales as more processors are added. The total amount of memory needed in the machine for the pointer/link store is proportional to the total amount of cache in the system. Since the amount of cache is much smaller that the amount of main memory, the size of the pointer/link store is sufficient to maintain full caching information, as long as the loading on the different memory modules is uniform. When this uniformity does not exist, a node can run out of pointer/link storage. While a detailed discussion is beyond the scope of this paper, several heuristics can be used in this situation to ensure reasonable performance. Overall, the directory occupies 7% to 9% of main memory, depending on system configuration.

Apart from the data structures used to maintain directory information, the base cache-coherence protocol is similar to the DASH protocol [LLG+90]. Both protocols utilize separate request and reply networks to eliminate request-reply cycles in the network. Both protocols forward dirty data from a processor's cache directly to a requesting processor, and both protocols use negative acknowledgments to avoid deadlock and to cause retries when a requested line is in a transient state. The main difference between the two protocols is that in DASH each cluster collects its own invalidation acknowledgments, whereas in FLASH invalidation acknowledgments are col-

---

2. The base cache-coherence protocol relies on replacement hints. The protocol could be modified to accommodate processors which do not provide these hints.

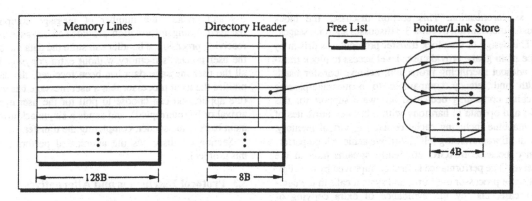

**Figure 3.1. Data structures for the dynamic pointer allocation directory scheme.**

lected at the *home* node, that is, the node where the directory data is stored for that block.

Avoiding deadlock is difficult in any cache-coherence protocol. Below we discuss how the base protocol handles the deadlock problem, and illustrate some of the protocol-independent deadlock avoidance mechanisms of the MAGIC architecture. Although this discussion focuses on the base cache-coherence protocol, any protocol run on FLASH can use these mechanisms to eliminate the deadlock problem.

As a first step, the base protocol divides all messages into requests (e.g., read, read-exclusive, and invalidate requests) and replies (e.g., read and read-exclusive data replies, and invalidation acknowledgments). Second, the protocol uses the virtual lane support in the network routers to transmit requests and replies over separate logical networks. Next, it guarantees that replies can be *sunk*, that is, replies generate no additional outgoing messages. This eliminates the possibility of request-reply circular dependencies. To break request-request cycles, requests that cannot be sunk may be negatively acknowledged, effectively turning those requests into replies.

The final requirement for a deadlock solution is a restriction placed on all handlers: they must yield the protocol processor if they cannot run to completion. If a handler violates this constraint and stalls waiting for space on one of its output queues, the machine could potentially deadlock because it is no longer servicing messages from the network. To avoid this type of deadlock, the scheduling mechanism for the incoming queues is initialized to indicate which incoming queues contain messages that may require outgoing queue space. The scheduler will not select an incoming queue unless the corresponding outgoing queue space requirements are satisfied.

However, in some cases, the number of outgoing messages a handler will send cannot be determined before-

hand, preventing the scheduler from ensuring adequate outgoing queue space for these handlers. For example, an incoming request (for which only outgoing reply queue space is guaranteed) may need to be forwarded to a dirty remote node. If at this point the outgoing request queue is full, the protocol processor negatively acknowledges the incoming request, converting it into a reply. A second case not handled by the scheduler is an incoming write miss that is scheduled and finds that it needs to send N invalidation requests into the network. Unfortunately, the outgoing request queue may have fewer than N spots available. As stated above, the handler cannot simply wait for space to free up in the outgoing request queue to send the remaining invalidations. To solve this problem, the protocol employs the *software queue* where it can suspend messages to be rescheduled at a later time.

The software queue is a reserved region of main memory that any protocol can use to suspend message processing temporarily. For instance, each time MAGIC receives a write request to a shared line, the corresponding handler reserves space in the software queue for possible rescheduling. If the queue is already full, the incoming request is simply negatively acknowledged. This case should be extremely rare. If the handler discovers that it needs to send N invalidations, but only M < N spots are available in the outgoing request queue, the handler sends M invalidate requests and then places itself on the software queue. The list of sharers at this point contains only those processors that have not been invalidated. When the write request is rescheduled off of the software queue, the new handler invocation continues sending invalidation requests where the old one left off.

## 3.2 Message Passing Protocol

In FLASH, we distinguish long messages, used for block transfer, from short messages, such as those required for synchronization. This section discusses the block transfer mechanism; Section 3.3 discusses short messages.

The design of the block transfer protocol was driven by three main goals: provide user-level access to block transfer without sacrificing protection; achieve transfer bandwidth and latency comparable to a message-passing machine containing dedicated hardware support for this task; and operate in harmony with other key attributes of the machine including cache coherence, virtual memory, and multiprogramming [HGG94]. We achieve high performance because MAGIC efficiently streams data to the receiver. The performance is further improved by the elimination of processor interrupts and system calls in the common case, and by the avoidance of extra copying of message data.

To distinguish a user-level message from the low-level messages MAGIC sends between nodes, this section explicitly refers to the former as a *user message*. Sending a user message in FLASH logically consists of three phases: initiation, transfer, and reception/completion.

To send a user message, an application process calls a library routine to communicate the parameters of the user-level message to MAGIC. This communication happens using a series of uncached writes to special addresses (which act as memory-mapped commands). Unlike standard uncached writes, these special writes invoke a different handler that accumulates information from the command into a message description record in MAGIC's memory. The final command is an uncached read, to which MAGIC replies with a value indicating if the message is accepted. Once the message is accepted, MAGIC invokes a *transfer handler* that takes over responsibility for transferring the user message to its destination, allowing the main processor to run in parallel with the message transfer.

The transfer handler sends the user message data as a series of independent, cache line-sized messages. The transfer handler keeps the user message data coherent by checking the directory state as the transfer proceeds, taking appropriate coherence actions as needed. Block transfers are broken into cache line-sized chunks because the system is optimized for data transfers of this size, and because block transfers can then utilize the deadlock prevention mechanisms implemented for the base cache-coherence protocol. From a deadlock avoidance perspective, the user message transfer is similar to sending a long list of invalidations: the transfer handler may only be able to send part of the user message in a single activation. To avoid filling the outgoing queue and to allow other handlers to execute, the transfer handler periodically marks its progress and suspends itself on the software queue.

When each component of the user-level message arrives at the destination node, a *reception handler* is invoked which stores the associated message data in mem-

ory and updates the number of message components received. Using information provided in advance by the receiving process, the handler can store the data directly in the user process's memory without extra copying. When all the user message data has been received, the handler notifies the local processor that a user message has arrived (the application can choose to poll for the user message arrival or be interrupted), and sends a single acknowledgment back to the sender, completing the transfer.

Section 4.3 discusses the anticipated performance of this protocol.

## 3.3 Protocol Extensions and Alternatives

MAGIC's flexible design supports a variety of protocols, not just the two described in Section 3.1 and Section 3.2. By changing the handlers, one can implement other cache-coherence and message-passing protocols, or support completely different operations and communication models. Consequently, FLASH is ideal for experimenting with new protocols.

For example, the handlers can be modified to emulate the "attraction memory" found in a cache-only memory architecture, such as Kendall Square Research's ALL-CACHE [KSR92]. A handler that normally forwards a remote request to the home node in the base cache-coherence protocol can be expanded to first check the local memory for the presence of the data. Because MAGIC stores protocol data structures in main memory, it has no difficulty accommodating the different state information (e.g., attraction memory tags) maintained by a COMA protocol.

Another possibility is to implement synchronization primitives as MAGIC handlers. Primitives executing on MAGIC avoid the cost of interrupting the main processor and can exploit MAGIC's ability to communicate efficiently with other nodes. In addition, guaranteeing the atomicity of the primitives is simplified since MAGIC handlers are non-interruptible. Operations such as fetch-and-op and tree barriers are ideal candidates for this type of implementation.

FLASH's short message support corresponds closely to the structuring of communication using active messages as advocated by von Eicken et al. [vECG+92]. However, the MAGIC chip supports fast active messages only at the system level, as opposed to the user level. While von Eicken et al. argue for user-level active messages, we have found that system-level active messages suffice and in many ways simplify matters. For example, consider the shared-memory model and the ordinary read/write requests issued by compute processors. Since the virtual addresses issued by the processor are translated into physical addresses and are protection-checked by the TLB before they reach the MAGIC chip, no further translation or protection checks are needed at MAGIC. By not allowing user-level handlers, we ensure that malicious user-level handlers do not cause deadlock by breaking resource consumption conventions in the MAGIC chip. The MAGIC chip architecture could be extended to provide protection for user-level handlers (e.g., by providing time-outs), but this change would significantly complicate the chip and the protocols. Instead, we are investigating software techniques for achieving the required protection to allow user-level handlers to execute in the unprotected MAGIC environment. Overall, we believe the disadvantages of providing hardware support for user-level handlers in MAGIC outweigh the advantages. Operations that are truly critical to performance (e.g., support for tree barriers and other synchronization primitives) usually can be coded and provided at the system level by MAGIC. Disallowing user-level handlers should lead to a simpler and higher-performing design.

While the inherent complexity of writing handlers may be small, it is important to realize that errors in the MAGIC handlers directly impact the correctness and stability of the machine. We consider the verification of handlers to be analogous to hardware verification, since MAGIC handlers directly control the node's hardware resources. As a result, although new protocols may be simple to implement, they must be verified thoroughly to be trusted to run on MAGIC.

## 4 MAGIC Microarchitecture

Fundamentally, protocol handlers must perform two tasks: data movement and state manipulation. The MAGIC architecture exploits the relative independence of these tasks by separating control and data processing. As messages enter the MAGIC chip they are split into message headers and message data. Message headers flow through the *control macropipeline* while message data flows through the *data transfer logic*, depicted in Figure 4.1. Data and control information are recombined as outgoing message headers are merged with the associated outgoing message data to form complete outgoing messages.

### 4.1 The Data Transfer Logic

Both message-passing and cache-coherence protocols require data connections among the network, local memory, and local processor. Because the structure of these connections is protocol-independent, the data transfer logic can be implemented completely in hardware without causing a loss of overall protocol processing flexibility. The hardwired implementation minimizes data access latency, maximizes data transfer bandwidth, and frees the protocol processor from having to perform data transfers itself.

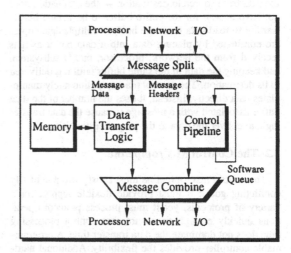

**Figure 4.1. Message flow in MAGIC.**

Figure 4.2 shows the data transfer logic in detail. When messages arrive from the network, processor, or I/O subsystem, the network interface (NI), processor interface (PI), or I/O interface (I/O) splits the message into message header and message data, as noted above. If the message contains data, the data is copied into a *data buffer*, a temporary storage element contained on the MAGIC chip that is used to stage data as it is forwarded from source to destination. Sixteen data buffers are provided on-chip, each large enough to store one cache line.

Staging data through data buffers allows the data transfer logic to achieve low latency and high bandwidth through data pipelining and elimination of multiple data copies. Data pipelining is achieved by tagging each data buffer word with a valid bit. The functional unit reading data from the data buffer monitors the valid bits to pipeline

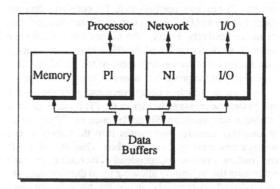

**Figure 4.2. Data transfer logic.**

the data from source to destination — the destination does not have to wait for the entire buffer to be written before starting to read data from the buffer. Multiple data copies are eliminated by placing data into a data buffer as it is received from the network, processor, or I/O subsystem, and keeping the data in the same buffer until it is delivered to its destination. The control macropipeline rarely manipulates data directly; instead, it uses the number of the data buffer associated with a message to cause the data transfer logic to deliver the data to the proper destination.

## 4.2 The Control Macropipeline

The control macropipeline must satisfy two potentially conflicting goals: it must provide flexible support for a variety of protocols, yet it must process protocol operations quickly enough to ensure that control processing time does not dominate the data transfer time. A programmable controller provides the flexibility. Additional hardware support ensures that the controller can process protocol operations efficiently. First, a hardware-based message dispatch mechanism eliminates the need for the controller to perform message dispatch in software. Second, this dispatch mechanism allows a speculative memory operation to be initiated even before the controller begins processing the message, thereby reducing the data access time. Third, in addition to standard RISC instructions, the controller's instruction set includes bitfield manipulation and other special instructions to provide efficient support for common protocol operations. Fourth, the mechanics of outgoing message sends are handled by a separate hardware unit.

Figure 4.3 shows the structure of the control macropipeline. Message headers are passed from the PI, NI and I/O to the *inbox*, which contains the hardware dispatch and speculative memory logic. The inbox passes the message header to the flexible controller — the *protocol processor* (PP) — where the actual protocol processing occurs. To improve performance, PP code and data are cached in the MAGIC instruction cache and MAGIC data cache, respectively. Finally, the *outbox* handles outgoing message sends on behalf of the PP, taking outgoing message headers and forwarding them to the PI, NI, and I/O for delivery to the processor, network, and I/O subsystem.

As soon as the inbox completes message preprocessing and passes the message header to the PP, it can begin processing a new message. Similarly, once the PP composes an outgoing message and passes it to the outbox, it can accept a new message from the inbox. Thus, the inbox, PP, and outbox operate independently, increasing message processing throughput by allowing up to three messages to be processed concurrently; hence the name "macropipeline." The following sections describe the operation of the inbox, PP, and outbox in greater detail.

### 4.2.1 Inbox Operation

The inbox processes messages in several steps. First, the *scheduler* selects the incoming queue from which the next message will be read. Second, the inbox uses portions of the selected message's header to index into a small memory called the *jump table* to determine the starting PP program counter (PC) appropriate for the message. The jump table also determines whether the inbox should initiate a speculative memory operation. Finally, the inbox passes the selected message header to the PP for processing.

The scheduler selects a message from one of several queues. The PI and I/O each provide a single queue of requests issued by the processor and I/O subsystem, respectively. The NI provides one queue for each network virtual lane. The last queue is the software queue. Unlike the other queues, the software queue is managed entirely by the PP. The inbox contains only the queue's head entry; the remainder of the queue is maintained in main memory, though in many cases it also will be present in the MAGIC data cache.

The scheduler plays a crucial role in the deadlock avoidance strategy discussed in Section 3.1. Each incoming queue has an associated array of status bits which the PP can use to specify the queue's relative priority, indicate whether messages on the queue require outgoing queue space for servicing, or disable scheduling from the queue completely. By initializing these status bits appropriately, the PP can ensure that all handlers can run to completion,

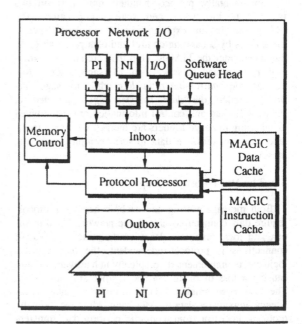

**Figure 4.3. Control macropipeline.**

that request messages are selected only when sufficient outgoing queue space exists, and that reply messages are selected regardless of the state of the outgoing queues.

By providing programmable, hardware-based message dispatch, the jump table frees the PP from having to perform an inefficient software dispatch table lookup before processing a message. A jump table entry contains a pattern field, a speculative memory operation indicator, and a starting PC value. The inbox compares the pattern field of each jump table entry to the message type, several bits of the address contained in the message, and other information to determine which entry matches the message. The matching entry's speculative memory indicator specifies whether to initiate a speculative read or write for the address contained in the message. The starting PC value specifies the PC at which the PP will begin processing the message. When the PP requests the next message from the inbox, the inbox inserts the starting PC value associated with the new message directly into the PP's PC register. The PP can program the jump table entries to change the particular set of handlers in use.

### 4.2.2 Protocol Processor Operation

Each protocol requires different message types, state information, state formats, and handlers. To accommodate this variation in processing needs, the PP implements a subset of the DLX instruction set [HP90] with extensions to accelerate common protocol operations. These extensions include bitfield extraction and insertion, branch on bit set/clear, and "field" instructions which specify a mask under which the operation is performed. Additional instructions implement the interface between the PP and the other MAGIC functional units, such as issuing message sends to the outbox, requesting new messages from the inbox, and programming the jump table. Thirty-two 64-bit general-purpose registers provide scratch space for use by PP code during protocol processing.

The PP itself is a 64-bit, statically-scheduled, dual-issue superscalar processor core. It fetches an instruction pair from the MAGIC instruction cache each cycle and executes both instructions unconditionally. The PP does not support interrupts, exceptions, pipeline interlocks, or hardware address translation. Although these features can simplify some aspects of protocol processing, we elected to eliminate them to reduce design and implementation complexity. Hence, because the PP lacks many of the resource conflict detection features present in most contemporary microprocessors, the burden of avoiding resource conflicts and pipeline interlocks falls on the PP programmer or compiler.

### 4.2.3 Outbox Operation

The outbox performs outgoing message sends on behalf of the PP. It provides a high-level interface to the PI, NI,

and I/O, relieving the PP from many implementation-specific details such as outgoing queue entry formats and handshaking conventions.

To initiate an outgoing message send, the PP composes the outgoing message header in its general-purpose registers. Next, the PP issues a "message send" instruction. The outbox detects the message send, makes a copy of the message header, inspects the destination of the outgoing message, and passes the message to the PI, NI or I/O, as appropriate. Copying the message header requires only one cycle, permitting the PP to proceed almost immediately with additional message processing while the outbox formats the outgoing message and delivers it to the proper interface unit.

### 4.2.4 Interface Units

In addition to actual message processing, MAGIC must interface to the network, processor, and I/O subsystem. The three interface units — the PI, NI, and I/O — implement these interfaces, isolating the rest of the chip from the interface details. This isolation is another component of MAGIC's flexibility, since it limits the amount of hardware modifications required to adapt the MAGIC design for use in other systems.

## 4.3 Putting It All Together

To make the discussion in the previous sections more concrete, this section summarizes the interaction of the data transfer logic and the control macropipeline and presents cycle counts for common protocol operations.

To achieve system performance competitive with a fully-hardwired design, MAGIC must minimize the latency required to service requests from the main processor. Minimizing main processor request latency requires MAGIC, internally, to minimize the data transfer logic time and, at the same time, ensure that the control macropipeline time is less than the data transfer time. Overall, MAGIC's performance can be measured both by the total time to process a message (the latency) and by the rate at which sustained message processing can occur (the occupancy).

To demonstrate that MAGIC can achieve competitive performance, we present the latency for servicing a processor read miss to local memory. Table 4.1 lists the latency through each stage of the data transfer logic and control macropipeline for this operation, assuming that the MAGIC chip was initially idle. The cycle counts are based on a 100 MHz (10 ns) MAGIC clock rate and are derived from the current Verilog models of the various units.

One cycle after the miss appears on the processor bus, the PI places the message in its incoming queue. After three additional cycles, the inbox has read the message from the PI queue, passed the message header through the jump table, and initiated a speculative memory read. At this point, state manipulation and data transfer proceed in parallel. The PP requires 10 cycles to update the directory information and forward the data to the processor (assuming all accesses hit in the MAGIC caches). The memory system returns the first 8 bytes of data after 16 cycles and the remaining 120 bytes in the next 15 cycles. Four cycles after the first data bytes return from the memory system, the PI issues the response on the processor bus and begins delivering the cache fill data to the processor.

**Table 4.1. Cycle Counts for Local Read Miss**

| Unit | Control Macropipeline Latency, 10 ns Cycles | Data Transfer Pipeline Latency, 10 ns Cycles |
|---|---|---|
| PI, incoming | 1 | 1 |
| Inbox, schedule and jump table lookup | 3 | 3 |
| PP | 10 | — |
| Outbox | 1 | — |
| PI, outgoing | 4 | 4 |
| Memory read, time to first 8 bytes | — | 16 |
| Memory read, time for remaining 120 bytes | — | 15 |
| TOTAL | 19 | 24 to first word, 39 total |

This example illustrates several important MAGIC architectural features. First, the speculative memory indication contained in the jump table allows the memory read to be started before the PP begins processing the message, thereby reducing the cache fill time. Second, the data transfer proceeds independently of the control processing; thus, at the same time the memory system is reading the data from memory into the data buffer, the PP is updating directory state and composing the outgoing data reply message. Third, the valid bits associated with the data buffer allow the PI to pipeline the data back to the processor, further reducing the cache fill time. Fourth, the separation of data and control processing eliminates multiple data copies: the data flows, via the data buffer, directly from the memory system to the PI while the control processing flows through the entire control macropipeline. Finally, as Table 4.1 demonstrates, the control macropipeline time is less than the data transfer time, indicating that the flexible protocol processing is not the limiting factor of MAGIC's performance.

The previous example focused on the latency required to service the processor's cache fill request. As noted above, the occupancy of message processing is also important. The occupancy is determined by the longest suboperation that must be performed. Again, competitive performance requires that the control macropipeline not be the longest suboperation. Table 4.2 lists PP occupancy cycle counts for some of the common handlers in the base cache-coherence protocol; the occupancies of the other units are insensitive to the type of message being processed. (Of course the data transfer logic time is eliminated for messages that do not require data movement.) The first three entries are operations that require local memory access; the final two entries require the PP to pass a message between the network and local processor. For all operations with a local memory access, the control macropipeline time is less than the data transfer time. Hence, as would be the case in a fully-hardwired controller, the sustained rate at which MAGIC can supply data is governed by the memory system.

**Table 4.2. PP Occupancies For Common Handlers**

| Handler | Occupancy (cycles) |
|---|---|
| Local write miss (no shared copies) | 10 |
| Local write miss (shared copies) | 7 + 13 per invalidation |
| Remote read miss, clean | 14 |
| Outgoing pass through on remote miss | 3 |
| Incoming pass through on remote miss | 3 |

The PP cycle counts for the operations in Table 4.1 and Table 4.2 assume that all PP loads and stores hit in the on-chip MAGIC data cache. Our initial studies, based on address traces collected from the DASH machine and on small executions of SPLASH [SWG92] applications, show that the PP reference stream has sufficient locality to make this a reasonable assumption.

We have coded a C version of the block-transfer protocol in our system-level simulator and, for performance studies, have hand-coded some of the critical handlers in PP assembly language. Our preliminary studies, based on these handlers, show that the initiation phase of the protocol takes approximately 70 cycles until the processor can continue from a non-blocking send. After performing transfer setup for 30 additional cycles, the PP begins the user message transfer. Once the transfer has started, MAGIC is capable of transferring user data at a sustained rate of one 128-byte cache line every 30 – 40 cycles, yielding a useful bandwidth of 300 – 400 MB/s.

## 5  System Software Strategy

As noted in Section 1, our goal is for FLASH to operate well both in a traditional supercomputer environment and in a general-purpose, multiprogrammed environment. The latter environment poses significant challenges since general-purpose environments typically contain large numbers of processes making many system calls and small I/O requests. In addition, users expect good interactive response, fair sharing of the hardware, protection against malicious programs, and extremely rare system crashes. The combination of workload characteristics and user requirements rules out using a standard supercomputer operating system for FLASH. Scalability and fault containment requirements rule out using a general-purpose operating system designed for small-scale shared-memory multiprocessors. To address these issues, we are designing a new operating system for FLASH, called *Hive*.

Beneath a standard shared-memory multiprocessor API, Hive organizes the hardware nodes into groups called *cells*. Each cell runs a semi-autonomous NUMA-aware operating system. The division into cells provides the replication needed for a highly-scalable operating system implementation and allows for fault containment. Cells interact as a distributed system internal to Hive, using the firewall and message-passing mechanisms of the MAGIC chip for fault isolation. The number of nodes per cell can be configured for different workload and availability requirements.

Hive supports shared memory between applications on different cells, and can allocate processor and memory resources from multiple cells to a single application. This support allows flexible, fine-grained sharing of the machine by large and small applications, despite the fault containment partitions. A more detailed discussion of Hive's design is beyond the scope of this paper.

## 6  Implementation and Status

FLASH will use the MIPS T5, a follow-on to the R4000, as its primary processor. Like the R4000, the T5 manages its own second-level cache. The target speed of the node board and the MAGIC chip is 100 MHz. The multiply-banked memory system is designed to match the node's bandwidth requirements and is optimized for 128-byte transfers, the system cache line size. FLASH will implement the PCI standard bus for its I/O subsystem and will use next-generation Intel routers for the interconnection network. The initial FLASH prototype will contain 256 processing nodes. We plan to collaborate with the Intel Corporation and Silicon Graphics on the design and construction of the prototype machine.

We currently have a detailed system-level simulator up and running. The simulator is written in C++ as a multi-

threaded memory simulator for Tango-Lite [Golds93]. The entire system, called FlashLite, runs real applications and enables us to verify protocols, analyze system performance, and identify architectural bottlenecks. We have coded the entire base cache-coherence and base block-transfer protocols for FlashLite, and have run complete simulations of several SPLASH applications. The FlashLite code is structured identically to the actual hardware, with each hardware block corresponding to a FlashLite thread. To aid the debugging of protocols implemented in FlashLite we have developed a random test case generator, the FLASH Protocol Verifier.

On the hardware design front we are busily coding the Verilog description of the MAGIC chip. To verify our hardware description we plan to have FlashLite provide test vectors for a Verilog run, and to run real N processor applications with N–1 FlashLite nodes and one Verilog node. Since the FlashLite code is structured like the Verilog description, we also plan to replace a single FlashLite thread with the appropriate hardware block description to allow more efficient and accurate verification.

Software tools for the protocol processor are another major effort. We are porting the GNU C compiler [Stall93] to generate code for the 64-bit PP. We have also ported a superscalar instruction scheduler and an assembler from the Torch project [SHL92]. Finally, we have a PP instruction set emulator ported from Mable. This emulator will help us verify the actual PP code sequences by becoming the PP thread in FlashLite simulations.

Operating system development is proceeding concurrently with the hardware design. Hive's implementation is based on IRIX (UNIX SVR4 from Silicon Graphics), with extensive modifications in progress to the virtual memory, I/O, and process management subsystems.

## 7  Related Work

The architecture of FLASH builds on the work of many previous research projects. In this section we compare FLASH to several existing and proposed machines.

The Alewife [ACD+91, KA93] machine from MIT shares with FLASH the goals of providing a cache-coherent single-address-space machine with integrated message passing. It is also similar to FLASH in that the directory information for coherence is kept in a reserved portion of the distributed main memory. However, it is different in that the common cases of the coherence protocol are fixed in hardware finite state machines, and therefore the base protocol cannot be changed significantly. The Alewife machine also does not support virtual memory, and as a result, many of the issues that arise in doing user-level protected messaging in the presence of multiprogramming are currently not addressed. FLASH directly addresses these issues.

The J-machine project at MIT [NWD93, SGS+93] has also focused on supporting multiple communication paradigms within a single machine. A key difference in the approaches, however, is that while the J-machine uses the same processor for both computing and protocol processing, FLASH uses separate compute and protocol processors. Although a single processor obviously costs less, our experiences with DASH in supporting cache coherence suggest that, if the protocol and compute processor were one and the same, the sheer number of protocol processing requests would cause the compute performance to degrade considerably. Furthermore, we believe that the task requirements for the compute processor and the protocol processor are fundamentally different, and therefore the two components need to be architected differently, especially if one relies on an off-the-shelf compute processor. For instance, our compute processor is designed for throughput on code optimized for locality, while the protocol processor is optimized to process many very short handler sequences, with successive sequences bearing little relationship to each other. Another difference is that whenever the compute processor makes a memory request, it does so with the intention of using the data returned for further computation. In contrast, when the protocol processor makes a memory request, it directly passes the data returned by memory to the network or to the local processor; the data need never go to the protocol processor's registers or through its memory hierarchy. This data handling method leads to significant differences in the capabilities of FLASH and the J-machine. For example, the J-machine processor, the MDP, has neither the throughput of our compute processor (e.g., it does not have caches or significant number of registers), nor does it have the extra hardware support for data transfer provided in MAGIC to handle remote requests efficiently.

The Thinking Machine's CM-5 [TMC92] provides user-level access to the network so that short user messages can be sent efficiently by the source processor. However, in contrast to FLASH, the main processor is involved in all transactions on both the sending and receiving ends. As discussed for the J-machine, we believe this can considerably reduce the communications and computation throughput when supporting shared memory.

To address the throughput and overhead issues discussed above, the Intel Paragon machine provides a second processor on each node to act as a messaging processor. The messaging processor is identical to the compute processor, and it resides on a snoopy bus along with the compute processor and the network interface chip. Unfortunately, because Intel's messaging processor is coupled to the compute processor through the snoopy bus, it will be unable to support FLASH's goal of supporting cache coherence. (It needs to be able to observe all requests issued by the compute processor.) MAGIC's tight coupling to the compute processor, the memory system, and the network allows it to support both cache coherence and message passing efficiently.

The recently-announced Meiko CS-2 [HM93] machine incorporates a processor core in its network interface. While the CS-2 is similar to FLASH at a high level, the processor core and the surrounding data path are not powerful enough to be able to implement a cache-coherence protocol efficiently (e.g., there is no on-chip data cache, so all directory data would have to come from main memory). Even messaging is done using a separate DMA controller in the network interface chip. In contrast, in FLASH all messaging and coherence are handled directly by the MAGIC protocol processor.

The *T machine proposed by MIT [NPA92] is in some ways closest to FLASH. *T proposes to use a separate remote-memory processor and a separate synchronization processor in addition to the main compute processor. While the remote-memory and synchronization processors in *T are similar to the MAGIC chip in FLASH, the *T paper discusses them only at a high level, giving the instruction set additions but no hardware blocks. *T also does not have effective support of cache coherence as a goal, and consequently does not discuss the implications of their design for that issue.

In a paper related to *T, Henry and Joerg [HJ92] discuss issues in the design of the network-node interface. They argue that most protocol processing for handling messages can be done by a general-purpose processor. Hardware support is needed in only a couple of places, namely for fast dispatch based on type of incoming message and for boundary-case/error-case checking (for example, the processor should be informed when the outbound network queue is getting full to help avoid deadlock). Our general experience in the design of MAGIC has been similar, although the specifics of our design are quite different.

Finally, the most recent addition to the array of large-scale multiprocessors has been the Cray T3D. The architecture supports a single-address-space memory model and provides a block-transfer engine that can do memory-to-memory copies with scatter/gather capabilities. T3D differs from FLASH in its lack of support for cache coherence and in its support of a more specialized bulk data transfer engine.

## 8 Concluding Remarks

Recent shared-memory and message-passing architectures have been converging. FLASH is a unified architecture that addresses many of the drawbacks of earlier proposals — it provides support for cache-coherent shared memory with low hardware overhead and for message passing with low software overhead. The goal of supporting multiple protocols efficiently and flexibly has to a large extent driven the architecture of FLASH. To achieve this goal, we made a set of hardware-software trade-offs. For flexibility, MAGIC includes a programmable protocol processor and a programmable hardware dispatch mechanism. In addition, MAGIC uses a portion of the local main memory for storing all protocol code and data instead of employing a special memory for this purpose. For efficiency, MAGIC has hardware support optimized to handle data movement in a high-bandwidth, pipelined fashion, as well as on-chip caches for high-bandwidth, low-latency access to protocol state and code. The result is a single chip that efficiently and flexibly implements all of the functionality required in a scalable multiprocessor system.

## Acknowledgments

We would like to thank Todd Mowry for his help in adapting the FlashLite threads package to Tango-Lite and Stephen Herrod for his help with FlashLite development. We would also like to acknowledge the cooperation of the Intel Corporation, Supercomputer Systems Division. This work was supported by ARPA contract N00039-91-C-0138. David Ofelt, Mark Heinrich, and Joel Baxter are supported by National Science Foundation Fellowships. John Heinlein is supported by an Air Force Laboratory Graduate Fellowship. John Chapin is supported by a Fannie and John Hertz Foundation Fellowship.

## References

[ACD+91]  Anant Agarwal et al. The MIT Alewife Machine: A Large-Scale Distributed-Memory Multiprocessor. MIT/LCS Memo TM-454, Massachusetts Institute of Technology, 1991.

[Golds93]  Stephen Goldschmidt. Simulation of Multiprocessors: Accuracy and Performance. Ph.D. Thesis, Stanford University, June 1993.

[HGG94]  John Heinlein, Kourosh Gharachorloo, and Anoop Gupta. Integrating Multiple Communication Paradigms in High Performance Multiprocessors. Technical Report CSL-TR-94-604, Stanford University, February 1994.

[HJ92]  Dana S. Henry and Christopher F. Joerg. A Tightly-Coupled Processor-Network Interface. In *Proceedings of the 5th International Conference on Architectural Support for Programming Languages and Operating Systems*, pages 111-22, Boston, MA, October 1992.

[HM93]  Mark Homewood and Moray McLaren. Meiko CS-2 Interconnect Elan–Elite Design. In *Proceedings of Hot Interconnects 93*, pages 2.1.1-4, Stanford University, August 1993.

[HP90]  John Hennessy and David Patterson. *Computer Architecture: A Quantitative Approach*. Morgan Kaufmann Publishers, San Mateo, CA, 1990.

[KA93]  John Kubiatowicz and Anant Agarwal. Anatomy of a Message in the Alewife Multiprocessor. In *Proceedings of the 7th ACM International Conference on Supercomputing*, Tokyo, Japan, July 1993.

[KSR92]  Kendall Square Research. KSR1 Technical Summary. Waltham, MA, 1992.

[LLG+90]  Daniel Lenoski et al. The Directory-Based Cache Coherence Protocol for the DASH Multiprocessor. In *Proceedings of the 17th International Symposium on Computer Architecture*, pages 148-59, Seattle, WA, May 1990.

[LLG+92]  Daniel Lenoski et al. The Stanford DASH Multiprocessor. *IEEE Computer*, 25(3):63-79, March 1992.

[NPA92]  Rishiyur S. Nikhil, Gregory M. Papadopoulos, and Arvind. *T: A Multithreaded Massively Parallel Architecture. In *Proceedings of the 19th International Symposium on Computer Architecture*, pages 156-67, Gold Coast, Australia, May 1992.

[NWD93]  Michael D. Noakes, Deborah A. Wallach, and William J. Dally. The J-Machine Multicomputer: An Architectural Evaluation. In *Proceedings of the 20th International Symposium on Computer Architecture*, pages 224-35, San Diego, CA, May 1993.

[SGS+93]  Ellen Spertus et al. Evaluation of Mechanisms for Fine-Grained Parallel Programs in the J-Machine and the CM-5. In *Proceedings of the 20th International Symposium on Computer Architecture*, pages 302-13, San Diego, CA, May 1993.

[SHL92]  Michael D. Smith, Mark Horowitz, and Monica Lam. Efficient Superscalar Performance Through Boosting. In *Proceedings of the Fifth International Conference on Architectural Support for Programming Languages and Operating Systems*, pages 248-59, Boston, MA, October 1992.

[Simoni92]  Richard Simoni. Cache Coherence Directories for Scalable Multiprocessors. Ph.D. Thesis, Technical Report CSL-TR-92-550, Stanford University, October 1992.

[Stall93]  Richard Stallman. Using and porting GNU CC. Free Software Foundation, Cambridge, MA, June 1993.

[SWG92]  J.P. Singh, W.-D. Weber, and Anoop Gupta. SPLASH: Stanford Parallel Applications for Shared-Memory. *Computer Architecture News*, 20(1):5-44, March 1992.

[TMC92]  Thinking Machines Corporation. The Connection Machine CM-5 Technical Summary. Cambridge MA, January 1992.

[vECG+92]  Thorsten von Eicken et al. Active Messages: A Mechanism for Integrated Communication and Computation. In *Proceedings of the 19th International Symposium on Computer Architecture*, pages 256-66, Gold Coast, Australia, May 1992.

# About the Authors

**Jelica Protić** is currently with the department of computer engineering, School of Electrical Engineering, University of Belgrade, Serbia, Yugoslavia, where she received her BS and MS in computer engineering, in 1987 and 1994, respectively. From 1987 to 1990 she was with the LOLA Institute, where she has been involved in a project of networking programmable logical controllers using a DSM-like paradigm. Shared-memory multiprocessors, distributed computing, local area networks, and system software in general are her current research interests. Distributed shared memory is her primary field of interest; together with the same coauthors she presented several preconference tutorials on this subject, and she is currently in the final phase of finishing her PhD thesis in this field. (Protić's home page: *http://ubbg.etf.bg.ac.yu/~jeca/*)

**Milo Tomašević** is currently with the department of computer engineering, School of Electrical Engineering, University of Belgrade, Belgrade, Serbia, Yugoslavia. He received his BS in electrical engineering, and MS and PhD in computer engineering, from the University of Belgrade, in 1980, 1984, and 1992, respectively. Previously he was with the Pupin Institute, Belgrade, where he was involved in several large research projects. His PhD research dealt with the cache coherence problem in shared-memory multiprocessors. His current research interests cover computer architecture, especially parallel and distributed systems. He has received awards for some of his conference papers. (Tomašević's home page: *http://ubbg.etf.bg.ac.yu/~etomasev/*)

**Veljko Milutinović** (Senior Member, IEEE) received the PhD degree from the University of Belgrade, Yugoslavia, in 1982. He has been on the faculty of the School of Electrical Engineering, University of Belgrade, Serbia, Yugoslavia since 1990. Prior to that, he was a faculty member of the School of Electrical Engineering at Purdue University, West Lafayette, Indiana. His R&D results include a commercial 16-node MISD machine for DFT processing developed at IMP, the architecture of an early 200-MHz RISC microprocessor for RCA, several multimedia PC-oriented multiprocessor concepts for NCR, and several DSM system-level solutions for Encore. He has been actively researching distributed shared memory computing since the early 1990s, when he was a part of the team that developed a board that turns a personal computer into a DSM node based on the reflective memory approach. He has authored more than 50 papers in IEEE periodicals and presented more than 200 invited lectures worldwide. His work has been extensively referenced in textbooks on computer architecture. (Milutinović's home page: *http://ubbg.etf.bg.ac.yu/~emilutiv/*)